THE NAVAL ARISTOCRACY

PETER KARSTEN

The Naval Aristocracy

The Golden Age of Annapolis and
the Emergence of Modern American Navalism

THE FREE PRESS · New York

COLLIER-MACMILLAN, LTD · London

1972

The Free Press
A Division of The Macmillan Company
866 Third Avenue, New York, New York 10022

Collier-Macmillan Canada Ltd., Toronto, Ontario

Library of Congress Catalog Card Number: 76-136609

printing number
1 2 3 4 5 6 7 8 9 10

For
*my mother and father
and the memory of my uncle*

Contents

A curious ethnological specimen, [the U.S. naval officer] is developing artificially in the direction of sleekness and culture. . . . The world, pondering on the great part of its own future which is in his hands, contemplates him with wonder as to what the devil he will evolve into in another century or two.

George Bernard Shaw, *Captain Brassbound's Conversion* (1899)

An Introduction

Recent events involving the character of the U.S. Navy and her officers—events such as the *Pueblo* incident, the Arnheiter case, and a number of fires and collisions at sea[1]—might have served as the impetus for this study. They did not; the first draft was complete before Lieutenant Commander Arnheiter was relieved, before the *Pueblo* was seized, before any of the recent naval disasters. But these incidents, accenting the problems attendant upon the maintenance of a vast naval force in command of the world's seas, serve to illustrate the need for Americans to ask themselves what this mighty Navy, with its hoary traditions and strict codes of behavior, is all about.

My own investigation began along fairly mundane lines. As a one-time junior naval officer turned historian, I took, at the outset of my historical studies, what might be regarded as a natural interest in the Navy's famous officer-historian-strategist, Captain Alfred Thayer Mahan. After wrestling for some time with the question of Captain Mahan's historical role, I finally decided that it was necessary to know more of Mahan's messmates—the U.S. naval officers active in the Navy that Mahan knew—men who were captains when he was a midshipman, and men who were midshipmen when he was a captain. In order to fully understand Mahan, I had to understand the two generations of officers born between roughly 1810 and 1870 and active from the 1840s to the 1920s.

Mahan was born in 1840 and died in 1914, but the 1845–1925 dates seemed preferable for several reasons. First, to understand Mahan's own historical role, it seemed appropriate to extend the sphere of analysis beyond the simple limits of Mahan's years of active or retired service (1856–1914) in order to provide sufficient background and continuity and to avoid chronological artificiality. Second, the founding of the Naval Academy in 1845 and the creation of a permanent naval reserve officer corps in 1925[2] provided just such a time span, a kind of "Golden Age" of Annapolis, which facilitated the drawing of limits to the analysis. Third, and independently significant, the period from the 1840s to the 1920s was the richest in terms of available source materials. Data on U.S. naval officers active prior to the 1840s are relatively sparse; data on officers active after the 1920s are often classified or simply uncollected. Eventually these eras would be explored as well, but it seemed reasonable to tackle this era first.

Numbered footnotes for the Introduction begin on page xv.

The available sources on U.S. naval officers are relatively rich, but they are not without limits. In the first place, by the time I began my research the primary subjects of my study were either dead or senile; interviewing was out.[3]

In the second place, only about one in every ten officers active in these years appear to have left any private records of their views. Correspondents were rarely able to save mail. Vice Admiral Stephen Rowan told the daughter of Matthew Fountaine Maury in 1873, "I have never had a settled home until now and having no place to preserve papers [I] was compelled to destroy all letters except official ones for want of room to keep them." And Fleet Admiral Ernest King explained that his own shortage of personal manuscripts was due to the fact that most naval officers "travel light" and don't "accumulate any substantial body of personal papers."[4]

In the third place, those manuscripts that have been preserved may not be altogether representative. Many of these private papers consist of letters to female relatives (mothers, sisters, wives, or daughters). There are fewer letters addressed to other officers, brothers, fathers, or sons. Perhaps male recipients were simply less inclined to save their private exchanges than were wives or sisters. In any event, naval officers may have been unwilling to reveal their inner world and thoughts to the gentlewomen in their lives.[5]

Finally, those private records (letters, journals, diaries, manuscript autobiographies, and the like) that were deliberately or inadvertently preserved have not always been transmitted to the public in their original form. All too often the wives or daughters who have passed these materials over to public repositories[6] have stripped them of much of their value to researchers. Thus Mrs. Captain John Leonard insured her husband's permanent obscurity when she sent the Naval Historical Foundation her husband's journals from 1882 to 1901. She left the numerous records of weather conditions, soundings, and the like untouched, but razored-out dozens of other pages, explaining to the N.H.F. curator, Commodore Dudley Knox, "sometimes personal expressions were in a separate page (these latter records I have removed carefully)."[7] Apparently only items considered inoffensive were preserved (though some of the material that survived on page *x* is so revealing as to make one long to see the item that was snipped out of page *y*).

But having noted these limitations on the data, I none the less feel that an accurate and clear portrait of the American naval officer of the "Golden Age" can be limned, and I have done what I can to render such a portrait and to breathe as much life into it as I could, and no more than it initially possessed.

Eventually I became less concerned with Mahan and more concerned with his messmates. This "strategic elite"[8] seemed most worthy of special attention, as a number of scholars have observed. Armin Rappaport has recently called for more inquiry into the "why and how" of late nineteenth-century naval professionalism and the relationship between the officer corps and Walter Herrick's "naval revolution." "What of the geographic, social, economic, and political background of the officers and of their education?" Rappaport asks. What of "the ideological background" of the "naval revolution"? James Merrill, surveying American naval history since the days of Mahan, recently noted the lack of attention to naval discipline, naval-business relations, and the Navy's role in diplomacy: "To what extent does the Navy serve as a pressure group?" he asked. "What is the relationship of the [naval] establishment to scientific advancement?" As Alfred Vagts has pointed out, little is known of the "sociology of the officers or the crews" of the pre-1940 U.S. Navy, which "leaves unanswered" several questions "highly important for the societal interpretation of sea strategy." Charles Coates and Roland Pellegrin have called for "further basic studies" to provide "sociological knowledge" of U.S. naval institutions and life, but George Davis' 1940 remark that "as yet there has been no first-rate study of the philosophic inspiration of modern navalism" provoked no studies.[9]

The naval officers of this era were central figures in U.S. foreign relations. Many were at least as articulate and thoughtful as their more famous colleague, Mahan. And it is in the story of these two generations of officers that one finds the wellspring and "philosophic inspiration of modern navalism." This study of the "naval aristocracy" is concerned with all the questions raised by Messrs. Rappaport, Merrill, Vagts, Coates, Pellegrin, and Davis, as well as a number of other issues. It is not, I submit, a muckraking diatribe directed at the Navy and its officer corps but an effort at analysis, from both static and dynamic perspectives, of this key profession. None the less, my findings reveal racism, authoritarianism, warmongering, navalism, and a number of other unattractive qualities in the officer corps that old-time liberal anti-militarists such as Charles Beard, Oswald Garrison Villard, and John Swomley often claimed were there.[10] For several decades now defenders of the military have pooh-poohed such claims. This study was not *intended* to be a broadside against such defenders of "the system" (in fact, I originally felt that my research would inevitably prove that scholars such as Charles Beard and William A. Williams had misread the record of American diplomacy), but it has in part become one. The material speaks for itself, but some readers may be offended by some of it. So was I, which is why I have reserved the right (or fulfilled my responsibility) to offer a set of critical observations in a final chapter, based on my analysis of the officer corps and the emergence on navalism, and reflecting my own judgments and values.

These officers were not an aristocracy in the strictest sense of that word. They ruled only in the Service; within the halls of government they were subordinate to elected authority. The power they wielded was delegated, not supreme. They were the naval elite servants of the ruling upper class.

None the less, they were predominately well born, a fact which constituted their chief claim to preferment until well into the twentieth century. And they did tend to propagate—to breed their own successors. A "naval gentry" or "strategic elite" they certainly were (indeed, it could be argued that this account of naval officers describes as well *all* upper and upper-middle class society and thought in the United States from the 1840s to the 1920s), but they eventually acquired the more exalted epithet that I will use—that of "naval aristocracy." And they acquired this epithet because men like Naval Surgeon William Wood, Senator John Logan, Navy Secretary Josephus Daniels, and many others came to regard the officers and gentlemen of the naval service as a largely self-generating elite, complete with aristocratic traditions and codes of behavior and armed with a self-serving philosophy.

The first five chapters are essentially ahistorical—that is, generalizations are offered that are designed to apply to virtually any officer from America's naval past. Obviously, many practices, roles, and functions changed over these years. These changes are dealt with in subsections or are reserved for the next three chapters, which are primarily concerned with certain professional anxieties and the resulting innovations, with particular focus on the years from 1880 to 1915. Obviously, not every officer thought, lived, and behaved like every other officer; and exceptions to my "ideal type" are noted wherever I have found them. But, all things considered, I still maintain that this virtually timeless "ideal type" of naval officer actually existed. In an era of considerable social change the naval aristocracy was a strikingly homogeneous socio-professional group, with a remarkably stable pattern of thought and behavior. Every line (and engineering) officer could expect duty assignments that were virtually identical to those of every other line (and engineering) officer—several years at sea in junior billets, followed by a tour of duty ashore, possibly at the Academy; then back to sea for several more years, in somewhat more senior billets such as navigator or executive officer; command of one's own ship; thence rotation to a bureau or yard for a tour or two; command at sea once again; and finally flag rank and the command of a bureau, yard, or squadron. The *time* spent on each rung of the rotation ladder might vary from generation to generation, a fact which tended at times to create profound intraservice tensions and career anxieties (see Chapter 6), but the actual duty *experiences* on each rung of the ladder were basically the same for all.

Collective biography is, I submit, both possible and useful with such a group. Doctors, lawyers, businessmen, engineers, and other professionals *can* be examined as independent groups, but with such professions the analysis tends to be one-dimensional. Doctors, for example, may be posh specialists or humble G.Ps. They may think themselves Sons of the American Revolution or Sons of Italy, conservative or radical, atheistic or pious. For many professionals, whatever professional similarities exist may well prove to be less significant than their other interests and identifications. But the naval aristocracy not only came from similar social, ethnic, and economic backgrounds and acquired similar values, it also attained a greater cohesiveness than did the membership of other less integral professions. Its primary loyalty was to the Service—"the Navy, first, last, and always." Its secondary loyalty was to the Nation—"my country, right or wrong."

In serving these abstractions the naval aristocracy was rarely disinterested, but always enterprising and zealous. Its enterprise appeared excessive to some, and its zeal somewhat suspect to others, but the naval aristocracy made certain that it could count on an ever-growing host of civilian navalists who were well-advised as to what really mattered.

Notes

Introduction

1. For a listing of some of the Navy's most recent headaches see *"Esquire's* Official Court of Inquiry into the Present State of the United States Navy," *Esquire* (July 1969), 86–88.

2. 43 *U.S. Stat.* 1080 (Act of Feb. 28, 1925).

3. However, I interviewed some officers who had *known* these men, and I made use of Columbia's Oral History interviews with naval officers.

4. King and Walter Whitehill, *Fleet Admiral King: A Naval Record* (N.Y., 1952), vii–viii; Rowan to Mary Maury, Aug. 29, 1873, Rowan Papers, R. G. 45, National Archives. Similarly the ex-U.S. Minister to Korea, Hugh Dinsmore, told an archivist in 1923 that several of Ensign George Foulk's letters to him in the 1880s "were destroyed with some other papers of no value." Dinsmore to Victor Paltsits, June 15, 1923, George Foulk Papers, Mss. Div., New York Public Library (hereafter referred to as N.Y.P.L.).

5. Possible exceptions are Edwin Anderson, Charles Sperry, and Robert W. Shufeldt, whose letters to wives and daughters seem remarkably frank.

6. In trying to track down relevant collections still in private hands, I have found only two. The Naval Historical Foundation and its Naval History Society predecessors did a remarkable job of ferreting out manuscript collections.

7. Mrs. Leonard to Knox, Oct. 24, 1938, Captain John Leonard "Papers," Naval Historical Foundation, Washington, D.C. (hereafter referred to as N.H.F.).

8. The term is Suzanne Keller's, in *Beyond the Ruling Class: Strategic Elites in Modern Society* (N.Y., 1963.)

9. Rappaport, in a review of Walter Herrick's *The American Naval Revolution* in *U.S. Naval Institute Proceedings,* XCIII (December 1967), 129; Merrill, "Successors to Mahan: A Survey of Writings on American Naval History, 1914–1960," *Miss. Valley Hist. Rev.,* L (1963), 79, 99; Vagts, "Fears of an Amer.-German War, 1870–1915," *Political Science Quarterly,* LV (1940), 55*n.*; Coates and Pellegrin, *Military Sociology: A Study of American Military Institutions and Military Life* (College Park, Md., 1965), ix; Davis, *A Navy Second to None: The Development of Modern American Naval Policy* (N.Y., 1940), 420.

10. See, for example, Beard, *The Navy: Defense or Portent?* (N.Y., 1932); Villard, *Our Military Chaos* (N.Y., 1939); Swomley, *The Military Establishment* (Boston, 1948).

THE NAVAL ARISTOCRACY

part one

The Naval Aristocracy
A COMPOSITE PORTRAIT

A privileged class has been instituted, to whom a large share of the
wealth and honors of the country belong, irrespective of any claim of
merit or service. The general character of our institutions has been
departed from, and as positive a nobility created, as though its
members received the titles of Lord, Earl, Marquis, or Duke. . . .
A subordinate instrument of the government has thus become an
independent institution, and without altering one word of the constitution of our country, principles have grown up contrary to its
whole spirit and purpose.

Surgeon William M. Wood, U.S.N., on naval officers, in "The Naval Institutions
of a Republic," in *A Shoulder to the Wheel of Progress* (Buffalo. 1853)

chapter 1

Where They Came From: The Social Origins of the Naval Aristocracy

> Oh, I am a merry sailor lad,
> With heart both light and free;
> I highly prize my gallant ship;
> I love the deep blue sea.
> Hurrah! Hurrah! Hurrah!
> I love, I love, I love the dark, blue sea;
> I love, I love, I love the dark, blue sea.

Anonymous nineteenth-century naval ballad, printed in Robert Neeser, *American Naval Songs and Ballads*, 312.

The British Backdrop

The early modern navies—those of the early sixteenth century—were generally officered by "tarpaulin" sailors, men who worked their way up to command through the ranks and who were thoroughly familiar with spar and sail. But as the size and significance of navies swelled, an increasing number of "gentlemen" officers were appointed. This was particularly so in the British Empire where the "levelling" effect of "tarpaulins" was greatly feared. As George Saville, Lord Halifax, put it in 1694:[1]

> If the maritime force . . . should be wholly directed by the lower sort of men, with an entire exclusion of the nobility and gentry, it will not be easy to answer the arguments supported by so great a probability, that such a scheme would not only lead toward a democracy, but directly lead us into it.

Halifax probably did not intend to eliminate the tarpaulin officer altogether, but it is a fact that these professional sailors found preferment more difficult in

Numbered footnotes for Chapter 1 begin on page 19.

4   the eighteenth-century Empire than had their ancestral counterparts. Thomas Macaulay's quip that the navy of Charles II contained gentlemen and sailors, but that "the gentlemen were not sailors, and the sailors were not gentlemen," was also true of the navies of the Georgian Age. Merchant captains could secure commissions, and often did, but only with abundant political influence. By 1773 only the sons of the nobility or gentry could gain admission to the Royal Navy Academy at Portsmouth. The Napoleonic wars forced the government to commission more tarpaulins, but only for the duration. The "lower class" echelon of Royal Navy officers fell from 6.7% to o between 1800 and 1850, while the percentage of noble- and gentle-born rose correspondingly. The British Navy was once again a closed society.*

In the days before the U.S. Naval Academy (1798–1844), the recruitment of U.S. naval officers somewhat resembled that of Great Britain. The initial warships of the War of Independence were officered by veterans of the Royal Navy or the merchant service, some of whom were low or middle-born; but thereafter the "tarpaulin" officer became an increasingly rare phenomenon. The Federalist founders of the U.S. Navy in 1798 heeded the advice of men like the proper Bostonian and navy agent, Stephen Higginson, to name only "proper characters" such as had "right habits, principles and feelings" to positions of honor and authority in the federal naval service.[2] Prospective officer candidates, virtually all from the upper echelons of American society,† were first created midshipmen. In the words of Seaman Jacob Hazen, midshipmen of the early nineteenth century "commonly looked upon themselves as being somebody":

> Much regard is paid among them to birth, and their characters and abilities are too often weighed, by even their superiors, in proportion to the positions occupied by their fathers in government and society. Hence their very messes become seasoned with a strong smell of aristocracy. . . .

Another proper Bostonian Higginson, Thomas Wentworth Higginson, referred to one of these "proper characters," Samuel F. DuPont, who had risen to flag

* On the other hand, many "tarpaulins" apparently were successfully integrated into the British naval aristocracy, for many of their sons became officers. The percentage of officers whose fathers had been naval officers rose from 25% in 1800 to 33⅓% in 1850.

Michael Lewis, *The Navy in Transition, 1814–1864* (London, 1965), 21; Henry L. Burr, *Education in the Early Navy [1775–1845]* (Philadelphia, 1939), *passim*; *Select Naval Documents*, ed. H. W. Hodges and E. A. Hughes (Cambridge, England, 1922), 131; *Dictionary of American Biography* (for 114 eighteenth- and early nineteenth-century American and British naval officers). Cf. Michael Lewis, *A Social History of the Navy, 1793–1815* (London, 1960).

† To cite but two examples: Midshipman James Biddle's brother was Nicholas Biddle of the National Bank. His uncles were prominent in law and politics. His father was a sea captain, a politician, and a prominent merchant. Other brothers were lawyers and statesmen. Nicholas B. Wainright, "Commodore James Biddle and his Sketch Book," *Pennsylvania Magazine of History and Biography*, XC (January 1966), 4. Midshipman John D. Henley's mother was Martha Washington's sister. Robert E. Johnson, *Rear Admiral John Rodgers, 1812–1882* (Annapolis, 1967), 5. Cf. George H. Preble, *Rear Admiral Henry K. Thatcher* (Boston, 1882), and *Dictionary of American Biography* entries for U.S. naval officers born between 1775 and 1825.

rank by 1862, as "that stately and courtly potentate, elegant as one's ideal French marquis."[3]

When these men rose to command, they often brought their nephews, sons, or grandsons into the service with them.[4] Apparently a midshipman's commission was deemed to be quite a prize; in 1833 Navy Secretary Levi Woodbury reported that, with no more than 35 midshipman vacancies each year, there were more than 1,300 applications on file.[5]

Political Influence

By 1845 the federal government had moved to institutionalize the recruitment of naval officer candidates with the creation of the U.S. Naval Academy at Annapolis, Maryland. Appointments to the Academy were to be made from the states and territories in proportion to their representation in Congress. Appointments were thus controlled by Congressmen and territorial representatives. Each "owned" an opening, and as soon as his previous appointment had completed midshipman training or had "bilged" (failed), he let it be known that applications for replacements would be considered. In the event that no candidates were forthcoming, the control of the appointment reverted to the Secretary of the Navy. Ten appointments for the sons of servicemen were controlled by the President.[6]

Until the outbreak of the Civil War the states of the eastern seacoast monopolized Academy appointments. Over 80% of the midshipmen appointed before 1860 came from one of the original 13 colonies. By 1866 43% were from the Middle Atlantic states, 25% from New England, 26% from midwestern states and only 5% from the South. But the latter regions sent increasingly larger percentages of candidates to the Academy over the ensuing decades until by 1896 the Middle Atlantic states were sending 32% of the total, New England only 10%, and the West and Old South had risen to 36% and 22% respectively.[7] The rise in the number of southern midshipmen *may* have been due, in part, to that section's "militant" tradition, but it may also have been a function of the economic decline of the southern upper and middle classes. As one naval officer of southern origin who attended the Academy in the Reconstruction period recalled: "Our parents at that time were so poor that they had to send their sons to some free institution in order to enable them to get an education."[8] Thus, for southerners like Hilary P. Jones and Holden Evans the Navy Academy was less a gangway to the quarterdeck than it was a means of obtaining a decent training as an engineer.* The rise of the number of candidates from western states was doubtless a result of the general shift in population, but here the figures can be deceiving. Many candidates appointed from western states were born in the east, often in New York or the District of Columbia; it is likely that

---

* Marcus Cunliffe is skeptical, but he has suggested the possibility of just such a relationship between Southern penury and the availability of inexpensive education at a service academy in explaining the presence of southern cadets at West Point. *Soldiers and Civilians: The Martial Spirit in America, 1775–1865* (Boston, 1968), 362.

6   they secured their appointments directly (as did Robley D. Evans, who traveled to Utah to establish overnight "residence" before returning to the east as a candidate from that territory) or indirectly, through the Secretary of the Navy, whenever western Congressmen and territorial representatives proved unable to fill their openings.[9]

The control of naval commissions had always been in the hands of politicians. In 1841, with the influx of Whig office-holders, a record 223 midshipmen were created![10] As Rear Admiral Stephen B. Luce, himself appointed in the boom days of 1841, later recalled, it took "influential friends" to secure an appointment. John Sanford Barnes was appointed in 1851 as a reward to his father, who had been associated with Navy Secretary William A. Graham in the construction of the Seaboard and Roanoke Railroad.* Charles Graves' father was a personal friend of Alexander H. Stephens. William F. Halsey's father secured his son's appointment from his old law partner, Navy Secretary George Robeson. John Crittenden Watson's grandfather was Senator John J. Crittenden. C. C. Todd's uncle was Supreme Court Justice Thomas Todd. John Grimes Walker was the nephew of Senator John Grimes of Iowa. Cornelius Schoonmaker's uncle was his Congressman; Fredrick McNair's and Alexander Habersham's fathers were theirs, and many others had political relatives.[11] Harris Lanning obtained his appointment because his father, a bank president, was sufficiently prominent to be offered the use of one, unsolicited, by his Congressman. Winfield Scott Schley, Albert Barker, Charles E. Clark, Caspar Goodrich, Franklin Hanford, Robley Evans, and George Remey, to name but a few, all left records of the use of political influence in the securing of their appointments. The list could be extended virtually at will.[12] The point is that political patronage was absolutely essential to a young man who hoped to embark on a career as an officer in Uncle Sam's Navy.†

During and after the Civil War the granting of appointments as political patronage continued, by this time extended to Senators as well. The value of this patronage to a Congressman in 1873 may be sensed in the fact that in that

---

* Army Lieutenant Duane M. Greene may have described the situation that guaranteed John Sanford Barnes an appointment when he wrote: "It often happens that an overseer on public works who controls a large number of votes, is given a cadetship for his son in consideration of his influence in the election of a Congressman." He added that "Congressmen frequently exercise their prerogative to their own political advantage." Greene, *Ladies and Officers of the U.S. Army: American Aristocracy* (Chicago, 1880), 156–157.

† John M. Clayton wanted a purser's commission for Charles I. Du Pont, Jr., not a midshipman's warrant, but his argument before Navy Secretary William Graham was just as political as those who secured line commissions for constituents. Du Pont's father was a planter, a banker, and a key figure in Delaware affairs. Clayton felt a "deep anxiety" over the son's appointment. "The family of the Du Ponts has been the main stay and principal support of the Whig party in Delaware ever since its origin. . . . I know that the Whigs of this section of the country would feel the appointment as one of the most gratifying to their wishes that could possibly be conferred. The office is a small one, but the gratitude which would be felt by us all, for such a favor to one of the Du Ponts, would be measured, not merely by the extent of the benefit it would bring with it to him, but by the high estimate placed upon his merits and those of his relatives." Clayton to Graham, October 5, 1851, *The Papers of William A. Graham*, ed. J. de R. Hamilton, IV, 207–208.

year one man paid no less than $1,700 to secure an appointment for his step-son.[13] Future naval officers learned, as one lieutenant put it in 1882, "the necessity of having influential (*Anglice*, political) friends on the same day that they sought appointment to the Academy." Unsuccessful applicants, such as young William Horn, learned that lesson as well. In 1862 Horn applied to his Congressman for an appointment to Annapolis and was told by that public servant that he had "promised his most intimate friends to use his influence to get appointments for their sons." Disappointed, Horn appealed to the Secretary of the Navy, Gideon Welles, for one of the "at large" appointments.[14] But the lack of political power on the local level could not be overcome by a similar lack of influence in Washington, and young Horn was compelled to choose another career.

Needless to say, there were complaints. The dispensing of appointments troubled those who favored a more competitive selection process. In 1872 Henry Barnard recommended competitive entrance examinations. Several years later Captain Richard W. Meade, 3rd, complained that the absence of such an apolitical selection process resulted in low admission standards, "much lower than they should be in justice to the country and the amount of money annually disbursed. . . . " But neither Barnard, nor Meade, nor anyone else could shake the patronage system of recruitment in the Gilded Age. As one such reformer put it in 1879:

> To argue that cadets should be appointed to the Naval Academy upon competitive examinations is to waste breath in asserting what everyone knows to be true, and what everyone also knows political patronage will never permit.

As late as 1890 Senator John Logan could still charge that the result of the government's system of officer candidate selection had been to constitute the Navy and the Army "the closest corporations in the country."[15] In the twentieth century competitive exams became the rule, but Congressmen often used them as only one of many criteria. Patronage is still an important consideration. The naval aristocracy has become more of an aristocracy of merit than one of upper class wealth or family, but wealth and family often amount to "merit"; the sons of upper-middle-class doctors, lawyers, businessmen, or government officials have an obvious cultural and educational edge on their less advantaged competitors.

The Social Origins of the Candidates

Samuel Huntingdon and James D. Atkinson have claimed that cadets and midshipmen of the nineteenth century were "a cross-section of middle-class America," a "mirror of the nation." "Representative of everyone," the Academy was "affiliated with no one."[16] These statements require considerable qualification.

When each candidate entered the nineteenth-century Naval Academy, his home town and his father's occupation were entered opposite his name in a

8   formal Academy Register of Candidates. These registers, along with nomination and testimonial letters for "at large" candidates, have been deposited with the National Archives. I compared the size of each candidate's home community and the occupation of his father to similar data for mature heads of households contained in nineteenth-century census returns, and the results do not bear out the claims of Huntington and Atkinson—at least not for the Naval Academy.

Only about one in every ten Americans in the mid-nineteenth century lived in a metropolitan center of over 100,000 population. But more than 30% of officer candidates entering the Academy between 1847 and 1880 were from such communities, and they were *rarely* from "the other side of the tracks."

Nearly half had attended private schools before reaching Annapolis.[17] Their parents could easily afford it, for over half of those who entered Annapolis between the Mexican War and World War I were the sons of bankers, manufacturers, merchants, judges, Congressmen, diplomats, and attorneys. Another one in every six was the son of a physician, dentist, druggist, civil engineer, educator, artist, or clergyman. And about one in every ten was the son of an officer himself. Another one in ten was the son of a planter, farmer, or rancher, often in years when agrarian heads of household outnumbered the rest of the population (see Table 1-1). Only about one in every seven nineteenth-century and one in every five twentieth-century Annapolites were the sons of small shopkeepers, salaried clerks, mechanics, or artisans who had not yet made their

Table 1-1   Officer candidates from agricultural backgrounds, 1847–1925, compared to percentage of all heads of household in nation engaged in agricultural pursuits*

Inclusive years	(no. sampled)** (less widows)	Percentage entering	Number	National percentage
1847–1860	(258)	14.7	(38)	61
1861–1865	(519)	7.1	(37)	55.8
1866–1884	(491)	9.8	(48)	50
1885–1900	(292)	13.3	(34)	37.5
1901–1925	(483)	8.5	(41)	18.8
Average, 1847–1925	(2,043)	9.7	(198)	44.6

* U.S. Bureau of Census, *Historical Statistics of the United States, Colonial Times to 1957* (Wash., 1960), 72.
**These and similar samples in other tables throughout Chapters 1 and 2 have been drawn from Register of Candidates, U.S. Naval Academy, R.G. 405, N.A.

way into the ranks of the commercial or manufacturing elite. And less than one in a hundred was the son of an unskilled factory operative or unpropertied agricultural laborer, although these were the livelihoods of no less than 51% of mature American males in 1870. When the fathers of candidates entering between 1847 and 1900 are compared with a cross-section of mature American heads of household drawn from the 1870 census (see Table 1-2), it becomes clear that the commercial, manufacturing and professional classes were overrepresented at Annapolis, and that the agricultural interests and the working classes were underrepresented.

William A. Williams has recently argued that agricultural interests were in the vanguard of the expansionist movement of nineteenth-century American diplomatic and naval policies.[18] While Williams has clearly demonstrated that many *leaders* of the agricultural community favored the expansion and protection of American markets overseas, he has not demonstrated that the *typical* farmer was especially concerned with such matters. It may have been in the nature of farm society for local matters to have counted for a great deal more than international affairs—even those international affairs which ultimately

Table 1-2   Officer candidates, 1847–1900, segregated by fathers' occupation, compared to cross-section of mature* male national work force, drawn from the 1870 census**

Fathers' occupation Total sample: 1,560 (widows are excluded)	Percentage of candidates appointed	Percentage of Mature male work force, 1870	Ratio of columns 2 & 3
Officer (161)	10.3	.03	343.3
Banker (86)	5.5	.15	36.6
Attorney, judge (194)***	12.4	.5	24.8
Manufacturer (114)	7.3	.5	14.6
Government official (123)***	7.9	.6	13.1
Physician, druggist, civil engineer (150)	9.6	1.1	8.7
Merchant (282)	18.1	2.5	7.2
Clergyman, educator, artist (80)	5.1	1.1	4.6
Shopkeeper, agent,*** hotelkeeper (111)	7.1	2	3.6
Artisan, clerk (104)***	6.5	skilled—10 unemp. &—30.2 unskilled total—40.2	.65
Planter, farmer,*** rancher (157)	10.0	prop. farmers—30 agri. laborers—21 total—51	.30 .19

* Extrapolated from census figures for males 16 years of age and older, and adjusted for occupations such as physician, judge, or manufacturer with a greater proportion of older members, and for occupations such as artisan, clerk, or agricultural laborer, which contained a disproportionate number of younger persons.
** U.S. Bureau of Census, *Ninth Census*, Vol. III, *The Statistics of the Wealth and Industries of the United States* (Wash., 1872), 797–843.
*** Analysis of the 483 officer candidates appointed in 1915 and 1925 reveals a slight decrease in the percentage of those whose fathers were farmers (corresponding to the general decrease in the national percentage of farmers), attorneys, and government officials, and a virtual doubling of the percentage (from 14.2 to 25.4) of those whose fathers were artisans, clerks, or shopkeepers. Perhaps the tripling of the size of the Academy between 1900 and 1920 resulted in a saturation of the upper and upper-middle class sources of officer candidates; perhaps the increased use of competitive exams explains the increases in middle and working class origins. I don't know which is more likely.

affected farm prices. It may also have been that the levels of educational and occupational aspirations among nineteenth-century small-scale farmers and their sons were lower than those of large-scale agribusinessmen or those of more urban youths and their parents, a phenomenon that Lee Burchinal has documented in the mid-twentieth century.[19] In any event, comparatively few farm boys sought, or were encouraged to seek, appointment to the Navy, the

10   Guardian of American overseas commerce. Large-scale farmers, planters, and ranchers, integrated with the modern financial, technological, and commercial ways of the national and international marketplace, appear to have looked upon the Navy with favor,[20] and it seems reasonable to suppose that it was the sons of these agribusinessmen who were drawn to Annapolis. It is what one would expect given the social origins of the rest of the student body at that institution.*

⟩   This brings me to my next point: The midshipmen of nineteenth-century Annapolis were drawn from the commercial, industrial, and professional elite of the nation. As one officer candidate put it to his younger brother in 1847, Academy appointments were "conferred upon the sons of influence and wealth" as "a natural consequence." Lieutenant John T. Wood, an Academy instructor, noted in his diary in 1860 that "the sons of quite a number of prominent men are now entering the Academy." Typical was the "young gentleman" whose father was styled "dealer in ivory," "grain merchant," "cotton textile manufacturer," "bank president," "M.C. [Member of Congress]," or, in the case of Herbert Woodman of the class of 1875, simply "capitalist."[21]

Sons of hotelkeepers, clerks, railroad agents, jewelers, machinists, wheelwrights, and postmasters there were, to be sure, though these may have been from the elite of their particular field. Not every Congressional district had a plethora of bankers' sons in pursuit of a naval commission. Many communities had a surplus of more mundane middle- and upper-middle class occupations to be recognized. Stuart Blumin and Michael Katz have analyzed urban (Philadelphia) and small town (Hamilton, Ontario) occupations in the 1850s and '60s and have found that several theoretically "middle-class" and "working-class" occupations like "brickmaker," "cabinetmaker," "hotelkeeper," "jeweler," "druggist," "agent," and "machinist" contained a considerable number of wealthy members. It is quite possible, and I think likely (though I have only traced a few dozen such individuals and consequently cannot claim a sufficient sample to constitute proof), that the hotelkeepers and brickmakers who sent their sons to the Naval Academy (and there were many in these prestige trades) were often just as wealthy as their banker-attorney-importer counterparts.

Applications and nominations of boys of more humble homes *can* be found, in the Secretary of the Navy's "at large" file, but relatively few such requests were honored. Their fathers (or, more often, their widowed mothers) simply didn't have sufficient political pull. Unless they were officers' sons, "at large" applicants were not likely to be invited to report to Annapolis, and if an occasional son of the "common folk" *did* manage to secure an appointment, upon his arrival at the Academy he faced an interviewing board in search of "good moral character" during which "the personal impression counted heavily."[22] He then faced a demanding Academy Board entrance exam, similar

---

* It is also what one would expect by analogy to the officer corps of other modern navies. For example, the social origins of Prussian and late nineteenth-century German army officers are clearly agrarian, whereas those of German naval officers in the same years are more commercial and professional. See Jonathan Steinberg, *Yesterday's Deterrent: Tirpitz and the Birth of the German Battle Fleet* (London, 1965).

to the competitive examination offered in the early twentieth century. Those
unversed in algebra, geography, grammar, and the like—a function of their
social background—rarely passed. No less than one in every seven who had
secured appointments failed to pass the entrance exams and were sent home,
and those who failed were disproportionately agrarian, middle class, or working
class (see Table 1-3).

Table 1-3 Percentage of officer candidates, 1847–1880, who received letters
of appointment but failed to pass Academy entrance exams, ranked by fathers'
occupation (based on a sample of 1,307)

Overall average failing entrance exams (191)   14.7%

Fathers' occupation	Percentage failing entrance exams	
Artisan, clerk (78)	29.5	(23)
Shopkeeper, agent, hotelkeeper (83)	20.5	(17)
Widow (142)	20.4	(29)
Farmer, planter, rancher (112)	17.9	(20)
Clergy, educator, artist (64)	14.1	(9)
Manufacturer (88)	13.6	(12)
Doctor, druggist, civil engineer (117)	12.8	(15)
Government official (96)	11.5	(11)
Merchant (218)	11.5	(25)
Officer (126)	11.1	(14)
Banker (66)	7.6	(5)
Attorney, judge (153)	7.2	(11)

One means of measuring the status of Annapolis students would be to compare them to the nation's business and political elite of their age. Frances
Gregory, Irene Neu, and William Miller have provided profiles of the social
origins of these elites in mid- and late nineteenth-century America,[23] and their
findings may be compared to my own. Business elites, political leaders, and
prospective naval officers were all more Northern than the national average (a
function of the Civil War), but business elites and Annapolis students were
more urban than were their political counterparts.* Alfred Vagts has suggested
that naval officers were a reflection of the social class of the political men from
whom they secured appointments, and he is probably very close to the mark,
though it may be possible to get a little closer. The fathers of naval officers were
more professional than were those of either late nineteenth-century business or
political elites, and they were more commercial and less agrarian than were
political leaders, though the differences are less significant than the differences

* No less than 31% of Annapolis students, entering between 1847 and 1880, and "more
than 20%" of William Miller's business leaders of 1900 were from cities with a mid-
nineteenth century population of 100,000 or more, whereas 75% of his political leaders in
1900 were from rural communities with populations of less than 2,500. Miller, ed., *Men
in Business* (N.Y., 1962), 324.

between all three groups and the cross-section of the mature male population in 1870 (see Table 1-4). Apparently naval officer candidates were drawn from a particularly "Navy-minded" elite that possessed many of the qualities of business and political elites, but was somewhat distinct from both.

Another means of measuring the status of nineteenth-century Annapolis students would be to compare their parents' wealth with data compiled by Merle Curti, Michael Katz, Roberty Doherty, and Stuart Blumin on the amount of wealth held by different layers of society in a variety of mid-nineteenth century American communities. I have traced about a dozen fathers of nineteenth-century Annapolites through the census to determine what they were

Table 1-4 Business leaders, naval officer candidates, and political leaders by fathers' occupation, compared to cross-section of mature male work force, 1870

Fathers' Occupation	National Profile, 1870	Miller's Political Leaders 1900	Officer Candidates (1847–1900)	Gregory-Neu "Industrial Elite," 1870	Miller's Business Leaders 1900
Businessman	5.5%	33%	37.7%	51%	55.5%
Professional	2.7	18	27.4	13	22.5
Farmer	51	38	10.0	25	13
Government Official	.6	9	18.2	3	7
Worker	40.2	2	6.5	8	2

worth, but I suspended that frequently unrewarding* pastime when it struck me that I might be able to use the rankings of occupation-by-wealth-holding compiled by Blumin, Doherty, and Katz to extrapolate an approximate wealth-holding profile for the fathers of Academy appointees. This extrapolation, when coupled with the bits and pieces of "hard" data I was able to uncover, appears to be directly correlated to the wealth-holding profiles (see Table 1-5). That is, those with certain "prestige" occupations who tended to monopolize their communities' wealth also possessed and exercised an ability to acquire for their sons a comparably disproportionate share of Annapolis appointments. In *that* sense Samuel Huntington was right; the Academy *was* a "mirror of the nation." But it reflected property, not people.

However, I don't know whether the typical appointee's father belonged to the upper 1%, the upper 5%, or only the upper 10% or 15% of the nation's wealth-holding families. More significant than the precise degree of wealth are the occupations themselves. It matters little whether a naval officer was the son of a merchant, manufacturer, judge, or banker worth $50,000 or $500,000. What is significant is that he was *rarely* the son of a grocer, clerk, or small-scale farmer worth $500 or $5,000 and that he was almost *never* the son of a factory operative or agricultural laborer worth nothing beyond his take-home pay. It would be interesting to know whether the naval aristocracy were the scions of the upper classes or of the upper-middle classes in the nineteenth century, but

---

* I had very few street addresses, and most census data are not alphabetical.

it seems more important to know that they were the sons of merchants rather than farmers, cosmopolitans rather than locals.

Annapolis has been called "the gangway to the quarterdeck," and indeed it was. But for many years it was the *only* gangway to the quarterdeck. Harold Langley has intimated that an enlisted man was free to rise to commissioned rank after 1862, but this was true only of the 1860s. Several enlisted men and civilians were given temporary or "acting" appointments during the Civil War in accordance with the Act of July 16, 1862, but this practice was formally abolished by the Act of July 15, 1870, by which time most of the temporary appointments had already been withdrawn. These volunteers were regarded by naval aristocrats as "*outsiders,* that no power can make officers of," "*tres communs et inferieurs.*"[24] The 1879 "act to abolish the Volunteer Navy of the United States" eliminated most of the rest of these "mustangs." A handful of "Navy apprentice boys" were given appointments to the Academy during the administration of Navy Secretary Gideon Welles, from 1863 to 1868. A total of nine of these individuals graduated, and three later rose to flag rank. But this exception appears to have been a war measure and was discontinued in 1869. Less than 1% of U.S. naval officers between 1845 and 1915 rose from the ranks. The Spanish-American War brought a number of volunteer or "militia" officers into the Service for the duration, but their careers were extremely precarious—and brief. One such volunteer recalled that "every [regular line] officer in the service had a kind of dread of us." Regular Annapolis graduates regarded the slightest Congressional consideration shown these volunteers as "manifestly an unjust discrimination against [Annapolis officers and officer candidates]." Enlisted men were clearly excluded from this small coterie of 1898 "mustangs." As late as 1898 an observer noted that "no enlisted man" in America could ever "hope to become a commissioned officer." British and European navies commissioned a number of exceptional tarpaulins in the nineteenth century; it was only republican Uncle Sam who denied Jack a commission.[25]

As the ships of the "new Navy" began sliding off the ways at the end of the century, however, it became more difficult for the naval aristocracy to justify the exclusiveness of its membership, though it tried. Ensigns and rear admirals fought the common foe—those advocating opportunities for enlisted personnel to earn commissions. The first blow fell in March 1901, when the government provided that as many as six warrant officers might be appointed to the lofty rank of ensign each year, *if* vacancies existed in that rank after the commissioning of all Academy graduates. The more substantial breakthrough did not come until 1914, when the "democrat with the small 'd,'" Josephus Daniels, held the post of Secretary of the Navy. The *Army and Navy Journal* reminded Daniels of "the necessity of governing Navy appointments in some measure by the rules prevailing in social clubs," but Daniels ignored the advice; the "closed corporation" was compelled to open its doors. With the Act of June 30, 1914, provision was made for the selection of as many as fifteen enlisted men per year for

Table 1-5 Mid-nineteenth century wealth-holding profiles, rankings of occupations by wealth-holding, and profile of percentage of candidates by fathers' occupation (1847–1900)

	Curti's Trempealeau County, Wisconsin, 1860[1]		Doherty's 5 New England towns, 1860[2]		Katz's Hamilton, Ontario, 1852[3]		Blumin's Philadelphia, 1860[4]	
	Percentage of population	Percentage of wealth held	Percentage of population	Percentage of wealth held	Percentage of population	Percentage of wealth held	Percentage of population	Percentage of wealth held
			Top 1	25	Top 1	21.3	Top 1	50
					Top 5	46.8		
	Top 10	38.8	Top 10	70	Top 10	61.9	Top 10	89
	2nd 10	15.3	2nd 10	14	2nd 10	13.1	2nd 10	8
	3rd 10	11.4	3rd 10	10	3rd 10	8 (approx.)		
	Bottom 70	34.5	Bottom 70	6	Bottom 70	17 (approx.)	Bottom 80	3

Blumin's[5] ranking of occupations by wealth-holding, Philadelphia, 1860	Percentage of fathers of officer candidates, by occupation	Percentage of mature male work force represented in each group of fathers in 1870
1. Merchant	Percentage from top 7 of Blumin's occupations plus bankers — 47.2	4.75
2. Attorney		
3. Physician		
4. Jeweler		
5. Broker		
6. Manufacturer		
7. Druggist		
8. Agent	Percentage of officers & government officials — 19.0	.63
9. Saddler		
10. Tanner	Percentage of agents, clergy, teachers, shopkeepers — 12.2	3.10
11. Brickmaker		
12. Cabinetmaker	Percentage of planters, farmers, ranchers — 10.0	30
13. Grocer		
14. Bricklayer	Percentage of skilled artisans — 6.0	10
15. Stonekeeper		
16. Carpenter		
17. Teacher	Percentage of others — .5	51.2
18. Machinist and 33 others		

[1] *The Making of an American Community* (N.Y. 1959), Table 9.
[2] Robert Doherty, *Society and Power* (mss.). 96–108.
[3] M. Katz, "Social Structure in Hamilton, Ontario," in Steven Thernstrom & Richard Sennett, eds., *Ninteeenth Century Cities* (New Haven, 1969), 212.
[4] S. Blumin, "Mobility and Change in Ante-bellum Philadelphia," in Thernstrom & Sennett, *op. cit.*, 204.
[5] Blumin, 168–169. See also rankings in Doherty, 108; and Katz, 224–228.

16   admission to Annapolis; thereafter the number grew.* But the recruitment of naval officers remained in the Academy family—that is, until 1925. In that year the naval aristocracy was forced to accept the permanent establishment of the naval reserve officer. Mahan's messmates would never again be quite the same.[26]

By the twentieth century Congressmen had begun to offer competitive examinations as a criterion for entry into the Academy, and in 1940 Commander Leland P. Lovette, the Navy's Chief Public Information Officer, denied that there was any class consciousness at Annapolis. But the fact remains, as recent surveys of the social origins of twentieth century officers demonstrate, that Annapolis continues to attract a higher social class of candidates than the other services. And if the quarterdeck became somewhat less exclusive in the early twentieth century, the Academy still did not have a black or Jewish graduate when World War II began. Visitors to Annapolis in the 1880s were shown the spot in the Academy messhall where Midshipman Hood of Alabama had broken a chair over the head of one black midshipman in Reconstruction days. Hood had simply explained that the black midshipman had "sassed" him. When another Afro-American was nominated to the Academy in 1897, Captain Phillip Cooper, the Academy's superintendent at the time, advised Navy Secretary John D. Long that the candidate would "not of course be *persona grata* with other cadets," but would "lead a solitary and forlorn existence in social relations." No black candidate managed to survive such "coventry" and its attendant abuses. The Academy's Surgeon reported in 1895 that the "great majority" of Annapolis "naval cadets," or "midshipmen," as they were variously termed over the years, had been blond or brown-haired, blue-eyed, "Anglo-Saxon and Teutonic" specimens and they continued to bear those features for several decades thereafter.[27]

Choosing Annapolis

A consideration of the social origins of officer candidates suggests that financial, commercial, industrial, and professional parents provided a more appropriate milieu for the choice of a naval career than did agrarian, white collar, or working class families. But this does not explain why particular individuals chose to seek a commission rather than to pursue a career in business, law, or medicine. To understand individual career decisions requires the use of different and more complex information, information too often unavailable to the modern researcher—psychological data that I would not be qualified to evaluate even if it were to be made available. But persuaded as I am that psychohistory has few qualified practitioners at present anyway, I am willing to venture a few tentative observations concerning the nature of the process of choosing Annapolis.

* Daniels may have been taking a page from the British; The Admiralty began commissioning ex-enlisted personnel on a regular basis in 1912. Stephen Roskill, *Naval Policy Between the Wars* (London, 1968), 120n and 121n.

Unlike British experience, wherein the gentry and nobility continued to send second sons into military service or the ministry, Annapolis never became a haven for younger sons. Primogeniture being neither law nor custom in mid-nineteenth-century America, the order of birth was irrelevant. In several instances, families dispatched the sum of their male offspring to the two warrior colleges. The brothers of William Reynolds went to West Point; he joined the Navy as a midshipman. Both Sands brothers, Benjamin and Joshua, became naval officers. Albert Kautz's brother became a general; he became an admiral. All three Remey brothers went to Annapolis. Alfred Mahan and one younger brother went to the Academy; another younger brother stayed with his father at West Point and became an Army officer. Arthur MacArthur, Jr., became a midshipman; his brother Douglas followed in his father's footsteps as a West Point cadet. Charles Sperry went to Annapolis; his brother Mark went to West Point.[28]

Unless the father was a naval officer or an impoverished postbellum Southern aristocrat there was no obvious reason that a family would want to send its son to Annapolis. Often the parents disapproved of the move, considering a naval career to be somewhat below their expectations for their sons.[29] Apparently the candidates made the choice themselves in many cases. (Only two officers later recalled that God had suggested Annapolis, or had helped them win entry.)[30]

The reasons given for choosing Annapolis were generally militaristic, in Alfred Vagt's sense of the meaning of that word. Many had experienced brief contact with ships, sailors, or naval officers. William Parker visited a ship at the age of 14 and was attracted to the uniforms and the aroma of pitch and tar. James H. Clark sought an appointment because "I had relations that have fought in every great war the United States ever fought." William C. Cramer explained:

> My father having command of a barque, I often during vacation take a voyage with him, & endeavor to imitate & inure myself to the life of a sailor. I am sixteen years old. . . .

John Sanford Barnes was similarly impressed by "all the splendor of gold lace and gilt buttons." Others, like George W. DeLong, Charles Stewart, John McIntosh Kell, Alfred Mahan, and French Endor Chadwick, "fell in with some tales of naval exploits of the War of 1812, which recounted the heroism of young midshipmen," or read the novels of Captain Frederick Marryat, R.N., particularly his *Peter Simple* (1834) and *Mr. Midshipman Easy* (1836). "Marryat's novels made me yearn for . . . the Navy," George DeLong, for one, recalled. Many read the *Lives of Distinguished American Naval Officers* and the *Naval History of the United States*, both by James Fenimore Cooper, himself an ex-midshipman, in one of their several editions. Commander Allan Brown's fictional hero, "Jack Haultaut, Midshipman, U.S.N.," read both Marryat and Cooper "on the sly," and "Jack" was probably characteristic. But Cooper and

18   Marryat were not the only authors of the early and mid-nineteenth century to intone the virtues of naval life. There were many inexpensive novels of naval duty and histories, such as "Flexible Grummet's" *Log* or Barber Badger's *Naval Temple*. Alfred Mahan, whose father was a professor of Army Tactics and Engineering at West Point, may have been unique in finding the Britisher Colburn's *United Service Magazine* available, but he was not unique in his recollection of how he had been "possessed" by "the sight of all things naval" as a boy. Francis Chew remembered that accounts of Commodore Perry's trip to Japan had first stirred him to interest in the Navy. His "head was completely turned" by illustrations of warships and "showy uniforms." And Ernest J. King recalled that a story in *Youth's Companion* of life at the Naval Academy had prompted him to seek an Annapolis appointment.[31]

Some who went to the Naval Academy during the Civil War, when it was moved temporarily to Newport, Rhode Island, later recalled that "the determining motive" in their choice of college and subsequent profession had been "the immediate chance of getting into active service against the rebels,"[32] but since this action tended to take them *away* from the war for at least three years and does not explain why they did not select West Point or join the volunteer army or navy, these explanations seem inadequate.

Perhaps the lure of the bounding main and a gold-braided sleeve was the key.* According to Charles H. Coates and Roland J. Pellegrin, teenagers impressed by the glamor of a military career tend to place naval officers on a higher level of status than do middle-aged persons.[33] Surely Admiral David D. Porter, who had been Superintendent of the Academy after the Civil War, was not far off the mark when he wrote in 1879 that "young men [enter] the navy . . . to obtain a livelihood in a pleasant profession [and] to obtain glory and promotion." But it is also possible that Commander Frederick Sawyer sensed a more basic motivation when he described "the secret ambition" of his 1898 messmates in Phillipine waters as the desire "to be a pirate."[34]

For some the Navy may have been the lesser of evils. Speaking from the hindsight of forty years of military judgments, Bowman McCalla claimed that he entered Annapolis because he felt he would "never have succeeded as a merchant." Others, like George Remey, may never have considered a naval career until their fathers were offered appointments for their sons.[35] In some cases the choice was undoubtedly made by the family rather than the son alone. And since the mother was primarily responsible for the education of her son, the decision often devolved upon her. This appears to have been the case with John Barnes, Bowman McCalla, and George Perkins and was probably true of others as well. Perhaps in these instances the naval career may have been considered a

---

* It isn't known how many twentieth-century midshipmen were raised on steady diets of such magazines as *Army and Navy Life* (1905–1908), *Uncle Sam's Magazine* (1909), or the various editions of the Navy League's *Journal*, but for those who were, the numerous short-stories, particularly in the first two publications, of young men giving their lives for their country with the name of their beloved on their lips, and of rich suitors rejected in lieu of navy lads, must have had an impact.

means of upward mobility,* while to clearly upper-class parents its was not so   **19**
much a step up or down as it was the assumption of a rigorous, low-income
profession that many may have been uncertain their sons would not eventually
tire of.† But since few records of this decision exist, we may never know why
many chose Annapolis, and we will have to be satisfied with understanding why
Annapolis chose them.

* For example, John Barnes (b. 1836) recalled that his mother "was proud of my Naval
career, my uniform, and the certain distinction which her mother's heart foresaw for me."
"My Egotistography," p. 118, Barnes Papers, N.Y.H.S. Cf. McCalla, "Memoirs," Ch. II, i;
Alden, *Perkins*, 10–11; Burchinal, *op. cit.*, 116, 118.

† Thus Mrs. Sarah Brown, upon hearing that her son Hamilton A. Brown had accepted
appointment to the Naval Academy, wrote him on February 16, 1854: "It has filled my
heart with the deepest sorrow, to part from my Dearest Boy for such a hazardous life
attended with so many trials and difficulty, dangers seen and unseen, and when there is no
nesesity [sic] now call for it." The boy's mother urged him to stay at home and manage his
father's vast estates. Hamilton Brown Papers, Southern Historical Collection, U. of N.C.
Library.

Chapter 1

1. Norbert Elias, "Studies in the Genesis of the Naval Profession," *British Journal of Sociology*, I (1950), 291–309; Halifax, *Rough Draught of a New Model at Sea* (London, 1694), *passim*.

2. Higginson to Treasury Secretary Oliver Wolcott, July 13, 1798, cited in Marshall Smelser, *Congress Builds a Navy, 1787–1798* (Notre Dame, Ind., 1959), 178.

3. Hazen, *Five Years Before the Mast* (2nd ed., New York, 1856), 283; T. W. Higginson, *Army Life in a Black Regiment* (Boston, 1870), 67.

4. See, for example, the careers of David Porter and his sons David Dixon Porter and William Porter and protege David Farragut, or the Bainbridge, Preble, Rodgers, or Trenchard families in the *Dictionary of American Biography*. Cf. Charles O. Paullin in the *Proceedings* of the United States Naval Institute [hereafter cited as *PUSNI*], XXXIII (1907), 632.

5. *American State Papers, Naval Affairs* (Wash., G.P.O., 1861), IV, 295–296.

6. Park Benjamin, *The United States Naval Academy* (New York and London, 1900), 350–353; 5 *U.S. Stat.* 788 (at 794) [Act of 3 March 1845]; 10 *U.S. Stat.* 100 (at 102) [Act of 31 Aug. 1852]; *Revised Statutes of the United States . . .* (Washington, G.P.O., 1875), Title XV, Chapter 5; 28 *U.S. Stat.* 136 [Act of 26 July 1894]; 12 *U.S. Stat.* 585 [Act of 16 July 1862]; 32 *U.S. Stat.* 1197 [Act of 3 March 1903, which increased the figures to two for each Congressman, Senator, and territorial representative.]

7. These data are drawn from the U.S. Naval Academy Graduate Association, *Register of Graduates* (Annapolis, 1916) and from *The Records of Living Officers of the U.S. Navy . . .*, ed. Lewis R. Hamersly (Philadelphia, 4th ed., 1890). Cf. Samuel P. Huntington, *The Soldier and the State* (Cambridge, Mass., 1954), 214; and Morris Janowitz, *The Professional Soldier: A Social and Political Portrait* (Glencoe, Ill., 1960), 86–88.

8. Rear Admiral Hilary P. Jones, cited in Rear Admiral Robert E. Coontz, *From*

20

the *Mississippi to the Sea* (Philadelphia, 1930), 56. See also Holden Evans, *One Man's Fight for a Better Navy* (New York, 1940), 5ff.

9. Robley D. Evans, *Captain's Log*, 12; *Records* . . ., ed. Hamersly, *passim*; Benjamin, *op.cit.*, 293. Rear Admiral John Hubbard of the Class of 1870 may have made a voyage similar to that of Evans: Hubbard was born and raised in Maine, but his appointment was from the Arizona Territory.

10. Among them, Francis A. Roe, Stephen B. Luce, Oscar Badger, William Truxton, James Jouett, Samuel Franklin, and the ill-fated Philip Spencer, hanged for his part in an alleged conspiracy to commit mutiny in 1843. *Complete Army and Navy Register* . . ., ed. Thomas Hamersly (N.Y., 1888); Burr, *Education*, 54. In 1842 Congress consequently provided legislation prohibiting the creation of further midshipmen until their number was reduced to 260. 5 *U.S. Stat.* 500 [Act of 4 Aug. 1842].

11. U.S. Naval Academy Association, *3rd Annual Reunion*, 1888 (Baltimore, 1889), 31; John S. Barnes, "My Egotistigraphy," typescript copy in J. S. Barnes Papers, New York Historical Society Manuscript Division [hereafter referred to as N.Y.H.S.], 21; Alice Trabue, *A Corner in Celebrities* (Louisville, Ky., 1922), 36; William F. Halsey, Jr., *Admiral Halsey's Story* (N.Y., 1947), 4. Cf. Marius Schoonmaker, "34 Years in the U.S. Navy: Life and Correspondence of Cornelius M. Schoonmaker," p. 5, Boxes 152 and 153, Naval Historical Foundation [hereafter referred to as N.H.F.], Manuscript Division, Library of Congress. Seventeen naval officers listed in the *Dictionary of American Biography* are described as having relatives in politics.

12. "An Admiral's Yarn" [Lanning autobiog.], 12, Naval War Coll. Archives; Denis Hart Mahan to Representative A. S. Murray, ?, 1856, Mahan Papers, N.H.F.; Captain Robley Evans, *A Captain's Log* (N.Y., 1901), 10; Rear Admiral Albert S. Barker, *Everyday Life in the Navy* (Boston, 1928), 1; Rear Admiral Charles E. Clark, *My Fifty Years in the Navy* (Boston, 1917), 1–30; Rear Admiral Caspar Goodrich, *Rope Yarns from the Old Navy* (New York, 1931), 2–4; Rear Admiral Franklin Hanford, *How I Entered the Navy* (Walton, N.Y., n.d. [in Rare Book Room, Navy Department Library, Washington, D.C.]), 14; Charles Mason Remey, *Reminiscences of His Childhood* (n.p., n.d., 4 typed volumes [copy in the State Historical Society of Wisconsin]), I, 14; General

Holland M. Smith, *Coral and Brass* (N.Y., 1948), 38.

13. 43rd Congress, 2nd Sess., *House Report No.* 124 [1875], 12.

14. Lieutenant "A. P. Mantus," *United Service*, V (1881), 52. Horn to Welles, ?, 1862, "At large" testimonials and letters, Correspondence concerning midshipmen, 1862–1911, R.G. 405, National Archives.

Commander Allan D. Brown's fictional character, "Jack Haultaut, Midshipman, U.S.N.," won his appointment to the Academy because "fortunately, Jack's father was well acquainted with Colonel Arkwright, the representative." *United Service*, XII (1882), 33.

15. Assistant Navy Secretary Gustavus V. Fox to Senator John W. Grimes, September 11, 1862, and September 22, 1862, in *The Confidential Correspondence of Gustavus Vasa Fox*, ed. Richard Wainright and J. Thompson (2 vols., N.Y., 1918–1919), II, 375, 386; Henry Barnard, *Military Schools and Courses of Instruction in the Science and Art of War* (New York, 1872), 922; Meade, "Essay on Naval Education," p. 12, Box II, R. W. Meade, 3rd, Papers, N.Y.H.S.; Goodrich, "Naval Education," *PUSNI*, V (1879), 327; Stephen Ambrose, *Duty, Honor, Country: A History of West Point* (Baltimore, 1966), 215–216.

16. Huntington, *op. cit.*, *227*; Atkinson, *The Edge of War* (Chicago, 1960), 63; U.S. Bureau of the Census, *Historical Statistics of the U.S.: Colonial Times to 1957* (Washington, G.P.O., 1960), 74. Morris Janowitz has also disagreed with Huntington on this score. See *The Professional Soldier: A Social and Political Portrait* (Glencoe, Ill., 1960), 80–81.

Atkinson's data on the occupations of fathers of West Point candidates between 1842 and 1925 refute his own claim. Fully 70% of these candidates were sons of business, government, or professional men in years when only about 1 of every 12 American breadwinners were so employed.

17. The pre-Academy midshipmen were also given a liberal dose of private education. (See Burr, *Education in the Early Navy*, 35ff., 147–165.) They were considered the "sons of gentlemen." Captain Charles H. Davis, *Life of Charles Henry Davis, Rear Admiral 1807–1877* (New York, 1899), 5–6.

18. W. A. Williams, *The Roots of the Modern American Empire* (N.Y., 1970).

19. Lee Burchinal, "Differences in Educational and Occupational Aspirations of

Farm, Small-Town, and City Boys," *Rural Sociology*, XXVI (1961), 107–121.

20. See Williams, *op. cit.*, *passim*; Thomas Coode, "Southern Congressmen and the American Naval Revolution, 1880–1898," *Alabama Historical Quarterly* (1968), 89–110; O. L. Burnette, "John T. Morgan and Expansionist Sentiment in the South," *Alabama Review* (1965), 163–182; and forthcoming dissertations by Gerald Burns and William Gay of the University of Pittsburgh, who are both analyzing a variety of social, economic, and legislative data relevant to an understanding of the nature of nineteenth-century American foreign policy.

21. West Point Cadet J. H. Duncan to his brother, W. P. S. Duncan, Sept. 17, 1847, William P. S. Duncan Papers, William Perkins Library, Duke University; Lieutenant John T. Wood Diary, Vol. I, p. 76a, University of North Carolina Library. Davis, *Life of Davis*, 4; Emma M. Maffitt, *The Life and Services of John Newland Maffitt* (New York and Washington, 1906), 30–31; Alfred Pirtle, *Life of James E. Jouett, Rear Admiral, U.S.N.* (Lousville, Ky., 1896), 1–10; Carroll S. Alden, *George H. Perkins, Commodore, U.S.N.* (Boston, 1914), 1; Rear Admiral Seaton Schroeder, *A Half Century of Naval Service* (New York, 1922), 2ff.; Rear Admiral Bowman McCalla, "Memoirs of a Naval Career," Unpublished autobiography, Navy Department Library, Washington, D.C., Chapter 1, 5; Rear Admiral Charles S. Sperry to Secretary of the Navy Meyer (personal), 27 January 1908, Sperry Papers, Library of Congress, Manuscript Division; Luis Kutner & Laurin Healy, *The Admiral* (Chicago, 1944), 301; Rear Admiral Hugh Rodman, *Yarns of a Kentucky Admiral* (Indianapolis, 1928), 14; *D.A.B.*, *passim*.

During the Civil War the Prince de Joinville, the son of ex-King Louis Phillipe, sent his son to the Academy. John C. Pegram, "Recollections of the U.S. Naval Academy," *Personal Narratives* of the Soldiers and Sailors Historical Society of Rhode Island, 4th Series, No. 14 (Providence, 1891).

The hero's father in Navy Chaplain Henry H. Clark's *The Admiral's Aid: A Story of Life in the New Navy* (New York, 1902), 15, was a prominent New York City investment banker with "European connections."

22. C. H. Foster, "The Requirements for Admission to the Naval Academy: An Historical Review," *PUSNI*, XLIV (1918), 339–353.

23. Gregory and Neu, "The American Industrial Elite in the 1870s: Their Social Origins," in *Men in Business*, ed. William Miller (Harper Torchbook ed., 1962), 194–211; Miller, "Historians and the Business Elite," *op. cit.*, 322–328; Vagts, *op. cit.*, 55n. Cf. C. Wright Mills, *The Power Elite* (New York, 1956), 181–182.

24. Captain William D. Puleston, *Annapolis: Gangway to the Quarterdeck* (New York, 1924); Harold Langley, *Social Reform in the U.S. Navy, 1798–1862* (Urbana, Ill., 1967), 279, 127; 16 *U.S. Stat.* 334 [Act of 15 July 1870]; Rear Admiral S. F. DuPont to his wife, Aug. 24, 1862 and Feb. 24, 1863, in *Samuel Francis DuPont: A Selection of His Civil War Letters*, ed. John D. Hayes (3 vols. Ithaca, 1969), II, 199, 452.

George Westinghouse (1844–1914), the famed inventor-entrepreneur, began his career as an acting 3rd assistant engineer in the Navy in 1864, but was mustered out after the war ended in 1865 because he was not of the "regular" Navy. "Westinghouse, George," *D.A.B.* His experience was typical of most Civil War "mustangs."

25. 20 *U.S. Stat.* 294 [Act of 15 February 1879]; U.S. Naval Academy Alumni Association, *Register of Alumni* (Annapolis, 1960), 23–30; Harold T. Weiand, "The History of the Development of the U.S. Naval Reserve, 1889–1914, Unpublished Ph.D. dissertation, University of Pittsburgh, 1953, 63; Captain John C. Watson to Senator William Lindsay, Feb. 10 and 14, 1899, John C. Watson Papers, Naval Historical Foundation; Duncan Cumming, "Promotion in the U.S. Navy," *Chambers's Journal*, 6th Series, LXXV (1898), 643. Cf. Letters of Resignation of Volunteer Officers, 1866–1875, Entry 85, Record Group 45, National Archives.

26. Ensign Nathan Twining to his brother Walter, ? 1901, Nathan Twining Papers, Manuscript Room, State Historical Society of Wisconsin; *The Papers of John Davis Long*, ed. Gardner Allen, Massachusetts Historical Society Collection, Vol. LXXVIII (Boston, 1939), 375n; 31 *U.S. Stat.* 1129 [Act of 3 March 1901]; 38 *U.S. Stat.* 410 [Act of 30 June 1914]; 43 *U.S. Stat.* 1080–1090 [Act of 25 Feb. 1925]; Wm. Braisted, *The U.S. Navy in the Pacific, 1909–1922* (Austin, 1971), 124.

The Marine Corps apparently was not as exclusive as the Navy. In 1916 as much as 17% of the officer corps had risen from the ranks. *Hearings before Committee on Naval Affairs of the House of Representatives on Estimates Submitted by the Secretary of the Navy, 1917* (Wash., G.P.O., 1917), 301.

27. Lovette, *School of the Sea* (Annapolis, 1940), 123–124; Janowitz, *Professional Soldier*, 90, 209; Robert Coontz, *True Anecdotes of an Admiral* (Philadelphia, 1935), 48; *Papers of Long*, ed. Allen, 18–19; Surgeon Henry G. Beyer, "The Growth of U.S. Naval Cadets," *PUSNI*, XXI (1895), 298; D. Edwin Lebby, "The Professional Socialization of the Naval Officer: The Effect of Plebe Year at the U.S. Naval Academy," unpub. Ph.D. dissertation, Univ. of Pennsylvania, 1970.

28. J. G. Rosengarten, *William Reynolds, Rear Admiral, U.S.N.* . . . (Philadelphia, 1880), 1–5; Albert Kautz Papers, Alfred T. Mahan Papers, and Charles Sperry Papers, L. of C. Twelve naval officers listed in the *Dictionary of American Biography* had brothers who were naval officers; four had brothers who were army officers. Apparently about one in every thirteen officers had a service brother.

29. In 1862 Midshipman Cornelius Schoonmaker boasted to his mother of the fine reputation his profession was enjoying and chided her: "Mother, what do you think of the Navy now? You never wanted me in it." Schoonmaker, "Life of Schoonmaker," p. 50, N.H.F. Cf. Emma DeLong, *Explorer's Wife* (N.Y., 1938), 7; *The Voyage of the "Jeanette": The Ship and Ice Journals of [Lieutenant] George DeLong*, ed. Emma DeLong (2 vols., Boston, 1883), I, 2; Commander Allan Brown, "Jack Haultaut, Midshipman, U.S.N.; or, Life at the Naval Academy," *United Service*, XII (1882), 32; "Reminiscences," p. 3, Francis T. Chew Papers, Southern Historical Collection, U. of N.C. Library.

30. Barker, *Everyday Life*, 1; Edward Arpee, *From Frigates to Flat-Tops* (privately printed, Lake Forest, Ill,. 1953), 8.

31. Captain William H. Parker, *Recollections of a Naval Officer, 1841–1865* (New York, 1883), 2; Barnes, "My Egotistography," p. 21, Barnes Papers, N.Y.H.S.; "At large" testimonial and nomination letters, 1862–1911, BuNav, R.G. 405, N.A.; *Voyage of "Jeanette,"* ed. DeLong, I, 2; DeLong, *Explorer's Wife*, 6; Charles Stewart to the Class of 1881, *4th Annual Report of the Class of 1881* (Baltimore, 1888), 56; Brown, *United Service*, XII (1882), 32; Albert Johannsen, *The House of Beadle and Adams* (2 vols. Norman, Okla., 1950), I, xxiv; Burr, *Education in the Early Navy*, 38–41; John McIntosh Kell, *Recollections of a Naval Life* (Washington, D.C., 1900), 136; "Chadwick, French Endor," *Dictionary of American Biography;* Rear Admiral Alfred Thayer Mahan, *From Sail to Steam* (New York, 1907), 71; "Reminiscences," p. 2, Francis Chew Papers, S.H.C., U. of N.C.L.: King, *King*, 14; Rear Admiral Rufus Zogbaum, *From Sail to "Saratoga": A Naval Autobiography* (Rome, 1961), 12, 20. Similarly John Lejeune, who was commissioned a marine officer upon leaving the Academy, recalled that he had been impressed by the spiffy appearance of the marine uniforms on a visit to a warship at the age of 13. Major General John Lejeune, *The Reminiscences of a Marine* (Philadelphia, 1930), 30. Cf. James Field, *America and the Mediterranean World, 1776–1882* (Princeton, 1969), 60.

32. Hanford, "How I Entered the Navy," p. 4, Navy Department Library; Goodrich, *Rope Yarns*, 2–4.

33. Coates and Pellegrin, *Military Sociology: A Study of American Military Institutions and Military Life* (College Park, Md., 1965), 46.

34. Porter, "Naval Education and Organization," *United Service*, I (1879), 471; Sawyer, *Sons of Gunboats* (Annapolis, 1946), 18. Cf. Henry H. Clark, *Admiral's Aid*, 14.

35. McCalla, "Memoirs," Ch. III, 3; Remey, *Reminiscences*, I, 14. For more on the naval officer's dissatisfaction with the world of the merchant see Chapter 5.

chapter 2

The Education of the Naval Officer*

My honor's free from stain or speck,
With pride I walk the quarter-deck;
The fore-most hands are at my beck,
For I'm a smart, young midshipman.

'The Young Midshipman," anonymous nineteenth-century naval song,
printed in Neeser, *American Naval Songs and Ballads.*

Hither we came with hearts of joy; with joy we now depart,
And give to each the honest grasp, which speaks a sailor's heart;
United all in solemn vows which can no breaking know,
For midshipmen can ne'er forget their Alma Mater, O!
One cheerful chorus, ring loud, we'll give before we go,
To the memory of Annapolis and our Alma Mater, O!

"The Naval Academy Graduate's Song," Robert Neeser, *American Naval
Songs and Ballads.*

The U.S. naval officer's "education" was a lifetime affair, but the training that
he received at the U.S. Naval Academy was particularly significant. At that
institution young men from every section of the country were shorn of local
and regional patterns of behavior and thought and clad indistinguishably in
new, more cosmopolitan ones, a process accelerated by the midshipmen themselves through the practice of "hazing." "Practical" know-how was crammed
into the midshipman's head. By the time he and his classmates joined their first
ships an unmistakable "esprit de corps" had developed.

*   *   *

* Since this chapter deals only with the education received by midshipmen at the
Naval Academy, some of the behavioral traits discussed herein will be treated at greater
length in a later chapter when the "naval mind" of the mature officer is examined.

Numbered footnotes for Chapter 2 begin on page 46.

Prior to 1851 the recruitment and training of officers was a business largely consigned to the commanders of the operating forces. "Young gentlemen," as midshipmen were called throughout the nineteenth century by their superiors, were assigned to ships subject to the whims of the Commanding Officers. Reporting in their early teens, they messed together in the stern and occupied an ambiguous position between commissioned officers and crew. Sometimes their duties consisted of little more than messenger of the watch for years until one of the ship's regular line officers was promoted, resigned, or died, at which time one of the ship's midshipmen was examined and "ranked". Promotion was speedier during the War of 1812 and the Mexican War than in peacetime. These pre-Academy officer candidates were "rough, riotous, and to the newcomer, merciless. If he didn't have a strong arm and a ready fist, woe betide him; for nothing but the law of might makes right prevailed."[1]

In 1845, largely through the efforts of Navy Secretary George Bancroft and Lieutenant Matthew Fountaine Maury, Congress created a naval school at Annapolis, Maryland. The first students, drawn from the existing body of midshipmen, arrived the same year. But it was not until 1851 that the four-year course was established for new recruits.[2] We are primarily concerned here with the post-1850 Naval Academy.

The Naval Academy, like the Military Academy at West Point, was an educational institution with a set of characteristics that immediately distinguished it from the civilian colleges of the mid-nineteenth century. At their inception West Point and Annapolis were quite similar in many ways to other existing academic institutions. But they had less propensity, or ability, to evolve. Service academy authorities saw no need for such innovations as elective courses. As one Army officer put it in 1917, "the great charm of West Point is that so many things never change." The service academy superintendent's primary mission was to create right-thinking military and naval leaders, not bachelors of art.[3]

Assimilation : A New Loyalty

The first thing the authorities sought to make clear to Naval Academy candidates and their parents was that acceptance of an appointment to the Academy was an act tantamount to a permanent severing of all civil and parental ties. John McIntosh Kell's mother was told by her Congressman upon Kell's acceptance of an appointment: "He now belongs to his country." Lieutenant Commander Francis A. Roe remarked in his 1865 textbook *Naval Duties and Discipline* that the young officer candidate had been "given away by the parent to the nation in tender years. . . . The child is literally given away to the State." In 1884 one father was told by the Academy's superintendent: "You have given up your son to the United States."[4]

Since many "young gentlemen" were not over-anxious to yield to this arrangement, the authorities at the Academy provided them with considerable encouragement to do so. The initial shock of isolation from familiar surroundings, coupled with the abrupt introduction to the routine of naval life, complete with identical quarters, cuisine, uniforms, and discipline, was fully exploited.[5] In the eyes of their mentors, the freshmen, or "4th classmen," were "strangers in a strange land," saplings "fresh from the nursery taking root in a new soil and gradually becoming acclimated in a wonderful garden not at all . . . like that to which [they have] been accustomed, but one wherein the twig will be uncommonly bent so as to insure an exceptional inclination of the tree."[6]

Service, Glory, Honor

Thereafter the authorities proceeded with indoctrination. Inasmuch as the Navy conceived of the candidate as "a grateful beneficiary of a government which has selected him for its present care, future honors, and lifelong consideration," simple obedience and subordination were expected and demanded.[7] The ultimate mission of the Academy was to provide the operating forces with leaders of unswerving loyalty prepared to carry out to the letter, if not beyond it, the naval policies of the Federal Government. To this end the midshipmen, or "naval cadets" as they were known for much of the late nineteenth century, were told that they were being "trained for no other purpose than to defend the tenets of the American way" and were imbued with the ceremonial symbols of "pure and holy patriotism." "From the time I came in as a plebe until I graduated," one officer recalled, "I was taught [that] that flag waving outside there was the only thing."

The candidate was "early impressed with the fact that his life is dedicated to his country, first and foremost," and that he had "renounced wealth and material gain." If the verb "renounce" connotes to some an action akin to religious celibacy, the connotation is not unwarranted, for the same officer who used it went on to say that the strong bond between Annapolis men was "based on a spirit similar [to] that [which] binds orders of priesthood together— a disciplined life maintained by regulations, customs, traditions, and devotion to a common cause. It is authoritarian," he added, somewhat unnecessarily.[8] Similarly Rear Admiral Albert P. Niblack told his son:[9]

> The naval profession is much like the ministry. You dedicate your life to a purpose. You wear the garb of an organized profession. Your life is governed by rules laid down by the organization. You renounce your pursuit of wealth. In a large measure you surrender your citizenship; renounce politics; and work for the highest good of the organization.

A number of officers conveyed the same impression when they suggested that they had been "called" to the Service, or that they viewed the Navy as their 'calling."[10] "To the Navy the uniform is its vestment and ceremony," Commander W. W. Phelps maintained. Rear Admiral David Potter claimed that a "Gospel" of governmental service had been created at Annapolis. And the personal correspondence of Rear Admirals George Balch and A. H. Johnson in the 1870s jocularly confirmed this. These two admirals addressed one another

26   as "Episcopal Bishop," and spoke of naval officers as "our good missionaries, now scattered over the habitable globe." When Balch was named Superintendent of the Naval Academy in 1879, there came a letter from Johnson, congratulating him on his being named to preside over "the renowned seat of learning of our Church of the Propaganda." Captain E. P. Jessop described the "soul of the service" in these same religious terms when he urged that the midshipmen be given still additional training in order to inspire "that indefinable something which lifts [the Navy] above greed, avarice, self-seeking, all commerciality, and makes us glad to take as our reward for services rendered the approbation of the cloth."[11]   ✓

For naval men "of the cloth," who viewed themselves as "called" to a life of "Service," wealth and material gain were not only "renounced," but generally unavailable.[12] Accordingly, the business world was frequently juxtaposed to the world of naval service. Thus Lieutenant Commander Roe described the dichotomy in terms of the special training naval officers had received at the Academy which set them "apart from . . . other men. And hence it is," he added, "that the naval officer is rendered so unfit for the pursuits and business of civil life."[13] While this was not exactly true—officers who resigned or were retired often did very well in commerce and industry—the point is that it was believed to be the case by the priesthood of the sea.

In place of the dollar, the midshipman was told of other virtues. Captain Mahan, discussing "The Navy as a Career," admitted that "[i]n no event will there be money in it," but spoke of "honor and quietness of mind and worthy occupation" which, he maintained, were "better guarantees of happiness." Similarly Rear Admiral Yates Stirling, in explaining "How to be a Naval Officer," described the life as "one vague, romantic jumble," but warned that those in search of a life of wealth or contemplation "might as well forget about the Navy." The Navy's system of promotion by seniority and the relative security of one's commission were stressed. In the days before the 1946 Maximum Employment Act, when many viewed job security as a key factor in the choice of a career, Admiral Stirling's assurance— "You can be dismissed neither by politics nor business conditions"*—must have been gratifying.[14] One anonymous naval cadet, writing in 1882, boasted that his future in the Navy would be "certain, for with ordinary good health [I am] almost sure to reach positions of honor, trust, and responsibility. . . . How many in civil life," he asked, "however fair their prospects, can say as much?" And there were those who regarded with awe the prestige attendant on the bearer of a naval commission. In 1854 one officer candidate was told that there was "not much prospect of a young man's getting rich" in the Service, "but it always insures him a position in good society."[15]

Academy authorities did what they could, then, to make the midshipman

---

* Stirling went on to say that "world disarmament alone can affect you," which goes a long way toward explaining the naval officer's attitude toward disarmament and arbitration, a subject we will deal with in a later chapter.

conscious of his other-worldliness. Commander Benjamin Totten's *Naval Text-Book . . . for the use of the Midshipmen of the U.S. Navy* drew a "wide distinction" between the civilian world, with its rhetoric of egalitarianism, and the military world, with its authoritarianism and rank. As one student of the Naval Academy put it:

> You listened to so many lectures admonishing you *not* to consider yourself superior to a civilian that you found yourself feeling that you really *were* a cut above, but it would be improper to show that you thought so.

Midshipman Alfred Mahan was speaking only partly in jest when he wrote to a friend from the Academy: "My military imagination rarely permits me to recognize, or rather, to realize, the existence of such an order of beings as civilians."[16]

Much of this value transmission occurred as a result of in-class contact between midshipmen and officer instructors and out-of-class contacts with these officers and their families at their Academy homes, but the task was not left to the Service alone. Impressive speakers could always be counted on to appear regularly at the Academy to tell the young "naval aristocracy"[17] of the grand "fraternity and affection springing from comradeship in arms" or of the respect in society for "a fine military air" or of their satisfaction that the naval officer's career was "beyond barter and above price, what no multi-millionaire could purchase and no 'trust' could own. . . . "[18] As one officer explained:[19]

> It makes a great impression upon youth when a man like Theodore Roosevelt tells the midshipmen . . . "No other body of young men has . . . as great a chance as each of you to lead a life of honor to himself and to be of benefit to the country at large."

Self-distinction, or "glory," and identification with a grand institution and its traditions may have been the Navy's best substitutes for wealth. Admiral David D. Porter, it will be recalled, felt that young Americans sought "glory and promotion" at the Academy; and Porter, who was the superintendent of the school himself in the late 1860s, considered these motives quite appropriate. As early as 1862 he wrote of his hope to "get the right set of officers into the Navy" after the war ended. "A new era should be instituted," he told Assistant Secretary Gustavus Fox, and added, "we need fearless, dashing men."[20] Captain Reginald R. Belknap felt that the young Annapolites should realize that they had become "members of a distinct race of high traditions, which they are expected to know and fulfill," and Captain Augustus P. Cooke told an 1889 reunion of the Naval Academy Graduates Association: "The birthright of the graduates of the Naval Academy is an immortality of fame." The Navy's hallowed dead—John Paul Jones, Stephen Decatur, James Lawrence, William Bainbridge, David Porter, Oliver Hazard Perry, John Rodgers, and after the Civil War, William Cushing and David Farragut—a litany of saints, were constantly exalted.[21] In fact, in 1905, what were believed to be the remains of John Paul Jones were shipped to Annapolis for interment in the new Academy

Left—The U.S. Navy's officer-gentlemen were sometimes styled "the naval aristocracy," partly because of their self-perpetuating habits, lampooned in this caricature by Midshipman George Gibbs, class of 1890, from an 1889 Academy yearbook (George Gibbs, ed., *Junk*, Baltimore, 1889).

Above—One version of "hazing" (midshipman-controlled value inculcation see page 39) in the late nineteenth century as depicted by Midshipman Gibbs (George Gibbs, ed., *Junk*, Baltimore, 1889).

Prominent national figures played a significant role in the process of midshipman socialization. Here President Theodore Roosevelt addresses the assembled officer candidates, circa 1905 (BuShips 9860, National Archives).

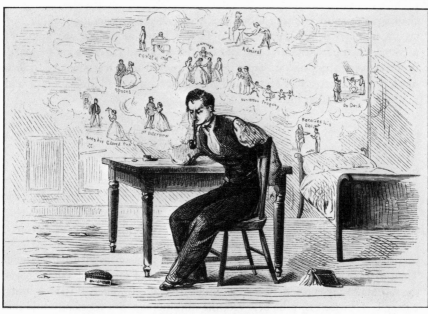

Day-dreams. The Pleasures of Hope,

This midshipman, dreaming of the life before him in the Service, is already thinking of keeping Navy blood in *his* family; note the presence of the Middy-clad tot among his "numerous progeny" (from an 1867 Academy yearbook, *Shakings*).

Below—Rear Admiral and Mrs. W. S. Sims and "numerous progeny," complete with nautically togged tot (Courtesy of Mrs. Robert H. Hopkins).

30   chapel-mausoleum where a more direct and effective veneration might pro-
ceed.* In 1866 newly-commissioned Ensign Douglas Roben was aping his
mentors when he wrote his classmate Charles Sperry: "Now we are to engage
in the *earnest* battles of life, stepping manfully into the great arena of strife to
pluck the laurel wreath of fame," and when he accompanied this harangue with
Longfellow's familiar lines:

> Lives of great men oft remind us
> We can make our own sublime
> And departing leave behind us
> Footprints on the sands of time

But Roben must have anticipated with a thrill the very "earnest battles" and
"the laurel wreath of fame" which he mimed. The letter's style, as well as its
author's hand, betrayed a real excitement that was a product of his Academy
education.[22]

Along with Service and Glory the midshipmen were imbued with Honor.
Their indoctrination into the rites of this third part of the Naval Trinity began
the moment they entered the Navy, with their oaths of office. If Rear Admiral
Henry L. Howison is to be believed, the midshipman was constantly told that
his oath of office was "something different from most other people's oaths."
The inculcation of a strong sense of personal honor was deemed essential to the
making of fearless leaders. "The best way to train a man to be brave," wrote
Rear Admiral Bradley Fiske, "is to cultivate his self-respect and a desire to have
the respect of his fellowmen; and to foster the idea that he will lose both if he
acts in a cowardly way." As these qualities were deemed indispensable to a naval
officer, Rear Admiral Bowman McCalla recalled that the midshipmen were
taught "especially to guard their own honor and the honor of the service."
When Midshipman Mahan was directed by Superintendent George Blake to
give the name of a midshipman whose store of tobacco had been discovered
during Mahan's watch, Mahan at first declined, "through ideas, perhaps mistaken, of honor." But when warned of possible dismissal if he persisted in his
crime of silence, Mahan told all. His fear of dishonorable "dismissal from a
Government institution" was "too heavy to be lightly encountered." The last
lines of the last verse of "Anchor's Aweigh," the Annapolite's "Alma Mater,"
composed by Midshipman Alfred Miles in 1907, reflect his training, for they
read:[23]

> Faith, Courage, service true
> With honor over, honor over all

This sense of obligation to the protection of one's own self-esteem, and to the

---

* In 1905 Acting Midshipman John Stone actually held the hand of Jones during the
autopsy. See the frontispiece and autopsy report in *John Paul Jones Commemoration at Annapolis, April 24, 1906*, ed. Charles W. Stewart (Wash., G.P.O., 1906, reprinted for some
mysterious reason in 1966).

esteem of the Navy and the nation, was to be extremely important in the unfolding of the mature officer's career, as we shall see.

Class and Manners

Simultaneously, the candidate was taught the meaning of rank. Newly arrived 4th classmen quickly learned of their standing in the Navy's social order. In the words of one graduate of the Academy, midshipmen "surrender the privileges of a birthright of equality in favor of the doctrines of an organization in which the knee must be bent in pagan-like adoration of a uniform worn by they know not whom."[24] If nineteenth-century American youth were imbued with a high "need for achievement," as David McClelland has suggested,[25] then reaction of the hero of Lieutenant Commander Edward Beach's novel, *An Annapolis First Classman*, to the news that he had been named cadet company commander is understandable. "Robert's heart commenced: a thump," Beach wrote:[26]

> the blood rushed to his head and he felt a surging of happiness within that seemed almost overwhelming. He was like a thirsty man in a desert unexpectedly finding water. Until this moment he had never known how much cadet rank meant to him.

Similarly, one learned the difference between "young gentlemen" and enlisted men, particularly Academy servants. "One must never call the midshipmen boys," Naval Constructor Holden Evans noted. "It is an insult to the Corps. Only the Negro servants at the Academy are 'boys.'" Thus Charles Sperry wrote home to his sister, warning her of the proper terminology, and explaining the difference between "boys ('negro')" and "young men." [27]

The authorities were well aware that, in spite of the fact that the candidates were referred to as "young gentlemen," they were not necessarily so. They cultivated the social graces in these Penrods with a passion and deemed it their "definite mission" to "train the midshipman for a life with formality." Balls, formal dinners, informal calls on members of the faculty and their families, and all forms of "social functions" were encouraged by successive administrations at the Academy (see illustrations). Fencing was taught, not because the middies would ever have to lead a boarding party, but simply because the art of the sword was considered to have the property of developing grace and poise. Dancing was also required. As Rear Admiral Edward Simpson told the first reunion of Academy graduates in 1886, "Show me the man who can't dance, and you point to a man who is not up in all branches of his profession. . . . The dance is a necessary part of his education."[28] All were required to seal their oaths of office by kissing the Bible and were required to attend daily chapel and Sunday church services, both of the Episcopal rite, to help each candidate to "realize that he is not merely an individual but is a member of an organization even in his devotions. . . . "[29] In the words of one Academy graduate, recalling life at Annapolis in the late 1870s, middies were "full of the idea of 'officers and gentlemen'; the idea of *noblesse oblige* was in the air."[30] In 1882 an anonymous

Midshipmen deemed themselves and were accepted as natural members of "high society," as these illustrations for two late nineteenth-century Naval Academy yearbooks suggest (from *Junk* and *Fag Ends from the U.S. Naval Academy*, Baltimore, 1878).

" Washington beauties there, by the score,"
Yfe with the belles of Baltimore."

NAVAL CADET—BEGINNING OF LEAVE.

Moving in the highest circles of society.

middie bragged that his forthcoming commission would "of itself [be] a pass-
port to good society everywhere." When his sister suggested that he might be
sorry some day for having chosen the naval service as his career, Midshipman
Charles Sperry defended his profession-to-be with these words:

> I could not have chosen a more tasteful or exciting profession. In the navy you are
> treated as a gentleman; you have some chance of satisfying your ambition.

This "chance" clearly had something to do with becoming a "gentleman." A
naval officer "must be a man of the world," Midshipman Mahan told his friend
Sam Ashe. "It is the good effect of the Institution [the Academy] and the [naval]
Profession. When I graduate I am going to make it a point always to kiss a lady's
hand. . . . I have heard that it is the custom on the continent of Europe and it is
certainly a beautiful one."[31] If nineteenth-century America could in any sense be
regarded as democratic, classless, anti-institutional, individualistic, pacifistic, or
any of the foregoing, then the Naval Academy was clearly out of step. If the
American Frontiersman was creating new customs, the American Midshipman
was relearning the old ones.

The Curriculum

The curriculum, quite predictably, reinforced the rest of the
training program. While anxious to impart practical "know-how" to its
neophytes, the Navy made an effort to avoid giving Annapolis the air of a trade
school. As one disgruntled instructor remarked, "The Naval Academy is the
only technical school in the world where the students are allowed to believe that
manual labor is undignified."[32] Gentlemen, by nature, were leaders—not
laborers.*

The result was that more time was spent with mathematics, mechanics, and
classroom seamanship and navigation than with shipboard training cruises.
Flag Officer David Farragut once told his superiors in the Navy Department:

> Gentlemen, you can no more make a sailor out of a land-lubber by dressing him up
> in sea-toggery and putting a commission into his pocket, than you could make a
> showmaker of him by filling him up with sherry cobblers.

Farragut had in mind volunteer officers, but his analogy could have applied to
Annapolites as well. The Academy imparted a certain amount of "know-how"
to each midshipman, to be sure. But the Annapolite's shiphandling could not be
compared to that of Farragut, David D. Porter, "Mad Jack" Percival, or
Stephen Luce, men of the "old school" of shipboard training, who could
throw a flying moor with abandon in any port. Luce's *Seamanship* served as the
textbook in that subject for two generations of Academy graduates; Luce's

---

* This disdain for manual labor could be attributed to Admiral David D. Porter and his
hand-picked successors at Annapolis. Porter detested naval engineers. But it may also have
been the fault of the engineering officers themselves, who disdained manual labor once they
had tried their hand at the gentler art of supervision. Monte Calvert, *The Mechanical
Engineer in America, 1830–1910* (Baltimore, 1967), 259.

HOW TO DISPOSE OF THE REMAINS OF OUR NAVY.

The shore-bound Academy may not have prepared midshipmen in navigation or seamanship as well as had the pre-Annapolis system of shipboard officer apprenticeship. This 1880's *Puck* cartoon depicts a disastrous series of expeditions dispatched to aid the shipwrecked U.S.S. *Jeanette.*

textbook had been the broad expanse of ocean and its myriad nooks and crannies. After a conversation with Lieutenant Samuel Magaw, one of "these lieutenants of the old school," Midshipman A. T. Mahan advised an ex-classmate that Magaw and his associates

> dislike the midshipman of the present day because they are not like those of their own time. They dislike to see the steerage of a man of war change; it is like the loss of an old friend. The great faults they find really are, that midn. now are cleaner, fare better, and are older than formerly, and instead of being cheek by jowl with the men, they prefer to tête-à-tête with a lady. . . . Those little points of seamanship that those officers talk of . . . don't do them a damned bit of good and never will.

Mahan must have lived to regret his disdain for the ways of the "old school"; he was a poor sailor and, after being involved in several minor groundings and collisions, lived in mortal fear of a more serious mishap.[33] Mahan was characteristic of the Annapolis breed in this respect; the Academy education made gentlemen of the neophytes, but it did not necessarily make them skilled sailors (see illustration).

Mathematics, gunnery, seamanship, navigation, tactics, engineering, and mechanics were given the most attention, but the midshipmen also received some instruction in drawing, French, Spanish, and "Ethics and Law."[34] In this last department the basic text was that of Chancellor James Kent on International and Federal Law. In the 1865 introduction to the Academy's own edition of the published views of this famous American arch-conservative, the anonymous editor praised "the true idea of that highest of earthly institutions, The State," and proceeded, in "An Outline of the Course of Study in Political Science," to announce that "The State," being "ordained by God," was "no soulless aggregate of individuals, but is itself a noble life, in which, and out of which, men live. . . . The theory that the State is founded on the mere consent of the people is false and fatal. . . . It was the *DIVINE WILL's* not man's . . . hence . . . our obligation of obedience to the State." This Hegelian view, characteristic of post-Civil War American writing,[35] concluded with the observation that the naval officer's mission in the world was "to carry forward the progress of the [Anglo-Saxon] race" and thus "to execute the Divine Will." Readers of this text were warned to beware of the arguments of "agrarians, socialists, and some dreamy philosophers." If the State *was* to be "carr[ied] forward" by the Navy, the midshipman would have to be made to understand that it was Industrial Capitalism, not Agrarian Socialism, to whom all loyalty was due.* Thus the 1865 official textbook informed the officer candidate of the enormous importance of this facet of his mission:[36]

> To maintain the untarnished honor of the government and of the nation and, at the same time, promote its commercial interests in peace, is an obligation upon the Naval Officer equal with his obligation to defend his ship to the last moment in the hour of battle.

Perhaps the naval officer's identification of American foreign trade and investments with American national interests and honor in his mature years, a phenomenon of which we will have more to say later, had its root in just such an academic merging of "commercial interests" and "untarnished honor" as we find here.

Other texts also tended to develop in the midshipman a high respect for order, race, nationalism, obedience, and rank. The 1862 revised edition of Commander Benjamin Totten's *Naval Text-Book . . . for the Use of Midshipmen of the U.S. Navy* reminded its youthful readers that their oaths bound them "unreservedly" and by "every moral and sacred obligation" to the Union and charged them to display "unbending discipline" and "unhesitating subordination." Edward A. Freeman's *General Sketch of European History*, used at the Academy in the late nineteenth century, was an exercise in nation-ranking by "racial" characteristics. "Aryan" nations were ranked above "Semitic," Oriental, and African states. Samuel Eliot's *Manual of United States History*, though described as "objective," tended to defend aristocratic institutions, such as the Anglican church of the pre-Revolutionary War era and the Society of the Cincinnati of the Federalist

---

* Agrarian Capitalism, the dominant philosophy of U.S. farmers, was an altogether different matter, of course. The Navy was quite prepared to guard and aid agricultural exporters.

36   Age. Eliot (1821–1898), an Episcopal Bostonian, spoke out vigorously against partisanship in government, a view most naval officers would also hold in later life.[37] In French class the "young gentlemen" read Alexander Dumas' life of that idol of many late nineteenth-century warriors, Napoleon.[38] And in "Ethics" they read Francis Wayland's *The Elements of Moral Science* (1837 edition). Wayland (1796–1865) was, among other things, something of a pacifist, which may explain why he was considered an "Old Prude" by the middies and why his *Elements* was formally buried by each class at the year's end for as long as the text was used.[39] But many of his views were in complete accord with those of the naval establishment. Wayland denigrated materialism, just as the midshipman was 'told at the outset that he has renounced wealth and material gain." His *Elements* also warned the officer candidates that, as mere executors of the national will, they had "no right to question the *goodness* or *wisdom* of the law."*

Apparently the Scotch common-sense philosophy of Thomas Reid, popular in many nineteenth-century American college curricula, served as the midshipman's sole introduction to that subject; it is clear that the authorities were not disciples of John Locke.[40] Our anonymous editor of the selections of James Kent also quoted at length from Reid's treatise *On the Mind*, which may explain why Alfred Mahan believed that there were "certain moral faculties" which were "not acquired by practice, though they may by it be improved and enlarged," but were rather "gifts from Nature." It may also explain why Richmond Hobson believed that the "upper brain" was the seat of "the will, of the consciousness of God, of the sense of right and wrong, [and] of ideas . . . that make character,"† and why Stephen Luce believed that education involved the "developing of the God-given qualities in man," and that the faculty which orders a muscle to act was called "the Will."[41] Conceivably Reid's notion that certain chosen individuals were born with latent virtues squared admirably with, and tended to buttress, the quasi-aristocratic view of the world projected by Academy authorities. In any event, the midshipman acquired a picture of a ship-shape universe, of a harmonious "chain-of-being." Perhaps the best illustration of this world-view may be found in a line from an essay entitled "Nature" which Midshipman Louis Kimberly penned for one of his Academy classes: "Every thing seems in order, and has its own functions to perform."[42] With this

---

* Wayland, 294, 332. For more elaborate explications of this and other themes in the mature officer, see Chapter 5, "The Naval Mind."

† The Act of 20 May 1886 (24 *U.S. Stat.* 69) provided for instruction at the two National Academies of the evil effects of liquor. If we may judge from the example of Richmond Hobson, this training was most effective; in 1919 Hobson recalled its impact: "Though abstemious myself, the thought that intoxicating liquors were really built up of the excretions of living organisms removed all glamour from the cup, and produced a reaction of loathing. Soon I was shocked to find that this toxin causes degeneracy in all living things, disrupts the germ plasm, blights offspring, and, in the end, entails sterility and extinction. I saw at once that . . . its handling was the most fundamental and organic question confronting society, involving not only the integrity of free institutions, but the lives of nations, and the perpetuity of the race." Hobson, *Alcohol and the Human Race* (New York, 1919), 8.

Academy experience in mind, perhaps the social attitudes of officers like Kim- **37**
berly in their adult years will be more intelligible.

Learning to Obey

Thus far we have had little to say about the nature of the candidate's education in discipline or sanction; inasmuch as each of these factors played
an essential part in the midshipman's life at the Academy, each must presently
be considered. Since one specified objective of the Academy was to "delineate
and enforce patterns of behavior" not readily acceptable to many entering
candidates, strict regulatory measures were deemed necessary. Academy
authorities were exacting. In fact, according to an 1864 report of a British naval
observer, Americans were considerably more severe in their treatment of midshipmen than was the Royal Navy. Discipline, or "organized living" as one
officer in authority preferred to call it, provided the "condition of living right,
because without right living civilization cannot exist." While this generalization
sounds almost like a truism, it must be remembered that it was *naval* civilization
that the writer had primarily in mind and that the "condition of right living"
often amounted to whatever the authorities wished it to be. There were no
restraints on Academy authorities other than those provided in the existing
Navy Regulations (which were supervised and administered by the authorities
themselves) or the consciences of the individual officers involved. And given the
nature of "naval civilization," these checks were not always the most effective.
As one officer confessed, "subconsciously officers sometimes oppress midshipmen because . . . it is the easiest thing in the world to do."

Upon such "misguided individuals" as those who failed to "live right" the
authorities "placed restraints."[43] Among them were the demerit system, "extra
instruction," the "unwritten regulation," and hazing. Demerits, the most common medium, was probably the least effective. Given for the most trivial misdemeanor, the demerit often served the opposite function of serving as a badge
of merit. As Midshipman Albert Caldwell explained to his father in 1863, the
middies tended to interpret this form of punishment as a status symbol:[44]

> a moderate lot of demerits don't do the least harm, but show that you are not quite
> subdued. As a general thing you will find that those who run a whole year without
> them are the outcasts of the institution, who are spiritless as well as friendless. . . . Too
> many demerits however show a rash hairbrained youth.

Where demerits proved insufficient, "extra instruction" might follow. This
category, less frequently resorted to but nevertheless omnipresent, intimidating,
and consequently more potent, included such practices as mass or individual arms
drill after hours, lining middies up all night until many collapsed from fatigue,
marching them in freezing weather in their underwear, and moving them to the
"prison-ship," *Santee*.[45] Lieutenant Commander J. D. J. Kelley explained the
"unwritten regulation" when he described how the Academy's earliest athletic
association operated:[46]

38   The contests . . . are financ[ed] . . . by a tax which is ingeniously raised through the proposition that all [naval] cadets who do not wish to contribute towards a new boat (for example) will please leave their names with the officer of the day! Need it be added that . . . the officer of the day's aged and mouldy list has been in all these years a *tabula rasa?*

The least official, and probably most effective, means of achieving "right living" at the Naval Academy was not even supervised, except indirectly, by the authorities themselves. This was hazing, the quasi-official, informal device by means of which the Corps itself provided for the assimilation of new candidates and the enforcement of "unwritten regulations."*

If one were to take the word of the Navy's own semi-official historian of the nineteenth-century Academy, Park Benjamin, of the class of 1867, there had never been any hazing to speak of, other than the blandest of juvenile pranks, until the 1871–72 appointments of a black youth and a New York street tough. "Then for the first time in its history vicious hazing ensued." (Benjamin did not spell out exactly which parties conducted the hazing, but it seems safe to assume that the two "boys of more or less doubtful antecedents" were recipients, rather than benefactors. Neither graduated. As a matter of fact, the authorities had, in somewhat malignant humor, arranged that the two outcasts be roommates, and predictably, they made life miserable for one another, with or without hazing.)[47] But, Benjamin's claim notwithstanding, wherever one looks, be it to autobiographies, private correspondence, diaries, or Congressional investigations, the evidence suggests that hazing was both real and vicious long before 1872.

Hazing had two shapes—mental and physical. The former, often more cruel than its counterpart, was known as "coventry." This was social ostracism, informally enforced by one's classmates as punishment for an unsanctioned act. Midshipman 1st Class Alfred Mahan, for example, suffered in "coventry" for his entire final year at the Academy because he had reported a classmate for "talking in ranks."[48] The important thing to note here is that this loss of standing represented peer disapprobation; Academy regulations might be in issue, but not necessarily. As one character in one of the Lieutenant Commander Beach's stories of life at Annapolis says:[49]

> If a fellow would cheat or do anything dishonorable, none of his classmates would speak to him; but if he were to "French" [climb over the wall to spend an evening in

---

* Cf. C. J. Lammers, "Midshipmen and Candidate Reserve Officers at the Royal Netherlands Naval College: A Comparative Study of a Socialization Process," *Sociologia Neerlandica*, II (1965), 114–115: "The initiation rites of the midshipman corps and social control as regards deviant behavior among the midshipmen erase initial cultural differences among the professional officers-to-be."

Hugh Mullan, "The Regular Service Myth," *American Journal of Sociology*, LIII (January 1948), 280, takes the view that hazing represents an expression of "pent-up sadism," and little more. Sanford M. Dornbusch, "The Military Academy as an Assimilating Institution," *Social Forces*, XXXIII (May 1955), 318, disagrees, and argues that hazing is little more than an assimilating device. Actually both interpretations of this phenomenon would appear to describe hazing at the nineteenth-century Naval Academy. Assimilation was achieved, and informal rules enforced, but often by the most brutal measures and with tragic results.

the town] as I have done, he would not lose caste. There are many offenses here of military nature that a midshipman might commit which would be severely punished by the authorities if he were detected, and yet at which most midshipmen would smile.

Physical hazing had early origins as well. In 1859 Midshipman Henry D. Foote—thoroughly unpopular—was actually tarred and feathered by his classmates! While Mahan was in coventry, young George Dewey was being hazed.[50] Uppity, or "gally," 4th classmen were the targets—youngsters who were reluctant to surrender their "birthright of equality." Hazing served as an unofficial means of preserving class rank, deference, and possibly some decade-old Academy "traditions." Radical alterations to the institutional fabric, such as the removal of the Academy to Newport during the Civil War or the "confusion" that resulted from the Academy's expansion in the first decade of the twentieth century, with unfinished buildings, increased enrollment, and the presence of many civilian workmen on the hallowed grounds, necessitated a more vigorous enforcement of candidate-made sanctions and rules. The alternative was a lowering of the veil of the temple. "One can have very little veneration for an institution knocking around as ours has been for the past four or five years," Midshipman Charles Sperry wrote from Newport in 1865. Since veneration was essential, hazing was probably more pronounced in these troubled years. Bowman McCalla and Richard Wainwright remembered "frequent and brutal" hazing at Newport.[51]

By the 1880s a pattern had appeared. The 3rd classmen, supervised by 1st classmen, hazed 4th classmen "in alphabetical order." Franklin Moeller, for example, was made to drill in his night-shirt, to "stand on his head," and to lie between two mattresses while upperclassmen jumped on him. The experience permanently injured him, both physically and professionally; he was himself eventually dismissed for going beyond the accepted limits in hazing underclassmen.[52] By 1906 Congressional inertia could no longer prevent an investigation into conditions at the Academy.[53] Thereafter hazing received less sanction from the authorities and probably became less dangerous.*

Much hazing was undoubtedly quite harmless and was probably not a phenomenon unique to the service schools.[54] But since the establishment of class distinctions (rank) and the inculcation of service traditions and respect for discipline were more important to the life of Annapolis than, let us say, to the University of Wisconsin, another Federally-endowed school that emerged in the mid-nineteenth century, it should not be surprising to find that the practice of hazing incoming candidates was looked upon by upperclassmen as one of their primary missions or that the form of this indoctrinating was

* Midshipman Henry A. Wiley, *An Admiral from Texas* (New York, 1934), 14–16, was dismissed in 1885 for being caught in the act of hazing, but was reinstated with the help of political friends, among them Senator John Morgan of Alabama. Political influence did not stop with the mere appointment. Cf. the Letterbook of Rear Admiral C. R. P. Rodgers, Entry 395, Subentry 119, R.G. 45, for examples of Secretarial clemency for political appointees.

often as brutal as it was. "Standing on the head," for example, might be perfectly innocuous, unless done, as it sometimes was, for hours on end, while the victim fainted repeatedly.[55]

A variation of hazing was fighting, generally between members of different classes. Midshipmen, it will be recalled, were instructed to "guard their own honor," and in the process of doing so, they frequently came to blows with one another. John Lejeune recalled many fistfights, as did Robert Coontz and Cyrus Brady. In fact, Coontz was not himself satisfied in one altercation until he had challenged his adversary to a duel—this in 1883. It was the death of Midshipman James Branch, slain in a fight with Midshipman Minor Merriweather, that finally provoked the Congressional investigation of the Academy's "self-regulating" practices.[56]

Obviously, the Academy's superintendents were well aware of the hazing and fighting going on throughout the nineteenth and early twentieth centuries, and many gave these customs their unofficial endorsements.[57] The incoming class of "plebes" in one of Lieutenant Commander Beach's novels was told by the authorities to "be careful of your conduct to [sic] the upper classes so as not to provoke hazing," but they were *not* told to report incidents of hazing. In 1873 Midshipman William Green resolved to endure hazing since, as he explained to a hometown friend, "There is no use in appealing to the officers, as the whole class will go for you then," and the officers would be of little help. Cyrus Brady noted, with a certain amount of satisfaction, that fighting at Annapolis was "encouraged by the officers" in defense of one's honor. Richmond Pearson Hobson's hero in *Buck Jones at Annapolis* declined to tell the superintendent the names of those who had hazed him, and Hobson's superintendent (a figure who strongly suggested Francis Ramsay, superintendent during the 1880s when Hobson attended the Academy) revealed considerable pleasure at "Buck's" reluctance to speak. Hobson's suggestion that Ramsay condoned hazing may have been unfair to that superintendent, whose official attitude toward the practice was critical. But not all superintendents were as upset about it. In 1906, when a real midshipman, Ronan C. Grady, president of the senior class, asked a real superintendent, Rear Admiral Benjamin Sands, to investigate and curtail hazing at the Academy, Sands refused and reprimanded him. This same Rear Admiral told the House Subcommittee investigating the fatal Branch-Merriweather fight the same year, "I am the personification of discipline, you know."[58] Not all officers approved of these unofficial methods of candidate self-discipline and assimilation, but apparently a good many did. And it is clear that a mild form of hazing continues, in a form apparently palatable to the public today—the "running" of 4th classmen by their seniors.

The End Product: "A Band of Brothers"

In a very real sense, the process by which naval officers were educated could be described as a dehumanizing process. Withdrawn from familiar surroundings, disciplined and hazed, taught to "function as part of a machine,"[59] little wonder that many felt an intense longing for liberty. "You can't imagine what a pleasure it will be," Albert Caldwell wrote home in anticipation of his forthcoming leave, "to be loosed from 2 years of severe military discipline." Nine years later Midshipman Mason Shufeldt told his father, Navy Captain Robert Shufeldt, of his certainty that there was "no place in the world except it be West Point" where young men were "kept in such an iron grasp" as at the Academy. "This system tends to make [us] sombre, haughty, aristocratic and overbearing," he confessed.[60] In some cases the dehumanization may have resulted in pathological mistrust of one's own friends and classmates and in secret hatreds for members of other classes.[61] The zealous and disciplined life was a most demanding one.

Many found the academic side of Academy life insufficiently demanding. In the words of one graduate who had become the principal of a village school, the Academy's instructors did little more than "turn the crank and grind out mechanical results." In 1912 Midshipman Ernest Small made the same charge publicly, in the pages of the Naval Institute's *Proceedings:*

> Specially prepared text books in "tabloid" form are issued to midshipmen, and they are required to accept fact after fact, because "the book says so." The valuable training given by modern education in weighing evidence is missed altogether, and the student develops a slavish adulation for the book.

In 1917 the Academy's Board of Visitors would claim that the institution's administrators displayed an "unspoken willingness to use the subjects of instruction as a means of discipline," rather than "as a quickening of the intelligence." "The remarks and questions of the instructors," the Board's report continued, "seem directed less toward inspiration and guidance than toward finishing a basis for grading."[62]

What the 1917 Board of Visitors tended to overlook was that the Academy's academic objectives differed strikingly from those of the established liberal arts colleges at which most of the Board's members had been schooled. While other American institutions of higher learning moved toward academic excellence in the late nineteenth and early twentieth centuries, academic conditions at the Naval Academy remained relatively static. The Academy's staff was ill-trained in the methods of "modern education"; in 1902 only 12% of the staff were civilians. But this statistic only reflects the policies of the Navy itself. Ships required masters—not philosophers-in-residence. The Academy's curriculum was chiefly designed to provide the former; it had little room for the latter. Failure of English, history, or a foreign language did not necessarily lead to repetition of the course, but failure of a purely professional subject, such as navigation, could well result in dismissal. Until 1908 the physical science course had always provided the theoretical background to lessons that were then given practical application, but after 1908 the pressure of more and more technical data to be "taught" to the fledgling Farraguts temporarily drove theory from

42 the classroom. Park Benjamin could boast that "young gentlemen" of "practical" temperament—whose minds didn't boggle at the vision of applied engineering, technical inventions, and the application of available formulae—would find true bliss in the Service, while adding:[63]

> The intellect which seeks to originate, which recoils from details, which is essentially constructive, will find in the Navy no proper field for its exercise. It may work harm.

This educational approach may explain why Rear Admiral Daniel Ammen attributed Commander William Cushing's insanity to "a lack of rigid early training, [so] necessary to healthy thought." It may also explain why Midshipman Charles Blake was worried about not achieving anything in life. "Here I am," he wrote in his diary in December of 1864, "drifting on and on, to—nowhere. I wish I were away from this Academy." (And Blake was not alone in these sentiments.)[64] It certainly explains why Lieutenant William Fullam considered the curriculum repressive. "Individuality and independence are constantly discouraged," he wrote in 1890, adding that "in his relations with his seniors" the midshipman always feared that he might "assert himself too much."[65]

Fullam's critique actually amounted to an indictment of an "inefficient" system; he was not really arguing for radical educational innovation. But his observations certainly resembled those of Midshipmen Perry and Small and the 1917 Board of Visitors. Instead of opening the candidate's mind, the Academy was rigidly confining it—and "inefficiently" to boot.[66]

Obviously, given all that we have had to say of Academy life thus far, not every candidate to matriculate survived, or wanted to survive. Many departed the sacred groves. Some "bilged" (failed academically); some were expelled for disciplinary breaches; and some resigned (though this required the Navy's permission since, as we have noted, the candidate "belonged" to the Service). Between 1850 and 1894 fewer than half of the appointees actually received commissions, and in some years, as shall be seen, the percentage was considerably smaller. Consequently, when an anonymous lieutenant, writing in 1881, spoke of the study of mathematics at the Academy as a means of insuring "the survival of the fittest" and two years later Captain Augustus Cooke claimed that "the fittest only survive" the system of discipline and academic exams, none rose to disagree.[67] Only those "adaptable" to the peculiar nature of life in the naval service were left standing when the day of final reckoning, and commissioning, dawned. Only those who, in the words of Midshipman Alfred Thayer Mahan, were possessed of the "fortitude" to "patiently submit to privations and woe and injustice" and emerge in a state of "uncomplaining, noble self-abnegation" were given rank in the Navy of the United States Federal Government.[68] In short, the militaristic prevailed.

Did it make any difference whether one was the son of a banker or the son of a wheelwright, whether one was from New England or the Old South, from a city or the countryside? It certainly did. The sons of officers, professionals, and businessmen *increased* their lion's share of officer billets during the Annapolis years; they were far more likely to survive the process of assimilation than were the sons of artisans or shopkeepers (see Table 2-1).* It would seem reasonable to assume that the same forces that had generated the desire on the part of the scions of business and professional people to seek a naval commission in the first

Table 2-1 Percentage of sample* passing the Academic Entrance Exam Boards between 1849 and 1880 who successfully completed the program, ranked by father's occupation

Father's occupation	Percentage graduating	Numbers
Officer (112)	67.9	(76)
Banker (61)	55.5	(35)
Doctor, druggist, civil engineer (102)	51	(53)
Clergyman, educator (55)	51	(28)
Planter, farmer, rancher (92)	51**	(47)
Widow (111)	47.5***	(52)
Manufacturer (76)	46.1	(35)
Government official (85)	45.8	(39)
Merchant (197)	43.1	(85)
Attorney, judge (142)	40.8	(58)
Shopkeeper (66)	37.8	(25)
Artisan, clerk (55)	34.6	(19)
Average of all (1,133)	47.2	(535)

* Drawn from Register of Candidates, U.S. Naval Academy, R.G. 405, N.A.
** The high percentage of farmers' sons *who had passed the Academic Boards* suggests that the sons of more localistic, small-scale farmers were screened out at the Academic Boards level, leaving more cosmopolitan. better-equipped sons of larger scale agricultural entrepreneurs.
*** The similarity of this percentage of widows' sons graduating to that of the overall average suggests that their homes were as cosmopolitan as those of the typical candidate.

place were being reinforced at Annapolis. But since I can't tell which students "bilged," which ones were dismissed on non-academic grounds, and which ones tended their resignations for personal reasons when they concluded that they had made a mistake, I find it impossible to say whether middle or lower class youths discovered something fundamentally repulsive about the ways of the Navy, or whether it was the other way around. Perhaps the feeling was mutual.

The Academy functioned brilliantly as an assimilating institution. The fact that the naval officers of the late nineteenth and early twentieth centuries were the children of well-to-do parents is important to remember in assessing the social attitudes they bore in their mature years. But their experience at Annapolis amounted to a good deal more than mere social-class reinforcement. Loyalty to

* Since business and professional people tended to be located in cities in the Northeast, urban and Eastern candidates were more successful than Southerners and small-town or rural candidates. New England's clear edge (53%) over the South (34%) and West (34%) must have been a function of the superiority of its school system, and the lack of such educational opportunities in the other two regions.

44   State and Service was emphasized at the expense of other loyalties.* "You have left behind a *local point of view*, and have acquired, perhaps unconsciously, a *national point of view*," Academy Instructor H. C. Washburn told a 1917 class. Similarly, in 1883 Captain Cooke boasted that each new group of plebes "soon lose all local prejudice and sectional feeling in a broad sentiment of patriotism and love of country."[69] The plebe's first opportunity to visit his family, often no less than a year from his matriculation, must have been mutually disconcerting. If the experience of the Coast Guard Cadet resembled that of his naval brethren, then discussion among 3rd classmen upon returning from their first home leave was chiefly "concerned with the way things at home [!] ha[d] changed." And if Herman Melville's entertaining description of the midshipman's homecoming in *Pierre* resembled reality, then the shock of the candidate's new visage and attitude must have given his family and friends something to talk about as well.[70]

Lieutenant Commander Roe's Academy textbook provides an interesting illustration of the metamorphosis that was sought. Roe described to the novitiate the proper sentiments of the typical green graduate's return to his home after his parents as having passed away, as indeed they were intended to, symbolically. After a visit to the tomb of his physical parents, Roe's model "feels a secret, passionate longing to get away again on the broad bosom of his [new] mother ocean, where he can draw a sigh from the deepest depths of his soul." He feels that he is now "the child of the ocean, and the orphan of the land."[71] first tour of sea duty. It is interesting to note that he conceives of the graduate's

If, as was hoped, the ocean did become the new mother of the novitiates, then the Academy, the site of their proselytization, or fertilization, was now considered their Mecca, or womb (depending on the individual's own idiosyncracy). According to Rear Admiral R. H. Jackson, for example, the Academy was the midshipman's "foster-mother," while Rear Admiral Edward Simpson considered it "our Mecca," to which he and his comrades made "our yearly pilgrimage for devotion and praise."[72]

Whatever their nature might be, the graduate generally bore fond memories of his days at the Academy. As one junior officer told his wife:[73]

> I used to think that Waterbury [Connecticut] was my natural home, but now the sleepy red streets of Annapolis are very dear to me and I find all my affections center there.

* Roe and the Academy authorities were not altogether successful in cutting the Annapolite free from his parental bonds, of course. Lieutenant Albert Caldwell maintained to his mother that he always looked upon word from home "with a kind of holy awe and reverence," and that he constantly strove to please his parents and to "enhance the value of life to the family." Caldwell to his mother, December 3, 1862, and October 20, 1869, Caldwell Papers, Indiana His. Soc. Lib. Similarly, Academy graduate Cadet Midshipman Frank Bunts wrote home to his brother in 1882: "Although I have the misfortune to be so far from home and separated from you all, I still regard myself as one of the family and desire to be well informed in anything relating to their interest or detriment." *Letters from the Asiatic Station, 1881–1883*, ed. Alexander Bunts (Cleveland, Ohio, 1938), 98. But Bunts resigned within a year of his writing this letter.

If loyalty to their institution was any measure of the effectiveness of their indoctrination, then the Academy authorities must have had frequent cause to feel that their efforts had been enormously successful.

But loyalty to Annapolis was without meaning in itself; what was far more significant was the loyalty to the Service and to the "band of brothers" that grew up behind the Academy walls. Commander Fredrick Sawyer recalled the intimacy "which existed among classmates of the Naval Academy in those [fin-de-siècle] days when classes were so small that we knew each other often better than brothers." Midshipman Mahan was sure that the associations formed at Annapolis would be "far more lasting than those made elsewhere, for here we are from every cause brothers: our association, our hopes, our profession all the same." When Midshipman Samuel Ashe of Mahan's year found he was unable to win the battle with seasickness and returned to North Carolina, Mahan sent him long, pathetic letters that open a window onto one Academy relationship. Several weeks after Ashe's departure, Mahan wrote to him:[74]

> I have not yet fully realized that you are gone, it seems only as if you were not in my room; if I could feel it in its full length and breadth it would almost kill me. . . . I lay in bed last night, dear Sam, thinking of the gradual rise and growth of our friendship. My first visit to your room is vividly before me, and how as I went up from there from night to night I could feel my attachment to you growing and see your own love for me showing itself more and more every night. After all, what feeling is more delightful than that of loving and being loved, even though it be only man's love for man? And then our visits to Cenas and Claiborne's room, where our dear friend Kelley was present . . . you will ever be first, and never less than second, in my heart.

If this situation was at all representative, as I suspect it was, then Academy "esprit de corps" ran deep, to say the least, and classmates could be counted on to act in accord unstintingly. In the language of the behavioral scientist, the "primary group" relationships at Annapolis were strong.

This commonality of profession, this ease and depth of identification among Academy graduates, this "common cause," was perhaps the most profound and lasting thing the candidate acquired.[75] As the naval officer matured, his identification with the Service was to become self-justifying and central to his daily life, his "raison d'être."

Is there irony or justice in the fact that it was not the monarchical Alexander Hamilton, but Thomas Jefferson, himself an admirer of the "common sense" school of thought, who dreamed of rearing a "natural aristocracy" and signed West Point into existence? And, similarly, is there some lesson in the fact that the second school for America's "natural aristocrats" was built on the banks of the Severn, not under the administration of a Whig or an unreconstructed Federalist, but in the years that the arch-democrat George Bancroft was Secretary of the Navy? George Fredrickson has found that military experience during the Civil War changed individualistic, anti-institutionalists into men who took great "pride in a life of service—professional skills and professional

46   objectives."[76] But this also describes the proselytism taking place at the Naval Academy, yesterday and today.

Chapter 2

1. Benjamin, *U.S.N.A.*, 52ff.
2. Edward C. Marshall, *History of the United States Naval Academy* (New York, 1862), 34. In *re* private naval schools for midshipmen before 1845 (a sorry lot) see Henry Burr, *Education in the Early Navy* (Phil., 1939), 35, 147–165.
3. Stephen Ambrose, *Duty, Honor, Country: A History of West Point* (Baltimore, 1966), 191–193, 197, 203.
4. Kell, *Recollections*, 9; Roe, *Naval Duties and Discipline* (New York, 1865), 214; P. W. Moeller, *The Naval Academy at Annapolis and Hazing* (New York, 1884), 8.
5. For an account of this phenomenon at the modern Coast Guard Academy see Sanford M. Dornbusch, "The Military Academy as an Assimilating Institution," *Social Forces*, XXXIII (May 1955), 316–317.
6. [Lieutenant] Ridgely Hunt [Ret.], "Education at the Naval Academy," United States Naval Institute, *Proceedings* [hereafter cited as *PUSNI*], XLII (May 1916), 736, 702–703. Hunt readily admitted that this "bending process" significantly distinguished the Naval Academy by the late nineteenth century from the "less exacting" colleges.
7. [Lieutenant Commander] James Douglas Jerrold Kelley, *The Ship's Company* (New York, 1897), 77.
8. Commander Benjamin Totten, *Naval Text-Book . . . for the use of Midshipmen of the U.S. Navy* (2nd ed., N.Y., 1862), 14; Lieutenant Ellery Stone, *PUSNI*, XLVI (1920), 368; [Commander] Leland P. Lovette, *The School of the Sea* (Annapolis, 1940), 124, 131, 206. For a similar statement by a West Point educator see Colonel Charles Larned, "Modern Education from a Military Standpoint," *North American Review*, CLXXXVIII (April 1908), 507. Lieutenant Ridgely Hunt, U.S.N. (Ret.),

compared Larned's description of West Point's retraining program to that at Annapolis. "Alma Mater," *PUSNI*, XXXIV (Sept. 1908), 761. In another reference, Colonel Larned compared West Point to "theological seminaries of the most orthodox type." *Centennial of the United States Military Academy* (Wash., G.P.O., 1904), i, 467. For a discussion of the role of "tradition" in the training of naval cadets see Lieutenant (junior grade) H. H. Frost, "The Traditions of the Naval Service," *PUSNI*, XLII (1916), 1509–1543.
9. Niblack, "The Letter of a Retired Rear Admiral to his Son at the Naval Academy," *PUSNI*, XLI (1915), 841.
10. See, for example, Mahan, *From Sail to Steam*, 11; Rear Admiral Stephen B. Luce, "Naval Training," *PUSNI*, XVI, No. 3 (March 1890), 389; Phelps, *PUSNI*, XXXIX (1913), 509ff.; Fiske, *From Midshipman to Rear Admiral*, 397.
11. Potter, "The Training of a Government Official," *PUSNI*, L (1924), 1983; Johnson to Balch, ? 1873, and August 8, 1879, George B. Balch Papers, S.H.C., U. of N.C. Library; Captain E. P. Jessop, "The Soul of the Service," *PUSNI*, XLVII (1921), 362.
Midshipman Harris Lanning's grandmother, "a pillar of the [Episcopal] Church," told him "she had always hoped I would be . . . a bishop . . . but thought that the next best thing for me was to be an officer in the U.S. Navy." "An Admiral's Yarn," p. 15, N.W.C. Archives.
12. There were exceptions; during the Civil War several officers, such as Captain William Walker and Rear Admiral David D. Porter, reaped lucrative bounties for prizes heavily laden with raw cotton.
13. Roe, *Naval Duties*, 215.
14. Mahan, "The Navy as a Career,"

The Forum, XX (1895), 277–283; [Rear Admiral] Yates Stirling [Ret.], *How to be a Naval Officer* (New York, 1940), 10–11.

15. [anonymous], "A Midshipman's Views on Marriage in the Navy," *The United Service*, VII (Sept. 1882), 279; J. B. Gordon to Hamilton A. Brown, January 18, 1854, Hamilton Brown Papers, S.H.C., U. of N.C. Library.

16. Totten, *Naval Text-Book*, 16; [anonymous], "You'll never get rich," *Fortune* (March 1938), 67; Mahan to Samuel A'Court Ashe, 1 January 1859, "The Letters of Alfred Thayer Mahan to Samuel A'Court Ashe, 1858–1859," Duke University Library, *Bulletin*, No. 4 (Durham, North Carolina, 1931), 58. The Navy man's renunciation of wealth and sense of moral superiority to civilians may be reflected in the way in which Naval Cadet Bradley Fiske was hazed; he was made to assume the appearance of an idiot on the command, "Jim Fisk, strike your attitude!" Walter Norris, *Annapolis; Its Colonial and Naval History* (New York, 1925), 285.

17. Hunt, "Education . . .," 736. In this regard, Morris Schaff also uses the expression "aristocracy" to describe the Corps of Cadets at West Point in his *The Spirit of Old West Point, 1858–1862* (Boston, 1907), 80–89. Cf. *Wash. Rep.*, Jan. 9, 1882.

18. Frank W. Hackett, *Deck and Field* (Washington, 1909), 90ff.; Charles W. Jones, *Address to the Naval Academy . . .* (Washington, G.P.O., 1882), 4; Midshipman Charles Sperry to his sister, 28 May 1862, Charles Sperry Papers, Manuscript Division, Library of Congress (Edward Everett had impressed Sperry); Navy Secretary Charles Bonaparte (grand-nephew of the Emperor) to the graduating class of the Naval Academy in 1906, cited in *Army and Navy Journal*, XLIII (Feb. 17, 1906), 697.

19. Lovette, *School of Sea*, 125.

20. Porter to Fox, "Private and Confidential," 28 March 1862, *The Confidential Correspondence of Gustavus Vasa Fox*, ed. Rear Admiral Richard Wainwright *et al.*, (New York, 1918–1919), II, 95.

21. Belknap, "Military Character," *PUSNI*, XLIV (1918), 7; U.S. Naval Academy Graduate Association, *4th Annual Reunion, 1889* (Baltimore, 1890), 17; Frost, "Traditions of the Naval Service," *op. cit., passim;* Ensign Roger Welles to his mother, 1 Sept. 1901, Roger Welles Papers, Naval Hist. Found.; Horace Porter, "Account of

the Recovery of the Body of John Paul Jones," *Century Magazine* (Oct. 1905), *passim.*

22. Roben to Sperry, 18 September 1866, Sperry Papers. Similarly, Midshipman Alfred Mahan hoped one of his classmates might "leave his name behind him." Mahan to Ashe, April 1, 1859, *Letters*, ed. Chiles, 104–105.

23. Rear Admiral Henry L. Howison before a Court of Inquiry in 1901, *Record of the Proceedings of a Court of Inquiry in the Case of Rear Admiral Winfield Scott Schley, U.S.N.* (2 vols., Washington, G.P.O., 1902), I, 22; Fiske, *The Navy as a Fighting Machine* (New York, 1917), 243; McCalla, Memoirs," ch. III, 41; Acting Midshipman Mahan to Captain George Blake, Dec. 7, 1857, Naval Academy Letterbook No. 8, Correspondence of the Superintendent of the Naval Academy to the Secretary of the Navy, R.G. 24; Lovette, *School of Sea*, 366–367.

24. Hunt, "Education . . .," *op. cit.*, 736.

25. *The Achieving Society* (Princeton, 1961).

26. Beach, *An Annapolis First Classman* (Philadelphia, 1910), 39–40.

27. H. Evans, *One Man's Fight*, 34; Sperry to Mary Sperry, 3 October 1862, Sperry Papers.

28. Lovette, *School of Sea*, 192; Antoine Corbusier, *Theory of Fencing* (Annapolis, 1873); U.S. Naval Academy Graduates Association, *Minutes of the 1st 4 Annual Reunions* (Annapolis & Baltimore, 1886–1890), 12–13.

29. Charles Sperry to Mary Sperry, December 1862, Sperry Papers; *Regulations for the Government of the Naval Academy* (Washington, 1851), 22; Barnard, *Military Schools*, 916; [Commander] Ralph Earle, *Life at the U.S. Naval Academy* (New York, 1917), 99, 162–163.

30. This is not to say that the concept of *noblesse oblige* was not active in other cultural institutions in late nineteenth century America as well. The Naval Academy, to be sure, reflected the mood of elitist American leadership.

31. A. B. Clements [Class of 1879], "Forty Years After," *PUSNI*, XLVI (1920), 88; [anonymous], "A Midshipman's Views . . .," *op. cit.*, 279; Sperry to Mary Sperry, 15 March 1863, Sperry Papers; Mahan to Ashe, November 7, 1858, and April 1, 1859, *Letters*, ed. Chiles, 21–22, 104. See also the curious columns, "Notes from Annapolis," in the *Army and Navy Register*

throughout the late nineteenth and early twentieth centuries for amusing glimpses of Academy social life.

32. Lieutenant Paul Foley, "The Naval Academy Practice Cruise," *PUSNI*, XXXVI (1910), 246.

33. The sailor-cobbler analogy may be found in Loyall Farragut, *The Life of David Glasgow Farragut* (New York, 1879). For evidence of Mahan's poor seamanship, see Adm. W. V. Pratt,"Autobiography," p.174, Pratt Papers, Bldg. 210, Wash. Navy Yard; Zogbaum, *From Sail to "Saratoga,"* 65; Rodman, *Yarns of a Kentucky Admiral*, 30; and correspondence of Commander Mahan to the Secretary of the Navy, throughout 1881–1885, Letters From Commanders, R.G. 45. Cf. Captain Robert Brent, "Mahan—Mariner or Misfit?" *PUSNI*, XCII (April 1966), 92–103.

34. Alden, *Perkins*, 18–19; Barnard, *Military Schools*, 900–903. For a good account of the midshipman's daily routine see Barnard, 907–908.

35. Merle Curti, *The Growth of American Thought* (2nd ed., New York, 1951), 482, and "Francis Lieber and Nationalism," *Huntington Library Quarterly*, IV (1941).

36. *Acts for the government of the U.S. Navy Together with an outline of the course of study in Political Science* (Newport, Rhode Island, 1865), 4–5, Lecture III, 5–8. Cf. Jones, *Address*, 2; Rear Admiral C. R. P. Rodgers to Navy Secretary Robert Thompson, June 23, 1877 [copy], Rodgers Letterbook, p. 33, Entry 295, Subentry 119, R.G. 45, N.A.

37. Totten, *Naval Text-Book . . .* (2nd ed., N.Y., 1862), 14; Correspondence of the Superintendent of the Naval Academy, Vol. 67, p. 147, R.G. 24, N.A.; Freeman, *General Sketch . . .* (3rd ed., London, 1873, 2–4, and *passim;* Eliot, *Manual of United States History* (Boston, 1861 [originally published in 1856]), 164–66, 269, 329, 369; *D.A.B.*

38. Barnard, 900.

39. Francis Wayland, *The Elements of Moral Science*, ed. Joseph L. Blau (Cambridge, Mass., 1963), 360–363; Sperry to Helen, May 27, 1865, Sperry Papers.

40. The passages I have quoted that relate to the Academy view of the State would indicate as much, but it is also important to note that the Academy's Library sources throughout the nineteenth century were devoid of any Lockean works, such as those of Locke, Sidney, Jefferson, Paine, or Price, a fact which immediately

distinguishes it from almost any American library which had its origins in the eighteenth century (see H. Trevor Colburn, *The Lamp of Experience: Whig History and the Intellectual Origins of the American Revolution* [Chapel Hill, 1965], 199–232). On the other hand, there were several copies of the works of such men as Chancellor James Kent and Thomas Carlyle on hand. *Catalogue of the Library of the U.S. Naval Academy* (Annapolis, 1860). Whoever was responsible for the creation of the library for Secretary Bancroft's Naval Academy must have had some very conservative ideas.

41. *Acts . . . Together with . . . Political Science*, 5–6; Mahan, "Rear Admiral William T. Sampson," *Fortnightly Review*, LXXVIII (1902), 234; Hobson, *Alcohol and the Human Race*, 69; Rear Admiral Stephen B. Luce, *United Service*, I (1879), 433 and *PUSNI*, XVI, No. 3 (1890), 372. Cf. Louis Kimberly, "Our Navy" [a mss. article], p. 16, Kimberly Papers, Chicago Hist. Soc.

42. "Nature" in the Louis A. Kimberly Papers, Chicago Historical Society.

43. Lovette, *School of Sea*, 118; Earle, *Life at the Academy*, 165 (first cited in Mills, *Power Elite*, 194); Roe, *Naval Duties and Discipline*, 188; Mahan, "The Military Rule of Obedience," in *Retrospect and Prospect* (Boston, 1902), 283; Hunt, "Education . . .," *op. cit.*, 720; Captain James Goodenough, R.N., "The Navy at Newport: A British View, 1864," ed. Frank Merli, *Rhode Island History*, XXV (1966), 110–116. Captain Goodenough particularly objected that "gun exercise" was "made to take the place of play" (114), but the introduction of football after the Civil War alleviated this deficiency.

44. Caldwell to "Papa," 13 March 1863, Albert Caldwell Papers, John Caldwell Collection, Indiana Historical Society Library.

45. *Hearings before a Subcommittee of the House Committee on Naval Affairs . . . on the Subject of Hazing at the Naval Academy* (Washington, G.P.O., 1906), 311.

46. J. D. J. Kelley, *The Ship's Company* (New York, 1879), 91.

47. Benjamin, *U.S.N.A.*, 373. See also Benjamin, "The Trouble at the Naval Academy," *The Independent*, LX (1906), 154–156.

For a similar example of racial ostracism at West Point see Lieutenant Henry O. Flipper, U.S.A., *The Colored Cadet at West Point* (New York, 1878). See also Stephen

Ambrose, *Duty, Honor, Country*, 231–237. In contrast to the service academies, Harvard admitted blacks and graduated them after the Civil War on a regular basis. Samuel Eliot Morison, *Three Centuries of Harvard (1636–1936)* (Cambridge, Mass., 1937), 416–417.

48. "Mahan-Ashe Letters," *op. cit.*, 107n. See also Beach, *Annapolis First Classman*, 182: "No organized 'coventry' was declared against him, but a most effective, far-reaching one existed."

49. Beach, *Annapolis First Classman*, 327.

50. "Mahan-Ashe Letters," *loc. cit.; The Life and Adventures of Jack Philip, Rear Admiral, U.S.N.*, ed. Edgar S. Maclay (New York, 1904), 58; Kutner & Healy, *The Admiral*, 39.

Foote [or "Foot"] had apparently behaved in such an outrageous manner, lying, stealing, drinking, and abusing female slaves, that he drew the wrath of the Brigade of Midshipmen upon himself. See Letter of "90 Midshipmen" to the Secretary of the Navy, April 8, 1859, copy in U.S. Naval Academy Letterbook, No. 10, pp. 89–92, Correspondence of the Superintendents of the Naval Academy to the Secretary of the Navy, R.G. 24., National Archives.

51. Benjamin,"Trouble at the Academy," *op. cit.*, 156; Sperry to his sister, Oct. 11, 1865, Sperry Papers; McCalla, "Memoirs," Ch. III, 33; Captain Damon E. Cummings, *Rear Admiral Richard Wainright and the United States Fleet* (Wash., 1962), 9.

52. Vice Admiral Harold Bowen, *Ships, Machinery, and Mossbacks: The Autobiography of a Naval Engineer* (Princeton, 1954), 3; P. W. Moeller, *The Naval Academy and Hazing . . .* (New York, 1884), 6, *passim*.

Professor Stephen Ambrose tells me that West Point never dismissed anyone for hazing. In this sense, then, Naval Academy authorities in the late nineteenth century were less sympathetic toward hazers than were those at the Point.

53. *Hearings on . . . Hazing, passim.*

54. On the other hand, hazing died out at Harvard by the 1870s, and civilian hazing was rarely as severe as the service academy brand. Samuel Eliot Morison, *Three Centuries of Harvard, 1636–1936* (Cambridge, Mass., 1937), 312.

55. See the 1906 Congressional Investigation (*Hearings . . .*) for details; see also Ethelbert D. Warfield, *Joseph Cabell Breckenridge, Jr., Ensign, U.S.N.* (New York, 1898), 32; Richmond D. Hobson to Elihu S. Riley, 5 May 1906, Naval Museum

Miscellaneous Manuscripts; Lejeune, 37–38; Cyrus T. Brady [Class of 1883], *Under Tops'ls and Tents* (New York, 1901), 23.

56. LeJeune, 39–40; Coontz, 71; Brady, 20n; Warfield, 30–31; Beach, *An Annapolis Plebe* (New York, 1907), 78. There appears to have been an unusual amount of hazing and fighting in the early 1880s, as these references indicate, a fact which will prove particularly significant when we examine those years in greater detail in a later chapter.

In the pre-1851 era, before less individualistic measures of redress were available, midshipmen duels were more frequent. See *The Papers of Francis G. Dallas . . .*, ed. Gardner W. Allen (New York, Naval Hist. Soc., 1917), 25–26, 38–39. Dueling did decline after the Civil War, possibly as a result of "the exodus of Southern officers" from the service, as Charles Sperry suggested to his cousin Helen, 10 June 1870, Sperry Papers. In light of the evidence offered by John Hope Franklin, *The Militant South, 1800–1861* (Beacon paper ed.), 44–62, this explanation seems quite feasible.

57. There were a few exceptions. Superintendent C. R. P. ("Alphabet") Rodgers, for example, was critical of hazing. See his letter to Navy Secretary William Hunt, Nov. 10, 1881, Correspondence of the Superintendents of the Naval Academy, R.G. 24.

58. Beach, *An Annapolis Plebe*, 70; Midshipman 4th Class William Green to "Hunt" Priddy, 1 October 1873, Naval Museum Miscellaneous Manuscripts; Brady, 20n; Hobson, *Buck Jones at Annapolis* (New York, 1907), 93–94; *Hearings . . .*, 12, 116.

Concurrently, General William T. Sherman, the Commanding General of the U.S. Army in the 1880s, also condoned hazing at West Point. Stephen T. Ambrose, *Duty, Honor, Country: A History of West Point* (Baltimore, 1966), 200, 222.

59. Benjamin, *U.S.N.A.*, 376; Major General LeJeune, one of the "tougher-minded" marines in America's past, remembered the Academy as a "great Machine," void of all human appeal. *Reminiscences*, 48.

60. Caldwell to his father, 13 March 1863, Caldwell Coll., Indiana Hist. Soc. Lib.; Mason Shufeldt to his father, 15 March 1872, Robert Shufeldt Papers, Naval Historical Foundation. Cf. Captain Shufeldt in testimony before the House Naval Affairs Committee, 44th Cong. 1st Sess.,

H. of R., Misc. Doc. 170, Pt. 5, *Investigation* . . . [1876].

61. See, for example, Beach, *Ralph Osborn—Midshipman at Annapolis* (Boston & Chicago, 1909), 223 & *passim*.

62. G. E. Perry to the Class of '81, 6 February 1890, *6th Annual Report of the Class of 1881* (Baltimore, 1890), 95; Midshipman Ernest Small, "The U.S. Naval Academy: An Undergraduate's Point of View," *PUSNI*, XXXVIII (Dec. 1912), 1398; Ensign Winston Folk, "Basic Education of Officers," *PUSNI*, LI (1925), 274; William Simons, *Liberal Education in the Service Academies* (Teachers College, Columbia, 1965), 95–100. Cf. Roger Nye, "The U.S. Military Academy in an Era of Educational Reform," unpub. Ph.D. dissertation, Columbia University, 1968. For a recent critique of Air Force Academy academics see J. Arthur Heise, "Why the Cadets Cheat," *Nation*, CCIV (May 15, 1967), 622–626.

63. Simons, *Liberal Education in the Service Academies*, 67, 72, 95; Benjamin, *U.S.N.A.*, 361–362. Cf. Fredrick Rudolf, *The American College and University: A History* (New York, 1962), 221–306; Laurence Veysey, *The Emergence of the American University* (Chicago and London, 1965); and Morison, *Three Centuries of Harvard*, 326–364, 400–436.

64. Ammen, "A Naval Hero," *Chicago Inter-Ocean*, 20 June 1886; "The Journal of Charles F. Blake, 1862–64," Naval Historical Foundation, 72, 94, 153, *passim*. See also Charles Sperry to his sister, 27 January 1864, Sperry Papers; and the Naval Academy Letterbook of Commander Louis Goldsborough, *passim*, Louis Goldsborough Papers, Manuscript Division, Library of Congress. Goldsborough, superintendent of the Academy in its early years, was chagrined at the degree of drinking midshipmen did when given permission to leave the Academy grounds, and he occasionally speculated as to the cause of this phenomenon. To the best of my knowledge, however, he never supposed that they may have been suffering from what Park Benjamin was later to call "intellectual indigestion." Benjamin, "The Trouble at the Naval Academy," *op. cit.*, 156.

65. Fullam, "The System of Naval Training and Discipline Required to Promote Efficiency and Attract Americans," *PUSNI*, XVI, No. 4 (1890), 481, *passim*. For similar critiques of the West Point

curricula by Army officers see Ambrose, *Duty, Honor, Country*, 212–214.

66. For a similar critique of the modern Academy see J. Arthur Heise, *The Brass Factories* (Wash., 1969).

67. *Register of the Alumni of the U.S. Naval Academy, 1846–1965* (Annapolis, 1966), *passim*; Barnard, 932; Lieutenant "A. P. Mantus," "Gentility in the Navy," *The United Service*, V (Sept. 1881), 347; Cooke, *PUSNI*, IX (1883), 204.

68. Mahan to Ashe, 1 April 1859, "Mahan-Ashe Letters . . .," *op. cit.*, 107.

69. Washburn, "What it Means to be an Officer in the U.S. Navy Today," *PUSNI*, XLII (1917), 2897; Captain Augustus Cooke, *PUSNI*, IX (1883), 204.

70. Dornbusch, *op. cit.*, 320; Melville, *Pierre; Or, The Ambiguities* (Signet paper ed. [orig. pub. 1852]), 50–52. (Two of Melville's cousins were naval officers.) Cf. Lieutenant Charles Flusser to his mother, February 27, 1861, Flusser Papers, "ZB" File, Naval History Division, National Archives.

71. Roe, *Naval Duties*, 218. Compare the views of Roe's budding professional to those of diplomat Joseph Grew: "I feel gathered once again in the arms of my father and mother, the Diplomatic Service." Grew to J. B. Wright, Jan. 18, 1920, cited in Warren Ilchman, *Professional Diplomacy in the United States, 1779–1939* (Chicago, 1961), 137n.

72. Jackson, "Loyalty," *PUSNI*, XLVII (1921), 878; Simpson, in U.S. Naval Academy Graduate Association, *3rd Annual Reunion, 1888* (Baltimore, 1889), 28. See also W. S. R. Emmet to the Class of 1881, 14 November 1887, *4th Annual Report of the Class of 1881*, 24: "I would like very much to make an occasional pilgrimage to Annapolis."

73. Lieutenant Charles Sperry to his wife, 24 August 1884, Sperry Papers. See also Silas Wright to the Class of 1881, 31 Oct. 1886, *3rd Annual Report* . . ., 52.

74. Commander Fredrick Sawyer, *Sons of Gunboats* (Annapolis, 1946), 16; Mahan to Ashe, 20 Oct. 1858, *Mahan-Ashe Letters*, 9, 18–19. See also Mahan to Ashe, 23 Oct. 1858, *Ibid.*, 8.

75. See Rear Admiral R. H. Jackson, *PUSNI*, XLVII (1921), 878; and, more recently, Rear Admiral James Calvert, *The Naval Profession* (N.Y., 1965), 73.

76. George Fredrickson, *The Inner Civil War* (N.Y., 1965), 175–176.

chapter 3

Naval Life and Society

Men go into the Navy . . . thinking they will enjoy it. They do enjoy it for about a year, at least the stupid ones do, riding back and forth quite dully on ships. The bright ones find that they don't like it in half a year, but there's always the thought of that pension if only they stay in. So they stay. . . . Gradually they become crazy. Crazier and crazier. Only the Navy has no way of distinguishing between the sane and the insane. Only about 5 per cent of the Royal Navy have the sea in their veins. They are the ones who become captains. Thereafter, they are segregated on their bridges. If they are not mad before this they go mad then. And the maddest of these become admirals.

Attributed to George Bernard Shaw

The midshipman who left the Academy with visions of future distinction and illusions of grandeur was swiftly disappointed. Instead of leading the column that crossed the enemy's "T" or the landing party that stormed the wicked pirate's citadel, the young graduate found himself directing more mundane matters, and taking more orders than he gave. And the bounding main, medium of his daydream glories, often grew less attractive, and more tiresome, with each passing day. Moreover, the ranking midshipman at the Academy suddenly found himself the junior officer aboard his first ship, with attendant discomfitures, especially if he were an engineer.

The close nature of shipboard life meant that each officer had to "give" a little to insure the composure of steerage or wardroom society, but the holders of commissions could always draw a sigh of relief as they considered that their sheepskin insured better living conditions than those of the crew. If the distinctions that rank caused between officers were great, the distinctions between "officers and men" were enormous. Essentially, there were two naval societies—

Numbered footnotes for Chapter 3 begin on pages 93, 117, and 136.

that of the officers and their wives and sweethearts, and that of the men and their sweethearts and wives. The gulf between the two was unfathomable.

Abroad, as in the States, the officer was granted an entrée into upper class circles. Whenever it could afford to, his family followed him to Europe or the Far East and established residence in a pleasant Anglo-American enclave. But many families remained in their permanent quarters in the States, where the officer's wife supervised the nurture of fledling Farraguts and many of their future spouses.

To the officer on shore duty in the States, shipboard life was approximated by the close society of the naval yard or base. The officer's rank largely determined his, and his family's, social position. Off-base social contacts with political, social, and business elite were not uncommon, but more often than not they were made by senior officers, whose rank, salaries, and official positions allowed for greater social indulgences than did those of the midshipman or lieutenant.

Retirement, which generally didn't come until one was well into his sixties, after 40 or 50 years of naval service, was a sad moment for most officers. But even then naval society persisted. Retired officers often settled in close proximity to one another and retained increasingly fond memories of the "band of brothers" and the Service.

As in life, many officers gathered in death, at Arlington National Cemetery.

UNDERWAY

The Romance of the Open Sea

Throughout the nineteenth century most naval vessels were propelled primarily by sail, and seafaring people were familiar with the lore of canvas and halyard. Half a century later, when the primary motive power was steam, naval officers recalled with nostalgia the thrilling ring of storm-preparation orders under sail: "Let fly to'gallant and royal halyards! Stand by the topsail halyards! Main topmast staysail downhaul!" etc. "One looks with as much pride and affection upon his ship," Midshipman William Cushing wrote his cousin, "as he would upon his wife." If, as Perry Miller has suggested, the American Dream may be viewed as a quest for the sublime, then Cushing's remark that he could "imagine no place where sublimity lies more grand than in a storm at sea" takes on special meaning.[1]

But spiritual or no, the adventure of sea life, with all its attendant dangers, was both "mysterious" and exciting to the young men of the naval cloth. "I love the sea," Captain Robert W. Shufeldt explained to a puzzled friend, "because it brings into play that part of my being nearest akin to *Power*." Midshipman Mahan imagined that his early passion for the open sea did "not arise from romance," for he believed that the "buoyancy in the sea air that elevates me" could be accounted for "chemically by the greater quantity of oxygen" than the atmosphere of Annapolis or inland communities he thought it contained. But for whatever reason, Mahan looked upon life at sea as "the most happy, carefree & entrancing life that there is," and confided that "[i]n a stiff breeze, when the ship is heeling over, there is a wild sort of delight that I have not experienced before." To officers like Mahan the romance of the open sea was a lifelong affair, shaping their image of the service and giving color to the ways in which they visualized the naval career. Note, for example, the intoxicated tone of Mahan's 1901 account of the Battle of Quiberon Bay:[2]

> Forty-odd tall ships, pursuers and pursued, under reefed canvas, in fierce career drove furiously on; now rushing headlong down the forward slope of a great sea, now rising on its crest as it swept beyond them; now seen, now hidden; the helmsmen straining at the wheels, upon which the huge hulls, tossing their prows from side to side, tugged like a maddened horse, as though themselves feeling the wild "rapture of the strife" that animated their masters, rejoicing in their strength and defying the accustomed ruin . . . the roar and flashes of the guns, the falling spars and drifting clouds of smoke, now adding their part to the wild magnificence of the scene.

Quiberon Bays were rare, but worth waiting for.

While awaiting the storm and strife of such a day, one might admire the more contemplative grandeur of the sea's usual, placid face. Midshipmen who dreamed of the rugged beauty of a Trafalgar or Camperdown learned to settle for the serene charm of fleet maneuvers under steam in sheltered waters. Rear Admiral Mahan recalled his first impression of such a scene when he described in his autobiography his thoughts on witnessing the motions of the French Mediterranean steam fleet in 1871:

> The bay . . . was as quiet as a millpond, and it needed little imagination to prompt recognition of the identity of dignified movement with that of a swan making its leisurely way by means equally unseen; no turbulent display of energy, yet suggestive of mysterious power.

In 1871 Mahan, by then a lieutenant commander, was writing to his bride-to-be of "the soft romance of the ocean" and of how pleasant life was in the solitude of his stateroom at sea.[3]

Disenchantment

Many naval neophytes, such as Mahan's classmate Samuel Ashe, discovered to their regret that the bounding of the main disagreed with their constitutions and left the service. But the seasick were not the only disenchanted. Many a "young gentlemen" who had envisioned himself immediately assuming responsibilities of momentous character was swiftly disabused of all such notions and put to work learning the routine duties of the deck and watch officer. Most of the time on board a naval vessel was spent in eternal preparation for a situation—be it collision at sea, man overboard, a fire in the powder room, or war—that might never take place. Drills, routine upkeep, and watches filled the naval day. Even in wartime, the only activity for months might be the steady motion of the ship. "The ship has done nothing but roll, roll all the time," Lieutenant Commander George Perkins wrote his sister during the Civil War. For officers caught on the blockade of the Confederacy, as many with whom we are concerned here were in their early careers, the "monotony of existence" was stupifying. "Dull! Dull!! Dull!!!" Navy Surgeon Samuel Boyer complained to his diary in November, 1863. "It seems like a living death to be on the blockade," Perkins wailed. "We get talked out on board ship, and sometimes a week passes & I do not speak a word except those which my duty requires."[4] "Mr. Roberts" was not the first U.S. naval officer to spend his days sailing from tedium to apathy.

Graduates of the Academy learned to put up with the boredom of habit. "My life is *so* monotonous!" Midshipman Charles Sperry had groaned to his sister from the Newport Academy in 1864, but Sperry stayed on to command the Round-the-World cruise of the Great White Fleet in 1908. The naval officer came to accept with grace and philosophic composure Joseph Conrad's judgement—that the only thing one might say in praise of the sea was that it is big. Thus when Lieutenant Charles Sperry's ship lay becalmed in 1868, he could write home:[5]

> I don't care much for we have three years to put in some way, and we may as well be here as anywhere else.

But philosophic composure is a long way from the excitement of anticipation, such as that exhibited by Ensign Douglas Roben.* That officer's second thoughts are not recorded, and it may be that his early career was more soul-stirring than were most. But even excitement was found to have its defects. The "romance poetry" of the naval life were "all very well in the right place—before a big warm fire by the side of a pretty girl," Passed Midshipman Charles Graves advised his cousin,

> but I can tell you, cousin Mag, they *won't do* on deck during a mid-watch on a December when you have to hold on to the rigging to keep from being washed overboard and the sea breaking over you every few minutes.

Disenchantment was demoralizing and widespread. Listen to Midshipman John Grimball's pathetic lamentation in his diary:

> I am leading a dog's life—I have been in the service over four years and I have never heard a man say that he likes this life yet. There must be a reason for this.

And so there was.

Actually, there were a number of reasons why Grimball and his messmates might have felt dissatisfied. Among them one might list the monotonous routine, the long periods of absence from home and family, the rigors of shipboard discipline and life, and the stultifying effect of promotion by seniority.

* See Chapter 2, note 22.

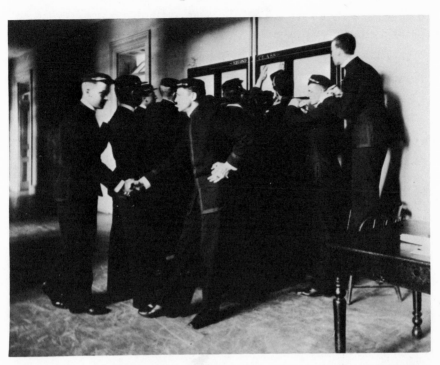

A "Band of Brothers." Middies pose before "class standing" lists, *circa* 1890 (Naval Photographic Center).

Budding naval aristocrats embarking on a summer training cruise in the 1890s (Detroit Collection, Library of Congress).

Summer cruises disabused some Annapolites of a few of their more unlikely pipedreams (see pages 53 58), as this page from an Academy sketchbook verifies (*Junk*).

Midshipmen man the rigging of the Academy's sail training-ship, U.S.S. *Chesapeake* (later renamed U.S.S. *Severn*), 1904 (Bu Ships 12154, National Archives).

The bachelor officer looked upon himself with alarm as one who had become a "celibate, living in an unnatural state." The married officer bemoaned the three-year separations from his family. Thus Commander Louis Goldsborough groaned to his wife in 1853, "I am getting terribly homesick! Heavens! What an unnatural profession mine is!!" And Commander John Winslow wrote his wife in 1854 of the great effort of "self denial" required "to be away from you all" and confessed that he had "missed my profession. I am not fit to remain away." And Lieutenant Cornelius Schoonmaker, later a victim of the Samoan hurricane that destroyed his ship, the *Vandalia*, in 1889, declared in late 1865 that he "would rather live ashore, be my own master, and not be subjected to the hardships and privations of a Naval officer."

> Our pay is small, . . . promotion is very slow, and though I am on the eve of promotion [to Lieutenant Commander], it will take ten or fifteen years to reach the grade of Commander. . . . What is this but life thrown away?. . . . All this I should have foreseen twelve years ago [when Schoonmaker accepted an appointment to the Academy], but I was too young and enthusiastic and head strong.

Commander William Temple confessed to Commander Henry Wise in 1866 of how very "glum & down-in-the-mouth" he had become after several unsuccessful attempts to obtain orders to shore duty. "Have I got to go *all* the way to Heaven by water?" he asked. "Am I not to be permitted to make a *portion* of the journey overland?" Commander John G. Walker was "convinced that a man happily married should not follow the sea," or so he told his new bride in 1869. Paymaster John Tarbell was disappointed by orders to report to the *Gettysburg* in 1876, for, as he told his diary, "I had no desire to go to sea." Commander Charles O'Neil owned to a friend in 1877 that "nothing can compensate for the long separation we have to put up with from time to time, from [homes?], family & friends." In his seaborne stateroom Lieutenant Charles Sperry dreamed of "the exquisite beauty of the woods" and "positively long[ed] for a white house with green blinds, or anything else," and "a drive . . . over the hills of Connecticut" throughout the early 1880s. And from Sitka, Alaska, Midshipman Roger Welles asked his mother in 1888, "Has spring come yet in Connecticut?" An understandably anonymous lieutenant told a Washington *Star* reporter in 1890 of the rigors of life at sea, adding that for his own part he would "rather live on land." And, concurrently, Lieutenant (junior grade) Albert Gleaves noted in his private journal: "It seems incredible that men can be found who are fools enough to go to sea," and confessed, "I am developing into a chronic growler." Lieutenant Edwin Anderson, in command of a busy China Patrol gunboat, told his wife in 1903:

> I am getting mighty sick of this Navy business; it is hustle, hustle, all the time; no comfort and worse than all no happiness because no wife and child. . . . if I could get [a comparable] living any other way . . . I would quit tomorrow, but I am too old now to commence life over again with any chance of success.

58   Ensign Edward Dorn confided to his diary his sense of failure, depression, "vain dreamings," and thoughts of leaving the service. Some, like Ensign Louis Belrose, eventually decided "the life of a naval officer" was "distasteful" to them and resigned. Others, like Lieutenant Samuel Wilson and Rear Admiral John B. Clitz, remained in the service and "contracted habits of intemperence and dissipation" which drove them to an early grave or to a court-martial and disgrace.[6] In short, there were many officers who found sea duty to be objectionable and had second thoughts about the romance of their profession's medium.

Simply because one disliked sea duty did not necessarily mean that resignation followed. Most officers reasoned, by the time they discovered that they hated the sea, that the time had passed for them to reconsider their career. Moreover, there were other bonds, such as a deep-rooted love of the service, that offset the irritation one might feel at times for shipboard life. With the exception of Belrose, none of the officers mentioned in the preceding paragraphs chose to leave the service voluntarily. All felt a certain ambivalence about shipboard duty, but none rejected the naval life as a result.

None the less, there were some officers whose dislike of sea duty became so great that they broke tradition and turned their sons away from naval careers. Commodore Charles Elliott, for example, insisted that if he "had a dozen sons" he would "gladly see them all in their graves sooner than at sea." And while *Midshipman* Mahan was certain that his "affections" would "never suffer any rude shock by my naval career, and the separations consequent upon it," *Captain* Mahan was of a different mind. Frequently he expressed his chagrin at the long separations from his wife and family, and on one occasion confided to his wife, "I hope our dear laddie will not be such a fool as to take up this absurd profession."[7] (He wasn't.) As we shall see, such reluctance to see a son follow in the wake of his father was somewhat uncommon, but the mere fact that there were any who felt this way is evidence of the disenchanting powers sea duty had for some.

Still, shipboard life *could* be made bearable to the naval officer. Black and oriental servants relieved him of the burdens of housekeeping. Rear Admiral Samuel Francis DuPont's steward "boys" were "faithful and genteel" mulattoes. As a lieutenant and the ship's navigator, Charles Sperry had a personal servant, and Navy Regulations provided (and still provides) that a captain, commodore, or rear admiral be assigned a personal steward, mess attendant, and cook. Wardroom officers had their own coterie of servants and, until 1914, their own "wine mess."[8]

The wardroom was the social heart of the ship to her officers, and meals were formal and often sumptuous. While in port, the wardroom mess might entertain a variety of visitors at dinner parties attended by the band if one were embarked. At sea, messing was less elaborate, but formalities were always observed. Seating was prescribed, and any change in the routine merited mention. "Did I tell you I had changed my seat since my reelection to the catership and now sit on [the Executive Officer's] left?" wrote Lieutenant

Admonishing the "boy" in the midshipmen's mess (from an 1867 Academy year-book, *Shakings*).

A typical officer's stateroom. Paymaster Edward Whitehouse of the U.S.S. *Maine*, 1896 (Detroit Collection, Library of Congress).

Captain Colby Chester's cabin, U.S.S. *Kentucky*, *circa* 1900 (Detroit Collection, Library of Congress).

Wardroom scene, U.S.S. *Maine*, 1896. Note the greying temples of the "junior" officers, and note the presence of Filipino, black, or Chinese servants in this and other wardroom photos (Detroit Collection, Library of Congress).

U.S.S. *Newark* messmates pose in the traditional Saturday toast to "Sweethearts and Wives," *circa* 1895 (Detroit Collection, Library of Congress).

Captain Alexander Rhind lounges comfortably in the company of Lieutenant George Dewey and two messmates while on blockade duty, 1865 (Brady Collection, 599, National Archives).

Charles Sperry to his wife in 1880. A complete account of wardroom amenities is not called for here, but one illustration is offered. On Saturday evenings throughout the service it was the custom, until 1914, for wardroom messmates to rise and drink a toast: "Wives and sweethearts, bless them." "It is a fine old custom and does us good," Charles Sperry wrote home. "[s]ome of the married men take their portion with a solemn and thoughtful gulp."[9] Built-in restraints —such as the curb on all discussion of religion, women, or politics—insured that wardroom officer relations were almost universally close and cordial, and the "band of brothers" solidarity was reinforced. The officer who compared "the separation of the officers at the close of [a] voyage" to "the breaking up of a family" wasn't overdrawing the scene. Officers could become as attached to their messmates and ship as they had to their classmates and Annapolis. On approaching his "old ship" U.S.S. *Minnesota*, "every line of her as familiar to me as the outlines of our house," Rear Admiral S. F. DuPont told his wife, "... I felt a very deep emotion which required an effort to repress."[10]

Pay and Rank

Naval officers may have been less concerned with material rewards than were their civilian counterparts, but they took a healthy interest

62 in the state of their pay none the less. Before the Civil War a naval officer's pay was relatively good. But prices rose 100% and salaries were cut 15% during the War, and by 1866 a lieutenant's pay was $1,875 per year for "sea duty," $1,500 for "shore duty," and $1,200 if he were placed on "leave," as many were. The difference between sea, shore, and leave pay was often sufficient reason for an officer to put up with the hardships of shipboard life, especially if he were a family man. "For a commander with [a] wife and children to support," a senior officer once explained to the Secretary of the Navy, "the hardship lies . . . in going off duty and losing pay at the rate of twelve hundred dollars a year." In 1866, sea duty or no sea duty, naval officers memorialized Congress "for an increase of their pay." They argued as a body that, as a result of their relative pay decrease, they had lost ground to other professional men, while merchants, landlords, mechanics, laborers, and other meaner men had improved their standing in relation to the naval aristocracy. A pay increase was necessary "to preserve the appearance of officers" and "to maintain the position required of us by public sentiment."[11]

> The condition of a naval officer is peculiar: at home he is expected to maintain among his countrymen the social standing which their commission has conferred upon him; abroad he is regarded as a representative of his countrymen, and our people demand that he shall, at any cost, maintain such a position that they shall not be estimated at less than their exalted place among the nations of the earth.

Congress did not immediately accept the naval aristocracy's argument, either because it felt that the Annapolites, like the diplomatic corps, could rely upon outside income to "maintain position" or because it did not fully accept the naval aristocracy's version of its "social standing" and obligations; but in 1870, with Grant in power, his old Vicksburg partner, Admiral David D. Porter, managed to push a 33% pay increase past Congress. It was the last one the Navy was to see for many years; but, when coupled with the deflation of the currency throughout the late nineteenth century, it brought better times to naval officers, except during a spate of high-price years in the early 1880s. None the less, things weren't as they had been before the Civil War, as senior officers never ceased to remind Congressmen, and ten years after the 1866 memorial to Congress there were still to be heard on Capitol Hill complaints that the officer's "social standing" made "respectable" life difficult "for the higher grades of officers," who felt compelled "to provide for two separate establishments [domiciles]." Wartime bounty and prize monies had enriched a number of commanders. Lieutenant Cushing had been voted $50,000 for sinking the rebel ram *Albemarle*, and commanders like Samuel Barron, David Porter, his son, David D. Porter, and David Farragut had won several times that sum in prize monies as their share in the seizure of enemy merchantmen and their cargoes. Post-1865 commanders achieved no such feats, and in 1899 prize and bounty rewards were abolished by act of Congress.[12] A few officers, like Commander Thomas Eastman, were unable to stay within their means and had to be refused promotion for "moral unfitness" (excessive indebtedness). If Ensign Worth Bagley is at all representative, then junior officers found the life they hoped to lead painfully expensive. After expending his monthly income in short order, Ensign Bagley complained to his sister in 1895 that he was rendered "as poor as the outer fringe on the outer circle of the stragglers of Coxey's army." However, except for the early 1880s, the late nineteenth and early twentieth centuries were respectable years, from a financial point of view, for most naval officers.[13]

The most orthodox manner by which one's pay was increased was the process of promotion to the next higher naval rank. But cash was only one of the rewards of promotion, and it was usually less important than other considerations.

Rank was its own reward. No added emoluments were needed to induce men to seek it. In the words of Flag Officer Louis Goldsborough, "Rank is the dearest object on earth to an officer" and "the most glorious reward to confer for merited services." To Captain French E. Chadwick it was "of fundamental importance" to the naval officer. And this was true not only because of added pay but also because of the added prestige and responsibilities it afforded its holder. When offered the command of the Mediterranean Squadron, Commodore Matthew C. Perry was offended, feeling that such a placid command was an insufficient challenge to "Old Bruin." "Advance in rank and command is the greatest incentive to an officer," he advised Navy Secretary William Graham. Perry would wait for an invitation to perform "some more important service." "Few men outside of military government can appreciate the importance of rank to a man under its control," Passed Assistant Engineer J. P. Stuart Lawrence told his mother. "Rank means power, honor and influence. The higher the one, the more abundant the others. When a man fights for rank it is for no shadow he contends."[14]

Within each rank there was (and is) a pecking order as well. The *Navy Register*, where each officer's assigned place in the naval hierarchy was recorded, was on a par with *Navy Regulations* in the officer's official athenaeum. And rare was the officer who was satisfied with his niche. "The struggle for rank with which Congress is regularly annoyed at each recurring Session, in the way of lengthy petitions begging special legislation to promote certain officers, has become a national nuisance," one observer wrote in 1874.[15] Relative rank defined one's shipboard quarters, one's seat at the mess table, one's duties, one's social habits, indeed, often one's very friends. And elevation from commander to captain, or captain to rear admiral, after a decade or more in the old rank, was a cataclysmic, though "long-looked-forward to," event certain to inspire a spate of congratulatory letters from old shipmates and their wives. Every officer preceding one in the *Navy Register* was scanned for signs of physical debilitation or indications of retirement plans, since only by death, disability, departure, or dismissal was room ever made in the upper ranks for advancement in times of peace. Thus the passing away or retiring of old classmates and

64   friends, distressing as their departure from the active list might be, was also the occasion for a certain amount of temperate and private rejoicing to those whose "inordinate lust for rank" would be partially satiated as a result of the removal of their names from the *Register*. When news came of the retirement of the Navy's greatest publicist and apologist, Captain A. T. Mahan, the only comment that the wife of Captain George C. Remey (whose name had followed that of Mahan for some 35 years in the *Register*) had to offer to her son regarding the event was to announce that "[t]his makes your father number three on the list of captains." The Remeys of the Navy were not necessarily "lustful" for rank, but they were particularly interested in its disposition. When several new rear admiral billets were created by the Naval Personnel Act of March 3, 1899, elevating younger captains to the long sought-after flag rank, the Remeys were hurt; Captain Remey now looked upon his own elevation to Flag rank as a somewhat less exclusive event.[16]

Remey's anxiety over his status in the naval hierarchy was not unique. It pervaded the naval aristocracy, from top to bottom. Seniors feared the ambitions of juniors; juniors the ambitions of peers. In 1889 Rear Admiral A. E. K. Benham, Commandant of the Mare Island Navy Yard, refused to fire a 13-gun (rear admiral's) salute to Temporary Rear Admiral, Permanent Commodore, George Brown, Commander of U.S. Naval Forces on the Pacific Station. Brown was Benham's junior in the *Register* by some 30 numbers, and Benham was not about to recognize Brown's premature elevation. Brown appealed to Washington for justice, however, and Benham grudgingly recognized Brown's equality with the proper number of puffs and booms. Although his views may have been unjustified, Admiral Dewey was certain that his subordinate, Rear Admiral William Benson, was seeking to depose him from the presidency of the Navy General Board in 1915. "How dare you to offer to speak to me," he roared at Benson in the presence of Navy Secretary Josephus Daniels, "you damned hypocrite and snake who has been seeking to undermine me, you blankety-blank God damned blankety-blank." Fifty years earlier, Midshipman Albert Caldwell poured out his own grief and ire to his mother over the "Despotism" of the Navy Department for its failure to promote his class at the same time that previous classes were being advanced, "and thus the gap between us and the class ahead of us is terribly widened." Momentarily, Caldwell lost all hope. "If ever you see a chance at home where you think I could do better say the word and I will come without any regret ... seniors have ceased to feel for their inferiors."[17] Shortly thereafter, Caldwell's class was advanced, and, qualms mollified, he remained loyal to the Service. But his generation was among the last to be so graced with preferment and career security. Midshipmen in the early 1880s were less fortunate.* And during World War I, when detachments of reserves were dispatched to the Navy Academy for special training, the Academy's professor of English recalled that

---

* This story is too involved and fraught with external significance to be treated here. It is fully explored in Chapter 6.

the regular Academy midshipman's chief worry during the war "seemed to be **65** not whether we should be able to beat the Germans but whether these reserves were going to stand in the way of promotion."[18]

Other forces motivated the naval officer—among them, love of country, defense of personal and service honor, fear of peer disapprobation, want of peer approbation, and lust for glory. But the high esteem each officer cherished for personal advancement was clearly a force that bears consideration and weight as well in evaluating any officer's personality and behavior. Commander W. W. Phelps surely spoke for many of his messmates when he wrote: "To each of us, his naval title is his hallmark in life, and after—will be his epitaph."[19] The naval officer probably couldn't manage to carry his rank with him to heaven, but he took it as far as the grave.

The Staff-Line Controversy

Some officers had no "rank" whatsoever, a fact that proved to be a constant irritant to their sensibilities. Naval constructors, surgeons, paymasters, and engineers were identified by their functional title—e.g., "Passed Assistant Engineer X," or "Acting Assistant Surgeon Y." These "staff" officers were not permitted to use the same symbols of rank as the line officer—e.g., "Lieutenant Z" or "Commander A"—until the twentieth century. Without these symbols, or a clear statement to the effect that the functional title implied "relative rank," the staff officers felt themselves devoid of dignity. Chief Constructor Francis Bowles, Chief of the Bureau of Construction and Repair in 1901, insisted that his office entitled him to the use of the rank of Rear Admiral:[20]

> There is no doubt that in the public mind, and also in social life, the title of rear-admiral, however ill applied, does in reality add honor and dignity to the office I occupy & serves to class it in relation to other positions in the naval service. No matter what his title, my experience from the Naval Academy through the various grades of the construction corps teaches me that the chief of the bureau of construction must have *rank* with other officers.

Line officers, jealous of their prerogatives, defended them against claims for either absolute or relative rank, concepts that struck them as "rampant 'sans culottism' run mad." In late November 1860, when the rest of the country hummed with talk of secession, the primary concern of line officers at the Naval Academy was to insure that line officers should have priority over all levels of naval pursers in obtaining quarters. When President Theodore Roosevelt named a naval medical officer to the command of the hospital ship *Relief*, Rear Admiral Willard Brownson, Chief of the Bureau of Navigation, resigned in protest. After all, as Commander A. T. Mahan once put it, it was the line officers, "who have some familiarity with sea life," who fought and navigated the ship while staff officers were "snoring away below."[21]

Of all the staff officers to voice their grievances it was the naval engineer who posed the greatest threat to the "supremacy of the line." In the 1840s when

66 steamships were first used in the U.S. Navy, the skilled engineer, fresh from the machine shop, was highly respected by line officers. But as the Navy became more dependent upon steam engineering for propulsion, the engineer began to insist on higher status—equivalent rank, equal berthing facilities, wardroom privileges, and the like. The line officer, "clinging to the traditions of his calling, jealously refused to surrender his privileges and prerogatives to the engineer."[22]

With the Civil War the quality of naval engineers fell as less qualified mechanics had to be recruited to man the new warships, and with the decline in quality came a slump in the effectiveness of the engineer's quest for status. In 1865 Chief Engineer Benjamin Franklin Isherwood asked for a reorganized and strengthened Corps of Engineers and, with the assistance of Naval Constructor John Lenthall, pushed forward work on the advanced design steam cruiser, U.S.S. *Whampanoag*. But the line officers, led by Vice Admiral David D. Porter, declared war on Isherwood and his engineers. "Isherwood has put in a claim to be made rear admiral," Porter explained to one friend, "and to punish him for his folly we intend not only to strip him and the engineers of all honors, but to make them the most inferior corps in the Navy." The "staff" were to be kept "in their proper places." Porter's "factious clique aims to govern the Navy," Navy Secretary Gideon Welles wrote in his diary; and Welles, seeing the rivalry of line and engineers develop, was unable to quell it.[23]

The struggle was brief and unequal. The Act of July 25, 1866, had made promotion of young line officers rapid and easy (for a few years); it fixed the number of line officers allowed at a figure higher than the actual number in the service, but made no comparable readjustment for any of the staff corps. Porter, a more genial and skilled courtier than Isherwood, ingratiated himself with key Republicans and, with the election of U. S. Grant, assumed control of the Navy Department. Grant's official Secretary, Adolph Borie, was little more than window-dressing. In March of 1869 Porter issued a general order, over Borie's signature, that all commands were henceforth "to recognize all orders coming from Vice Admiral Porter, as orders from the Secretary of the Navy." Isherwood's masterpiece, the *Whampanoag*, which had made a fast 17.1 knots in its trials, was partially disabled and berthed, rotting, until 1885, when it was sold. The "smooth-water Navy" of the era of reconstruction had no need for *Whampanoags*, and little need for engineers (see illustration, p. 68).[24]

Porter dealt the Corps of Engineers a terrible blow, permanently preventing their posing any threat to "the supremacy of the line," but he did not dispose of them altogether. Rather, in 1866, while Porter was superintendent, the grade of cadet engineer was added to that of midshipman at the Naval Academy, and thereafter the Navy trained its own engineers. Staff-line relations remained poor, however. Engineers, sensitive about their second-class officership and conscious of their special skills and training, continued to fume. Every warship was "a battleground for Staff and Line." The chief engineer of many a vessel told his assistants "never to let them [the line officers] know what was going on in the

Engine Room," and at least one assistant considered this "nothing but right." As one engineer-authored pamphlet maintained, the corps of naval engineers, "specially educated," were vital to the "Navy of the future."[25] Steam was the force of progress; the engineers its masters. Most line officers didn't see things that way at all and continued to check the ambitions of their brethren in the engine spaces. In 1876 they created a "line fund" to provide constant support in Washington to lobbyists who defended their command prerogatives against the "aggressive movement" of the Corps of Engineers.[26] And on shipboard they continued to favor line midshipmen over cadet engineers. As one young engineer put it, naval engineers "have no rights or place assigned to them aboard ship" that they could be certain of retaining. "They have no one to take their part; the Chief Engineer can't do anything and, of course, the Captain always sides with the midshipmen. . . ." Elderly engineers (and their assistants) found it galling to be obliged to take orders from the line officers of the deck, "a young fellow" twenty or thirty years their junior, "and salute him as a superior." They compared the line's control of the Service to "the vested interest of an arrogant and greedy aristocracy."[27]

Other staff officers advanced in relative rank at a somewhat faster rate, which was particularly irritating to the junior engineering officers. In 1881 one wrote home:[28]

> Dr. Baldwin has just joined the ship. I ranked him all to pieces out in China but now he ranks me and has two stripes on his arm to my one. Well!

The next year, in 1882, the cadet midshipmen and cadet engineers were merged—the first tentative step toward final consolidation of the two rival branches of the Service. Only one engineer was commissioned with the next class; the general officer reduction was in part responsible, but, more significantly, the final qualifying exam stressed navigation and seamanship, skills cadet engineers had never been required to learn. Those cadets of later dates who had entered as engineers rose to the top of their classes and remained there, but the machinery set up to provide the Academy with an annual handful of engineer candidates was disbanded, and by the late 1880s all Annapolites were receiving a uniform training curriculum.[29]

Line-Engineer hostility in the upper grades continued throughout the 1880s and 1890s; in 1891 Chief Engineer George Melville, Chief of the Bureau of Steam Engineering, wrote an extensive critique of the line's treatment of engineers aboard U.S. warships and demanded wardroom equality and an increase in engineer status. In a showdown case, one assistant engineer who refused to allow his men to obey the orders of deck personnel was adjudged by a court martial to have violated a lawful order. Engineers like Asa Mattrice continued to inveigh against the injustices perpetrated on their associates by the line, but after 1882 they were fighting without hope of reinforcements. The number of naval engineer officers fell from a wartime high of 2,277 in 1865 to 173 in 1896; the Act of August 5, 1882, set a final goal of 100 officers. With the

Chaplain Alexander A. McAllister conducting religious services on board U.S.S. *New York, circa* 1898 (Detroit Collection, Library of Congress).

When Admiral David D. Porter and line officer colleagues demanded legislation that would reduce engineers, doctors, paymasters, and other "staff" officers to second-class officer-citizenship, Thomas Nast of *Harper's* lampooned "The Academy of Naval Snobs," its Superintendent, Porter, and the rest of the "naval aristocracy" (Harpers *Magazine*, 1869).

merging of Academy line and engineer candidates an important source of   **69**
engineer officers dried up. Eventually the younger line and engineer officers
joined forces to terminate the controversy that had racked the Service for half
a century. In 1899 Congress ordered the merging of commissioned engineers
and line officers. Engineers were given absolute rank; the Bureau of Steam
Engineering was abolished, "the wind being taken out of its rotten sails," as one
line officer curiously put it.[30]

Shipboard Diversions and Cultured Naval Gentry

Officers spent their free time on board in a number of ways.
"During the evenings," Charles Sperry wrote home, "all hands, officers and
men, amuse themselves by singing everything they can think of."[31] The "old
Navy" loved pets. In a regular three-year cruise, a ship might acquire cats,
dogs, parrots, monkeys, a pig, a bear, a lemur, a penguin, a guanaco, several
chameleons, a tortoise or two, a mongoose, a hedgehog, an ostrich, a crow, some
guinea pigs, a number of caged white mice, rabbits, hens, or a snow-white goat.
All good sailors knew of Noah and his ark, and apparently some interpreted
the motto "Be Prepared" quite broadly.

A more important diversion for the officers involved the "cultivation of the
mind," an objective of the corps ever since Navy Secretary George Bancroft
directed the first Academy superintendent to train the midshipmen in matters
that might enable them to "make themselves as distinguished for culture as
they have been for gallant conduct." Acculturation was not immediate. Commander George Blake, superintendent when Mahan entered the Academy, was
mortified when an American officer "excepted" the dinner invitation of a
British official. And Midshipman Charles Sperry was offended in 1863 by the
"wretched bad grammar" he observed about him.[32] But the naval authorities
had the ship and the sea on their side. The monotony of existence underway
turned many an officer's fancy to reading and writing. Most important in this
regard was one's correspondence with family and friends. Letters often began
the day one's ship left one mail port and ended the day she reached the next,
additional paragraphs often being added with each day, in the manner of a
diary. But since the ship might be two weeks or more between mail pick-up
and deliveries, and since a month or more passed before one's questions about
the family finances or the children's welfare might be answered, letters necessarily involved few of an officer's spare hours.

Reading was a better way to pass the time. George Perkins mastered the
boredom of the blockade, for example, by the ingestion of a steady diet of
books. "I do nothing but read & build castles in the air," he told his sister. Some
officers, such as Perkins and Dewey, seemed to prefer novels, such as those
of Captain Frederick Marryat, William Makepeace Thackeray, or Charles
Dickens;[33] others, such as David D. Porter, Seaton Schroeder, and Foxhall
Parker, found history and biography more compelling.[34] Scientific and professional tracts were, of course, studied, as was the Bible. It isn't clear how

70   prevalent such a practice was throughout the service, but Lieutenant George
Preble and his wife mapped out a joint scriptural reading plan. With a three-
year tour of duty confronting him in 1853, Preble arranged with his wife to
read numbered chapters of the Bible each Sunday so that each would be reading
the same chapter at the same time. "It will be pleasant aforetime to know [that]
our thoughts, as well as our hearts, are united," he explained.[35]

More ambitious were those officers who spent their free hours sketching,
creating poetry, writing novels, historical works, or professional treatises,
draughting plans for their retirement dream house, or, if a senior officer,
planning a volume of memoirs or an autobiography. Thus Commander
Washington Irving Chambers, one of several who planned their own retirement
home, sent the editor of *Craftsman* magazine an elaborate blueprint of a two-
story, perfectly cubical house, in which each member of the household, including
the servants, was confined to his own "stateroom," quite unlike the liberating
spatial quality of homes Frank Lloyd Wright was designing concurrently.[36]
J. D. Jerrold Kelley, Charles Blake, David D. Porter, and Montgomery Sicard,
to name but a few, sketched, painted with oils or watercolors, and wrote songs.[37]
William Gibson, Robert Townsend, Casper Schenck, J. D. Jerrold Kelley,
Thomas H. Stevens, Henry Clay Taylor, Washington Irving Chambers, F. S.
Bassett, and Charles H. Rockwell, among others, wrote and published poems,
generally for the *United Service Magazine*, a late nineteenth-century monthly
designed for military belles-lettres, and each of the graduating classes of
midshipmen published a few of their own poetic offerings in their annual yearbooks and, after 1924, in the Academy's Literary Society publication, *The
Trident*.[38]

Naval officers were novelists as well. Captain Richmond P. Hobson wrote
a series of novels about Academy life, as did Commander Edward L. Beach.
Lieutenant Commander Yates Stirling, Jr., published five novels that took his
midshipmen from the Academy to Japan, the South Seas, the Philippines,
China, and Europe, while Lieutenant Cyrus Brady restricted the scope of his
novel to naval duty in the Pacific. Lieutenant Mason Shufeldt wrote short
stories of exploring in Africa. Ensign Frank Bunts wrote ghost stories. Paydirector Shenck wrote short stories "of love and faith." Captain Henry Clay
Taylor wrote a novel of the East Indies, "Navoonya," somewhat in the style
of *Lord Jim*. Commander Henry Wise wrote several respectable novels, among
them *The Story of the Gray African Parrot* (1859) and *Captain Brand of the "Centipede"* (1864). Acting Ensign Grattan, David D. Porter's Civil War aide, wrote
stories of the war, "Under the Blue Pennant, or Notes of a Naval Officer."
Lieutenant William Lynch's *Naval Life; or Observations Afloat and on Shore:
The Midshipman* (1851), in the turgid style of the day of Herman Melville, was
one of many anecdotal, novel-like productions of Mahan's messmates, as was
Rear Admiral Edward Simpson's *Yarnlets: The Human Side of the Navy* (1934).
Commander Arthur Nazro was remembered as being "a little of an author."
Commander Homer Blake appears to have begun a Victorian novel, as did

Commander Nathan Sargent. Admiral D. D. Porter was probably more   **71**
prolific than any of the others excepting only Hobson, Beach, or Stirling; he
published several novels and left several others in manuscript form.[39] Other
examples might be offered of the literary disposition of naval officers (not all
of which was limited to the stateroom or cabin, of course), but perhaps the
point has been made. Commodore Francis Ramsay's alleged remark to the
contrary notwithstanding, it seems that it *was* "the business of naval officers
to write books."*

Nowhere will one find in the poems or tales of Mahan's messmates the kind
of critique of American society so evident in much of the work of certain of
their contemporaries, such as Samuel Clemens, William Dean Howells, Upton
Sinclair, or Theodore Drieser, but this is understandable. The naval officer's
sense of art and cultural trappings were in the upper-class tradition described
by Neil Harris: conservative and ideologically committed to the preservation
of the existing framework of "social control."[40] The naval officer hoped "to
cultivate the pursuits of science, literature, and art . . . to expand the mind."
He conceived of himself as one having "a higher mission than that of waging
war."[41] An Academy graduate, the novelist Winston Churchill, described the
sort of literature that he and his naval colleagues produced as "mid-Victorian,"
with little respect for the relativity of pragmatic ethics. Plots concerned the
honorable and glorious conduct of gentlemen, many of them English, some
American. Naval officers were the heroes of works by men like Richmond
Hobson, Yates Stirling, Jr., Edward Beach, and Charles Rockwell,[42] but other
naval novelists, like Porter and Nathan Sargent, virtually ignored America or
dismissed it as "a land of a thousand cities and vast wilderness." Both Porter's
Arthur Merton and Sargent's "Donihle; or an American Baronet" (an unpublished novel) have their setting and action in England.[43] And while this practice
was somewhat common to the "genteel tradition," it may also serve to illustrate
the distinctly English quality of much of naval society and culture, the roots
of which we will explore in a later section.

Without entering into any extensive critique or analysis of the style or art
of the fiction and poetry penned by our star-spangled sailors, a few observations
may, I think, be made. To begin with, few, if any, of the naval literati wrote
what could be called graceful prose or polished verse. For example, David D.
Porter, in speaking of death, decay, and flux, conjured up in a manuscript
story, "An Ancient City," this ungainly image:

In a loaf of bread, unknowingly, we'll gulp down the essence of a once loved wife,
who shared our joys and sorrows!

* Ramsay is reported to have said of Captain Mahan's work: "It is not the business of
naval officers to write books." Puleston, *Mahan*, 115. The remark may be spurious, or it
may be that Ramsay meant that writing books was not the primary business of naval
officers. In any event, as the preceding pages and a later chapter ought to indicate, the remark
is in no way descriptive of what naval officers actually did.

which may have caused some editor to murmur, "Indeed!" Richmond Hobson's description of the death of a young marine officer with the familiar naval name, "Preble," may not have been as awkward, and was quite acceptable to most readers, but probably wouldn't be regarded by a "new critic" as very elegant. Hobson wrote:[44]

> The dying youth's eyes seemed to look into the depths of space. Now his voice was scarcely audible. A sweet smile came over his face.
> "God is good."

Marine and naval officers did compose themselves to die in just such a fashion,[45] but there were times when the naval authors strayed from a strict rendition of the dialect or sentiments of their subjects. Captain Robert Townsend praised Commander Henry Wise's stories of naval life, but he pointed out that Wise had drawn "old Jack" (the mature enlisted man) as he "would have been, had he enjoyed the advantages of early education and breeding." Populated by bumbling "Stepin Fetchit" servants, salty but courteous old tars, handsome young officers or English gentry, gracious belles, and evil bankers or their corrupt sons, the naval officers' novels were brimming with hearts and flowers. Listen to this randomly-selected passage from Porter's manuscript novel, "The Convict":[46]

> A year had nearly gone by since the engagement of Julia and Eustis and they seemed wrapped up in each other. Life was all *couleur de rose* and there was not a cloud visible in their sky; the stars shone brighter. . . .

Porter was a contemporary of Oliver Wendell Holmes, Sr., Nathaniel Hawthorne, Walt Whitman, and Herman Melville, but regrettably neither he nor any of his fellow officers ever managed to rise above a level of rather hackneyed banalities. None the less, if no better, the naval author was certainly no worse than the *typical* novelist of his genre and era.

Of a higher quality and quantity were the professional nonfiction books and articles naval officers produced in these years. (Since these are discussed in a later chapter, their existence is simply noted here.) The United States Naval Institute, founded by naval officers in 1873 and modelled after the British United Service Institute, began publishing, in 1874, a quarterly (eventually a monthly) journal, the *Proceedings* of the U.S. Naval Institute. This publication was filled with articles of a professional or historical nature written by the officers themselves. It served as the naval officer's primary vehicle for nonfiction expression. But prolific officers found other publishers as well. Midshipman Alfred Mahan cursed his studies in 1858 and swore that if he were "not in the Navy but in some profession that would require continual book-worming I should go nearly crazy and shoot myself I am sure." But Commander Mahan wrote essays for the *Proceedings*, and by 1894 Captain Mahan was referring to "my literary career" and speaking of his wish to devote all his energies to the writing of a biography of Lord Nelson and other historical works.[47] Mahan preferred to write ashore. But if the percentage of naval officers who wrote poems, novels, and essays (from 15 to 20% of the total corps) was higher than the percentage of diplomats or businessmen or doctors or lawyers of the late nineteenth century who wrote for publication or private gratification, then the monotony of shipboard existence may have been the cause of the literary activity of many of his messmates.

The Religion of the Commissioned

As a group, naval officers were probably less pious than some of their countrymen, more pious than others. Their piety is difficult to measure. Outwardly, many appear to have rejected the spiritual leadership of Academy Chaplain "Holy Joe" Nourse in the 1850s and '60s, but one can find examples of inbred piety among Annapolites.[48] Once at sea Mahan and his messmates may have turned to religion as a relief from monotony, as a measure of their awe and respect for the overwhelming presence of nature as it lay about them in every direction, or out of fear (the sea and the diseases man bore on it killed with regularity in the nineteenth century).[49]

Whatever their motives, the naval aristocracy could often be counted on to display becoming religiosity on the appropriate occasion. Thus Captain Jack Philip persuaded his crew to praise God on their knees after the Battle of Santiago. More mundanely, most commanding officers required that all off-duty members of the crew attend Sunday church services. One chaplain described the ceremony:[50]

> Sunday . . . the men were ordered to dress in their white trousers and frocks. . . . At ten o'clock, the shrill pipe of the boatswain and the hoarse voices of the boatswain's mates sounded over the decks of the frigate [*Cumberland*]: "All hands to muster." The marines in their full dress, the seamen in their clean white trousers and frocks, and the band in their crimson costume, with the officers in their uniform dress, occupied their several positions. The deck having been thus arranged, I advanced, with the Captain, to the capstan, and commenced the usual services of the [Episcopal] Church.

Not all officers approved of "this *compulsory* way of *forcing* men to hear a sermon preached by a chaplain, under a military order." And not all chaplains approved of the exclusive use of Episcopal rites at all shipboard religious services. Chaplain Joseph Stockbridge, a Baptist, fought "a long & fierce struggle" with naval authorities over the use of the Prayer Book, frock, and other orthodox accoutrements, and lost. "That controversy [sic]," he told Hannibal Hamlin, "brought me into disfavor at the Navy Dept."[51]

Chaplain Stockbridge's vexation was understandable; the nineteenth century U.S. Navy was dominated by Episcopalianism. Better than 40% of the U.S. navy chaplains[52] and approximately 40% of the naval officers were Episcopalians. In 1850 only about 14% of Americans were Episcopal, Unitarian, Presbyterian, or Congregationalist; no less than two-thirds of all officer candidates belonged to these upper-class, conservative faiths. Only about 22% belonged to the Methodist or Baptist Churches, or to evangelical sects (less than 1%), although more than half the nation belonged to one of these religious groups (see Table 3-1). C. Wright Mills maintained that nineteenth-century naval officers were "definitely Protestant."[53] Actually Catholics were reasonably well represented. But Catholicism has much in common with Episcopalianism. The most striking feature about the religion of the commissioned is not that it was "definitely Protestant," but that it was "high church."

Morris Janowitz maintains that "there is good evidence that a substantial minority [of U.S. military officers] adopted the Episcopal faith, rather than having been born into it." Perhaps officers favored the church "frequented by the right sort of people;" it may have been that some nineteenth-century officers also adopted Episcopalianism, though I failed to find evidence of any naval officer in the period from 1845 to 1925 who discarded the faith of his fathers for that of the Episcopal Church. Of several hundred naval officers listed in the *Dictionary of American Biography*, only six biographies include an indication of the parents' religious affiliation. Five were sons of Episcopalians; one of Catholics. Given the upper or upper-middle class origins of those naval officers born in the nineteenth century, their "high church" religious affiliations should not be surprising. My view is that it was not necessary for nineteenth-century naval officers to "adopt" the Episcopal faith. Conservative churches generated disproportionate numbers of officer-servants of the State.[54]

The nineteenth century Episcopal tradition in the Service may account in part for the liveliness of Episcopalianism in today's Navy, but, as Professor Janowitz has observed, the ideological compatibility of the two "services" is also important. The Episcopal catechism's maxims ("To submit . . . to my governors . . . to order myself lowly and reverently to all my betters and to do my duty. . . .") were consistent with the naval aristocracy's own precepts. Thus Rear Admiral David Potter argued that the naval officer's respect for discipline and order was "only a symbol" of his respect for "that higher power which has established the order of the Universe." When Rear Admiral A. T. Mahan's Trinity Church pastor appointed a workingclass layman to the parish board as a democratic measure, board member J. Pierpont Morgan confined himself to a written protest of this sanscullotism, but board member A. T. Mahan felt compelled to resign.[55] The Episcopal service was "prescribed" by Academy regulations for the Naval Academy Chapel, which has been described by one officer as "the heart of the Naval Service."[56] Contact with Royal Navy Church of Englanders and British society throughout the world led Mahan and his messmates to "these English chapels . . . scattered from pole to pole."[57] If there were officers who had been born into a fundamentalist faith, there were many reasons for them to feel uncomfortable as members of the naval aristocracy.

The Crew

No account of naval officers would be adequate without a look at Jack Tar and officer-enlisted man relations. A look it will have to be, how-

Table 3-1 Religion of naval officers, compared to business and political leaders and a national profile for 1850 and 1900

	Nationwide, 1850[1] (estimating "others" to be 30% of nation)	304 Annapolis[2] students, 1885–1895	Miller's 165[4] political leaders in 1900	Gregory-Neu's 217[4] "industrial elite" in 1870	Miller's 174[4] "business elite" in 1900	Nationwide,[1] 1900 (estimating "others" to be 30%)	1,129[2] Annapolis students, 1900–1920
Episcopalian	1.8%	40.1%	16.0%	26.5%	30.0%	2.2%	28.0%
Unitarian	.4	3.5	[3]	10.5	7.0	.2	2.2
Congregational	3.2	7.5	[3]	23.5	[3]	2.3	6.5
Presbyterian	8.0	11.3	22.5	14.5	25.0	7.0	15.5
Lutheran	2.2	2.0	[3]	[3]	[3]	6.3	3.0
Catholic	10.4	11.1	4.0	0.0	7.0	13.5	12.5
Jewish	.4	0.0	2.0	0.0	3.0	2.5	1.3
Methodist	27.5	14.0	17.5	6.0	11.0	20.0	16.5
Baptist	16.0	7.3	9.5	4.0	6.0	18.0	8.5
Others (evangelical sect, agnostic, etc.)	30.0	3.0	27.0	15.0	11.0	30.0	5.8

[1] Calculations extrapolated from church membership figures in Edw. Gaustad, *Historical Atlas of Religion in America* (N.Y., 1962), 52ff; and Bureau of Census, *Historical Statistics*, 228. The figures for Catholics are probably too low, and there is really no way of knowing the correct percentage of "others," but church membership figures are useful measures of the comparative degree to which churches have found roots among *established* members of a community.
[2] Register of Candidates, U.S. Naval Academy, R.G. 405, N.A. (religious affiliation available only after 1880).
[3] Not specified.
[4] Distributing "unspecified Protestant" proportionately among specified Protestants in the fashion of William Miller, *Men in Business*, 334.

ever, since sailors wrote no official reports and few private accounts of their naval careers or personal lives, and left no manuscript collections to fill the shelves of public or private repositories. To a certain extent this is undoubtedly due to the fact that enlisted men were simply less articulate than their officer superiors. But it may also reflect a difference in what the two groups believed to count in life. To many officers the preservation of personal and official correspondence seems to have been viewed as vital to the proper development of one's career. Rear Admiral S. F. DuPont, for example, expressed real concern about his "archives." His letter books as a squadron commander were the embodiment of his "professional *life*," and he regarded his private correspondence as extremely important and worthy of preservation as well. In a social role constructed of such material as honor, fame, and glory, the guarding of sources that might aid one to reconstruct the past may have been deemed axiomatic. The noncommissioned naval man may have regarded himself in less exalted terms, which might explain why no known sailor managed to insure the security and future availability of any body of private manuscript records. Officers clearly regarded the crew in such light, for while they frequently praised their officer subordinates in official combat reports, they rarely mentioned enlisted personnel. It is unlikely that *all* sailors carried on as faithful and active a correspondence with their families as did their captains and lieutenants, but there were undoubtedly *some* who did. The preservation of such a series of letters would have helped to reconstruct a more rounded picture of the crew than the one offered here, but the contours of that picture can be traced; and with the jigsaw pieces that are available, we can venture some educated guesses at what the remaining pieces would look like. As Jesse Lemisch has put it, "we cannot with any validity conclude anything about the inarticulate . . . until we actually study them."[58]

To begin with, few sailors appear to have entered the naval service for the same reasons as the officer candidates. Undoubtedly there were some, like Josiah Cobb or Samuel Leech, who became "enamoured with the idea of a sea life" after the visit of some "reckless" sea-going relative to the family home, or who found in the smell of the sea and the pitch and tar of the waterfront a romantic perfume too heady to give a wide berth to.* But unlike the officer, whose training provided him with a heroic image and whose commission assured him high social standing, opportunity for leadership, and security to boot, the apprentice or landsman who enlisted for one tour of duty was assured low status, little opportunity to exercise authority, and no guarantee that he would not be discharged at the end of his tour. As one observer remarked, the

* According to Michael Lewis, a most thorough historian of the Royal Navy, the sailor of the British Navy of the mid-nineteenth century was the son of a seafaring father. This may have been true of the American bluejacket (several autobiographies indicate that the seafaring tradition often ran to three generations), and no less than 50% of all sailors enlisting in the U.S. Navy at East Coast rendezvous in 1880 listed their former occupations as "mariner," but these may simply have been reenlistees. Cf. John Laffin, *Jack Tar: The Story of the British Sailor* (London, 1969).

American bluejackets had "little to bind them to the Service, and a man who is a **77**
bluejacket this year may conceive that he had better be a dentist the next."[59]
Throughout the late nineteenth century U.S. warships were manned by a wide
spectrum of human types; thieves who accepted service rather than jail;[60] seafarers who had been "crimped" (ensnared) by flop-house landlords; eager
young apprentices; native-born farmhands and mechanics down on their luck;
immigrants clustered in urban areas such as Boston, New York, or Philadelphia;
Chinese recruited in the Far East; black men from the States or the West Indies;
and, fortunately from our point of view, a few articulate adventurers such as
Herman Melville and Charles Nordhoff.

The most unfortunate of these, of course, were those whose enlistment was
not even voluntary. "Shanghaiing" was not practiced in the U.S. Navy in its
most aggravated form, impressment. But involuntary enlistment in other forms
was common. In the 1830s slaveowners leased their property to the Navy for
use on board warships or within navy yards,[61] but emancipation of the slaves
did not abolish the practice of leasing humans for naval service. Unscrupulous
waterfront landlords ensnared seafaring boarders and "sold" them to a naval
receiving station, where they presented exorbitant bills and collected part or all
of their victim's bounty and first three months' wages. Of the sailor thus saddled
with a "dead horse," Admiral Porter wrote sympathetically in 1885:

> Poor wretch! he soon gets himself put in double irons, and only awakens to a con-
> sciousness of his folly next morning when he finds himself handcuffed, and hears that
> he has sold himself to Uncle Sam.

"The Government," Porter charged, "encourages . . . the landlord system, by
which the very life-blood of a sailor is sucked out of him before he goes on
board ship."[62] It was not so crude a recruiting device as the press gang or the
"shanghai," but the end result was the same.

Voluntary enlistment did not necessarily indicate a love for the sea, the naval
service, or the country (though, of course, it might). Carter Goodrich and Sol
Davidson have demonstrated that the western frontier did not act as a significant
"safety-valve" for urban laborers hit hard during depression years,[63] but the
naval and merchant services may have provided minor "safety-valve" relief
for skilled craftsmen. In every period of depression throughout the nineteenth
and twentieth centuries, the U.S. Navy and merchant marine were able to
improve the overall quality of enlisted personnel whenever the depression was
so complete that the recruiting officer acquired considerable choice of candidates.
Thus Seaman Jacob Hazen maintained that "the best remedy for hard times"
was "to go to sea," and Rear Admiral Thomas Washington, Chief of the
Bureau of Navigation in 1921, told the House Naval Affairs Committee that
more and better men applied for naval service after mid-November of 1920
"due to the economic depression" during which "they could not hold their
jobs ashore. . . ." As Marine Brigadier General George Barnett told the same

78   committee several years earlier, there was "no better [economic] barometer of
the times than a [service] recruiting record."[64]

In boom times, the enlistment of skilled native-born craftsmen fell off, and
the recruitment of foreign-born was required to fill the vacancies. The law
required that two thirds of each ship's complement be composed of American
citizens, and indigent immigrants were obliged to falsify their nationality to
pass as Kinderhook Dutch or Pennsylvania German.[65] By 1878, in spite of the
panic of '73, 60% of the Navy's enlisted personnel were foreign-born. Most
recruiting in the 1870s took place in New York City, and in 1879 Navy
Secretary Richard Thompson attempted to increase the percentage of native-
born by sending new recruiting teams to the Midwest. Undoubtedly these
teams recruited some Midwesterners, but the step was no panacea. When the
U.S.S. *Ashuelot* sank in 1883 in the China Sea, 92 of her 111-man crew were
foreign-born, twenty different nationalities having been represented. At the
same time the *Monocacy* housed natives of 21 different nations. Of 105 men only
20 were U.S. citizens. Foreign-born held the ship's key enlisted posts: master-
at-arms, captain of the foretop, chief boatswain's mate, and so on. The only
Yankee aboard was the ship's cook. The *Ashuelot* and *Monocacy* were permanent
China station gunboats, likely to draw on foreign sources to fill their comple-
ments, but in 1887 the *Enterprise*, a more typical warship that drew its crew
from domestic stations, was 47% manned by foreign-born. In fact, in 1890,
better than 55% of the complement of American warships were still foreign-
born, compared to the national level of 26% of 21 year-olds or over. Since
approximately half of the foreign-born residing in the United States at any
point in time in the late nineteenth century were naturalized citizens, one might
suppose that about 28% of the crews of American warships from the Civil
War to the Spanish-American War were citizens of foreign powers. And a
British contemporary observer tells us that in 1894 some 30% of the enlisted
personnel in the U.S. Navy *were* foreign nationals.[66]

This same observer offered an intriguing addendum to his figures when he
noted that some 40% of these foreign nationals had declared their intentions
of becoming U.S. citizens. If this be true, and if it be characteristic of earlier
periods as well, then Passed Assistant Engineer Frank Bennett's remark that
most foreign-born tars were long-timers in the service may tell us much of the
process of enlisted recruitment. Since most of the crew of the steam-sail warships of the late nineteenth century was assigned to the vessel for the duration
of what was normally a three-year tour of duty, it would seem likely that the
30% who were foreign citizens were recruited in Boston, New York, Philadelphia, or a foreign port and that a significant proportion of these men,
perhaps as many as 40% of their total figure, reenlisted at the end of their tour,
thus helping to keep the total figure of foreign-born sailors at the 55–60%
level.[67]

British and Northern Europeans outnumbered all other foreign-born on
American warships unless the vessel was one, like the *Monocacy*, permanently

assigned to Chinese waters. Figures for the *Monocacy* and the *Enterprise* for 1883 **79**
and 1887 respectively reveal a profile of national origins for their crews which
may be compared to the U.S. population profile at that time (see Table 3–2).[68]

Germans and Canadians were less likely to enter the naval service than were
Scandinavian-born, who had a greater nautical tradition than did their inland
counterparts. The high numbers of Japanese and Chinese among the crew
should not necessarily be read as an indication of the nautical tradition of these
nationalities, for virtually all enlisted Orientals were (and still are) accounted
for as stewards, messmen, or cooks—functionaries on the lowest level of naval

Table 3-2 Ethnic Composition of U.S. Warship Crews in late Nineteenth Century

	East Coast· Enlistments. 1880	Enterprise (1887)	West Coast¹ Enlistments, 1880	Monocacy (1883)	Mature Males in U.S., 1890
U.S.-born	48.5%	53%	40%	20%	74%
Foreign-born	51.5	47	60	80	26

Analysis of Foreign-born by National Origin:

	East Coast	Enterprise	West Coast	Monocacy	U.S. (1885)
British	24.5%	8.0%	14%	15.0%	12.5%
Irish	23.5	25.5	28	10.5	24.5
Scandinavian	31.0	23.7	18	26.2	8.0
Central Europe	9.0	10.9	13	15.9	29.0
Canadian	6.0	9.3	0	3.3	21.0
Asiatic	0	16.0	21	24.7	1.5
Other	3.0	8.0	6	8.4	3.5

¹ Weekly Returns of Enlistment at Naval Rendezvous, R.G. 24, N.A.

society—"boys."* Their appearance on the spar deck for quarters, "armed with
boarding-pikes," has been recorded by one who considered their presence to
have "introduced an element of opera bouffe" to the business of shipboard drills.
It was their function aboard the *Monocacy* to "repel boarders" should such a
necessity arise,

> and when this Mongolian horde rushed madly from one end of the deck to the other,
> brandishing their spears and yelling "hi-ya!" their long cues [sic] and light-blue
> garments fluttering in the breeze behind them, the remainder of the crew did well to
> flee to the paddle-boxes, whence one could contemplate the Oriental spectacle and
> think of Kublai Khan and his "ancestral voices prophesying war" in comparative
> safety.

A different view of these Chinese "boys" was taken by one who affectionately
remembered their personal loyalty. Their stipend, Rear Admiral David Potter
recalled, was "next to nothing a month." Their food was "only a fragment
from [their] master's [!] table." Their bed was "only a mat on the hard deck

* On the other hand, Richard McKenna's account of the ability and rapidity that
Chinese "boys" demonstrated in assuming critical shipboard duties on the Yangtze patrol
gunboats is surely accurate. See *The Sand Pebbles* (New York, 1962), *passim*.

80   outside [his] door."[69] They took over the duties slaves had performed before
1865.

What of black Jack Tar? He had difficult beginnings. Orders issued by the
first Navy Department, during the quasi-war with France, prohibited the
enlisting of Negroes. The War of 1812 swept these bans away; by 1816 one
of every seven tars on the *Java* was black. Black sailors participated in an 1837
naval exploring party in Florida. According to one British account in 1842,
recently reprinted in the Navy's quasi-official publication, the *Proceedings* of the
U.S. Naval Institute, there were as many as 40 free blacks on the *Brandywine*
in 1842 who, according to the ship's first lieutenant, "received exactly the same
bounty, the same wages, and the same privileges as the whites; . . . in their
duty . . . no distinction was made between black & white, but each were
mingled indiscriminately, and classed only by their relative degrees of seamanship. In this," the first lieutenant was reported to have said, "the blacks were
not at all inferior to the whites, either in their skill, readiness, or courage."
None the less, by mid-century naval authorities were making efforts to hold
black enlistments down to 5% of total complement. Remarkable West African
seafarers, Kroomen, were frequently hired on for part-time duty on Africa
station vessels in the 1850s, but few, if any, were asked to stay when the vessel
returned to the States. One anonymous sailor complained in 1856 of being
obliged to salute certain colored Brazilian officers, "which was peculiarly
unpleasant to us." While free blacks on the *Brandywine* in 1842 *may* have been
treated like whites, "contraband" blacks a score of years later were not. These
ex-slaves were initially allowed "no higher rating than 'boys' . . ." by Navy
Secretary Gideon Welles. The exigencies of the war forced the authorities to
waive temporarily their racially restrictive enlistment policies. One authority
has argued that by 1865 fully 25% of the complement of Union warships were
black. None the less, blacks were often segregated on these ships, a policy that
appears to have been continued for nearly a century. More than one bluejacket
reported "intense race hatred" and "open hostility" between black and white
sailors in the late nineteenth and early twentieth century Navy. In 1883 the
Monocacy's apothecary was black, but he was the only Negro aboard, and he
was from Martinique.

The popular mulatto, Gunner's Mate "Dick" Turpin, was exceptional. In
the early 1890s racial fights definitely occurred on the *Charleston*, the *Boston*,
and the *Independence* and may have broken out on other vessels as well. White
personnel told *Army and Navy Journal* readers how they detested blacks and
disliked having them as shipmates. By 1913 black tars had been totally segregated and their enlistments restricted to the rank of messman. All but a handful
of the 10,000 black naval volunteers in World War I served in this capacity;
each officer had his own. After the war black enlistments fell off still further
as Filipinos replaced them as messmen. In 1921 only 2.1% of whitehats had
black skin, and this percentage fell steadily over the next two decades. By June
1942, the Navy had only 6 rated Negroes (other than messmen) in the regular

Navy, and a committee of senior naval officers and department officials defended **81** their policy with the remark that "the enlistment of Negroes (other than as mess attendants) leads to disruptive and undermining conditions."[70]

Why is it that native-born white Americans could not be attracted into enlisting in their Navy in the nineteenth century? Or, to put the question differently, what might have induced them to join? Good pay? An opportunity to see the world? Good food? Pleasant working conditions? Opportunities for rapid job advancement? Any of the above?

In addition to the hazards of maintop life, one had to be able to bear the effects of the rise and fall of the sea. "Some suppose that sailors are never seasick after the first time at sea," Samuel Leech wrote. "This is a mistake." Then there was the matter of pay; $8.00 per month for "green hands" in 1870, $10.50 by 1878. Farm laborers were doing better as late as 1890, and industrial and railroad workers averaged from 50% to 80% more pay than their naval counterparts.[71] "Liberty" was severely restricted for "Jack" in foreign ports, making it next to impossible to claim that one might "see the world" by joining the Navy. "Born in a land as free as the air they breathe, used to liberty of conscience, freedom of thought and liberty of action," nineteenth century white Americans were reluctant to "submit to the incarceration of a man-of-war life," or so "Marlinspike" advised the editor of the *U.S. Nautical Magazine and Naval Journal* in 1856.[72] Moreover, the cuisine served Jack Tar compared unfavorably to that offered the average American, or even the well-kept American hog. A diet of tinned beef, "bully" (mutton), "salt horse" (corned beef) or salt pork, beans, fresh fruits and vegetables while in port, coffee, and molasses sustained the wardroom officers, while the crew messed on a paste made of boiled dough, bacon fat, and molasses, and on salt pork, worm-and-weevil-ridden hardtack, and cockroach-ridden coffee, with enough lime juice to prevent scurvy. Spoiled rations, poorly ventilated living quarters,* and foul water tanks were common affairs, but conscientious officers duly registered their protests. Commander Thomas Turner, for example, complained to Captain Thomas A. Dornin, Commanding Officer of the Norfolk, Virginia, Navy Yard in 1858:

> It would be impossible to exaggerate the condition of the water in some of these tanks [on the U.S.S. *Saratoga*]; in point of the most offensive filthiness, it was as bad as it could well be.

Turner held Dornin's shipyard personnel responsible for the "immense quantity of refuse matter" found in some of the tanks, "emitting the most unpleasant odor," and noted that he "was almost [!] afraid to issue it for use." But even when provisions were wholesome, there was no guarantee that they would be put to good use. The Navy's chefs did not always enjoy as creditable a rating

---

* On the U.S.S. *Swatara* in 1877, for example, the officers' staterooms allowed them 324 cubic feet per officer, whereas the sailors' quarters allowed only 58 cubic feet per man. Drake, ". . . Shufeldt. . .," 300.

as they do today in some circles. "The devil certainly sends the navy its cooks," Lieutenant Commander Caspar Goodrich wrote in 1879, "for they make Jack's grub as indigestible as possible."[73]

Promotion was slow in the officer corps but even slower in the enlisted ranks. It was not until 1904 that enlisted men became eligible for commissions, as Chief Warrant Officers or line officers. The twenty year retirement at half pay provision did not become law until 1925. Less than 1% of all enlisted personnel were warrant officers in 1894, and of these only 10% were appointed from the ranks. But even if one did become the one in a thousand who advanced to warrant-officer status, the commissioned officer always stood one rung above. Several tars were irritated by the comparatively high pay of midshipmen— four times the pay of an able seaman in 1845. The naval apprentice system, established in 1837, was designed to provide the Navy with career-minded sailors, but few sons of the Age of Jackson were willing to settle for the life of Jack Tar. Articulate sailors like Jacob Hazen warned parents against embarking their sons on the stultifying apprentice system. "Six years to become an ordinary seaman!" complained one pair of tars in 1857. Harold Langley has intimated that the 1850 and 1855 Congressional modifications to the apprentice system laid a foundation for a sound body of career enlistees, but his estimate is fifty years premature.[74]

"SEMPER FIDELIS"

Guarding the pale separating the lower deck rabble from officer country stood the marine sentry. If we were to accept Lieutenant Commander Roe's contemporary account of the marine's role, one might suppose that marines were among the most beloved of Jack Tar's shipmates. "The sailor loves to see [the marine's] stiff, erect form pacing up and down on his post," Roe wrote in 1865. "They [sic] feel a sense of security to see him there." Marines, with "their bright but pitiless bayonets," were "great preservers." A warship would lose "her true character without a marine guard." Roe's officer candidates were reminded that the marine guard was the Executive Officer's "right arm." "Remember," he added, "they are the 'ever faithful'." Was it really true that sailors loved marines? Why was it necessary to remind the future officer of the loyalty of this sea-borne soldiery? Was the marine's only mission that of storming citadels? What was meant by Roe's reference to their being required in order to "preserve order and maintain the peace of the ship?"[75] Could it be that marines were actually a kind of police without which the nineteenth-century American naval society might disintegrate?

In the first place, it was not true, as Roe had claimed, that sailors felt any pleasurable "sense of security" in observing the marine at his post. As Herman Melville put it, "the man-of-war's-man casts but an evil eye on a marine." Later observers explained in detail why it was that "Jacky does not love the marines." It appears that the marine's duty was "chiefly that of a policeman. He stands guard and sees that Jacky does not misbehave himself." Marines were "soldiers" designed "to watch, and search, and discipline the sailor." This was the ground on which the keeping of marines on board ship (and consequently out of the reach of the U.S. Army) was defended in 1864, 1876, and 1890. And while naval officers were interested in preserving their own "army," the primary argument that those who opposed the abolition of the Corps offered at these times was not a wish to conserve a colorful and traditional arm of "the Service" but rather sheer necessity. Grog was abolished in 1862, but there was plenty of liquor smuggled aboard in bladders and dufflebags and much violence and fighting. "The only way to gain prestige among [the crew]," one tar recalled, "was to fight and win a battle." And keeping men aboard was just as important as keeping them subdued. If marines were withdrawn from warships, the argument went, "there would be a great many desertions." Passed Assistant Engineer J. P. Stuart Lawrence summed up the feelings of many officers on the matter in a letter to his mother in 1876. Without the marine guard, Lawrence asked rhetorically, "who is going to prevent the sailors from running away?" Who, indeed? But the more central, and all too often unposed, question was: Why should anyone who had enlisted want to "run away" at all? Many officers appear to have accepted such a paradox as a fundamental axiom of enlisted society and ratiocination. In the words of one Commanding Officer, "If you freighted a ship for heaven, and was [sic] obliged to touch in at hell for wood and water, half the boat's crew would desert."[76] And while this remark may hold a kernel of truth, it is probably more important to know something of the conditions of life that the men would have had to put up with on that celestial journey, conditions as concrete and urgent as the destination was unearthly. If, as one observer suggested, the bluejacket's dream was primarily for "shore-liberty, a river of grog, and a mountain of tobacco,"[77] simple enough pleasures as they were, they were out of Jack Tar's reach in the late nineteenth century.

Officer-Enlisted Relations

Part of Jack Tar's dilemma was that most naval officers never seemed to comprehend the fact that the autocratic and imbalanced society of the warship was not always as acceptable to the bluejacket as it was to his officer. The officer believed himself to be "the beau ideal of young Naval heroes" to his men. "No class of men living appreciate the genuine qualities of a cultivated gentleman as the American sailor," proclaimed Lieutenant Commander Roe. According to Commander Richard Wainwright, sailors earnestly hoped their officers might always "appear well beside foreign officers." Undoubtedly there was some truth to these remarks. Many officers *did* gain the respect and affection of their men. The exploits of men like Lieutenants Uriah P. Levy and William Woodhull, both of whom drew their swords on separate occasions to defend bluejackets being pursued by Argentine soldiers and police, and the reluctance of men like Commodore Robert Stockton to flog offenders before the lash was outlawed in 1850 undoubtedly won the huzzahs of Jack and

84   his shipmates.* But one wonders whether sailors were as delighted as the midshipmen who "loved" the officer who seized a drunken black sailor by the collar,[78]

> whirled him about, rushed him forward over the deck, and pitched him bodily down the fore hatch before the man knew what had happened to him, [and after adjusting his gloves] went quietly off to the [dance] hall.

The "voice from the main deck" on the subject of crew-officer relations is, of course, a faint one, but one can detect certain strains that distinguish its melody from that of the voice from the quarterdeck. Consider, for example, the charge of the member of the crew of the U.S.S. *Wabash* in 1872 who wrote to the editor of the New York *Sun*:

> We are cursed and d——d by every man that wears a piece of gold lace, and as they wear that gold lace, they think they should be worshipped by every man that wears a blue shirt. . . . Even the lowest grade of officers, the midshipmen, call the men: "You d——d dogs, come here, or I will help you!"

Or listen to the "voice from the main deck" himself, Samuel Leech, who complained that officers "do not treat with a sailor as with a *man*."

> They know what is fitting between each other as officers; but they treat their crews on another principle; they are apt to look at them as pieces of living mechanism, born to serve, to obey their orders, and administer their wishes without complaint.

"Don't stop to think," a bluejacket told young Stephen Blanding, a fresh enlistee in 1863. "Your superiors will do all the thinking, and you will do all the work." Sailors maintained that they were not looked upon as altogether sentient beings but as cogs in the naval gear.† In one of Lieutenant Commander Beach's novels, a characterization is offered of one old tar who had read *Roughing It* and *Babes in the Wood* "with solemn graven face," and had finally decided they were too deep for him. "'It would take a gentleman to understand them books,' said he." It mattered not that many sailors were no less well-read than their superiors; few officers saw them in terms other than of the carefree, simple, grog-and-tobacco "Jacky" of folklore. Lieutenant Commander Roe's query: "Have petty officers rights?" was offered in deadly earnest, as was his revealing self-response: "I am aware that the word [rights] has a fearful sound, and a portentous significance to a good many officers. But the age [1865] has

---

* Robert E. Johnson (*Rear Admiral John Rodgers, 1812–1882* [Annapolis, 1967], 93) believes that the bluejackets "regretted the passing of the cat-o'-nine tails." It may be that some did, but Johnson does not cite any of them, and it seems more likely that Johnson is simply adopting the opinion of his subject, Rodgers, who himself regretted the abolition of flogging.

† For a similar critique of U.S. Army officers of the late nineteenth century, see ex-Lieutenant Duane M. Greene, *Ladies and Officers of the U.S. Army: American Aristocracy* (New York, 1880), 103–104: "Rank is the shield behind which they stand to heap tyranny upon insult and wrong. They do not regard inferiors as having rights which they should respect, and by the tyrannical exercise of authority, they exhort a slavish obedience from those over whom they are placed. They look upon a private soldier as a machine—animate, yet without sense of injustice or wrong; exacting of him the offices of a menial—a serf—degrading him even in his own estimation."

declared that all men have rights, and the fact may as well be admitted grace- **85**
fully."[79] The plight of the navy bluejacket was partially rectified in the 1850s,
as Harold Langley has demonstrated,[80] but, Roe's advice notwithstanding, the
quality and status of bluejacket life throughout the late nineteenth century still
left much to be desired.

SHIPBOARD DISCIPLINE

Nowhere are these shortcomings more evident than in the state
of naval discipline in the era between 1850 and 1900. Flogging was outlawed
by 1851, but the rationale that had produced and permitted it continued in the
minds of many officers. Branding and tattooing were not abolished as punishments until 1872, and until 1878 sailors could be forced to testify against themselves. If sailors fought, drank, swore, or deserted, harsh corporal punishment
was deemed an excellent remedy—not an underlying cause. When word that
flogging had been abolished reached one vessel, its Commanding Officer
punished the next offender by double-ironing his hands behind his back and
placing him in front of the bilge pump, "from which a stream of water was
turned on his face until he became unsensible." Each time he recovered consciousness the operation was repeated until the doctor reported that further
punishment might endanger his life. In another instance, an Executive Officer
disregarded one man's plea of illness. For sweeping the deck improperly, he
triced him up by the wrists from the main rigging "with his arms fully extended laterally" and left him there "until he begged for mercy." Both the
man's collarbones were broken in the process. One officer killed an intoxicated
seaman when he forced a mop into his mouth. A common form of punishment
(after the abolition of flogging), considered quite mild, consisted of lashing a
man's thumbs behind his back, passing the lashings over a hammock hook, and
tricing him up "till his toes were just clear of the deck." Thieves were punished
by being compelled to promenade the deck with a strait jacket made of canvas
upon which was painted in large letters "Thief" and were thereafter set ashore
at the ship's next port of call. In 1882 Navy Secretary Hunt complained, in
General Order 287, of the excessive use of the sentence of solitary confinement
on bread and water for thirty days at a crack.

The Navy may have helped to carry American culture to the Orient, but it
didn't depart altogether empty-handed. Naval officers adopted the "sweat-box"
punishment, whereby victims were incarcerated in separate iron boxes "to
remain without either food or drink until they make a confession" or until their
spirit was broken. Where the "sweat-box" failed, a suspect might be hung by
the neck from the spanker boom for short periods of time or restricted indefinitely to the limits of the ship. Eventually a general order was issued prohibiting
"sweat-boxes," but while the leadership remained unchanged, the labelling of
one form of punishment as cruel or "unusual" only meant that a new one
would come into vogue. And as late as 1897 there were officers who advocated
a return to flogging.

86   Occasionally an officer might be brought to the bar of justice for cruelties inflicted on his charges, as in the cases of Commander Alexander H. Semmes in 1871 and Commander Bowman "Billy Hell" McCalla in 1890, but the punishments failed to fit the crime. Semmes, whose cruelties had made him feared and hated among sailors everywhere, was suspended from duty for one year. McCalla, found guilty by a jury of his peers of having badly cut a member of his crew with his sword, the man having been "in a kneeling position on the deck" of the *Enterprise* "and in double irons, with his hands ironed behind his back," and of lashing men to Jacob's ladders, ironing them together for days on end, strait-jacketing them for 6 days at a time, and failing to enter any of these acts in the ship's log, was punished with a brief suspension from duty and the loss of several numbers in the navy register.

To be sure, such punishments were considered severe by the officers concerned. McCalla, for example, worked for ten years to erase the stain of suspension from his escutcheon and to have his name restored to its former position in the register. (His manuscript autobiographical apologia, wherein these efforts are recorded, is an illuminating document; nowhere therein does he deny the truth of the charges.) But there were many at the time, civilians as well as sailors, who considered them inadequate penalties.

If punishment of over-exacting officers was light, an important factor contributing to this situation was the complexion of the tribunals that tried the cases of the accused martinets. Naval courts-martial, not very surprisingly, were composed entirely of naval officers. The corps judged itself, and that which was one man's cup of tea was not likely to become another's cup of hemlock. "I see they are after you again because you added irons to a bread and water diet," Commander Charles Clark wrote to Commander Caspar Goodrich in 1894 and added, "I know you won't let this trouble you since it is an oversight common in the service." After Commander Bowman McCalla's unsuccessful bout with a court-martial, a number of officers wrote letters in his defense and argued (successfully, as it turned out) for his complete exoneration.[81]

The "whitewash" was commonplace wherever the officer corps sanctioned disciplinary forms not legally allowed, but this was not the only reason that the disciplining of officers appeared less severe than that of the crew. The naval aristocracy was a small body throughout the late nineteenth century, and men who had been classmates at Annapolis or who were navy yard neighbors or shipboard messmates were unwilling, and somewhat inappropriate, judges of one another. Thus the "band of brothers" were (and still are) less willing to charge their own membership with offenses for which bluejackets were punished daily. The sailors who wrote to the editor of the *United States Nautical Magazine and Naval Journal* in 1856, complaining that drunken sailors received severe penalties, "but let an officer come on board dead drunk—which has often been the case this cruise—and nothing is said to him,"[82] could have been written one hundred-odd years later.

Still another reason that officer disciplining seemed insignificant compared to that of enlisted men may be found in a simple reading of the table of maximum punishments itself. As late as 1917 the maximum punishment for "swearing" that might be levied on an officer was "a public reprimand," while an enlisted man might be sentenced to solitary confinement in double irons on a bread and water diet for 30 days. For "irreverent behavior during church" an officer might lose three numbers on the navy register; an enlisted man might find himself confined in double irons for three months for similar behavior. For the military crime of "carelessness" an officer could not be punished with anything more grievous than the loss of ten numbers; an enlisted man might be confined for six months for the same offense. For the unlawful possession of liquor on board ship, or for smuggling liquor aboard, an officer might lose as many as three numbers and suffer public reprimand; for similar conduct an enlisted man could expect as much as six months confinement and a dishonorable discharge. And so on.[83] Given the nature of rank and status in the service, it would be asking too much to expect that an officer might suffer confinement without subsequent loss of all standing and prestige among the crew, which explains why officer confinement was not provided for. And it is true, as has been suggested, that officers looked upon reprimands, suspensions, and the loss of numbers as anathema. But it is also likely that the loss of numbers, or a one-year suspension from duty, did not strike many sailors as sufficient retribution for the mistreatment of Jack Tar.

"The Captain is King" and "The King Can Do No Wrong"

If, as has been suggested, enlisted men were frequently mistreated in the nineteenth century, if commanders were inclined to consider their men at times to be little more than "pieces of living mechanism," surely the traditional concept of shipboard sovereignty was at the heart of the problem. Under the impact of the reform movement of the 1830s and 1840s the Navy was forced to dispense with the cat, but it did *not* cease to function autocratically. The abolition of flogging was no panacea. When the young Herman Melville and other anti-institutionalistic Brahmins mounted an assault on the naval aristocracy, they were met full force by the fury of men like Louis Goldsborough and Thomas O. Selfridge, Sr. Captain Selfridge, for example, attacked Melville's *White Jacket* and its assumptions, while defending flogging. "He would have laws, democratic in all respects, for the rule of our [sic] Navy. What absurdity!" "Democratic" laws implied the disintegration of order in "their" Navy to Mahan's messmates; the defense of command prerogative was looked upon as one of the first orders of the day. In Mahan's Navy a warship at sea was "a complete system in itself. The captain is king, and as absolute a monarch as ever lived. The officers are his house of lords, and some five hundred men his subjects." "The captain passes for a religious character," one bluejacket observed, while a distraught lieutenant complained that he appeared "always [to] maintain the role of an absolute monarch. What he says is law." Or, as another officer put it, "The line of demarcation between the cabin and elsewhere is feudal in

88   character."[84] Thus when one uninformed chaplain began the service, before the Commodore had taken his seat, with the traditional Episcopal passage: "The Lord is in His holy temple, let all the earth keep silence before him," he was interrupted by the Commodore, who strode up the aisle in a huff and exclaimed: "Sir, I would have you understand that the Lord is not in His holy temple until I have taken my seat!" And just as today, when the sun crosses the noon meridian, the officer of the deck must first ask permission of the captain to strike eight bells before noon is officially declared to have arrived, so in the late nineteenth century permission had to be secured "from the proper authority" before the sun could officially be declared to have set—enveloping darkness notwithstanding.[85]

Jack Tar was not the only one to feel tyrannized by his commanding officer. Midshipman Francis Roe's bitter entries in his private journal in 1859 tell a typical story of the junior officer's feeling of persecution ("I am in his power!"). The "band of brothers" code was not the only force that prevented one officer from accusing another of misdeed. Fear of reprisal was also a powerful deterrent. In the words of Lieutenant Commander Kelley, "The lieutenant or junior officer who reports his commander [for misconduct] has but a slim chance for the good things of the service. Such an act is looked upon as insubordination."[86] The first maxim one learned: never inconvenience the Commanding Officer. Thus Midshipman Stephen Luce was advised that he might "drown a dozen sailors with impunity, but never, under any circumstance . . . lose a single chicken belonging to the Captain." And courts-martial convened by senior authority were (and still are) understood to be warrants for conviction. The second maxim: never disagree with your Commanding Officer. Lieutenant Commander J. Ogden Hoffman thus repeated to the "band of brothers" the advice he had received from "a very wise captain":[87]

> If the captain reproves you for something you have not done, or your superior officer finds fault with something that you know is absolutely right, just stand and take it, and keep quiet unless your opinion is asked. In either case, if you were right, the other will soon find out, and his opinion of you will rise, as he then knows that you knew he was wrong and did not tell him so.

Not the kind of advice that produces risk-takers like Lord Nelson or internal critics like Admirals William Sims and Hyman Rickover, but advice consistent with what most officers then believed to be "the military way of doing things."

Jack Tar and the "New Navy"

By 1875 naval officers and Congressmen alike had become conscious of the fact that the naval service was not a popular one. The apprentice system, reinitiated in that year, was designed to provide the Navy with career-oriented seamen, and was modelled somewhat after the British example, but as late as 1893 only 10% of these apprentices remained in the service.[88] All things considered, the Navy's unpopularity among bluejackets should not be surprising. Too many ex-sailors had warned "youth, whose sole aim is reckless adventure and romantic daring," to beware of rushing headlong "into degradations he knows not of," and rather to "pause in his mad career, before he makes his desperate plunge" into Uncle Sam's naval service. And too many apprentices had discovered that "common seamen" led "at best a dog's life" in the nineteenth-century Navy.[89] A fullscale change in attitude was necessary before the Service was to become more attractive to a superior class of sailor.

By the fin-de-siècle the dilemma intensified by the growing need for seamen to man the cruisers, battleships, and dispatch vessels of the "new Navy"[90] had made itself felt among a number of officers, most of them of junior rank, who sought a number of reforms. They advocated, first, the extension and improvement of the apprentice system; second, the restriction of recruitment to native-born Americans;[91] third, the withdrawal of all marines from warships; fourth, the tempering of discipline by the addition of incentives, such as higher pay and greater promotion opportunities; and fifth, the improving of the quality of life on board ship for members of the crew. Of the first two objectives we will have more to say in chapter five. Of the third—the question of marines on warships— it is not enough to say that their efforts came to naught, nor to say that the movement was as much a function of the desire to inculcate a more military spirit among bluejackets as it was a sincere effort to relieve the condition of inferiority and coercion under which Jack Tar had worked for years. The fact is that younger officers began to sense that the bluejacket's status had been lowered by the presence and behavior of marine "policemen." As one ensign remarked in 1890: "The presence of the marines on shipboard is almost as un-American as would be the control, by troops, of citizens already provided with their legal and efficient authorities." Thenceforth sailors were increasingly employed to displace marines in landing parties. The drive, spearheaded by Lieutenant (later Rear Admiral) William F. Fullam, faltered when President Theodore Roosevelt's last Congress did not take the necessary steps to withdraw the marines from warships, but in the interim much was done to buttress the pride and esprit-de-corps of the bluejacket.*

Similarly, enlisted pay, promotion opportunities, and retirement benefits

* The first effort to withdraw the marines from ships appears to have come in 1852 (Langley, *Social Reform*, 118). For the best illustrations of the struggle to drive marines off, see the W. F. Fullam Papers, Naval Historical Foundation, and Fullam's article, with attendant discussion by Ensign A. A. Ackerman and others, "The System of Naval Training and Discipline Required to Promote Efficiency and Attract Americans," *PUSNI*, XVI, No. 4 (1890), 473–536, esp. 475 and 505. Commander Fullam took great pride in the fact that his landing parties from the *Marietta* that kept the Nicaraguan and Honduran armies apart in 1906–1907 (see chapter 4) were entirely composed of bluejackets. See his official and personal correspondence on the subject, circa 1907. The discussion in 1890 of Lieutenant Fullam's paper showed that 13 officers agreed with him while only 6 disagreed, 3 of whom were marines and 2 of whom were senior officers. Thus of 14 junior officers who spoke out on the subject of marines, et al., only one sided with the senior officers. We will have more to say of this junior–senior rift in a later chapter. Cf. Smith, *Coral and Brass*, 57; Lieutenant C. C. Todd, *United Service*, VI (1882), 261; J. D. J. Kelley, *The Ship's Company* (N.Y., 1897), 182.

"Many races and many tongues" in the old navy. Mizzentopmen of the U.S.S. *Galena* with pets, in 1877 (Naval Photographic Center).

"Native-born" recruits for the "new navy.' Naval apprentices assigned to the U.S.S. *Brooklyn, circa* 1905. Note the sharp decline in the proportion of blacks in blue. (Detroit Collection, Library of Congress).

"Young Turk" officers and enlisted men had different motives, but both groups were opposed to the continued presence of marines on the vessels of the "new navy." Here marines of the U.S.S. *Kentucky* form the square, *circa* 1900 (Detroit Collection, Library of Congress).

The "Young Turks" sought to substitute naval personnel for marines as the primary servants of the empire builders of "the American century." Here sailors of the "new navy" learn the marine's trade in an 1887 mock amphibious assault in the vicinity of the Naval War College (from *Squadron Evolutions*).

92   improved moderately, as these issues won the support of the junior officers throughout the 1880s and '90s. Who were more qualified and capable of sympathizing and identifying with Jack Tar than men who themselves had been years without hope of promotion or reward? Who but a junior officer might write in 1881: "reward should be the right hand of discipline in the new navy, as punishment was in the old"? Older officers saw little sense in this attention to the crew's wants. "What a hell of a pass the Navy's come to," one Rear Admiral remarked at the turn of the century, "with enlisted men being allowed to write home." When Jack received a 10% pay-raise in the May 13, 1908, Naval Appropriations Act, his old friends, the junior officers of the 1880s and '90s, had the conn in the naval establishment.[92]

The quality of enlisted life improved with the change in attitude on the part of the officer corps. At the time of the founding of the Naval Academy the sailor had few, if any, means of securing wholesome recreation. Public restaurants and hotels posted signs: "No dogs or sailors allowed." And efforts by bluejackets to provide for their own diversions, such as the Seaman's Amateur Theatre organized at the Port Mahon Navy Yard in 1845, often met with disapproval from senior officers like Captain John Dahlgren, who viewed the Port Mahon theatre with alarm. "My belief is that any association in a military body is likely to mar discipline," he wrote at the time. "Therefore I object to them. It matters little whether the object be good or bad. The law is sufficient to insure order, religion, and morality, each being provided for in separate clauses. . . ." However, by the turn of the century, with professional skills counting for more due to the increasingly technological nature of the steam and steel warships of the "new Navy," enlisted retention had become essential. Naval authorities were willing to make a greater effort to make the life of the enlisted man attractive. With the pay raise came better food and better cooks. As early as 1903 movies were being shown to the crew on a regular basis. Rear Admiral Charles Sperry, Commander-in-Chief of the "Great White Fleet" in 1908, spoke for the "band of brothers" when he told the Secretary of the Navy of his hope that the warship might increasingly serve as "a home to the sailor."[93]

It is difficult to decide which factors were more important in producing the change that came over the enlisted ranks with the turn of the century—the economic depression of the '90s, the movement to improve the image and conditions of life of the bluejacket, or some other set of conditions. But change there was. By 1897 the foreign-born percentage of enlisted personnel had fallen to 25%, below the national level, and by 1904 it had dropped still further to 9%. By 1906 crews were younger and perhaps a bit more genteel. When the North Atlantic Fleet visited New York in 1906, hundreds of sailors independently visited the Metropolitan Museum of Art. Then the Great White Fleet sailed around the world, and the sailor's life become more respectable.[94]

Chapter 3 (Underway)

1. Schroeder, *Half Century of Naval Service*, 65ff; Perry Miller, *The Life of the Mind in America: from the Revolution to the Civil War* (New York, 1965); Cushing to his cousin, Mary Edwards, May 20, 1860, in Edwards, *Cushing*, 60.

2. Mahan to Ashe, February 7 and June 1, 1859, *Letters*, ed. Chiles, 84 and 120; Mahan to Miss ——, October 16, 1857, in Ellen K. Mahan [a daughter], "Some Recollection of Alfred T. Mahan," in Mahan Papers, L. of C.; Mahan, *Types of Naval Officers* (Boston, 1901), 139–140; Shufeldt, cited in Fredrick C. Drake's fine study of that officer: " 'The Empire of the Seas': A Biography of Robert W. Shufeldt, U.S.N.," unpub. Ph.D. dissertation, Cornell Univ., 1970, p. 166.

3. Mahan, *From Sail to Steam*, 29; Mahan to Miss Ellen Evans, April 3, 1871, Mahan Papers, L. of C.; Mahan to his sister, Jenny Mahan, January 13, 1868, Mahan Papers, L. of C. See also Rodman, *Yarns of a Kentucky Admiral*, 48.

4. I. E. Vail, *Three Years on the Blockade* (New York, 1902), 37; *Naval Surgeon: Blockading the South, 1862–1866: The Diary of Dr. Samuel P. Boyer*, ed. Elinor & James Barnes (Bloomington, Ind., 1963), 215; Perkins to his sister, cited in Carroll S. Alden, *George H. Perkins, Commodore, U.S.N.* (Boston, 1914), 165, 171.

5. Sperry to his sister, January 21, 1864, and Sperry to his cousin Helen, May 7, 1868, Sperry Papers, L. of C.

6. Graves to "cousin Maggie," December 23, 1859, Charles Graves Papers, S.H.C., U. of N.C.L.; Fitzpatrick & Saphire, *Navy Maverick*, 232; Lieutenant Harry Rochester, "A Bachelor Looks at the Navy Pay Bills," *PUSNI*, LI (1925), 1455; Goldsborough to his wife, July 12, 1853, Louis Goldsborough Papers, W. R. Perkins Library, Duke U.; Lieutenant John M. Ellicott, *The Life of John A. Winslow, Rear Admiral, U.S.N.* (New York, 1902), 66; Schoonmaker, "Schoonmaker," Box 152, N.H.F.; Temple to Wise, April 21, 1866, Wise Papers, N.Y.H.S.; Thomas, *Career of Walker*, 32; Tarbell, "Journal on *Gettysburg*, 1876–1877," Naval Historical Foundation, 1; O'Neil to "Mrs. Smith," September 15, 1877, Box 340, Charles O'Neil Papers, Naval Histori-cal Foundation; Sperry to his wife, Edith, January 23, 1879, and to his brother, Mark, April 21, 1885, Sperry Papers, L. of C.; Welles to his mother, May 23, 1888, Roger Welles Papers, N.H.F.; Portage (Wisc.) *Daily Register*, 3 July 1890; entry for February 19, 1890, in "Private journal," Box 20, Albert Gleaves Papers, Naval Historical Foundation; Anderson to his wife, January 15, 1903, Rear Admiral Edwin Anderson Papers, S.H.C., U. of N.C.L.; 1878 diary, *passim*, Captain Edward Dorn Papers, in possession of Mrs. C. G. Halpine, Annapolis; "Resignations of officers, 1866–1877," Entry 65, R.G. 45; Lieutenant Leonard Chereny to Mrs. Mary Doneyson, September 4, 1879, ·Lieutenant Samuel L. Wilson Papers, N.H.F.

7. Charles Nordhoff, *Life on the Ocean* (Cincinnati, 1874), 20; Mahan to Ashe, October 29, 1858, *Letters*, ed. Chiles, 10, Mahan to his wife, March 18, 1894, Box 21, Mahan Papers, L. of C.

8. *DuPont Letters*, I, 186; Sperry to his wife, June 22, 1879, Sperry Papers, L. of C.; McCalla, "Memoirs," Ch. XXIX, 10. One can get some sense of what ratio of servants to wardroom members the officers expected from the remarks of Rear Admiral John Ford in 1905 about the "almost worthless Japanese . . . servants" his squadron had acquired: "One boy to look after a dozen of us!" Ford, *An American Cruiser in the East: Travels and Studies in the Far East* (New York, 1905), 6.

Warrant officers and junior officers had separate wardrooms. By one account, the warrants never socialized with the regular commissioned officers, either on board or ashore. Franklin, *Memoirs of a Rear Admiral*, 268.

9. Sperry to his wife, June 10, 1880, Sperry Papers. See also the entry on page 103 of "The Journal of Charles F. Blake, 1862–64," Naval Historical Foundation; Master Charles Sperry to cousin Helen, March 26, 1871, Sperry Papers; Paydirector Caspar Schenck, "Sweethearts and Wives" [a poem], *United Service*, V (November 1881), 642–643; and the letters of Commander Nathan Sargent to his wife in 1905, Box 361, Naval Historical Foundation.

10. [Volunteer officer] Israel E. Vail,

94

Three Years on the Blockade (New York, 1902), 72; DuPont Letters, I, 174–175.

11. See for example, Commander D. M. Fairfax to Commander Henry Wise, January, 1862, Wise Papers, N.Y.H.S.; Bureau of Census, Historical Statistics of U.S., 115; Folder 40, Box 211, Naval Historical Foundation; Captain Caspar Goodrich to Navy Secretary John Long, Papers of Long, ed. Allen, 39; The Memorial of the Officers of the United States Navy for an Increase of their Pay with Documents Setting forth and Sustaining the Same (New York, 1866), 5–6, 17; Captain Edward Nichols to Captain George H. Preble, Feb. 9, 1866, and March 27, 1866, Box 1, Preble Papers, Mass. Historical Society.

12. The abolition of bounties and prize monies prevented the kind of intraservice disputes as the one Lieutenant Commander John Upshur and Lieutenant Commander William Cushing engaged in after the Civil War. See "The Civil War Journal of William B. Cushing," p. 79, Entry 392, Subentry 99, Vol. II, R.G. 45.

13. 16 U.S. Stats. 321; Jewell, Among Our Sailors, 233; 44th Cong., 1st Sess., House Miscellaneous Document No. 170, Pt. 8 [Investigation by Naval Affairs Committee] (1876), 86; John M. Batten, Reminiscences of Two Years in the United States Navy (Lancaster, Pa., 1881), 60; Lieutenant Commander William G. Temple to Commander Henry Wise, November 2, 1863, Wise Papers, N.Y.H.S.; 30 U.S. Stats. 1007; Bureau of Census, Historical Statistics, 115–117; Thomas Eastman file, Box 11, NI, Entry 464, R.G. 45; Bagley to his sister Edith Bagley, October 21, 1895, Bagley Family Papers, U. of N.C.L. See also Evans, Admiral's Log, 25.

In 1925 agitation for a stipend for each dependent drew criticism from a bachelor officer as a "communistic" measure, but the proposal eventually became law. Lieutenant Harry Rochester, "A Bachelor Looks at the Navy Pay Bills," PUSNI, LI (1925), 1457.

14. Goldsborough to Assistant Secretary Fox, June 16, 1862, Confidential Correspondence of Fox, I, 291; Chadwick, PUSNI, XXCII (1901), 27; Perry to Graham, Dec. 3, 1851, Graham Papers, ed. Hamilton, IV, 221–222; Lawrence to his mother, April 23, 1876, Lawrence Papers, Naval Museum, Annapolis. Cf. Fortune (March 1938), 66; and Commodore A. S. Crowninshield, Chief of the Bureau of Navigation, to a House committee: ". . . I feel jealous of my

title and rank. . . ." Congressional Record, XXX, 669.

15. Jewell, Among our Sailors, 251. See, for example, [Captains in the U.S. Navy], Memoranda showing why Captain J. E. Jouett should not be promoted over the heads of his fellow officers (Washington, D.C., 1880).

16. See, for example, Mrs. Remey's Letters, X, 550, XI, 789, 810, passim; Admiral Roger Welles Papers, N.H.F.; Jewell, Among our Sailors, 252; Commander Louis M. Goldsborough to his wife, September 25, 1852, Goldsborough Papers, Perkins L., Duke U.: "the moment poor Upshur either dies . . . or gets well enough to be removed from his ship . . . I shall doubtless find myself duly installed on board of her. I go with great cheerfulness. . . ."

Actually, the creation of new upper-echelon ranks was a goal most officers had sought for years as a means of placing the squadron and fleet commanders on an equal footing with those of foreign navies and to provide for greater promotion possibilities and incentive for junior officers. See, for example, Goldsborough to Fox, June 16, 1862, Confidential Correspondence of Fox, I.

17. Lott, A Long Line of Ships, 122–123; Daniels, The Wilson Era: Years of Peace, 505; Caldwell to his mother, August 21, 1866, Albert Caldwell Letters, J. C. Caldwell Collection, Indiana Hist. Society Library.

18. Professor William Stevens, "The Naval Officer and the Civilian," PUSNI, XXVII (1921), 1728.

19. Phelps, PUSNI, XXXIX (1913), 526. The naval officer's pride in the amount of gold on his sleeve explains why photos of high-ranking Army and Navy officers generally catch the members of the different branches in different poses. The Army (and Air Force) officers let their hands fall naturally into their laps or by their sides; their rank is displayed on the epaulets. Navy officers wearing blues, on the other hand, tend to hold or fold their hands in front of them—whereby their rank becomes visible.

20. Bowles to Navy Secretary John Long, Dec. 6, 1901, Papers of Long, 408. For a similar argument by a Naval surgeon, see Surgeon Ruschenberger, "Naval Staff Rank," U.S. Service Magazine, III (1865), 356–368. And for good accounts of the naval constructor-line controversy see Arnold Lott, A Long Line of Ships, and the autobiography of Naval Constructor Holden

Evans, *One Man's Fight for a Better Navy* (N.Y., 1940).

Even some chaplains felt the need for "relative rank" in the late nineteenth century, so crowded were the quarters on steam-sail men-of-war. See U.S. Navy, Bureau of Naval Personnel, *The History of the Chaplain Corps, U.S.N.*, by Clifford M. Drury (Nav Pers 15807, 1948), I, 105–107, 130.

21. Vol. I, p. 91, John T. Wood Diary, Southern Historical Collection (S.H.C.), U. of North Carolina Library, "Passed Midshipman," *Assimilated Rank in the Navy* . . . (Wash., 1850), 2; (anon.), *Assimilated Rank in the Navy: Its Injurious Operation upon the Discipline, Harmony, and General good of the naval service* (Wash., 1850), *passim;* (anon.), *A Few Thoughts Upon Rank in the Navy* (Phil., 1850), *passim;* Commander A. T. Mahan to Samuel Ashe, Jan 27, 1876, Ashe Papers, Duke University Library; Charles E. Neu, *An Uncertain Friendship: Theodore Roosevelt and Japan, 1906–1909* (Cambridge, Mass., 1967), 241.

22. McCalla, "Memoirs," Ch. IX, 20; "Naval Engineers," *D.A.B.;* Calvert, *Mechanical Engineer in America,* 19–23; "Living Conditions of Naval Personnel, 1860–1910," Box 274, NL, Entry 464, R.G. 45; Long, *New American Navy,* I, 87. For the best treatments of naval engineers in the nineteenth century see Passed Assistant Engineer Frank Bennett, *The Steam Navy of the United States* (Pittsburgh, Pa., 1897, 2 vols.); Monte Calvert, *Mechanical Engineer in America, 1830–1910: Professional Cultures in Conflict* (Baltimore, 1967); and Edward W. Sloan, III, *Benjamin Franklin Isherwood: Naval Engineer* (Annapolis, 1965).

23. Calvert, *Mechanical Engineer,* 246–247; Porter to Surgeon Ninian Pinckney, Dec. 31, 1867, Porter Papers, L. of C.; Porter to Commodore Henry A. Wise, Dec. 20, 1867, Wise Papers, New York Historical Society (hereafter referred to as N.Y.H.S.), cited in Swann, *Roach,* 38; *Diary of Welles,* ed. Beale, III, 248–249, 253–254, 596.

There is a parallel to the line-engineer controversy in the resistance of the Diplomatic Corps in the early twentieth century to a proposed amalgamation of that elite corps and the less prestigous consular corps. See Warren Ilchman, *Professional Diplomacy,* 151.

24. Bennett, *Steam Navy,* II, 6–7; Sloan, *Isherwood,* 231, 234.

For a wise and readable discussion of the reasons that the *Whampanoag* was unacceptable to the senior line officers see Elting E. Morison, *Men, Machines, and Modern Times* (Cambridge, Mass., 1966), 112–119. See also my chapters 6 and 7. The best account of the Porter era, however, is Lance Buhl, "The Smooth Water Navy: American Naval Policy and Politics, 1865–1876," Harvard Ph.D. dissertation, 1968.

25. Calvert, *Mechanical Engineer,* 255; Acting Assistant Engineer J. P. Stuart Lawrence to his mother, Nov. 13, 1875, and April 9, 1876, Lawrence Letters, Naval Museum, Annapolis; [anon.], *Stictly Private and Confidential!* [n.p., n.d., circa 1880], 22–26.

26. "Olimgus," *Naval Rank* [n.p., n.d.]; *Naval Personnel, Line and Staff, Memorial to the Secretary of the Navy* (Wash., 1878), 8–9, 271. [This pamphlet is a combination of three statements—an original line statement, answered by the engineers and rebutted by the line in two sets of footnotes.] *Strictly Private,* preface.

27. Lawrence to his mother, Feb. 5, Nov. 12, Aug. 6, and March 5, 1876, Aug. 2, 1877; and Rear Admiral J. P. Stuart, Lawrence Letters, Nav. Museum; *Strictly Private,* 39. Cf. Surgeon Wood in the frontispiece.

28. Lawrence to his mother, Oct. 19, 1881, J. P. Stuart Lawrence Letters, Nav. Museum.

29. For a sample Academy engineering course in 1905 see *PUSNI,* XXI (1905), 851–943.

30. Bennett, *Steam Navy,* 7ỉ3, *passim;* Benjamin, *U.S.N.A.,* 356; Commander French E. Chadwick to Commander Frederick Rogers, April 6, 1886, Chadwick Letterbooks, N.Y.H.S.; 52nd Cong., 1st Sess., House Exec. Doc. 1, Pt. 3, *Report of the Secretary of the Navy, 1891,* 435; Mattice, *Queer Doings in the Navy* (n.p., n.d., circa 1895), 4, *passim;* Calvert, *Mechanical Engineer,* 225–258; Chadwick to Commander Folger, June 19, 1886, personal copybook, Chadwick Papers, N.Y.H.S.

The Royal Navy managed to avoid the integration of line and engineering officers until after World War II. Roskill, *Naval Policy,* 123.

31. Sperry to his cousin, Helen, June, 1867, Sperry Papers; Louis A. Kimberly Papers, Chicago Hist. Society; Lieutenant William H. Beehler, *The Cruise of the U.S.S. Brooklyn* (Philadelphia, 1885), 329–330; Rear Admiral Daniel Ammen, *The Old Navy and the New* (Philadelphia, 1891), 366;

Lieutenant Commander J. D. Jerrold Kelley, *The Ship's Company* (New York, 1897), 210–220.

32. Lovette, *School of Sea*, 59, 209; Sperry to his sister, February 8, 1863, Sperry Papers, L. of C.

33. See, for example, Alden, *Perkins*, 165; Mahan to Ashe, October 29, 1858, *Letters*, ed. Chiles, 14–15; Fredrick Palmer, *With My Own Eyes* (Indianapolis, 1933), 114; Sperry to his cousin, Helen, April 7, [1871?], Sperry Papers, L. of C. Sperry claimed that he became thoroughly familiar with the city of London before visiting it by reading several of Dickens's novels.

34. Thus Mahan's favorite was Macaulay; Sperry read Carlyle; and Porter, Schroeder, and Parker read widely in naval history and biography. Puleston, *Mahan*, 239; Sperry to his wife, April 4, 1886, Sperry Papers; Porter to Barnes, March 8, 1875, Porter Papers, N.Y.H.S.

It is always dangerous to infer much from the contents of one's library shelves, but the compendium of some 1,200 volumes belonging to Rear Admiral Thornton Jenkins in 1872 is of interest. Jenkins purchased treatises on philosophy, military affairs, history, and political and physical science, as well as many novels. (*Catalogue Sale of . . . the Library of Admiral Thornton A. Jenkins*) (n.p., 1872 [L. of C. has a copy]).

35. *Preble Diary*, ed. Szczesniak, 12.

36. Chambers to Mr. Stichley, October 1906, Box 6, Chambers Papers, Naval Historical Foundation (N.H.F.). See also Rear Admiral Daniel Ammen, *Country Homes and Their Improvement* (Washington, 1885); and Captain Nathan Twining to his brother Walter, January 3, 1917, Twining Papers, St. Hist. Soc. of Wis.

37. See, for example, Box 557, Rear Admiral Montgomery Sicard Papers, N.H.F.; Charles Blake Papers, N.H.F.; Grattan Papers, N.H.F.

38. See, for example, Lieutenant Commander William Gibson, "Faith Militant," *The United States Service Magazine*, I (New York & London, 1864), and Captain Robert Townsend, "To my Wife at Parting, 1861," *Ibid.*, II, 281; Paydirector Casper Schenck, "Sweethearts and Wives," *United Service*, V (Nov. 1881), 642–643; Gibson and others in *United Service*, II (1880), 326; III (1880), 34, 541; V (1881), 285–286, 745; Rear Admiral Thomas H. Stevens, "Faith, Hope & Charity," *United Service*, 2nd Series, I (1889), 190; Lieutenant F. S. Bassett [Retired], "The Spectral Sealer,"

Ibid., II (1889), 31–36; Commander C. H. Rockwell, "The Boatswain's Call," *Ibid.*, VIII (1892), 65–66; and "Recollection," IX (1893), 38–39; Commander William Gibson, *Poems of Many Years and Many Places* (Boston 1881). Captain Henry C. Taylor's love poems are in the Taylor Papers, N.H.F.; Captain Washington I. Chambers' efforts, some of which are published in various issues of the Navy League's official publication in the 1910s, are in Box 7 and Box 148 of the Chambers Papers, N.H.F. Most of these are vitriolic attacks on the barbarities of Hun "Kultur." See also Nathan Sargent's "Class of '70" Academy classbook in Box 148 of the Sargent Papers, or any of the yearbooks of the late nineteenth century.

For an example of a literary publication for local consumption see The *"Idaho" Idler*, (1867), Box 274, NL, Entry 464, R.G. 45.

39. See, for example, the novels, poems, and stories cited in the bibliography. See also Box 38, Commodore Robert Shufeldt Papers, N.H.F.; Rear Admiral David Potter (SC), *Sailing the Sulu Sea* (N.Y. 1940), 22; Item 24, Box 148, Nathan Sargent Papers, N.H.F.; Letterbook, 1869–1872, p. 187, Homer C. Blake Papers, N.Y. Public Library; "The Convict" and several other manuscript novels, poems, and stories in Boxes 28 and 29 and Volumes 9–13 in the David D. Porter Papers, Mss. Div., L. of C.

This is to say nothing of the literary works of James Fenimore Cooper and Winston Churchill, both of whom had been midshipmen on board naval vessels in their youth, or the several novels of Academy life from the pen of Academy Chaplain H. H. Clark.

40. Harris, *The Artist in American Society: The Formative Years, 1790–1860* (New York, 1966). See chapter 5 for more analysis of the naval officer's social ideas.

41. Admiral David D. Porter, "Naval Education and Organization," *United Service*, I (1879), 473–474. Porter went on to discuss the merits of education at Exeter, Harrow, Eton, Yale, Harvard, Oxford, and Cambridge. Apparently he drew the line on certain popular contemporary musical instruments. As Superintendent of the Academy in 1867 he insructed Midshipman Robert Thompson (later President of the Navy League) "who plays so abominably on the fish horn" to practice outside of the school limits "or he will find himself coming out of the little end of the horn."

Porter to Thompson, October 25, 1867, Naval Museum, Annapolis.

42. Churchill, in the introduction to a late edition of *Richard Carvel* (New York & London, 1953 [orig. pub. 1899]), ix; Rockwell, "The Captain's Story," *United Service*, 2nd Series, VII (May, 1892), 494–503.

43. Porter, *Allan Dare and Robert le Diable* (New York, 1884), 78; *Arthur Merton* (New York, 1889), 328; Sargent, Item 24, Box 148, Sargent Papers, N.H.F.

44. Porter, "An Ancient City," p. 34, Box 30, David D. Porter Papers, L. of C.; Hobson, *In Line of Duty*, 325.

45. See "The Pursuit of Glory," in Chapter 5.

46. Townsend to Wise, September 15, 1863, Henry Wise Papers, N.Y.H.S.; Hobson, *Buck Jones*, 1–45 & *passim;* Porter, "The Convict," Chapter II, p. 24, Box 28, Porter Papers, L. of C.

47. Mahan to Ashe, December 19, 1858, *Letters,* ed. Chiles, 54–55; Mahan to his wife Delda, May 9, 1894, and January 13, 1895, Mahan Papers, L. of C.

48. See, for example, *Mahan-Ashe Letters,* ed. Chiles, *passim;* and Arpee, *Frigates to Flat-Tops,* 28.

49. "My greatest interest is in religious or church matters," Lieutenant Commander Mahan told his mother in 1868. "I am very short of good reading, and should like to have a volume of really good sermons." Admiral David D. Porter hoped that the study of the sea would prove God's laws. And Rear Admiral Louis Kimberly attributed the death by drowning of a sailor who broke an oath to stop gambling to "a visitation of Providence." Mahan to his mother, Feb. 20, 1868, Mahan Papers, L. of C.; Porter, *United Service,* I (1879), 479–480; Kimberly, "Reminiscences," Kimberly Papers, Chicago Hist. Soc.

50. *Life and Adventures of Jack Philip,* ed. E. S. Maclay (New York, 1904), 37; Herman Melville, *White-Jacket, or the World in a Man-of-War* (Boston, 1892, [orig. pub. 1850]), 149; Chaplain Fitch W. Taylor, *The Broad Pennant* (New York, 1848), 134–136.

51. Private journal of Passed Midshipman Francis A. Roe, entry for April 3, 1859, Box 143, N.H.F.; Benjamin, *U.S.N.A.,* 380; Drury, *History of Navy Chaplain Corps,* I, 98–99; Richard West, Jr., *Mr. Lincoln's Navy* (New York, 1957), 88; Lieutenant William H. Beehler, *The Cruise of the U.S.S. Brooklyn, 1881–1884* (Philadelphia, 1885), 28.

52. In 1881, of 101 navy chaplains whose ordination can be determined, 42 were Episcopalian, 22 Methodist Episcopalian, 14 Presbyterian, 12 Baptist, 7 Congregationalist, 3 Unitarian, and 1 Universalist. The first Catholic chaplain was not commissioned until 1888; the first Jewish chaplain, not until well into the twentieth century. Drury, *Hist of Chaplain Corps,* I, 117. Cf. Rt. Rev. W. Lawrence, Episcopal Bishop of Massachusetts, to Navy Secretary John Long, Jan. 27, 1902, *Papers of Long,* 416.

53. Mills, *Power Elite,* 182.

54. Janowitz, *Professional Soldier,* 98–99. Cf. John Lovell, "The Professional Socialization of the West Point Cadet," in Janowitz, ed., *The New Military* (N.Y., 1964), 137–138; Baltzell, *Philadelphia Gentlemen,* 226.

Thus in George Bernard Shaw's *Captain Brassbound's Conversion* the pirate chief is converted to Episcopalianism by a U.S. Navy chaplain. *Works,* IX (1930), 281.

55. Potter in *PUSNI,* L (1924), 1988; Baltzell, *Philadelphia Gentlemen,* 233. The only emblem ever allowed to fly above the national ensign on a U.S. man-of-war is the church pennant.

56. Sperry to Mary, Nov. 15, 1866, and Oct. 11, 1865, Sperry Papers, L. of C.; *Conf. Corr. of Fox,* II, 395–396; Rear Admiral Bruce McCandless, *et. al., Service Etiquette* (Annapolis, 1959), 313.

57. *Diary of Preble,* ed. Szczesniak, 73; Elliott, *Winslow,* 101; Sperry to ?, April 20, 1868, Sperry Papers, L. of C.; *Naval Surgeon; Blockading the South, 1862–1866: The Diary of Dr. Samuel P. Boyer,* ed. Elinor and James Barnes (Bloomington, Ind., 1963), 363; Mahan to Ashe, April 25, 1871, Ashe Papers, Duke U. Library. Cf. Mrs. Dahlgren, *South Sea Sketches,* 29; Lieutenant John O'Neil to his father, October 8, 1862, O'Neil Papers, Perkins L., Duke U.; Eva Dahlgren to Rear Admiral John A. Dahlgren, December 29, 1867, Dahlgren Papers, Perkins L., Duke U.:

"Yesterday Aunt Pattie, Mrs. Read, & myself went to the English [Anglican] Church here [in Livorno, Italy] and after service to our surprise 3 American [naval] officers stepped up and shook hands most cordially with us."

At least one Episcopal Church school in China was named after a U.S. naval officer. See John W. Wood to Mrs. E. T. Mahan, July 1, 1922, Mahan Papers, L. of C.

58. Lemisch, "The American Revolution

98   seen from the bottom up," in *Toward a New Past: Dissenting Essays in American History*, ed. Barton Bernstein (N.Y., 1968), 40–41; *DuPont Letters*, II, 535.

59. Leech, *Thirty Years from Home; or, a Voice from the Main Deck* (Boston, 1843), 25; Josiah Cobb, *A Green Hand's First Cruise* (Boston, 1841), I, 13; Fredrick T. Jane, *Heresies of Sea Power* (London, 1906), 329.

60. McCalla, "Memoirs," Ch. III, 1–2; Harold Langley, *Social Reform in the U.S. Navy, 1798–1862* (Urbana, Ill., 1967), 71–72.

61. [ex-Gunner] William McNally, *Evils and Abuses in the Naval and Merchant Services Exposed* (Boston, 1839), 127.

62. *Ibid.*, 19–20, 44; Porter, *The Adventure of Harry Marline; or, Notes from an American Midshipman's Lucky Bag* (New York, 1885 [N.Y.P.L. has copy]), 79–80. Cf. Langley, *Social Reform in the U.S. Navy*, 61, 74–78.

63. Goodrich and Davidson, "The Wage-Earner in the Westward Movement," I: *Political Science Quarterly*, L (June, 1935), 161–185; II: *Ibid.*, 51 (March, 1936), 61–116. See also Murray Kane, "Some Considerations on the Safety Valve Doctrine," *Mississippi Valley Historical Review*, XXIII (Sept., 1936), 169–188; and Fred A. Shannon, "A Post-Mortem on the Labor-Safety-Valve Theory," *Agricultural History* (Jan. 1945), 31–37.

64. Herman Melville, *White-Jacket, or the World in a Man-of-War* (Boston, 1892 [orig. pub. 1850]), 74; Hazen, *Five Years before the Mast* (2nd ed., Phil., 1856), 13; U.S. House of Rep., *Hearings on Bill H.R. 13706 before Committee on Naval Affairs* (G.P.O., 1921), 168–186; and *Hearings before Committee of Naval Affairs [House] on Estimates Submitted by the Secretary of the Navy, 1917* (G.P.O. 1917), 345. For a similar explanation of U.S. enlistments in this same period see Don Rickey, Jr., *Forty Miles a Day on Beans and Hay: The Enlisted Soldier Fighting the Indian Wars* (Norman, Okla., 1963), 19, 22, 29.

65. McNally, *Evils and Abuses*, 44ff.

66. 45th Cong., 2nd Sess., *House Report No. 432*, "Enlistments in the Navy," (1878); Charles Roll, *Colonel Dick Thompson: The Persistent Whig* [Indiana Historical Collections, XXX] (Indianapolis, 1948), 237; John H. Paynter, *Joining the Navy* (Washington, 1911), 40; Passed Assistant Engineer Frank M. Bennett, "American Men for the American Navy," *United Service*, 2nd Series, XI (February, 1894), 99–100; 51st Cong., 1st Sess., House Committee on Naval Affairs, *Report No. 1255* (1890); U.S.

Bureau of the Census, *Historical Statistics of the United States, Colonial Times to 1957* (Washington, 1960), 65; 736; Duncan Cumming, "Promotion in the U.S. Navy," *Chambers' Journal*, 6th Series, LXXV (1898), 641.

67. Cumming, *loc. cit.;* and Bennett, *loc. cit.* Cf. Quarterly Returns on Enlistments on Vessels, and Weekly Returns of Enlistments at Naval Rendezvous, 1845–1900, R.G. 24, and Muster Rolls of U.S.S. *Kearsarge*, 1876, and U.S.S. *Ohio*, 1845, Entry 90, R.G. 45.

68. Bennett, *loc. cit.;* Census, *Historical Statistics*, 65–66.

69. Bennett, *op. cit.*, 102; Potter, *Sailing the Sulu Sea*, 127; W. J. Henderson, "Warship Community," *Scribner's Magazine*, XXIV (1898), 286.

70. Langley, *Social Reform in the Navy*, 74, 92–95; Dennis D. Nelson, *The Integration of the Negro into the U.S. Navy* (New York, 1951), 4, 6–8; *Journey into Wilderness: An Army Surgeon's Account of Life in Camp and Field During the Creek and Seminole Wars, 1836–1838*, by Jacob Rhett Motte, ed. James F. Sunderman (Gainsville, Fla., 1953), 169; Herbert Aptheker, "The Negro in the Union Navy," *Journal of Negro History*, XXXII (April, 1947), 169–200; W. S. Hammond, "Attempt of members of the crew of the U.S.S. *St. Mary's* to run her aground in Valparaiso [1865]," p. 4, Box 7, NJ. Entry 464, R.G. 45; Bu-Nav (Pers-A 212), "U.S. Naval Administration in World War II: The Negro in the Navy," pp. 1–4, copy in possession of Professor Richard Dalfiume, S.U.N.Y. Binghamton; "Marlinspike," *U.S. Nautical Mag. and Naval Journal*, V (1856), 295–296; John S. Buckingham, *The Slave States of America* (London, 1842), II, 470–471, cited in *PUSNI*, XCIII (January, 1967), 144; Boynton, *History of the Navy During Rebellion*, I, 29; Bennett, *loc. cit.;* Lieutenant George Steunenberg (U.S.A.), "Negroes in the Navy," *Army & Navy Journal*, XLIV (1907), 563; and L (1913), 1296, 1140; World War I Diary, p. 17, Timothy Brown Papers, State Hist. Soc. of Wisc. Marv Fletcher supplied the *A. & N. J.* citations, for which I am grateful.

71. Roland Gould, *The Life of Gould, an Ex-Man-of-War's Man* (Claremont, N.H., 1867), 170; 45th Cong., 2nd Sess., House Rpt. No. 432 [1878]; 21 *U.S. Stat.* 331; Bureau of Census, *Historical Statistics*, 91–92.

72. *U.S. Nautical Mag. and Naval Journal*, V (1856), 295–296.

73. Leech, *Thirty Years from Home*, 249;

Charles Nordhoff, *Life on the Ocean* (Cincinnati, Ohio, 1874), *passim;* Rodman, *Yarns of a Kentucky Admiral*, 55–65; James Durand: *An Able Seaman of 1812*, ed. George S. Brooks (New Haven, 1926), 32; Stephen Blanding, *Recollections of a Sailor Boy*, 66; Turner to Dornin, September 8, 1858, 1858–1860 Letterbook, Rear Admiral Thomas Turner Papers, Mss. Div., N.Y.P.L.; Goodrich, "Naval Education," *PUSNI*, V (1879), 333. On poor living conditions see also Surgeon A. N. Bell, "The Ship and the Sailor," *U.S. Nautical Mag. & Naval Journal*, III (1856), 194–198; and Blochman, *Doctor Squibb*, 29–35. Bluejackets were not the only ones whose pantries were invaded by insects. Cockroaches know no rank, and officers held cockroach races in the wardrooms. Rodman, 70; Charles McVay Manuscript Autobiography, McVay Papers, N.H.F.

74. Jacob Hazen, *Five Years before the Mast*, 228; Gould, *Life of Gould*, 170, 190, *passim;* Langley, *Social Reform in U.S. Navy*, 98–106, 206, 280; *U.S. Nautical Magazine and Naval Journal*, V (1857), 296; Cumming, *op. cit.*, 643; Bennett, *op. cit.*, 105; 33 *U.S. Stats.* 346 [Act of April 27, 1904]; *Army & Navy Journal*, LI (1913), 363; 43 *U.S. Stats.* 1080 [Act of Feb. 28, 1925]. Warrant officers did not necessarily want social equality, of course, and some tended to look upon members of their class who did seek elevation to line status as pariahs. Ex-Warrant Officer William McNally wrote of one carpenter's mate who secured an appointment as a marine Second Lieutenant through political influence: "His commission will not bring him a greater salary than his former warrant, but some men have little minds, and Wm. L—— can now mess with the wardroom officers, and sport a green coat instead of his former blue one . . . he may now forsake [midshipmen and warrant officers] for something higher." McNally, *Evils and Abuses*, 7n.–8n.

75. Roe, *Naval Duties and Discipline*, 151–152.

76. Melville, *White Jacket*, 352; Passed Midshipman Charles Graves to his cousin Maggie, February 18, 1860, Graves Papers, S.H.C., U. of N.C. Library; W. J. Henderson, "War-ship Community," *Scribner's Magazine*, XXIV (1898), 291; *Letters from Naval Officers in Reference to the United States Marines*, ed. Colonel John Harris, U.S.M.C. (Washington, 1864), *passim;* Lawrence to his mother, March 12, 1876, Rear Admiral J. P. Stuart Lawrence Papers, Naval

Museum, Annapolis; Lieutenant William F. Fullam, "The System of Naval Training and Discipline Required to Promote Efficiency and Attract Americans," *PUSNI*, XVI, No. 4 (1890), 473–536; Captain Robert Blake, U.S.M.C., "The Marine at Sea," *The Marine Corps Gazette*, X (1925), 1–14; W. P. Marshall, *Afloat on the Pacific, or Notes of Three Years Life at Sea* (Zanesville Ohio, 1876), 129; Evans, *A Sailor's Log: Recollections of Forty Years of Naval Life* (New York, 1901); Stanton H. King, *Dog Watches at Sea* (Boston, 1901), 225; Captain Charles H. Davis, Jr., *Life of Davis*, 108–109; Commander Francis O. Davenport, *On a Man-of-War: A Series of Naval Sketches* (Detroit, 1878), *passim.* For good accounts of whiskey smuggling see Langley, *op. cit.*, 211–213.

77. Henderson, *op. cit.*, 295.

78. "The Journals of David Noble Johnson (1822–1863), United States Navy," ed. Mendel L. Peterson, *Smithsonian Miscellaneous Collections*, CXXXVI, No. 2 (1959), 148; Roe, *Naval Duties*, 86; Wainwright, "The New Naval Academy," *World's Work*, IV (1902), 2272; Saphire and Fitzpatrick, *Navy Maverick*, 200ff; Woodhull to Benjamin Yancey, U.S. Minister to the Argentine Confederation, August 23, 1859, "U.S.S. *Bainbridge* Letterbook, 1859–1860," U.S. Navy Miscellaneous Collection, Mss. Div., L. of C.; Cyrus T. Brady, *Under Tops'ls and Tents* (New York, 1901), 118–119.

79. Jewell, *Among our Sailors*, 260; Leech, *Thirty Years from Home; or, A Voice from the Main Deck*, 123; Blanding, 19; Roe, 120; Beach, *An Annapolis Plebe*. See also the sailor characterizations in Richmond Hobson's *Buck Jones at Annapolis* and H. H. Clark's *Joe Bently, Naval Cadet.* Cf. Durand, 32; "Journals of Johnson," *op. cit.*, 149; Hazen, *Five Years before the Mast*, 230.

80. Langley, *Social Reform in the Navy*, *passim.*

81. For pre-1850 abuses see James Durand, *An Able Seaman*, 18; Burr, *Education in the Early Navy*, 190–191; Langley, *Social Reform*, 131–206, esp. 181; McNally, *Evils and Abuses*, 86, 107, 124–127; Rear Admiral H. O. Dunn, "Discipline in the 'Old Navy,'" *PUSNI*, XLII (1916), 16 ff.; Richard Sewell, *John P. Hale and the Politics of Abolition* (Cambridge, Mass., 1965), 138; Surgeon John A. Lockwood, *Flogging in the Navy* (Wash., 1849), *passim;* and Rear Admiral Louis Kimberly, "Reminiscences," Kimberly Papers, Chicago Hist. Soc. On the

abolition of branding and tattooing see 17 *U.S. Stat.* 261 [Act of June 6, 1872] and 20 *U.S. Stat.* 30 [Act of March 16, 1878].

For post-1850 abuses see the Kimberly Papers; Admiral William Sims, "Military Character," *PUSNI*, XLIII (1917), 447–448; *Naval Surgeon . . . Japan*, 234–237, 316, 148–149, 108–110; J. Grey Jewell, *Among Our Sailors* (New York, 1874), 253, *passim*; Standley and Ageton, *Admiral Ambassador*, 12; Kelley, *The Ship's Company*, 157, 178; McCalla, "Memoirs," Ch. XIV, 31; General Court-Martial Order No. 29, Navy Department, May 15, 1890, copy in Meade Papers, Miscellany, Box III, N.Y.H.S.; Clark to Goodrich, August 11, 1894, Goodrich Papers, N.Y.H.S.; *Cabinet Diaries of Daniels*, entry for May 21, 1917, p. 155; NO (Navy Personnel—Courts-Martial, 1860–1910), Entry 464, R.G. 45, *passim*; Connolly, *Navy Men*, 286–302; Commander Edward M. Blackwell, *Blackwell Genealogy* (Richmond, 1948), 22.

82. *The United States Nautical Magazine and Naval Journal*, V (1857), 296. Cf. Fred Buenzle, *Bluejacket* (N.Y., 1939), 42–44.

Similarly, whenever officers faced civilian tribunals, their station, income, and self-possession placed them in a position superior to that of a bluejacket in similar straits. See, for example, the case of Commander George Dewey in West, *Admirals of American Empire*, 66.

83. United States Navy Department, *Naval Courts and Boards* (Washington, G.P.O., 1917), 37, 218–224. Section 8 of the Act of February 16, 1909 (35 *U.S. Stat.* 623) abolished irons as a punishment except when imposed by a General Court-Martial. Under the 1951 Uniform Code of Military Justice irons are abolished altogether as a form of punishment.

84. Melville, *White Jacket;* Selfridge, mss. review of *White Jacket*, dated July, 1850, in the Thomas O. Selfridge Collection, Box 168, Naval Historical Foundation; Passed Midshipman William B. Cushing to his cousin, May 20, 1860, Edwards, *Cushing*, 60; Mrs. Madeline V. Dahlgren, *South Sea Sketches* (Boston, 1880), 98; Portage (Wis.) *Daily Register*, 3 July 1890; McNally, *Evils and Abuses*, 106; Kelley, *Ship's Company*, 179.

85. Rear Admiral A. Farenholt, "And There Were Giants in the Earth in Those Days," Box 274, NL, Entry 464, R.G. 45; Rear Admiral George Belknap, "The Old Navy," in *Naval Actions and History, 1799–1898*, Vol. XII of *Papers of the Military*

Hist. Soc. of Mass. (Boston, 1902), 36; Sims, "Military Character," *PUSNI*, XLII (1917), 451.

86. Entry for August 31, 1859, Private Journal, Francis A. Roe Papers, Box 143, Naval Historical Foundation; Kelley, *Ship's Company*, 179.

87. Lovette, *School of Service*, 238; Mahan to his wife, December 19, 1894, Mahan Papers, L. of C.; Hoffman, "Tact in Relation to Discipline," *PUSNI*, XLVI (1920), 1206.

88. See, for example, Bennett, *op. cit.*, 105; Captain Stephen B. Luce, "The Manning of our Navy and Merchant Marine," *PUSNI*, I (1874), 1ff; "U.S. Training-Ships," *United Service*, I (1879), 425–435; "Naval Training," *PUSNI*, XVI (1890); and Lieutenant Aaron Ward, "Naval Apprentices," *United Service*, III (1880), 740–755.

In the first half of the nineteenth century Britain's recruitment policy shifted from impressment to long-term career enlistment (Lewis, *Navy in Transition*, 180–188). Admiral Luce advocated the British system in "How Shall we Man Our Ship?" *North American Review*, CLII (1891), 64–69.

89. Cobb, *Green Hand's First Cruise*, I, "to the reader"; Midshipman Cushing to Mary Edwards, May 20, 1860, in Edwards, *Cushing, loc. cit.;* Hazen, *Five Years before the Mast*, 278; Melville, *White Jacket*, 366; Buenzle, *Bluejacket*, 14, 17.

90. In 1891 the Navy's enlisted population stood at 7,737; by 1897 it had risen to 10,586; and by 1904 the figure stood at 30,144. (U.S. Bureau of Census, *Historical Statistics*, 736). George Davis, *A Navy Second to None*, 469, gives slightly different figures. Although I consider Davis' study to be both useful and careful, I have in all cases chosen to use the Census Bureau's figures.

91. This is not to say that early nineteenth-century officers did not also regret the high numbers of foreign-born in the service in their day; they did. See Langley, *Social Reform in the Navy*, 90.

92. Connolly, *Navy Men*, 286–287; Passed Assistant Engineer Bennett, *op. cit.*, 106–115; and Lieutenant Theodorus Mason, "Desertion in the Navy," *United Service*, V (1881), 260, 262; Lieutenant Commander Roy Smith, "The Recruiting of the Naval Personnel," *PUSNI*, XXVIII (1902), 214; 35 *U.S. Stats.* 127.

93. Madeline Dahlgren, *Memoir of John A. Dahlgren* (Boston, 1882), 112; King, *Dog*

Watches, 250, 246; Lieutenant Commander T. P. Magruder, "The Enlisted Man," *PUSNI*, XXXVI (1910), 380ff; Drury, *History of the Chaplain Corps*, 149; Sperry to Secretary Meyer, January 27, 1908, Sperry Letterbook, Sperry Papers, L. of C.; Theodore W. Koch, *Books in the War: The Romance of Library War Service* (Boston, 1919), 123–143.

If warships were becoming "homes," however, they were still a bit like "prison homes"; as late as 1925 enlisted men's liberty in foreign ports was severely restricted. Connolly, *Navy Men*, 297.

For a good set of photos of the crew of one vessel of the "new Navy" see *Scribner's Magazine*, XXIV (1898), 286ff.

94. *PUSNI*, XL (1914), 686; Long, *New American Navy*, I, 92; King, *Dog Watches*, 230; Captain Marbury Johnston, "Discipline in the Navy," *PUSNI*, XXXVIII (1912), 851–852.

Similarly, the Marine Corps enlisted complement jumped from 2,000 to 10,000 men between 1890 and 1915, and 39,000 applicants competed for 4,000 openings in 1915. U.S. House of Representatives, *Hearing before the Naval Affairs Committee, Estimates submitted by the Secretary of the Navy* Washington, G.P.O., 1916), II, 2249.

IN FOREIGN PORTS

It is ironic that the naval officer, unrepresentative as he was of much that was transpiring on the American frontier and the nitty-gritty, rough-and-tumble commercial life of the more settled areas, was often the only American many foreign people ever saw. As one officer put it, he was "a sort of world-pervading Bedouin," often visiting places as yet ungraced by an American consular flag. One lieutenant, in command of a gunboat on the China station at the turn of the century, recalled later that wherever he went he was "kowtowed to and feted." His lowly rank was less significant than his station. As commander of a U.S. warship he "represented the great United States, and so, important people all along the [Yangtze] river—rich merchants, local governors, mandarins—came to do honor. . . . It was all very pleasing to a fellow in his middle twenties." Even where consuls were in residence, officers often saw themselves as superior deputies of the Democracy. For example, one officer described the U.S. Consul at Canton and his family as "cattle." "They are not recognized anywhere," he told his wife, and added, "I don't care to have anything to do with such people." Another claimed:

It often happens that the sole means possessed by the inhabitants of foreign places of judging of Americans is through their acquaintance with our naval officers. . . . They . . . regard [the Navy] as [an] indice of the character of our people, rather than . . . our Consular representatives, whom they consider to be . . . uneducated men (in their sense of the word), possessing little or no refinement, and altogether undesirable acquaintances.

This officer was particularly irked by the fact that most consuls had acquired their posts as "rewards for minor services rendered in the field of politics," and he was not alone in his condemnation of these "accidents of party supremacy."[1]

To the extent that naval officers were critical of consuls, actual experiences with consuls abroad were at least as important as the naval aristocracy's disdain

102   for the consul's social standing.* Thus, when the U.S. Minister[2] to Korea, W. H. Parker, couldn't maintain a presentable state of sobr iety with sufficient frequency, Ensign George Foulk was obliged to relieve him. In the 1880s naval commanders operating in the Indian Ocean were actuall y directed to evaluate American consulates in East Africa and South Asia. In 187 0 the Hawaiian Queen died, and all the consulates in Honolulu except that of t he United States half-masted their ensigns. Six months earlier a false rumor of the Queen's death had caused the American Consul no slight scandal when h e half-masted his flag prematurely. This time he had determined to await orders from proper authority, fully confirming the death of the monarc h, before acting. The Commanding Officer of the U.S.S. *Jamestown,* at anchor in Pearl Harbor, however, took a different view of the sit uation. Considering it imperative that the U.S. flag join all others at half-mast to avoid national embarrassment, he ordered a detachment of marines ashore and for ced the U.S. consul to set the ensign at half-mast, violating Hawaiian sovereig nty in the act. The ensuing repercussions revealed no love lost between naval officers and consuls.

In 1874 several "outrages" were reported to nav al authorities by the manager of a U.S. and British silver mine near La Paz, M exico. Rear Admiral John J. Almy, Commander of the North Pacific Squadron, authorized Captain Walter W. Queen in the *Saranac* to aid the mine's manager, Mr. Henry Brooks. In the process of settling the claim with the Mexican authorities, however, Captain Queen and his Executive Officer, Lieutenant Commander William Bainbridge-Hoff, "seemed to have forgotten the existence of the U.S. Consul at La Paz; at least they entirely ignored his presence," or so the Consul, David Turner, reported to his superiors in Washington. Concurrently U.S. Naval Forces on the Asiatic Station were confronted with a formidable enemy—the newly arrived U.S. Consul-General at Yokohama, Thomas B. Van Buren—who immediately began to arrest and punish mischievous and intransigent officers and sailors, believing he had the authority to do so. Before he could be convinced of his error, he had jailed and fined several bluejackets, and had threatened to "slap Surgeon King, U.S.N., in jail" or "to deport him."[3] No love was lost here either.

There is no reason to suspect that Consul-General Van Buren fabricated any of the charges of misbehavior. He may have discovered the miscreants in attendance at a local "Johnnie Nookee" (or "John Nugi"), a popular pastime of naval officers in Japanese ports in the late nineteenth century. And had he done so, his threats of jailing and deportation might be explicable, for a "Johnnie Nookee" was a wild and woolly affair. Naval Surgeon Samuel Boyer described one that many of Mahan's messmates on the *Iroquois* and *Idaho* attended in 1868–1869. Eighteen naked women, "dancing in the most voluptuous manner,

---

* But some officers found the company of even the lowliest of U.S. Consular Corps officers, the commercial agent, delightful. Commander John Rodgers, for example, found the commercial agent at Batavia to be gracious, with several "exceedingly well bred children" and "refined ladies." Johnson, *Rodgers,* 106. See pp. 172–174 for more on Navy-State relations.

placing themselves in all the different kinds of attitudes that one might imagine **103** men and women would take whilst having carnal communication with each other," caroused about one room and then proceeded to lead individual guests into separate rooms for further entertainment. "In short," Boyer confided to his diary, "the whole is one carnival of sin and iniquity; the passions of both sexes aroused to the highest pitch." Needless to say, Boyer considered the affair "well worth the time and money spent in beholding it," and added: "To say that you were in Japan without seeing a 'Johnnie Nookee' is the same as saying that you were in Italy without seeing Venice." Boyer and his friends were wardroom officers, but the inhabitants of the squadron's cabins apparently did not consider such entertainment below their station, for Boyer noted that "our old Admiral and all the Captains had a 'Johnnie Nookee' a few days ago." Several years before, Lieutenant George Preble had written to his wife that he found Japanese bi-sexual bathing to be "disgusting," and he probably did; but one wonders whether Preble or Boyer was more illustrative of the attitude of naval officers towards such jollifications as the "Johnnie Nookee." The kind of letters of Mahan's messmates that have been saved, most of them letters to wives, female cousins, sisters, or mothers, are something less than ideal windows into the hidden lives of their senders. But there are a few indications therein that there were a number of officers who equated "Johnnie Nookees" with Venice. For example, Lieutenant Charles Sperry told his wife of the "great many honest, clean handed, pure hearted gentlemen" he had associated with "in knocking about the world as I am doing now," but he added that he had seen "beastliness that beggars description" as well. Surgeon Boyer's frequent entries relating to the treatment for venereal disease of sailors and officers alike who had suffered a rendezvous with "Miss Placed Fortune"[4] would appear to require some qualification of the genteel image of the naval officer that some of our earlier observations may have created. Not all officers succumbed to temptations, but apparently a good many did.

But one could indulge in only so many "Johnnie Nookees" in one port. Most of one's time was spent in more civilized fashion. If the visit was one's first, a dignified tour of the hinterland or city sights was generally the first order of business. In addition to "seeing Venice," more ambitious officers on the European station might take a week's leave and tour France, Switzerland, Germany, or the Austro-Hungarian Empire, where one might feel a surge of "stern pride" over the "great respect" shown one's "Republican uniform." Thereafter one might retire to the city's sedate English Club (most ports had one by the late nineteenth century) where naval officers socialized with officers of British and other foreign services, played whist, or caught up with the news of the world in the club's quiet library. If the port was not too far from a golf course, and many "English" ports were not, naval officers could be found on the links and in the clubhouse. In the words of one newspaper correspondent who served with the Navy in the First World War, "No history of the Navy would be complete without a word about golf. It is *the* Navy game. Golf clubs are to be

Artist Rufus Fairchild Zogbaum (father of Admiral Zogbaum) depicts one young officer-and-gentleman meeting guests in the 1890s, and another joining guests for luncheon in the captain's cabin (New York Public Library Picture Collection).

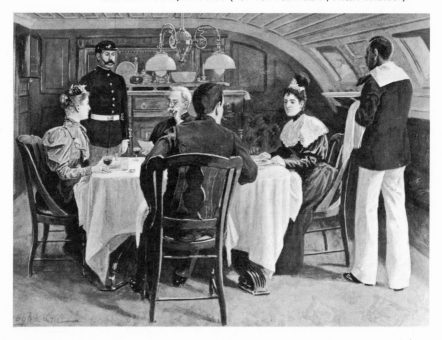

Officers of the wardroom mess, U.S.S. *Solace,* and their guests pose for the photographer, *circa* 1900 (Detroit Collection, Library of Congress).

The British Community
request the honour of the Company of
The Captain + Officers U.S. "Baltimore"
Saturday
on ~~Tuesday~~, the 12th of May, 1900, at a Fête
on the Cricket Ground to meet
Captain Percy Scott, R.N. C.B.,
and the Officers of H.M.S. " Terrible."

H. E. POLLOCK,
Hon. Secretary,
For the Committee.

9.30 to 11.30 p.m.

...men of Manila request
...ur Company at a Ball
...at the Club House,
...the 21st December 1900.
Dancing to commence at 9 p.m.

R.S.V.P. to   C. Kingcome
Hon Secy

Admiral Remey & Staff
U.S. Flagship "Brooklyn"

In foreign ports the naval aristocracy was well received, particularly in English circles, as these invitations, retained by their recipients, suggest (from various manuscript collections, Library of Congress).

106   found in every cabin; in the tiny libraries Harry Vardon rubs shoulders with naval historians and professors of thermodynamics." Officers also socialized with the officials of U.S. and British firms located in foreign ports. These social relations were not always the best, but they occasionally revealed the common backgrounds of the two professions. Lieutenant Edwin Anderson, in command of a South China Patrol gunboat at the turn of the century, discovered that "the head manager of the Standard Oil Co. out here," John Bolles, was his second cousin and childhood playmate.[5] It's quite possible that this sort of co-incidence was common.* In the evenings there were dinners and dances with "the best officers" Europe had to offer, "as well as with people of so many highly civilized courts."[6]

For social events and pleasant ports, England and the Mediterranean stations were generally considered unsurpassed by most officers. But to the recent graduate of the Academy, finally realizing the high standing in society promised him as an officer in the fleet, virtually any port in the world became impressive. "To travel in 'foreign parts' on board a mighty man-of-war is some pumpkins," Passed Midshipman J. Laurens Read wrote his sisters in 1858. "Just think of me, trotting myself out at Havana with sword and belt on! Ahem!" Similarly, Ensign Albert Caldwell wrote his mother from northern Europe in 1867, "How we apples do float! Sure is a Honour taking tea with the nobility of Brittany— the uniform does wonders over here."[7]

The warships themselves "did wonders" for the officer's social life abroad. In the words of Passed Assistant Engineer J. P. Stuart Lawrence, there was nothing in the late nineteenth century "that the average girl enjoy[ed] to such an extent as a dance aboard a man of war." Officers lavishly entertained the gentry, nobility, and civil-military officialdom of each and every "civilized" port of call.† In 1853 Commodore Matthew C. Perry described to his wife one party the Asiatic Squadron had just given in Hong Kong: "The Governor, [the British] Admiral, and many others of the elite were present and the affair went off splendidly."[8]

Parties, dinners, and dances were looked upon as a well-earned and welcome relief after a week or two at sea. Squadron commanders and captains of vessels operating independently often arranged their port schedules to coincide with the leading social events of the season in each port. In fact, there were times when some rear admirals, commodores, and captains appear to have allowed their pursuit of pleasantries to distract them from their basic missions. For those fortunate enough to be assigned the duty of transporting a V.I.P. from port to port, the social calendar was particularly heavy. In 1868–1869, for example, the *Franklin* carried Admiral and Mrs. David Farragut about on a grand tour of the

---

* For example, Annapolite William V. Pratt's father worked for Russell and Co. in Shanghai.

† The court-martial of the bandits in George Bernard Shaw's *Captain Brassbound's Conversion*, conducted by officers of an American warship, is spoofed as a social event. Apparently some U.S. naval officers had impressed Shaw and his countrymen with the etiquette of extravagance.

Continent, where the ship's officers joined the Farraguts at receptions in their honor held by the courts of France, Portugal, Denmark, Sweden, Russia, Italy, and the Ottoman Empire, and entertained lords, princes, and empresses on board the flagship. Several years later, when ex-President Grant made his curious tour of the world, U.S. naval commanders vied for the honor and pleasure of escorting their former Commander-in-Chief on different legs of his journey. As one officer explained to his wife back in the States, Grant's presence on his ship would "decidedly improve our chances of a good time."[9]

Naval officers were always well received by men of their own station, cloth, or predilections—from the days when Spanish and Brazilian naval officers entertained officers of the U.S. Africa squadron in the late 1840s to the days when British and European navalists and imperialists welcomed Mahan and his officers of the *Chicago* in the early 1890s and officers of Dewey's squadron hobnobbed with the Spanish colonials they were displacing in the Philippines. Thus Ensign William Standley and his messmates on the *Olympia* were well received at the turn of the century by Russian officers and civil dignitaries in Vladivostok. To Standley the socializing, which ran from early afternoon to the wee hours of the morning, was "the introduction to a new way of life":[10]

We were young and the tinsel glamor of the society of the local government officials was very appealing.

But it was the British whose hospitality seemed the most genuine.

Anglo-American Naval Rapport; or, Victorians Rule the Waves

As early as July 4, 1825, when British and U.S. naval officers celebrated American Independence off the west coast of South America, the relations between naval officers of the two services in foreign ports were "very intimate." And they became more intimate as the century wore on. Whether is was in Rio de Janeiro, the Canary Islands, the Mediterranean, or the Africa or China coast, wherever two warships of Britain and the U.S. met there was sure to be a "jollification." And if the port harbored a naval and diplomatic set as well, so much the better. "English women prefer to dance with Americans," Lieutenant Charles Sperry explained to his bride in 1880. While it is possible that this was the case, what may be more likely is that Sperry and his messmates simply welcomed the opportunity to hold an Englishwoman in their arms. "It makes me feel as if I belonged to the world to dance with an English woman," Sperry owned to his wife in 1884.[11]

A visit of a British warship to the States or an American warship to Britain was an event particularly looked forward to by officers of both services. "The Navy people" in England "always treated me in the best style," Assistant Navy Secretary Gustavus Vasa Fox, himself an ex-naval officer, told Captain Henry Wise in 1867. "The middle classes and the Navy people cannot do too much for us." U.S. naval attachés in London were made honorary members of the

108   Royal Navy Club, where Captain Mahan was feted and given three heartfelt cheers during his triumphant visit to England in 1894.[12] Navy Secretary Josephus Daniels was quite convinced of the strong friendship between British and American naval officers, though he thought there was "none between sailors of the races." At least one U.S. sailor also felt a tension between "Limey" and "Jack." But those who witnessed the dinner given to 2,400 British and American sailors in 1906 would certainly have disagreed, as would Lieutenant Commander H. B. Hird, who remarked in 1924 that "the spirit of comradeship is strong between the [British and American] fleets."[13]

At sea, on station, U.S. and Royal Navy vessels demonstrated this camaraderie in a variety of engaging ways. For example, whenever Britisher and American served together, as did H.M.S. *Cyclops* and U.S.S. *Perry* on the Africa station in the 1850s, the departure of one was certain to result in an exchange of three rousing cheers. Another British-American post-1815 naval practice was that of unauthorized, and often, unplanned, joint belligerent naval action. This cooperation appears to have had its symbolic, if not its actual chronological origin in the aid that the American Commodore Josiah Tattnall offered to the British Rear Admiral Hope and his battered squadron in 1859, when Hope, who had hoped to batter certain Chinese forts into submission, was in immediate peril of being battered into submission himself. Tattnall's use of Sir Walter Scott's expression, "Blood is thicker than water," as he offered his ships to Rear Admiral Hope became a celebrated adage, cited often by officers of the two fleets at banquets throughout the world for three-score years or more. Thus when Captain Mahan was entertained in St. James' Hall in May 1894, a huge banner, bearing the legend "BLOOD IS THICKER THAN WATER" surmounted the orchestra stand. And when the fictitious commander of a U.S. Yangtze patrol gunboat in Lieutenant Commander Yates Stirling's 1909 novel, *A U.S. Midshipman in China*, was in need of support, his fictitious British counterpart assured him "we've not forgotten Tattnall's 'Blood is thicker than water.'"[14]

Tattnall's act appears to have served as a model for both officer corps. To cite but a few examples: in 1866 Commodore John Rodgers, U.S.N., and Rear Admiral Joseph Denman, R.N., planned joint naval action against a Spanish ironclad off the coast of Chile; in 1867 Captain C. Murray Aynesley, R.N., in H.M.S. *Jason*, joined Commander Francis Roe, U.S.N., in the *Tacony*, to test the late Emperor Maximillian's Imperialist Army's control of the stronghold at Vera Cruz. "A shot fired at one ship," Aynesley assured Roe, "will be answered by both." In 1873 Captain Lorraine in H.M.S. *Niobe* threatened to bombard Havana if the Spanish authorities did not cease their execution of *Virginius* passengers;* in 1874 Commander Theodore Jewell, U.S.N., in U.S.S. *Tuscarora* and his British counterpart in H.M.S. *Portsmouth* landed armed forces

---

* Moreover, to complete the cycle, prominent citizens of Virginia City, Nevada, sent Captain Lorraine a solid silver brick as a "token" of their esteem, with the inscription "Blood is thicker than water" engraved thereupon. Ralph Roske & C. Van Doren, *Lincoln's Commando* (N.Y., 1957), 293.

at Honolulu to place Prince David Kalakaua on the Hawaiian throne; in 1882 **109**
U.S. Marines were landed to aid in the British occupation of Alexandria;*
during the Philippine insurgency U.S. naval leaders borrowed landing craft
from Royal Navy well-wishers to carry out amphibious operations against
Aguinaldo's men; and, on at least one occasion, a British gunboat was the
actual instrument that forced the surrender of a Filipino city to U.S. representatives. At the turn of the century both fleets worked closely together to
forestall any German or Japanese interference or threat to British or American
property in Hawaii, Manila Bay, Samoa, or Haiti, and to crush the Boxers in
China; many a British-American naval friendship made on the road to Peking
was later refreshed when the two fleets anchored together in the North Sea
in 1917; and in 1924, when the American manager of Arnold & Co. was
murdered by Chinese at Wanhsien, Lieutenant Commander Ivan Whitehorn
in H.M.S. *Cockchafer* and his Annapolite counterpart demanded an apology and
the execution of the culprits and threatened to shell the town, ignoring the
objections of Prime Minister Ramsay MacDonald.[15] Lieutenant Rufus F.
Zogbaum, U.S.N., captured precisely the mood of his age in a scene in his
novel, *The Junior Officer of the Watch*. His hero, "Midshipman James Pickins of
the U.S.S. *Dearborn*" and a British naval officer came to the rescue of an English
merchant captain and his lovely daughter who were threatened by dastardly
Arab pirates:

> Fierce yells from Berber throats, hoarser Teuton shouts, the spitting of revolvers. . . .
> All was over in a minute. . . . The bodies of the Riffians were thrown into the water,
> their boat smashed and stove in by axe-blows; the English officer . . . turned to Jim,
> who silently gripped the proffered hand, and the two young men, "Britisher" and
> "Yankee," smiled grimly one into the other's eyes.

Vincent Davis tells us that World War II naval commanders had a "positive
dislike for fighting alongside the Royal Navy"; but if this was so during
World War II, it was less often the case in earlier days.[16]

With or without belligerent naval intervention, each service could always
count on the other to man the rails, at the very least. Thus when British warships
shelled Alexandria in 1882, French naval elements stood off from the scene,
but the American rear admiral steamed his cheering ships around the British
fleet at the close of the action. Reciprocally, when Commodore Dewey's
squadron left Hong Kong upon news of the U.S. declaration of war with
Spain, patients on a British hospital ship gave them a rousing send-off. And
when U.S. sailors and marines were landed at Vera Cruz in April 1914, the
British squadron of Rear Admiral Sir Christopher Craddock manned the rails
and cheered them on.[17]

Until the 1920s, at the very earliest, American naval power never matched
that of Britain. But British naval authorities, apparently convinced that they

---

* See Thomas Nast's cartoons celebrating the incident in illustration sections in this
chapter and in Chapter 4.

British and U.S. naval forces often went to one another's aid, officially and unofficially, between the 1840s and the 1940s. This 1882 Nast cartoon depicts one such occasion, off Alexandria, where a U.S. naval squadron "covered" British warships shelling the port (*Harper's Magazine*, 1882).

Another act of Anglo-American naval camaraderie: the crew of U.S.S. *Olympia*, enroute to the Battle of Manila Bay, returns the cheering of a British hospitalship in Hong Kong harbor, as seen by an artist on board the *Olympia* (*Harper's Magazine*, 1898).

U.S. gunboats *Monocacy* and *Palos*, with British gunboats *Wigeon* and *Teal*, on the Yangtze, standing off a Star.dard Oil regional headquarters building (marked on photo), *circa* 1910 (Naval History Division, Navy Department).

In 1898 a naval "Britannia" was shown greeting her American counterpart, "Columbia" in the pages of *Puck*. The cartoon, entitled "After Many Years," bore the following exchange of dialogue: "Mother!" "Daughter!" (*Puck*, 1898).

World War I allies. Admiral David Beatty, R:N., Rear Admiral Hugh Rodman, U.S.N., King George V, Vice Admiral William S. Sims, U.S.N., and Edward, Prince of Wales, in 1918 (Naval History Division, Navy Department).

Note the anchor in this enterprising 1898 ad (*Harper's Magazine*, 1898).

Pears' Soap
AND AN
ANGLO-AMERICAN ALLIANCE
WOULD IMPROVE
THE COMPLEXION
OF THE
UNIVERSE

112   could always count on U.S. naval friendship, actively and frequently lent their
administrative and technical skills and plans to Mahan's messmates. Commencing in 1879 the top Annapolis graduates were sent to the Royal Naval College,
Greenwich, to study British naval construction techniques and to make detailed
sketches—virtual blueprints—of the turrets of such class vessels as H.M.S.
Inflexible, Devastation, Ajax, Colossus, Collingwood, and *Warspite.* British constructors like Josiah McGregor were hired as "consulting engineers" to the U.S.
Navy on the invitation of the U.S. naval attaché in London, who also advised
the U.S. Navy Department to treat all blueprints of British warships confidentially, in order to protect their British friends. The coordinated-fire-control
gunnery theory of Captain Percy Scott, R.N., and Lieutenant William S. Sims,
U.S.N., tested on the Asiatic Station in the opening years of the twentieth
century, was simply the most spectacular of a variety of joint enterprises, such
as the improved fire control system plans passed to Rear Admiral Caspar
Goodrich on a 1905 visit to Britain or the report Sims later made to his superiors
in Washington, with British approval, on H.M.S. *Dreadnought* capabilities. All
were kept strictly confidential. As Sims warned the U.S. Naval Institute's
Board of Control in 1902, any release of Scott's gun-training techniques would
be "unfair to our British friends," inasmuch as they had not been shown to
French or any other naval powers. World War I only legitimatized the exchange
of professional secrets, and after the war the exchange continued, now on a
somewhat more equal footing.[18]

Trade secrets were not the only things the two navies shared; they shared
heroes as well. To Mahan and his messmates all the great British naval heroes
were the most admirable souls, and Nelson and Collingwood were nothing short
of sublime. The British might not have been quite as generous in their regard
for Paul Jones, but they were happy to claim Decatur, Hull, Farragut, and men
of their ilk as honorary members of their honorable society. And for every
Britisher like First Lord of the Admiralty "Jackie" Fisher, who hung a steel
engraving of George Washington in his cabin and feted Rear Admiral William
Sampson, U.S.N., on Washington's birthday after the battle of Santiago, there
were Americans like Commander Charles Sperry, who hung a copy of Kipling's
"Recessional" in his cabin and told his friends to pray for Queen Victoria, and
Captain Washington Irving Chambers, who rephrased "God Save the King"
to read:[19]

> Just monarch of the sea!
> Bulwark of Liberty!
> of thee I sing
> . . .
> Guardian of many lands,
> Mother of many bands
> . . .
> Long live thy lusty sons!
> God bless them all!

Given the fact of common heroes and common naval secrets, one might expect that the two services had in mind other modes of reciprocity. And of course they did. The Civil War temporarily soured naval relations,[20] but feelings mellowed with the passage of the years. By 1868 British officers were toasting their American counterparts as members of "our own race." In the 1870s some U.S. officers proposed to join England to crush a German "Armada," should such a fleet be flung at the Royal Navy, and to brandish Old Glory on behalf of the mother country: "Its stars for England, its stripes for England's foes!" By the 1880s talk of the confederation of "the whole Anglo-Saxon race" was "a popular idea with many" at British, U.S., and Commonwealth naval gatherings. In 1885 Commander Albert Barker advised Secretary of the Navy William Whitney as much from Australian and New Zealand waters, and in 1889 Commander Bowman McCalla similarly informed Whitney's successor, Benjamin Franklin Tracy, of the Royal Navy's great affection for the United States. "We have endeavored," he explained, "to express our appreciation, believing this feeling to be mutual."[21]

The experiences and sentiments of McCalla and Barker were typical. Captain Francis Roe met an unidentified British naval officer in Naples in the 1890s, and the two cheerfully exchanged daydreams of the glories and virtues attendant to the future union of British and American naval power. Concurrently, Captain Caspar Goodrich discussed with Sir George Clarke a plan to marry the two fleets into one floating World Police Force. Admiral Philip Colomb, R.N., confessed his hope to his fellow naval historian, Captain A. T. Mahan, U.S.N., that "we may make a league to keep the rest of the world in order between us." Mahan, Colomb, Admiral Lord Charles Beresford, James Bryce, and Major Sir G. S. Clarke all contributed articles to the *North American Review* throughout the 1890s on "a naval union" and "imperial federation." Then, at the close of the Spanish-American War, came congratulations from Royal Navy Admirals like Sir Nowell Salmon, who welcomed Rear Admiral George Belknap, U.S.N., into the imperial club. "I feel sure," Salmon told Belknap, "we would rather see you in the Philippines than ourselves." "I believe you are on the road to . . . Imperial Democracy." Rear Admiral Mahan responded to one British well-wisher: "We are much the same; and I believe in it as inevitable." And in April 1899, after successful settlement of the Samoan partition crisis, during which British and U.S. naval forces had demonstrated considerable harmony, the daily paper on American Rear Admiral Albert Kautz's flagship in Apia, Samoa, editorialized on "the Anglo-American Alliance":[22]

At last has come to pass that; which was looked forward to with hope by Americans and English, . . . the union of the two great English speaking nations of the earth.

Why should the Anglo-Saxons be divided? Ours, the most numberous and enlightened race of all have but to speak together and none dare dispute. . . . We can lick the world. Let this war in Samoa be our example for future actions.

Despite these awesome predictions of "union" and federated "Imperial Democracy" no formal reunion followed this fin-de-siècle vision of joint

114   omnipotence. Some U.S. naval officers appear to have been relieved that it was so. Commander Francis Barber, for example, wrote critically to Navy Secretary John D. Long in early 1899 of the "tommyrot" he had been hearing of "an Anglo-Saxon alliance." Barber was naval attaché to the Triple Alliance, and he may have acquired his distrust of Britain in Berlin or Vienna. But he and the few who agreed with him in the Service were unrepresentative.[23] Many Annapolites, far from being discouraged, remained in the van of the movement for federation and did what they could to "contribute to the cause of Great Britain." Numerous examples of this could be offered;[24] perhaps a few will make the point. First, there were the letters of Rear Admiral Charles Sperry, American representative to the Second Hague Conference, to General Horace Porter, President Theodore Roosevelt, and the President's sister, Mrs. Rear Admiral W. S. Cowles, in 1908. Sperry had conferred extensively with Captain Ottley, the Royal Navy's representative to the Conference, and he pointed out to his distinguished correspondents the virtues of an Anglo-American naval union. "The control of the Pacific lies with us," Sperry explained. Americans should realize their opportunities and responsibilities and throw their lot in permanently with the British. Sperry's sentiments were echoed fictionally the same year by Lieutenant Rufus Fairchild Zogbaum, whose hero in *The Junior Officer of the Watch* won the hand of the English girl whom he had saved from Berber pirates. Zogbaum achieved a kind of symbolic federation in the story's concluding lines:

> Arms drooping and hands thrown out, sideways, with a pretty gesture of self-abnegation and surrender, softly the red lips parted, and in a voice sweet and clean and low, Beatrix uttered the words coming down through the ages: "Thy people—shall be *my* people, Jim."

Two years later Commander William S. Sims, U.S.N., told a London Guildhall audience of his conviction that, if the British Empire were ever "seriously menaced by an external enemy," Englishmen could "count upon every man, every dollar, and every drop of blood of your kindred across the sea." Sims' sentiments were seconded by Chief Boatswain's Mate Carl Benzon, U.S.N., but Commander-in-Chief William Howard Taft found them censurable, none the less; he reined Sims in.* Apparently concurrent remarks by Rear Admiral Seaton Schroeder went undetected; Schroeder, in command of the U.S. North Atlantic Squadron, told Admiral of the Fleet Sir Edward Seymour and a host of banqueters that "the armament of the world" ought to be "dictated by the reciprocal attitude of Yankee and Briton."

With the outbreak of World War I the naval aristocracy intensified its efforts on behalf of the Royal Navy. The October 1914 issue of *The Navy*, the U.S.

---

* According to Josephus Daniels, Sims "paid very little attention to the views of others, unless they happened to be British," and "wanted an organization like the British Admiralty." *The Wilson Era—Years of Peace*, 270. These charges were made after Sims had attacked Daniels for incompetence in the administration and strategic planning during the war, but they were probably accurate none the less.

Navy League's journal, which closely reflected Service sentiment, was styled
"Anglo-Saxon Naval Supremacy" and was an obvious effort to identify U.S.
and British naval aims and leadership. The Wilson Administration did what
it could to prevent Mahan and his messmates from issuing "unneutral" statements, but it had its hands full. And when the United States entered the war,
the Department dispatched Rear Admiral William S. Sims, the 1910 Guildhall
culprit, as naval liaison to London. Many American officers found British
wartime blockade policies somewhat offensive,* and Britons were similarly
upset about American wartime penetration of traditional British markets, as
well as the rise to parity with the Royal Navy of President Wilson's "navy
second to none," but the differences were eventually resolved; a new naval
equilibrium was established by 1930. The "naval disarmament" arms race of
the 1920s pitted the two naval aristocracies against one another, but only on a
professional level. Each service had to warn of the dangers the other posed to
their nation's interests in order to hold their own in the annual Army–Navy
appropriations campaigns. Off-duty, Rear Admiral W. V. Pratt, U.S.N., told
the Council on Foreign Relations in 1923 of his pleasure with "the establishment
of a stable balance of sea power between the two great English-speaking
nations." "The United States and the United Kingdom must stand firmly side
by side . . . 50–50 in all things," Pratt later advised the Secretary of the Navy in
1933. "The mutual interests of Great Britain and ourselves in sea power will
draw us inevitably closer together provided we take care not to let economic
and other matters drive a rift between us."[25] The rivalry was only skin-deep.

One may well wonder at the intensity and virtual uniformity of this rapport.
Why were American officers so united in their praise of the "refinement" and
"Christian civilization" of their "wonderful" friends from "Great-heart
England?" Why did they boast of being "frankly" and "particularly pro-
English?" Why did they find the hatred of Englishmen among some Americans
(many of them probably Irish-Americans) to be "strange" and "senseless?"
Why did they "grieve" over this disaffection "more . . . than . . . anything
else?"[26]

Certainly the common historical and cultural tradition was in the forefront
of their reasons. Upper-class American society in the mid-nineteenth century
was, in the words of Henry Cabot Lodge, "essentially English in its standards
and fashions. . . . Our literary standards, our standards of statesmanship, our
modes of thought . . . were as English as the trivial customs of the dinner-table
and the ballroom." The naval officer who preferred to dance with an English
girl was not cultivating a new taste; he was rediscovering an old habit. As

* Thus in mid-1918 Captain W. V. Pratt, U.S.N., feared that the two nations might
come to blows over trading disputes, and hoped that his British counterparts would quit
what he called their "damned way of paternalism." And, parity once achieved, Rear
Admiral Josiah McKean, U.S.N., expressed a reluctance henceforth to "having the American Eagle second to the British Lion under any conditions in relation to any questions, at
any time, in any place in the world." (Braisted, *U.S. Navy in the Pacific, 1909–1922*, 308,
417, 424, 455.) Cf. "Rem. of Adm. Th. Hart," p. 57, Oral Hist. Res. Office, Columbia U.

116   midshipmen, Mahan and his messmates had received what one superintendent called "an English education." They spoke and wrote "in the manner of English gentlemen." According to Navy Secretary Gideon Welles, writing in his diary in 1869, the senior officers and their lieges were thought "to ape, imitate, and copy the English."* All had great interest in the detection and proper eulogism of any and all English forebearers to be located in their geneological past.[27] The fact of a common language and a common Episcopal religion must have accented this Anglophilia in foreign ports, when the two services entertained one another among peoples of different tongues and cultures. And the vitality of the British Empire, so omnipresent to the late nineteenth and early twentieth century traveller, profoundly impressed Mahan and his colleagues; as one officer put it, "When compared with our own penny policy, there is something grand in the display England makes."[28] In short, the U.S. naval officer was an Anglophile because he identified with his British colleague in every imaginable way—socially, professionally, ideologically, culturally, historically, and racially.†

In spite of the excellent relations officers had with most foreign officials and social elite, they drew the line when it came to the "inferior" peoples of the world. Officers and their wives had little or no contact with Chinese or Filipino society, a fact that one observer attributed to "the English tradition of having nothing to do with the natives . . . in the Orient." But while this may explain the American naval officer's slighting of the Filipino elite, it does not explain why the same thing happened in Haiti, when the families of the naval and marine occupation forces began to arrive in that land in 1916. There a distinctly "American social group" emerged, "centering in the American Club," and a "line of social cleavage" appeared "because of the color prejudice."[29] Obviously, just as "race" was at the heart of the British segregation policies, so it was at the heart of American naval social alignments abroad. Naval officers, like their contemporary WASP countrymen, had a fine sense of racial discrimination.[30]

Family Life Abroad

The families of naval officers were not always required to remain in the States while father roamed the seven seas. Wives who could afford to, followed their naval husbands about, and George Dewey recalled that "there used to be a saying" among the officers in the 1880s "that we went from port to port to meet our wives . . . and get letters from our sweethearts." (In fact, the wives of some admirals, commodores, and captains were actually taken aboard for the duration of the cruise, until in 1881 Navy Secretary William Hunt ordered that practice to cease.) If father's ship was ordered to the Mediterranean

---

* Sailors referred to Rear Admiral David Harmony, U.S.N., as "His Lordship" because of Harmony's heavy British accent. Buenzle, *Bluejacket*, 265.

† For a discussion of the U.S. naval officer's concept of race and the role of "Anglo-Saxonism" within that concept, see "Racism" in Chapter 5.

squadron, mother might pack the family up for a year or more in Europe, **117** summering in Switzerland or Baden-Baden and wintering in Paris, where the children might continue their schooling or, more likely, she might report directly to Villefrance on the Riviera, unofficial headquarters for the American Mediterranean squadron, where temporary residence would be established. If, on the other hand, father was ordered to the Asiatic squadron, mother established residence in Yokohama (before 1900) or Manila (after 1900). As early as 1882 at least a fifth of the wardroom officers of each Asiatic squadron warship had wives living ashore in Yokohama, and by 1920 an even greater percentage of families set up housekeeping in Manila and summer quarters at Chefoo.

Not all wives found the experience exhilarating. Lieutenant Roger Welles' bride found the constant pursuit of the fleet tiring and the heat, lizards, insects, and customs of the Orient oppressive, and confided to her diary:

> The family of any girl who *thought* of marrying into the Navy should make her take a position for one year with a fly-by-night, one-day-in-a-place theatrical company.

Marine officer Holland Smith considered the wives of officers who set up a household abroad "sturdy pioneers." But most wives reveled in the experience of having two servants in the Philippines and "a Chinese Amah" or a special tutor at the Bishop Brent Episcopal School in Manila for the children. Mrs. Roger Welles hated Manila but loved its Polo Club. After one long tirade in her diary about the filthy conditions in the city, she praised the Island's governor for preserving the polo fields and clubhouse. After all, her world was not the malaria-ridden world of the Old City. One "Navy wife" recalled that "in the good old days everyone looked forward to duty on the Asiatic Station. . . . The exchange was splendid. . . . Most Americans lived in luxury with flocks of servants and wonderful food and drink. What a Navy wife . . . couldn't buy in China on her Ensign husband's pay wasn't worth buying."[31] Under such conditions it was possible to view orders returning papa to shore duty in the States, or to a warship operating in home waters, with regret or even alarm.

Chapter 3 (In Foreign Ports)

1. Benjamin, *U.S.N.A.*, 357; Ensign Winston Folk, *PUSNI*, LI (1925), 275; Connolly, *Navy Men*, 51; Lieutenant Edwin Anderson to his wife, March 16, 1903, Anderson Papers, S.H.C., U. of N.C. Library; Lieutenant A. P. Mantus (pseud.), "Gentility in the Navy," *United Service*, V (1881), 345–346.

2. *Korean-American Relations*, Vol. I, ed. George McCune and John Harrison (Berkeley, 1951), 43.

Parker was probably exceptional. State Department officers of ministerial rank were generally well regarded; many were of a slightly higher social class than the naval aristocracy itself.

3. Jewell, *Among our Sailors*, 239–241 (Jewell had been U.S. Consul at Singapore and was not an admirer of naval diplomacy); Turner to Second Asst. Sec. of State, Oct. 30, 1874, dispatches from U.S. consuls at La Paz, Mexico, Microcopy T–324, Roll 2, N.A.; Captain Edward McCauley, commanding U.S.S. *Lackawanna*, to Rear Admiral A. M. Pennock, commanding U.S. Naval Force on the Asiatic Station, Sept. 18, 1874, Letterbook, 1873–1877, p. 251, Edward McCauley Papers, N.Y.H.S. Cf. Sir Rutherford Alcock, *The Capital of the Tycoon* (2 vols., N.Y., 1863), I, 42, 156. The story of the naval inspection of American consulates on Indian Ocean stations is to be found in Kenneth Hagan's forthcoming study of American naval diplomacy from Hayes to Harrison.

When an ex-naval officer, David Porter, was named to the Ottoman court in the 1830s, Navy-State relations in the Eastern Mediterranean reached a new low, but the fact that several of the officers who had cashiered Porter a decade before were in command of U.S. naval forces in the Mediterranean was probably the key to that feud. "Porter, David," *D.A.B.;* James Sens, "United States Relations with Turkey, 1831–1843," unpublished master's essay, Ohio University, 1964.

4. *Naval Surgeon in Japan*, ed. Barnes & Barnes; 102–103, *passim*; *Preble Diary*, 183; Sperry to his wife, Oct. 3, 1879, Sperry Papers.

5. Anderson to his wife, Oct. 2, 1901, Anderson Papers, S.H.C., U. of N.C. Library.

6. See, for example, the letters of Ensign Robert McNeely in the first decade of the twentieth century to his sister Fannie McNeely concerning travel in Europe in the Macay-McNeely Family Papers, S.H.C., U. of N.C. Library; the long account of parties attended by Belgian, Turkish, or British royalty in Rear Admiral Andrew T. Long, "Around the World in Sixty Years," pp. 220–230, Long Papers, S.H.C., U. of N.C. Library; Sperry to his wife, Jan. 7, 1880, and Sept. 4 and Oct. 3, 1885, Sperry Papers; Mahan's letters to his mother, his

wife, and his friend Samuel Ashe, circa 1868–1870 and 1894–1895; Mahan, *From Sail to Steam*; Franklin, *Memories of a Rear-Admiral*; McCalla, "Memoirs," *passim*; Henry B. Beston, *Full Speed Ahead: Tales from the Log of a Correspondent with our Navy* (Garden City, 1919), 94; Midshipman Francis Roe's Private Journal, entry for Jan. 20, 1860, Box 143, N.H.F.; Madeline Dahlgren, *Life of Admiral Dahlgren*; the N.H.F. papers or autobiographies of Rear Admirals Hugh Rodman, W. S. Schley, Robert Coontz, and many others.

7. Mahan to his wife throughout 1893–1894, Mahan Papers, L. of C.; West, *Admirals of American Empire*, 78–79; Read (or possibly John Maffitt) to his sisters, July 2, 1858, John Newland Maffitt Papers, S.H.C., U. of N.C. Library, also cited in Emma Maffitt, *Life and Services of John Newland Maffitt*, 202; See also the manuscript autobiography in the Charles McVay Papers, N.H.F., and Ensign A. A. McKethan to his mother, October 31, 1893, A. A. McKethan Papers, Perkins Library, Duke U.; Caldwell to his mother, Sept. 7, 1867, Caldwell Papers, Indiana Hist. Soc.

8. Lawrence to his mother, Nov. 18, 1880, Rear Admiral J. P. Stuart Lawrence Papers, Navy Museum, Annapolis; West, *Admirals of American Empire*, 78–79; Morison, *Perry*, 352. The practice of entertaining distinguished guests aboard on warships, known now as the "Fo'c's'le Frolic," is as alive today as in the days of Farragut and Fiske.

9. James E. Montgomery, *Our Admiral's Flag Abroad: The Cruise of Admiral D.G. Farragut* . . . (New York, 1869), 29–31, 35–40, 61, 122; Lieutenant Charles Sperry to his wife, March 25, 1879, Sperry Papers.

10. See, for example, Edward Billingsley, *In Defense of Neutral Rights* (Chapel Hill, 1967), 198; Foote, *Africa*, 369–370; Sperry's letters to his wife in 1886; Mahan's letters to his wife in 1894; Potter, *Sailing the Sulu Sea*, 250–310; Admiral William H. Standley and Rear Admiral Arthur A. Ageton, *Admiral Ambassador to Russia* (Chicago, 1955), 4, 9.

11. *Memoir and Correspondence of Charles Steedman*, 86; Lynch, *Naval Life*, 98; Foote, *Africa*, 369–370; Paymaster John F. Tarbell's "Journal of the Gettysburg, 1876–1877," Naval Historical Foundation, 2 and *passim*; Sperry to Miss Marion Carter, January 11, 1880, and to his wife, January 7, 1880, and November 15, 1884, Sperry Papers, L. of C.

12. Fox to Wise, May 1, 1867, Wise Papers, N.Y.H.S.; Commander F. E. Chadwick to Henry Kelly, Esq., R.N., July 17, 1886, Personal copybook, Chadwick Papers, N.Y.H.S.; Mahan to his wife, September 13, 1894, and July 8, 1894, Mahan Papers, L. of C. While Mahan was being feted in London, Herbert Spencer was being regaled in America. And when Mahan returned to America, his messmates welcomed him home with verse such as Rear Admiral George Belknap's, intoning the "happy days" at Annapolis over the "scholastic bays" Mahan had "grandly won" from "mother England." Belknap, "Old Navy," *Naval Action and History*, 72.

13. *Cabinet Diaries of Daniels*, ed. Cronon, August 17, 1919, entry, 431; p. 196, WWI diary, Timothy Brown Papers, State Historical Society of Wisconsin; Evans, *Admirals Log*, 358; Hird, *PUSNI*, L (1924), 1865.

14. Foote, *Africa*, 337; N.Y. *Tribune*, May 25, 1894; West, *Admirals of American Empire*, 155; Barker, *Everyday Life in the Navy*, 88; Evans, *Admiral's Log*, 358; Macartney, *Mr Lincoln's Admirals*, 122; Stirling, *Midshipman in China*, 100ff. Scott's phrase appeared in Chapter 38 of *Guy Mannering*. Cf. McKenna, *Sand Pebbles*, 429. For the best account of the Tattnall-Hope liasion see Curtis T. Henson, "The U.S. Navy and China, 1839–1861," unpub. Tulane Ph.D. thesis, 1965, 320–337.

Rear Admiral Henry Erben, U.S.N., may have been using a variation of the Tatnall-Scott expression when he told Mahan's St. James' Hall hosts that "blood was the thing that told" in U.S.-British naval relations. *Army and Navy Journal*, XXXI (1894), 775.

15. Johnson, *Rodgers*, 285–292; Lieutenant Seaton Schroeder, *The Fall of Maximillian's Empire as Seen from a U.S. Gunboat* (New York, 1887), 110–111; Captain Richard S. Collum, U.S.M.C., *History of the United States Marine Corps* (Philadelphia, 1890), 219; William A. Russ, Jr., *The Hawaiian Revolution: 1893–1894* (Selingsgrove, Pa., 1959), 18, 42; Robert Heinl, ed., *Dictionary of Military and Naval Quotations* (Annapolis, 1966), 179; Bradford Perkins, *The Great Rapprochement: England and the United States, 1895–1914* (N.Y., 1968), 50; Roskill, *Naval Policy*, 434–435; Colonel Roger Willock, "Gunboat Diplomacy: Operations of the North America and West Indies Squadron, 1875–1915," Part 2, *American Neptune*, XXVIII (April 1968), 107; Rear Admiral Albert Kautz, U.S.N., "Our

Flag," I, No. 4 (U.S.S. *Philadelphia*, Apia, Samoa, April 1899), General August V. Kautz Papers, L. of C.; Franklin, *Memories*, 337; McCalla, "Memoirs," Ch. XXVII, *passim*; Braisted, *Navy in Pacific*, 49, 63, 70, 75, 85; Rear Admiral William S. Sims & Burton J. *The Victory at Sea* (Garden City, 1920), 54, 55; *PUSNI*, L (1924), 1522–1523. Cf. Braisted, *U.S. Navy in the Pacific, 1909–1922*, 97, 318.

16. Zogbaum, *The Junior Officer of the Watch* (N.Y., 1908), 146–147; Davis, *Postwar Defense Policy and the U.S. Navy, 1943–1946* (Chapel Hill, 1966), 29.

17. *United Service*, VII (1882), 454–455; Surgeon Charles P. Kindleberger, U.S.N., "The Battle of Manila Bay," *The Century Magazine* (August 1898), 620; West, *Admirals*, 200; Thomas, *Old Gimlet Eye*, 179; *Army and Navy Journal*, XXXVII, 152.

18. See, for example, "Study to Reorganize the U.S. Naval Medical Corps Along Lines of the Royal Navy," Box 1, Surgeon Ninian Pinkney Papers, N.H.F.; Lovette, *School of Sea*, 104, 295; Lieutenant M. H. Bixby Papers, U.S. Navy Miscellaneous Mss., L. of C.; Commander French Chadwick to the Secretary of the Navy, Oct. 3, 1885, "Letters from Commanders," Entry 23, R.G. 45; Rear Admiral Caspar Goodrich Papers, N.Y.H.S.: Lieutenant Commander William Cowles to Assistant Navy Secretary James R. Soley, Aug. 18, 1894, and Cowles to Messrs. Laird Bros., Sept. 27, 1893, Cowles Naval Attaché Letterbooks, Entry 301, R.G. 45; Sims, "Roosevelt and the Navy," *McClure's Magazine*, LIV, Pt. 2 (1923), 62; Sims to the Board of Control, U.S. Naval Institute, Sept. 8, 1902, copy in Sims Papers, N.H.F.; Captain W. A. Egerton, R.N.—Commander D. C. Bingham, U.S.N. Correspondence, 1917–1919, Box 493, N.H.F. Lieutenant Commander Cowles was a close friend of Captain Percy Scott as early as 1895, Cowles to Scott, May 30, 1895, Cowles Letterbooks, Entry 301, R.G. 45.

19. Mahan, *Types of Naval Officers*, *passim*; Zogbaum, *The Junior Officer of the Watch*, 41; "An Ex-staff Officer," *An Appeal on Behalf of the Navy . . .* (Washington, 1886), 21; Goodrich, *PUSNI*, XXIV (1898), 12; *Conf. Corr. of Fox*, II, 98; Mahan, *From Sail to Steam*, 321; McCalla, "Memoirs," Ch. XXIV, 33, Fisher, *Memories and Records*, I, 22; Sperry to Mary, April 20, 1868, and to his wife, May 16, 1899, Sperry Papers, L. of C.;

Chambers, "God Save the King! as Written By An American," Box 48, Chambers Papers, N.H.F.

Mahan's *Nelson* and his "The Neopolitan Republicans and Nelson's Accusers," *English Historical Review*, XIV (1899), 471–501, are good examples of thoughtful paeans to this Englishman by an American. The fictional lieutenant in Academy Chaplain H. H. Clark's *Joe Bently, Naval Cadet* named his three children after British warships (201).

20. See, for example, Davis, *Life of Davis*, 292, 300–301; John M. Brooke to Captain George Belknap, July 30, 1879, Box 423, N.H.F.; and General Miscellany, Box 20, Robert Shufeldt Papers, N.H.F.

21. James E. Montgomery, *Our Admiral's Flag Aboard: The Cruise of Admiral Farragut, 1867–1868* (New York, 1869), 187, 191; Foxhall Parker, *The Fleets of the World: The Galley Period* (New York, 1876), 227–228; Barker to Witney, November 4, 1885, "Letters from Commanders," Entry 23, Record Group 45, National Archives; McCalla, "Memoirs," Ch. XVI, 15–16.

22. Belknap, "Old Navy," in *Naval Actions and History*, 69; *Army and Navy Journal*, XLVI (Jan. 16, 1909), 541; Colomb to Mahan, April 26, 1891, Mahan Papers, L. of C.; Mahan, "Motives to Imperial Federation," in *Retrospect and Prospect*, 130ff; Clarke, "A Naval Union with Great Britain," *North American Review*, CLVIII (March, 1894), 353–365; Beresford, "Possibilities of an Anglo-American Reunion," *North Am. Review*, CLIX (Nov. 1894), 564–573; Mahan, *loc. cit.*, 551–563; Beresford, "The Future of the Anglo-Saxon Race," *North American Review*, CLXXI (Dec., 1900); James Bryce, "The Essential Unity of Britain and America," *Atlantic Monthly*, LXXXII (July, 1898), 22–29; Colomb, "The U.S. Navy under New Conditions of National Life," *North Amer. Rev.*, CLXVIII (Oct., 1898), 434–444; Salmon to Belknap, July 8, 1898, Aug. 14, 1898, and April 18, 1899, R. R. Belknap Papers, Box 424, N.H.F.; Taylor, *Mahan*, 182; Kautz, "Our Flag," I, No. 4 (U.S.S. *Philadelphia*, Apia, Samoa, April, 1899), 2, in August V. Kautz Papers, L. of C.; Pratt, *PUSNI*, XLIX (1923), 1084. Cf. B. Perkins, *Great Rapprochement*, 245–246, 271; Arthur Marder, *British Naval Policy, 1880–1905* (London, 1940), 442–455.

In light of the above, Richard Hofstadter's remark that "even the navalist Mahan approved of the British" appears to be some-thing of an understatement. (Hofstadter, *Social Darwinism*, 183.)

23. Barber to Long, Jan. 23, 1899, cited in Alfred Vagts, *The Military Attaché* (Princeton, 1967), 197. Robley Evans and Hugh Rodman were torn between their admiration of Germany and their respect for Britain. See their autobiographies.

24. See, for example, H. H. Clark, *Admiral's Aide*, 149; *Army and Navy Journal*, XLII (Oct. 15, 1904), 161; (Feb. 11, 1905), 624; XXXVIII (Mar. 23, 1901), 701; XL (July 25, 1903), 1186; XLV (June 27, 1908), 1181; L (April 12, 1913), 955; XLVI (Jan. 16, 1909), 541; (Nov. 21, 1908), 308; XLVIII (Dec. 24, 1910), 473; LI (Nov. 29, 1913), 404; Fiske, *From Midshipman to Rear Admiral*, 528; Mahan to F. Maxse [editor of the British *National Review*], Dec. 9, 1901, Mahan Papers, L. of C.; "Notes of Conversation with Cpt. Otterly, R.N. . . ." Sperry to Roosevelt, Sept. 12, 1908, Sperry to Mrs. A. R. Cowles, Dec. 10, 1908, and Sperry to General Porter, Dec. 4, 1908, Sperry Letterbook, Sperry Papers, L. of C.; Zogbaum, *Junior Officer*, 311; Sprout and Sprout, *Rise of Naval Power*, 286; Schroeder, *Half Century of Naval Service* (N.Y., 1922), 401; *The Navy*, VIII (Oct. 1914); Herman F. Krafft & Walter B. Norris, *Sea Power in American History* (New York, 1920), xv. For a somewhat different view of the strength of this federation sentiment, see Kenneth Bourne, *Britain and the Balance of Power in North America, 1815–1908* (Berkeley, 1967), 319–323.

25. Roskill, *Naval Policy*, 21–25, 433–434; Raymond G. O'Connor, *Perilous Equilibrium: The U.S. and The London Naval Conference of 1930* (Lawrence, Kansas, 1962), 13–14; Roskill, *PUSNI*, XCVI (Mar., 1970), 90.

26. James M. Hoppin, *Life of Andrew H. Foote, Rear Admiral, U.S.N.* (New York, 1874), 126; G. V. Fox to Commodore Henry Wise, May 1, 1867, Wise Papers, N.Y.H.S.; Captain Nathan Twining to Walter Twining, Jan. 3, 1917, Twining Papers, St. Hist. Soc. of Wisc.; Cornelius Schoonmaker, "Life and Letters of Captain Schoonmaker," p. 143, Box 152, Schoonmaker Papers, N.H.F.; Mahan, *From Sail to Steam*, 223; *PUSNI*, V (1879), 365; Sperry to his wife, Mar. 25, 1879, Sperry Papers, L. of C.; Edward McCauley [a retired naval officer] to Rear Admiral Albert Gleaves, July 25, 1923, Gleaves Papers, Box 3, N.H.F.; Rodman, *Yarns of a Kentucky Admiral*, 275, 280; Captain W. I.

Chambers, "What Has England Done?" Box 48, Chambers Papers, N.H.F.; Rear Admiral F. A. Roe, to Rear Admiral George Belknap, Oct. 30, 1897, and Nov. 25, 1897, R. R. Belknap Papers, Box 424, N.H.F.

27. See, for example, Lodge, *Early Memories* (New York, 1913), 203–204; Captain C. R. P. ("Alphabet") Rodgers to Lieutenant Commander Henry Wise, May 17, 1861, Wise Papers, N.Y.H.S.; Holden Evans, *One Man's Fight for a Better Navy*, 150; *Diary of Welles*, ed. Beale, 588; Davis, *Life of Davis*, 3; Niblack, *Why Wars Come*, 17.

28. See, for example, Nelson Ferebee to "Mattie," March 31, 1895, Ferebee–Gregory–McPherson Papers, S.H.C., U. of N.C.L.; Mahan to his sister, April 17, 1868, Mahan Papers, L. of C.; Sperry to his wife, Nov. 15, 1884, Sperry Papers, L. of C.

29. *Fortune* (March, 1938), 164; Dr. Carl Kelsey, cited in McConklin, *Garde D'Haiti*, 139.

30. See "Racism" in Chapter 5.

31. Dewey, *Autobiography*, 159; Mont-gomery, *Our Admiral's Flag, passim*; Hunt, *William Hunt*, 251; Remey, *Reminiscences of Boyhood*, I, 48; Sperry to brother Mark, April 2, 1885, Sperry Papers; "Schoon-maker," 190–194; Smith, *Coral and Brass* (New York, 1948), 45; Hunts, *Letters from the Asiatic Station*, 145; October 3, 190? entry, Mrs. Roger Welles Diary, Welles Papers, Box 202, Naval Historical Foundation; *Fortune* (March, 1938), 164; Anne B. Pye and Nancy Shea, *The Navy Wife* (New York, 1942), 270. The society pages of the *Army and Navy Journal* generally included a column devoted to the movements and activities of officers and their families assigned to foreign stations. Some of the observations made in the preceding para-graphs rest on a sampling of these columns from about 1870 to 1920. For other interest-ing accounts of navy family life abroad see Mrs. Henry A. Wise, "Our Home Abroad" [unpub. mss.], Box 274, NL, Entry 464, R.G. 45; or the 1877 diary of Mrs. Rear Admiral Charles Steedman, Steedman Papers, Perkins L., Duke U.

NAVAL LIFE IN THE STATES

Eventually every naval officer got to see a bit of the United States. "Shore duty," the answer to the waterlogged officer's prayers, came about once in every three tours of duty. "Coburgers," or officers who managed to remain on shore duty indefinitely, were rare, but a number of senior officers did manage to retain Navy Department Bureau assignments for a decade or more. Each of the bureaus required a number of officers, as did each navy yard and the Academy, and a number of officers were usually assigned to munitions, armorplate, and shipbuilding establishments as well. In the yards and factories officers often found it necessary to rub shoulders with supply merchants such as Phelps, Dodge, & Co., marine engineers, and yard employees; and there were those such as Commander William Grenville Temple, Captain David Farragut, and Captain Percival Drayton who looked upon such work as "a disgusting business altogether" and considered it "a pity that any gentleman should be obliged to dirty his fingers with it."[1] But "shore duty" had redeeming advantages.

For the married officer, the most obvious advantage was the opportunity to live with one's family for a long enough period to get to know one's children —and one's wife. But since officers began their social lives as bachelors, any discussion of "shore duty" should begin with a few words about the social life of the naval officer before proceeding to a treatment of family life.

The "naval aristocracy" probably had a better chance to shine abroad than

122   in the States. Most of their countrymen appear to have taken somewhat less of an interest in bemedalled and bespangled warriors than did foreigners. But if the social whirl of the average officer was less dizzying at home than abroad, it was still quite active.[2]

Norfolk, Virginia, appears to have been the center of naval society before the Civil War, but in 1886 it was reported to be "a dreary place." "The inhabitants of Norfolk hold themselves studiously aloof from us," Captain Christopher Raymond Perry "Alphabet" Rodgers wrote Commander Henry Wise, adding "but then . . . I have the agreeable society of my colleagues." Ex-naval constructor Holden Evans may have been oversimplifying naval society when he remarked that "the naval set lives within itself"; but the fact was that navy yard life, complete with stately white-pillared mansions and Chinese or black "houseboys,"[3] permitted the officer to withdraw from the external community in times of ill-feeling such as prevailed at Norfolk during the era of "reconstruction."

Norfolk never recovered its former status, and Annapolis—aside from its professional and sentimental appeal—slowly became less and less attractive to bachelors as the century wore on. By the turn of the century Washington, Philadelphia, New York, Boston, and Portsmouth, New Hampshire, vied for popularity on the east coast, and San Francisco, where officers were "in unusually high favor," was the desirable west coast naval base. Rear Admiral Daniel Ammen, who was critical of the "constant struggle for position" in New York and Washington society of the late nineteenth century, longed for the Norfolk of the 1840s, which he recalled as being considerably more dignified. Ammen, Admiral William Standley, and Lieutenant Cornelius Schoonmaker favored the life of the small town or country estate, where families had "lived together for centuries" and life was less "commercial." But many officers accepted less grudgingly "the march of improvement and modern civilization" and settled their families in navy yards located in urban areas.

The Washington Navy Yard, nesting on the bank of the Potomac, was "socially . . . very pleasant," or so Commodore William Folger advised Commander Charles O'Neil's wife in 1890.[4] For the Commandant of the Yard there were a horse, a carriage, and a coachman, as there were in every yard, and all three were frequently put to use.* All navy yards were walled, virtually self-contained units in spite of the fact that most were in the immediate vicinity of the urban core. The Washington Navy Yard, a full two to three miles from the city's residences and boarding houses, was somewhat more isolated,† but "a certain amount of social activity" none the less existed between officers and

---

* One sailor-newsman later wrote that he could not recall ever having seen "an old-time admiral or naval captain moving up Atlantic Avenue [in Boston] under his own power," so common was the use of carriages. James B. Connolly, *Navy Men* (New York, 1939), 28.

† Yards had their advantages, though, in maintaining "esprit de corps," a fact made evident by the loss of "esprit de corps" today with those navy families who cannot find quarters in the crowded yards and are obliged to settle in the suburbs where they tend to compare themselves unfavorably to civilian counterparts. *PUSNI*, XCV (1969), 64.

"uptown Washington in spite of the long distance and slow transportation between these centers."[5]

Officers stationed ashore in the States generally found that "the doors of society" were thrown open to them, and took advantage of this opportunity "of taking the place within [society's] magic precincts to which the highest gentility entitles them!" The "social cachet" of junior officers were "taken up by well-to-do civilians," and the graduates of the Academy, trained in the gentle graces, responded with élan. Not all the social meetings resulted in firm friendships, but some did. "Your official and social position afford you the desirable freedom of approach to the magnates of the State Department," Pay Inspector Thomas Caswell remarked to Rear Admiral Charles Steedman, who was residing temporarily at Washington's weighty Metropolitan Club. And social contacts were by no means restricted to government officials and lobbyists. Some of Alexander Hamilton, Jr.'s, most frequent correspondents were naval officers, among them David Farragut, David D. Porter, John Rodgers, and Hamilton's close friend, Percival Drayton. Less intimate—but none the less genuine—social ties were more common, such as the one between Commander Albert Grant and John Jacob Astor. Thus when Grant was Commanding Officer of the Philadelphia Navy Yard, Astor dispatched John, Lord Heffernan, to him with a letter of introduction, begging that Commander Grant "introduce him to Phila. society," an act Astor apparently felt Grant highly qualified to perform. Similarly, the "fleet captain" of the prestigious New York Yacht Club, Commander J. D. Jerrold Kelley, was in charge of all receptions for visiting royalty.[6]

Members of the "naval aristocracy" quickly learned to discriminate between "high" and "middle" social classes. Thus Midshipman Charles Sperry advised his sister that the Academy had taught him to despise "a society whose members have rec'd only a slight education at best and who have never been brought up with any great refinement." And twenty years later he sympathized with his wife's complaint of the quality of society in the Cape May, New Jersey, summer resort area:[7]

> It must be stupid at Media if the people are uncouth and I can understand the advantages of Idlewild where the people are somewhat more select.

Morris Janowitz has found that naval officers outnumbered army and air force officers in the social registers of 5 out of 6 cities examined from the 1920s through the 1950s,[8] and, as Janowitz suspected, the naval officer's social standing was always greater than that of the other services throughout American history. Nevertheless, there were moments when Mahan and his messmates wished that they might receive more social recognition. A few examples should suffice to illustrate these.

One may be seen in the naval-marine tension in the late nineteenth century over the issue of marines on ships. The naval aristocracy had always considered marines a slightly inferior breed, certain as they were that the Marine Corps'

124   social position was "not equal to that of the [naval] Line." And in 1882, when Congress ordered that henceforth vacancies in marine officer ranks were to be restricted to graduates of the Academy, some feared that they would be forced into a less eminent career than they had anticipated. But as pressure was brought to bear upon the Navy Department and Congress to order the withdrawal of marines from ships, the Marine Corps responded with "a regular campaign of entertainment" and made themselves "solid with those who are in power." Naval officers eventually felt themselves to be "on the defensive and losing side" in the skirmish.⁹ By 1910 the issue had been largely resolved in favor of the marines, and with its passing, social lobbying returned to a more normal level—once again to the slight advantage of the Navy.*

Another example of the social anxiety of naval officers may be the case of the officer who "was very much aggrieved" to learn that the Assistant Navy Secretary had not been invited to a White House reception. Apparently some naval officers identified their social standing with that of the Department.¹⁰

Still another example is that of Captain Mahan. The publication of *The Influence of Sea Power Upon History, 1660–1783* brought Mahan less recognition in the United States than he had hoped. "Except [for Theodore] Roosevelt," he told his wife in 1893, "I don't think my work gained me an entree into a single American social circle." Mahan was of the opinion that one's reputation rose only "when rammed home by a certain amount of attention from people in position." Thus he was delighted when first the British, and then the American, elite finally crowned his efforts with testimonial dinners and a cluster of honorary degrees, but now he was disappointed at his inability to afford the high cost of fin-de-siècle social life. In part motivated by a desire to preserve his newly acquired fame, Mahan joined the expensive but prestigious New York Yacht Club.¹¹

Marriage in the Navy

Naval officers courted after the fashion of true Victorians—they sought brides who might "help them on the road to fame" and would "indelibly impress the stamp of lofty character upon the proud achievements of their lords." It was assumed that an educated and cultivated gentlewoman could not help but improve the moral fibre of her nautical mate. As shall be seen, the naval officer had little use for Man; but, as one officer put it, "although my faith in man is weak, my faith in woman is not." Midshipman Charles Graves had just such a romantic view of the female of the species. In speaking to his brother of his love, Fannie, Graves graphically observed:

> Sometimes when I get so enraged with some of the sailors that I can hardly keep from knocking them down, *her* image flits before me, and I immediately become as calm, quiet, and serene as a dying Muscovy duck.

---

* None the less, the Marine Corps continues to wield the public-relations mace with considerable skill. In the words of President Harry Truman, "they [the marines] have a propaganda machine that is almost equal to Stalin's." Truman to Rep. Gordon McDonough, August 29, 1950, cited in Heinl, ed., *Dictionary*, 184.

"Man" was "a growling, discontented animal"; "woman" was "always patient & uncomplaining." The female of the species possessed the necessary inborn traits required to raise the future Farraguts of the Republic in the proper manner. "The recollections of a mother's loving arms and the prayers they have said together have turned back many a heart and hand from wicked deeds," Lieutenant Charles Sperry maintained. Captain Washington Irving Chambers observed, in a poem addressed to his niece, "Katharine (expecting) Xmas 1916":[12]

> Tis those who watch at the cradle
> Who guide the great deeds of the world . . .
>
> In mother's love there lies the seed
> Of all that's good and great and blest.

A cultured mate was desirable. But so was a wealthy one, for two reasons. First if the wife's family or friends were "people of influence and power," the likelihood of which was greater if she were "of parts," she thus became a useful "acquisition to the service, for these will become valued allies to the [Navy's] cause." Second if the wife possessed an outside income "the equivalent of $60,000 in government bonds," she thus matched her husband's salary and enabled him to "maintain an establishment and social status commensurate with his position under the government." Culture, wealth, and other less tangible qualities such as disposition, beauty, or grace were all sought. But many officers probably married women who failed to meet one or another or several of these criteria, "if for no other reason than to keep up the old navy name."[13]

Statistical evidence of the social origins of naval brides is not abundantly available, but some observations may be made, with less plenary certitude than some social scientists would like, but with as much heft as the data permit. The *Army and Navy Journal* carried announcements of most service marriages, but it is difficult to ascertain the bride's social background from these items alone. Personal correspondence, diaries, autobiographies, reunion books, and the like are more useful in this regard.

C. Wright Mills maintained that in the late nineteenth century the U.S. naval officer "married within his own class level," and for the great majority of officers this was probably the case. Men like Stephen Luce, John Rodgers, John D. Henley, Alexander Wadsworth, George H. Perkins, John G. Walker, Samuel Jackson, C. C. Todd, John Crittenden Watson, and James Cresap, and an indeterminate number of others married the daughters of "very rich" financiers, merchants, and industrialists whom they had met socially or professionally. A writer for *Fortune* magazine observed in the 1930s that many naval officers "seemed to have outside income or moneyed wives."[14] About one officer in every five, men like Bowman McCalla, Robley Evans, Perrin Busbee, Theodorus B. M. Mason, and Seaton Schroeder, married within the Service to the sisters, daughters, or widows of naval (and occasionally Army) officers.

126   Of forty-eight officers listed in the *Dictionary of American Biography* for whom information on their wives is available, twenty-three married women in high social positions, twenty married the daughters, widows, or sisters of naval officers, and five married into Army families. Others for whom no information about their wives was offered may have married less affluent and less conspicuous women.[15]

Only one class of Academy graduates, that of 1871, collected marriage data from its members some thirty years after graduation. Of 38 active-duty graduates, 31 married, generally from 10 to 15 years after graduation. Since several of the remaining 7 died within a decade of graduation and since the Navy's "unwritten law" at that time discouraged marriage before age 30 or 35, it seems safe to say that marriage (at a mature age) was quite an accepted social exercise among Mahan's messmates. In fact, in the early 1880s Congress was asked to consider a bill designed to prevent the "young and, consequently [!], irresponsible naval officer" from marrying "unless he proposes resigning directly afterwards. The risk of injuring the navy" by early marriage, it was argued, was "too great." But it was not great enough to persuade Congress to legislate. Naval society frowned upon early marriage, but not with Congressional endorsement or sanction.[16]

Of the 31 active naval graduates of the class of '71, 5 indicated that they had married into service families, and 5 gave evidence of having married into "prominent" non-service families. The other 21 gave no information about their wives, and we can assume that most of these married, as Mills suggested, within their own upper-middle class. "Very few naval men, in spite of their education," Charles Sperry told his wife, "marry far from their native condition —either above or below." Only thus could Lieutenant Sperry account for "some of the people they pick up as wives." His verdict may have been too harsh; several years later he reported a number of good matches classmates and messmates had made.[17] But many who married women of parts were not marrying above their class at all. Many officers, it will be recalled, were of prominent families themselves.

The Naval Family

Of this same class of 1871, 86% of those who married reared their own or adopted children. No class, regional, or career pattern can be attributed to those whose families were childless, and it would appear that the vast majority of naval families sought to have children. The naval officer responded to the loss of his wife in the same fashion as any widower of his culture. When Commander William Sampson's first wife died in 1878, he married again in order that his children should not be motherless. When Lieutenant Commander George Dewey became a widower, his children were reared by his aunt and maternal grandmother.[18] But in other matters the similarity of the naval officer's family to that of the average well-adjusted upper-middle class genteel American of his age is less marked.

From abroad, and during his occasional visits with his wife and children, the naval officer exercised a significant measure of social and physical control over his family. Charles Mason Remey recalled that while a boy he had seen very little of his naval dad. In fact, "father was away from home so much of the time that when he came home I felt a bit strange with him . . . we had to get acquainted as it were." Under these conditions young Remey made the mistake of assuming that his father had little to say of family affairs. "I didn't pay much attention to him until one day I discovered that he really did have authority in the household." The naval parent was a strict disciplinarian, often critical of the lack of adequate discipline in other American homes. And the wife was expected to be subordinate as well. Those were the conditions of life in Alfred Mahan's household and in John Dahlgren's, George Remey's, Charles Sperry's, and every other naval family whose behavioral patterns can be ascertained from existing evidence.[19] Everyone in the Mahan household remained subordinate to him. His wife never questioned his views, and one daughter wrote that she could never remember "ever wanting to disobey." Mahan's letters to his wife all began: "Dearest Deldie"; all were signed: "A. T. Mahan." "It would be a dreadful thing for you," Mahan told his "Deldie," "if you were to lose me" (as indeed it was; with all his writing, Mahan managed to leave his family but a cottage home in southeastern Long Island and a few hundred dollars in the bank). Lieutenant Charles Sperry assured his wife that he considered her "a strong and self reliant woman," but explained that "it pleases the lords of creation to think their women need petting." And Sperry continued to refer to himself throughout the years, half jokingly, but also half seriously, as "your Lord." Arthur Calhoun spoke of "the passing of Patriarchism and Familism" in late nineteenth century America, but he could not have had the naval officer's family in mind.[20]

Obviously the naval officer's absence from the household for three years or more at a clip prevented him from exerting any continuing, daily influence on family affairs. Absence probably did make many naval hearts grow fonder, as eulogists of the naval family liked to say,* but father's primary commitment was to his profession, as he was quick to point out.[21] Thus "Patriarchism and Familism" had to be preserved by the surrogate lord of the hearth, mother. Charles Remey remembered his father as a man "very much afraid of anything

---

* "This absence, this utter sundering from social life and home, brings a well of everlasting love in [the naval officer's] heart," Lieutenant Commander Francis Roe wrote in 1865. *Naval Duties and Discipline*, 218. Similarly, Anna A. Rodgers, writing in 1898, praised "those strangely happy homes in the Navy . . . where reigns good love . . . preserved by . . . separation and the ever-haunting element of danger." "Mutiny on the Flag-ship [a short story]," *Scribner's Magazine*, XXIV (1898), 297. See also Lieutenant Edwin Anderson to his wife, from the Yangtze, March 24, 1903, Anderson Papers, S.H.C., U. of N.C. Library: "How I would have liked to have [had] you in my arms, felt your sweet, warm body next to mine and whispered in your ear . . . [sic] and seen the color mount in your cheeks and the lovelight shine in your perfect eyes and have you slip your arm around my neck and answer 'Yes!'" Anderson's memory and imagination were more concrete and specific than those of his more romantic, vague colleagues—unless these are the sorts of passages that were carefully snipped out of their letters home.

128   touching on the emotional side of life. At times he just held himself in and assumed a silence that I never felt I could encroach upon. Fortunately, I had my mother to open my heart to."²²

Naval parents took their responsibilities for the rearing of their children most seriously. Papa may have had Francis Wayland's charge in mind: "to teach [the] child its duties to God and to man, and produce in its mind a permanent conviction of its moral responsibilities." In any event, these were the educational goals of naval parents. To Lieutenant Sperry marriage gave a woman a "kind of occupation," though he apparently felt the husband was a kind of employer, since he instructed his wife (as did most officers) in detail as to the training their children were to receive and then drove his instructions home with the comment: "I would brand my words in your memory so that you may never forget them as long as there is breath in your body." With or without her husband's coaching, Rear Admiral John Dahlgren's wife Madeline stated the case of the naval mother with particular clarity. In her view—and I found no naval wives who disagreed with her—"the chief function of woman in the State—and what a grand mission it is!—is as educator of the children." As wife and mother, woman was "queen of the most holy aspirations." A proper Victorian, Mrs. Dahlgren had nothing to say of breast-feeding or the proper care of infants, but "infancy passed," she was filled with admonitions. Mother's role was that of an on-going builder, moulding the "awakening intelligence to the child," who then, "instructed by her pious precepts," went forth "to mould other citizens." "Home virtue" implied and involved the creation of an atmosphere wherein it would be possible to "perpetuate [the State's] institutions." Such was "God's [and Mrs. Dahlgren's] ordering" of the naval wife's role as tutor and guide.²³

Sons were more central to the family plan than were daughters, for obvious reasons. Sons would carry the family name; they would require more formal education and greater self-reliance; they would eventually be called upon to offer more vivid "proof" of their virtue and abilities than their sisters, for whom "neatness," "cultivation," "Dignity of Character," "prudence, and kindness of heart, together with a pure heart," would suffice. The daughter was given such negative advice as the admonition not to "go *below*" her own "level for companions," but she received little or no positive advice—such as might create in her a "need for achievement." Daughters were taught only "to be useful and contented in the sphere in which they [were] placed." It was left for the sons to be inspired by ambitious parents to be always "industrious" in assaulting all "unclimbed heights above you." "Oh! my son, do not disappoint the hopes and expectations of your Father," Commander Louis Goldsborough frequently begged. Goldsborough insisted that his son conduct himself "in a manner worthy of the son of a gentleman," but he also insisted that if the boy had "a spark of nobility and proper pride in his nature," his mother was to fan it into a blaze of that "laudable pride and ambition which should stimulate every noble boy to exertion!" Just as the naval officer looked upon his own stainless honor with a becoming reverence, so he expected the same of his son. "We **129** must teach him to fear nothing but dishonor, or the very shadow of it—to be a gentleman with clean hands and a pure heart," Lieutenant Charles Sperry told his wife, "and being such a gentleman, and *looking* such a one, it will be easy for him to be a Christian." Piety (or its appearance) was deemed to be the safest road to salvation and renown. "When the fire is well stacked," Mahan told his wife, concerning his son Lyle's piety, "it is ready for the kindling when the flame falls from Heaven." In the meantime, naval mothers warned their sons to "beware of bad companions," especially female ones, and to "do well" in school, for, as Mrs. Remey told her son, "my heart is set on my children."[24]

Some sons, such as Louis Goldsborough, Jr., Charles Remey, and Robert Lowell, were sent to such fashionable and proper colleges as St. John's, Harvard, and Princeton. But most naval fathers, probably well over half of those with sons, sought to place at least one of their sons in the Naval Academy.[25] "I have a young Commodore just 2 & ½ month old now, who will probably be 'hustling' for a 2.5 [the passing grade at Annapolis] some of these days," Edward Capehart boasted to his classmates several years after their graduation. "My only child is a Naval Officer," Admiral Charles B. McVay told a friend, "and I hope that at least one of my grandsons will follow the same profession." Unless someone else's Congressman could be persuaded to sponsor a naval officer's son, the only opportunity officers had of securing appointments for their sons was by personal appeal to the Secretary of the Navy or the President, who controlled a number of naval cadetships theoretically set aside for such purposes. Thus Captain George Henry Preble solicited an appointment for his "*only* son" from President U. S. Grant. "His claims for such an appointment," Preble advised Grant, "consist in my own thirty-eight years service in the Navy . . ., and his name which in a few years with my retirement from active service will be unrepresented upon the active list of the Navy." Preble then proceeded to tick off a list of ancestral naval heroes as long as Grant's arm, hoping to add substance to his argument. As Admiral David D. Porter advised President Grover Cleveland, naval officers were extremely fond of "perpetuating their names in the service." Thus the caricature of a "Plebe" in a collection of Academy songs and poems published in 1889 was entitled: "Bound to keep Navy Blood in the Family" (see page 28). Thus the remark of the anonymous "ex-staff officer" in 1886:

> I may claim to have been born in the Navy. The blood of one of Decatur's officers flows in my veins, and in all my earlier years I breathed the atmosphere of Navy tradition, and while still a child lived in the cabin of the noblest frigate of them all [U.S.S. *Constitution*].

And thus the appearance in the late nineteenth century of young Stephen Decatur, VII![26]

The securing of an appointment to the Academy was a major task, requiring great resourcefulness. Mother might be brought into the act at an opportune moment if the circumstances so required. When Charles Sperry, Jr., came of age, his father arranged for Mrs. Sperry to descend upon their Congressman in his summer retreat to cop the prize. "This is the critical time and if we fail to move now we may get another chance but I doubt it," the Commander fretted to his wife. "Your going may turn the scale." A small handful of desperate Navy families may have risked dishonor, as did Commander John H. Upshur, who was court-martialed for trying to buy his son an appointment.[27]

Understandably, the securing of an appointment did not necessarily cinch the matter. There were entrance exams to be passed,* and mother often trundled off to Annapolis "to be near our boy" and offer moral, and any other, support deemed necessary to help the future Farragut over that first hurdle. Once the Academy gates closed on the accepted candidate aid was more knotty a business to arrange and was consequently more spotty in arriving. Obviously nothing could, or would, be done if Junior were caught "violating his sacred trust" (lying) or "sullying his sacred honor" (cheating), but less nefarious deeds such as "Frenching" (absenting himself briefly from the grounds without leave), drinking, hazing, or failing a non-professional course that led to dismissal were often contested by parents such as Captain C. B. Sedgwick, who had "set [his] heart on his [son's] being an Officer of the Navy," and couldn't "bear to see him fail."[28]

In addition to Sedgwick, McVay, Sperry, Preble, Aaron Weaver, and H. W. Lyons, there were many others whose sons became naval officers. Christopher R. Perry, Matthew C. Perry, David Porter, John C. Watson, Thomas Selfridge, and Alexander S. Mackenzie each reared at least two additional members of the naval aristocracy; Foxhall Parker, Somerville Nicholson, George Belknap, William Sampson, John Rodgers, Thomas Truxton, Victor Blue, W. F. Halsey ("Bull" Halsey's father), Richard Meade, 2nd, Elie A. A. LaVallette, Richard Wainwright, Charles Davis, George T. Winston, George Colvocoresses, John Downes, his son, John Downes, Jr., and his son, John Downes, III, Thomas H. Stevens, and his son, Thomas H. Stevens, II, Edward Simpson, Robley Evans, William Bainbridge-Hoff, Percival Drayton, William Maxwell Wood,† Louis Kempff, Robert Shufeldt, David McDougal, and Austin Knight (to name only those whom my research has uncovered) all had to settle for one; and Captains William Bainbridge and Theodorus Bailey were reduced to boasting of a nephew in the blue and gold of an officer of the line.[29] These examples are but

---

* Recently the Navy Department "informally" took under advisement the suggestion of Captain Paul Harrington (whose son, Paul Harrington, Jr., is also a naval officer) that the sons of Academy graduates be afforded some special consideration on the competitive entrance exams now in use. Harrington's argument was that Navy sons would be more highly motivated and would be more likely to make a career of the Service than the sons of non-Academy people. (*Shipmate*, XXXI [1968], 13.) The hypothesis seems quite reasonable—indeed, likely, given the naval aristocracy's past performance—but such inbreeding may be undesirable.

† Wood, it will be recalled, was the officer who had expressed vehement disapproval of U.S. naval officers as a "privileged class" (see the frontispiece to Part One), 15 years before he sent his own son to Annapolis.

a sampling of a much larger body; the similarity of names at thirty-year inter- vals indicates that there were a great many other family successions in the Service, but confirmation was difficult, given the limitations of the source material.[30]

It may be recalled that many officers had brothers who had attended West Point. A few sons of naval officers undoubtedly chose to follow the example of their army uncles rather than their naval fathers. For whatever reasons, there appear to have been several instances of service-hopping. Naval officers such as George T. Winston, Robert W. Shufeldt, John Almy, Francis Roe, C. R. P. Rodgers, Benjamin Sands, James Jouett, and John C. Watson sent sons to West Point, and sons of Watson, Matthew C. Perry, Purnell Harrington, and David Porter became marine officers.[31] Lieutenant Commander Ira Harris told his colleague, Lieutenant Charles MacGreggor, in 1868 of how "nice" it was "to have some families where a number of members are in the services. They can pull together better & keep up more influence for the common cause."[32]

"Navy girls," as the daughters of naval officers were known, obviously could not attend Annapolis, a disappointment to those who had learned to hum the Navy Yard bugle calls before they could talk or had played "Captain and crew" in nursery school. Some, like Marine Major General Smedley Butler's "Marine girl," were "christened and adopted" by their father's ship or regiment at birth or an early age. A most effective means of showing their loyalty, one frequently taken, was that of marriage to a dashing young (or middle-aged) lieutenant. This is what Smedley Butler's daughter eventually did, as did the daughters of Robley Evans, Charles Clark, Christopher R. Perry, Matthew C. Perry, John Worden, John Rodgers, Charles Sigsbee, Hiram Paulding, and an unidentified messmate of Charles Sperry,[33] to name but a few. "Navy Blood" was thus so thick in some circles that it became possible for the naval aristocracy to produce such people as John Downes, III, Class of '71, whose father and grandfather had been naval officers, whose wife was the sister of a naval officer, and whose son became a naval officer; or Oliver Hazard Perry, II, whose father, both uncles, and paternal grandfather had been naval officers, whose brothers were naval and marine officers, whose nephew was a naval officer, and whose sister married the son of a naval officer! [34]

The life of the Navy wife was a parochial one in the late nineteenth and early twentieth century. When her husband was at sea, she might retire with her family to her home town, but was more likely to remain in whatever navy yard or base in which she had been most recently deposited. There she found well-furnished quarters and others patiently awaiting the return of their spouses, and there created a pleasant society, though virtually devoid of male members. If, as Christopher Lasch has suggested, the role of women in the American families of the late nineteenth century was changing with the rise of industrially-made goods and state-operated schools, the role of the Navy wife was less altered than that of her contemporaries. The Navy wife remained at the center of family life. The emergence of public schools had little impact on

132   the family of the naval officer; his children generally attended private schools. The relief from certain household chores did not spell the collapse of the Navy mother's function; she already had part- or full-time help, and as surrogate lord of the hearth she was obliged to handle much of the family's finances, though most officers put their wives in touch with a trusted lawyer before sailing.[35]

Socially, her days were as active as could be expected under the circumstances. Calls were frequently exchanged, where "many an observant young Navy wife" took advantage of the opportunities "to note those customs of decor, taste, and conversation which make up one of the intangible legacies passed on from Navy family to Navy family."[36] Navy yard socializing among the families of officers stationed at the yard was, of course, most lively. What follows is a random selection from the correspondence of the wife of the commandant of the Portsmouth, New Hampshire, Navy Yard in 1897. It could have been selected from the correspondence of a Navy wife at the Washington Navy Yard in the 1850s, or the San Diego Naval Base in the 1920s. Nothing I might say would give a better picture of navy yard society than such a passage; hence a page is cited in its entirety:[37]

> . . . I find the day long enough for me.
> John has been attending Miss Woodbury's Kindergarten this week and enjoys it. He has just gone with Jecky; a diminutive basket of sandwiches in her hand. She has begun music lessons with Miss Betty Foster, who comes from Boston once a week to the school. The latter wears a magnificent ring (so Jecky says) but the marriage is not to take place until the young man is established in business.
> We had quite a gay time yesterday, many coming to call, after our luncheon. Alice Higgins among them. She assured me she was quite overcome when your Father took her out to the dining room that day, having forgotten that she was the guest of honor. Capt. Reisinger has been away for a few days, and as a reminder of his return, sent me a large bunch of white and pink carnations, which decorate the tea table.
> Last week Jecky, Mary, and I went over to a Church social, at the Woman's Exchange. Mrs. Hovey read us a description of her ascent of Vesuvius and Miss Spaulding gave us her experience of a Christmas in England. There was music and Mr. [William] Buehler [a naval officer] recited poems, which he did admirably. It was a very pleasant affair.
> Your Papa and I are asked to tea at the Rectory, on Saturday, to meet the Bishop. . . .

When father set sail for foreign seas, mother continued to cultivate her mind and read Samuel Smiles' *Self-Help*, which she adored, and a volume of Lord Byron, whom she was less inclined to praise. "Do you think him a noble man?" Captain George Belknap's wife asked her mother. He was "so varied in his temper and public career" that she had "no sympathy" for him. Yet there were moments when Byron and men of his ilk sounded a mite like her husband. It was all very confusing. "There is so much to remember."[38] Under such strain the Navy wife might set her reading material aside and return to the family

project—tracking down important ancestors.* A noble pedigree, it seems, was   **133**
most useful in gaining father entrée into the hereditary organizations naval
officers were joining, among them the Sons of the American Revolution and the
Society of the Cincinnati. Quasi-military organizations, such as the Order of
the Red Eagle, the Grand Army of the Republic, the Loyal Legion, the Imperial
Order of the Dragon, the Military Order of Foreign Wars, the Army and Navy
Union, and the Spanish-American War Veterans Association, to name but a
few, were somewhat less esteemed, but still quite popular.[39] An ex-army officer
described the U.S. Army in 1880 as "a little domain of its own, independent and
isolated by its peculiar customs and discipline; an aristocracy by selection and
the halo of tradition," its interior "an unexplored region to the mass of the
people." He added that the wives of army officers were "inflated with aristocratic ideas, to which they had previously been utter strangers."[40] Navy wives
were not necessarily utter strangers to aristocratic ideas, but otherwise this might
have passed for a description of naval society in the same age.

The Navy wife's identification with the Service was virtually as strong as
that of her officer husband. Love for the Navy was "evident in her every action,
while understanding of its traditions and procedure practically ooze[d] out of
her pores." Needless to say, "Navy girls" accepted rank as an appropriate
symbol of social rank, with all its attendant obligations. "Loyalty to your
husband's Commanding Officer includes loyalty to his wife as well," one manual
for Navy wives maintained. The wife of Commander Roswell Hitchcock
recalled that "Mrs. Admiral" always expected the wives of officers in her
husband's squadron "to touch their bonnets to her. She demanded the most
obsequious attention." When Mrs. Rear Admiral Robley Evans approached
Mrs. Admiral George Dewey at a White House reception in 1905 she was
observed to have "curtsied low to Mrs. Dewey" and to have "said in a loud
voice, 'I salute my chief!' "[41] Mrs. Dewey's name did not appear on any
official "chain of command" register, but "what every woman knows" was
just as clear then as it is now; the Navy wife has always been an active agent
behind the scenes in her husband's life.†

Retirement and Beyond

Before the mid-twentieth century few retired officers managed
to launch a second career. Mahan and his messmates saw forty to fifty years of
service and retired in their sixties. Some, like Captain William Cronan, "condemned and surveyed by hard-hearted doctors," went to the "side-lines"

* For example, Rear Admiral Albert Barker could, and frequently did, trace his ancestry
to the Mayflower. Barker, *Everyday Life, passim.*

† The reader may be aware of the fact that in the early 1960s the Navy actually added a
section to the form for the report of fitness of officers, a section to be given over to the
evaluation of the officer's wife. The change was withdrawn after several days of severe
criticism and public ridicule, but it serves as evidence of an enduring sense in naval circles
that the Navy wife plays an important role in her husband's professional affairs. Cf. Calvert,
Naval Profession, 90.

134   several years before their normal retirement dates but retained their "great love for the Navy" for many years thereafter. Few looked with pleasure on the ending of their days of active service. As the day of one rear admiral's retirement approached, his wife wrote, "I can realize that it is a great trial for any officer to give up active duty." Senior officers waged a perennial battle with the Congress, the Department, and their consciences to stay on the active list. They were reinforced by a set of devoted and equally concerned senior officer's wives. Navy Secretaries from Gideon Welles to Josephus Daniels have left a record of the fury of the officer's wife whose husband was being unwillingly retired. The wife of Captain John Gibbons, for example, ruthlessly berated Secretary Daniels on hearing that her husband had been "plucked" for inadequate time at sea. If it were not for her husband's counsel of restraint, she advised Daniels publicly, "I would . . . with my own hands tear and rend those miserable men who denied my husband what was his right" (appointment to rear admiral and several more years of active service).[42] The wrath of the Mrs. Captain Gibbons notwithstanding, the retirement laws remained, and Mahan and his messmates were all eventually turned out to pasture.

Retirement was not altogether unpleasant, of course. One might winter in Washington, New York, Baltimore, or Philadelphia and summer at Annapolis, Newport, or the Maryland or New York family farm, and one was always among old service friends for much of the year. "Admiral Farquhar is at the hotel opposite our own [at Jamestown, Rhode Island]," Mrs. Remey wrote her son, "and he and your Father meet every day, often for a walk . . . Admiral Erben is also at Jamestown, and Admiral Selfridge at a cottage a mile off, so there is no lack of acquaintances."[43] There were those, like Admirals Daniel Ammen and William Standley and Commodore George Perkins, who tried to make a go of operating a farm or ranch. Perkins, for one, was not very popular with his farm hands, since he seemed to see no difference between porch and quarterdeck, and demanded "unhesitating obedience," but he was satisfied with the results; he raised horses profitably and predictably lived a life "very much like that of an English country gentleman." Others, like Admiral George Dewey, moved about a good deal, staying at Saratoga Springs one season and the Breakers in Palm Beach the next.[44] One officer suggested in 1881 that retired senior officers be created consuls and sent abroad to live out their final years in further service to the Republic, but between Andrew Jackson's appointment of David Porter in the 1830s and Franklin Roosevelt's appointment of William Standley in the 1940s I could find no more than one appointment of a naval officer as Minister or Consul-General anywhere.[45] Perhaps Edward M. Earle put his finger on one reason that administrations might have been reluctant to dispatch retired senior naval officers on diplomatic missions not unlike those they had performed daily throughout their lives, when he argued in 1926 that

> Retired Admirals not infrequently constitute themselves unofficial spokesman for the nation in questioning the good faith and pacific intentions of other peoples and

Governments, thereby offering the jingo section of the press in our own and other countries sensational copy, calculated to promote international distrust.

But since Porter, Shufeldt, and Standley were all outspoken jingoes, it does not appear that moderation and restraint were prerequisites to diplomatic posts. It is more likely that naval officers simply disliked the thought of leaving friends and fatherland behind for the dubious virtues and virtual exile of consular duties. They appeared to prefer to settle comfortably stateside, where they might put the last hand to their memoirs and give their favorite after-dinner address a whirl before a variety of patriotic societies, veterans groups, fraternal organizations, ladies clubs, and chambers of commerce. In the words of one officer, "the Navy remain[ed] in the blood" of retired "high old salts," and in 1909 enough of them felt a stirring of the saline in their veins to provoke the creation of the Naval History Society, an organization modeled deliberately after the British Naval Records Society. As one of the founders explained, he could think of no "more interesting and useful occupation" during retirement "than a pleasant connection with subjects of naval interest."[46] And, of course, there was always the hope that one might be recalled to active duty, as were Montgomery Sicard, Alfred Mahan, and Washington Chambers, in the event of war—something to look forward to in one's old age.

Many naval officers selected their burial plots at Arlington National Cemetery, though some preferred interment in a family plot. Exceptionally prestigious individuals, such as Admirals Farragut, Porter, or Dewey, might be given permission to raise a tomb larger than regulation size, and some subordinates sought to be placed as close as possible to their former chief. Rear Admiral Charles Sperry, who had requested a lot near that of Admiral Dewey, must have been disappointed when Dewey's wife decided to inter the Admiral in Washington's Episcopal Cathedral instead, after the fashion of British royalty. Rear Admiral Charles Sigsbee feared with the "pride of position and reputation" that his somewhat eccentric wife might "introduce some contretemps" over his funeral arrangements, but Sigsbee's case was exceptional; most wives shared their husband's sense of propriety to the bitter end.[47]

Just as naval officers felt "called on" to work for the welfare of the widows of their brother officers, so Navy wives offered heartfelt condolences for their bereaved sisters of the service. "He is only a little way off," Mrs. Mildred [Admiral George] Dewey wrote to Mrs. Captain Nathan Sargent on the occasion of that officer's untimely death. "I try to think he is gone on a cruise." Mrs. Dewey's advice to Mrs. Sargent, to "[h]old fast to the Navy" that her husband had "loved" and for whose "interests" he had "worked loyally," is perhaps the best illustration of the closeness of naval life and society that could be offered to conclude this chapter.[48] And the Mildred Deweys of the Navy were legion.

Chapter 3 (Naval Life in the States)

1. See, for example, Lott, *Ships*, 18; Temple to Commander Henry Wise, May 7, 1862, and Drayton to Wise, October 31, 1863, Wise Papers, N.Y.H.S.; Temple had been Ordnance Officer at the New York Navy Yard; Drayton was his relief. Farragut was Commandant of the Mare Island Navy Yard in the 1850s.

2. Mills, *Power Elite*, 181; "Mantus," *United Service*, VI (1882), 207; *PUSNI*, XLII (1916), 736. For examples of the naval officer's social routine in the States see the diaries of Nathan Sargent, 1888–1902, Box 149, Naval Historical Foundation; the diaries of John Leonard, Captain John Leonard Papers, N.H.F.; Franklin, *Memories of a Rear Admiral, passim*; Francis Leigh Williams, *Mathew Fontaine Maury: Scientist of the Sea* (New Brunswick, N.J., 1963), 328; and the social pages of the *Army and Navy Journal*.

3. Burr, *Education in Early Navy*, 107; Rodgers to Wise, January 21, 1866, Wise Papers, N.Y.H.S.; Evans, *One Man's Fight for a Better Navy*, 148; Lott, *Ships*, 137, 153.

4. Winston Churchill, *Richard Carvel*, vii; Commander Louis M. Goldsborough's letters to his wife in the Louis Goldsborough Papers, Perkins L., Duke U.; Lieutenant Charles Sperry to his cousin Helen, October 8, 1870, Sperry Papers; Ammen, *The Old Navy and the New* (Phil., 1891), 31; Ammen, *Country Homes and Their Improvement* (Wash., 1885), 4, 22; Standley, *Admiral Ambassador*, 58; "Schoonmaker," p. 184; Ensign Albert Caldwell to his mother, Sept. 7, 1867, Caldwell Papers, Indiana State Hist. Soc. Lib.; Folger to Mrs O'Neil, February 20, 1890, O'Neil Papers, Box 340, N.H.F.

5. Remey, *Reminiscences of Boyhood*, I, 79. See also *The Public Service* I, No. 4 (N.Y., 1887), 56, for data of social life in navy yards.

The Brooklyn Navy Yard was less attractive. Consequently, Captain Percival Drayton, its Ordnance Officer during the Civil War, preferred to take up residence with his friend, Alexander Hamilton, Jr., at 18 Washington Square, where the social life was more agreeable. Drayton to Captain Charles Steedman, August 11, 1863, Steedman Papers, Perkins F., Duke U.

6. *United Service*, V (Sept. 1881), 345; *Fortune* (March 1938), 161; Lawrence G. Blochman, *Doctor Squibb: The Life of a Rugged Idealist* (New York, 1958), 59ff; Caswell to Steedman, November 27, 1884, Steedman Papers, Perkins Library, Duke U.; Nathalie J. Kelley Cook, *J. D. J. Kelley, Commander, U.S.N.* (n.p., 1942), Chapter 3; Alexander Hamilton, Jr., Letters and Papers, N.Y.H.S.; Astor to Grant, Jan. 2, 1912, Box 1, Vice Admiral Albert W. Grant Papers, Div. of Archives and Mss., State Hist. Soc. of Wisc. (This was probably John Jacob Astor [1864–1912], son of William B. Astor [1829–1892] and victim of the *Titanic* disaster, but it may have been John Jacob Astor, son of William Waldorf Astor [1848–1919], who had become a British subject by 1912.) Cf. DuPont to Drayton, Dec. 26, 1864, *DuPont Letters*, III, 416–417. Nearly all the manuscripts of these naval officers are replete with invitations to dinners, balls, and receptions, indicative both of their acceptability to high society and of their sense of pride in having been so accepted.

7. Sperry to Mary, December 22, 1865; Sperry to his wife, August 9, 1884, Sperry Papers.

8. Janowitz, *Professional Soldier*, 209.

9. Cadet Midshipman F. Bunts to his mother, February 1, 1883, *Letters from the Asiatic Station*, 203; Lejeune, *Reminiscences, passim*; Commander [?] P. F. Harrington to Lieutenant Commander W. F. Fullam, May 5, 1896, Box 1, Fullam Papers, N.H.F.

10. *America of Yesterday as Reflected in the Journal of John Davis Long*, ed. Lawrence S. Mayo (Boston, 1923), 159.

11. Mahan to his wife, May 13, 1893, and Oct. 19, 1894, Mahan Papers, L. of C.; Edward Arpee, *From Frigates to Flat-tops*, 34n.

12. Lieutenant "A. P. Mantus," "Marriage in the Navy," *United Service*, VI (1882), 208; Harry R. Cohen to the class of '81, Dec. 7, 1886, *3rd Annual Report of the Class of 1881*, 14; Commodore James Biddle to his niece, Adele Biddle, Dec. 5, 1847, cited in Nicholas B. Wainwright, "Commodore

James Biddle and his Sketch Book," *Pennsylvania Magazine of History and Biography*, XC (1966), 48; Charles Graves to his brother, February 13, 1857, Graves Papers, S.H.C., U. of N.C. Library; Blochman, *Squibb*, 79; Sperry to his wife, Dec. 26 and 28, 1880, Sperry Papers, L. of C.; Chambers, "To Kathrine (expecting) Xmas 1916," Box 48, Chambers Papers, N.H.F. Cf. G. B. Shaw, *Captain Brassbound's Conversion*, in *The Works of . . . Shaw*, IX (London, 1930), 288.

13. Lieutenant "A. P. Mantus," "Marriage in the Navy," *op. cit.*, 207.

14. Mills, *Power Elite*, 181–182; Commander Louis Goldsborough to his wife, Jan. 13, 1853, Goldsborough Papers, L. of C.; Miss Helen MacLachlan to the author, Dec. 4, 1963; Alden, *Perkins*, 217; Thomas, *Career of Walker*, 8; Johnson, *Rodgers*, 5; Sperry to his wife, May 2, 1886, Sperry Papers, L. of C.; *Fortune* (March, 1938), 161; Trabue, 36. Lieutenant Commander William Cowles married Theodore Roosevelt's sister, Anna.

15. McCalla, "Memoirs," Ch. IX, 7; Braisted, 117; Ensign Nathan Twining to his brother, Oct. 10, 1898, Twining Papers, State Hist. Soc. of Wis.; *PUSNI*, LXXVII (March, 1952), 266; Cummings, *Wainwright*, 37; *Class of '71, United States Naval Academy* (privately printed, New York, 1902), *passim*.

16. *Class of '71*, *passim*; Lieutenant "Mantus," "Marriage in the Navy," *op. cit.*, 199, 202, 208. As late as 1921 Captain Thomas Hart was to recommend that naval officers be prohibited from marrying until they were named Lieutenant (j.g.). Hart to the President of the Personnel Board, Aug. 17, 1921, Hart Papers, Bldg. 210, Wash. Navy Yard.

17. *Class of '71*, *passim*; Sperry to his wife, June 23, 1879 & May 2, 1886, Sperry Papers, L. of C.

18. West, *Admirals of Empire*, 119–120, 140.

19. Apparently this martinet mode of child-rearing was not unique to Mahan's messmates. One thinks of the family of the Austrian naval captain in *Sound of Music*.

20. Charles Remey, *Reminiscences of Boyhood* (n.p., n.d. [copy 8 at St. Hist. Soc. of Wis.]), III, 220; Roe, *Naval Duties and Discipline*, 185; Puleston, *Mahan*, 218–219; Mahan to his wife, March 4, 1895, Box 21, Mahan Papers, L. of C.; Sperry to his wife, November 26, 1880, & March 23, 1885, Sperry Papers, L. of C.; Arthur Calhoun,

A Social History of the American Family (New York, 1946 [orig. pub. 1919]), III, 157–178.

21. "Mantus," *op. cit.*, 202; Mahan in an introduction to The *Life and Adventures of Jack Philip, Rear Admiral, U.S.N.*, ed. Edgar Stanton Maclay (New York, 1904), 29.

22. Remey, *Reminiscences of Boyhood*, I, 41. Thereafter Charles Remey had very little to say of his father at all.

23. Wayland, *Elements of Moral Science*, 291–293; Sperry to his wife, June 25, 1880, and October 3, 1879, Sperry Papers; Madeline V. Dahlgren, *Thoughts on Female Suffrage and in Vindication of Woman's True Rights* (Washington, 1871), 5–6, 9–11.

24. See, for example, Commander Louis Kimberly to his niece Zoe, January 27, and November 1, 1863, and December 30, 1870, Kimberly Papers, Chicago Historical Society; Mrs. Remey to her son Charles, December 31, 1899, *Mrs. Remey's Letters*, XII, 838–839; Captain Charles Sperry to his son, Charles Sperry, Jr., Feb. 15, 1902, and to his wife, April 20, and January 23, 1879, Sperry Papers, L. of C.; Goldsborough to his wife and son, November 1, 1852, and January 13, and February 5, 1853, Goldsborough Papers, L. of C.; Lewis, *Farragut*, II, 385; Mahan to his wife, August 24, 1893, and March 4, 1895, Box 21, Mahan Papers, L. of C.; Mrs. Remey to her son Charles Remey, Nov. 12, 1896, Sept. 2, 1892, Dec. 27, 1896, and Feb. 21, 1897, and Mary Remey to her brother, March 12, 1893, *Mrs. Remey's Letters*, VIII, 224, 253; VII, 3; X, 548, 566. Mrs. Remey's anxiety was such at times that she dreamed of her son embarrassing the family by failing to complete prep school. VIII, 224.

25. Fifty-three out of 90 nineteenth and early twentieth century officers for whom information of their son's education is available in the *D.A.B.* sent their sons to the Academy.

26. Goldsborough to his wife, July 1854, Goldsborough Papers, L. of C.; Capehart to the class of '81, Nov. 15, 1888, *5th Annual Report*, 5; McVay to Dr. S. C. G. Watkins, Dec. 27, 1929, McVay Papers, N.H.F.; Preble to Grant, Jan. 22, 1874, George Henry Preble Collection, Maine Historical Society; Admiral Porter to President Cleveland, Jan. 3, 1887, Commodore Aaron Weaver Papers, U.S. Navy Collection, Manuscript Div., L. of C.; *Junk: A Collection of Songs and Poems by Cadets at the U.S. Naval Academy*, ed. George F. Gibbs (Wash., 1889); Kutner & Healy, *The*

Admiral, 174–175; "An Ex-Staff Officer," *An Appeal on Behalf of the Navy and its Personnel* . . . (New York, 1886 [copy in N.Y.P.L.]), 24.

One Senator favored an 1852 bill to give none but Congressmen the control of appointments because he was "against all monopolies on behalf of families or individuals in appointments in the Navy." *Congressional Globe*, XXI, Pt. 3 (Aug. 30, 1852), 2443.

27. Sperry to his wife, June 30, 1898, Sperry Papers; "Upshur, John Henry," *D.A.B.*

Rear Admiral John Rodgers may have hired additional Democrats at his Mare Island Navy Yard command in 1874 in order to induce the area's Representative, John Luttrell, to offer an Academy appointment to his son. Johnson, *Rodgers*, 346.

28. Captain H. W. Lyons to Navy Secretary Long, Jan. 29, 1902, *Papers of Long*, 421; Captain Sedgwick to Commander Henry Wise, Oct. 26, 1863, Wise Papers, N.Y.H.S.

29. Morison, *Perry*, 25, *passim*; Langley, *Social Reform in the Navy*, 115; Sperry to Mary, Oct. 11, 1865, Sperry Papers, L. of C.; Cummings, *Wainwright*, 4; *Class of '71*, 3; Lott, *Ships*, 86, 126, 128n; Falk, *Fighting Bob Evans*, 95; Connolly, *Navy Men*, 195; *United Service*, XI (Sept. 1884), 304; Thomas H. Stevens, II, Papers, Perkins L., Duke U.; Rear Admiral Andrew T. Long, "Around the World in Sixty Years," p. 10, Long Papers, S.H.C., U. of N.C.L.

30. From the 1840s to the 1920s the U.S. Navy's officer complement increased tenfold (Bureau of Census, *Historical Statistics*, 736–737). Thus the percentage of midshipmen whose parents were naval officers cannot serve as an indication of the percentage of officers from a previous generation who sent sons to the Academy.

31. George W. Cullum, *Biographical Register of Officers and Graduates of the U.S. Military Academy* (3rd ed., Boston, 1891), *passim*; Morison, *Perry*, appendix; Winston Papers, S.H.C., U. of N.C.L. (Winston's first son went to Annapolis; his second to West Point); Trabue, *Corner in Celebrities*, 21. I am indebted to James Bouma for the information about Watson, and to Kenneth Hagan for the information about Shufeldt and Jouett.

32. Harris to MacGreggor, Oct. 16, 1868, Folder 12, Box 209, N.H.F.

33. See, for example, Remey, *Reminiscences of Boyhood*, I, 34; Morison, *Perry*,

appendix; *Mrs. Remey's Letters*, VII, 253; Lowell Thomas, *Old Gimlet Eye: The Adventures of Smedley Butler* (New York, 1933), 116; Franklin, *Memories of a Rear Admiral*, 84–85; Sophie R. De Meissner, *Old Naval Days: Sketches from the Life of Rear Admiral William Radford, U.S.N.* (New York, 1920), 54, 195–200; Langley, *Social Reform in the Navy*, 115; Sperry to cousin Helen, May 12, 1872, Sperry Papers, *Class of '71*, *passim*; "Biographical Sketch of R. W. Meade, 3rd," Box I, Meade Papers, N.Y.H.S.; Evans, *Admiral's Log*, 84; Clark, *Fifty Years in the Navy*, 197.

T. O. Selfridge's daughter married a Russian naval officer, (Lott, *Ships*, 83). Seven of seventy of the daughters of other officers listed in the *D.A.B.* are said to have married naval officers; this figure may be incomplete. Commander William Herndon's daughter married President Chester Arthur, and others, such as the daughters of Matthew C. Perry, who married Belmonts and Hones, also made prominent matches.

34. Perhaps the most striking Navy family tree is that of the Rodgers family, which spanned a century and a half of naval aristocracy. See the biographies of Commodore John Rodgers and his son by Oscar Paullin and Robert Johnson, the articles on the Rodgers naval men in the *D.A.B.*, and the Rodgers Family Papers in the Mss. Div., L. of C., and in the Hist. Soc. of Pa. Cf. C. B. Otley, "Militarism and the Social Affiliation of the British Army Elite," in J. Van Doorn, ed., *Armed Forces and Society* (The Hague, 1968), 105–106.

35. Lasch, *The New Radicalism in America, 1889–1963: The Intellectual as a Social Type* (New York, 1965), 46–48; Charles Remey, *Reminiscences of Childhood*, IV, 311. For good examples of the kinds of everyday expenses incurred by naval officers and their families see the volume of receipt invoices marked "For Personal Expenses, 1879–1881," in the Samuel Dana Greene Collection, N.H.F.

36. Calvert, *Naval Profession*, 93. See also his instructions on social protocol (*Ibid.*, 93–98) and similar instructions in Florence R. Johnson, *Welcome Aboard*, *passim*; and Anne B. Pye and Nancy Shea, *The Navy Wife* (New York, 1942), *passim*.

37. *Mrs. Remey's Letters*, X, 588. See also the letters of Mrs. Robert Shufeldt in Box 9 of the Commodore Robert Shufeldt Collection, N.H.F.

38. Captain George Belknap's wife to

her mother, Aug. 31, 1879, R. R. Belknap Papers, Box 423, N.H.F.

39. See, for example, John A. Riddle to Mrs. M. M. A. Belknap, Feb. 10, 1879, Lieutenant Charles Belknap to Captain George Belknap, Dec. 18, 1880, and many other 1881 letters, Belknap Papers, Box 423, N.H.F.; McCalla, "Memoirs," title page.

A few naval wives tried their hand at creative writing. See for example, the essays of Madeline Dahlgren, *op. cit.*; the manuscript travelogue of Mrs. Henry Wise, "Our Home Abroad," Box 274, NL, Entry 464, R.G. 45; or the manuscript novel of Mrs. George Balch, "Old Naval Academy Days," Balch Papers, S.H.C., U. of N.C. Library.

40. Duane M. Greene, *Ladies and Officers of the U.S. Army; or, American Aristocracy: A Sketch of the Social Life and Character of the Army* (Chicago, 1880), 3, 38.

41. Pye and Shea, *Navy Wife*, viii; *Welcome Aboard*, 242; Mary Hitchcock, *Tales Out of School About Naval Officers* (N.Y. 1908), 87–88; Kutner and Healy, *The Admiral*, 291. Cf. *Society of Sponsors of the U.S. Navy* . . . (n.p., 1915 [copy in the State Hist. Soc. of Wisc.]), *passim*, for the views of Navy wives on naval affairs. Marine General Holland Smith wrote of his wife, "With her, the Marine Corps has come first." Smith, *Coral and Brass*, 50.

42. Cronan, *PUSNI*, LV (1929), 113; *Mrs. Remey's Letters*, XII, 952; *Diary of Welles*, I, 532; Langley, *Social Reform in the Navy*, 33–34; 44th Cong., 1st Sess., House Misc. Doc. 170, Pt. 5, *Investigation by the Naval Affairs Committee*, 144–146; *Diary of Welles*, III, 107–108; Daniels, *Wilson Era: Years of Peace*, 286–287. Cf. "Dedication to the Navy" in "The Inner World" in Chapter 5.

43. Volume 19 [1870–1872], Louis Golds-borough Papers, L. of C.; *Mrs. Remey's Letters*, XII, 956, 969. See also the *D.A.B.* and the society pages of the *Army and Navy Journal*.

Old enlisted men were sent to the Sailor's Home at Philadelphia until the early twentieth century, when enlisted men became eligible for retirement pay as well.

44. Standley, *Admiral Ambassador*, 58; Alden, *Perkins*, 265–267, 269–272, 291. Cf. Ammen, *Country Homes*, *passim*; Dewey file, Mss. Collections, Carnegie Library, Syracuse University.

45. Robert W. Shufeldt was U.S. Consul-General at Havana from 1861 to 1863, and was offered the post of Minister to China in 1889 (he declined).

46. Lieutenant R. M. G. Brown, "The Commercial and Naval Policy of the United States," *United Service*, IV (May 1881), 606; Earle, "The Navy's Influence in Our Foreign Relations," *Current History*, XXIII (1926), 648; Standley, *Admiral Ambassador*, 55; Lovette, *School of Sea*, 272; John F. Meigs to Caspar Goodrich, March 26, 1908, & January 6, 1909, and John S. Barnes to Goodrich July 2, 1909, Goodrich Papers, N.Y.H.S. See also Goodrich to Rear Admiral Willard Brownson, Oct. 14, 1903, *PUSNI*, XXIX (1903), 824; and Commander Horace Mullan (Ret.) to Rear Admiral Charles O'Neil, Dec. 12, 1898, O'Neil Papers, R. B. Hayes Library, Fremont, Ohio.

47. Sperry to the Quartermaster General, May 18, 1906, Sperry Papers, L. of C.; Daniels, *The Wilson Era: Years of Peace*, 509–510; Folder A, Box 1, Charles Sigsbee Papers, N.Y. State Library, Albany, N.Y.

48. Commander D. M. Fairfax to Captain Henry Wise, Oct. 15, 1867, Wise Papers, N.Y.H.S.; Mrs. Dewey to Mrs. Sargent, Feb. 4, 1908 Box 560, Nathan Sargent Papers, N.H.F.

chapter 4

What They Did: The Navy's Role in Diplomacy

> Yankee ships are building fast,
> Their Navy to increase
> . . .
> They will enforce their commerce
> The laws by Heaven were made
> That Yankee ships in time of peace
> To any port may trade.
>
> From a nineteenth-century naval chanty, printed in *Naval Songs,*
> ed. Stephen B. Luce (N.Y., 1883)

> A man-of-war is the best ambassador.
>
> Oliver Cromwell

The Navy's mission has always been to carry out the policies of the U.S. government. This much is evident. But there appears to be some disagreement among historians as to precisely what these policies were. Some, such as Fletcher Pratt, Dudley Knox, Samuel Eliot Morison, McGeorge Bundy, and Armin Rappaport, have tended to portray the Navy as a wise instrument of an "innocent" American diplomacy, "protecting peaceful traders from murderous onslaughts by natives," defending American honor, freedom, and rights, punishing aggression, surveying the deep for posterity, and rescuing shipwrecked mariners. And there is considerable truth to their interpretations—the U.S. Navy *did* guard the nation's "honor" and "rights"; it *did* survey the seas—for the benefit of American commercial posterity; and it *did* take a real interest in the fate of shipwrecked mariners of all nationalities (excepting perhaps only "Bolsheviks"). Another group of historians, among them Charles Beard and

Numbered footnotes for Chapter 4 begin on page 178.

140

Walter LaFeber, has tended to stress the active role naval force played in protecting American traders and investors abroad. This school inadequately describes the outlook and behavior of the naval officers themselves, matters with which we will concern ourselves in the next several chapters. But this does not detract from what Beard and LaFeber claim that the Navy of the late nineteenth and early twentieth centuries was actually doing abroad. That is, if Charles Beard had little to say of what was going through the *minds* of Navy captains as they kept "the fires of Federalist *Machtpolitik* . . . glowing throughout the years,"[1] his notion of how the Navy managed to keep those fires alive was a good deal closer to reality than was the picture painted by Admiral Morison.[2]

We want to have a clear picture of the duties American men-of-war were ordered by their government to perform between the 1840s and the 1920s. U.S. warships could not be deployed everywhere with impunity in these years to secure American diplomatic objectives. No Administration was so reckless as to order a squadron to stand into the Thames or the Elbe without first securing the permission of London or Berlin. But different standards could be applied in less fortified regions. American men-of-war were deployed in all non-North Sea waters in this period, and they were deployed for a reason—to conduct the business of the United States abroad. But they were not deployed recklessly; only a serious problem required a naval or marine solution. Warships were only used in situations that mattered. By investigating the missions these warships performed, we reveal the basic contours of American foreign policy.

Exploring, surveying, fighting Indians in Oregon, and rescuing shipwrecked mariners and beleaguered missionaries were among these missions, and they should not be forgotten or disregarded. But one must keep in mind that all of these matters were related in one important sense—they all served to aid the expansion of the American economy into foreign lands.* Thus Navy Secretary

* Obviously the protection of missionaries was not fundamentally an economic measure. But, as one naval officer put it, the American missionary was an important means of "developing the commercial resources of the countries where he has been stationed." Commander A. H. Foote, *Africa and the American Flag* (New York and London, 1854), 76. Paul Varg has indicated that missionaries "never argued that their work would lead to an expansion of trade. . . ." *Missionaries, Chinese, and Diplomats: The American Protestant Missionary Movement, 1890–1952* (Princeton, 1958), 84–85. But see the remarks of one missionary, cited in La Feber, *New Empire*, 307–308: "If I were asked to state what would be the best form of advertising for the great American Steel Trust or Standard Oil or the Baldwin Locomotive Works . . . or the Singer Sewing machine [Co.] . . ., I should say take up the support of one or two or a dozen mission stations. . . . Everyone thus helped would be, conspicuously or inconspicuously, a drummer for your goods, and the great church they represent at home would be your advertising agents." And see also the negative response of the U.S. Minister to China, Charles Denby, in 1895, to a suggestion by the Commander-in-Chief of the U.S. Asiatic Squadron that all U.S. missionaries in inland China be recalled "until conditions settle down": "Missionaries are the pioneers of trade and commerce. Civilization, learning, instruction breed new wants which commerce supplies. . . ." (Thomas McCormick, *The China Market: America's Quest for Informal Empire, 1893–1901* [Chicago, 1967], 65–66).

On Indian fighting in Oregon, see Letterbook of Commander Guert Gansevoort (Herman Melville's cousin), Commanding U.S.S. *Decatur*, 1855–1856, Subentry 30, Entry 395, R.G. 45.

142   Mahlon Dickerson outlined the "primary object" of what was to become the famed Wilkes Expedition to Captain Thomas ap Catesby Jones as "the promotion of the great interests of commerce and navigation. The advancement of science is considered an object of great, but comparatively of secondary importance." Navy Secretary William A. Graham ordered Lieutenant William Herndon to explore the upper reaches of the Amazon watershed specifically in order to ascertain what trading and planting opportunities might exist in those inner regions of South America. Graham allowed Herndon "to make such geographical and scientific observations by the way as may be consistent with the main object of the expedition, always bearing in mind that these are merely incidental, and that no part of the main objects of the expedition is to be interfered with by them."

Thus it is not surprising that Commander Cadwalader Ringgold, in command of the North Pacific Surveying and Exploring Expedition in the 1850s, simply ceased his "scientific" activities and remained in South China waters when Taiping rebels threatened U.S. merchants in that region. Surveying and exploring were the expedition's expressed objects, but as Lieutenant Alexander Habersham, the expedition's chronicler, put it, the expedition "was originated by the necessities of commerce." And Assistant Navy Secretary Gustavus Vasa Fox, himself a veteran of both the Navy and the merchant service, explained the function of the newly-created Bureau of Navigation to its first chief, Rear Admiral Charles H. Davis, by pointing out the "grand opportunity" to make this bureau" useful to the whole mercantile community." C. Wright Mills described the U.S. Navy of the late nineteenth century as "a gentleman's club, which occasionally went on exploring and rescuing expeditions." While the Greely relief expedition and the deLong exploring expedition, among others, were of this nature, Mills' description of the Navy's role and mission is inadequate. The U.S. had naval vessels in Asiatic, Latin American, and Mediterranean waters at all times in these years. Obviously the Navy had a far greater mission to perform than that of explorer or surveyor—for its vessels were armed with smooth-bore cannon and later with breech-loading rifles, which proved handy whenever a coast did not want to be surveyed, but which served other purposes as well. Weaponry, which distinguishes the man-o'-war from the merchantman, is the key to the Navy's special mission in American diplomacy. It is the use—or, to be more precise, the deployment or threatened use—of weaponry (including embarked Marines) that constitutes the Navy's role in American diplomacy. The Navy was often the "cutting edge" of that diplomacy; this chapter is designed to demonstrate what it was that the Navy cut.[3]

Obviously, a navy has a vital role in the defense of a nation's coastal territories. Any number of Congressmen who rose in the nineteenth century to argue for greater naval appropriations invoked the spectre of a hostile fleet bombarding New York, New Orleans, or San Francisco, landing a party of armed men, and burning and looting commercial houses and public buildings. Most of this anxiety reflected a concern for these vital coastal organs of domestic and foreign trade, but the fact remains that, in the words of Lieutenant Commander J. D. Jerrold Kelley, "the first duty of a navy is to guard the territory of its people."

How much of American naval policy does this truism explain? Were American solons and statesmen really fearful of the devastations of the Turkish or Chilean navies, as their statements sometimes lead one to believe? To a certain extent this may have been the case, but much of this rhetoric was more ceremonial than earnest, intended as much for one's constituents as for one's colleagues. The policymaker's words of concern for national defense masked the more important half of his case for a greater navy—his appreciation of the role that a navy played in the defense and development of American trade and investment abroad.[4]

Whatever the feelings and intentions of Congressmen might have been of the Navy's role in coastal defense, few members of the naval aristocracy itself believed that such a role was really critical. Mocking just such a doomsday prediction of gutted ports and burning warehouses, Commander Caspar Goodrich sarcastically remarked to his peers in 1896:

> . . . the wonder arises as to how we have managed to escape a direful fate during the twenty-five to thirty years following the late war, when our navy was a negligible quantity.

Publicly Goodrich and his colleagues might warn of "the daily jeopardy of national humiliation," chiefly for appropriation purposes. They were not unconcerned about coastal defense, to be sure, and if the proper public attention to such matters resulted in more funds for naval affairs, so much the better. But privately several, including Rear Admiral Mahan himself, expressed doubts that the Navy would ever be called upon to repel an invasion of the U.S.[5]

In any event, of all the naval powers of the middle and late nineteenth century, only Spain threatened U.S. seaports with a hostile fleet. And that rusty sea power had to be virtually forced to do so by the actions of the U.S. Congress itself. Three thousand miles of bounding main separated America from potential plunderers. Relations with Great Britain were generally good after 1815. And by 1850 it was clear that steam engineering, with its unquenchable thirst for coal, posed new hazards for any nation intending to conduct extended naval operations in American waters.

One must look elsewhere, then, to discover the truly significant function the Navy performed in the 1845–1925 era. Territorial integrity had been Lieutenant Commander Kelley's first "duty of a navy"; close on its heels was a duty "to protect [America's] natural commerce; *and then*, in the general interest of humanity, to police and survey the seas."[6] And according to Navy Secretary Paul Morton, Kelley's second point was the more important one. In Morton's words, the Navy's mission was that of "the watchdog of American commerce

144   everywhere on the high seas." It was to be "the policeman by day and the watchman by night of our foreign trade."[7] And by then (1904) it had established itself in another role as well—that of advance man.

Ever since the early days of the Navy, U.S. ship-owners and export–import firms had lobbied for naval protection and had received a fair measure of it. Consequently, when in 1858 a New York meeting of merchants complained that the protection the Navy afforded merchant shipping was inadequate, Commander Thomas Turner sent a furious missive to Navy Secretary Isaac Toucey in defense of the Service. Turner considered the charges of inadequate aid "so eminantly [sic] unjust and untrue as the experience [sic] of the whole navy afloat will attest (Our merchant vessels being constantly relieved in one way or another by our cruisers on foreign service). . . . It would be impossible for me to remember the innumerable instances during my last cruise for relief afforded our merchantmen on several occasions." Turner went on to suggest that the Department order all vessels to retain "an abstract of all such service performed" in order to provide "full and ample refutation" of any such charge, and thus "to vindicate [the] honor and character of the service." Turner did not seem to realize that a charge of inadequacy might have, in fact, been little more than a plea for more ships. But his response is instructive, none the less. No one knew better than the naval officer himself of the manifold ways that the Navy aided American shipping and commerce.

Commander Turner said nothing of the aid merchantmen received from the Navy in naval shipyards, but if the Mare Island Navy Yard was at all exemplary, this aid was considerable. In its first days in the 1850s, and for many years thereafter, the Mare Island Navy Yard overhauled many more privately-owned brigs, barques, sloops, schooners, ships, clippers, and steamers than it did vessels of the U.S. Navy, Revenue Service, or Coast Survey. U.S.S. *Cyane*, U.S.S. *Massachusetts*, and other Asiatic or Pacific Station vessels shared the drydocks with merchantmen such as *Five Yankee*, *Golden Gate*, *America*, *Success*, *Uncle Sam*, *Western Continent*, *Spirit of the Times*, and *Dictator*. Mare Island was not just a *navy* yard.[8]

For years naval officers collected and reported information on commercial opportunities throughout the world to U.S. chambers of commerce. In 1892, Lieutenant Commander J. D. J. Kelley maintained that "[e]very warship should be a commercial agent, and the dissemination of information upon the resources of the country, the prices and values of our commodities, the advantages inuring to foreign merchants by dealing with us, ought to form an essential part of the orders of cruising men-of-war." And in 1922 Lieutenant Commander Fitzhugh Green, in an article in the Naval Institute's *Proceedings* entitled "Science and the Navy," urged naval officers to provide marketing and investing data "to thousands of waiting investors, industries, and utilities." Naval officers often learned of the quality and availability of profitable natural resources in the lands their ships visited. "What we gather in the distant markets of the world may seem silly and insignificant to us. To the right person at home it may mean everything."[9] And a reading of naval archival records clearly indicates that Kelley's and Green's advice was widely followed.

In the same manner, the Office of Naval Intelligence published a general policy statement throughout the 1920s of the ways that the Navy served the nation. This remarkable document, entitled *The U.S. Navy as an Industrial Asset*, maintained that in addition to its role as commerce protector, the Navy furnished American businessmen transportation "to various places" and provided them with "all information of commercial activities." When business opportunities arose, American firms were notified by the Navy "and given full information on the subject."[10]

Policeman, repairman, watchman, advance man, the naval officer was a vigorous ally of the U.S. businessman abroad—in Asia and the Pacific, in Latin America and the Caribbean, and in Europe, Africa, and the Mediterranean.

Asia and the Pacific

Good people of America, the day is drawing near,
When to more genial latitudes our gallant ship must steer;
For our orders are imperative, to cruise in distant seas,
To watch the long-tailed Chinamen and crafty Japanese . . .

From a nineteenth century naval song, printed in George R. Willis, *The Story of Our Cruise in the U.S. Frigate "Colorado", . . . 1870–1872* (n.p., n.d., *circa* 1873) .

The history of U.S. Navy activities in Far Eastern waters from 1845 to 1925 is an almost constant record of involvement in the affairs of other peoples on behalf of American merchants and investors. A measure of this involvement was somewhat understandable; contracts or treaties were sometimes broken; the property of U.S. citizens or corporations was sometimes pirated; American traders were, now and then, unjustly encumbered. But there were also many instances of naval involvement on behalf of U.S. business interests that bore many of the marks of impropriety or sheer bullying.

The more celebrated examples of aid involved the use of naval force to open Asian lands to American trade. By 1860 a host of ports in China, Micronesia, the Sandwich Islands, Formosa, and Japan had been compelled by U.S. warships to admit American export–import merchants and merchantmen. Lieutenant George Preble, who served with Commodore Matthew C. Perry in Japanese waters, thought that the treaty Perry's warships had compelled the Japanese to sign was a great waste of energy, as he had doubts that the Japanese would ever consume significant quantities of American produce. But his was not to reason why, and so he dutifully inscribed on several fans that Japanese visitors offered the motto: "Commerce and Agriculture tend to unite America and Japan." Commander John Rodgers, who may have been dubious too, nevertheless described Shanghai to Navy Secretary James Dobbin as "the Chinese Emporium of American Commerce."[11]

In 1870 Commander W. T. Truxton was dispatched in the *Jamestown* to the islands now known as the Gilberts, the Marshalls, and the Marianas to negotiate executive agreements between the local chieftains and "the King of the United States," in much the same way that U.S. Army officers were concurrently dealing with Indian tribes in the American West. Truxton's addresses to "the People of Tarawa" are fascinating documents worthy of special attention. He recounted the history of U.S.–Tarawa relations, beginning with the typical (and possibly justifiable) claim that the natives had abused shipwrecked American sailors, thus provoking the wrath of "the King of the United States." But since the Tarawans were "a poor and small people and without the true God," Truxton explained, the American king had sent his missionaries to them "to tell you that you must not murder and steal." Apparently the missionaries had not sufficed, for Truxton had now been sent to insure the safety of American merchantmen, who continued to stand into the island harbors in moments of distress. The Tarawans must not have been very centralized, for Truxton insisted that they "acknowledge one Head and appoint his successor, while I am here," in order to guarantee "a stable government under which you can make laws to regulate your [!] trade," and, what was more important, to provide greater security for American trade.[12] The similarity between this microcosm of American diplomacy and Spanish–American exchanges in the 1890s over the Cuban revolution, as described by Walter LaFeber, are striking.[13] Truxton expressed no interest in the calibre of the ruler he hoped might emerge. His only concern was with American trade, for which tranquil, stable rule was required.

A less successful example of the use of American naval force to open the doors of an Asian nation was the case of Korea. As early as the 1830s U.S. policymakers had expressed an interest in the Hermit Kingdom. Lincoln's Secretary of State William Seward was particularly hopeful of opening the kingdom to American trade, and in 1866 he saw his chance. U.S.–Korean relations had been placid, and shipwrecked U.S. sailors had always been afforded succor by Korean authorities, but in that year a spectacular incident gave Seward and his ideological successors an extraordinary opportunity. The U.S. merchantman *General Sherman* had, without Korean permission, stood into the closed port of Pyongyang. Its ultimate purpose was trade, but its hostile attitude provoked its own destruction by Korean authorities. In time, a punitive naval expedition was dispatched, ostensibly to insure the safety of American sailors, but designed as well to jar the door open, if possible. The bloody work of that expedition in destroying the barrier forts in 1871 failed in both regards, but it was somewhat rectified by the efforts of Commodore Robert Shufeldt in 1882, and that officer's more amicable negotiation of a treaty with officials of the Hermit Kingdom. And it was a naval officer, Ensign George Foulk, who, as naval attaché to Korea and personal confidant to the Korean monarch, wrote an Academy classmate in 1884 of his hope that with a little personal effort "the tide of Korean purchasing can be very easily turned American-wards."[14]

In order to operate in Far Eastern waters the Navy, and the merchantmen, needed coaling stations. This is why Captain "Mad Jack" Percival was dispatched in the *Constitution* in 1844 for the South Pacific. His instructions were to "secure a coal station" on the island of Borneo, and if he saw fit to land his marines at Danang to punish some obstreperous Vietnamese, well, that was why he was called "Mad Jack." Apologies could always be made, as they were, some four years later.[15] In 1864 the Japanese leased port facilities for a coaling station at Yokohama, which was quickly sublet by the Navy Department to the Pacific Mail Steamship Company and was used by both institutions long into the twentieth century.[16] In 1872 Commander Richard Meade, 3rd, was dispatched in the *Narragansett* to arrange the lease or purchase of a coaling station at Pago-Pago "at the earliest possible moment."[17] It was not until 1878 that a treaty with the Samoan chief was actually signed, but by 1884 the Navy had stations at Pichilingue (in Lower California), Yokohama, Tutuila (in Samoa), and Pearl Harbor, and Secretary Chandler was asking for additional stations at the Panamanian isthmus, Korea, the Straits of Magellan, Haiti, Curaçao, Brazil, Madagascar, Liberia, and Fernando Po.[18]

It was not enough to open ports and establish coaling stations. The ports had to be kept open and commercial interests protected constantly. A few examples should illustrate these duties. In 1856, when local unrest threatened the property of American merchants in Canton, Commander A. H. Foote, like Commander Ringgold before him, landed sailors and marines to guard the American factory and later shelled the Chinese Barrier Forts between Canton and Whampoa. In 1863, while civil war raged in American waters, Secretary of State William Seward authorized the U.S. Minister to Japan to unleash Commander David McDougal in the *Wyoming* on the Shogun's forts and vessels, "if necessary," to "redress wrongs." Within a month McDougal was unleashed and the *Wyoming* sank two Japanese warships, silenced several shore batteries, and collected $12,000 in penalties for Japanese damage to U.S. property. In 1866 Chinese pirates threatened to seize opium belonging to the American owners of the S.S. *Parsee*, and Captain Robert Shufeldt was dispatched in the U.S.S. *Wachusett* to protect the American traffic in the opium trade. The *Wachusett* did the job, and the next year it was sent up the Yangtze to Hankow to guard an exclusive American franchise, the Shanghai Steam Navigation Co.

In 1868 when news of the ill-fated revolution in Spain reached Rear Admiral Stephen C. Rowan, Commander-in-Chief of the Asiatic Squadron, he sensed that the revolt might cause tremors in the Spanish-held Philippines and dispatched Commander Earl English in the *Iroquois* to Manila to look after American commercial interests "in case of disturbance." From Manila, Commander English assured his chief that "American merchants here were much pleased at the arrival of one of our men of war, so soon after the appearance of indications of trouble." Commander Truxton had directed the Tarawans to pay a fine of 100 casks of cocoanut oil, but within a year they had "again become insolent"; in December, 1871, the U.S. Minister to Hawaii, Henry A. Pierce, asked the commander of the South Pacific Squadron, Rear Admiral John A. Winslow, to send a vessel to Polynesia to follow up on Commander Truxton's demands and to visit several guano islands being mined by American firms.

By 1870 Americans had extensive business interests in South China (Amoy, Hong Kong, Canton) and on the Yangtze river. Two venerable gunboats, *Ashuelot* and *Monocacy*, had been assigned Hong Kong and Shanghai respectively as their "headquarters." And in November of 1870 Rear Admiral John Rodgers sent Commander Homer Blake up the Yangtze in the gunboat *Alaska* to show the flag. Blake reported that the trip had "a most salutary effect" on the natives, demonstrating that American warships were capable of ascending the Yangtze to "redress any wrongs which they, the Chinese, may inflict upon our people. The trade of the Yangtze is very large," Blake continued, "and daily increasing; in fact, it is almost an American monopoly." He concluded with the opinion that "no more important duty could be performed by one of the smaller vessels of this [Asiatic] squadron than to be employed cruising in the [Yangtze] river." Eventually Commander Blake's recommendation was realized. Patrolling of the Yangtze and South China seas was sporadic in the late nineteenth century, though there were several times in these years when U.S. naval commanders won the praise of American and other western businessmen in China for their willingness to land sailors and marines on indications that the natives were restless.* Naval activity in these regions increased in the first decade of the twentieth century. In the words of one officer, "as more ports in the Orient were opened for trade purposes the need for [additional] naval squadrons became greater." The South China Patrol was created in the early twentieth century, and by 1921 the U.S. gunboats plying China's main artery were formally known as the Yangtze Patrol. The gunboat *Panay*, attacked by Japanese aircraft in 1937 as it was convoying Standard Oil tankers on the Yangtze, was the last of a long line of descendants of the *Alaska* and Commander Blake's suggested policy.[19]

Naval aid to American business interests in Hawaii is still another example of how the "cutting edge" of U.S. diplomacy was wielded. In 1874, when forces from the *Tuscarora* were landed in Honolulu, their commander received the thanks of that city's chamber of commerce. Nineteen years later, in 1893, when American businessmen seized control of the island, and Captain Gilbert Wiltse landed marines from the U.S.S. *Boston*, these same businessmen thanked

---

* Richard McKenna, *The Sand Pebbles* (N.Y., 1962), 20–21, gives brief attention to the role of American businessmen in Sino-U.S. relations, but his own portrayal of a Yangtze Patrol gunboat offers few allusions to the Patrol's role in the protection of American economic interests and focuses rather on the protection of missionaries. There was a good deal of this, to be sure, but this otherwise excellent historical novel is somewhat weakened by its omission of any substantial account of the naval-business relationship on the river. Lieutenant Commander Yates Stirling's novel, *A U.S. Midshipman in China* (Phil. 1909), which frequently reveals the primacy of things economic in America's relations with China, deserves a new edition.

Wiltse and Rear Admiral John Walker, who had appeared with his squadron in Pearl Harbor at the first indication of trouble. The deposed royalists were constantly threatening to regain power, and the insurgent merchants and planters, who had little use for Hawaiian independence after the McKinley Tariff, deemed it "obvious" that a "a feeling of unrest and disquiet" would result "if the naval forces now in Hawaiian waters" were to be "abruptly withdrawn."[20] Walker remained until President Sanford Dole's revolutionary government was secure.

If one accepts Walter LaFeber's account of the causes of the Spanish–American War, as I am inclined to do, then it becomes clear that the Navy served to "clear the air" of a Spanish colonialism incompetent to deal with a revolution that had obtusely disrupted the American economy. But even if one rejects Professor LaFeber's presentation, even if one chooses to view the war as a war of humanitarian liberation or a "Great Aberration," one must still deal with the record of American diplomacy that presses in on each chronological side of the "Splendid Little War." If the war *was* an "aberration" from the normal state of foreign policy, wouldn't it be important to know something of what it was an aberration from?

Once again, the study of naval officers before and after war with Spain in the Pacific suggests that the primary mission of the operating forces in the Far East was to serve as the shield and sword of American economic expansion. A look at the correspondence of the U.S. commander in the Pacific, George Dewey, should serve as an illustration. Three months before war was declared, Commodore Dewey wrote to his sister of the deployment of his ships in Chinese and Korean waters where they were "looking out for a right to protect American interests, of which there are many more than is generally known." Clearly Dewey was not referring to missionaries, for his next sentence read: "What we all want is Chinese trade, and we are gradually getting more and more of it, all of which we would lose were it not well known that we are ready and will[ing to] protect it." Dewey's son was a New York export–import merchant. He wrote to his father: "I see an unusually large quantity of American cloth has been exported to China and Japan lately," and added that "you of course are directly responsible for this good turn." The son of the future hero of Manila Bay then spoke of his ambition to sell cotton prints in the Orient.[21]

Four months *after* Manila Bay Dewey sent a long report to Navy Secretary Long, in which he set forth his case for the retention of the Philippine archipelago or, at the very least, the island of Luzon. Dewey had nothing to say of the "white man's burden," nor the Protestantizing of the Catholic Filipinos. He talked about the possibilities of the tobacco trade on Luzon. This staple, Dewey argued, could be produced in "large quantities." The interior of the island had "as yet not been developed." There were other potential resources to be developed: timber, minerals, and sugar. And Luzon was "nearest the great centres of trade in the Far East" and well located on the trade routes "from the United States and Honolulu to these centres." Its ports were vital to American

150   control of the western Pacific.[22] President McKinley spoke of instructions from the Lord, but inasmuch as the instructions he gave to the American delegates were to accept nothing less than Luzon, one suspects that George Dewey, tobacco, and Manila, "the Liverpool of the Pacific," had more to do with his decision than he let on to the delegation of leaders of the Methodist Episcopal church in 1899. But then there has always been something doctrinal, evangelical, and heavenly about economic expansion to American statesmen.

After the treaty ending the war had been signed and the Filipino insurrection had been quelled, U.S. warships returned to their old stations and took up their old duties. In Canton, when two enterprising Kwantung merchants threatened Standard Oil's virtual monopoly of the fuel market by refilling that company's distinctive five-gallon tins with less expensive Russian oil, the American consul, with several U.S. naval officers in tow, demanded and received redress. And in 1905, when, after much haggling, Chinese officials at Chinkiang refused to grant Standard Oil Company agents permission to build oil tanks and rail facilities on properties where they maintained they had legally acquired a lease, Commander Nathan Sargent was dispatched with three warships to the area. His report to the Asiatic Fleet commander is worth citing, so illustrative is it of the nature and function of gunboat diplomacy:[23]

> The unexpected appearance of our three vessels and the uncertainty of their intentions were sufficient to [arrest the flow of events]; the decision of the Taotai . . . was reversed at once and the representative of the Standard Oil Company is now free to improve his property and by so doing to enlarge the trade of this American corporation.

Ten years later, when the World War drew western power home into the European maelstrom, Commander S. E. Moses told his colleagues of the need for more U.S. warships "off the coast of China" to fill the void. "Now is the time. Opportunity knocks."[24] If Chinese reared in the age of Sargent and Moses are now teaching their young that Americans are imperialist, capitalist warmongers, they did not have to go to *Quotations from Chairman Mao Tse-tung* for their inspiration.*

Latin America and the Caribbean

All that we have said of the Navy's role in Pacific diplomacy may be said of the Caribbean and South American waters as well. Since the days of the Monroe Doctrine, U.S. policy-makers had hoped these seas would be highways for U.S. trade. The Navy was crucial to the success of this policy; its special arbiters between the 1840s and 1920s were two generations of U.S. naval officers.

In Central America, however, the Navy assumed unique duties. Even before

---

* In this context, it seems to me that the view of U.S. diplomacy and naval development in these years taken by Soviet historians in *A Soviet View of the American Past*, ed. O. Lawrence Burnette, Jr., and William C. Haywood (Madison, Wisc. 1960), 35–37, is closer to reality than are the annotations of Mr. Burnette. For evidence of the imperialistic and warmongering facets of the naval officer's mind, see the relevant sections of Chapter 5.

the days of the California Gold Rush diplomats had taken an interest in the possibilities of a trans-isthmian canal. In 1866 Rear Admiral Charles H. Davis recommended such a project to Congress as a boon to trade, and throughout the latter half of the nineteenth century federal surveying expeditions, staffed and led by American naval officers and enlisted personnel, were dispatched with regularity to Central America.* The 1846 treaty with Columbia for the protection of Panamanian transit was regularly invoked. Commodore William Mervine landed sailors and marines there in 1856, as did Commander William D. Porter in 1860 and Rear Admirals Steadman and J. J. Almy and Commander W. B. Cushing, in 1873.[25]

In 1885 still another revolution endangered the transit of commerce on the trans-isthmian railway, and Commander Bowman McCalla was ordered to command a large detachment of sailors and marines to "keep the transit open." His instructions advised him to:[26]

> Enforce the regulations of the railway company, consult with Mr. [George] Burt, the superintendent of the Panama Railroad, and do anything in your power to aid him and the officials of the trains in guaranteeing safe conduct to passenger and freight.

None of this was extraordinary; the landing of armed U.S. troops on foreign soil to "do anything" to insure the safe and regular course of commerce was fairly commonplace. What made this particular expedition interesting were the secret orders McCalla received from the Chief of the Bureau of Navigation,

* Lieutenant I. G. Strain was the first naval officer to lead an expedition. He explored the Isthmus of Darien in 1854. Lieutenant T. T. Craven followed him in 1861. Commander Fredrick Engle surveyed the Isthmus of Chiriqui (north of Panama) in 1860. Strain, *Paper on the History and Prospects of Interoceanic Communication by the American Isthmus* (New York, 1856); 39th Cong. 1st Sess., Senate Ex. Doc. No. 62, *Letter . . . in relation to the various proposed lines for interoceanic canals and railroads between the waters of the Atlantic and Pacific Oceans* [1866], 5–15. Commander Thomas Selfridge led one group in 1871; another in 1873. Selfridge Papers, Letterbook No. 4, "Miscellaneous U.S. Navy," Box. 158, Naval Historical Foundations; *PUSNI*, LI (1925), 171. Robert Shufeldt took a deep interest in such projects and led a group to the Tehuantepec region in 1870. Lieutenant Fredrick Collins led an 1875 expedition to the Atrato region, as did Commander Edward Lull in 1871. Lull later surveyed Lake Nicaragua. Commander Alexander F. Crossman drowned while exploring the San Juan del Norte region in 1872; Commander Chester Hatfield finished the survey. Bowman McCalla, Donald Craven, and W. A. L. Gresham all slashed their way through the underbrush and scaled the mountain ranges in Nicaragua or Panama as young officers. *5th Annual Report of the Class of 1881*, 15, 17. A 1914 Office of Library of Naval War Records survey offered a partial list of 85 officers who had participated in various isthmian surveys. Entry 464, R.G.45, N.A.

Apparently William Goetzmann's army officers were not the only nineteenth century U.S. military men to engage in exploration and surveys of the continent, nor were overseas ventures such as the Wilkes, Habersham, Rodgers, and DeLong expeditions the only types of surveying parties that U.S. naval officers were deemed qualified to lead. Cf. Goetzmann, *Army Exploration in the American West, 1803–1863* (New Haven, 1959), 61; and *Exploration and Empire* (New York, 1966).

It is also clear that the U.S. government took a considerable interest in the nineteenth century in railroads and canal-planning in Central America, as well as in the U.S. and its territories. Cf. Carter Goodrich, *Government Promotion of American Canals and Railroads, 1800–1890* (N.Y., 1960).

152   Captain John G. Walker (who was later named President of the State Department's Isthmian Canal Commission in 1901). The Pacific Steamship Company had acquired several off-shore islands in the Bay of Panama for use as coaling and supply depots. McCalla was ordered to seize these islands, and any others in the vicinity that appeared strategically attractive, and to "occupy them with a permanent force," if he felt they would prove useful to his mission. "I write you all this confidentially," Walker told him. "There will be no record of it in the Navy Department, but you may consider it as an order to be carefully carried out." Fortunately, from our point of view, a copy of this order *was*, perhaps inadvertently, retained.[27] But one wonders how many similar orders to naval commanders *were* disposed of without a record for posterity of their issuance and nature.

Later, in 1901, Captain Thomas Perry was dispatched to the Isthmus in the *Iowa* to protect railway transit from insurgent activity, as was Rear Admiral Silas Casey in 1902. When President Theodore Roosevelt ordered Commander John Hubbard in the *Nashville* to prevent Columbia from landing a force at Colon to quell another revolt in 1903, he was making use of a Navy that had had considerable experience in such matters.*

The dream of an isthmian canal was a function of the general thrust of American economic expansion. It was not primarily designed to facilitate the movement of Oriental tourists or immigrants to the Eastern United States, or vice versa. The canal's adherents—among them many naval officers[28]—had in mind the movement of freighters, not passenger liners or aid missions.† But the Navy's mission in Latin American waters was by no means limited to the gaining of the Panama Canal in the period from the 1840s to the 1920s.

Throughout these years warships were widely used to aid American business interests in Latin America. Ever since Captain David Porter sailed around Cape Horn in 1812 to prey on British merchantmen and to protect those of his own country, American naval officers had been conscientious in their regard for the property of their countrymen on the west coast of Latin America. Their concern for American commerce in the Caribbean had considerably earlier origins.[29] And both concerns continued unabated. A few examples from the nineteenth century should illustrate the point. In 1846, when war with Mexico was declared, Commodore Robert Stockton, commander of U.S. Naval Forces on the Pacific Station, advised President Polk that he intended to put to sea immediately to protect Americans "engaged in commerce" and their property. Stockton's successors were similarly inclined. When San Juan del Norte (Greytown) authorities attempted to drive the Accessory Transit Company, a

* In fact, Rear Admiral Colby M. Chester claimed that the *Nashville* had simply carried out a "traditional policy." *Army and Navy Journal*, LII (Sept. 26, 1924), 102.

† Many naval officers were more concerned with the strategic value of a transisthmian canal that would link Atlantic and Pacific fleets than they were with American commerce, to be sure, but if one keeps in mind that one of the primary missions of these fleets in these years was to guard and aid American businessmen abroad, then the "strategic" value of a canal takes on added meaning.

Vanderbilt Line auxiliary, out of certain leased properties in 1854, Captain George Hollins was dispatched in the *Cyane* to support the demands of the U.S. consul there for reparations. Hollins burned the town "to make the punishment of such a character as to inculcate a lesson never to be forgotten . . . and [to] satisfy the whole world that the United States have the power and determination to enforce that reparation and respect due them. . . ." In 1855 the Paraguayan dictator Lopez first attracted and then apparently confiscated the property of American merchants. Three years later, after Paraguay had fired on a warship sent to "survey" Paraguayan waters, a squadron of nine vessels was sent to the Rio de la Plata. The squadron succeeded in forcing Paraguay to open its doors to commerce and trade with the United States, and insuring that trade's security. And later, when Civil War wracked the U.S. and ships were badly needed for the blockade, Flag Officer Charles Bell cruised in South American waters "to give security to our countrymen engaged in business."

Naval power was occasionally wielded in Latin America to guard seagull dung. In 1858 Commander Thomas Turner was ordered to Haiti to "look after the interests of a company of American citizens" who claimed to have discovered a guano island off the coast of Haiti. The Haitian government pressed its own claim, which Turner ignored, referring the Haitian Minister of Foreign Relations to an 1856 U.S. statute which authorized the use of naval force to protect the claims of U.S. citizens to any guano island they might "discover." However unattractive this particular mission may have been to some officers, it seems to have been a fairly common one. For example, in 1885 Captain Charles Norton in the *Shenandoah* was frequently directed to Mollendo, Peru, where it appeared that the inhabitants were unwilling to acknowledge that Grace & Co. were the sole beneficiaries of the generous local seabirds, who themselves were probably unaware that they were depositing their capital in a remotely regulated bank.[30]

Naval aid to American economic expansion in Latin America was not restricted to warship activity alone. While the Senate of the United States debated the annexation of Santo Domingo in 1869, Vice Admiral David Dixon Porter circulated a pamphlet that celebrated the virtues of this sun-drenched isle. His argument for annexation referred to the "rich land," the copper mines, the orderly, disturbance-free government, and the excellent harbor, Samana Bay. All that was needed to fill out the picture, he suggested, was Yankee leadership:[31]

> If the resources of the country were once developed by such men as would come from the United States, there would be no end to the wealth that could be obtained from that island; and I am quite satisfied you could export more and better sugar in ten years, after the labor of the country was once set in motion, than is now imported from the island of Cuba . . . what a misfortune that [Santo Domingo] is not in the hands of somebody to develop its resources.

If Charles Sumner was able, as chairman of the Senate Foreign Relations Committee, to prevent the annexation of the Dominican Republic, David D.

Naval force was frequently offered to clear trading lines, to open doors, and to keep them open. Gatling gun mounted in whaleboat, *circa* 1870, for use in support of landing parties and in shallow-draft patrolling (U.S. Naval Institute).

Less frequently, but occasionally, naval forces were dispatched "to insure domestic tranquility." U.S. naval personnel commanding a street intersection in "mob tactics" formation somewhere in the domestic United States in 1888 (*American Magazine* 1888).

Personnel of the 1872 Selfridge surveying expedition to the Isthmus of Darien, one of a number of nineteenth century naval surveys. The expedition's leader, Commander Thomas O. Selfridge, stands in the foreground, rifle on his shoulder with the mien of a "mountain man" (Naval Photographic Center).

Thomas Nast may have had a low opinion of the quality of America's warships in 1882, but he was satisfied that they were doing the job of guarding American commercial privileges abroad (*Harper's Magazine*, 1882).

U.S. sailors and marines guarding the American-owned Panama R.R. Co. during an 1885 revolution in the Isthmus, as seen by a *Harper's* artist (*Harper's Magazine*, 1885).

In 1871 a U.S. naval squadron battered on the door of "the Hermit Kingdom," Korea. Here Rear Admiral John Rodgers and his commanders plan the bloody but futile destruction of several Korean coastal forts (Naval History Division, Navy Department).

Officers and men of the landing party pose amid the ruins of one fort (Naval Photographic Center).

Fallen defenders of Kwang fort, renamed "Fort McKee" on the Navy's post-operation battle map (Silas Casey Papers, Library of Congress).

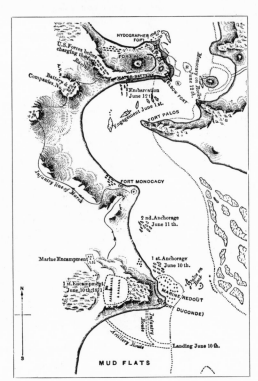

Map of "Fort McKee" (Silas Casey Papers, Library of Congress).

A 1931 Navy poster praising the Yangtze Patrol. See p. 148 for discussion of the "Yangpat" (Naval History Division, Navy Department).

YANGTZE RIVER GUNBOATS

U. S. S. Oahu Patrolling the Yangtze River

Powerful light draft naval vessels protect American lives, alleviating distress and assisting commerce on the upper Yangtze River. These gunboats penetrate regions over 1300 miles from the sea in a land where transportation and communication is primitive.

Artist Henry Reuterdahl's impression of the U.S.S. *New Orleans* in Shanghai harbor *circa* 1900 (from J. D. Long, *The New American Navy*).

Emilio Aguinaldo, Filipino nationalist revolutionary, at the gangway of the U.S.S.
Vicksburg after his capture in 1900 (Naval Photographic Center).

U.S. and other officers of empire, Peking, *circa* 1910 (Naval History Division, Navy
Department).

American sailors "showing the flag" in China during the revolutionary era in the mid-1920s (Bu Ships 12230, National Archives).

Counter-insurgency, 1919 vintage. A landing party of the U.S.S. *Olympia* near the contested city of Murmansk during the Russian Civil War (Naval Photographic Center).

Porter, the most powerful officer in the Navy throughout the late nineteenth century, was not to blame.

The United States never annexed Santo Domingo, but this did not keep investors and traders from its shores. And consequently the Navy made more than one stop at the city of Santo Domingo to help make the island safe for American dollars. Thus Rear Admiral C. H. Poor was dispatched in 1870 with a squadron of seven warships to patrol the Dominican coast on behalf of a dictator friendly to U.S. investments. And in 1893 unrest sent Rear Admiral Oscar Stanton's squadron to the island to protect the interests of such chaps as Nathaniel McKay, who wrote to Stanton:[32]

> I trust that you will not spare a shell to fly into that old City of Santo Domingo. That is the only [thing?] which will bring those Spanish people to terms. . . . The American flag should be protected, and I know you are just the man to do it. . . . I know them well at San Domingo, as I have about $50,000 invested there at San Domingo City in a bridge across the Ozama river. : . . They [the Dominican authorities] are very desirous to defraud me out of my bridge. . . . There is nothing that will bring these people to terms, as I said before, but a shell. . . . American interests abroad would be much better protected by our Navy if [it] were given more power.

Apparently McKay associated—indeed, equated—the defense of "his" bridge with the defense of the America flag; Stanton probably did too. But otherwise perceptive historians of American diplomatic and naval affairs have failed to make such association. They have made much of the nation's defense of its honor or "strategic interests" without noting that when "patriots" rose to call for greater naval expenditures to defend "the flag" or "the national honor" or "the national interests," they often had more tangible things in mind. These symbols—flag, honor, interest—generally represented one or another facet of the nation's economic fortune, the defense of which, to use Senator Lodge's phrase, was all that the national leadership wanted.[33] This does not necessarily mean that the Nathaniel McKays, steel-city Congressmen, U.S. consul-generals, or Navy League officials who utilized these symbols were deceitful phonies, speaking of honor and meaning only profits. They usually had both in mind, and the profits often were not even their own. America's elite are business enterprise-oriented. Their perceptions of national interest, their concept of "the flag," their sense of national honor, indeed, their very image of America has always been, in large part, one of economic activity and growth; and any felt threat to the health of the system appears also as a threat to all of the other elements and symbols of the American dream.[34]

Regardless, as we have said, of what view one takes toward the "Great Aberration," the fact is that after the Spanish–American War the Navy was used in Latin American waters in much the same way that it was in prewar years, with this exception—it was used more frequently and with more telling effect. By 1900 Americans had acquired a taste for chocolate, sweets, and bananas. The invention of the internal combustion engine put a premium on Latin America's oil resources. Developers engaged in a wide search for the

162   "black gold." And the Navy, with a vested interest in fuel oil sources, lent a hand here too. In 1901, for example, Captain Nathan Sargent was ordered by the Department to Venezuela's Orinoco River in an appropriately named warship, *Scorpion*, to investigate the region's investment potential and to confer with agents of the Orinoco Shipping and Trading Company, a firm in the area with American connections. By 1910 U.S. investments in Mexican oil fields near Tampico had acquired such diplomatic importance that Secretary of State Philander Knox arranged for the stationing of a squadron of warships off that port; as Knox put it, they were to keep any Mexican revolutionary forces in the area, whose movements might imperil U.S. oil interests, "in a salutary equilibrium, between a dangerous and exaggerated apprehension and a proper degree of wholesome fear." President Woodrow Wilson continued Knox's policy, and by early 1914 the U.S. naval forces off Tampico outnumbered the combined forces of Britain and the European powers in the area.

Most historians regard the administration of Wilson, Secretary of State William Jennings Bryan, and Navy Secretary Josephus Daniels as one in which American investments abroad received less attention than they had under previous administrations and would under subsequent ones. The usual device employed to establish this distinction is the passage in Daniels' autobiography in which the Navy Secretary related with relish the confrontation he claims to have had with a group of Americans who had considerable investments in oil in the Tampico region. Daniels criticized these investors for having taken their dollars out of the United States to avoid taxes and to seek higher returns. There is no doubt that Daniels, War Secretary Newton D. Baker, and other members of Woodrow Wilson's cabinet were largely out of sympathy with American investors in Mexico,[35] but this lack of sympathy did not produce an unsympathetic policy; American warships continued to stand guard over American oil investments in Mexico.

Robert Quirk claims that the American warships off Tampico in 1914 were on the scene as a "constant reminder" to the government of Mexico of President Wilson's displeasure with General Victoriano Huerta, head of the Federal government. He may be right, but he offers no evidence to support this claim. Actually Rear Admiral Henry Mayo, in command of U.S. naval forces off Tampico, advised the commanders of Huerta's forces and those of his opponents in the area on April 1, 1914, that his warships were present "for the sole purpose of affording protection to American and foreign lives and non-military American and foreign property" and warned all parties specifically to avoid or respect the valuable American-owned oil properties in the vicinity of Tampico. Less than a week later, in concert with British and German naval commanders in the area, Mayo repeated his warning, and on April 7 he sent Lieutenant Commander Ralph Earle, Commanding Officer of U.S.S. *Dolphin*, to the Federal headquarters to prevent the shelling of Constitutionalist forces that had taken up positions in the immediate vicinity of several American-owned oil storage tanks. Mayo later complained to General I. Morelos Zaragoza, Federal Commander at Tampico, after a shell from the Federal gunboat *Veracruz* hit a Standard Oil Company tank. The next day, April 9, Federal authorities briefly detained a U.S. naval officer and the *Dolphin's* whaleboat crew, and the "affair of honor" had begun. President Wilson may not have *intended* that Mayo act so vigorously to safeguard Standard Oil in Mexico, but he did nothing to prevent Mayo's presence there, and he wholeheartedly supported Mayo when the chips were down.[36]

Increasingly, American inland investment in foreign countries became more important than coastal trading posts. Thus, in 1910, while the Honduran government arranged for the sale of Honduran natural resources to American investors and negotiated a loan with J. P. Morgan, other Hondurans revolted. Commander George Cooper in the *Marietta* advised the Secretary of the Navy to authorize the use of naval and marine force to crush the revolution and protect the loan and monopolies. The revolt *was* crushed, with the aid of carefully deployed naval forces, but the commanders of these same warships were concurrently directed to *aid* revolutionaries in neighbouring Nicaragua! There an employee of the Pittsburgh-based United States–Nicaraguan Concession, a mining concern, was being installed in the presidency with considerable aid from U.S. naval forces and U.S. marines under Major Smedley Butler, all under the watchful direction of that firm's ex-legal counsel, Secretary of State Philander C. Knox.[37] Naval expeditions, such as were dispatched to Cuba, Honduras, Nicaragua, Haiti, and Santo Domingo between 1906 and 1915, became more and more elaborate, involving greater degrees of persuasion and greater use of punitive and occupation forces, generally U.S. Marines.

In 1915 Marines occupied Haiti. The next year Marine officers went before the House Naval Affairs Committee to defend appropriations for the occupation forces. Colonel L. W. T. Waller explained that Americans hoped to "develop the country" but that they would be unable to do so "unless there is the proper protection." The presence of the marines would be "the only insurance they have" until a Haitian gendarme could be trained. When Congressman Ernest Roberts of Massachusetts wanted to know why the Haitians were not being required to pay "the whole expense" of this training program, Major General George Barnett, Commandant of the Marine Corps, responded with remarkable frankness:

> ... the American Government is not entirely philanthropic in this matter ... they are doing this business in Haiti for some future gain to themselves too. They want order, and they have been paying a large sum for it already.*

When the marines left these lands in the 1920s and '30s, their withdrawal by no means constituted a basic change in the nature of American Caribbean

---

* Naval Affairs Comm., House of Representatives, *Hearings . . . on Estimates Submitted by the Secretary of the Navy, 1916*, 64th Cong., 1st Sess. [1916], II, 2266, 2153. Representative Roberts, it must be understood, was haggling over only the price of imposing and guaranteeing order, not the principle involved. Thus his response to Barnett's remarks was: "And is it cheaper to do it in that way?"

164   diplomacy, for the Trujillos, Batistas, and Somozas were trained and ready to provide better, and cheaper, protection for American capital. And U.S. sea power was never more than a hop, skip, and a jump away. Admiral Robert E. Coontz, chief of Naval Operations, spoke reassuringly on this theme to the National Association of Manufacturers in 1922:[38]

> Naval forces are maintained throughout the Caribbean Sea for the purpose of keeping down revolutions, protecting life, and protecting our commerce. Our trade could hardly exist throughout the West Indies, but for the protection given it by our Special Service Squadron. Our fruit trade throughout the West Indies is enormous. . . . If a revolution is brewing in the vicinity of [a] fruit plantation . . . our naval commander at Panama has only to dispatch a gunboat and the appearance of our flag is usually sufficient to relieve the situation.

Present-day statements of U.S. policy toward Latin America are generally more subtle than this; there are more vague expressions of regard for the "Free World" or "world order." But it is difficult to believe that policies that sent troops into Santo Domingo, overthrew the Guatemalan government, and trained the Bolivian junta's counterinsurgency forces are substantively different from those of the fin de siècle.*

Europe, the Mediterranean, the Near East, and Africa

Naval force was less frequently called for in the "Old World," and the deployment of U.S. naval forces in these waters is not the best guide to U.S.–European relations. Koreans, Samoans, Hondurans, and Haitians had no comparable naval forces and could be cowed by American sea power, but the same approach would not do for Italy, France, Germany, Britain, or Russia, or even for Spain, Austria-Hungary, or the Scandinavian countries.† Professional cutaway-and-top hat diplomats, armed with tariffs, reciprocal trade agreements and the like, wielded the "cutting edge" in Europe.

However, in many regions of the Mediterranean and the Near East, where power was diffused and political conditions often unstable, American naval

---

* Apparently the "Good Neighbor Policy" of F. D. R. had its imperial overtones too. Shortly after its annunciation, Roosevelt quietly ringed the island of Cuba with warships and eventually brought about the fall of the government of Grau San Martín. Williams, *Tragedy*, 174. Marine and naval landing parties continued to land on the island throughout the blockade to protect U.S. planters and merchants, but they were now logged ashore as personnel attending "social affairs," instead of being described as what they were—armed guards. (I am indebted to Professor Robert F. Smith for this information.)

Actually the shift to "good will" began in the 1920s with Secretary of State Charles Evans Hughes and President Herbert Hoover. See, for example, the editorials in *The Big "U"* [newspaper of the U.S.S. *Utah*], I, No. 10 (Jan. 5, 1929), 2, *passim.*

† U.S. sea power stood behind that of Britain through most of this period; it was about on a par with that of Germany, France, Russia, or Italy. Neither Spain, Austria-Hungary, nor any other European power had quite as much naval power in the years from 1845–1925 as did the U.S. But the "Monroe Doctrine" was somewhat reciprocal in this regard; due to the nature of European power balances, even the weakest European naval power usually could count on the support of a more formidable naval ally.

power appeared when it was needed to protect American business interests and missionaries. The American Navy was created, after all, to defend American shipping in the Mediterranean from Tripolitan privateers, and the concern for American commerce in this region continued. In 1849, for example, vessels of the U.S. Mediterranean Squadron were being dispatched to such ports as Tunis, Venice, Smyrna, Istanbul, Livorno ("Leghorn"), Tripoli, Haifa, Naples, and Alexandria to insure the safety of American citizens and commerce in those ports. In November 1862, while Civil War raged at home, Union warships sailed from port to port in the Eastern Mediterranean, their "paramount object" being that of "the efficient protection of our commerce and citizens who are engaged in commercial pursuits." And they continued to visit most of these ports, and many others, to the present day.

When Greeks and Turks met in bloody tugs of war, U.S. warships were right on hand. Admiral Edward Eberle, chief of Naval Operations in 1924, boasted that when "American interests in oil, tobacco, flour, and other commodi[ties] of everyday necessity" in the region "were jeopardized," the forerunners of the present-day Sixth Fleet steamed into view "to see that fair play and justice was [sic] accorded us. Our tobacco warehouses in Turkey and Greece, for example, contained hundreds of thousands of dollars worth of American-owned tobacco," but "invariably" the Navy's "presence had a most stabilizing influence."[39]

The Bolshevik Revolution appeared to some naval officers to present unusual opportunities for the American economic penetration of North and South Russia. From 1918 to 1924 officers such as Rear Admirals Newton McCully and Mark Bristol, Lieutenant Commander George M. Tisdale, and McCully's aide, an ensign with the appropriate name of Jay Gould, busied themselves in preparing recommended steamer routes for U.S. shipping, dispatching information on resources and market potentials, providing port officers in the White and Black Seas, and aiding the agents of American Car, Singer Sewing Machine, and International Harvester. Bristol and Tisdale did argue for material support to the White armies in South Russia; they had no love for the Bolsheviks. But they justified their anti-Red argument by pointing out that a non-Bolshevik South Russia might want to use American threshing machines, railroad cars, and dollars.[40]

The U.S. naval presence in African waters was also less formidable than it was in Asian or Latin American waters. But it served its purpose, for American economic interests in Africa were less extensive than in Asia or Latin America. A few examples illustrate that U.S. warships in African waters were performing functions virtually identical to those operating elsewhere. A naval counterpart in Africa of Truxton at Tarawa or Rodgers in Korea was Commander William Pearson in U.S.S. *Dale*. In 1851, at the bequest of the State Department, Pearson was sent to the island of Johanna, one of the Comorros, in the Mozambique Channel, off the east coast of Africa. Johanna's ruler, King Selim, had imprisoned the captain of an American whaler for 9 days on a misdemeanor.

166 Upon his release, the enraged skipper demanded retribution, and Pearson's visit was an accommodating home government's response. After shelling Johanna's main port, Pearson compelled Selim to pay 30 bullocks and one thousand dollars to the local U.S. consul and to sign a "most favored nation" executive agreement, which opened the island to American trade on the best of terms. This agreement stipulated, among other things, that, "in the event of disputes arising between the Natives of this Island and any American citizen, the matter is to be referred to the U.S. Government, which will act as it may judge proper. . . ." In 1851 Commander Andrew Foote in the *Perry* met with local potentates in West Africa "to encourage trade with the American merchants in gums, copper, and the products of the country. . . ." Similarly, in 1873 the visit of the U.S.S. *Yantic* to Zanzibar, off the east coast of Africa, was designed to persuade the natives to experience the benefits of trade with American merchants. The celebrated world-wide cruise of Commodore Robert Shufeldt from 1879 to 1882 was primarily designed to secure favorable trade agreements with African and Asian potentates, and it was remarkably successful. But it was only the most spectacular example of the sort of thing that many other officers were now and then called upon to do. Nearly a decade after Shufeldt had met with the Sultan of Zanzibar, Commander Bowman McCalla in a well-named man-of-war, U.S.S. *Enterprise*, showed the flag there again to encourage a promising cotton trade that was being captured by German and Italian entrepreneurs. And a decade later the *Army and Navy Journal's* Liberian correspondent begged the Navy Department to "allow one of its vessels on the Atlantic Station to call" once every several months to check the lead that Germany was building up "in the commercial race in Liberia."

Samuel P. Huntington has claimed that U.S. businessmen "made no effort to utilize the military for its own purposes" in these years;[41] but it is not clear how he hoped to sustain this claim. It is off the mark, to say the least, as a description of the relations of many a businessman with the Navy.*

The U.S. Navy in War and Peace : Some Observations

With every-day duties such as those just described, it's not surprising that many officers viewed Germany as America's most dangerous commercial enemy. Confrontations with German naval forces at Apia, Samoa, in 1889, Manila Bay in 1898, and Venezuela in 1903 accented this rivalry. The first serious, sustained, and formal efforts by U.S. naval leaders to design naval war plans, originating in the Bureau of Navigation's Office of Naval Intelligence in the early 1880s, further developed at the Naval War College after 1885, and perfected within the Navy's General Board after the turn of the century, included plans for war with Great Britain, Japan, and other naval powers but

* On the other hand, Mira Wilkins has argued that the typical U.S. overseas company was "on its own" in the nineteenth and early twentieth century (*Emergence of Multinational Enterprise*, 37), and I don't intend to dispute her. Policymakers were generally reluctant to apply force, preferring non-military solutions to diplomatic problems. But this is not to say that businessmen did not *seek* naval support; they did.

focused most attention on the growing German–U.S. naval and commercial **167**
rivalry, In 1913 the Navy General Board formally assembled the "Black War
Plan" based on theoretical war at sea with Germany, a war which they conceived of as having emerged from a struggle over commercial trading rights
and routes.* All of which leads us to a consideration of World War I.

Thus far I have said little of the two great wars between 1845 and 1925—the
Civil War and World War I. Since enormous amounts of naval force were used
in both, they deserve consideration. The Civil War, from the Navy's point of
view, should be viewed in large measure as a struggle to protect the commerce
of those loyal to the Federal Government (thus the destruction of the C.S.S.
Alabama by the U.S.S. *Kearsarge* and the variety of measures taken to insure the
safety of Union shipping), to proscribe or destroy the commerce of those who
seceded from the Federal Government (thus the "Anaconda" blockade of
Confederate ports), and to deny the enemy the opportunity to achieve either
objective himself.[42] Naval power was used to support Union ground forces
and to deprive the rebels of seaborne means of relief, supply, or communication,
to be sure. But efforts taken to protect the Union's wheat and to blockade the
Confederacy's cotton were also important.

Similarly the use of naval force in World War I was predicated on the fact
that the U.S. economy would suffer greatly from a cessation of trade with the
Allies. To Ernest May the rediscovery of the administration's attitude toward
the submarine neatly disposes of the unflattering economic "causes" for war
invoked by the Nye Committee's investigation of the munition and financial
magnates. But what is rarely mentioned is the fact that the submarine need
not have offended anyone's sensibilities if Wilson, as Thomas Jefferson (whom
Wilson's party's convention invoked in 1916) had done over a century before,
been willing to withdraw American goods and shipping from the seas. Had
Wilson *really* been "too proud" to fight, this alternative always remained
available. Daniel M. Smith is surely correct in concluding that the United
States went to war in defense of her "strategic interests," but what must be
made very clear is that the most strategically vital of all interests in Uncle Sam's

---

* See, for example, LCDR Charles Cullen, "From the *Kriegsacademie* to the Naval War
College," *Naval War College Review* (Jan. 1970), 6–18; and Warner Schilling, "Admirals
and American Foreign Policy, 1913–1919," Unpublished Ph.D. dissertation, Yale University,
1953.
Navy Secretary Benjamin F. Tracy's "secret strategy board" of 1890–91 and the 1898
Naval War Board were short-range projects, though they yielded interesting results. See
for example, Kenneth Bourne and Carl Boyd, "Captain Mahan's 'War' with Great
Britain," *PUSNI*, XCIV (1968), 71–78. More useful were the plans for a naval assault on
Spanish forces at Manila Bay, drawn up by the O.N.I.'s Lieutenant William Wirt Kimball
and Lieutenant Commander Richard Wainwright, among others. These were first brought
to light by William Braisted in 1958 in his *The U.S. Navy in the Pacific, 1897–1909*, 21–
23, and discussed again in 1966 by John A. S. Grenville and George B. Young in their
Politics, Strategy, and American Diplomacy: Studies in Foreign Policy, 1873–1917. Cf. Grenville,
"American Naval Preparations for War with Spain, 1896–1898," *Journal of American
Studies*, II (April 1968), 40–48; Ronald Spector, "Who planned the Attack on Manila Bay?"
Mid-America, LIII (1971), 94–102.

168 nest was the economy. Woodrow Wilson would never had to defy German "aggression," defend American "prestige and honor," or assume the burden of reestablishing a world "balance of power" had it not been for the intimate relationship between American prosperity and allied military fortunes.[43]

Most accounts of American diplomacy and naval history, in dealing with the period from 1850 to 1925, focus unnaturally on the Civil War, the Spanish–American War, and World War I. Obviously something must be said (and has been, *ad nauseam*) of these three periods of warfare. But in saying more of these exceptional moments, when the normal, peaceful diplomatic channels were disrupted and inadequate, the historian creates a false impression of the nature of American diplomacy and of the Navy's mission in that diplomacy, in these years. To read Ernest May's analysis of the diplomacy of these years, for example,[44] one would never know that, in acting to provide security for American business interests abroad, the Navy came into hostile contact with armed forces of foreign states on at least 44 different occasions between 1865 and 1927. And Milton Offutt, who came up with this figure in 1928, was not counting the instances when force was merely threatened.[45] If one were to add such data to the list of times that foreign powers made the grievous error of attempting to defend their sovereignty, the rate of force-deployment per year would be considerably higher. Instead of repeatedly attempting to "revise" one another's interpretations of the wars with Spain, and the Central Powers, students of American diplomacy might more fruitfully explore and analyze the assumptions inherent in such decisions as the one that sent three warships to Chinkiang in 1905 to protect the property of Standard Oil. They might also analyze the implications in Lieutenant Alexander Habersham's remark in 1857 when, discussing U.S. naval diplomacy in Japanese waters, he wrote: "The only way we ever got along there was to do what we wished to without asking questions and then refer [the Japanese] to the treaty for our authority."[46]

Historians might inquire into such restrictions on national sovereignty as the disarming of (removing the firing pins from) the lone Chinese cruiser at Taku Bar, port of entry for Tientsin, during the Boxer rebellion, inasmuch as the cruiser was loyal to the Empress.[47] They might read and reflect on William Braisted's account of the three-power struggle over the control of Samoan naval bases in 1898, when Rear Admiral Albert Kautz shelled the popular Samoan forces who were driving the British- and U.S.-supported claimant to the Samoan throne quite literally into the sea.[48]

Or they might consider the significance of the use of naval force on the Mosquito Coast in 1907. When fighting broke out early in that year between Honduran and Nicaraguan forces, Commander William Fullam was ordered to land several detachments of sailors from the *Marietta* to prevent the firing of several coastal towns in which U.S. and British "legitimate business interests"*

---

* Virtually all U.S. business interests that Washington was asked to aid were referred to as "legitimate." But what may be legitimate to statesmen in Washington may appear altogether illegitimate in a foreign capital. I have said little here of the means employed

were established. After having warned the two commanding generals not to conduct hostile operations in the vicinity of these towns, Fullam proudly informed the Secretary of the Navy that both commandants had "freely admitted the truth of the argument that these constant wars would permanently paralyze all business in this part of the world if the Republics were permitted to exercise the full rights of belligerents under the ordinary provisions of International Law." And what was more, the opposing Generals had not only admitted this, but they had *accepted* "a very decided limitation on their rights as belligerents" and a corresponding extension of "neutral" rights, amounting to the protection of all "business interest." Fullam concluded his report with the remark: "Each side at present seeks to prove its superior liberality in this respect, and to claim credit for such a humane motive!"[49] And he could well have afforded to add the touch of sarcasm one detects in these final words, for what he had managed to do was to oversee the physical imposition of an abridgement of the sovereignty of two American nations, on behalf of "legitimate business interests." The forces of Nicaraguan General Juan Estrada were severely handicapped by this bar on hostilities in the vicinity of commercial ports, where the Honduran troops were quartered.[50] Hence it was not correct to say, as Fullam said, that the United States was "neutral." True neutrality simply was never considered. Nor was it considered in China in 1923, when Lieutenant Leland P. Lovette in the *Pampanga* compelled General Guai Bong Ping and his adversary to suspend their military operations in the vicinity of Wuchow when hostilities threatened the security of American-owned property.

John Braeman, while recently criticizing those who tend to illuminate the economic bases of American foreign policy in the years under consideration, asked: "Should we *not* want overseas trade? Should the U.S. Government *not* protect its citizens abroad?"[51] Clearly these questions get us nowhere, for even if we answer as Professor Braeman intends us to, we must still deal with ethical questions: In the capturing of markets and sources of raw materials, are there any acts which can be regarded as unconscionable or unjustifiable? In the "protection of American citizens" abroad, how far may one go before one violates the rights of other sovereign states? *These* questions deserve at least as much consideration as those of Professor Braeman.

William A. Williams has suggested that there is often a wide breach between what he calls "the actuality" and "the rhetoric" of American diplomacy. The record of naval diplomacy seems to confirm such a breach. The public statements of U.S. diplomats and politicians are often brimming with generous intentions and disinterested concern, but words and deeds are different animals. Thus while American politicians and statesmen expressed their sympathy and interest in the Latin American wars of liberation in the early nineteenth century,

by merchants in securing leases or franchises in foreign lands, a subject which would make an interesting study in itself. An admirable departure for such a study is Mira Wilkins' *The Emergence of Multinational Enterprise: American Business Abroad from the Colonial Period to 1914* (Cambridge, Mass., 1970).

170   American naval officers on Latin American stations concerned themselves solely in breaking the Patriot paper blockade of Spanish Peru, opening the ports of new Republics, carrying American merchants from one Spanish-held port to another, and allowing them to set up displays of their ginghams and silks for Spanish buyers in the cabin of the commanding officer! As the Chilean Patriot ambassador to the court of St. James put it, the United States sent its "merchant ships to our ports as [it] would send them to an uninhabited coast, threatening us with [its] warships as [it] would the blacks of Senegal." In the 1830s the Navy did it again, this time protecting American trade with Mexico from cruisers of the Texas Navy!

Similarly, while American politicians hailed the Greek struggle for independence, officers such as Admiral David Farragut coolly rebuffed Greek patriots. Naval vessels throughout the 1850s acted as counterrevolutionaries in the Caribbean and Central America. Commander Henry Clay Taylor rebuffed overtures from natives seeking to oust Spain from the Caroline Islands in 1890. "I said to all around me that the United States was a friend of Spain and would so remain. . . ." And several years later, when U.S.S. *Maine* stood in to Havana harbor and exchanged honors with Spanish authorities, Cuban patriot-rebels were enraged. Commander Duncan Ingraham did order an Austrian warship to release one of Louis Kossuth's Hungarian patriot colleagues in 1853, but this individual had become a "first paper" American and had gone to Smyrna "for the purpose," in Commander Ingraham's words, "of establishing himself in business." Thus when he was seized by Austrian naval authorities, Commander Ingraham's assistance was comparable to that afforded all American businessmen abroad. And if Ingraham secretly *was* motivated by a concern for the quest for Hungarian independence, Commodore Matthew C. Perry, who felt no sympathy with "the cause of Hungarian liberty (alias socialism & Red republicanism)," was probably more typical of the naval aristocracy.[52]

Perhaps the best example of this phenomenon of a two-faced America, of rhetoric and reality, was the case of Samoa. And since it is also a good illustration of the closeness of naval–business liaison in these years, it will require a somewhat detailed analysis.

Marilyn Blatt Young has recently maintained that in the decade after the close of the Civil War the close cooperation between businessmen, foreign-policy-makers, and naval officers "had yet to evolve," and she offers, as proof of this contention, the view of Charles Beard that the expedition of Commander Richard Meade to Samoa in 1872 was undertaken on Meade's own "blind" initiative "without any authority from his government, entirely on his own motion."[53]

This is far off the mark. American citizens had long sought Samoa as a coaling station and a source of raw materials. By 1870 there were over 50 U.S. citizens living in Samoa, most of them traders, in addition to a U.S. Commercial Agent at Apia and a Vice-Commerical Agent at Pago Pago. These agents constantly begged the State Department to send a U.S. warship, and insisted that independent Samoa was "unmistakeably" ready to be granted "a pure   **171** republican" form of government by the Great American Republic. In 1871 William Webb, the great shipping entrepreneur, sent ex-merchant skipper Edgar Wakeman to Honolulu with orders to arrange the lease of Samoan port facilities and the purchase of any attractive Samoan plantation lands. Webb and a number of other investors had created the Great American Land and Steam Company, a San Francisco-based corporation, in hopes of capturing a monopoly of what they imagined would be a great deal of U.S.–Australian shipping, and they regarded the lease of Samoan port facilities as essential to their operation.

Wakeman quickly made contact with Navy and State officers in Honolulu, and in July, 1871, he was taken to Samoa on U.S.S. *Nevada*, "in pursuance with [Webb's] instructions." His report to Webb in September of that year was highly enthusiastic; Pago Pago was a fine coaling station, and Samoa was a planter's paradise.

Upon his return to Honolulu, Wakeman accompanied Rear Admiral John Winslow, commander of U.S. Naval Forces on the South Pacific Station, and Commander Richard Meade, 3rd, commanding officer of U.S.S. *Narragansett*, to the office of the Resident U.S. Minister to Hawaii, Henry Pierce. Pierce agreed to provide a formal request to Winslow and Meade for the dispatch of Meade the following January to Samoa for the purpose of securing a treaty with Samoan authorities that would provide for exclusive U.S. control of Pago Pago and something short of a U.S. protectorate for the entire island chain.

On January 19, 1872, Pierce formally requested that Meade visit Samoa. "In view of the future domination of the U.S. States [sic] in the N. & S. Pacific Oceans," Pierce wrote, "it is very important that the Navigator [Samoan] Islands should be under American control, ruling through native authorities." Any treaty Meade might arrange "would receive, no doubt, the approval of our government," but "if otherwise, time would [have been] gained by such a treaty." Pierce reminded Meade that although the treaty Commander Thomas ap Catesby Jones had arranged with the Hawaiian authorities in 1826 never won Senate approval, it gave the U.S. a "binding" claim until an acceptable treaty was negotiated in 1849.[54]

The rhetoric and the reality of this Samoan adventure were worlds apart. Wakeman gave Commander Richard Meade two very different letters for transmittal to officials in Samoa. One was addressed to a certain Reverend Powell, "the Missionary," who "almost entirely governed" the Pago-Pago natives. This one was obviously intended for public consumption. It guaranteed that the Samoan "wilderness" would be "made to blossom like a Rose" in a few years, and promised that "a new order of things" would "shine upon your good people," who were soon to "experience from the hands of the American People a liberality that will excell that of any other people in the world."

The other letter was addressed to the British Consul at Apia and was clearly

172 intended for the eyes of island potentates alone. Therein Wakeman affected that his company hoped to organize the island "on the Great American Principal [sic] of Republicanism," but he must have been thinking of his company's principal, as he went to special pains to disarm that principle of "Republicanism" of all substance. The Spectre of the Paris Commune must have troubled such men as Wakeman and the British Consul, Mr. Williams, for Wakeman's letter continued: "Just as all Europe is on the Eve of throwing Kings & Imperialism to the dogs don't allow any one at your point to indulge in any such absurd notion. You have great power with the Chiefs and you must tell them that they must unite their future with the U.S. Government at Washington. . . ." Meade's treaty was recommended to the Senate by President U. S. Grant, and though it failed to receive approval in 1872, some six years later a Samoan Chief left for Washington to sign a treaty with the Great American People whose "liberality" could make the wilderness blossom with coffee, cotton, sugar, "and many other valuable articles of commerce," without disturbing Kings & Imperialism.[55]

*   *   *

American economic interests appear to have dominated U.S. diplomacy in the Golden Age of the Annapolites, a judgment that becomes particularly defensible when rendered in such a case as I have been presenting, involving evidence drawn solely from the record of U.S. naval operating forces. This concern with economic interests throughout the world was not something that developed when America passed, in Mr. McGeorge Bundy's phrase, "from Innocence to Engagement." America was always "engaged." The offer of naval forces abroad was as old as the U.S. Navy itself. If the tempo increased somewhat over the years, the cause for this increase lay in the increased tempo of American economic "engagement" abroad—*not* in any vague but abrupt "emergence of America as a world power." America's emergence as a world power was a steady, dynamic affair; the warship only policed the process.

Naval commanders were capable of initiating action, but they generally operated in response to appeals for aid from American citizens abroad, and these appeals generally were channeled through U.S. consulates or ministries. Naval officers occasionally made the first contact with Americans abroad who feared for their property rights or lives. Some regions in Africa, Southeast Asia, and Polynesia were, for many years, without adequate U.S. diplomatic representation. In these regions the warship constituted a kind of floating embassy. Usually Navy and State collaborated in the dispatching of warships to "hot spots." As Secretary of State William Seward put it in 1867, "There is no subordination of the ministers to the commander of a squadron, and no subordination of the commander of the Squadron to a minister." Cooperation was stressed.[56]

But this was a difficult balance to maintain, and now and then the Navy

simply ignored the local State Department representatives. Thus Commodores
John Aulick and M. C. Perry regarded Humphrey Marshall, U.S. Commissioner
to China in the early 1850s, and other diplomats in the Far East as "assistants
to the naval diplomatists," and longed to leave Marshall, China, and the Taiping
Rebellion for Japan, "where as yet there are no American merchants or diplomatic agents."[57]

If naval officers believed they had prior claim to the disposition of an incident,
if they felt themselves more capable of handling the problem than the local
State Department authorities, or if they simply disapproved of the local U.S.
consul or commercial agent, then they might be inclined to take matters into
their own hands. Many officers would take to heart Assistant Navy Secretary
Theodore Roosevelt's curious remark to the Naval War College in 1897: "The
diplomat is the servant, not the master, of the soldier."

For example, State and Navy Department authorities do not appear to have
made the U.S. Consul at Bluefields, Thomas Moffat, altogether privy to their
plans to support a Diaz–Estrada revolution in Nicaragua in 1909. Moffat told
a Senate investigating committee of his alarm at the prompting and encouragement naval officers had offered the revolutionaries.

But Moffat appears to have been left out of the picture by his own department.
A more striking case of naval side-stepping of consular authority was that of
the Triunfo affair. In 1868 Joseph H. Dulles, President of the Triunfo Silver
Mining and Commercial Company, a Philadelphia-based firm, asked Rear
Admiral Thomas Turner, Commander of the North Pacific Squadron, to
watch over the company's valuable silver mine near La Paz, Mexico. Several
of the investors, Dulles explained, were "your personal friends." When Turner
gave up command of the squadron, he passed the Dulles letter on to his relief,
Rear Admiral Thomas T. Craven, and asked Craven to take a special interest
in the safety of the mine and to advise him personally of measures taken to
safeguard the mine from "a rude people like those in Mexico." Several years
later, in 1874, the mine's manager, angered by some of the policies of local
Mexican officials, armed his workers, contacted naval authorities, and persuaded
Captain W. W. Queen in the *Saranac* to negotiate directly with Mexican
authorities. The U.S. consul at La Paz was outraged that Captain Queen
"seemed to have forgotten his existence," and "entirely ignored his presence."
But it is more likely that Queen simply assumed that the protection of the mine
was fundamentally a naval matter with which the U.S. consul need not overly
concern himself.[58]

Moreover, communications were so poor prior to World War I that individual commanders often found themselves virtually on their own for days at
a time. For example, Commander George Dewey considered the two-month
communications lag with Washington in 1875 as sufficient cause for his assumption of the initiative in his own effort to protect the Triunfo mine. Similarly,
in 1914 Clarence Miller, U.S. Consul at Tampico, Mexico, disagreed with Rear
Admiral Henry Mayo's handling of the *Dolphin* whaleboat incident and

174 disapproved of Mayo's blustering demands, but he was forced to communicate with the State Department on Mayo's radio set. Even when the U.S. consulate was readily available, as had been the case with the Triunfo mine incidents, or when time permitted the receipt of specific instructions from Washington, the naval aristocracy generally had its own way. Secretaries of State such as Frederick Frelinghuysen, Walter Gresham, John Hay, and Philander Knox, as well as most members of the diplomatic corps itself, generally considered the intelligence reports of naval officers on the scene to be "more reliable" than those of "green" consuls and frequently consulted Navy Department files. "I . . . leave it . . . entirely to your discretion, without any suggestion of mine," the U.S. Minister at Vienna, J. Glancy Jones, put it to the Mediterranean Squadron Commander Commodore E. A. F. LaVallette, "knowing that your long experience and thorough knowledge will prompt you to do what is right and proper [at Trieste]."[59]

American policymakers rarely hazarded the use of naval force carelessly or willfully. To men like Grover Cleveland, William Howard Taft, Woodrow Wilson, and Calvin Coolidge the use of bluejackets or marines indicated a failure of the preferred, non-military management of a politico–economic situation. Moreover, naval officers generally made considerable efforts to keep their actions within the bounds of the international law of their day, as it was perceived by themselves, their Washington colleagues, and their Western counterparts. But whether hazarded with propriety or no, the mere presence of men-of-war was intimidating. Warships were more than guns and marines to foreign potentates. They represented *more* ships, *more* guns, and *more* marines. The heads of foreign states realized that the appearance of a warship of the Mighty Republic to the north or east meant business—Uncle Sam's business— and that further haggling with a local U.S. consul now involved greater risks. Ernest May has recently claimed that there was "very little connection between foreign affairs and naval policy" in the late nineteenth century. Unless May were to define his terms very narrowly, I would not be inclined to agree with him.

Communication facilities improved after World War I, and by 1925, with the implementation of the Diplomatic and Consular Act of May 24, 1924, the independent decision-making powers of naval officers were largely displaced by standing orders referring all non-emergency problems to Washington for disposition.[60] The tactical ground rules were altered, but not the overall strategic objectives. In 1930, as in 1830, the Navy worked closely with American businessmen abroad.

Some Ancestors of the Military-Industrial Complex

Thus far we have described the "public" record of the relationship between the Navy and business. But there is a "private" side to this story as well. Occasionally naval officers who saw an opportunity to "pick up a buck on the side," and who were willing to be tainted by a little material gain, left a record of their transactions. In the early nineteenth century naval commanders frequently contracted with merchants from many countries to carry their bullion from place to place for a 3% fee. These floating banks could also become display counters, as in the case of U.S.S. *Dolphin*, when her Commanding Officer, Lieutenant David Conner, invited Yankee merchant Eliphalet Smith to come abroad, sail from port to port, and exhibit his ginghams and silks to prospective buyers in the captain's cabin. Conner's aid to American business with this gesture apparently struck the Secretary of the Navy as a bit too personal and suspicious, for he was reprimanded for "prostituting" his warship "to purposes of private trade and traffic." Navy Purser Rodman Price and his senior Commodore Thomas ap Catesby Jones, made fortunes speculating in gold dust and San Francisco real estate, disposing of naval surplus, and misusing naval funds and material while stationed off California during the gold-rush years. Officers sometimes smuggled dutiable goods into the country. Others left their speculative capital abroad. Lieutenant George Henry Preble bought land "dog cheap" in the Bonin Islands along with Commodore Perry and several other officers when Perry's expedition visited Iwo and Chici Jima in 1854. Lieutenant Commander Thomas H. Stevens, II, acquired title to a small American Honduras Company banana plantation in 1890, and others bought mining properties in Alaska and elsewhere.[61] It would be interesting to know how widespread this practice of land speculation was among naval officers, for if Price, Preble, and Stevens were at all typical, one would then be expected to ask whether the actions naval officers took in protecting "American interests" in distant ports were altogether disinterested.

Since many officers were financially unable to engage in any large-scale ventures on their own, the most common private arrangements with the world of business were those in which a naval officer accepted a position as an agent of a firm. In the Bonin Islands enterprise noted above, Commodore Perry also bought some land for the New York shipping firm of Howland & Aspinwall, apparently as their agent. Twelve years later ex-Captain Gustavus Vasa Fox accepted a permanent position with this same firm at a salary of $10,000 per year plus expenses.[62] Commodore Robert Shufeldt was offered a position as "Commodore of the Fleet" of Russell Sage's Pacific Mail Steamship Company in 1868 at a salary of four thousand per year. Shufeldt's leadership abilities were needed, Sage told Navy Secretary George Robeson, to reorganize the firm, an act which would enhance its "commercial value and national importance." When Robeson declined to grant Shufeldt the necessary year's leave of absence, Shufeldt gave the names of a number of other officers who he was sure would help the firm become "the standard bearer of our commercial supremacy in the East" to Sage's managing director, Rufus Hatch. Lieutenant Z. L. Tanner's name may have been one, for he commanded the Pacific Mail S.S. *City of Pekin* in 1877. In 1879 Captain John Grimes Walker took a position with the C. B. & Q. railroad, which served him in good stead when he later was named Chief of the Bureau of Navigation. Several years later the Union Iron Works

176   of San Francisco, a firm interested in Asian mines and sales, authorized Shufeldt to act on its behalf during that officer's round-the-world cruise, and in 1883 Shufeldt and Walter Townsend, another Union Iron Works' agent, negotiated a trade agreement with Korean authorities for their San Francisco employers.[63] Two years later Ensign George Foulk, while chargé d'affaires at Seoul, closed a pearl-fishing agreement with the Korean government for the American Trading Company and helped that company land contracts for a coastal vessel, a palace electric-power plant, and a water-powered mill. By 1889 Foulk was out of the Navy, living in Tokyo as the American Trading Company's Asiatic agent.[64]

With or without government sanction, naval officers were widely employed by shipping, ordnance, munitions, and armor industries. In 1848 Commodore M. C. Perry was named General Superintendent of Mail Steamers and assigned the duty of supervising the construction of the new government-subsidized lines. According to Captain Percival Drayton, Captain John Rodgers was accorded numerous favors by the "iron interest" for having "assisted" these interests "in making money."[65] In 1874, while on active duty, Lieutenant William Folger went to work for the Gatling Gun Company in Fitchburg, Massachusetts. Twelve years later he became the part-time employee of another Fitchburg ordnance firm, the Simonds Rolling Machine Company. With this experience behind him, Navy Secretary Benjamin Franklin Tracy elevated him in 1890 to the office of Chief of the Bureau of Ordnance, where he might oversee the arming of the "new Navy." Three years later Folger left the Bureau of Ordnance, but, while still in the Service, he accepted a position with the American Projectile Company of Lynn, Massachusetts. Ensign Ira N. Hollis was detailed as professor of marine engineering at Union College, Schenectady, in 1883. From there he went to a naval advisory board to plan the "new Navy's" white squadron, and from 1887 to 1890 he was assigned to the Union Iron Works to supervise the construction of the *Charleston*. In the mid-1880s Lieutenant Commander F. M. Barber became the exclusive agent for the French armor firm, Schneider-Creusot, in the United States, with the approval of the Navy Department. In 1883 Lieutenant William Jaques was named secretary to the Naval Gun-Foundry Board and was sent to Great Britain to study Sir Joseph Whitworth's hydraulic forging press. He became Whitworth's exclusive agent in the U.S. Upon his return to the States Jaques was sent to the Bethlehem Iron Company to supervise the construction of a forging plant; eventually he left the Navy and went to work for Bethlehem. Concurrently, Commander Robley Evans worked four months in Pittsburgh testing structural steel for the B. & O. Railroad. Later he and Commander Caspar Goodrich headed two papermill plants belonging to Navy Secretary William Whitney's company! Lieutenant C. A. Stone was sent to the Carnegie Steel Corporation in 1891 by Secretary Tracy where he served as Carnegie's "ordnance officer" for two years while on leave from the Navy. When he retired in 1893 for physical disabilities, he stayed on at Pittsburgh with Carnegie. Lieutenant John Meigs was retired

for color-blindness in 1891. He went to work for Bethlehem Steel, as an ord-   **177**
nance engineer and became a "merchant of death," selling ordnance abroad.*
J. W. Powell rose to the presidency of the Fore River Shipyard after his naval
career ended. During World War I he managed five Bethlehem shipyards and
served as president of the Emergency Shipbuilding Corporation. Charles
Schwab, first president of U.S. Steel and later president of Bethlehem Steel,
"liked to employ Naval Academy graduates, for they carried out his order with
implicit attention to the spirit and the letter." When Navy Secretary John Davis
Long credited the Navy's high standards for domestic steel fixed by the Department in 1883 with the "phenomenal growth" of the steel industry in the late
nineteenth century, he omitted to note that the Navy's role in this industrial
"take-off" was highly personal. Pittsburgh met the Navy's standards because
the Navy's top ordnance experts *recommended* high-priced contracts in order to
spur the creation of basic forgings for structural tests and thus saw the Steel
City through.[66]

Other ex-naval officers became prominent figures in the business world.
Robert Thompson, for many years a leader in copper and nickel smelting and
long head of the Navy League, was one. Lewis Nixon, who resigned in 1891
to join Wm. Cramps & Sons and helped to construct the battleships of the
"new Navy," was another. In 1895 Nixon started his own firm, the Crescent
Shipyard at Elizabeth, New Jersey, where he built 100 vessels in six years.
Still another prominent Academy graduate was Homer Ferguson who became
president of the Newport News Shipbuilding Company and president of the
U.S. Chamber of Commerce in 1922. Willard Brownson became director of
International Nickel upon retirement. Francis T. Bowles became president of
the Fore River Shipbuilding Company shortly after leaving his bureau post as
Chief of Construction and Repair. James Russell Soley, long a professor of
International Law at the Naval Academy and Naval War College, left the
service in 1892 to join the law firm (Coudert Brothers) of ex-Navy Secretary
Tracy, ex-President Benjamin Harrison, and New York "boss" Thomas Platt.
Lieutenant Alexander Habersham, assigned, as Preble had been, to a warship
in Japanese waters in the 1850s, had more faith than Preble in the future of trade
with the Orient. He resigned in 1860 to establish a trading company in Baltimore, with branches in Japan, and became a leading importer of Oriental
goods. Similarly, Lieutenant Zachariah Nixon took leave from the Navy to
command the merchantman *Warrior*, and four years later, still on leave,
established himself in Lima, Peru, as head of Nixon and McCall, a shipping
firm. Rear Admiral Colby Chester was sent to the Ottoman Empire in the early
twentieth century, where he became enthusiastic about the possibilities for
American businessmen in that part of the globe. He and his son, ex-Lieutenant

---

* A fascinating example of the liaison between naval officers and their businessmen allies
in these years is the case of naval support to Bethlehem Steel efforts to sell warships to China
in the early twentieth century. See William Braisted, "China, the U.S. Navy, and the
Bethlehem Steel Company," *Business History Review*, XLII (May 1968), 50–66.

178 Arthur Chester, later organized the Ottoman-American Development Company and lobbied with some success for Turkish contracts.

In short, it is clear that the business transactions of many naval officers with industry and commerce were "wide, important, and varied."[67] Something that is less clear is whether these transactions caused members of the naval aristocracy to compromise their public positions of trust. Since officers assigned to industrial plants saw themselves as defenders of the national interest, they were often very demanding inspectors of the armor plate, cannon, and shells produced—at least as long as they remained in the Service. In any event, the interrelationship of the Navy and the American economy, similar to what some are now calling the "military-industrial complex," was central to the Navy's mission in the Golden Age of the Annapolites.

Chapter 4

1. Beard, *The Idea of National Interest: An Analytical Study in American Foreign Policy* (New York, 1934), 106. See also Ernest May, "Emergence to World Power," in *Reconstruction of American History*, ed. John Higham (New York, 1962), 180–196; Fletcher Pratt, *The Compact History of the U.S. Navy* (N.Y., 1951); Dudley Knox, *A History of the United States Navy* (N.Y., 1936); McGeorge Bundy, "Foreign Policy: From Innocence to Engagement," in *Paths of American Thought*, ed. Arthur M. Schlesinger, Jr., and Morton White (Boston, 1963), 293–308; Armin Rappaport, *The Navy League of the United States* (Detroit, 1962); and Walter LaFeber, *The New Empire: An Interpretation of American Expansion* (Ithaca, N.Y., 1963). The "peaceful traders" and "murderous . . . natives" citation is from Samuel E. Morison, "*Old Bruin*": *Commodore Matthew Calbraith Perry* . . . (Boston, 1967), 262. Cf. Morison, *Bruin*, 429.

2. Beard, *Idea of National Interest*, 60ff.; *The Navy: Defense or Portent?* (New York, 1932).

3. Dickerson to Jones, circa 1837, cited in W. P. Strauss, "Preparing the Wilkes Expedition: A Study in Disorganization," *Pacific Historical Review*, XXVIII (1959), 223; Graham to Herndon, Feb. 15, 1851,

Papers of Graham, ed. Hamilton, IV, 35–36; 33rd Cong., 1st Sess., House of Representatives, Exec. Doc. No. 53, *Exploration of the Valley of the Amazon . . . by W. R. L. Herndon and Lardner Gibbon, Lts., U.S. Navy* (2 vols., Wash., 1854), I, 20, 22; Johnson, *Rodgers*, 109; Habersham, *The North Pacific Surveying and Exploring Expedition* (N.Y., 1857), 507; Fox to Davis, 2 October 1862, *Confidential Correspondence of Gustavus Vasa Fox, Assistant Secretary of the Navy*, ed. Robert Thompson (N.Y., 1918), II, 68–69; Mills, *Power Elite*, 181. See also Article 1536 of the *Revised U.S. Statutes* (1875) for a description of the duties of naval vessels toward distressed navigators, and the chapter on the late nineteenth century in (Captain) Dudley Knox, *History of the U.S. Navy* (New York, 1936). Cf. Edward Towle, "Science, Commerce, and the Navy on the Seafaring Frontier: The Role of Lt. Matthew Fontaine Maury and the U.S. Naval Hydrographic Office in Naval Exploration, Commercial Expansion, and Oceanography before the Civil War," unpub. Ph.D. dissertation, Univ. of Rochester, 1966.

I make no claim that this account of the Navy in American diplomacy from the 1840s to the 1920s is in any sense exhaustive. A definite study would, for example, make more complete and detailed use of the naval sources in the National Archives than I have. My own interest in the naval officer lies primarily in matters often unrelated to most of those records. But a healthy sampling of Archival materials, heavily supplemented with data obtained from a variety of other sources, has persuaded me to believe that this account is representative.

4. Kelley, *Our Navy* (New York, 1897), 9. Cf. Harold & Margaret Sprout, *The Rise of American Naval Power, 1776–1918* (Princeton, 1946), *passim*; and Robert Seager, III, "Ten Years Before Mahan: The Unofficial Case for the New Navy, 1880–1890," *Mississippi Valley Historical Review*, XL (Dec. 1953), 497ff; Albert C. Stillson, "The Development and Maintenance of the American Naval Establishment, 1901–1909," unpublished Ph.D. dissertation, Columbia, 1959, 17–20.

5. Goodrich, *PUSNI*, XXII (1896), 553; Mahan to "Mr. Fitz-Hugh," March 9, 1912, Folder 18, Box 209, N.H.F.; Rear Admiral A. M. Knight, president of the Naval War College and member of the Navy General Board, before the House Naval Affairs Committee, 64th Cong., 1st Sess., *Hearings . . . on Estimates Submitted by the Secretary of the Navy* (3 vols., Wash., G.P.O., 1916), II, 2082. See Chapters 6 and 7 for further discussion of the willingness of naval leaders to tell Congressmen what they felt Congressmen wanted to hear during appropriations hearings.

6. My italics. Kelley, *Our Navy*, 9.

7. From a speech before the Merchant's Club of Chicago in 1904, cited in the *Army and Navy Journal*, XLI (23 July 1904), 1220. I am indebted to Richard Werking for this citation. Obviously, this function of naval power was not something performed solely by U.S. warships. All navies were so employed in these years.

8. Turner to Toucey, 23 June 1858, Letterbook of Commander Thomas Turner, 1858–1860, Rear Admiral Thomas Turner Papers, Manuscript Room, New York Public Library; Arnold S. Lott, *A Long Line of Ships: Mare Island's Century of Naval Activity in California* (Annapolis, 1954), 36, 62. For other examples of naval aid to trade in the Pacific in these years see *Letters of Captain George H. Perkins, U.S.N., 1858–1880*, ed. Susan Perkins (Concord, N.H., 1886), 169 (for Indo-China); Commander Albert Barker to the Secretary of the Navy, 4 November 1885, "Letters from Commanders," Entry 23, Record Group 45,

National Archives (for Australia); *The Life of an American Sailor: Rear Admiral William H. Emory, U.S.N.*, ed. Rear Admiral Albert Gleaves (New York, 1923), 90–91 and *passim* (for Alaska); and Boxes 1 and 2, SS (Naval Assistance to Merchant Ships), Entry 464, R.G.45.

9. Kelley, *Our Navy*, 9; U.S. Navy, Bureau of Navigation, Cipher Dispatch Records, 1892–93 and *passim*, National Archives; Green, "Science and the Navy," *PUSNI*, XLVIII (1922), 1703–1706. Green offered dozens of examples of foreign trade and investment opportunities.

10. U.S. Office of Naval Intelligence, *The U.S. Navy as an Industrial Asset: What the Navy has done for Industry and Commerce* (Wash., G.P.O., 1923), 5. For a more complete account of the Navy and business in the 1920s see Charles Beard, *et al.*, *The Idea of National Interest* (rev. ed., Quadrangle Paper, Chicago, 1966), 322–327.

Another "aid" to the business community may have been the Congressional act that provided for the enrolling of several Japanese midshipmen at Annapolis in the 1870s. The Academy's superintendent, Rear Admiral John L. Worden, predicted "the best results to American interests in Japan" from this experiment. 42nd Cong., 2nd Sess., U.S. Senate, *Letter from the Superintendent of the Naval Academy*, Senate Document No. 77 [1872].

11. Beard, *Idea of National Interest*, 61; Samuel Bryant, *The Sea and the States: A Maritime History of the American People* (Apollo ed., 1967), 238–239; Rosengarten, Reynolds, 6; *The [Diary of George H. Preble] in the Far East, 1853–1856*, ed. Boleslaw Szczesniak (Norman, Okla., 1962), 120, 144, 152; Rodgers to Dobbin, 23 June 1855, *Yankee Surveyors in the Shogun's Seas*, ed. Allan Cole (Princeton, 1947), 128; Foster R. Dulles, *America in the Pacific: A Century of Expansion* (Boston and New York, 1932), 62–79.

12. Truxton to the People of Tarawa, 19 May 1870, copy in the R. W. Meade, 3rd, Mss., New York Historical Society (N.Y.H.S.).

13. LaFeber, *New Empire*, 284–418.

14. Peter Karsten and Thomas Patterson in *PUSNI*, XCV (February 1969), pp. 112–114; Foulk to Ensign Washington I. Chambers, 11 September 1884, W.I. Chambers Papers, N.H.F.

15. Benjamin F. Stevens to Navy Secretary John D. Long, 29 July 1898, in *The Papers of John Davis Long, 1897–1904*, ed.

180

Gardner Allen (Mass. Hist. Soc. Coll., Vol. 78, 1939), 168–169. The late professor Bernard Fall first related the Danang incident in *The New Republic*, 17 December 1966, and I subsequently found mention of it in Gustavus V. Fox to Issac Barnes, 25 March 1850, G. V. Fox Bound Volume, "Cruise to China," Fox Manuscripts, New York Historical Society.

16. Seward W. Livermore, "American Naval-Base Policy in the Far East, 1850–1914," *Pacific Historical Review*, XIII (1944), 113–135.

17. Meade to the People of Samoa, 2 March 1872, House Exec. Doc. No. 161 enclosure D; George H. Ryden, *The Foreign Policy of the U.S. in Relation to Samoa* (New Haven & London, 1933), 66; Edgar Wakeman, *The Log of an Ancient Mariner* (San Francisco, 1878), 342–358, and Samoa, 1887–1902, Boxes 640 & 641, VI, Entry 464, R.G. 45.

18. Charles O. Paullin, "A Half Century of Naval Administration in America, 1861–1911," *PUSNI*, XXXIX (1913), 1494.

In 1900 the Navy sought bases in North and South China, but the government's efforts to secure such ports were insufficient, or simply unsuccessful. McCormick, *China Market*, 192.

19. Charles O. Paullin, "Early Voyages of American Naval Vessels to the Orient: The East Indies Squadron in the Waters of China and Japan, 1854–1865," *PUSNI*, XXXVII (1911), 387–417; Captain Arthur C. Hansard, R.N., "Early Days in Japan," *PUSNI*, XXXVII (1911), 151–156; Seward to his minister, July 7, 1863, and passim., Microcopy No. 77, Roll 104, Records of the Department of State, Diplomatic Instructions, Japan, I, 101, National Archives (N.A.); *Naval Surgeon: Revolt in Japan, 1868–1869* (the diary of Samuel P. Boyer), ed. Elinor & James Barnes (Bloomington, Ind., 1963), 128; Pierce to Winslow, Dec. 30, 1871, U.S. Legation, Hawaii, Letters Sent, 1865–1897, Box 30–18, R.G. 84, N.A.; see also Commander Richard Meade to Pierce, July 27, 1872, and Jan. 23, 1872, U.S. Legation, Hawaii, Miscellaneous Letters Received, 1868–1872, R.G. 84, N.A.; Blake to Rodgers, 24 November 1870, Homer Blake Letterbook, 1869–1872, p. 71, Homer Blake Papers, Manuscript Room, New York Public Library; Rear Admiral Stephen Rowan, Commander, Asiatic Squadron, to Commander Somerville Nicholson, July 31, 1870, Nicholson Papers, N.H.F.; U.S. Vice Consul-General, Shanghai, to Rear Admiral

John L. Davis, Commander, Asiatic Squadron, and Foochow Chamber of Commerce to Davis, Nov. 19, 1884, Asiatic Squadron Letters, Microcopy 89, Roll 270, R.G. 45, N.A.; Lieutenant (j.g.) Wallace S. Whaiton, "Our Chinese Navy," *PUSNI*, LI (1925), 69. See also Copybooks of Rear Admiral Thornton Jenkins and others, Commanders of the Asiatic Squadron, 1871–1872, and of Rear Admiral Earl English, Commander South Atlantic Squadron, 1885, Entry 30, R.G. 45; Te-Kong Tong, *U.S. Diplomacy in China, 1844–60* (Seattle, 1964); E. M. Tate," U.S. Gunboats on the Yangtze. History and Political Aspects, 1842–1922," copy in the Division of Naval History Office, N.A.; Susan Kleinberg, "The Yangtze Patrol, 1910–1915," unpublished M.A. seminar essay, Univ. of Pittsburgh Dept. of History, 1969; Fredrick Drake, " 'The Empire of the Seas' . . ., "177, 204; Esson Gale, "The Yangtze Patrol," *PUSNI*, LXXXI (1955), 317–332; and James Merrill, "The Asiatic Squadron, 1835–1907," *The American Neptune* XXIX (1969), 106–117. Cf. C. J. Bartlett, *Great Britain and Sea Power, 1815–1853* (Oxford, 1963), 260–267.

20. Walter Herrick, Jr., *The American Naval Revolution* (Baton Rouge, 1966), 104; *Report of the Secretary of the Navy, 1874*, 43rd Cong., 2nd Sess., House Exec. Doc. 1, Pt. 3, 180–197; *Letter from the Secretary of the Navy . . . transmitting . . . letters sent to the Department by Rear Admiral J. G. Walker relating to the Sandwich Islands*, Senate Exec. Doc., No. 16, 53rd Cong. 3rd Sess. (1894); Russ, *Hawaiian Revolution*, 75–111, 261–262.

21. Dewey to his sister, Jan. 30, 1898, *Life and Letters of Admiral Dewey*, ed. Adelbert M. Dewey (Akron, Ohio, 1899), 194; Dewey to his father, Jan. 18, 1898, George Dewey Papers, Library of Congress.

22. Captain Royal Bradford, U.S. naval attaché to the Peace Commission, presented a similar argument in a brief drafted within days of the arrival of Dewey's report and argued as well for the annexation of *all* of Spanish Micronesia (Carolines and Ladrones as well as the Philippines). McKinley settled for the Philippines and one coal-cable station, Guam. Dewey to John D. Long, 29 August 1898, *Papers of Long*, 188–190; Earl S. Pomeroy, *Pacific Outpost; American Strategy in Guam and Micronesia* (Stanford, 1951), 5–12; McCormick, *China Market*, 120. For a similar naval view of the Philippine question, see the remarks of Rear

Admiral Joseph Coghlan in the *Army & Navy Journal*, XLV (7 March 1908), 704.

McKinley probably read Dewey's report to Secretary Long; Professor Thomas McCormick of the University of Wisconsin tells me that McKinley read and initialed copies of the correspondence of every Pacific Fleet Commanding Officer to the Commander-in-Chief of the Asiatic Fleet in these years.

23. Sawyer, *Sons of Gunboats*, 145–147; McCalla, "Memoirs," Ch. XXVII, 5–10; Sargent to the Commander-in-Chief of the Asiatic Fleet (carbon), 17 December 1905, Nathan Sargent Papers, Naval Historical Foundation; Ronald Boggs, "American Diplomats, Naval Officers, and Businessmen: China, 1903–1905," unpublished seminar paper, Dept. of History, University of Pittsburgh, 1968.

24. Moses, "The Orient in 1916: Its Interest to the United States," *PUSNI*, XLIII (1917), 78. Naval officers were not the only public officials to feel this way, nor were they acting in a void when they steamed into Chinese ports with guns bristling, cleared for action. Their favorite Commander-in-Chief, President Theodore Roosevelt, made clear to J. Pierpont Morgan in July 1905 that he intended to keep the door to China open so that "American commercial interests could prosper" (cited in Howard K. Beale, *Theodore Roosevelt and the Rise of America to World Power* [Baltimore, 1956], 207). Similarly, Roosevelt's colleague, Senator Henry Cabot Lodge, told a friend in the diplomatic service that he hoped the U.S., Great Britain, and Japan might "prevent the absorption of China by Russia and keep the Empire open for our trade and commerce, which is all we want." (Cited in Ray Ginger, *Age of Excess* [New York, 1965], 357.) And, in spite of what has been said of President Woodrow Wilson's handling of the banker's consortium in 1913, Martin Sklar and William A. Williams have demonstrated to my satisfaction that both Wilson and his Secretary of State William Jennings Bryan were vitally interested in investments and trade in Asia. Williams, *The Tragedy of American Diplomacy* (rev. ed., N.Y., 1962), 67–78.

25. *Army and Navy Journal*, LII (Sept. 26, 1914), 102. In 1867 Secretary of State William Seward hoped to take advantage of a revolution in the Isthmus of Panama to land marines and sailors and ask the Senate to approve the annexation of the Isthmus, June 14, 1867, entry, *The Diary of Gideon*

Welles, ed. Howard K. Beale (3 vols., New York, 1960), III, 107.

26. See "Correspondence relating to the Naval Expedition to the Isthmus of Panama, 1885," Entry 25, Appendix A, Item 13, R.G. 45, N.A.; and McCalla to Lieutenant Theodorus B. Mason, 16 April 1885, in R. S. Collum, *History of the United States Marine Corps* (Philadelphia, 1890), 228.

27. Walker to McCalla, 6 April 1885, John Grimes Walker Papers, Box 595, Naval Historical Foundation.

28. When Congress incorporated the Maritime Canal Company of Nicaragua in 1889, Rear Admiral Daniel Ammen, Captain A. S. Crowninshield, and Civil Engineer A. G. Menocal, U.S.N., were among the 20 original board members. Miles P. Duval, Jr., *Cadiz to Cathay* (Stanford, 1940), 84. See also Rear Admiral Daniel Ammen, *The Old Navy and the New* (Philadelphia, 1891), 470–500; *Letter . . . in relation to . . . interoceanic canals*, 17–18; and Commander H. C. Taylor, "The General Question of Isthmian Interest," *Nicaragua Canal Discussion before the American Association for the Advancement of Science*, 36th Meeting (New York, 1887), 12.

29. For a good recent account of this concern see Edward B. Billingsley, *In Defense of Neutral Rights: The U.S. Navy and the Wars of Independence in Chile and Peru* (Chapel Hill, 1967). The best general account for the entire period is Robert E. Johnson, *Thence 'Round Cape Horn: The Story of U.S. Naval Forces on the Pacific Station, 1818–1923* (Annapolis, 1963).

30. Beard, *Idea of National Interest*, 366; Donald Griffin, "The American Navy at work on the Brazil Station, 1827–1860," *American Neptune*, XIX (1959), 241; Henry Wriston, *Executive Agents in American Foreign Relations* (Baltimore, 1929), 665–670; Turner to the Haitian Minister of Foreign Relations, 16 August 1858, Turner Letterbook, 1858–1860, Rear Admiral Thomas Turner Papers, Manuscript Room, New York Public Library. See the correspondence of Rear Admiral John H. Upshur, commanding U.S. Naval Forces on the Pacific Station, and Captain Charles Norton, *Shenandoah*, 1884–1885, Squadron Letters—Pacific Station, Record Group 45, National Archives. See also Johnson, *Thence 'Round Cape Horn*, 81, 106, 117. The naval protection of guano (a fine fertilizer) and the search for new deposits seems to have begun in 1854.

31. Porter, *The Island of San Domingo*

(n.p., n.d. [copy in University of Wisconsin Memorial Library]), 3–4. See also Rear Admiral Daniel Ammen, *The Old Navy and the New* (New York, 1891), who, with Porter, hoped that President Grant, their old wartime friend, would approve the annexation of Santo Domingo. Allen Nevins, *Hamilton Fish* (New York, 1936), I, 263–269. I am indebted to Richard Werking for this latter citation.

32. Captain Paul Ryan, "The Old Navy and Santo Domingo," *Shipmate* (Feb. 1967), 4; Nathaniel McKay of 15 Whitehall Street, New York, to Stanton, 30 September 1893, Rear Admiral Oscar Stanton Papers, G. W. Blunt White Library, Mystic, Connecticut. As an American investing in the construction of bridges, McKay must have been aware of the Charles River Bridge case and its implications regarding the mutability of the rights of the bridge owners, but either his possessive instinct led him to ignore these implications or he sensed that the federal government drew the line at the water's edge. In any event, I could not ascertain Stanton's action in this matter from perusal of either his personal papers or archival records of the Stanton visit to the Dominican Republic.

33. Lodge, cited in Ginger, *Age of Excess*, 357. Cf. Norman Risjord, "1812: Conservatives, War Hawks, and the Nation's Honor," *William and Mary Quarterly*, XVIII (1961), 196–210; Armin Rappaport, *The Navy League of the United States* (Detroit, 1962).

34. I refer the puzzled or skeptical reader to Beard, *Idea of National Interest, passim,* and Kenneth Boulding, *The Image* (Ann Arbor, 1956).

35. See, for example, *The Cabinet Diaries of Daniels*, ed. Cronon, 461.

36. Milton Offutt, *The Protection of Citizens Abroad by the Armed Forces of the United States* (Baltimore, 1928), 158; Sargent to the Secretary of the Navy, 6 February 1901, and adjacent dates, copies in Box 146, Captain Nathan Sargent Papers, Naval Historical Foundation; Howard F. Cline, *The U.S. and Mexico* (Cambridge, 1953), 155; Josephus Daniels, *The Wilson Era: Years of Peace, 1910–1917* (Chapel Hill, 1944), 185–186; Robert E. Quirk, *An Affair of Honor: Woodrow Wilson and the Occupation of Vera Cruz* (Lexington, Ky., 1962), 8, *passim*; "Admiral H. T. Mayo's Reports," Box 659, WE-5, Subject File, 1911–1927, R.G. 45, N.A. See also Naval Affairs Comm., House of Representatives, *Hear-*

ings . . . on Estimates Submitted by the Sec. of the Navy, 1919, Pt. 2, 66th Cong. (1919), 856; Marine Major General George Barnett: "We keep [Marines] at Tampico, because [of] the danger of the oil business. . . ." Cf. Kenneth Grieb, *The U.S. and Huerta* (Lincoln, Neb., 1969), 40–50, 142–158; Wilkins, *Emergence*, 164.

37. See Cooper to Secretary of the Navy (Aide for Ops.), January 11, 1911, and *passim*, Honduranean Correspondence, 1910–1911, Entry 310, R.G. 45, for the Honduran case. Charles Beard has an excellent summary of the Nicaraguan affair in *Idea of National Interest*, 170–182, but see also Nicaragua Correspondence, 1909–1910, Entry 309, R.G. 45, N.A. See also note 50 below.

38. Coontz, "The Navy and Business," *PUSNI*, XLVIII (1922), 991.

For earlier examples of this phenomenon see 56th Cong., 1st Sess., House Documents (Consular Reports), Vol. 46 [1899], 38: "During the years succeeding [Rear] Admiral [John G.] Walker's visit . . . to Brazil in 1890 . . . the increased respect commanded by the appearance of our vessels has been, I [Consul Hill of Santos] believe, a real and constant . . . commercial factor." (The foregoing consular report entry was literally selected at random.) See also Commander Thomas Turner to President Benito Juarez, 25 December 1858, 1858–1860 Letterbook, Turner Papers [for Mexico]; Navy Secretary William E. Chandler to Commander Alfred T. Mahan, 17 March & 27 March 1885, "Letters to Officers Generally," 1884–1886, Entry 18, R.G. 45, Nat. Arch. [for Guatemala]; RADM John G. Walker to his wife, 4 October 1892, in Frances Thomas, *The Career of Rear Admiral John G. Walker* (Boston, 1959), 58 [for Venezuela]; LaFeber, *New Empire*, 200ff. [for Brazil]; and Frederick B. Pike, *Chile and the United States, 1880–1962* (Notre Dame, 1963), 66–85 [for Chile].

39. See, for example, Captain John Gwinn, Commander, Mediterranean Squadron, to Lieutenant Commanding William W. Hunter, May 20, 1849, copy in Somerville Nicholson Papers, N.H.F.; Commander H. K. Thatcher to Assistant Secretary Fox, 3 November 1862, *Conf. Corr. of Fox*, II, 426; 44th Cong., 1st Sess., Ex. Doc. No. 170, *Protection of American Citizens in the Ottoman Empire* [1876]; Admiral Edward Eberle, "A Few Reflections on Our Navy and Some on its Needs," a 1924 address [mimeograph copy in the

files of the State Historical Society of Wisconsin], 3.

The Navy had a standing agreement with Standard Oil in Turkey (as elsewhere) throughout the post-World War I years for the storage of its fuel oil in Standard Oil Tanks in the Bosporus. Lieutenant Commander Richard S. Field, "A Destroyer in the Near East," *PUSNI*, LI (1925), 251.

Naval diplomacy in the Mediterranean involved a greater degree of individual protection (the safeguarding of tourists, missionaries, educators, vice-consuls—in addition to businessmen) than elsewhere in the world.

40. Henry P. Beers, *U.S. Naval Detachment in Turkish Waters, 1919–1924* and *U.S. Naval Forces in Northern Russia (Archangel and Murmansk), 1918–1919*, Admin. Reference Service Reports Nos. 2 and 5 (Office of Naval Records Admin., Navy Dept., 1943); Office of Naval Intelligence, "Possible U.S. Economic Intervention in Russia," Subject File, WA-6, 1918, R.G. 45, N.A.; Jeremy Thomas, "The U.S. in South Russia, 1919–1920: A Study in 'Neutral Involvement,'" unpublished seminar paper, Dept. of History, Univ. of Pittsburgh, 1968.

In these same years, U.S. naval forces dominated the northern Adriatic in an apparently selfless effort to prevent Italy from strangling a nascent Yugoslavia and to insure the Yugoslavs access to a good northern Adriatic port. See A. C. Davidonis, *The American Naval Mission in the Adriatic, 1918–1921*, Admin. Reference Service Report No. 4 (Office of Naval Records Administration, Navy Dept., 1943).

The Davidonis account of the Adriatic mission suggests that the U.S. had no ulterior designs in the region, and this may be. But Davidonis is biased; he regards all U.S. efforts to strengthen Yugoslavia at the sake of Italy as unadorned justice. Recent re-examinations of Wilsonian diplomacy with regard to Eastern Europe (to which Trieste and Fiume are access) cast some doubt on the selflessness of this mission. But even if this is a case of totally disinterested U.S. naval diplomacy, it is a rare one.

41. Huntington, *Soldier and the State*, 290. *Re* the Pearson visit to Johanna, see the relevant documents in the Papers of Rear Admiral E. A. F. LaVallette, Perkins Library, Duke U. See also Foote, *Africa*, 308–309; Clarence Clendenen, *et al.*, *Americans in Africa, 1865–1890* (Hoover Institute Studies, No. 17, 1966), 71–73; McCalla, "Memoirs," Cp. XV, 36–38; *Army and*

Navy Journal, XXXIX (1902), 332. Cf. Letters from Commander P. F. Harrington of U.S.S. *Juanita* on disturbances on the Island of Johanna, East Africa (involving a U.S.-owned plantation, in 1885), Entry 25 (14), R.G. 45, N.A.

Kenneth Hagan's forthcoming study of U.S. diplomacy from Hayes to Harrison has a good account of the African portion of Shufeldt's cruise as well as other naval activity in African waters.

42. See, for example, the correspondence of Allan McLane, president of the Pacific Mail Steamship Co., and the heads of August Belmont & Co., Wells Fargo & Co., W. F. Weed & Co., and 32 other firms to the Secretary of Navy during the week of April 18–24, 1861, all in *Official Records of the Union and Confederate Navies in the War of the Rebellion* (30 vols. & index, G.P.O., 1894–1927), I, 10–14; Welles to Flag Officer John Montgomery, April 27, 1861, cited in Johnson, *Thence 'Round Cape Horn*, 113; and the New York Chamber of Commerce to Captain John L. Worden, March 18, 1862, Worden Papers, Lincoln Memorial University, Harrogate, Tennessee. For a fine account of just such commerce protection during the Civil War see Benjamin F. Gilbert, "U.S. Naval Operations in the Pacific, 1861–1866," unpub. Ph.D. dissertation, Univ. of Calif. at Berkeley, 1951.

43. May, *The World War and American Isolation, 1914–1917* (Cambridge, Mass., 1959), and Smith, *The Great Departure: The United States and World War I, 1914–1920* (New York & London, 1965), 80–83.

44. May, "Emergence . . .," *Reconstruction of American History*, ed. Higham, *passim*.

45. Offutt, *Protection of Citizens Abroad*, Chapters 2 & 3. As the title suggests, Offutt's account is more factual than probing. Some of these "skirmishes" were not overtly commercial in nature (e.g., Valparaiso in 1891), but a little probing beneath the surface usually leads one back to the Almighty Dollar (e.g., what was the *Baltimore* doing in Valparaiso to begin with? For the answer see Pike, *Chile and the U.S.*, 66–85, esp. 69; and Herrick, *American Naval Revolution*, 115–116).

46. Habersham, *North Pacific Surveying & Exploring Expedition*, 250.

47. Standley and Ageton, *Admiral Ambassador*, 10. Thereupon, Ensign Arthur MacArthur was sent on board her with a U.S. naval guard "to make certain that the Chinese man-of-war observed strict neutrality [!]."

184

48. Eventually Britain, the U.S., and Germany agreed to partition Samoa and abolish Samoan self-rule altogether. Ironically, as Professor Braisted points out, the bases were never of any value, being too far from the main lines of communication (Braisted, *Navy in Pacific*, 58–63).

49. Fullam to Secretary of the Navy [copy], 26 March 1907, [Rear Admiral] William F. Fullam Papers, Naval Historical Foundation. See also Fullam's 1906 correspondence with the Secretary and his brother officers and Box 3 of the Washington Irving Chambers Papers, Naval Historical Foundation, for other examples of the Navy's role as guardian of U.S. business interests in the waters of Cuba, Santo Domingo, and Nicaragua.

50. Fullam to Estrada [translated copy], 24 March 1907 and 29 March 1907, Fullam Papers.

For other examples of U.S. naval infringement of Central American sovereignty see Commander John Shipley, commanding U.S.S. *Des Moines*, to American consul, Bluefields, Dec. 10, 1909, Nicaragua Correspondence, 1909–1910, Entry 309, R.G. 45; Harold Denny, *Dollars for Bullets* (N.Y., 1929), 260–262; and note 37 above. Naval forces such as U.S.S. *Des Moines, Yorktown,* and *Marietta,* and Major Butler's marines were all involved in keeping "anti-American" [!] Nicaraguan loyalists from resisting the U.S.-sponsored coup of United States-Nicaraguan Concession official Adolpho Diaz. Cf. Beard, *Idea*, 177–178; Dana Munro, *Intervention and Dollar Diplomacy in the Caribbean, 1900–1921* (Princeton, 1964), 175, 183, 225–229, 260, 352.

51. From a paper, "The Wisconsin School of Diplomatic History: A Critique," read before a meeting of the Organization of American Historians, Chicago, April 27, 1967.

52. Williams, *The Tragedy of American Diplomacy* (rev. ed., N.Y., 1962), 2; Billingsley, *In Defense of Neutral Rights,* 104 and *passim*; K. Jack Bauer, "The U.S. Navy and Texas Independence," *Military Affairs,* XXXIV (1970), 45–46; Montgomery, *Our Admiral's Flag Aboard*, 180ff; Taylor to the Secretary of the Navy, Oct. 28, 1890, Box 3, VP File, Entry 464, R.G. 45 N.A.; Louis Feipel, "The Navy and Filibustering in the Fifties," *PUSNI*, XLIV (1918), 767ff; Commander Wat Cluverius, "A Midshipman on the *Maine*," *PUSNI*, XLIV (1918), 241–245; Andor Klay, *Daring Diplomacy* (Minneapolis, 1957), 68; Morison, *Perry*, 273, 416.

53. Young in *Toward a New Past,* ed. B. Bernstein, 182; Beard, *Idea of National Interest,* 60, 63.

54. See Dispatches from U.S. Consuls in Apia, Samoa, Microcopy T 27, Roll 3, Vol. III, 1867–1875, N.A.; 42nd Cong., 2nd Sess., *Executive Letters (Confidential) to U.S. Senate,* May 22, 1872; Pierce to Meade, Jan. 19, 1872, U.S. Legation, Hawaii, Letters Sent, 1865–1897, Box 30–18, R.G. 84, N.A. Cf. George Rieman [Meade's Clerk], *Papalangee, or, Uncle Sam in Samoa: A Narrative of the Cruise of the U.S.S. "Narragansett" Among the Samoan Islands* (Oakland, Calif., 1874).

55. Wakeman to Reverend Powell [copy], 13 January 1872; and Wakeman to the British consul, "Mr. Williams," [copy], 13 January 1872, Rear Admiral Richard Meade, 3rd, Papers, Box I, New York Historical Society. The reference to coffee, cotton, etc., is from Wakeman to Meade, 13 January 1872, Meade Papers, Box I.

56. Seward to the U.S. Minister to the Argentine Republic, May 18, 1867, cited in John Bassett Moore, *Digest of International Law* (Wash., G.P.O., 1906), IV, 616–617; Beard, *Idea of National Interest,* 175–176.

57. Henson, "U.S. Navy and China . . .," 120–180, 355–460; esp. 179–180.

58. Dulles to RADM Thomas Turner, June 25, 1868, and Turner to Craven, July 11, 1868, Craven Papers, Manuscript Division, Carnegie Library, Syracuse Univ.; Consul David Turner to Second Assistant Secretary of State, October 30, 1874, Dispatches from U.S. Consuls at La Paz, Mexico, Microcopy T-324, Roll 2, R.G. 84, N.A. Cf. C. O. Paullin, "The U.S. Navy in Mexico," *PUSNI,* XLII (1916), 175; and note 2, Chapter 3, of this book.

One of the difficulties of gunboat diplomacy was that its effectiveness often varied inversely with the square of the distance of the gunboat from the "hot spot." The Triunfo Mine required the attention of Commander George Dewey in 1875 and, after his departure, that of the commander of the North Pacific Squadron himself, Rear Admiral Alexander Murray, in 1876. Dewey, *Autobiography*, 146–149; Consul Turner to Asst. Sec. of State, Oct. 19, 1876, La Paz Dispatches.

59. Dewey, *Autobiography*, 148; Quirk, *Affair of Honor*, 27; Hilary Herbert, "Grandfather's Talks About his Life Under Two Flags," p. 326, Herbert Papers, S.H.C., U. of N.C. Library; Jones to LaVallette, LaVallette Papers, Perkins Library, Duke

U.; Hay to Roosevelt, cited in *PUSNI*, XLVIII (1922), 548.

60. May, in John Garraty, *Interpreting American History* (N.Y., 1970), II, 76; Johnson, *Thence 'Round Cape Horn*, 10; *PUSNI*, L (1924), 5.

61. Billingsley, *In Defense of Neutral Rights*, 156–158; 1881 Folder, Box 13, N.J., Entry 464, R.G. 45; "Price, Rodman," *D.A.B.*; Gilbert Workman, "Forgotten Firebrand," *PUSNI* (Sept. 1968), 86–87; April 1854 entry, *Preble Diary*, 171. See deeds in Thomas H. Stevens, II, Papers, dated May 13, 1890, Perkins Library, Duke U.; and Ferebee-Gregory-McPherson Papers dated Jan. 17, 1881, S.H.C., U. of N.C. Library. Cf. Morison, *Perry*, 313–314.

62. *Preble Diary*, 171; Fox-Aspinwall correspondence in the Gustavus V. Fox Papers, New York Historical Society.

63. Hatch to Shufeldt, 17 July 1874, Sage to Robeson [copy], 17 July 1874, Shufeldt to Hatch, 18 July 1874, Shufeldt to Hatch, 31 July 1874, Box 11, and Box 24, [Commodore] Robert Shufeldt Papers, Naval Historical Foundation; Fred H. Harrington, *God, Mammon, and the Japanese* (Madison, Wisc., 2nd ed., 1961), 131.

64. Harrington, 128; Foulk to Lieutenant (junior grade) Washington I. Chambers, 23 March 1888, Chambers Papers.

The crew of naval vessels may have had similar pecuniary visions, but they were seldom given the opportunity to realize them. When the crew of the *New York* was landed in 1894 to "put an end to . . . looting" in Port-of-Spain, Trinidad, many returned the same evening "with all sorts of things," including 20 young goats; all were eventually returned. Evans, *Sailor's Log*, 366.

On the other hand, when Captain Charles Clark stripped the battered Spanish warship *Cristobal Colon* of its valuables, he carefully set aside the wardroom silver for his own disposition. Similarly, Ensign Hugh Rodman and his superiors, Captain Coghlan and Commodore Dewey, kept silver they took from the Spanish fleet at Manila. Clark, *My Fifty Years*, 299; Rodman, *Yarns of a Kentucky Admiral*, 257.

65. Morison, *Perry*, 257; Johnson *Rodgers*, 275.

66. U.S. Senate, Comm. on Naval Affairs, *Hearings of an Investigation . . . in Relation to Prices for Armour for Vessels of the Navy* (Wash., G.P.O., 1896), 294, 346–353; *Report of the Select Committee on Ordnance and War Ships* (Wash., G.P.O., 1886), 475–477; Frank B. Copley, *Fredrick W. Taylor: Father of Scientific Management* (2 vols., N.Y., 1923), I, 336, 378; "Hollis, Ira Nelson," *Dictionary of American Biography*; Lovette, *School of Sea*, 208, 305; John F. Meigs, *The Story of the Seaman* (2 vols., 1903), I, 37; 48th Cong., 1st Sess., House Ex. Doc. No. 77, "Report on the Gun Foundry Board." For good accounts of the Navy's relationship to the steel industry in the late nineteenth century see Herrick, *American Naval Revolution*, 64–66, 78–82; Dean Allard, "The Influence of the U.S. Navy upon the American Steel Industry, 1880–1900," Georgetown Univ. M.A. essay, 1959, 79; and Ensign J. B. Bernadou, "The Development of the Resources of the U.S. for the Protection of [Naval] War Material," in Office of Naval Intelligence, *Naval Mobilization . . .* (Wash., G.P.O., 1889).

67. *PUSNI*, XLVIII (1922), 1000; Paul T. Armistead, "Retired Military Leaders in American Business," unpub. Ph.D. dissertation, U. of Texas, 1967, 181–185; Walter R. Herrick, Jr., "General Tracy's Navy," Ph.D. dissertation, U. of Va., 1962, 311–312; Lovette, *School of Sea*, 272, 296, 298, 305; Billingsley, *Neutral Rights*, 158; Herbert Feis, *The Diplomacy of the Dollar, 1919–1932* (N.Y., 1966, paper ed.), 55–56.

During the Spanish-American War a group of Academy graduates who had resigned their commissions and entered the world of business offered their services as purchasing agents, inspectors of supplies, etc., in order (if we accept the word of Park Benjamin) to release active duty officers for combat service. Benjamin, "The Unused Products of the Naval Academy," *The Independent*, L (Oct. 27, 1898), 1181. These gentlemen, like Professor Rappaport's Navy Leaguers, claimed to be disinterested patriots. But there were Academy grads who renounced their vows of material celibacy when they left the service and told their classmates, "Our grand aim in life [now] is to make money. . . ." One such individual suggested that there was "potential energy" and "advantage of position" in the fellowship of Academy classmates, and that those who had resigned should form "a POWERFUL CORPORATION" to rival those emerging all about them. W. G. Ford, Jr., to the class of 1881. December 1886, *3rd Annual Report of the Class of 1881*, 53–54. Cf. Rappaport, *Navy League*, 54.

chapter **5**

Why They Did It: The Naval Mind

> The unquestioning obedience, the sense of duty, the methodical
> habits of an unvarying routine, the restriction when afloat to a
> society every member of which is cast in the same mould, necessarily
> sets an iron impress upon the character of the naval man, and makes
> him the pattern of conservatism which he is.
>
> Captain French E. Chadwick in *PUSNI*, XXVIII (1902), 252

The chapter title is no misnomer; despite claims to the contrary in some circles, naval officers were hardly mindless. As a group they held complex, albeit virtually identical, clusters of opinions on a host of subjects. For purposes of analysis, these opinions have been disconnected, isolated. But the officer made no such separation himself. Like every human being, the naval officer drew upon the sum of his convictions in conceptualizing a situation and in dealing with a problem. Sometimes one facet of his mental hardware might assume more prominence than others; sometimes another facet was presented. When faced with a situation involving the seizure of an American's property abroad, for instance, one officer might see the matter in terms of "national honor," another in terms of "national interest," still another as an opportunity to win some prestige for the Service or some glory for himself. Probably all these elements could be expected in one degree or another. Perhaps the officer's identification of one abstract concept, the Service and its values, with those of another abstract concept, the State and what he believed to be its proper role on the world scene, was at once the most curious and complex mental exercise performed and the most important one. But each facet deserves special consideration if one is to emerge with a reasonably complete image of the naval mind.

Numbered footnotes for Chapter 5 begin on pages 237 and 268.

Then under strong sail we laugh at the gale,
An' though landsmen look pale, never heed 'em;
But toss off a glass to a favorite lass,
To America, Commerce, and Freedom!

From a nineteenth century naval song, printed in George H. Preble,
Grog : A Mixture of Prose and Verse (Phil., 1884)

To say that the Navy was used to protect and assist American
businessmen at home and abroad is not the same as saying that naval officers
consciously and intentionally allied themselves with "Robber Barons" specifically to help those dauntless entrepreneurs stuff their pockets. The typical naval
officer aided businessmen but distrusted the world of corporate business, and
some officers despised all it stood for.[1] If there were officers hypnotized by the
dollar sign, they were deviants from the professional norm, and they eventually resigned or were dismissed, to continue their materialistic role in the more
accommodating atmosphere of civilian life.

In spite of their disdain for their wards, the naval aristocracy was quite willing
to act as guardians of business interests abroad, for two reasons: first, because
they considered themselves to be a kind of international policemen and, second,
because of their ability to identify American trade or investments with America's
"national interest."

Like many of their countrymen, the naval aristocracy felt a responsibility to
a high-Church God to see His will done throughout the world, but this mission
was understood to be indistinguishable from the expansion of American power
and prestige. "Anglo-Saxon" supremacists first, naval officers were humani-
tarians and Christians whenever such behavior did not jeopardize the efficient
diffusion of American influence. After all, was not America, despite the shortcomings of its democratic political system, the very seat of benevolence and
beneficence? How could the world then object to being policed by America's
Navy?

The Naval Critique of the Business World

Distrust of, and disdain for, the world of stock exchanges and
marketplaces are standard features of military men, and the U.S. naval officer
of the late nineteenth century was no exception. He and his messmates left a
trail of abuse for business civilization as long as their ink would permit. When
Samuel Coues, president of the American Peace Society, offered a critique of the
Navy in 1845, Commander Louis Goldsborough replied with a critique of
Coues' business profession. Commercial firms such as the one in Portsmouth,
New Hampshire, that Coues headed "induce falsehood, fraud, forgery, perjury,
hatred, malice, covetousness, and a host of other iniquities." Goldsborough had
little use for the "miserable mercenary" world he spent his life abroad pro-
tecting. In 1862 Rear Admiral Andrew Foote passed away in New York City

after a long, dutiful career, and his friend Rear Admiral John Dahlgren was
furious at the lack of attention paid to his comrade-in-arms. "The Admiral's
body was removed to his home in New Haven," he observed in his journal,
"but so quietly that no one knew it. So much for the fame of our best officer.
New York goes on and makes money, heedless of it all." Three years later
Lieutenant Commander Roe boasted that the Navy was free from the "profound arts of petty vices, such as nowadays taint the society of all men, especially
business men." Roe, like Dahlgren, was disgusted to find that naval officers
received little thanks from "a peaceful and prosperous people" who were
enjoying immunities the Navy had won.[2]

Similarly, Lieutenant Nathan Sargent had ugly things to say about the late
nineteenth century American's "materialistic outlook." Ensign Washington
Chambers felt that the nation was sinking into "a lethargic state of impotent
corpulency" in 1884. In 1907 Commander Chambers attributed the nation's
"effeminacy" to its wealth, and upon reading his unpublished poems it becomes
clear that, like Sargent, he viewed "materialism" as the enemy.[3] Commander
C. H. Rockwell sounded like a Populist in November, 1892, when he railed at
"the bursting coffers of vast and powerful corporations, while the nation is
dotted with freehold farms oppressed with burdensome mortgages."[4] In 1903
the Department received a complaint from Willis Gray, an official of the
Hankow Railroad at Canton, who criticized the official conduct of one of
Commander William Beehler's officers in South China waters. Beehler was
outraged by the attention given this complaint; criticism by a naval senior or
by a State Department official was one thing, but "by a 'civilian' Railroad
magnate!" The villains of two of Lieutenant Commander Edward Beach's
novels of life at Annapolis are fabulously wealthy young men whose parents
"surround" them "with comforts and luxuries" both at home and at the
Academy. The heroes expose their rich classmates as the authors of a variety
of nefarious schemes, and the miscreants are expelled. One naval officer character in Lieutenant Commander Yates Stirling's *A U.S. Midshipman in the
South Seas* complains that a political crisis in one of the Pacific islands is being
"brought about by these scheming, mercenary, merchants." Similarly, the
villain of Lieutenant Rufus Zogbaum's novel of Navy life acquires "something
shady about him" when he becomes rich.[5] A real midshipman, F. F. Foster,
welcomed America's entry into the war in 1917 because he felt that America's
"taste for luxury" was bringing her to the brink of the same ruin that befell
ancient Rome. Rear Admirals Bradley Fiske, William Wirt Kimball, and
Albert Barker all anathematized "the multi-millionaire manufacturer."[6] And
so on; the record could be expanded to record similar examples of naval
animosities toward the world of the marketplace almost indefinitely.

Paradoxically, Captain Alfred Thayer Mahan, some of whose books and
essays have all the flavor of a National Association of Manufacturers Annual
Report, is at other times the epitome of the antimaterialistic naval officer. In the
same days that he was putting the finishing touches to his masterpiece, *The*

Influence of Sea Power Upon History, 1660–1783, he wrote privately of his **189** impatience with the government for its tardiness in halting "the concentration of wealth and power in the hands of a protected few." He was a true son of Annapolis, with all the Academy disdain for those who "attach to the making and having of money" a value in excess of what Mahan thought proper. "Great and beneficent achievement," he believed, ministered to "worthier contentment" than "the filling of the pocket." He believed the British naval figure Admiral George Brydges, Lord Rodney, one of his heroes, to have been flawed seriously by his lust for wealth. Like Midshipman Foster, Mahan felt that Rome had collapsed when her "strong masculine impulse" had "degenerated into that worship of comfort, wealth, and general softness" that he considered characteristic of the "peace prophets" of his day.* Mahan, who felt called to a life of service to the State, often sounded like his more spiritual brethren while denouncing the world of Mammon that his Navy sustained. Listen to the High Priest of the Quarterdeck in one of his prophetic moments:[7]

> Ease unbroken, trade uninterrupted, hardships done away, all roughness removed from life—these are our modern gods; but can they deliver us, should we succeed in setting them up for worship? . . . If our civilization is becoming material only, a thing limited in hope and love to this world, I know not what we have to offer to save ourselves and others.

Clearly there was no love lost between trader and sailor.

To a certain extent naval officers tended to view the world of commerce and trade as a profession with a creed of its own that was in natural conflict with the service's creed. To men like Admiral Porter, for whom the austere Academy was "Mecca," there must have been something obscene and sacrilegious about men who viewed the California gold fields as "Mecca." Many officers feared that the Navy might be altogether ignored and disbanded in the great scramble for material gain. "Immersed as the people are in peaceful and material pursuits," Commander Mahan wrote in 1882, "the military establishment is necessarily one of our lesser interests." Similarly, Lieutenant J. D. Jerrold Kelley claimed that the country was "so enmeshed in the golden web of money-spinning that it thought little of service needs." He feared the effect of "foolish critics" who had begun "without rebuke to question" the need for a Navy and "to clamor for its extinction."[8] While the response naval officers made in the 1880s to the economy-minded critics will be given special attention in a later chapter, the thing that is important to note here is simply that naval officers often identified the world of commerce with their natural domestic enemies.

This tension between naval officers and the objects of their care may be elsewhere observable in the reaction of officers to incidents that caused the

---

* Thus he viewed the panic of some East Coast businessmen during the Spanish–American War to have been "due largely . . . to that false gospel of peace which preaches it for the physical comfort and ease of mind attendant, and in its argument against war strives to smother righteous indignation or noble ideals by appealing to the fear of loss—casting the pearls of peace before the swine of self-interest." Mahan, *Lessons of the War with Spain*, 45.

190   withdrawal of a vessel from other fleet elements actively playing at war games. The chief of the Bureau of Navigation, Commodore John G. Walker, displayed obvious impatience over the "picayune interests of Americans" that had obliged him to order the *Galena* to be detached from Rear Admiral Luce's North Atlantic "squadron of evolution" in 1888 to rectify the seizure of the *Haytien Republic* by Haiti. Luce recaptured the *Haytien Republic*, but wrote his wife of his disgust with the whole business; he had lost an entire season of war games as a result of the affair. A few years later Captain George Dewey protested to Navy Secretary Tracy the scattering of ships about the world to "show the flag" in foreign ports. Dewey hoped the fleets might be concentrated more frequently for operating maneuvers. Captain Mahan had the same opinion of "the picayune interests of Americans" abroad. In 1895 he complained to a British colleague, J. R. Thursfield, that the U.S. could never manage to hold a squadron together long enough to conduct the kind of exercises necessary if one were ever to contest the command of the sea. The trouble was that whenever the Navy was able to assemble for war games "a boobery starts up in Central or South America, or Hayti, or elsewhere, & away go one or two ships."[9] Such piddling affairs as those of Mr. Nathaniel McKay with his bridge across the Ozama River would have left Mahan unmoved. A bold fleet engagement in the style of Collingwood or Nelson was more like it.

The officer's Academy training and his renunciation of wealth and material pursuit served to bias him against those whose material interests he guarded, but frequently businessmen themselves didn't help matters.* Admiral Porter's recollection of the "Vandals" who descended upon California in the Gold Rush days was probably typical. The gold-dust field was their "Mecca"; the precious metal their "Prophet." Lieutenant J. W. Spaulding was offended by "the un-American [sic] manner, and the cockneyism," of U.S. merchants in the Far East in the 1850s. Commander W. T. Truxton reported the commercial agent of one firm operating in Melanesia to his employers in 1870 for breaking agreements with natives and generally abusing the firm's trading privileges. Four years later Commander Oscar Stanton wrote disapprovingly of a number of American merchants in Borneo to his senior, while Lieutenant Commander Charles Sperry reported to his wife a similar coterie of miscreants operating in Hong Kong in 1880. In both cases the traders were charged with abusing their hospitality. In an 1884 letter to his friend Samuel Ashe, Commander Alfred Mahan had some harsh things to say of American businessmen in Peru. The Commander had been ordered in the *Wachusett* to protect them, but he displayed little sympathy for his wards. They had taken the risks; they should be prepared to defend themselves. "Americans have opportunity enough in America." When Charles Sperry was ordered to the Orient again in 1899, this

* Commander Frederick Pearson claimed that the Alaskan traders, whose urgent appeals for naval relief often brought warships to Sitka, Anchorage, and Juneau, were more interested in the warships' payrolls than their aid, a charge quite similar to those that Army officers levied against western border towns in the same period. *Army and Navy Register,* III (August 12, 1882), 10.

time as a commander, he found another irritant, one Mr. Higgins, agent for an
American railway in the Philippines. Higgins, Sperry informed his wife, "was
simply all things to all men as his immediate interests dictated," a behavior that
Sperry found reprehensible. Consequently, Sperry confessed that he and his
fellow officers were "not particularly sorry to see the insurgents knocking the
stuffings out of his railway." When asked to help prevent the drafting of peon
laborers from U.S.-owned coffee plantations near Matagalpa, Nicaragua, in
1910, Rear Admiral William Kimball somewhat saracastically expressed a
willingness to help these "fine straightforward" planters "were it not that the
upholding of such [draft] exemption could be a support by the U.S. Government to the illegal peon slavery [used by the planters]."[10]

Some naval officers did what they could to counter what they deemed to be
the more striking examples of impropriety on the part of merchants and
speculators. In American Samoa, Commanders W. J. Terhune and B. F.
Tilley, successive U.S. Governors, successfully resisted the efforts of American
planter entrepreneurs to buy up the lands of native Samoans in the early
twentieth century, in spite of the fact that both of Terhune's Executive Officers,
one after the other, went over to the planter cause. (The fight cost Terhune
his sanity; when the strain on his resources grew too intense he took his own
life.) Other officers spoke out against the exploitation of Orientals by businessmen and consuls, though it is important to note that it was not so much
the materialistically based business civilization that troubled them as it was the
abuses these officers claimed to have observed within that civilization. The
former was fraught with much potential harm to man and state, to be sure, but
the latter were the sure signs of decay and iniquity revealed. The Annapolites
objected to "unjust" treatment, to treatment that "would not bear scrutiny
among fair minded people." But they did so chiefly because they feared a loss
of trading rights if such treatment of the natives and their governments continued. There was "a lot of money to be made in China" by businessmen "if
they go about it properly," as Captain E. T. Constien put it to Vice Admiral
Roger Welles in 1925.[11]

Many officers felt that business ethics in the U.S. were no more palatable
than they were in the Pacific. In 1885 Spencer Kase, Jr., one of the members of
the class of 1881 who had been forced to leave the service in 1883, expressed the
sentiments of those of his classmates who were thrust with him into the world
of buy and sell. In two years Kase had come to the conclusion that the only sort
of man who ever succeeded in business was

> the man who has good hard cheek, a very small conscience, or none at all, an utter lack
> of self-respect, and an ability to tell the most outrageous lies.

Kase was convinced that "the honest businessman" had existed in some sort of
state of nature but that by 1885 he was "a thing of the past."[12]

Even those business interests allied to the Navy could draw fire. Rear Admiral
S. F. DuPont often criticized "the *monitor* interest, a five-million contract,"

192 which he felt was "plundering the public treasury." DuPont's chagrin with "the looseness" of his era made him "rejoice at the stern and severe naval education we have passed through." In light of the evidence of some private naval-business arrangements cited in the previous chapter, DuPont's conviction that "no man has yet dared approach a *Navy* officer to offer a pecuniary advantage" is somewhat remarkable.[13] But DuPont was sincere; he and his professional colleagues felt themselves to be above reproach.

The exception proves the rule. In 1879 Lieutenant Commander Dewitt Kells, commander of the naval station at Brownsville, Texas, was dismissed from the service for conspiring with "a certain class of people" to provoke a war with Mexico that would "bring business to them." But Kells was only a "mustang," one of the few volunteer officers commissioned during the Civil War to have retained his rank until the late 1870s. He was not an Academy graduate and had thus never been a member of the inner priesthood of believers. Captain George Remey, a duly-anointed Annapolite who was dispatched to relieve Kells of command, was appropriately repelled by his behavior. In Remey's eyes mere money-making was an inadequate reason for mortal combat. He later refused to permit a wealthy cigar merchant to slip into Havana during hostilities in 1898 to look after his properties; this man may have had nothing to do with the cause of the war, but Remey was no more willing to permit profiteering in wartime than he was to let it lead to war.[14]

A sure irritant to the sensibilities of naval officers was the careless depletion or destruction of natural resources. As agents of the government naval officers felt obliged to protest whenever they considered that traders were endangering the future of the nation's natural wealth. The naval officer's attitude toward the seal industry in the Bering Straits is a good example. By the late 1880s American and foreign sealers were making such inroads into the population of that pelted creature that naval officers like Commander French Endor Chadwick, Captain Charles Clark, and Rear Admiral Stephen B. Luce entertained serious misgivings as to the fate of the trade. Sealers who killed unsystematically, with no thought of conserving sufficient young stock to insure future breeding, were looked upon as "piratical money making ruffians" by the very men whose warships stood guard over the American rights to the slaughter.[15] The Navy defended the interests of sealers, but not because it approved of their methods.

Here was an intriguing paradox. Naval officers aided and abetted businessmen abroad, but privately held many of them in low esteem. Was George Dewey behaving inconsistently when he threatened to shell a town to protect one businessman, and then threw another American mogul off his ship when that man suggested that his taxes were of sufficient magnitude as to give him a personal stake in the Navy? How do we explain Alfred Mahan's attitude in August, 1894, two months after he accepted honorary degrees from Oxford and Cambridge for his laudatory account of the role sea power played in advancing commercial interests, when he "backed out" of a party on board an American vessel because he heard that a member of the Jay Gould family, "a name . . . distasteful to me," would be present? Where did the naval aristocracy draw the line? Given their dislike of the more raw order of businessman, how could they bring themselves to lend such an individual, a type quite common abroad, any assistance at all? To preserve his own self-respect the naval officer must have had to do a good deal of rationalizing from time to time. But this process was not nearly as tortuous as one might suspect; in fact, it was a most natural act for these "Admirals of American Empire." Rear Admiral Robley "Fighting Bob" Evans summed up the feelings of his fellow officers in 1910 when he explained that "business methods" were "sometimes of such a questionable character" that naval force was "necessary to correct or unhold them."[16] Apparently naval officers looked upon their relationship to businessmen abroad as that of big brothers with responsibilities to act as staff and shield for vulnerable, and sometimes reprehensible, members of the national family—which tells us a good deal about what they considered their role to be.

"Police of the World"

Mahan's messmates took special interest in the welfare of Americans and American property and capital abroad, but as the "policemen of the seas" they often played no favorites, offering protection to all who ventured forth to ply the seas on honest business.* The suppression of piracy had long been one of the prime missions of western navies, and by the late nineteenth century American officers, who had helped extinguish North African and Caribbean marauders, were determined to take a greater share of the burden of policing the seas. In 1880, for example, Captain F. A. Roe insisted that the United States had a "duty of honor as well as morality" to "contribute its quota of service to the general police of the ocean. . . ." It was "full time," Roe insisted, that the United States bear its *burden of duty*, and not leave to Old Europe *the honor* as well as the *responsibility* of policeing [sic] the waters of the globe." And when pirates descended on merchantmen in the Sulu Sea and Yangtze valley in the early twentieth century, U.S. gunboats were often the first on the scene.[17]

From the policing of the high seas it was only a short step to the policing of the world's ports as well. Captain Roe, after all, had felt that America's obligation extended to the ocean's "marts of trade," its ports as well as its highways. Mahan's messmates frequently saw themselves as "the police of the world," empanelled "as jurors to decide the fact and sit in judgement upon wrongdoers," to protect sailors and others from hooliganism on land as well as sea. This was why George Bernard Shaw's American naval officer, "Captain

---

* Similarly, British officers in the 1890s "looked upon the Navy . . . as a World Police Force. . . . We considered that our job was to safeguard law and order throughout the world —safeguard civilization, put out fires on shore, and act as guide, philosopher and friend to the merchant ships of all nations." Vice Admiral Humphrey H. Smith, *A Yellow Admiral Remembers* (London, 1932), 54, cited in Arthur Marder, *The Anatomy of British Sea Power* (Hamden, Conn., 1964 [orig. pub. 1940]), 15–16. Cf. Grace E. Fox, *British Admirals and Chinese Pirates, 1832–1869* (London, 1940).

194   Kearney," sat in judgment on the pirate, "Captain Brassbound," and his cohorts; it was why Rear Admiral John C. Watson, commander of the Asiatic Squadron in 1899, ordered Commander E. H. Leutze, commander of the Naval Station at Cavite in the Philippines, to "arrest" insurgents in his area; and it was why "Lieutenant Commanding" John Rodgers considered the 1855 North Pacific Surveying and Exploring Expedition to be so essential. The increase of trade, a certain product of the expedition, was only "desirable," but the safeguarding of navigation and shipwrecked sailors was, to Rodgers, "a necessity." Similarly, Rear Admiral Oscar Stanton displayed no interest in the commercial value of the treaty Commodore Perry had secured with Japan and viewed the "Japan Expedition" solely in terms of the protection it afforded to sailors. The punitive expedition to Korea in 1871 was viewed as a blow for sailors' rights as well as an effort to provide an opening wedge for American trade, and the incidents at Valparaiso in 1891 and Tampico in 1914 both had their origins in the treatment of sailors ashore.

When trade was involved, naval officers conceptualized their mission in the same terms. To Lieutenant Commander Mahan the Japanese who fired upon the foreign concessions in 1868 were no less "scoundrels" because they had assaulted commerce ashore rather than on board the vessel that had carried the merchants to Osaka. Two months after he intervened in the Honduran–Nicaraguan war of 1907, Commander William Fullam explained to the editor of the New Orleans *Times-Democrat*: "We are sailors trying to suppress piracy on land." In fact, individual officers occasionally became so vigorous in their efforts to "suppress piracy on land" that they had to be held at bay by order of the Secretary. A case in point was that of Commander Joseph Hemphill in the *Detroit*, who became so aggressive in his treatment of Venezuelan rebels whose attacks on foreign businessmen he regarded as "lawlessness" and acts of "outlawry on mankind" that he had to be reminded by the Secretary of State that his mission was to protect U.S. property, not to hazard it.[18]

National Loyalty

Central to the officer's concept of his role as international policeman was his sense that his work was essential to the protection of the nation's "honor" and "prestige." At the heart of this conviction was his Annapolis-bred devotion to the nation-state. We have said something of the steps taken to inculcate this intense loyalty to the federal government in the chapter on the Naval Academy. It remains for us here to evaluate the success of that program by examining the attitude of the mature officer.

A cursory glance at virtually any remarks made by naval (or other service) officers* in this or for that matter any other era in American history might lead one to the conclusion that the military man is unquestioning in his loyalty to

---

* Enlisted men, in spite of poor treatment, were just as nationalistic as their officers. See, for example, Rodman, *Yarns*, 242–243; Hazen, *Five Years*, 443; *U.S. Nautical Magazine and Naval Journal*, III (1856), 194–198.

the State. And with certain qualifications[19] this conclusion would be entirely **195** correct. It was an American naval officer, after all, Stephen Decatur, "the very embodiment of chivalrous patriotic youth," who coined the phrase "my country, right or wrong," long before the Academy opened its doors. Throughout the nineteenth and early twentieth centuries wardrooms drank toasts to Decatur's adage; officers proposed its acceptance as the Academy's motto; Admirals ended addresses with ringing statements of their utter dedication to its premises. According to Lieutenant Ridgely Hunt, Decatur's motto had become the Navy's "own doctrine," revered "as the faith to uplift it through life unto death with a beatific satisfaction known only to martyrs."[20] It was (and apparently still is)* the naval officer's Golden Rule.

Translated into less spiritual rhetoric this meant that the naval officer would never fail to do his duty in any cause in which his nation was engaged, be it "righteous or unrighteous." In the words of Captain Francis A. Roe, it was enough for the naval officer "to know that his Country has Enem[ies] Afloat, and he knows well enough what to do." The challenging of a superior's orders was, of course, unthinkable. "No faults on the part of superiors," Captain William Sims maintained, could excuse "any failure of loyalty" on the part of a naval officer. Unflinching fealty was due to the federal leadership "under all circumstances." According to Rear Admiral Josiah McKean, no naval officer would ever allow his own attitude toward a policy of the federal government to obstruct his action under that policy.[21]

> That is not the way we are trained. . . . We have done as we were ordered. We *will* continue to do so. That is our job as we understand it under our system of government.

"Patriotism" was placed on a par with (and sometimes ahead of) religion as "the highest and most idealistic cause that can animate man." The flag was sacred cloth. "I tell you it gets you!" one Lieutenant Commander remarked. "That flag comes first with me—before everything else. I know we ought to have more pay, but believe me, I'm here to stay."† This kind of patriotism was incapable of producing anything but "good" results and was exonerated of all claims that its pursuit had "inculcated in anywise a warlike spirit for war's sake."[22]

---

* No less than 73% of our questionnaire sample of today's Academy midshipmen found Decatur's expression attractive (while only 23% of Pitt students approved of this pre-Nuremberg code of conduct). E. Berger, L. Flatley, J. Frisch, M. Gottleib, J. Haisley, P. Karsten, L. Pexton, and W. Worrest, "ROTC, My Lai, and the Volunteer Army," *Foreign Policy*, I (Spring, 1971), 144.

† Many enlisted men were similarly affected by their nautical doses of patriotic punch. One crew member of a minesweeper told Secretary of the Navy Josephus Daniels in 1919, "I never knew what patriotism meant before I learned it by service in the Navy. . . . I am a different man. Before the war . . . I felt no passion of patriotism. . . . But the Navy has taught me such reverence for the flag that I have a thrill every time it is raised, and somehow my country became something more than land and water and houses. It seems something holy to me. And that's what my naval service did for me." Daniel's comment on this was: "Such inculcation of love of country was the best by-product of the war." Daniels, *Our Navy at War* (New York, 1922), 314.

196   If all of this appears a mite uncritical, if it smacks at times of absolutism and ◦ the unblushing fealty of the Cavaliers, it is not surprising. The naval officer's mental furniture was distinctly Jacobite in style, with none of the philosophical underpinnings later demanded of his foes at Nuremberg.* For example, when Lieutenant W. O. Henry discussed what he called "the proper loyalty to seniors," he followed it with the parenthetical remark: "(That the King is King and that the King can do no wrong, etc.)." Naval officers were at home with this Tudor-English aphorism, as they were with its authoritarian rendering. When Midshipman Alfred Mahan offered his first account of the origins of "England's greatness," he turned, not to her "glorious navy," but to "the idea of obedience to the powers that be" which had been "born, bred, and nourished in an Englishman from his cradle to his grave."23

To the great regret of some officers, America had rejected the British royalty. Quite understandably, they tended to look upon the Chief Executive, their Commander-in-Chief, in prerogatival terms, but they were also capable of identifying their allegiance with the nation as a whole. Rear Admiral S. F. DuPont praised Congress for giving the President "tremendous power" in 1863:

> No monarch in Europe has greater [power]. . . . Eleven hundred millions of dollars voted!! A conscript bill which makes a militia *national* and not local and heaves the governors of the states and state's-rights nonsense overboard. . . .

Captain Caspar Goodrich felt that "love of country" ought to "supply the place of a feudal or monarchical loyalty and furnish an incentive to brave deeds and patient suffering" for all officers.24 And it did, of course; naval officers were arch-nationalists. But the interesting thing to note is that Goodrich considered nationalism to be a proper surrogate for a more attractive and deep-rooted "feudal or monarchical loyalty." It was a creed designed to "furnish an incentive" to Annapolites to emulate the Romance of the Rose! (Goodrich's reasoning should be kept in mind when we explore the naval officer's political and social predilections.)

---

* For those who object that I am passing judgment on men who were only behaving as their society expected them to behave instead of anticipating the ethical standards set at Nuremberg, my response is twofold. In the first place, I do not agree that it can be said that their "society" (outside of their own inner circle) altogether sanctioned the Decatur syndrome (see, for example, Henry D. Thoreau, "Civil Disobedience," *A Yankee in Canada, with Anti-Slavery and Reform Papers* [Boston: Ticknor and Fields, 1866], 123–151; and James Anson Farrer, *Military Manners and Customs* [New York, 1885], 257). And in the second place, I am less bent upon passing judgment on naval officers than I am on understanding them. It is true, that, upon understanding them, I often feel some revulsion and in the final chapter I try to point out that there were, and still are, alternatives to the Annapolite, but that is not the same thing as outright subjective condemnation. F. Scott Fitzgerald said of a particularly nasty character in his play *The Vegetable* (N.Y., 1923): "Frankly, I don't like her, though she can't help being what she is." You can understand how the naval aristocracy thought and acted as they did, but you don't have to like them for it, and once you have described these attitudes and actions, you don't have to pass the acquitting judgment of silence on them, their society, and its ethos.

!

Perhaps the naval officer's "love of country" is seen nowhere more clearly than in his response to the Civil War. According to Captain Roe the Navy man "cared not a whit about slavery, or the Negro! What he cared about was the Union; and the *integrity of the Union*! and he went into that war for the Union and for the Union only!" Similarly Rear Admiral Mahan testified that in "the stormy days which preceeded the War of Secession, no hatred of slavery, nor impulse of [material] interest, competed in power with the idea of national integrity to be asserted and preserved." "The Union" was "cherished almost to idolatry" by Northern-born junior officers and by virtually all senior officers, wherever they were from.* When one North Carolinian suggested to Mahan that the Union would not survive the 1860 election, Mahan was "as much aghast as though [he] had been told [his] mother would die within the term." The young Georgian or Virginian who left the service in the opening days of 1861 was treated respectfully by his ex-comrades but was criticized for having been "influenced by states-rights sophistry to foresake the flag under which he was born. . . ." And there were those who "inveighed fiercely, and even coarsely," against their Southern ex-colleagues, demanding that all traitors "be hanged."[25] When the Academy was moved to Newport in 1861 its commandant, Captain Christopher Raymond Perry ("Alphabet") Rodgers, was also moved—to tears—as he begged the departing Middies: "Be true to the flag, young gentlemen!" Lieutenant W. B. Cushing wrote his sister Mary at the outset of hostilities of his determination to "fight under the old banner of freedom" and of his readiness to die "under the folds of the flag that sheltered my infancy and while striking a blow for its honor" as well as his own. As the fighting dragged on, Midshipman Albert Caldwell fretted. "If the war goes on another year," he wrote his father in March, 1863, "we will lose our

---

* Many officers and officer candidates resigned and went south to fight for their states, but a greater percentage of southern Academy graduates (particularly older officers, who had agreeable careers to protect and whose identification with the Nation instead of their state was longer and stronger) remained loyal to the flag than did southern Harvard or Yale graduates. Cf. Morris Schaff, *The Spirit of Old West Point, 1858–1862* (N.Y., 1907), 233. In late December, 1860, Commander Charles Steedman's sister from Charleston, South Carolina, called him a traitor for his refusal to resign. Cousin James Steedman and nephew W. W. Smith wrote to the Commander a week later from the same secessionist hotbed: "There is not one of your relations but who are strong supporters of South Carolina; your father's *oldest* & *strongest* friends occupy the same position and we all expect you to do your duty to your God, your State, and Truth." Steedman stuck to the Union. Lieutenant John Taylor Wood's diary from 1860 and 1861, kept while an instructor at the Academy, reveals the inner turmoil of a southern-born member of the naval aristocracy. On November 8, 1860, the day after Lincoln's election, Wood resolved to "Hang firmly by the Union." Two weeks later he had changed his mind: "I must go with the South, let what will, come." The next month, while South Carolina was seceding, Wood was telling himself to "avoid political discussions" and to "do nothing rashly." Four months later he was still at the Academy, feeling "uneasy about my position here, for in these times we cannot say what may happen." Within a fortnight Sumter had been attacked and had fallen, Lincoln had called for volunteers, Virginia, North Carolina, Tennessee, and Arkansas had joined their southern brethren, and Lieutenant Wood had given up his "position" at the Academy and his commission in the Navy and was making his way to Richmond. Steedman Papers, Perkins Library, Duke U.; Wood Diary, Vols. I and II, S.H.C., U. of N.C. Library.

198 nationality"—which appears to have struck Caldwell as something akin to losing one's life, or faith, or virginity. Rear Admiral C. H. Davis's diary entry for April 12, 1863, is typical. Davis was troubled by the lack of support from many civilian Northerners "in the greatest of all contests, the contest for the life and existence of our common mother, our country." But his own faith was steady:

> I think more of death because life has now a new value derived from the possibility of being serviceable to the country. Oh, my country, my country! how my heart aches and all the pleasure of life is taken away by its distress! It grieves me so, beyond the utmost power of endurance, to hear some of my friends speak of its governments and its institutions as failures.

Davis and his fellow regulars were not the only Americans to write in this tone during the early 1860s.[26] That is not the point; I am not trying to suggest that the patriotism and nationalism of naval officers were unique to them. What I do submit is that their "love of country" was intense, and that although it burned bright enough during the Civil War for us to see over a century away, it burned just as bright in piping times of peace.

Morris Janowitz has argued that nineteenth century American nationalism was "not primarily a political concept for the military profession," but was "social and ethnic" in nature, emphasizing "Anglo-Saxon" ancestry as the bedrock of national loyalty among Army and Navy officers. This may have been true of some officers, for it is clear that "Anglo-Saxonism" was a pervading and profoundly influential mystique. Commodore Stephen Luce, for example, did hope that the "Anglo-Saxon race" would "continue to shape the destinies of these United States."[27] But it does not appear that the naval officer's *only* identification was with a social or ethnic concept of the state; they had their own views as to how the state should be run, to be sure, but when they spoke of their loyalty to the nation there was hardly a suggestion that the day might come when the social or ethnic complexion of the state would cause them to swerve in their loyalty to Old Glory. The naval aristocracy's reaction to the election of a Populist or of a Socialist such as Eugene Debs would have been interesting, for it would truly have tested their loyalty to the state and their Commander-in-Chief as abstractions.*

---

* Thus C. B. Otley maintains (*op. cit.*, 108) that British officers have remained loyal to their system of government essentially because they have seen no danger therein of truly radical steps that "seemed bent on reconstructing the basic social order or which seemed to threaten the corporate interests of the officer corps." Were such a radical transformation to *be* ordered, Otley (echoing Gaetano Mosca) doubts "that the [officer] corps would have remained in docile submission to its civilian masters."

I would say the same of the American professional officer corps. Many have argued that "it can't happen here," but when several of my students asked a random sample of Annapolis and University of Pittsburgh students if they "could imagine circumstances under which a military take-over of the U.S. government would be justified," we found that 34% of Annapolis students (but only 17.5% of Pitt students *could* imagine such circumstances. See E. Berger, *et al.*, *loc. cit.*

National Honor   **199**

The nation's "honor" or prestige was often at the heart of the naval officer's behavior as "international policemen." But it was also the reason for many actions, exclusive of those taken in policing the world's watery highways, in which naval officers claimed to have "guarded the nation's honor." This term was used by Commander Andrew Foote to defend his destruction of Chinese barrier forts at Whampoa in 1856. It was also the defense offered in 1871 when naval forces destroyed Korean forts to avenge an "insult to the flag" that the Koreans had offered when they opposed a party of armed U.S. sailors who had entered Korean inland waters in violation of Korean regulations. The anonymous "naval officer" contributor to the *United Service Magazine* in 1889 who wanted the U.S. to build additional gunboats to strengthen her position in the Chinese river valleys said nothing of the export-import markets, but he made much of the possibility that, without additional gunboats, America might be forced to "submit to some flagrant acts of discourtesy at the hands of insignificant but insolent nations." Rear Admiral Robley ("Fighting Bob") Evans looked upon the murder of a German missionary on the Shantung peninsula in the 1890s as a considerably less serious matter than the "insult to his government" inherent in the Chinese officialdom's tardiness in bringing the murderers to justice. Captain N. H. Farquhar described the Apia, Samoa, disaster, in which several U.S. warships (as well as British and German ones) were lost in a hurricane, to a reunion of Academy graduates in terms of national honor. The risks at that season of the year, Farquhar claimed, were great, "but the Honor of the country was at stake, and what sacrifice could be too great to maintain that?" It was Commodore Dewey's sensitivity over the nation's honor that caused him to stalk out of a dinner party at Hong Kong attended by the entire international "naval set" in the colony, when Germany's Prince Henry toasted the U.S. last. Oil was the prime mover, but it was Rear Admiral Henry Mayo's ultimatum to the Huerta forces at Tampico in 1914 that precipitated the "Affair of Honor" with Mexico. When Japanese forces began closing the door in China in the late 1930s, Admiral Harry Yarnell opposed all efforts from Washington to temper his vigorous defense of American businessmen there. Yarnell felt the honor of the nation and the Service demanded it. Support to these businessmen could not be withdrawn, as he put it, "without bringing discredit on the United States Navy."[28] "National honor," as Leo Perla has demonstrated, has often been the blister on the surface of international relations.

National Interest

"Honor" was often the surface issue, but, as Perla himself maintained[29] and the preceding chapter ought to have demonstrated, the Dollar lay at the heart of gunboat diplomacy. Naval officers were more than willing to strike a blow for national "honor" or "prestige," but, as the preceding pages suggest, they had little natural proclivity to go to the aid of the Dollar. Nevertheless they did, with tedious regularity. Naval officers often were responding to specific orders from Washington, which might explain matters, since disobedience of a direct order was unthinkable, regardless of what opinion one might hold of the merchant or investor whose business one had been ordered to aid. But officers frequently went a good deal beyond the terms of their orders and often acted without any special instructions whatsoever in helping men for whom they may have had little or no personal respect. How then are we to explain this ambivalence? How are we to understand the aggressiveness displayed by the Navy in defending its spiritual Nemesis? Could national "prestige" have had something to do with it? Theodore Roosevelt, it will be recalled, had told midshipmen of their opportunity "to be of benefit to the country at large." Might the defense and expansion of the trade and investments of *individual* Americans have been equated with the defense of *national* interests? The evidence clearly indicates that this was the case.

Long before the publications of Captain Mahan appeared, American naval officers advocated the development of a vast, modern, prosperous merchant marine—not necessarily because of any secret financial arrangement between the two interest groups but, in part, because naval officers considered it patriotic to help whiten foreign ports with American sails.* In 1845, for example, Commander Goldsborough attacked "the treasonable idea of conferring our carrying trade upon foreigners! Its very conception is shuddering; . . . its advocacy . . . absolutely abominable!" Commodore Shufeldt hoped to reorganize Russell Sage's Pacific Mail Steamship Company in 1874 in order to enhance its "national importance" and to enable it to act "as the standard bearer of our commercial supremacy in the East," but not because of Sage's salary offer of $4,000 a year, which was less than Shufeldt made in the Navy. To the naval officer, the Navy and the merchant marine were "inextricably associated in the economic progress and prosperity of the [American] people"; both were "essential conditions of national progress and prosperity."[30]

If the merchant marine was nationally important, how much more so were the goods and capital it carried to foreign lands? Some officers made less of "economic progress and prosperity" than they did of the less tangible factor of "prestige" abroad,[31] but the vast majority seem to have recognized that the prestige of the nation was somehow linked with its economic wellbeing and growth and that the defense of the nation's honor was usually a polite way of saying the defense of American trading rights or capital. Commander Andrew Foote made this abundantly clear in the concluding chapter of his 1854 account of the U.S. Navy in West African waters, and Commander John Rodgers recognized it in 1855 when he expressed sympathy for those American merchants who had been denied residence in Japan. Rodgers informed the hapless entrepreneurs that the Japanese action constituted "a public wrong, not a private

* This was not the entire story, by any means; the growth of the merchant marine service would necessitate further growth of the Navy itself, a more important objective to many officers.

For more on naval officers and the need for a merchant marine see pp. 302–303 in Chapter 6 and pp. 372–373 and 377–378 in Chapter 8.

one" (probably of slight consolation) and added that he was "American enough" to trust that their government would interpret the treaty with Japan to mean more than "wood, water, and shelter for ships." Washington was too slow in aiding its overseas agents of national prosperity to satisfy Lieutenant Alexander Habersham, who complained of the belated treatment of these traders.

Captain John Dahlgren took the same position as Rodgers and Habersham. In 1859 Dahlgren was at Tampico, Mexico, protesting the seizure of $12,000 worth of property belonging to a U.S. citizen. He construed the incident to be an insult to the nation itself and insisted on redress. Similarly, Ensigns Hugh Rodman and Roger Welles viewed the naval intervention in the Panamanian revolution of 1885 in terms of national interests. Properties built with "American capital" became "American property" in their eyes, and both naval neophytes felt it obvious that the U.S. would "protect her interests." Lieutenant Lucien Young regarded the landing of sailors and marines in Hawaii in 1893 as necessary because of the "American property" at stake. Rear Admiral John Edwards favored the sale of illuminants to China, not because he was "in league" with the Standard Oil interests (excepting, of course, the figurative sense of that phrase) but because the sale of lamp oil paved the way, he believed, for more substantial American trade. Commander Nathan Twining was critical of what he regarded as a reluctance on the part of the Wilson administration to dispatch additional warships to protect American oil interests in Mexico during the Carranza–Huerta power struggle. Rear Admiral William L. Rodgers argued for less arrogance in naval dealing with Chinese, not because he bore any affection for Orientals or particular respect for their feelings, but because Chinese good will was necessary to "maintain the open door" and "secure Chinese commerce."[32]

Commander Nathan Sargent served with Dewey at Manila and saw the issues there in remarkably clear terms. The Pacific Ocean was to be "the theatre of the twentieth-century struggle between nations for commercial supremacy," and Sargent felt that the nation that commanded the commerce of the Pacific would thus "control the commerce of the world." Consequently, he looked upon the Battle of Manila Bay and the conquest of the Philippines as measures to provide the United States with an "Eastern Empire" that would assure her "the trade routes" of Pacific commerce "for all time" (Sargent was no advocate of eventual Philippine independence).

In his daily duties Sargent also characterized the Navy's attitude toward overseas American economic interests. Sargent, you may recall, was the officer in charge of the expedition of five warships that forced the Chinkiang Taotai to honor a lease of land for storage tanks to Standard Oil in 1905. He described this act to his Commander-in-Chief as a measure that would help "enlarge the trade of this American corporation." The nationality of the firm was apparently at the heart of Sargent's zeal in the matter, for he had displayed considerably less interest five years before in helping the Orinoco Shipping & Trading Company in Venezuela. This company was not sufficiently American to spark

202 his patriotism. To Sargent the firm "represents American interests only indirectly; it would be more correct to say that it claims to represent American capital."[33] And this was not enough. The distinction Sargent made was important: Portfolio investment of American dollars abroad would not earn the respectful attention of naval officers (barring orders from Washington to the contrary) as readily as the dollars invested in an enterprise conducted by a legitimized "American corporation."[34] Only the latter fully qualified as "American property" worthy of special attention from the graduates of the Naval Academy.

One might be inclined to write off these expressions of concern for the welfare of "legitimate" business as polite public statements of sympathy from men who were merely doing their duty, were it not for the fact that naval officers spoke in the same terms while off duty. Shufeldt's correspondence with the Pacific Mail Steamship Company was, ostensibly at least, private; and Ensign Roger Welles' letter to his father was most certainly so. And the number of times that officers went out of their way to draw the connection between national policy and American business interests abroad, quite apart from those circumstances where such statements could be construed to be officious, formal, and devoid of personal conviction, makes it clear that they were sincere in identifying economic and national interests. Thus Captain Shufeldt felt that U.S. citizenship entitled businessmen to extensive assistance from the Navy. To be an American, in fact, was to be a citizen of the world, as far as Shufeldt and his colleagues were concerned. They spoke of the merits of Roman citizenship in the days of the Empire, "*Civis Romanus sum*," and swore to do their part to elevate "American sons" to the position of power of "the ancient Roman."[35] They looked upon European merchants as "sinners against our greatness." They visualized, quite reasonably, an intermeshing, public partnership in which "the capitalist forms trading companies and the naval officer seeks for coal ports upon favorable routes, while a wise government throws its protecting care over our citizens abroad by the presence of its navy and the building up of a worthy consular service...."* They went quite literally to the ends of the earth "to foster and to extend" American trade and investments that they deemed "essential factors of national happiness and prosperity." They hoped to insure that the American businessman would be free "to hold up his head proudly" anywhere in the world "and to stick out his chin with confidence at any power that rise to roughhouse American interests." For most officers, one principle dominated—"to inviolately protect under every circumstance, and with all the available power of the Nation, our citizens engaged in lawful and peaceful avocations abroad."[36] Many of these sons of planters, bankers, and merchants didn't have to be taught these maxims of "mercantil-

---

* Understandably, when naval officers such as Admiral Mark Bristol found American businessmen and missionaries "much divided" and unwilling to "pull together" for the greater good of the "national interest," they were disgusted. See, for example, Bristol to Lewis Heck, March 22, 1928, Bristol Papers, L. of C.

ism," but their Academy experience, you are reminded, must have helped to **203**
prepare them "to defend the tenets of the American way."* *to include business*

The Social and Political Ideas of American Naval Officers

Perhaps it would be more accurate to style this section simply "the social ideas of American naval officers," for the naval aristocracy had few political predilections. Officers moved about too often to develop any significant local outlook, and on the national level they looked upon themselves as "children of the Government" and were unquestioning in their fealty to "the Administration." The President was the Navy's Commander-in-Chief, and be he Theodore Roosevelt or Andrew Johnson, his will was law.[37] Small "d" democrats were "rare birds in the Navy," and large "d" ones were almost as rare. Republicans there were, in name, but the average officer saw little or no distinction between the parties and rarely voted. When one officer was pressed by a New York Republican to hire additional Republican navy yard workers, he informed the politician that he "did not care for politics, & was wholly unacquainted with the political opinions of any man in the Yard," and that such considerations would "not have the slightest weight" with him in any event. When further pressed with the charge that he was favoring Democrats, the naval aristocrat replied that, on the contrary, he was "an old-fashioned Federalist of the Hamilton School" and that he had never voted in his life. Such hoary apolitics may have disarmed local bosses, but voicing them rebounded on the officer if the Navy Secretary, generally an ex-ward heeler himself, considered the officer's interference in the control of patronage to have jeopardized the party's future in the area.[38]

Naval officers rarely entertained aspirations for political office. Once in a rare while a naval officer might become a public official. When this occurred, as it did in the case of Richmond P. Hobson, a Spanish-American War hero who was elected to Congress from his Alabama district, the officer's experience in the Navy as protector of American business interests tended to reappear—a case of the servant of the State directing affairs as he had been taught to implement them. Thus, Hobson, in 1915, argued that "America must control the sea" in defense of her "vital interests"—and the "vital interests" Hobson had in mind were cotton goods, of special interest to his Alabama constituents. Hobson's specific grievance was the loss of twenty million dollars of this trade in Manchuria as a result of the Japanese occupation of that area. And while it is safe to say that Hobson, as an Alabaman, might well have expressed alarm over the loss of this cotton market regardless of his prior career, the thrust of his message—for an "open door" one needs an "adequate Navy"—should at least partially be attributed to his experiences with the Asiatic Fleet from 1899–1901.[39]

* See Chapter 2, especially notes 7 and 36.
Inasmuch as the naval aristocracy spent a considerable portion of their lives protecting American commerce and investments abroad, one might expect that they conceptualized and even articulated their relationship to the national economy before Mahan. And they did. See "The Concept of Sea Power" in Chapter 6.

204   It took a hero's welcome to persuade Commodore George Dewey, fresh from his triumph at Manila Bay, to seek office. But even Dewey could win the nomination of no more exalted a body than the 4th Annual Convention of Hoboes, who made him their unanimous choice for President in 1900. Dewey announced his candidacy with the claim that he considered the office of the President "not such a very difficult one to fill" and topped that off with the admission, when asked to elaborate, that perhaps he had "said too much already." This interview turned out to be the high point in a brief but hilarious campaign. Unlike a more modern counterpart, Admiral Dewey neither faded nor floated away after his political rebuff; he remained a key figure in the Service. But he never dabbled in politics again.[40]

Most Annapolites deemed politics an ungentlemanly business, and most politicians were regarded as "vulgar dogs." Andrew Johnson, William Jennings Bryan, Woodrow Wilson, and Josephus Daniels appear to have received the most individual abuse, but naval officers collectively disliked the pork-barrel, wheeler-dealer Congressman. "I hate a politician worse than a snake," one officer wrote to his wife. Predictably, politics was not considered a proper subject for one's wife or family. "Politics is bad enough for men," the same officer continued, "but when women . . . meddle with it then they become, Oh, how disgusting." Another officer wrote home:[41]

> I hope that politics is not discussed at home—it . . . really is too dirty a subject for a conversation at table.

Woman suffrage was regarded by most officers and their wives as "the worst kind of communism" that would breach the "line of demarcation" between the sexes. Women were advised to concentrate their affection upon the home, since it was not considered advantageous to the State that they enter the political arena. Most officers felt that political rights should be confined to propertied men, to those who "regulate business, commerce, transportation, manufactures." Blacks, women, enlisted personnel, and paupers were not deemed worthy of a voice in the affairs of government. The enfranchisement of "great hordes of men" from the "lowest and basest slums of Europe and Asia" was deemed "a matter of the deepest national concern." Like the rest of the American "aristocracy" of their day, most naval officers were "nativists." It did not necessarily follow that the lower classes were unworthy of contributing to the expenses of government. The loss of political rights was not to be followed by a sundering of economic duties. On the contrary, the naval aristocracy felt the wealthy bore "unduly the burden of taxation and charitable contributions." As Rear Admiral French E. Chadwick put it, democracy had established in some communities governments operated "by the least educated, the least interested class of citizens," who dispensed the tax monies of those who had the community's "well-being most at heart."

> It stands to reason that a man paying $5,000 taxes . . . should be assured a representation in the Committee which lays the tax and spends the money which he contributes.

Captain Caspar Goodrich bemoaned "the steady loss of influence" of men of "birth, education, and moral elevation," who would "in the ideal community, be entrusted with the largest measure of the powers of government." Some, such as Captain Mahan, preferred a social class less financially bound to commerce and perishable goods. The British aristocracy, Mahan noted with satisfaction, had none of the "political timidity which characterizes those whose property is exposed and business threatened [by wars]—the proverbial timidity of capital."[42] But if Mahan and some of his messmates preferred a landed gentry, an aristocracy of "old" wealth, they were generally quite tolerant of the "new," commercial upper class, from which, after all, many of their colleagues had come.

There were "good" politicians and "bad" politicians, to be sure. The good ones, essentially, were those who stood selflessly and patriotically for the good of the nation, which, to the naval officer, was synonymous with the good of the Navy. The bad ones were those who fought increases in naval expenditures and were (thus) unpatriotic. After reading Chancellor James Kent's "Commentaries on International Law," as complete a collection of Federalist views on vested interests and the merits of aristocracy as one might hope to find, Midshipman Mahan bemoaned the fact that "the influence of gentlemen" had diminished and passed into the hands of "such scum as the mass of our politicians are." "Oh, ——!" he exclaimed to his ex-roommate. "The only foundation of all military greatness & discipline sapped, the axe laid at the root of the national defense! These [democratic] influences will be the bane of the country in war." Some thirty years later Captain Mahan was high in praise of the "wise" British system of class government, where the aristocracy was more sympathetic to "the spirit of military honor, which is the first importance," than were the elites in the United States. And by 1911 retired Rear Admiral Mahan had become confirmed in his belief that "external politics" were matters "of professional concern to military men" inasmuch as they affected naval expenditures.[43] Similarly Rear Admiral Bradley Fiske waged war on "the dangerous enemy of the United States," "the American politician . . . who prevents our getting an adequate army and navy." From the standpoint of "national longevity," Fiske insisted, politics was "a disease." Fiske called on his brother officers to continue to wage the battle "against the political influences that sap the strength of the nation." "Militarism does not menace the liberties of the people," he maintained, "but it does menace the irresponsible powers of politicians."[44]

The naval aristocracy's critique of "the *genus politicus*" was founded on three related postulates: first, that the democratically selected representative of the people harkened to the voice of the people "far more readily than he [would] to the advice of experts"; second, that the voice of the people was counsel inferior to that of experts; and third, that for matters related to the governing of naval affairs, naval officers were their own best experts and ought be given control of their own affairs.

The aristocracy's disdain for the common man was intense. "I think a man

206   must feel elevated," Midshipman Mahan joshed, "as he says, 'Fellow citizens,' and turns around to look at the motley crowd usually assembled on such occasions." Mahan delighted in Sir Walter Scott's contrasting of "gallant soldiers and noble gentlemen" on the one hand with "crack-brained demagogues and sullen boors" on the other, a distinction "between spilling a flask of generous wine, and dashing down a can full of base, muddy ale." Commander William Fullam regarded the efforts of Cuban Liberal politicians in 1906 to rally "the negroes and worst elements" of Cuba to their support as "proof of their lack of patriotism." A patriotic politician would never have stooped to such measures. The thought that "village churls, who are born but to plough," might have some voice in national, and naval, affairs was enough to make the average Annapolite's blood simmer; and both he and his wife had to be warned to "damn democratic institutions far from the civilian ear!" lest "the Peepul" get wind of the naval aristocracy's true sociopolitical aroma.[45]

Like many other "progressive" professionals active at the turn of the century, the naval officer felt that "the helm of state" should be "committed to experts" —that the machinery of government and diplomacy should be placed in "trained" hands—in order to increase "efficiency." "Executive efficiency," Captain Mahan argued, was the "most essential attribute of government." "Let your motto be 'Efficient,' without malice, greed, or hate/Co-operative-preparation, Service, Duty to the State," Captain W. I. Chambers rhymed in 1916. The warship was a perfect laboratory for social engineering. As Captain W. V. Pratt told a Senate subcommittee in 1920, the "habits of a life time" had forced the minds of naval officers to fix their attention "along the straight road of mechanical efficiency."[46]

The naval aristocracy favored civil service reform, and, understandably, they focused their assault upon the Navy Department itself. Publicly they objected to the control of naval affairs by politicos and non-professionals, but secretly officers resented all civilian control. Commander Francis Roe privately advised Captain Henry Wise of his conviction that the Navy Department's decisions were "invariably adverse to the interests of the Line, or in other words the interests of the Brain, the pluck, and the responsibilities of the Navy." An understandably anonymous officer complained publicly that the control of the Service by "half a dozen clerks" was "wrong from beginning to end. It is worse than wrong; it is a crying shame." Rear Admiral S. F. DuPont considered it fortunate that Navy Department civilians were "an official ephemera, who live between sunrise and sunset as compared with a Navy officer."[47]

Such professional distrust of civilian control eventually led to the creation in 1916 of the office of Chief of Naval Operations, a move designed to minimize civilian control. The move may have succeeded, but it did not necessarily improve the quality of the decisions emanating from Washington. During the 1920 Congressional investigation of the Navy Department's planning and fighting of the World War, Admiral William Sims argued that Navy Secretary Josephus Daniels had failed to respond adequately to exigencies demanded by the German submarine assaults on Allied shipping, in that Daniels had not acted immediately on Sims' recommendations from London for a shift to destroyer construction and convoy operations. But while Sims' indictment of Daniels has been read as evidence for a general critique of civilian control of naval policies,[48] it is important to note that several high-ranking naval officers who had been stationed at the Navy Department in Washington during the war disagreed with Sims. They had *advised* Daniels to pursue the very policies Sims. attacked as "civilian" in tone and quality. Moreover, Daniels appears to have lined up with the "progressives" more often than with the troglodytes.[49] Admiral David D. Porter took virtual control of the Navy Department for a brief period in 1869 upon the election of his old comrade-in-arms, U. S. Grant, but his efforts to reorganize the Navy Department of Gideon Welles should certainly not be viewed as substantive proof of the naval aristocracy's superior competence in the field of naval administration. Apparently "experts" could make mistakes as grievous as those of "village churls" and machine lieutenants.

Within the Service, officers strove to increase the efficiency and discipline of their ships and men. The indoctrination of Jack Tar, performed by the graduates of the Naval Academy under the direction of Uncle Sam, was most interesting. It was neither classical, nor terribly "practical" in nature, since education "beyond the barest elements" was looked upon as "overeducation," and officers admitted with disarming frankness that such "overeducation" would lead the naval apprentice "into disgust for routine and discouragement for rewards" and result, "in nine cases out of ten," in their leaving the Navy. "Overeducation" was deemed "neither right nor politic." Instead the band of brothers restricted their indoctrination to "citizenship training," which consisted in lessons in physical hygiene, the use of arms, and discipline. Citizenship training involved the inculcation of "patriotism," to be sure, but it meant much more—it was fundamentally an effort to improve the "productive capacity" of bluejackets, making them of "much greater commercial value to the economy of the nation." "Men and iron" were both "raw resources" to be developed, not only for peacetime commerce, of course, but to fashion the sinews of naval might. "When I see so many men in line," Ensign Roger Welles told his mother on witnessing an urban throng, "I think of what an immense number of men [the U.S.] *could* place in the ranks now in case of war." The inception of a disease which could have been prevented—and officers generally had in mind venereal diseases—was looked upon as "a crime both against ourselves and the State." It reduced "industry" and disrupted discipline and efficient shipboard operation. And these were intended to be the chief fruits of any indoctrination program.[50]

Commodore Luce's apprentice school system was at the heart of the naval aristocracy's citizenship-training program, but the aristocracy had its sights set on the general American populace as well. Annapolites saw "many indications that respect for authority might well be increased in the United States. Efficiency experts find this fault the hardest to remedy. . . ." Universal military

208   training was the answer. It would bring rich and poor together in a common atmosphere "to the benefit of both" and would overcome "a tendency to 'softness'" which was "becoming a grave symptom of national decadence; the need of restoring [sic] *American* militancy." This critique of "a new softness" was as old as George Washington and as modern as Eugene Kinkead and Lieutenant Colonel William E. Mayer,[51] but it may have had its greatest potency in the fin de siècle and the days of World War I. In any event, Mahan and many of his messmates were highly critical of the "natural man so to speak." The typical New England, Great Lakes region, Southern, or foreign recruit had to be "curried down & licked into shape before he [wa]s really good for much." American naval officers were "strenuous believers" in the German Army system of U.M.T. It had increased every German male's "productive capacity" by at least 5%, Commander French Chadwick maintained, and had resulted in German citizens with the capacity to "produce better children, govern their families better, and [prove] more stable in conduct." What more could any good servant of the State desire?[52]

      To say that naval officers took little or no part in the political debates of their day is simply to say that they did not consider that their positions as "children of the Government" permitted them openly to engage in the process of politics.[53] It is *not* to say that they did not hold any opinions regarding the qualifications deemed proper for high office, or the behavior expected of such individuals when elected. Mahan and his messmates, like their Hamiltonian brethren before them, favored strong, centralized government and the bold exercising of power. "A little despotism in government is a good thing,"[54] Captain Percival Drayton once remarked to a friend, and I have found none of his naval colleagues who disagreed.

      It may come as a surprise to those who hold Captain A. T. Mahan in high esteem to know that he, like his one-time Commanding Officer, Drayton, displayed a distinct preference for autocracy. While a student at the Naval Academy, he was critical, not only of democratic, but of republican forms of government as well. "Oh, Sam, say what you please, a republic is the damnedest humbug ever created for times when war is even a bare possibility," he wrote his ex-roommate. Like his messmates, Mahan's primary concern was with the fate of the Union—and the civil and political rights of its citizens necessarily were considered less important than the survival of the abstract life of the State. "Until the reign of peace, good-will to men comes, mankind must be subject to mankind, & for the preservation of the State this subjection must be absolute, perfect—a principle, a creed." Mahan feared that "American independence" had prevented the people (as indeed it had) from cultivating "the great virtue that alone will save us in the hour of danger, obedience—passive, unresisting obedience." He was pessimistic. "It requires virtue & high mindedness above an American youth to realize the beauty, the grandeur, of the sacrifice in a warrior." Young Mahan was probably unfamiliar with Alexis De Tocqueville's warning:

A democratic people must despair of ever obtaining from soldiers . . . blind, mute, **209**
submissive, and invariable obedience . . . the nation might be in danger of losing its
natural advantages if it sought artificially to acquire advantages of this particular kind.
But he could not have been expected to have sympathized with its sentiments
even if he had seen the passage. Mahan's respect was reserved for "the mighty
hand that crushes everything that stands in its way and the will that makes men
giants," for men like Napoleon and "those of unrelenting heart who tear away
and break down every obstacle." "Every great man that ever lived," he told a
bevy of young ladies, while a firstclassman at the Academy, "every great man
that ever lived had the nature of a despot."[55]

It would be relieving to brush these remarks aside as the product of boyish
exuberance, born in years of internecine politics and disorder. But these convictions survived the test of time and reappeared in Mahan's years of literary
activity in the late nineteenth and early twentieth centuries. Prior to the outbreak of World War I Mahan had many respectful words for "the submission
of the Prussians," whose lack of concern for popular legislative responsibilities
lent them "plastically to the moulding force of a strong government. . . ."
"Able" despots could provide "fortunate" government "independent of the
popular will." Free governments could not see their way to act in their own
best interests, "while, on the other hand, despotic power, wielded with judgment and consistency, had created at times a great sea commerce and a brilliant
navy with greater directness than can be reached by the slower process of a free
people." *This* was what Mahan had "learned" from his study of history, but it
was something he had suspected all along. A peaceful, gain-loving nation was
not sufficiently "far-sighted" for Mahan, and far-sightedness, he maintained,
was what was needed "for adequate military preparedness."[56]

Mahan did not specify the degree of preparedness that would prove "adequate," nor did he reveal the reason that popular government was not naturally
"imbued with the spirit of the people and conscious of its true bent." The
creation of a brilliant navy by means of despotic power was problematic, to
be sure; but the difficulty, as Mahan conceived it, didn't lie in the threat to
democratic institutions and human rights. Mahan had only scorn for those with
such "morbid distrust" of the military way of life. The difficulty lay in "insuring
the perseverance" of this brilliant navy after the death of the particular despot
who had brought it to life! For Mahan and his messmates "passionate devotion
to a Person, to a great Leader," became "that one supreme motive in human
action." It is no wonder that every officer whose sentiments could be determined on the matter adored the Navy's best friend in the White House, the
man on horseback, Roosevelt; hoped that "Teddy will get it again" in 1912;
and looked upon his passing in 1919 as a great personal blow.[57]

As we have seen, the naval officer's own concept of governing men was often
severe to extremity. "The military man's thought is aggressive," Captain W.
V. Pratt told a Senate subcommittee in 1920. "The world would be better,"
Commander Ralph Earle declared, if "people who will not live right" were

210 "made to feel the tyrannical, unyielding, and hard-nailed fist. . . ." Mahan and his messmates rarely qualified as savage beasts. They almost always kept their cool and acted with gentlemanly impartiality; but, because of the nature of their profession and the absence of immediate legal restraints that might have prevented them from abusing their position in the warship community, they often overstepped the legal limits of the disciplinary codes. The end result was a harshness that probably exceeded that of their civilian contemporaries. Consider, for example, their views on capital offenses and their punishment. Men like Mahan, who longed "to see a man's head taken off with a single blow of the sword," felt no compunction about meting out punishment themselves. Was Lieutenant Albert Caldwell merely trying to impress his aunt with his severity in 1878 when he told her

> I have not despaired of our institutions but we have got to do some hanging & build larger prisons or we too [as the British and European powers] will go to the bad. . . . We must hang forgers, defaulters, maim [?] murderers & the like or society will not be able to protect itself against the increasing swarm of them.

Or did he really hope the nation would reverse the direction of its prison reforms and return to the eighteenth century British model? It seems entirely possible that Caldwell was quite sincere, if we are to judge from the similarity of views one finds among his messmates. To cite but two other examples: When Leon Czolgosz shot President McKinley in 1901, Lieutenant Roger Welles wrote to his mother, "I really think hanging or electrocuting is too humane a manner of putting [Czolgosz] out of the way—he should be tortured in some way"; and when Captain Robert Coontz assumed his duties as Governor of Guam, he told the natives that he "would be a hanging governor. If the person who committed a crime were insane," Coontz explained, "it would be no harm to hang him." The naval aristocracy, with their unbounded contempt for "bleeding-hearts liberals" and "sentimental writers," had no qualms about spilling blood or employing newly-developed noxious gases in wartime and were just as "tough-minded" in peacetime.[58]

The naval officer's affection for authoritarianism, his sense of traditionalism, and his disdain for libertarianism, bred of a lifetime of military thought and behavior,[59] led him to favor strong government and exacting discipline. Thus the Navy's governing of Santo Domingo during the Wilson administration ignored legal process, freedom of press and of speech, and alienated every element of that nation's social order. They drew harsh criticism from authorities in Washington, but the officers in charge could see no reason to alter their course. Stability could only be secured, they maintained, in an atmosphere of order, system, regularity, obedience.[60]

Consequently, naval officers despised "radicals," "socialists," "anarchists," "bolsheviks," men who proposed a radical reordering of the social or economic system. Like many of their contemporaries, they had very little sympathy for "idlers," "misfits," or poor, deeming their plight to be the result of "moral torpor." Old-age pension plans and such general welfare schemes as took shape **211** in late nineteenth and early twentieth century America generally drew hostile fire from the naval aristocracy. Thus labor unrest such as that displayed in the strikes of 1877 made officers' "blood boil as it had boiled but once before," when the State had been threatened with a different form of "anarchy," secession. "The law-supporting and preserving instincts" that throbbed in the breasts of all the "young officers of the republic" in those tense months were contrasted with "the fiendish impulses of their fellow-citizens" and their "insane acts of destruction." One officer described the sentiments of one group of Annapolites and their men:

> Tears in several eyes showed the extent of the indignation which was prevailing . . . and the speedy adjustment of belts and arms exhibited the general impatience which was felt to be off for any point where law, order, and decency were dethroned and in need of succor.

Throughout the "doldrum years" of the 1870s and '80s, when appropriations were particularly hard to come by, naval officers sometimes reminded policy-makers that the Navy helped "a pigmy and widely-dispersed army" to protect the nation from rebellion and riots launched by international "anarchists" with "revolutionary ideas" that had to be fought, not with other ideas, but with "the bullet or bayonet." During the depression of the 1890s naval forces were deployed in riot-tactic formations (see photo, p. 154)—skills learned since 1877. With the nomination of William Jennings Bryan in 1896 there were officers who were convinced that the nation was on the verge of "*French Republicanism and Anarchism*," and in 1902, when Germany's Prince Henry paid a visit to the U.S., Rear Admiral Robley Evans saw to it that the "anarchists" in every naval port were interned until after his departure.[61]

By the second decade of the century other threats loomed on the naval officer's horizon—the I.W.W. and the "bolsheviks"—and officers who had managed to get along with labor organizers in the past grew distrustful of them by 1915, "believing they were in league with the I.W.W." "The Navy loathes the I.W.W.," one Admiral remarked in his autobiography; he might have added what others were to add—that the Navy loathed Bolshevism as well. "Wobblies" and communists, "secret incendiary organizations," "noxious bacilli," "the hoboes of the earth," were enemies of the State. On August 3, 1918, a landing party from the U.S.S. *Olympia*, Dewey's Manila Bay flagship, clashed with Soviet troops near Archangel—the first such shedding of blood to involve U.S. and Soviet combatants.* Simultaneously, the Navy was fighting

---

* Not all Annapolites favored intervention in Russia. Rear Admiral Newton McCully was uncertain of the wisdom of the occupation of Archangel and Murmansk (Tolley, *op. cit.*, 72). But most favored intervention. Between 1918 and 1920 Rear Admirals Austin Knight, William L. Rodgers, and Albert Gleaves all urged Washington to show more support for anti-Bolshevik forces in Vladivostok and Siberia. Knight exceeded his authority in joining his forces with those of Japanese and European powers to declare a protectorate over Vladivostok. Captain William Watts, commanding U.S.S. *Albany*, went so far as to

212   "Bolshevism" in this country as well. According to the Department of Justice's own investigator, the Seattle–Portland District Office of Naval Intelligence made 129 "indiscriminate arrests" of suspected radicals between October 1, 1917, and April 1, 1918. The O.N.I. was temporarily curbed, but six months later, in August, 1918, their Seattle agents seized 39 more suspects. The next year sailors were landed in Portland to break a Wobbly longshoreman's strike and the Chief of Naval Operations, Admiral Coontz, ordered the seizure of all ships with I.W.W. or Bolshevik crews operating in American waters. Contributors to the Naval Institute's *Proceedings* throughout the 1920s drew the conclusion that the emergence of a socialist government in Russia required the rebirth of American nationalism if international anarchism was to be avoided. Many officers saw the spirit of Bolshevism everywhere. Ensign Winston Folk, for example, described the "scoffing, anti-everything, young Bolshevik who prides himself on being the leader of the gang which loafs around the corner drug store [!]" Such unproductive, individualistic, opportunistic members of society were apparently anathema to the Ensign Folks of the world.[62]

One officer, Rear Admiral Albert Niblack, drew up an impressive list of "un-American" activities—activities tending to "weaken the obligation of the individual to the State." He included "Internationalism, Bolshevism, Radical Socialism, Pacifism, Trade Unionism, Judaism, Jesuitism, Hyphenism, Individualism," yet concluded that "the age of individualism has now passed" and that henceforth men would have to perform more functional duties within the corporate state. Rear Admiral Bradley Fiske agreed, but he warned that were the foreign trade of the nation to be suspended, "the greatest danger to the country would not be from the enemy outside, but the unemployed people inside. . . ." Only one officer seemed to sense the irony of this virulent assault on socialism by men who had long maintained that their own Service was itself "a socialistic organization whose motto might well be 'From each man according to his abilities, to each man according to his needs.' " But even this officer, Captain E. B. Fenner, did not intend that his parallel be read as a defense of socialism; he had in mind the increasing of military discipline, a phenomenon he vaguely associated with socialism, in order to "blot out petty and unessential individualism for the good of the service."[63]

To a considerable extent the "citizenship training" that enlisted men received from the naval aristocracy was designed to prevent the flight of Jack Tar to the ranks of socialism. What would be the fate of the nation's interests if sailors for whom Congress had neglected to vote appropriations in 1877 were to join the strikes? "One shudders at the bare thought," one contemporary officer wrote, "A commune? Horrible!" Later, when Russian and German sailors raised the Red Flag and struck blows for social and economic reform, the naval aristocracy quailed in its dress whites at the prospect of American *Potemkins*

---

land 100 sailors to help seize the Bolshevik-controlled Suchun coal mines. His only regret was that he had caused no Bolshevik losses. (Braisted, *U.S. Navy in the Pacific, 1909–1922*, 357, 385–399.)

steaming off to join their Soviet brethren and proposed more rigorous citizen-ship training programs. "Our men must be made to understand that the sane development of American institutions is the hope of humanity," wrote Captain Dudley Knox in 1920.[64] A century before, Thomas Jefferson had spoken of the need to water the tree of liberty every generation with the blood of revolution. Jefferson had never cared very much for the Navy or its methodology. But then twentieth-century naval officers were hardly alone in their dread of the "spectre of communism."

Racism

One element in the general critique of "radicalism" inevitably involved "internationalists and foreigners." Unchecked immigration had resulted in a "large heterogeneous foreign population comprising many elements of a most dangerous character" neither "of our race nor our ways of thinking." In the 1890s the naval aristocracy joined in the assault upon the "strangers in the land," who continued to constitute a disproportionate per-centage of the crews of American warships. Enlisted personnel should be of "*American birth, not citizens merely*," one officer insisted. "I am tired of Scandi-navian, German, and Irish-American naval sailors." The Navy now demanded, and eventually won, legislation permitting the restriction of enlistments in all ratings except that of steward to U.S. citizens (Filipinos, Chinese, and Japanese continued to serve as messmen). On the surface, this campaign to nativize the Service was military in nature—much was said of the danger of divided loyalties and the "vain attempts to arouse some national spirit and *esprit* in such [inter-national] crews." But it was also, in part, a product of the post-Haymarket anti-radical panic of the upper classes, and a function as well of the naval aristocracy's racist bent, a racism bred of social Darwinism. Thus one officer argued that under the pre-nativist system of recruitment the tendency was "towards the survival of the least fit," and another insisted that since "naval policy" was "largely the result of racial characteristics," the U.S. Navy needed "Anglo-Saxon" blood.[65]

Mahan and his messmates were quite familiar with "the Darwinian Theory," and found "very plausible" the notion that God's laws of creation were general and evolutionary rather than specific and static. After all, was not the "grandest," most "sublime" heritage of humanity the right of all to compete "freely" in the struggle for honor, fame, and wealth, to "become superior in position"? Naval officers were not Sumnerian social Darwinists; they had little faith in the sanctity or feasibility of an unadulterated laissez faire, of an unchecked socio-economic order. The naval mind was too Hobbesian in its premises to accept unbridled competition as a satisfactory principle. None the less, naval officers did espouse a form of social Darwinism. Irwin Wyllie has shown that business-men of the late nineteenth century did not employ social Darwinism as a rationale nearly so often as they did the older self-help notions of the Puritan ethos. Similarly, Samuel P. Huntington has argued that the military man's adherence to bellicose social Darwinism in this age was "rare," and Richard Hofstadter apparently agreed. But my own research forces me to conclude that the naval officers who made sure that the libraries of the Great White Fleet were well stocked with copies of the works of Herbert Spencer, John Fiske, and Rudyard Kipling before setting forth to circle the globe, officers who accepted "the struggle of life" and "the race of life" as "phrases so familiar that we do not feel their significance until we stop to think about them," officers whose philosophy was fraught with expressions such as "Struggle is a law of nature" and "Righteousness is evolution," who believed that "to cease struggling" was "to cease to exist," who worried constantly that their country was losing its "fighting spirit" and would degenerate in "race decadence," who argued that "'Might makes Right' is not a mere political theory but a biological fact,"— both accepted and vigorously and frequently employed much of the philosophy of social Darwinism.[66]

The observations Mahan's messmates made of the peoples of different races, religions, and nations are probably not unlike those made by most American travelers of their age, but they are no less a vital part of the naval officer's perception of the world around him for all their familiarity, and are consequently worthy of attention.

Highest in the esteem of the naval aristocracy were the English, Scottish, and Scandinavian peoples; there was "a manliness about them" which appealed "most strongly to Anglo-Saxon hearts." European and Russian culture was also impressive, but the "New World" spirit of the Annapolite was offended by some Continental life styles. Europe offered "a world rich in the accumulation of ages, and full of meat as a chestnut," but, like the chestnut, "sometimes a little worm-eaten and moldy."

Irish were "stupid turf-lumps" (unless one's messmate had Irish kinfolk), and, in the mid-nineteenth century, some thought Germans "smoke-dried, beer-soaked villains." By the turn of the century, Germans were more accepted. In October, 1898, one Lieutenant Commander hoped that America's next "antagonists" would be Germans, who would be "'foemen worthy of our steel' and not Spaniards." In 1906 Commander Nathan Sargent praised the Australians for excluding "Chinese, Japanese, Hindoos, Malays, Kanakas, etc.," but he was critical of their policy of discouraging the admission of Scandinavians, Germans, "and members of the Latin race, whose aid would be of infinite assistance. . . ." The assistance Sargent felt that Slavs and Latins could offer, however, was limited. He had in mind labor immigrants on a part-time basis to harvest the sugar cane, work that shouldn't be done by "an Anglo-Saxon." The French were deemed suitable masters of their Berber subjects, while the Iberian peoples, collectively referred to as "dagoes," were not. The Spanish, Portuguese, Italians, and Slavs were low men on the totem pole of the Western world, though there were gradations.[67]

Latin-Americans, from observation, were even less satisfactory than their Iberian ex-masters. Several felt that Latin-American police who could not understand drunken sailors were "stupid." Latin-Americans were "pitifully incompetent" to rule themselves, "which of course is no news to a naval officer," Captain Charles Sperry wrote to his son in 1906. Mulattos and mestizos were "retrograde people." Commander William Fullam believed that "the best remedy would be to submerge Central America for a sufficient time and then repopulate it" with worthier, more dynamic stock. Mexicans were better than their southern neighbors, but they could not be "compared to Anglo-Saxons."68

The Japanese were deemed the most admirable of the Eastern peoples. They were "yellow," and socially unsuitable; but they were also aggressive, ambitious, and imbued with a deference and a fine "sense of honor," not unlike the British or the naval aristocracy itself. Captain Louis Kimberly told his niece of a pretty Japanese child he had seen on the streets of Kobe and suggested that he would "have liked to have brought it up for a servant," but others, perhaps more impressed by the Japanese than Kimberly, resolved to treat them decently, "even if they *were* only half civilized." Commencing in 1868, one Japanese midshipman was admitted to the Naval Academy each year until the end of the century. By the twentieth century, however, the Japanese military and naval successes began to worry, as well as impress, the naval aristocracy. Commander Nathan Twining, for example, warned that the day would come when Anglo-Saxons and a "rejuvenated Teutonia" would have to "unite against the slav and other outer barbarians," among them the Japanese "ape of the Orient."69

Samoans and Tahitians were less ambitious than Japanese, but they were "veritable living bronze statues," of a higher racial order than other Pacific peoples. Filipinos were like children—"far superior in their intelligence and more capable of self-government than the natives of Cuba," and "an entirely different people from niggers"—but still children, and less attractive than Samoans or Tahitians. Some officers felt Hawaiians were somewhat below Samoans too, because of what was deemed their "negro-like features."70a In the 1870s an American warship's commander readily granted passage to an American citizen who wanted to desert his loving Hawaiian wife, and in the 1890s Queen Liliuokalani was dismissed as a "relic of barbarism." But Oceanic peoples were still one step above continental Orientals like the Koreans and the Chinese. "Don't get knocked over by those confounded Koreans," Lieutenant Commander William Cushing told Master Elliot Pillsbury, whose ship, the U.S.S. *Colorado*, was about to attempt to force open the door of the Hermit Kingdom. "It's better to be killed by white men." Similarly, Rear Admiral Robley Evans thought an American naval officer "worth any thousand Koreans in the country." Some officers regarded Chinese, "the outer barbarians," as a people beyond the pale of the civilized world, who deserved to be treated as such. When Rear Admiral John Rodgers visited Canton in 1872 he displayed his contempt for Chinese culture by using a Buddist altar joss stick to light his cigar. "Not that I wanted to smoke," he assured his friends. He had simply wanted to test the Chinese priests. To Rear Admiral Evans, the Chinese court's

216   "keen, tricky-looking eyes were set too close together" for his liking. He "positively distrusted, even disliked" the Empress' coterie from the moment he laid his own eyes on them, and, he maintained, "I found this was the feeling entertained by most of the officers who were with me." Lieutenant Commander Yates Stirling also found Chinese to be sneaky, but *he* thought they had "ignorant faces" and "simple minds." Colonel John Thomason, U.S.M.C., had one of his short-story characters rescue a Russian Bolshevik spy from Chinese assassins, in spite of the fact that Thomason disliked Bolsheviks, because, "after all, she's a white woman," and "none of these yellow babies" were going to be allowed to put their hands on a white while the U.S. Marines were around. Many officers saw little need to show the slightest consideration to the Chinese or other Oriental. He had to be "held with an iron hand and must be made to fully realize that the white man is his master; otherwise he appreciates what power lies in his immense numbers." "From my experience," wrote Rear Admiral "Billy Hell" McCalla, "I have observed that the use of artillery has a very great deterrent, moral effect upon the Chinese." When Chiang Kai-shek attacked the Chinese Communists in 1927, precipitating chaos throughout Central China, one senior American naval officer concluded that "a Chinaman respects force—nothing else, similar to the child that behaves in preference to punishment for his misdeeds," and suggested that if China could not "put her house in order, to see her lands yield their maximum possible products, and to furnish protection . . . to the foreigner residing within her territory,"[70] then others would have to do it for her.

A few officers, like Admiral David D. Porter and Lieutenant (j.g.) George Foulk, were highly respectful of Oriental civilization and culture, and others, like Cadet Midshipman Frank Bunts, recognized that, although they were deemed to be "no better than heathens," the Chinese themselves "consider us so immeasurably inferior to them." And the success of the Kuomintang in the 1920s impressed others with the latent strength and ability of Chinese civilization and compelled some to reevaluate the policies of gunboat diplomacy in East Asia. By 1930 many naval officers felt a paternalistic kind of respect for modern China.[71] Naval officers had little patience with archaic, inefficient, unstable governments, and they rarely associated the presence of foreign business, missionaries, or naval power with the instability of such governments. "Efficient organization" was deemed a "faculty wholly distinct from the personal qualities of the individual members of certain races," such as the Chinese or the Turks.[72] Unfamiliar religious or cultural traits drew criticism as well, as did differences in pigmentation and other physical features. But these last cannot simply be described as "racial prejudices," since the primary value judgments involved non-racial characteristics. The Chinese were not despised primarily for their physical attributes any more than the Japanese were admired for theirs. The naval aristocracy's observations of foreign cultures and peoples lacked sociological sophistication, to be sure, and consequently *led* to faulty assumptions and conclusions regarding physical characteristics, but they were no less sophisticated than most of their contemporaries, and more objective than some.[73]

Mahan's messmates were particularly negative toward black people. In 1940 the Navy's Director of Public Relations, Commander Leland Lovette, denied that naval officers held any convictions that a "superior race" existed or that the Navy restricted its membership to such a race. But there were no Chicano or black Annapolites in circulation at that date who could verify such a statement. Official Navy accounts have always explained that blacks were never graduated from Annapolis because their presence in the fleet would have created unrest among those who disapproved of their holding rank and thus would have lowered service efficiency and weakened the Navy's ability to perform its missions.[74] In spite of the fact that post-1950 naval experience has given the lie to these assumptions (or rationalizations), they appeared highly plausible in their day. And the "efficiency" argument was a more acceptable justification for bars on black midshipmen than the naval aristocracy's other one—prejudice. Mahan's messmates could argue for restrictions on grounds of "efficiency" because they had the same antipathies to the notion of black officers that they predicted would flare up among enlisted men. And these antipathies were probably more central to their opposition to desegregation of the "band of brothers" than was the "efficiency" rationale. To the average naval officer "all colored people" were "natural born thieves," and worse. With his African origins, the black man was an "absolute barbarian," not far in advance of the ape. Officers who had served in African waters testified to the black's physical stamina, but also to his "lack of inborn mental aptitude." Rear Admiral John Grimes Walker insisted on wearing gloves "for sanitary purposes" when black dignitaries came aboard in Haiti,[75] and Marine Colonel L. W. T. Waller told a House Naval Affairs Committee in 1916 that the Haitians would be "much better off" under "dictatorial military government."[76]

There was little change over the years in the attitude of naval officers toward the black man, though segregation was less pronounced prior to the fin de siècle.[77] At the end of the Civil War there were officers, like Captain Percival Drayton, who favored placing the black "on a perfect equality with the white." It was "very gratifying to some people to dominate an 'inferior race',," Drayton observed to Alexander Hamilton, Jr., "but it engenders the meanest and lowest passions, and invariably ends in the demoralization of the so called superior, and I for one want to see no such." But Drayton was unique. As in the days of slavery, individual blacks whose service had been long and faithful inspired their naval masters with affection and respect. Thus Admiral Porter was so impressed with one black tar's courage that he "took Bob home" with him after the war and made him his coachman. Similarly Captain Charles Sigsbee displayed profound affection for his black servant, as did others. But Porter's paternalism and Sigsbee's affection were not Drayton's egalitarianism. One officer recommended in 1910 that certain vessels be manned with blacks or Asiatics (with white officers and petty officers, to be sure) for "tropical service," and some vessels were so manned during World War II, but during the golden years of the Annapolites, from the founding of the Academy to the 1940s, the black man was rarely to be seen in the Navy.[78] Like many of their contemporaries, Mahan and his messmates also had a low opinion of Jews. They were "cruel," "sharp," "shifty," and "specious." Little wonder that a Jew who passed an open examination for assistant paymaster in August, 1917, was denied a commission by the aristocracy "because he did not look as if he would make a good naval officer." In my sampling of the religious affiliations of midshipmen from 1885 to 1920, out of a total sample of 1,433 Annapolites, 16 were Jewish. Of these, 8 graduated, but none of these 8 were still in the service 5 years later.[79] The presence of blacks and Jews might or might not have imperiled the "efficiency" of the Service, but the mere threat of their presence imperiled the morale of the naval aristocracy.

Man, Pacifism, and the Causes of War

Perhaps the most important social ideas of the American naval officers were those dealing with human nature and war. On these subjects the naval aristocracy differed radically from the members of peace societies and the advocates of international legal arbitration. From the 1840s to the 1920s (and beyond) naval officers frequently inveighed against the "piper of peace" whose "stentorian lungs" disturbed the social harmony. Owenites, Fourierites, Millerites, "these bastard bantlings of the brain of man," were deemed the arch-enemies of Navy and State. International lawyers were only slightly better. The "rose-colored representations of those who advocate arbitration" as a means of settlement of international disputes were mocked as fatuous. Both Mahan and his messmates had "very little, if any, sympathy" with the main purposes of the Hague Peace Conferences, the League of Nations, the Washington Naval Conference, or any other caucus of "international busy-bodies" who favored the sanctity of hospital ships, the outlawry of asphyxiating bombs, the settlement of disputes without recourse to war, and the disassembling of the U.S. Navy. Disarmament would result in "the release to a beneficiary system of the sums now spent on armament." And this would mean "a flood of socialistic [welfare] measures" which would "demoralize" the populace and be wealth lost "to the State." Arbitration interfered with "the free play of natural forces," and, like socialism, tended to eliminate competition between nations. Compulsory arbitration would create "a socialistic community of states, in which the powers of individual initiative, of nations and of men, the great achievement of our civilization," would perish, "having lost the fighting energy which heretofore has been inherent in its composition." "After all," as Commander John Rodgers explained in 1862, while seeking an opportunity to tackle the *Merrimac*, "man . . . is a fighting animal. Carnivorous and therefore with killing propensities. . . ." The very individualism that members of the naval aristocracy hoped to curb at home was seen as vital to the life of the nation in the international community. Officers went "by the book" within the national system, but they believed that, in the international world, "the book" could never be written that would not offend the sovereign rights of the State. "There is unquestionably a higher law than Law," Captain Mahan remarked, but his "higher law" was very different from that of William Lloyd Garrison or William H. Seward. It was the law of "force," which was "the basis of social order so long as evil exists to be repressed."[80]

Naval officers were rarely successful in obstructing peace conferences (though Captain Mahan managed to prevent the adoption of provisions calling for the referral of international disputes to compulsory arbitration and the outlawry of asphyxiating gases and attacks upon private property on the high seas at the First Hague Conference in 1899), but they consoled themselves by telling one another, and anyone else who would listen, of the absurdity of the pacifist-"international busybody" view of man.* In 1845 Commander Louis Goldsborough questioned the perfectibility of man, and he was echoed by his messmates for three-quarters of a century or more. "Unfortunately for the peace makers, the millennium has not yet come," Commander F. V. McNair wrote in 1874, "and whatever may be the indications of it in the heavens above, there are none whatever on the earth below." There was nothing, McNair concluded, to lead one to the belief that wars in the future would be any less frequent than in the past. Admiral Porter reiterated this antimillennial view in 1875, as did Commodore George Ransom in 1880, Lieutenant Richard Wainwright in 1882, Ensign W. I. Chambers in 1885, Lieutenant E. B. Barry in 1890, Commander C. H. Rockwell and Captain A. T. Mahan in 1893, Rear Admiral Daniel Ammen in 1891, Rear Admiral Bancroft Gherardi in 1898, Rear Admiral W. T. Sampson in 1889, Lieutenant Commander John Hood in 1902, Rear Admiral Stephen Luce in 1903, Captain John C. Wilson in 1914, ex-Captain Richmond Hobson in 1915, Rear Admiral Albert P. Niblack in 1922, Lieutenant Wallace Wharton in 1924, Lieutenant Leland Lovette in 1930, and God knows how many others in between. The millennium was out of reach, barring God's active intervention on its behalf; man was a "fighting animal." Disarmament was out of the question "till we have climbed much nearer to the stars." Future "problems in the destiny of man" would be worked out "through the instrumentality of the sword." There was "no escaping it." War was simply one of "the many evils flesh is heir to," and the only way to prevent war from breaking out, like a rash, was to keep a thick coat of armaments and battle readiness over every inch of the body politic. "If you wish to preserve the peace of the world give us more battleships and fewer statesmen," Rear Admiral "Fighting Bob" Evans told a San Francisco audience in 1908 at the height of the Japanese-American unrest prompted by that city's school segregation of Japanese-born. And Rear Admiral Albert Barker took a curious pleasure in pointing out that

---

* This section should not be understood to be a criticism of the naval officer's view of human nature. The author does not himself hold any particular view of man that he hopes to establish as having any more validity than that of his subjects. But this much can be said: the naval officer's preoccupation with the view of man as basically weak and evil may have clouded his ability at times to perceive other human potentialities.

war with Columbia over the Panama Canal Zone did not materialize because of America's "complete preparation" for such a meeting. (Barker apparently found nothing unsound in one's "preparing for defense" a navy that also justified one's assuming the offense.) Perhaps Passed Assistant Engineer Frank Bennett put the issue in the clearest terms when he argued that the battleship, "as an object lesson," was "better than the cathedral" for compelling nations to behave.[81]

Preparedness for war didn't always serve to prevent war, of course, and there *were* Americans who argued that the opposite was more often the case. The naval officer who argued, as did Commander Goldsborough in 1845, that the Navy was a key force in preventing war with Mexico was likely to be somewhat nonplused by the events of the following year. Similarly, Commodore Luce oversimplified matters when he argued that "the cloud of war which has so long been hovering over Europe" had not burst, simply because all the great powers were prepared for it. "It will be better to depend upon the great armaments, as institutions maintaining peace," wrote Rear Admiral Mahan in 1910, to prevent the outbreak of war in Europe. "At the present moment and for many years to come the great preparations for war are the surest guarantee for the continuance of *actual* peace & sec[urity] among the nations of our European civilization," he added in 1913. When the outbreak of war made somewhat less tenable the argument that armament races prevented war, one could always retreat to the more fundamental precept and point out that the very fact of the war was a "constant reminder that nations are beyond the domain of law and are subject to the impulses that sway human nature unrestrained."[82] From whatever perspective the naval officer might view human behavior, war and warships were always in the foreground.[83]

Naval officers had mixed feelings about the causes of wars. On the one hand, they knew from their own daily work the importance of business relationships in international politics, and the less tidy quest for power. On the other hand, few officers were willing to accept the notion that money-seeking or power-lust were as valid reasons for war as were "moral" ones.

When they spoke in general terms of war, Mahan and his messmates usually admitted the primacy of commercial forces. "History shows us plainly," wrote Captain William Sampson in 1889, "that even Christian nations who uphold the most advanced ideas of international law do not hesitate to disregard its plainest rules when the seeming prosperity of their country may be advanced thereby; and it is all done in the name of civilization and for the best good of the victims." Sampson's insistence that nearly all controversies arising between nations were traceable directly or indirectly to questions of commerce and trade was reiterated in 1892 by Commander C. H. Rockwell; in 1894 by Lieutenant Sidney A. Staunton; in 1902 by Captain French E. Chadwick; in 1907 by Admiral George Dewey, who doubted that the exclusion of the Japanese would result in war unless trade competition were to "accentuate the situation"; in 1910 by Rear Admiral Robley Evans; in 1911 by Captain Bradley Fiske;

again in November, 1914, by Fiske, when he accurately predicted to Navy **221**
Secretary Josephus Daniels that war was likely for the United States within the
next few years as a result of trade relations the United States would develop
while the war in Europe continued; and again in October, 1916, by Fiske, when
he wrote publicly that "of all the causes that occasion war the economic causes
are the greatest. For no thing will men fight for more savagely than money. . . ."
Fiske reiterated this view in 1921, as did Rear Admiral Albert Niblack in 1922
and Captain Frank Schofield in 1924, who also announced that "the Navy
believes that whether self interest is or is not a proper motive of conduct, it is
the real underlying nature of international conduct in general" and that "ideal-
ism pitted against commercialism and self seeking" was perpetually "bound to
lose." In January, 1926, Rear Admiral Thomas Plunkett warned the Republican
Club in New York City that war was imminent because of the reawakening
of America's merchant marine and the efforts of Americans to capture the
markets and raw materials of the world. With such a policy, "economic in its
origin," war was "absolutely inevitable."[84]

"Political" and "strategic" motives for war were given due consideration
and treatment, to be sure, but these factors were put in proper perspective,
which is to say that they were related and subordinated to economic stimuli.
"Economic disputes soon become political," Rear Admiral Harry Knapp
pointed out, and added, "in my opinion no greater nonsense has been uttered
of late than the attempt to differentiate between economic and political pre-
dominance. . . ." Captain French Chadwick told a 1902 War College class
that he and his colleagues had "come to see that it is commercial interest which
rule and not the mere dicta of governments." Nations might collide over the
control of a "strategic" position, such as Manila, Gibraltar, Hawaii, the Suez,
or Panama, but it was often their position on international trade routes that
made them "strategically valuable."[85]

Wealth, or the power derived therefrom, was deemed a primary motive for
wars—that is, all excepting *American* wars. Naval officers drew up war plans
to fit hypothetical trade controversies, but when war did come, as in 1861,
1898, or 1917, Mahan and his messmates justified their nation's action in high-
principled language. Thus Rear Admiral Francis Roe was highly incensed in
1897 by the French seizure of Madagascar, "an atrocious crime." The inhabitants
of that island were "*more than* half civilized, peaceful, and an inoffensive race. . . ."
The next year, however, Roe could call, along with many of his colleagues,
for the annexation of Hawaii and Puerto Rico, and the subjection of the
Philippine islanders.[86] Such a policy was defended on moral grounds. "Commercial considerations undoubtedly weigh heavily" in America, Captain Mahan
wrote at the turn of the century, "but happily sentiment is still stronger than
the dollar." Mahan insisted that a "mature consideration" of the causes of
America's wars would reveal that the motives driving the nation to war had
never been "aggression for the sake of increasing power, and consequently
prosperity and financial well-being," but rather "moral."[87] "The cause of war

222   is in the human heart, and its passions, more often noble than simply perverse." To regard the world in terms of self-interest alone was to do mankind a grave injustice. Thus Mahan attacked Norman Angell, whom he incorrectly understood to have claimed that economic interests were the sole causes of wars. It did no good for Angell to point out that he recognized many causes for wars or to cite earlier, often more thoughtful statements Mahan had himself made to the effect that "economical facts" were generally the primary causes of wars.* Mahan could not be moved from his late-in-life conviction that morals counted for more than money, especially where America was concerned.[88]

"Mission" and Missionaries

In many officers there was much of the same zeal that had driven missionaries to the far corners of the globe. Mahan and his messmates frequently looked upon their "calling," their professional mission, and the "national interest" in broader terms than those of trade and investments. As illustrated by their attitude toward the causes of American wars, Commerce was forced to share the naval officer's loyalties with Christ and Civilization.

With shot and shell the naval officer brought order to the sealanes, but he preferred to think of his role in terms of calming the waves. In the 1840s Lieutenant Andrew Foote entertained serious doubts about the propriety of a naval career; his father asked him whether the Navy was necessary to police the seas and whether it should be "in the hands of good or bad men." Since Foote accepted the need for naval power, he conceded that good men should control and elected to remain in the Service, where he might strike a blow for the Right. When the *Techumseh* hit a mine and sank in the opening moments of the Battle of Mobile Bay, Flag Officer Farragut hesitated for a moment and invoked God's counsel. He later claimed that a voice answered him, commanding him "Go on!" Farragut did, and his biographer, Captain Mahan, agreeably attributed the "Damn the torpedoes" decision to "sublime impulse." Similarly, Rear Admiral Bradley Fiske described Admiral Dewey's forces at Manila Bay as having been "pulled and pushed by some outside Force" and suggested that he himself had been "like a Whitehead torpedo, that seems to direct itself, but is really directed by a brain outside." Lieutenant Cameron McRae Winslow claimed that he had been afforded "the protection which God gives to those

---

* Had he seen it (he did not cite it) Angell must have found the following passage of Mahan's particularly appropriate: "Economical factors brought about the American Union and continue to build it. . . . Race, yes; territory—country—yes; the heart thrills, the eyes fill, sacrifice seems natural, the moral motive for the moment prevails; but in the long run the hard pressure of economic truth comes down upon these with the tyranny of a despot." Mahan, "The Practical Aspects of War," in *Some Neglected Aspects of War* (New York, 1907), 78–79.

Mahan's use of such an essentially negative expression as "the tyranny of a despot" to describe the primacy of economic causality suggests his latent disapproval of this economic primacy. When Angell threatened the future of the entire military establishment with his argument that wars were no longer economical, Mahan found it easy to shrug off the economic explanation and to assume one more likely to nullify Angell's argument. See Chapter 7 for more on Mahan's concern for the Service and its relation to his navalism.

who fight in a righteous cause" during the Battle of Santiago. Captain Bowman **223**
McCalla believed that he had been "but a humble instrument of the Divine
Will which works only for Good" when he and his troops captured the Chinese
arsenal at Siku during the Boxer Rebellion, a triumph "ordained by God."[89]

Like the missionary, many a naval officer thought of himself as an agent who
could "supply the conditions for the Lord's coming" and bring "the relief of
His Civilization" to the heathen. Commodore Oscar Stanton looked upon the
expedition of Perry to Japan not as a measure to aid American trade, which was
the way it was conceived in Washington, but as an effort to "restore Christianity" to the islands. Ensign J. B. Bernadou praised the work George Foulk was
doing in Korea in 1887 but said nothing of Foulk's fostering of commercial
relations with the Hermit Kingdom. "I look upon you as a kind of missionary
of Western civilization," he told his old messmate, Foulk. To Lieutenant
Commander J. D. J. Kelley the Navy projected civilization "into lands which
are benighted" and developed the "idea of republicanism" throughout the
world. Rear Admiral George Belknap viewed Rear Admiral A. E. K. Benham's
breaking of the rebellious Brazilian Navy's blockade of Rio in January, 1894,
not as a blow in behalf of American trade (which it was), but as a blow in
behalf of "human rights" and "the battle of freedom for the people of Brazil"
(which it was not). Retired Captain A. T. Mahan's 1902 intonation of the
virtues of "expansion" had none of the ring of the American Shipping and
Industrial League, but rather that of the Peace Corps or the Society for the
Propagation of the Gospel in Foreign Parts. Expansion constituted

> a regenerating idea, an uplifting of the heart, a seed of future beneficent activity, a
> going of the self into the world to communicate the gift it has so bountifully received.

Rear Admiral Albert Barker might object that in the naval intervention in
the affairs of Santo Domingo in the early twentieth century "there was no
such thing as high principle involved, such as liberty, or self government,
nothing at all except to get hold of the money." But such disavowals were rare.
"Naval power" was more frequently styled "the agency for regenerating and
redeeming the world." "I thought I was carrying out the expressed wishes of
the Christian people of America," Captain L. M. Overstreet remarked of his
past in the Spanish–American and First World Wars, adding that this feeling
had been formed "each Sunday morning" in the church of his youth.[90] Clearly
the Naval Academy indoctrination, designed to wipe the slate clean of many
other earlier experiences, carefully preserved religious memories and convictions.

Once again, like many missionaries, many naval officers looked down upon
non-Christians. They were heathens living in "ignorance and sin." Africans
were barbarians. Hindus were ridiculous. Buddhist theology was "loose."
Commodore M. C. Perry may have had no affection for Kossuth, but he was
full of praise for the neo-Christian Taiping rebels, "an organized revolutionary
army gallantly fighting for a more liberal and enlightened religious and political

224   position." Moslems were unworthy masters of the Holy Land. "It was certainly not an ignoble ambition to drive the Turk from the Holy Sepulchre," declared Lieutenant Charles Sperry. In 1940 Commander Leland Lovette denied that the naval officer had any sense that he was "God's anointed," but if this was true of the generation of 1940, it was less true of previous generations.[91]

With all of these similarities one might suppose that naval officers and missionaries would have been ideological and spiritual doubles, or at least friends. But often this does not appear to have been the case. One student of Korean–American relations has suggested that the relations between officers and missionaries were "generally good" in the late nineteenth century,[92] but my inquiry does not substantiate this view.

The protection of missionaries was not on a par with the fostering of trade and the safeguarding of investments. Nevertheless, it was often an important facet of the warship's routine on foreign station. And while the naval officer often *disliked* the American businessman abroad, he generally *despised* the American missionary. Commander Louis Goldsborough called them "blackguards," and damned "these turbulent, disturbful, dirty, Missionaries!!!" Captain Theodore E. Jewell repeatedly remarked that it was a "damned shame" to have to send a man off to war to protect "a half a dozen missionaries," and that if he were King of Korea he would "cut off the head of every damned missionary in the country." Rear Admiral William Kirkland actually took the side of the Turks in a dispute involving American missionaries and Turkish authorities in 1895. Captain Richard P. Leary, first naval Governor of Guam, banished Catholic missionaries, and gave no encouragement to Protestant propagandists who hoped to fill the vacuum. Admirals Henry Wiley and Hugh Rodman criticized American missionaries in China. But Lieutenant Edwin Anderson's experience and remonstrance was particularly noteworthy.

Anderson—the epitome of Richard McKenna's "Lieutenant Collins," fictional C.O. of the "U.S.S. *San Pablo*"—complained in 1903 of his orders to visit a missionary on the Yangtze. "This is a new role for me, to be protecting Missionaries," he observed to his wife. "You know how I love them!" Apparently Anderson's charge and his wife lived close to the Chinese peasantry, or their soil, for Anderson noted that "they certainly carried their real estate under their finger nails." To make matters worse, the missionary, Rev. Clarence E. Spere, was not a very attractive physical specimen. Anderson was outraged:[93]

> If I have to meet such things [missionaries] without shooting them I don't believe I can stand it. He has a retreating chin, goggly, watery eyes, long nose, and sits with his hands clasped and finger tips touching. And such a pious whine. I think if I could have given him a good kicking it would have done his soul much good. That sort of cattle makes me all wrong—Why don't they send *men* out here?

Not all missionaries were found wanting by their naval compatriots. As good Episcopalians, several officers hoped to "insure a due observance of the worship of the [Anglican] Church as one body throughout the world, with a

common thought and a common voice, as distinguished from the whim of   **225**
each several clergyman conducting the worship of particular congregations."[94]
Anglican-Episcopalians were not the only missionaries whom Mahan and his
messmates tolerated. Clergymen-businessmen-statesmen like Horace Allen,
whose general attitude Annapolites approved of, were highly regarded, as were
missionaries who lived among the natives, serving their temporal, more than
their spiritual, needs. This type of missionary was less likely to need naval
assistance.

It was the clergymen who came to evangelize rather than to fraternize, who
frowned on the customs of their new-found spiritual charges but refused to
remain within the confines of the Western concessions, who disrupted ancient
mores and life styles and brought disorder, who entered into the unpopular
business of landlordism, who hoped to alter the lives of "heathens" without
the use of force and then required force to support them, these missionaries
irritated naval commanders. Thus Lieutenant Edward Washburn, commanding
U.S.S. *Samar* on the Yangtze in 1911, was outraged by the American missionary
who flew the revolutionary flag of Sun Yat Sen's Republic from his mission
compound and delivered a lecture to the natives on "liberty and other inflam-
matory subjects." Such "trouble breeding" constituted a "menace" to American
interests on the Yangtze, and Washburn warned the miscreant man of God
to resume a neutral stance or prepare to suffer deportation.[95]

As was the case with their social peers in the U.S., Annapolites had a low
opinion of "priests, nuns, [and] monks," but they also disdained the less "established" of the Protestant sects.* Naval officers had little use for millenarians,
as we have seen, and they had even less use for pacifist churchmen or the
"conversion, revivals, *et id genus omne* of religious humbugging" often associated
with many of the missionary sects. Least popular of all were those who tried
to evangelize the Navy itself, such as the one who asked Lieutenant Commander
Charles Sperry if he had "many Christians on board" his ship. "I might have
told him," Sperry wrote his wife, "we have very few Turks." The typical U.S.
naval officer believed that if there *was* to be a second coming, a world-wide
Great Awakening, it would probably be heralded by battleships, not Baptists.
Undoubtedly it was this hostility of the men in blue cloth for those in black
that produced the verse popular in wardrooms in the late 1860s, a verse Charles
Sperry heard "shouted by a crew of mids at the tops of their voices":[96]

> Wish I were a Cassawary [sic]
> Upon the plains of Timbuctoo;
> Wouldn't I eat a missionary
> Arms and legs and hymn book too?!

* Baptists and Catholics were not the only subjects of criticism. One Annapolite mar-
veled that a female friend could have had anything to do with Presbyterians and was
stunned when she married a Presbyterian minister. "Imagine such a sweet creature, rich
too, throwing herself away on a *Presbyterian* parson. If he were a good high church Episcopalian I would not mind, though a naval officer would be better—but an old blue!" Mahan
to Ashe, January 1, 1859, *Mahan-Ashe Letters*, ed. Chiles, 64.

National Darwinism

The protection and promotion of the economic interests of American citizens were the most vital naval missions. But naval officers held other somewhat less official or operative missions in high regard as well. One of these was the conviction that America had a responsibility or "mission" to the world. The other was that she was destined to dominate the waves and the shores they lapped. The two had separate, but similar, origins. The former was the product of the naval officer's sense of morality; the latter a product of his social ideas. Officers looked upon their role in "civilizing" the external world as something no less important than economic expansion, to which it was related. They spoke of the righteousness of their work and the virtues of bringing republicanism to the uncivilized. But this was not the only language used to explain American policy, and it is important to consider the entire image officers held of world affairs in order to understand what they meant by disinterestedness and "righteousness."

Consider, for example, the expression Captain Mahan used to describe the conditions under which the United States might acquire strategic colonies: Such lands were to be taken "when it can be done righteously." Note also his claim: "to follow righteousness" was "the supreme moral choice" since it was "the expression of God's Being and God's Will." All history was a struggle of good and evil. There was "no middle path."[97] But wasn't anything "righteous" if one wanted it to be badly enough? How was one to distinguish "good" acts of acquisition from "evil" ones?

Apparently Rear Admiral Richard Meade, 3rd, thought he knew, for he advocated the diffusion "throughout the world" of the "principles which form the basis of American institutions" and the "great blessings that naturally spring therefrom" by "peaceful means if we can, but by a thoroughly warlike front, if we must." His concept of America's "mission" was "to tame the wild earth." But this meant the development of natural resources and the growth of the American economy through foreign trade.[98] To Meade, then, the "principles" to be diffused were the underpinnings for economic interests, and any measures taken to secure them were righteous.

Anything sufficiently "progressive" seems to have qualified as "righteous." Lieutenant Sidney Staunton felt that "the interests of civilization and commerce" demanded that the French "extend her influence beyond the boundaries of her immediate possessions" in Indo-China. Lieutenant Commander Kelley favored the "march" of "affirmative and sometimes aggressive ideas of freedom and progress," in spite of the fact that he recognized them to be "antagonistic to the traditions, customs, and practices" of the peoples upon whom they marched.[99]

Mahan himself tended to define morality in terms of brute strength. Like Louis Goldsborough, Bradley Fiske, and others, he turned to the Bible to establish that the Almighty had not only sanctioned, but also "intended," that "men should fight!" He frequently intermingled Biblical passages with the remarks of Napoleon Buonaparte, referred to "the dominion of Christ" as "essentially imperial," and argued that "Christianity and warfare" had a great deal in common. He viewed the British subjugation of Egypt and India, as did most Anglo-Americans, with pleasure and approval; and one is left with the distinct impression that he would not have regarded the liberation of those colonies and their return to a less "progressive" government with similar satisfaction.[100]

Commander Henry Clay Taylor publicly maintained in 1887 that the Navy's mission in Latin American waters was "that of defending, not oppressing, the brave and gentle nations to the south of us," and he vowed that the "autonomy of their governments" and the freedom of their citizens would never be "threatened" by the United States. Taylor utterly rejected the use of the expression "manifest destiny."

> That expression has been for centuries the excuse for cruel wars. That cry has too long indicated . . . might was stronger than right. Not thus do we look upon our destiny.

But Taylor doubted that the U.S. could "shake off at will" something he called "the natural and inherent responsibilities of its greatness." The subject of his remarks was the proposed canal across Nicaragua, which Taylor considered vital to support "the outpouring of our products, rapidly increasing." He visualized the use of Lake Nicaragua, at the center of a completed canal, as a staging area for American naval maneuvers. Squadrons "in the height of vigor and discipline" would issue periodically from the Lake, "striking rapid and effective blows in both oceans, and returning to refit in this sheltered stronghold, to draw from it nourishment and fresh strength for a renewal of hostilities." In later years, Taylor frankly admitted that when he spoke of *defending* the gentle Latin American neighbours what he really meant was *dominating* them, "whether that dominance be commercial and friendly" (the desirable sort) "or warlike." His earlier disavowal of "manifest destiny" before the American Association for the Advancement of Science was now significantly qualified, for he justified his new terminology with the remark that "we work with the current nature has caused to flow."[101]

"Manifest destiny" appears to have been a viable tenet with Taylor after all, just as it was with other officers. Captain Robert Shufeldt believed that the United States ought to be "mistress of Cuba's destiny." Captain Gilbert C. Wiltse, who landed sailors from the *Boston* at Honolulu in mid-January, 1893, thus insuring the success of the revolutionaries, was reported to have told a Congressional committee investigating the incident

> all this talk about who has a right to govern in these [Sandwich] Islands is bosh. I do not care a cent about that. The only question is, Does the United States want these Islands? If it does, then take them.

Commander French E. Chadwick and Captain Charles H. Davis, Jr., both felt, prior to the Spanish-American War, that the United States had an "obligation"

228   to use its power throughout the world as it saw fit.[102] By the testimony of these officers, either might made right, or the question of whether an act was "righteous" was altogether irrelevant, and the only question worth asking was whether or not the application of power produced the desired result.

As noted earlier in this chapter, naval officers were thoroughly familiar with "social Darwinism." Their translation of this concept into the international world, something we may refer to as national Darwinism, probably constituted the chief prop in their conceptualization of America's position in world affairs. The language of national Darwinism can be found at the crux of their thought. Ensign Washington Irving Chambers mixed his metaphors when he compared nations to humans and stars, rising "from weak infancy to a manhood of glory and power" and fading "until they have been swept into the gloom of eternal night," but his contemporaries knew what he meant. Captain Mahan spoke, as we saw, of the "struggle of life" throughout the world, going on to explain that nations were everywhere arrayed against nations, "our own no less than others." He then made his famous remark: "Whether they will or no, Americans must now begin to look outward. The growing productivity of the country demands it." Similarly, Lieutenant Commander Richard Wainwright, writing on the eve of the Spanish-American War, spoke of the rise and fall of great nations "in their struggle for existence" and warned that the United States "must expand in its growth, extend its interests, . . . or contract."

> The struggle for existence in nations, like that in individuals, is ceaseless, vigorous and relentless. The law of the survival of the fittest is as true for the political aggregation as for the individual.

Wainwright was not an evangelical imperialist. He, like Mahan, Taylor, and others, had something far more materialistic in mind when they set forth the frontier-expansionist ideology. They were concerned with the state of the economy. This was the key to the survival of nations. Wainwright was worried about the "financial depression of the 1890s," the industrial and agricultural overproduction, the shortage of U.S. merchant shipping, and the plight of America's markets in China and Latin America. "New markets are the road to wealth," Wainwright insisted, and only the wealthy survived. This was not to say that "money-getting" alone sufficed. It was simply one necessary ingredient. The other was a navy. And in order to survive, a nation needed both. As Captain Taylor put it, wealth and naval power were equally vital to "complete the national life." The Navy was "a component part of the organism which when completely developed is called a nation."[103]

Later, after the Spanish-American War had illustrated the importance of the Navy and the tempo of expansion had quickened, Mahan's messmates continued to urge their country to "accept her manifest destiny" and to "fulfill her mission." Rear Admiral Luce told students at his naval war college of the "continual struggle for supremacy" in the world, "before which barbarism is constantly retreating." America's mission was clear to Luce: It must press the uncivilized to "accept the bountiful gifts of nature, or make way for those who will." Luce warned all those in any way opposed to the tide of progress and added, for the benefit of his students of naval warfare and strategy: "This means much for us, here, today." Concurrently Captain Richmond P. Hobson, hero of Santiago, told his countrymen of the "mighty forces" at work in the world— "irresistible" forces "like the cumulative processes of nature." America, in the van, was divinely destined to be[104]

> the controlling World Power, holding the sceptre of the sea, reigning with the guiding principle of a maximum of world service. . . . The race will work out its salvation through the rise of America. I believe this is the will of God.

The God, that is, who spoke through Hobson, Mahan, Josiah Strong, Senator Albert Beveridge, and the rest of the Saints.

The War with Spain and the Philippines

Nowhere is this curious mix of attitudes toward, and concepts of, the external world—this blending of economic interests, moral fervor, and militant national Darwinism—nowhere is this mix more obvious than in the naval officer's conceptualization of the war with Spain in which he was so deeply involved. Some officers recognized the efficacy and importance of commercial considerations, at least in their official correspondence. But many viewed their work in moral, humanitarian, and/or *Machtpolitikal* terms.

The causes of the war were generally considered to be moral and humanitarian, in keeping with the naval aristocracy's reluctance to see themselves as anything less than crusaders. It was "a most righteous" war, waged to put a stop to intolerable "outrages." "If I were a religious man, & I hope I am," Commodore Dewey wrote in August, 1898, "I should say that [the victory over Spain] was the hand of God." And in 1907 Admiral Dewey declared with greater assuredness that the U.S. Navy had indeed been "the instrument in the hands of God for punishing Spain for her centuries of tyranny." Similarly Captain Mahan felt that by 1897 national interest had "made expedient, the acquisition of Cuba, if righteously accomplished," but, he continued, "Cuba would be Spanish now, if interests chiefly had power to move us."[105]

Later, when it came to drafting the peace, naval officers had a similar image of the meaning of their success. To be sure, Commodore Dewey's reports to the Secretary of the Navy focused on the economic vantages to be gained. But naval officers felt that Dewey's victory meant "a great deal more than mere commercial supremacy."

> It means that the higher civilization of the nineteenth century is to prevail [as well as] the extention of that principle of Benevolence and Charity. To do unto others as you would have them do unto you.

230   In language common to their social class naval officers called on compatriots to fulfill "the mission that Providence seems to have delegated to us." "The world is a vineyard and we . . . must assist in its Cultivation," wrote Rear Admiral Louis Kimberly. Dewey's suggestions regarding the possible cultivation of the Philippine Islands had been offered to his worldly superiors, but Kimberly's sense of responsibility went beyond the grave. He spoke for many officers in comparing their role to that of the stewards in the parable of the talents. "What report shall we make to the Master?" he asked his comrades-in-arms.

Similarly, to Rear Admiral Mahan victory meant that "the *mere* dollar and cents view, the mere appeal to comfort and well being as distinct from righteousness and foresight," were giving way to "nobler, if somewhat crude and even vainglorious, feelings":

> "Deus vult," say I. It was the cry of the Crusader and of the Puritan, and I doubt if man ever utters a nobler [one].

The "open door" meant more than economic expansion; it meant missions, schools, and political advisers. The domination of America's newly-acquired naval bases and colonial territories occasioned attendant duties. Mahan's overarching objective was to tie these outposts to the mother country with hoops of love as well as steel, in what he considered to be the manner of the British Empire. "Just dealing and protection" were not enough; "the firm but judicious remedying of evils, the opportunities for fuller and happier lives, which local industries and local development afford," were also obligations of sovereignty. To Mahan and many officers like him "self-interest and benevolence alike" demanded that "the local welfare be first taken into account." Any effort of mine to analyze the relative merits of "self-interest" and "benevolence" would probably yield negligible results. The two were generally indivisible, interdependent. But the point to note here is that the concept of stewardship was quite compelling.[106]

When it came to determining the substance of this "benevolence," naval officers were apt to be less precise. Mahan, who spoke convincingly of America's "duty" to others as a nation with "abundant surplus income," also maintained that a nation's leadership had no right to tax the strength or wealth of its own people. The chief of state was a "trustee" of the people; they were his "wards." Governments were "agents," not "principals." Thus arbitration could not "be embraced in that spirit of simple self-sacrifice" so admirable in individual human relationships. No government had any authority to limit or restrict the political sovereignty of its nation. Rather, rulers were obliged to "do their best, even to the use of force, if need be, for the rightful interests of their wards." Obviously this philosophy might conflict with the aspirations and "natural rights" of other peoples, especially if those other people were not exercising their own sovereignty with sufficient vigor. The failure of government to develop the resources of the land, for example, justified "compulsion from outside" to Mahan. "We meddle not," he wrote, in the affairs of China "until they become internationally **231** unendurable." Intervention was permissible, indeed, obligatory, whenever a nation's "stage of development" corresponded to that of "childhood or decay." Mahan's attitude toward the Philippines makes it clear that he did not feel that one of the "duties" of powerful states was to guarantee self-determination, or even to permit it.

Like most officers, Mahan was reluctant to spell out his philosophy in its simplest terms—"Might makes Right"—in spite of the fact that he and his messmates implemented this maxim daily on foreign stations. Perhaps the starkness of this "realism" troubled them, making it difficult for them to bring themselves openly to acknowledge it. Surely this was the case with Commander Taylor, who found himself unable to approve the expression "manifest destiny," in spite of the fact that he espoused expansionism and national Darwinism.*

But, on the other hand, this philosophy *was* occasionally articulated when it was demanded by the logic of the situation. Thus the "justice" of American expansion was seen as "the natural rights of the greatest number." Obviously "political independence," for Filipinos or anyone else, was irrelevant.† It was only "the personal liberty of the individual Philippine Islander" that Mahan took any interest in, and, of course, "personal liberty" was defined by Mahan, not Aguinaldo. The extent to which Mahan was unwilling or unable to correlate Aguinaldo's motives with those of his North American counterpart, George Washington, may best be seen in his choice of a word to describe the Filipino "insurgents." With ironic insight, he called them "refractory," a word that conveys an appropriate image of the insurgents as men whose fusion resisted the firing of their freedoms and resources in the furnace of American imperialism.[107]

Given these precepts, the attitude most officers took toward the Philippine annexation question is not surprising. Captain Taylor, for example, spoke of the new "responsibilities" that "the imperial republic of the world" had assumed in those islands—responsibilities to "protect their feeble peoples" and to "aid them in their efforts to secure a political happiness and freedom hitherto denied them." But neither he, nor Mahan, nor Lieutenant Bradley Fiske, nor Commodore Dewey, nor Rear Admiral Robley Evans, nor Captain Edward Beach, all of whom expressed similar views, included self-determination and Filipino independence in their explanation of what constituted "political happiness and freedom."

* But see *PUSNI*, XXXVIII (1912), 1243, for an example of an officer who did spell out "Might makes Right" as "a biological fact."

† American imperialists were by no means the first to take the position that "uncivilized" peoples had no political or sovereign rights. They had before them the entire record of European and British imperialism to substantiate their claim. Thus Sir John Knox Laughton, a British contemporary, spoke in the same language as Mahan and his messmates when he maintained that colonial peoples within the British Empire, such as the Maltese, had "not the slightest claim to political rights of any kind." Donald M. Schurman, *The Education of a Navy: The Development of British Naval Strategic Thought, 1867–1914* (Chicago, 1965), 102.

Dewey, who had a real opportunity to help shape an equitable U.S.-Philippine policy, failed to read insurgent General Emilio Aguinaldo's decrees, remarking later before a Senate committee investigating Philippine affairs that they were not of sufficient consequence to have required his attention. Thus Aguinaldo's declaration of Filipino independence was virtually ignored and wasn't even reported to Washington. But Dewey's ignoring of Filipino aspirations was not limited to his reluctance to consider Aguinaldo's behavior noteworthy. He also disdained to treat those Filipinos who *favored* U.S. dominance with any respect. When one Filipino newsman asked him why he had telegramed a request to Washington that the *Oregon* be sent to Manila, Dewey told him that the request had been made "for 'political reasons.'" There was going to be an election for Mayor of Manila, and Dewey told the Filipino that he wanted to see a "perfectly fair" election, "and then he laughed."[108]

Ensign Edward Beach was captured by Aguinaldo when fighting broke out between his troops and the Americans. His account of the friendly treatment he received was generous to the Filipinos. With obvious irony, he remarked that he had "completely lost confidence in Aguinaldo and the Filipinos as savages. They weren't living up to what was expected of them." He praised the insurgent government's organization and the bravery of its troops. "The course of the short-lived Republica Filipina was creditable and honorable," he reported in 1920, "and Filipinos for all time will regard their ancestors of 1898 with pride and affection." None the less, Beach considered the American suppression of the independence movement a "noble" act, "entirely unselfish." Once an officer swore allegiance in spirit to his government's executors, it became virtually impossible for him to take any *public* position other than one which held that the government always "did what was right and what it had to do."[109]

Occasionally a naval officer might let himself be drawn into a private debate on the Philippine counterinsurgency policy, with interesting results. Lieutenant Bradley Fiske recorded a lengthy conversation he held in 1899 with "a Filipino gentlemen of considerable education" regarding the suppression of the independence movement that is worth examining in detail here. The Filipino told Fiske of the chagrin his countrymen felt upon being ordered to lay down their arms. "We thought that we were going to have our independence," he said, to which Fiske replied, "You're going to have your independence; I mean in the way that Ohio has her independence, or any other state."* But the gentleman from Manila insisted that that was not what he had had in mind:

---

* Compare this to the remark of Rear Admiral George Remey: "We being in legal possession of the Philippine Islands, as a moral question, I do not see . . . why we are any more called upon to give up possession than of the State of Maine,. or the State of Florida, or the State of California, if at any time the inhabitants of either, or all of these states should desire to declared their independence of the United States.... The policy of our great country has . . . been one of expansion. . . ." *Life and Letters of Remey*, X, 943.

No, I mean *our* independence; I don't call belonging to the United States having our independence; we want to have our own government and to be a nation in the world, a real nation ourselves.

Fiske assured him that that was impossible, since the Philippines would never be strong enough to stand by themselves. But his adversary was unmoved; the United States could have insured the security of the islands with a guarantee of protection. Intervention and subjugation could not be justified by disguising them as protection. "You have no more right here than the Spaniards had." Fiske seemed to concede this point, for he threw it back at the Filipino himself. "What right would you Tagal[og]s have to govern these islands? The only 'right' you Tagals would have to govern them would be got by force. . . . you know perfectly well that the Tagals would have to . . . whip all the other tribes into subjection, and your right over the islands would be exactly the same right as that of every government in the world, the same right that the United States has here now."[110] Now the Filipino felt he had him: "Then you admit that you have no right here at all except the right of force. You admit that you come down here and take our islands away from us simply because you are strong enough to do it, and that you've no right to do it at all." But Fiske refused to accept this conclusion. The islands belonged to no one, he explained—or, rather, to whomever could govern them. The defeat of the Spanish had resulted in the destruction of "practically the only government that was here"—the only power that had protected lives and property. If the Americans were to leave the islands, they would be left "without an efficient government." The United States had an obligation to insure order "at least as good" as that of the Spanish.

> It would not be decent for us to give them to you, if we merely thought that perhaps you could govern them, because we are bound to be absolutely sure that you can and that you will; it would be a crime to allow a doubt to exist.

The two gentlemen then shook hands and parted, but Fiske went away with "a clearer idea . . . of how deep and determined was the Filipino feeling towards us"; the same evening he arranged for his wife and daughter to leave Manila by the next steamer.[111]

Rear Admiral Robley Evans, while Commander-in-Chief of the Pacific Fleet, visited the Philippines several years after the quelling of the independence movement and noted the "curious" distrust of Americans in Filipino circles. "It afterwards grew into a positive hatred," he recalled, "until today [1910] many of them do not hesitate to say they would be glad to have the Spaniards back in our stead." Evans attributed this hatred to the feeling of inferiority and dependence inherent in the position of the Filipino, with whom naval officers had minimal social contact, but he offered this analysis coolly and analytically, with little or no empathy. Like Fiske, Evans also debated the American presence with "a man of position in Manila," who told him that his

234   people disliked the Americans "more than they had the Spaniards." The American flag officer was annoyed and mystified:*

> I asked him if he would not admit that we had paved and cleaned the city, cut through the old walls, and let in air and light, thus improving the sanitary conditions. He admitted that we had done these things, but not with the consent of the people, who were satisfied with things as they stood. . . . One could not argue with such a fool. . . . Education will in time remedy this: If it does not, bullets and bayonets will.

Evans brings to mind the general characterized in *The Teahouse of the August Moon*, who insisted that his islanders would learn democracy if he had to "shoot every one of them."

Lieutenant Edwin Anderson, commanding a gunboat during the counter-insurgency operations off Samar and the Kanahuoan islands in 1901, was even more irritated than Rear Admiral Evans with the "lazy" and "insolent" natives, "ungrateful for everything we do for them." Anderson came to respect the former Spanish authorities who "knew best how to handle these cattle." Disgusted with the pro-American Filipinos, "paid large salaries for doing absolutely nothing," he soon became disgusted with the counter-insurgency policy itself. The burning of boats, houses, and crops, the "water cure" torture of village chiefs ("which I do not care to apply myself") troubled him. "The atmosphere around Samar is so hazy with smoke where the troops are burning villages and crops," he wrote his wife, "that the island can hardly be seen."

> I suppose that is the only way to put down this insurrection, but none the less it is a terrible thing to do as a great many of the inhabitants are well disposed and they are being ruined just as well as the evil ones.

Anderson saw no "earthly use of our trying to hold these islands" and maintained that most of his messmates "loathed the war as I do," but he and his messmates were all professionals—true Annapolites; they stayed at their posts and did their jobs. Anderson was delighted by his superior officer's praise "for my good work" in destroying 41 boats and 80 bancas in one day, especially when he was advised that his superior "would see that I got recognition." In the final analysis, Lieutenant Anderson's attitude toward U.S. policy in the Philippines contributed less to the shaping of his role in that policy than did his professionalism.†

* Evans, *Admiral's Log*, 96, 104, 221–223. Other officers were equally mystified at the reluctance of the Filipinos to appreciate their acculturation. After all, as Rear Admiral Kimball pointed out, "We have taught the savage Igorotes football!" *The Navy*, VIII (January 1914).

† Anderson to his wife, Oct. 21, Oct. 23, and Dec. 8, 1901, and undated file, Edwin A. Anderson Papers, S.H.C. ; U. of N.C. Library.

See *The Nation*, LXXVI (April 23, 1903), 324, for more remarks critical of the suppression of the insurgents, attributed to an unidentified "distinguished naval officer"and see the account of the suppression of the "*Republica Filipina*" in Ensign (later Fleet Admiral) William D. Leahy, "Diary, 1897–1913," State Hist. Soc. of Wis., Division of Archives and Manuscripts, 95. Leahy, a Catholic, may have identified with Filipino Catholics. In any

The Navy and the "Pax Americana"   **235**

We'll bear her flag around the world,
In thunder and in flame,

. . .

Columbia free shall rule the sea
Britannia ruled of yore.

From "Columbia Rules the Sea," a naval song printed in Robert Neeser,
American Naval Songs and Ballads.

Service in the U.S. Navy throughout the world gave naval
officers an inflated (but not necessarily unreal) sense of American power and a
passionate desire to see that power continue to grow. Three weeks before the
battle of Santiago, Roger Welles wrote home of his sense of certainty that Cuba
would "soon be under the Stars and Stripes," and observed: "Where old glory
is once raised it should never be hauled down." Rear Admiral Albert S. Barker
demonstrated it as well when he told the Society of the Cincinnati that wherever
the Navy planted the flag "there you will have just laws, there you will have
freedom." But it was Rear Admiral William W. Kimball's proud remarks
that best convey this sense of American sublimity. Speaking from experience,
Kimball maintained that it was[112]

> absolutely impossible to wear a sword and sail salt water in Uncle Sam's service for a
> half century or so without becoming imbued with the feeling that the United States
> of America is the finest and most glorious thing that ever happened and that it must
> lead in everything.

One of the results of this sense of transcendence was the conviction that the
U.S. Navy had a duty to help establish a peaceful condition of affairs throughout
the world. Only thus could American economic growth be assured; only thus
could American Christianity and culture reach the heathen and barbarian.
Ships policed the seas; marines and naval landing parties, the land. The British

---

event, he restricted his criticism to the *methods* used by certain individual army officers in
quashing the revolt—*not* the quashing itself. In 1905 army officer, Major R. L. Bullard,
claimed that several U.S. Army officers hampered effective control of the Philippines
because they were not "in sympathy with the government's policy in keeping these islands,"
but he did not elaborate. Bullard, "Cardinal Vices of the American Soldier," *Journal of the
Military Service Institution of the U.S.*, XXXVI (1905), 107.

See also the ambivalent views of Colonel Ethan Allen Hitchcock in the mid-nineteenth
century for another example of a professional officer who became disgusted with U.S.
military intervention into the affairs of other nations but remained in the Service none the
less. Hitchcock regarded both the Seminole War and the Mexican War as "wicked." "My
heart is not in this business," he noted in 1846. "I am against [the war with Mexico] from
the bottom of my soul as a most unholy and unrighteous proceeding; but as a military man
I am bound to execute orders. . . . Shall I resign? . . . I must be an instrument. . . . We
ought to be scourged for this. . . . I am losing everything valuable in my profession [by not
being in the thick of things]." Hitchcock, like Anderson, was too thoroughly committed
to a professional military career to resign or publicly rebel. Shortly after penning these
diary entries he joined General Winfield Scott's expedition to Vera Cruz. W. A. Croffut,
ed., *Fifty Years in Camp and Field: The Diary of General Ethan Allen Hitchcock*, 78–85, 94, 111,
123, 192, 198, 203, 213, 218, 225–229.

236   had been models; by 1920 they were somewhat subordinate allies. Mahan's messmates were advocates and heralds of the *Pax Americana*. In 1852 Lieutenant George Colvocoresses argued that the U.S. should conquer the Fiji Islanders "into subjection and order" as a means of insuring peaceful conditions in those islands and affording "encouragement to commerce." A generation later Lieutenant J. D. J. Kelley explained the need for U.S. naval squadrons in Latin American waters to put down business-unsettling "insurrections . . . at the shortest notice and with the greatest advantage." In 1911 Commander George Cooper told his superiors at Washington that it was "the imperative duty of the United States to prevent absolutely" the revolutions that had broken out in Central America, imperiling U.S., British, and European trade in that region. A month before American business leaders despaired of a peaceful solution to the Cuban insurrection and war was declared on Spain, Lieutenant Commander Wainwright asked his professional associates to "command peace" everywhere to insure prosperity, and to "command a speedy return to peace" in the event that revolution or war demanded it. Captain French E. Chadwick told the naval war college student body that the "mission" and "true strategy" of the United States was to guarantee peace throughout the world "by commanding it." America was "great and rich enough and fortunately so strategically placed, as to be able, if we desire, to do so." Concurrently, Captain Richmond Hobson, who was certain that America was an "innately peaceful" nation—indeed, the "only fundamentally peaceful people of the world"—wanted to "extend the Monroe Doctrine into an American Doctrine that would exert influence and lend a helping hand to all the less happy peoples of the earth, creating and exerting powerful influence for the oppressed of all lands, and for all the yellow and black peoples as they come under the dominion of the white race. . . ." White America was "constituted" by God "the advocate and champion of peace in the world."* Like Wainwright, Hobson hoped to prevent war. He was mindful of the fact that violence would only damage America's chances of securing her share of the "ocean of wealth" and "unmeasured virgin resources" in China and mindful that any war that injured the British or French, with whom Americans had over a billion dollars of commerce by 1902, would likewise injure America. In fact, Hobson saw that American trade and investments were becoming so extensive that "an injury to any part of the human race would be an injury to us. . . ."[113]

* This is not to say that all naval officers saw no boundaries to America's "sphere of influence" in the world. Mahan felt that "the Valley of the Amazon indicated a boundary south of which it seemed . . . unnecessary to carry our Monroe Doctrine." (Mahan to "Mr. Fitz-Hugh," March 9, 1912, Folder 18, Box 209, N.H.F.) Rear Admiral Charles H. Stockton criticized the application of the Doctrine to Haiti and South America. *The Navy,* VII (April 1913), 135–136. Captain Shufeldt felt that Panama ought to be "the extreme limit of American domination of the American continent." (Cited in Drake, "Shufeldt," Ph.D. thesis, 576n.) And Captain Chadwick argued that the Caribbean was "undoubtedly our sphere of influence." ("The Great Need of the U.S. Navy," *Munsey's Magazine,* XXXIII [1905], 643.) But all these self-limitations preceded the Great War. Such qualifications were less frequent after the creation of the "Navy second to none."

As America's Navy grew in dimensions and relative power, so did the **237** ambitions of its officers. Thus it is not surprising that we find naval officers implicitly rejecting the concept of a League of Nations on the eve of that institution's birth or demanding "a navy second to none" at the Disarmament conference tables in the 1920s. In spite of the seemingly humanitarian underpinnings to the views of men like Hobson and Taylor, it was men like Commander Nathan Twining and Lieutenant H. H. Frost who best typified the bedrock "tough-minded" philosophy of Mahan's messmates. Twining was highly critical of President Woodrow Wilson's "lofty attitude of solicitude for humanity." He argued that the U.S. should place its own economic interests before the interests "of humanity in general." Frost's defense of a "go-it-alone" foreign policy for the U.S. coolly blended nationalism and Darwinism:

> We must encourage the idea of competition with other nations and discourage the cosmopolitan idea that we are all citizens of the world and therefore should help all nations.

Like Hobson, Frost was willing to aid the French or British in the defense of international trade. He simply opposed giving something for nothing. If peace was to be imposed by American ships, it should be an American peace. Richard C. Brown has argued that U.S. Army officers of the early twentieth century were not imperialists. The same cannot be said of their compeers from Annapolis.[114]

Chapter 5 (The External World)

1. Cf. Samuel P. Huntington, *The Soldier and the State: The Theory and Politics of Civil-Military Relations* (Cambridge, Mass., 1957), 222–225, 267–268, 310; John P. Mallan, "Roosevelt, Brooks Adams, and Lea: The Warrior Critique of the Business Civilization," *American Quarterly* (1956), 216–230; Peter Karsten, "The American Citizen Soldier: Triumph or Disaster?" *Military Affairs*, XXX (Spring 1966), 39. None of these accounts deals with the critique of materialism by any naval officers but Mahan.

2. Goldsborough, *A Reply . . . to an Attack made upon the Navy of the United States by Samuel E. Coues, President of the [American]* Peace Society, in which a Brief Notice is taken of the Recent Fourth of July Oration delivered at Boston, by Charles Sumner (Portsmouth, N.H., 1845), 9; Madeline V. Dahlgren, *Memoir of John A. Dahlgren* (Boston, 1882), 395; Roe, *Naval Duties*, 138, 141.

Not surprisingly, Captain Shufeldt had harsh words for American opium traders such as he had been ordered to protect. Drake, "Shufeldt," Ph.D. thesis, 217.

3. Item 20, Box 147, Nathan Sargent Papers, N.H.F.; Chambers, "The Reconstruction and Increase of the Navy," *PUSNI*, XI, No. 1 (1885), 6; *PUSNI*, XXXIII (1907), 839. In an unpublished poem entitled "Painless Aviation, or Kultur

in the Future" Chambers attacked "luxury-loving" socialites who were "Without grit for the noble effort/In the service of the State." See also his "Literary Notes," "Preparedness, February 22, 1916, A.D.," and "Love, War, and Efficiency, or Naval Doctrine and National Character." All are in Box 48, W.I. Chambers Papers, N.H.F.

4. Rockwell, "Wanted—A Definite Policy," *The United Service*, 2nd Series, VIII (Nov. 1892), 413. See also Admiral David D. Porter's unpublished novel, "The Convict," Chapter II, page 18, where Porter rages against the tyrannizing of workers by capitalists. D. D. Porter Papers, Box 28, Mss. Div., L. of C.

5. Commander William Beehler to Rear Admiral Robley Evans, June 15, 1903, Box 3, Edwin Anderson Papers, S.H.C., U. of N.C. Library; Beach, *Ralph Osborn*; and *An Annapolis Plebe*; Stirling, *A U.S. Midshipman in the South Seas* (Phil., 1913), 230; Zogbaum, *The Junior Officer of the Watch* (New York, 1908), 170. Another Academy graduate, Winston Churchill, titled one chapter of his novel, *The Crisis* (1901), "Introducing a Capitalist," wherein he attacked war profiteering.

6. Foster, "War's Benefits," *PUSNI*, XLIV (1918), 1454; Fiske, *From Midshipman to Rear Admiral* (New York, 1919), 227; Kimball, in *The Navy*, VIII (Feb. 1914), 79; Barker, *Everyday Life in the Navy*, 377.

7. Mahan to Ashe, 10 August 1888, Ashe Papers; Mahan, "Personality and Influence," unpublished speech delivered at Dartmouth Navy School, England, Mahan Papers, L. of C.; Mahan, "The Navy as a Career," *The Forum*, XX (Nov., 1895), 283; Mahan, *Retrospect and Prospect*, 134; Mahan, *Types of Naval Officers*, 219; Mahan, *The Interest of America in Sea Power, Present and Future*, 121, 235.

On the other hand, Mahan was not above turning to J. P. Morgan in 1889 with a request for $2,000 to finance the publication of Mahan's first book. Perhaps there was poetic justice in the fact that Morgan offered to put up only $200; Mahan was forced to learn the ways of the salesman. Puleston, *Mahan*, 89–90.

8. Mahan to Ashe, 21 December 1882, Ashe Papers; Kelley, *Our Navy: Its Growth and Achievements* (Hartford, Conn., 1897 [originally published in 1892]), 7–8. Kelley was describing the 1880s.

9. Walker to Luce, 14 August 1888, and Luce to his wife, 18 January 1889, Rear Admiral Albert Gleaves, *Life and Letters of*

Luce, 216; Admiral George Dewey, *The Autobiography of George Dewey* (New York, 1913), 161; Mahan to Thursfield, 21 November 1895, Mahan Papers, Library of Congress.

10. Porter, "The Chinese in America," *The United Service*, I (1879), 302–303; Spaulding, *Japan and Around the World . . .* (New York, 1855), 177–178; Truxton to Messrs. Glover, Dow & Co., 27 June 1870 [copy], R. W. Meade, 3rd, Mss., Box I, N.Y.H.S.; Stanton to Rear Admiral Thorton Jenkins, Commander, U.S. Naval Force on the Asiatic Station, 2 January 1874, Letterbook 3, p. 119, Oscar Stanton Papers, Mystic; Sperry to his wife, January 7, 1880, Sperry Papers; Mahan to Ashe, July 26, 1884, Ashe Papers; Sperry to his wife, May 10, 1889; Kimball to the Secretary of the Navy, Feb. 24, 1910, Nicaraguan Correspondence, Entry 309, R.G. 45. See also Commander Andrew Hull Foote, *Africa and the American Flag* (New York, 1854), 71–73; Colonel John W. Thomason, U.S.M.C., — *and a Few Marines* (New York, 1945 [orig. pub. 1926]), 332, 576; and Eldon Griffin, *Clippers and Consuls: American Consular and Commercial Relations with Eastern Asia, 1845–1860* (Ann Arbor, Mich., 1938), 125–126: "Members of the Navy sometimes derided merchants."

11. Captain J. A. C. Gray (M.C.), U.S.N., *Amerika Samoa: A History of American Samoa and its United States Naval Administration* (Annapolis, 1960), 191–199; Rear Admiral W. L. Rodgers, "The Diplomatic Side of the Naval Officer's Profession," *The Marine Corps Gazette*, IX (March 1924), 42; Constien to Welles, August 4, 1925, copy in Welles Papers, Box 201, N.H.F. For a later example of the same attitude toward exploitation see Major Evans F. Carlson, *Twin Stars of China* (New York, 1941), 277–278, 298–299, 311–312.

12. Kase to the class of '81, 5 Oct. 1885, *2nd Annual Report of the Class of '81*, 23; see also Harry R. Cohen to the class of '81, December 7, 1886, *3rd Annual Report*, 14. Similarly, when George Foulk left the service in 1888 and took a business position, he confessed to an Academy classmate that he found it difficult to work with civilians. Foulk to Chambers, 23 March 1888, Chambers Papers, NHF.

13. *DuPont Letters*, II, 227; III, 11, 62, 76, 127.

14. *Remey Life and Letters*, VI, 523; IX, 836.

15. Chadwick to Representative Hilary

Herbert of Alabama, Chairman, House Naval Affairs Committee, 15 September 1888 [copy], Chadwick letter copybook, New York Historical Society; Clark, *My Fifty Years*, 256. See also correspondence between Treasury Secretary Hugh McCulloch and Navy Secretary Gideon Welles concerning the sealers in early 1869, copies in the T. T. Craven Papers, Syracuse; and *PUSNI*, XLIV (1918), 739.

For the "shock" officers expressed over the lease of the Teapot Dome oil reserves to the Sinclair interests, see Captain John Halligan to the Secretary of the Navy, 7 September 1923, *PUSNI*, 50 (1924), 1191.

16. West, *Admirals of American Empire*, 79; Mahan to his wife, 8 August 1894, Mahan Papers, L. of C.; Evans, *An Admiral's Log*, 442.

17. F. A. Roe, *Reasons why our Navy should not be Reduced!* (Washington, 1880), 10–11; Kelley, *Our Navy*, 10; Admiral David D. Porter, "Our Navy," *United Service*, I (1879), 3; Rear Admiral David Potter (SC), U.S.N., *Sailing the Sulu Sea* (New York, 1940), *passim*; Box 3, Edwin Anderson Papers, S.H.C., U. of N.C. Library.

18. Kelley, *Question of Ships*, 112; Shaw, *Captain Brassbound's Conversion*, in *The Works of George Bernard Shaw*, IX (L., 1930), 275; Watson to Leutze, Oct. 30, 1899, Entry 1, R.G. 313, N.A. Rodgers to Navy Secretary James Dobbin, 15 February 1855, in *Yankee Surveyors in the Shogun's Seas*, ed. Allan B. Cole (Princeton, 1947), 7, 45; Stanton, "The Japan Expedition," Stanton Papers, Mystic; Mahan to his mother, 20 February 1868, Mahan Papers, L. of C.; Fullam to the editor of the New Orleans *Times-Democrat* [copy], 31 May 1907, Fullam Papers, N.H.F.; Secretary of the Navy to Hemphill, 19 October 1899, Record Group 45, Subject File, VP, Box 7 (Protection of Individuals and Property), National Archives.

19. Although their loyalty is to the Constitution, many officers have expressed considerable disapproval of Congressional and (occasionally) Executive interpretations of the Constitution and of Congressional responsiveness to the "whims" of constituents.

20. Charles L. Lewis, *The Romantic Decatur* (Annapolis, 1937), 237; Rear Admiral David Porter (SC), *Sailing the Sulu Sea* (New York, 1940), 24; Hunt, "Alma Mater," *PUSNI*, XXXIV (Sept. 1908), 816; 5 July 1925 speech of Admiral Roger Welles, copy in Box 201, Welles Papers,

N.H.F.; Captain William Puleston, *The Influence of Force in Foreign Relations* (N.Y., 1955), 46; Hunt, "Education at the Naval Academy," *PUSNI*, XLII (May 1916), 736.

21. Untitled mss. by Roe (c. 1897), Box 424, R. R. Belknap Papers, N.H.F.; Sims in a 1916 address on "Military Character," cited in Elting E. Morison, *Admiral Sims and the Modern American Navy* (Boston, 1942), 59; U.S. Senate, Committee on Naval Affairs, *Naval Investigation* (Wash., G.P.O., 1920), II, 1760–1761. See also Rear Admiral French E. Chadwick, *The American Navy* (New York, 1915), 279.

22. Captain Dudley Knox, "The Elements of Leadership," *PUSNI*, XLVI (1920), 1896; Rear Admiral William Sampson, "Admiral Dewey as a National Hero," *The Century Magazine*, XXXVI (1899), 928; Fiske, *Navy as a Fighting Machine*, 113.

For more officer patriotism see Stone, "Moral Preparedness," *PUSNI*, XLVI (1920), 368; Rodman, *Yarns of a Kentucky Admiral*, 242–243; Mahan to his mother, 20 Feb. 1868, Mahan Papers, L. of C.; and Commander John L. Worden to the Secretary of State, New York, December 20, 1862, Worden Papers, Lincoln University Library, Harrogate, Tennessee.

23. Henry, "A Six-Year Course at the Naval Academy," *PUSNI*, XLVIII (1922), 727; Mahan to Ashe, 1 April 1859, *Letters*, ed. Chiles, 106.

24. *Du Pont Letters*, II, 481; Goodrich, "Esprit de Corps—A Tract for the Times," *PUSNI*, XXIV (March 1898), 8.

25. Roe mss., Box 424, Belknap Papers; Mahan, *From Sail to Steam*, 87; *The Interest of America in International Conditions* (Boston, 1910), 175; and "Motives to Imperial Federation," in *Retrospect and Prospect*, 95; Admiral David D. Porter, *Incidents and Anecdotes of the Civil War* (New York, 1886), 51; William H. Russell, *My Diary North and South*, ed. Fletcher Pratt (Harper paper ed., 1965), 30. See also Lieutenant George Perkins to his sister, May 1, 1861, in Carroll S. Alden, *George H. Perkins, Commodore, United States Navy* (Boston, 1914), 103; Foltz, *Surgeon of the Seas*, 140; Lieutenant Charles Flusser to his mother, Sept. 19, 1861, Flusser Papers, "ZB" File, Naval History Div., National Archives.

26. See, for example, Fredrickson, *loc. cit.*, or any one of a host of published Civil War diaries.

27. I.e., Clark, *My Fifty Years*, 34; Cushing to his sister, May 7, 1861; Edwards, *Cushing*, 89; Caldwell to his father, March

240

13, 1863, Caldwell Letters, Indiana Hist. Soc. Lib.; Captain C. H. Davis, Jr., *Life of Charles H. Davis, Rear Admiral, 1807–1877* (New York, 1899), 292; Janowitz, *Professional Soldier*, 137–138; Luce, "Naval Training," *PUSNI*, XVI (1890), 377. Cf. Niblack, *Why Wars Come*, 21.

28. C. E. Macartney, *Mr. Lincoln's Admirals* (New York, 1956), 85–86; Rear Admiral Andrew Foote Papers, letters for 1856, L. of C.; West, *Admirals of American Empire*, 74–75, 104, 199; George R. Willis, *The Story of Our Cruise in the U.S. Frigate Colorado . . . 1870–72* [n.p., n.d. (Library of Congress has a copy)], 68–80; "A Naval Officer," "A Plea for Gunboats," *United Service*, 2nd Series, I (Jan. 1889), 19, 95; Rear Admiral Robley D. Evans, *An Admiral's Log* (New York, 1910), 114; Farquhar, cited in Marius Schoonmaker's manuscript biography and edited letters of Captain Cornelius Schoonmaker, p. 20, Cornelius Schoonmaker Papers, Naval Historical Foundation; Josephus Daniels, *The Wilson Era: Years of Peace, 1910–1917* (Chapel Hill, 1944), 186–187; Robert E. Quirk, *An Affair of Honor: Woodrow Wilson and the Occupation of Veracruz* (Norton Paper ed., 1967), 25ff; Thaddeus Tuleja, *Statesmen and Admirals* (N.Y., 1963), 163; Leo Perla, *What is "National Honor"?* (N.Y., 1918).

29. Perla, *What is "National Honor"?*, 16.

30. Goldsborough, *Reply to Coues*, 12–13; *U.S. Nautical Magazine and Naval Journal*, V (1856), 119; Shufeldt to Rufus Hatch, 31 July 1874, Robert Shufeldt Papers, L. of C.; Admiral R. E. Coontz, citing the Navy General Board's report to the Secretary of the Navy for 1920, before the House of Representatives, Committee on Naval Affairs, *Hearing on Bill H.R. 13706 on Relief of Contractors . . . 1920* (Wash., G.P.O., 1921), 90.

31. See, for example, Commander Royal R. Bradford, "Coaling Stations for the Navy," *Forum*, XXVI (Feb. 1899), 738; and Rear Admiral Evans, cited in *Army and Navy Journal*, XL (Nov. 22, 1902), 281.

32. Foote, *Africa*, 379; Rodgers to American citizens in Hakodadi, Japan, 25 June 1855, *Yankee Surveyors*, ed. Cole, 119; Habersham, *Expedition*, 294; Madeline Dahlgren, *Memoir of John A. Dahlgren* (Boston, 1882), 214–216; Rodman, *Yarns of a Kentucky Admiral*, 215; Roger Welles to his father, 2 April 1885, Roger Welles Papers, Naval Historical Foundation; Young, "*Boston" at Hawaii*, 182; Rear Admiral John R. Edwards before a Pittsburgh meeting of Mining Engineers, cited in the *Army and*

Navy Journal, LII (Sept. 19, 1914), 83; Rodgers, "The Diplomatic Side of the Naval Officer's Profession," *Marine Corps Gazette*, IX (March 1924), 42; Twining to his father, May 29, 1914, Twining Papers, State Hist. Soc. of Wis. Cf. Drake, "Shufeldt," Ph.D. thesis, 115.

33. Commander Nathan Sargent, *Admiral Dewey and the Manila Campaign* [written in 1903] (Washington, 1947), 6. (Laurin H. Healy & Luis Kutner, *The Admiral* [Chicago, 1944], 147, incorrectly attributed this passage to Dewey himself.) Sargent to Commander-in-Chief, Asiatic Fleet, 17 December 1905 [copy], and Sargent to the Secretary of the Navy, 6 February 1901, Captain Nathan Sargent Papers, Box 146, Naval Historical Foundation.

34. Perhaps this distinction also helps to explain the oft-cited Woodrow Wilson–Josephus Daniel tift with American investors in Mexico in 1913–1914 and again in 1919. Daniels, *loc. cit.*; entry for 18 Nov. 1919, *The Cabinet Diaries of Josephus Daniels*, ed. David Cronon (Lincoln, Neb., 1962), 461.

35. Kelley, *Our Navy*, 11; Shufeldt, Mss. circa 1875, Box 20, General Miscellany, Shufeldt Papers; Captain N. H. Farquhar, cited in Schoonmaker, *loc. cit.*; Rear Admiral R. W. Meade, 3rd, "Some Suggestions of Professional Experiences in Connection with the Naval Construction of the Last Ten Years, 1884–1894," Box II, Richard Worsham Meade, 3rd, Mss. N.Y.H.S.

36. Lieutenant J. D. J. Kelley, *The Question of Ships* (New York, 1884), 45; Kelley, *Our Navy*, 10–11; Captain Henry Clay Taylor, "American Maritime Development," *Transactions of the Society of Naval Architects and Marine Engineers*, III (1895), 12; Captain Frank H. Schofield, "The Aims and Present Status of the Navy," (mimeo., Feb. 1924, copy in State Hist. Society of Wis.) 1; R. W. Meade, 3rd, "Some Suggestions . . .," 17–19.

37. J. S. Barnes, "My Egoistigraphy," 143, N.Y.H.S.; Ensign Douglas Roben to Ensign Charles Sperry, Sept. 8, 1866, Sperry Papers, L. of C. Cf. Huntington, *Soldier and the State*, 259, for similar contemporary Army officer views.

38. I.e., Fitzpatrick & Saphire, *Navy Maverick*, 184; Rear Admiral Charles Steedman to Dr. Lawrence Mason, Nov. 17, 1884, Steedman Papers, Perkins Library, Duke U.; Remey, *Reminiscences of Childhood*, IV, 302; Clark, *My 50 Years in the*

Navy, 223; *Naval Surgeon*, ed. Barnes, 62, 115; Lieutenant Charles Sperry to his wife, November 4, 1880, Sperry Papers, L. of C.; Lieutenant William G. Temple to Commander Henry Wise, May 7, 1862, Wise Papers, N.Y.H.S.; Mark D. Hirsch, *William C. Whitney: Modern Warwick* (New York, 1948), 261.

39. See, for example, Flag Officer Louis Goldsborough to Assistant Navy Secretary Fox, June 16, 1862, *Confidential Correspondence of Fox*, I, 291; Fox to Flag Officer Samuel P. Lee, Sept. 22, 1862, *ibid.*, II, 215; Hobson, *An Adequate Navy and the Open Door Policy* (Wash., 1915), 7, 11, and *passim*. Rodman Price (*b.* 1816) and Robert Stockton (b. 1795) also entered politics after naval service. The former became a Governor of New Jersey in 1853; the latter, a U.S. Senator from the same state in 1850.

40. Kutner & Healy, *The Admiral*, 304; Arthur Strawn, "Rise and Fall of a Hero," *American Mercury*, XV (1928), 346–354.

41. Commander C. B. Sedgewick to Commander Henry Wise, February 10, 1867, Wise Papers, N.Y.H.S.; Commander French E. Chadwick to "B," July 17, 1886, Personal copybook, p. 122, Chadwick Mss., N.Y.H.S.; untitled mss. of F. A. Roe (c. 1897), R. R. Belknap Papers, Box 424, N.H.F.; Zogbaum, *From Sail to "Saratoga,"* 138; Mahan to General Francis Greene, September 17, 1900, and to John M. Brown, August 31, 1896, Box 15, Mahan Papers, L. of C.; Mahan to Roosevelt, July 8, 1913, Theodore Roosevelt Papers, L. of C.; Warner Schilling, "Civil-Naval Politics in World War I," *World Politics*, VII (1955), 572–591. Daniels was styled "the dangerous element of *Populism*" by one anonymous officer. "Lo! a Daniel Comes to Judgement," unsigned mss. in Box 146 of the Nathan Sargent Papers, N.H.F., 4. Commander Nathan Twining considered Wilson's entire administration to be "somewhat socialistic" and too humanitarian to suit him. Twining to his brother Walter, Sept. 24, 1913, Twining Papers, State Hist. Soc. of Wis. Cf. Huntington, *Soldier and the State*, 259; Stillson, "Development . . .," unpub. Ph.D. diss., 92–158; Archibald Turnbull, "Seven Years of Daniels," *North American Review*, CCXII (1920), 606–617.

42. Lieutenant Commander George Bacon to his wife, May 16, 1863, "Civil War Letters of George Bacon," ed. John K. Mahon, *American Neptune*, XII (1952), 271–281; Ethel Harrington to her father, Captain

Purnell Harrington, Mar. 11, 1902, Harrington Papers, Arents Library, Syracuse U.; Albert Caldwell to his mother, November 5, 1876, Caldwell Papers, Indiana Hist. Soc. Library; Madeline Dahlgren, *Thoughts on Female Suffrage*, 7; Mahan, undated (1912?) speech on woman suffrage, Mahan Papers, L. of C.; Ensign A. A. McKethan to his mother, June 20, 1894, McKethan Papers, Perkins Library, Duke U.; Captain Percival Drayton to Alexander Hamilton, Jr., April 15, 1863, in *Naval Letters of Captain Percival Drayton, 1861–1865*, ed. Gertrude L. Hoyt (New York, 1906 [copy in N.Y.P.L.]), 36–57; Niblack, *Why Wars Come*, 17; Goodrich, *PUSNI*, XXIV (1898), 7; Mahan, *Influence of Sea Power Upon History, 1660–1783* (New York, 1962), 57–58; Marcus Benjamin, "Francis A. Roe," in *Memorial Papers of the Society of Colonial Wars in the District of Columbia* (November, 1903); Senior Naval Officer, Port Royal, to Commander T. H. Eastman, Nov. 3, 1876, "Living Conditions of Naval Personnel, 1871–1910," Box 274, NL, Entry 464, R.G. 45: "Liberty will not be granted to enlisted men on election day." Chadwick, cited in Samuel P. Hays, "The Politics of Reform . . .," *Pacific NWQ* (1964), 163.

43. Mahan to Ashe, February 14, 1859, *Mahan-Ashe Letters*, ed. Chiles, 86–87; same to same, April 1, 1859, *ibid.*, 104; *Influence of Sea Power*, 57–58; Huntington, *Soldier and the State*, 277.

44. N.Y. *Times*, August 20, 1916; Fiske, *From Midshipman to Rear Admiral*, 374; Brayton Harris, *The Age of the Battleship, 1890–1922* (New York, 1965), 25; Niblack, *Why Wars Come*, 6–7.

All of this disdain for politics did not prevent Annapolites such as F. V. McNair, George Dewey, and John A. Lejeune from using political influence to secure a desired billet. See the 1894 folder in the Charles I. Graves Papers, S.H.C., U. of N.C. Library; Dewey, *Autobiography*, 150ff.; and the folders for 1908–1913 in the Lejeune Papers, N.H.F.

45. See Foltz, *Surgeon of the Seas*, 84; Lieutenant Wallace S. Wharton, "The Navy—A National Investment," *PUSNI*, L (1924), 1833; Mahan to Ashe, March 23, 1859, & February 7, 1859, *Mahan-Ashe Letters*, ed. Chiles, 84, 103–104; Major Henry C. Davis, U.S.M.C., "Self-Discipline," *Marine Corps Gazette*, I (1917), 255; Professor William Stevens, U.S. Naval Academy, "The Naval Officer and the Civilian," *PUSNI*, XLVII (1921), 1727:

Fullam to Captain Richard Wainwright, October 9, 1906, Fullam Papers, N.H.F. 46. Mahan, *Interest of America in International Conditions*, 203; *Armaments and Arbitration*, 60; Fiske, *Invention*, 336ff.; Chambers, "Preparedness, February 22, 1916, A.D." Box 48, Chambers Papers, N.H.F.; *Naval Investigation: Hearings before the Senate Subcommittee on Naval Affairs* (1920), I, 1465; 44th Cong., 1st Sess., House Misc. Doc., 170. Pt. 5, *Investigation by the Committee on Naval Affairs, Appendix 18* (1876), 29n. Cf. John Peter Rasmussen, "The American Imperialist Elite: A Study in the Concept of National Efficiency," unpublished Ph.D. thesis, Stanford U., 1962.

More than one naval officer studied under the wizard of scientific management, Fredrick W. Taylor. Copley, *Taylor*, I, 336, 378–379, II, 300–303.

47. Roe to Wise, December 4, 1867, Wise Papers, N.Y.H.S.; *Army & Navy Journal*, V (1867–1868), 379, cited in Leonard A. Swann, Jr., *John Roach, Marine Entrepreneur* (Annapolis, 1965), 35; DuPont Letters, III, 290; Paul Y. Hammond, *Organizing for Defense* (Princeton, 1961), 74–77. Cf. Barker, *Everyday Life in the Navy*, 218; Evans, *One Man's Fight for a Better Navy*, 60; Admiral David D. Porter, *Memoir of Commodore Porter* (Albany, N.Y., 1875), 87. Cf. Rear Admiral Cagle, *PUSNI*, XCV (1969), 39.

48. Elting Morison, *Admiral Sims and the Modern American Navy*, 447ff.

49. See, for example, Innis LaRoche Jenkins, "Josephus Daniels and the Navy Department, 1913–1916: A Study in Military Administration," unpublished Maryland U. Ph.D. dissertation, 1960, *passim*; Ronald Spector, "Professors at War . . .," 272–275; Braisted, *U.S. Navy in the Pacific, 1909–1922*, 300.

50. Lieutenant Commander Caspar Goodrich, "Naval Education," *PUSNI*, V (1879), 338; Captain W. F. Fullam in *The Navy*, VII (Feb. 1913), 48, 61; Fiske, *Navy as a Fighting Machine*, 239; Janowitz, *Professional Soldier*, 115; O.N.I., *U.S. Navy as an Industrial Asset*, 11; "W.X." [a naval officer], *National Defense* [n.p., n.d., c. 1882], 4; Ensign W. I. Chambers, *PUSNI*, XI (1885), 52; Welles to his mother, August 9, 1885, Welles Papers, N.H.F.; McCalla, "Memoirs," Ch. XII, 25; Evans, *Admiral's Log*, 346; Commander French E. Chadwick, *Temperament, Disease and Health* (New York & London, 1892), 5. Cf. Bruce White, "ABC's for the American Enlisted Man:

The Army Post School System, 1866–1898," *History of Education Quarterly* (Winter, 1968), 491–492.

Chadwick also feared that vaccination for all diseases "would be at once destructive of the cultivation of the physique, which is one of the marks of the present age, as it was in the noble period of Greece. . . . We would soon be a world of weaklings instead of the strong." *op. cit.*, 72.

51. Karsten, "Democratic Citizen Soldier . . .," *op. cit.*, *passim*. Luce was, of course, only advocating the apprentice system first proposed by Lieutenant Matthew C. Perry in 1824. See Langley, *Social Reform*, 98–106.

52. See Luce, "The Manning of our Merchant Marine and Navy," *PUSNI*, I (1874), 1ff; "U. S. Training-Ships," *United Service*, I (1879), 425–435; "Naval Training," *PUSNI*, XVI (1890), *passim*; Aaron Ward, "Naval Apprentices," *United Service*, II (1880), 740–55; H. C. Washburn, "The American Blind Spot," *PUSNI*, XLIII (1917), 40–41; Chadwick to Colonel William Church (editor of the *Army & Navy Journal*), November 6, 1888, & to "Mr. Macgregor," October 31, 1887, copies in Chadwick's Letterbook, N.Y.H.S. Cf. Bowen, *Ships, Machinery and Mossbacks*, 6.

53. It is also true, of course, that Departmental regulations generally prohibited officers from speaking out on public questions without permission. Not all officers accepted this "muzzling" without a protest. See, for example, the exchanges between Secretary Chandler and Rear Admiral Case, in February 1885, Box 13, NJ, Entry 464, R.G. 45.

54. Drayton to Lydig M. Hoyt, June 19, 1864, *Naval Letters*, 60.

55. Mahan to Ashe, April 1, 1859, & March 23, 1859, *Mahan-Ashe Letters*, 60. Chiles, 104, 103; Tocqueville, *Democracy in America*, ed. H. S. Commager (New York, 1947), 459.

One startled young lady to whom Mahan had addressed his praise of despots remarked, "Mr. Mahan, you frighten me; what a tyrant you will be." *Mahan-Ashe Letters*, 103.

56. Mahan, *Interest of America in International Conditions*, 100, 203; *From Sail to Steam*, *passim*; *Armaments and Arbitration*, 16, 59; *Naval Administration and Warfare*, 136–137; *Influence of Sea Power Upon History, 1660–1783*, 51, 23. See also Mahan, "Twentieth Century Christianity," *North American Review*, CXCIX (April, 1914), 590.

Elsewhere he maintained that the rise of popular government in Great Britain, arising from the passage of the 1873 Reform Bill, would cause her to "drop behind" and lose the command of the seas (*Influence*, 58).

57. Mahan, *From Sail to Steam*, 196–197; "Misrepresenting Mr. Roosevelt," *Outlook*, XCVIII (17 June 1911), 357–358; *Influence* ...., 51; "Twentieth Century Christianity," *North American Review*, CXCIX (April 1914), 595; Captain William F. Fullam to Captain William Sims, January 11, 1912, Fullam Papers, N.H.F. Admiral W. S. Sims spoke, I think, for most of the "band of brothers" when he told Rear Admiral Dunn in 1919: "Theodore Roosevelt is dead. I have been able to think of nothing else for days." Morison, *Admiral Sims*, 179.

58. *Naval Investigation*, I, 1465; Earle, *Life at Naval Academy*, 165; Mahan to Ashe, August 12, 1868, Ashe Papers, Duke U. Lib.; Mahan's introduction to *Life and Adventures of Jack Philips*, ed. Maclay; Caldwell to his aunt, May 6, 1878, Caldwell Papers, Indiana Hist. Soc. Lib; Welles to his mother, September 15, 1901, Welles Papers, N.H.F.; Coontz, *From Mississippi to the Sea*, 334; Puleston, *Mahan*, 208.

59. "All the officers of the American Navy have grown into manhood . . . under a similar code of ethics, artificially administered and in sharp contrast with the laws of society based on public opinion." Lieutenant Ridgley Hunt (Retired), *PUSNI*, XLII (1916), 727.

60. Midshipman Charles Sperry to his sister, January 25, 1863, Sperry Papers; Midshipman Marius Schoonmaker to his parents, September 2, 1859, in Marius Schoonmaker, "Life and Correspondence of Schoonmaker," p. 22, Schoonmaker Papers, N.H.F.; Journal of Lieutenant Stephan Rowan, December, 1859, entry, Rowan Papers, National Archives; Rear Admiral F. E. Chadwick, *The Causes of the Civil War, 1859–1861* (New York, 1907), 124–125; Samuel Ashe, in *Southern Churchman*, January 8, 1921, 7; Munro, *Intervention and Dollar Diplomacy*, 315–323.

61. Lieutenant Albert Caldwell to his mother, May 16, 1878, Caldwell Papers, Indiana Hist. Soc. Lib.; Mahan to Ashe, February 7, 1859, *Letters*, ed. Chiles, 83; Mahan, *America's Interest in International Conditions* (Boston, 1910), 66; Captain H. C. Cochrane, U.S.M.C., "The Navy in the Labor Strikes of 1877," *The United Service*, I (1879), 115–129, 616–634, esp. 121; Lt.

T. B. M. Mason, "On the Employment of Boat Guns as Light Artillery for Landing Parties," *PUSNI*, V (1879), 207–230; Rear Admiral Alexander Murray to Navy Secretary Thompson, Aug. 1, 1877, North Pacific Squadron letters, Roll 60, Microcopy 89, R.G. 45; unidentified Lieutenant Commander to Navy Secretary Herbert, VP file, Oakland, Calif., Navy Base, 1894, N.A.; Jones, *Address to Naval Academy*, 2; "Mantus," "Uniformity in the Navy," *United Service*, V (1881), 144; Porter, *The Naval History of the Civil War* (New York, 1886), 831; LaFeber, *New Empire*, 99; Rear Admiral F. A. Roe to Rear Admiral G. E. Belknap, February 26, 1897, R. R. Belknap Papers, N.H.F.; Evans, *Admiral's Log*, 28–29. Cf. Davies, *Patriotism on Parade*, 339.

For examples of the use of U.S. marines and naval forces as strikebreakers see Captain Richard S. Collum, U.S.M.C., *History of the United States Marine Corps* (Phil., 1890), 186, 189, 205–217.

62. Daniels, *Wilson Era: Years of Peace*, 306; Rodman, *Yarns of a Kentucky Admiral*, 305; Fiske, *Invention*, 338–339; Fiske, *Art of Fighting* (New York, 1920), 325, 367–368; Captain Wat T. Cluverius, "The Array Against Sovereignty," *PUSNI*, LI (1925), 1916–1923; E. M. Halliday, *The Ignorant Armies* (New York, 1958), 29; Henry P. Beers, *U.S. Naval Forces in Northern Russia (Archangel and Murmansk), 1918–1919*, Admin. Ref. Service Report No. 5 (Office of Records Admin., Navy Dept. 1943), 3, 13, 17; William Preston, Jr., *Aliens and Dissenters: Federal Suppression of Radicals, 1903–1933* (N.Y., 1966 Harper Torchbook ed.), 161–162; Coontz, *From the Mississippi to the Sea*, 377–380; Captain Dudley Knox, "The Elements of Leadership," *PUSNI*, XLVI (1920), 1896; Folk, *PUSNI*, LI (1925), 276–279. Cf. Rear Admiral Kemp Tolley, "Our Russian War of 1918–1919," *PUSNI* (Feb. 1968), 58–72; Lieutenant Chester Jackson, "Mission to Murmansk," *PUSNI* (Feb. 1968), 82–89.

63. Niblack, *Why Wars Come*, 49; Fiske, *Navy as a Fighting Machine*, 70; Captain E. B. Fenner, "Discipline," *PUSNI*, XLVII (1921), 1385; Knox, "The Navy and Public Indoctrination," *PUSNI*, LV (1929), 490; Cf. Allen Guttman, "Political Ideas and the Military Elite," *American Scholar* (Spring, 1965), 221–237.

A top-level conference of naval leaders in May, 1932, recommended that naval reserve units be given training in riot tactics. Wiend, "Naval Reserve," Ph.D. thesis, 235.

64. Cochrane, *op. cit.*, 116; Knox, "The Elements of Leadership," *PUSNI*, XLVI (1920), 1897.

65. Captain Dudley Knox, *PUSNI*, LV (1929), 490; Lieutenant (j.g.) Matthew Radom, "The 'Americanization' of the U.S. Navy," *PUSNI*, LXIII (1937), 234; Lieutenant Fredrick Collins, "Naval Affairs," *PUSNI*, V (1879), 164; Captain Stephen B. Luce, "U.S. Training-Ships," *United Service*, I (1870), 425; Luce, "Naval Training," *PUSNI*, XVI (1890), 377; Lieutenant William Fullam, "The System of Naval Training and Discipline Required to Promote Efficiency and Attract Americans," *PUSNI*, XVI (1890), 479, 480, 485, *passim*; Passed Assistant Engineer Frank Bennett, *op. cit.*, *passim*; Lieutenant William Folger to Lieutenant Fullam, April 28, 1896, Box 1, Fullam Papers, N.H.F. There are many other letters from naval officers addressed to Fullam in Box 1, Fullam Papers, written throughout the 1890s, complimenting Fullam on his (and Rear Admiral Luce's) efforts to restrict enlistments to native-born. See also Chapter 3, "Jack Tar and the 'New Navy.'" Cf. John Higham, *Strangers in the Land: Patterns of American Nativism, 1860–1925* (New Brunswick, 1955).

66. *Letters of Perkins*, 37; Midshipman Charles Sperry to "Mary," December 9, 1866, Sperry Papers; Mahan, *From Sail to Steam*, 285; Roe, *Naval Duties*, 187, Wyllie, "Social Darwinism and the Businessman," *Proceedings of the American Philosophical Society*, CIII, No. 5 (1959), 629–635; Huntington, *Soldier and State*, 264, 497; Hofstadter, *Social Darwinism*, 184; Ensign W. I. Chambers, *PUSNI*, XI (1885), 5; Richmond P. Hobson, *Alcohol and the Human Race*, 143; Surgeon J. F. Leys, U.S.N., *PUSNI*, XXXVIII (1912), 1242; Hart, *Great White Fleet*, 67; Mahan, *Interest of U.S. in Sea Power, Present and Future*, 18, 21–22; Chambers, "Preparedness, Feb. 22, 1916, A.D." Box 48, Chambers Papers, N.H.F.; Niblack, *Why Wars Come*, 21. See also "National Darwinism" on pp. 226–229 of this chapter.

67. See, for example, Montgomery, *Our Admiral's Flag*, 129; F. E. Bunts to the class of '81, November 3, 1889, *6th Annual Report of the Class of '81*, 24; *U.S. Nautical Magazine and Naval Journal*, III (1856), 171; Rodman, *Yarns of a Kentucky Admiral*, 205; Lieutenant Commander Barber, cited in Alfred Vagts, "Hopes and Fears of an Amer.-German War, 1870–1915," *Political Science Quarterly*, LIV (1939), 527; Commander Nathan Sargent to the Commander-in-Chief, Asiatic Fleet, July 28, 1906, Box 146, and Item 20, Box 147, Nathan Sargent Papers, N.H.F.; Lieutenant James Reid, *PUSNI*, XXIX (1903), 10; Mahan to Ashe, March 6, 1870, Ashe Papers, Duke U. Library, *Life and Adventures of Jack Philip*, ed. Maclay, 203–204; Richmond Hobson, *In Line of Duty*, 236.

68. Undated mss. in Box 8, August V. Kautz Papers, L. of C., p. 18; Mahan to his father, July 30, 1867, Mahan Papers, L. of C.; West, *Admirals of American Empire*, 133; Lieutenant William H. Beehler, *The Cruise of the U.S.S. Brooklyn, 1881–1884* (Philadelphia, 1885), 34; Sperry to Charles Sperry, Jr., October 9, 1906, Sperry Papers, L. of C.; Fullam to the editor of the New Orleans *Times-Democrat*, May 31, 1907, [copy] Fullam Papers, N.H.F.; Cadet Midshipman W. I. Chambers to his parents, May 8, 1877, W. I. Chambers Papers, N.H.F.; Rear Admiral C. D. Sigsbee, Commander Caribbean Squadron, June 26, 1904, to Secretary of the Navy (Confidential), Letterbooks of Carib. Squad., 1904–1907, Entry 395, Subentry 132, Vol. II, R.G. 45.

69. Private journal, 1867–1869, "Asiatic tour," Papers of Vice Admiral Stephan C. Rowan, National Archives Microfilm No. 180; *Preble's Diary*, ed. Szczesniak, 141; *PUSNI*, V (1879), 347–348; Barker, *Everyday Life in the Navy*, 96; Rear Admiral George Belknap, "The Old Navy," in *Naval Actions and History*, 65; Kimberly to Zoe, November 20, 1870, Kimberly Papers, Chicago Hist. Soc.; Habersham, *North Pacific Surveying and Exploring Expedition*, 236; Evans, *Admiral's Log*, 21; *Compilation of Laws Relating to the Navy . . .*, ed. John W. Hogg (Washington, G.P.O., 1883), 51; Twining to his brother, Sept. 25, 1914, Twining Papers, State Hist. Soc. of Wis. Cf. Mahan, *The Problem of Asia and its Effect Upon International Policies* (Boston, 1900), *passim*.

For the most complete statements of the fear of Japan on the part of early twentieth century American naval officers see William Braisted, *U.S. Navy in the Pacific, 1909–1922* (Austin, Texas, 1971); and Gerald E. Wheeler, *Prelude to Pearl Harbor: The U.S. Navy and the Far East, 1921–1931* (Columbia, Mo., 1963).

70. Evans, *Admiral's Log*, 12, 166, 179, 259; Captain Edward Dorn to his nephew, T. E. Mayhew, 1918–1919, Dorn Papers, in possession of Mrs. C. G. Halpine, Anna-

polis, Maryland; Rear Admiral Dewey to Senator Redfield Proctor, January 7, 1899, Dewey Papers, L. of C.; Dewey to Navy Secretary Long, telegram, June 27, 1898, cited in Kutner & Healy, *The Admiral*, 224; Fiske, *War Time in Manila*, 89; W. P. Marshall, *Afloat on the Pacific; or, Notes of Three Years of Life at Sea* (Zanesville, Ohio, 1876), 105; Young, *The "Boston" at Hawaii*, 52; Cushing to Pillsbury, April 18, 1871, *PUSNI*, XXXVIII (1912), 925; Johnson, *Rodgers*, 336; Yates Stirling, *A U.S. Midshipman in China* (Phil., 1909), 57, 317; Lieutenant J. D. J. Kelley, *United Service*, I (1879), 264; Thomason, *—and a few Marines*, 8–10; Commander Nathan Sargent to the Commander-in-Chief, Asiatic Fleet, Dec. 22, 1905, copy in Box 146, Sargent Papers, N.H.F.; Captain Charles Hutchins, Why All This Chaos in China," *PUSNI*, LIII (1927), 422, 425; McCalla, "Memoirs," Ch. XXVIII, 15.

70a. When Lieutenant Tom Massie's wife was allegedly raped by a Hawaiian in 1931, Admiral William Pratt and Yates Stirling publicly urged Massie to take revenge. He did so, with relative impunity. See Peter Van Slingerland, *Something Terrible Has Happened!* (N.Y., 1966).

71. Porter, "The Chinese in America," *United Service*, I (1879), 315–319; Bunts to his brother, Jan. 17, 1883, *Letters*, 195; Rear Admiral George Melville, "The Important Elements in Naval Conflicts," *Annals* of the American Academy of Political and Social Science, XXVI (1905), 125–133; Captain E. B. Miller to Rear Admiral Edwin A. Anderson, Mar. 5, 1924, Anderson Papers, S.H.C., U. of N.C.L.; Captain E. T. Constein to Vice Admiral Roger Welles, Aug. 4, 1925, Welles Papers, N.H.F.; Admiral Charles B. McVay mss. autobiography, pt. 9, p. 14, McVay Papers, N.H.F. Cf. Paul Reinsch, *An American Diplomat in China* (Garden City, N.Y., 1922). Jim Sens' forthcoming study of changing perceptions of China in the 1920s among U.S. naval and marine officers on station there and their impact on U.S. policy toward the Kuomintang should be both interesting and useful in this regard.

72. Mahan, *From Sail to Steam*, 221–230, 234; *Armaments and Arbitration*, 163, 60; Mahan to Theodore Roosevelt, Dec. 2, 1911, Roosevelt Papers, Mss. Div., L. of C.

73. See, for example, Ensign Albert Niblack, "The Coast Indians of Southern Alaska and Northern British Columbia,"

Annual Report of the Smithsonian Institution (Wash., G.P.O., 1890), 226–386; Captain Edward Dorn, miscellaneous private papers relating to the Samoan Islanders, in possession of Mrs. C. G. Halpine, Annapolis; and Commodore Stephen Rowan's Private Journal, 1867–1869, "Asiatic Tour" (on the Japanese), Vice Admiral Rowan Papers, R.G. 45, National Archives, for three sociological commentaries on foreign cultures by naval officers with a degree of sophistication uncommon in their day.

74. Lovette, *School of Sea*, 123–124; D. Nelson, *Integration of Negro into Navy*, *passim*; U.S.N., Bu Nav (Pers—A212), "U.S. Naval Administration in World War II; The Negro in the Navy," p. 4, copy in the possession of Prof. Richard Dalfiume, History Dept., S.U.N.Y., Binghamton.

75. See, for example, Ensign Roger Welles to his mother, June 23, 1887, and Dec. 3, 1900, Welles Papers, N.H.F.; Rear Admiral Louis Goldsborough to his wife, Aug. 20, 1873, Vol. 19, Goldsborough Papers, L. of C.; Commodore Robert Shufeldt, "The Future of Cuba," undated mss., Box 20, Shufeldt Papers, N.H.F.; Barker, *Everyday Life*, 240; *Life of Philip*, ed. Maclay, 97.

In Admiral Porter's novel, *The Adventures of Harry Marline*, a tribe of imaginary African natives, the "Chatawees," are provided with tails! (126). None the less, Porter's hero arranges a treaty with these semihumans to "develop" their lands and to obtain railway rights.

76. When Representative Oscar Calloway asked Waller if he believed that all people would be better off with military dictators Waller replied, "No sir, . . . just these people." *Hearings before the House Naval Affairs Comm. on Estimates of the Sec. of the Navy, 1916*, II, 2268.

77. See material on black sailors in Chapter 3.

78. Drayton to Hamilton, July 16, 1865, Drayton Papers, U.S. Navy Collection, New York Public Library (N.Y.P.L.); Porter, *Incidents and Anecdotes of the Civil War*, 244; Sigsbee, *The "Maine"* (New York, 1899), 14–15; Lieutenant Commander T. P. Magruder, "The Enlisted Personnel," *PUSNI*, XXXVI (1910), 385–386.

79. Mahan to his mother, Aug. 21, 1867, Mahan Papers, L. of C.; Caldwell to his mother, Dec. 13, 1870, Caldwell Papers, Indiana Hist. Soc. Lib.; Commander Nathan Sargent to the Secretary of the Navy [copy], Feb. 6, 1901, Box 146, Sargent

Papers, N.H.F.; *Cabinet Diaries of Daniels*, ed. Cronon, 194.

The only pre-Civil War regular Navy Jewish officer of record was Uriah P. Levy (b. 1792), active in the 1810s, '20s, and '30s. His struggles with the anti-semitism of his day are recorded in Fitzpatrick and Saphire, *Navy Maverick*.

80. See, for example, Goldsborough, *Reply to Coues*, 3–5; Mahan, *From Sail to Steam*, 9; Lieutenant Commander G. E. Brandt, *PUSNI*, L (1924), 916; Captain Wat T. Cluverius, "The Array against Sovereignty," *PUSNI*, LI (1925), 1916–1923; Porter, *Incidents and Anecdotes of the Civil War*, 124; Rear Admiral S. B. Luce, *The Navy*, V (1911), 27; *PUSNI*, XIV (1888), 628, XXX (1906), 1367–86; and *North American Review*, CLII (1891), 672–673; Gleaves, *Luce*, 174, 297; Johnson, *Rodgers*, 196; Captain William Sampson, *PUSNI*, XV (1889), 171; Mahan to Theodore Roosevelt, June 11, 1911, Roosevelt Papers, L. of C.; Andrew D. White, *Autobiography* (2 vols., New York, 1904–1905), II, 319–320, 343, 347; Niblack, *Why Wars Come*, 144–145; Chambers, Box 148, Chambers Papers, N.H.F.; Captain Dudley Knox, *The Eclipse of Sea Power* (New York, 1922), 14–15; Puleston, *Mahan*, 171, 180, 210; Mahan, *Armaments and Arbitration*, 5–10, 13, 120, and *Lessons of the War with Spain and other Essays* (Boston, 1899), 227.

Andrew White was impressed with Mahan's arguments at the Peace Conference, but he feared that their logic "would oblige us, if logically carried out, to go back to the marauding and atrocities of the Thirty Years' War." *Autobiography*, II, 316–317.

81. Goldsborough, *Reply to Coues*, 22; McNair, *PUSNI*, I (1874), 163–176; Porter, *Memoir of Commodore David Porter* (Albany, N.Y., 1875), 103, 250; Ransom, *United Service*, II (1880), 206; Wainwright, *PUSNI*, VIII (1882), 134; *PUSNI*, XXIV (1898), 41; and *The Navy*, VII (1913), 44; Chambers, *PUSNI*, XI (1885), 3–43; Barry, *PUSNI*, XVI (1890), 521; Ammen, *Old Navy and the New*, 419; Rockwell, *United Service*, 2nd Series, X (1893), 14–16; Mahan to his wife, August 24, 1893, Mahan Papers, L. of C.; Gherardi, cited in *Army and Navy Journal*, XXXVI (22 October 1898), 185; Sampson, cited in *Army and Navy Journal*, XXXVI (27 May 1899), 922; Hood, *PUSNI*, XXVIII (1902), 196; Luce, *PUSNI*, XXXIX (1903), 543; and Gleaves, *Luce*, 297; Wilson, *The Navy*, VII (July, 1914), 298;

Lovette, *PUSNI*, LVI (1930), 430; Niblack, *Why Wars Come*, 2, 27; Wharton, *PUSNI*, L (1924), 1834; Edwin A. Falk, *Fighting Bob Evans* (New York, 1931), 442; Bennett, *Steam Navy*, II, 847; Barker, *Everyday Life*, 393. Cf. Huntington, *Soldier and the State*, 63–68. Mrs. M. V. Dahlgren, wife of the Rear Admiral, asked in 1881, "Has the world approached so much the millenial condition that we . . . can suppress our armies and let our navies die out?" *South Sea Sketches* (Boston, 1881), 28. And Andrew White, president of Cornell University, said of Captain Mahan, "When he speaks, the millenium fades, and this stern, severe, actual world appears." *Autobiography*, II, 347.

82. Goldsborough, *Reply to Coues*, 17; Luce, *PUSNI*, XVI (1890), 368; Mahan, *Armaments and Arbitration*, 13; Mahan to "Fitzhugh," Jan. 18, 1913, Folder 18, Box 209, N.H.F.; Hobson, *An Adequate Navy and the Open-Door Policy* (Washington, 1915), 5. Cf. Bengt Abrahamsson, "The Ideology of an Elite: [Military] Conservatism and National Insecurity [in Sweden]," in Jacques Van Doorn, ed., *Armed Forces and Society* (The Hague, 1968), 70ff.

83. This preoccupation with war and preparedness tended to provoke hostile reactions from superiors like Josephus Daniels who did not entirely share the naval aristocracy's views. Thus Rear Admiral Bradley Fiske, who hounded Daniels on preparedness matters and war scares in 1913, later recalled that Daniels "was always convinced in his own mind that there would never be any war. I found after a while that it was not a good thing to say anything to him about war. He did not seem to be ready to start on any subject connected with war at all. . . . I gave up using the word 'war' as much as I could." 66th Cong., 2nd Sess., U.S. Senate, *Naval Investigation, Hearings before the Subcommittee on Naval Affairs* (2 vols., Wash., G.P.O., 1921), I, 731.

84. Sampson, *PUSNI*, XV (1889), 171; Rockwell, *United Service*, 2nd Series, VIII (1892), 414; Staunton, *Harper's New Monthly Magazine*, LXXXVIII (1894), 653–668; Chadwick, *PUSNI*, XXVIII (1902), 263–264, 266; Dewey to Rear Admiral Willard, H. Brownson, Jan. 15, 1907; Evans, *Admiral's Log*, 445; Fiske, *PUSNI*, XXXVII (1911), 735; Stillson, "American Naval Establishment," Ph.D. thesis, 110; Fiske, *Navy as Fighting Machine*, 26; Fiske, "Disarmament and Foreign Trade," *PUSNI*, XLVII (1921), 1541; Niblack, *Why*

Wars Come, 158–159, 9, 11–14; Schofield, "The Aims and Present Status of the Navy" and "Incidents and Present day Aspects of Naval Strategy" (mimeo. copies, n.p., 1923 & 1924 [copies in State Hist. Soc. of Wisc.]), 1–2, 15, *passim*; Beard, *Idea of National Interest*, 236.

Stillson, *op. cit.*, 97, cites similar views of Rear Admirals William Folger, William Rodgers, and Charles Sperry.

85. Knapp, "The Naval Officer in Diplomacy," *PUSNI*, LIII (1927), 316; Chadwick, *PUSNI*, XXVIII (1902), 266; Fiske, *PUSNI*, XXXVII (1911), 713; Fiske, *Navy as Fighting Machine*, 312; Chambers, "Literary Notes," Box 48, Chambers Papers, N.H.F.

86. Roe to Rear Admiral G. E. Belknap, Nov. 25, 1897, and any of his 1898–1899 letters, Box 424, R. R. Belknap Papers, N.H.F.

87. Consider also Commander John Rodgers' explanation of the causes of the Mexican War to the Governor of Simoda, Japan, May 20, 1855: "Our citizens temporarily living in Mexico and carrying on trade there or living quietly for their pleasure were unjustly treated; for a long time we endeavoured to obtain what the treaty allowed. The Mexican government refused to listen to our remonstrances; many cases occurred. At last, after fruitless attempts to obtain justices, we made war. . . . The Mexicans . . . thought, because we were a very peaceable people, that we would not punish them." This thinly veiled threat to a Japanese official, who sought to interpret the U.S.–Japanese treaty strictly, said nothing of President James Polk's expansionist ambitions. *Yankee Surveyors in the Shogun's Seas*, ed. Allan Cole (Princeton, 1947), 108.

88. Mahan, "Sailing Home to War," *Harper's Weekly*, LI, No. 2 (5 October 1907), 1453; Puleston, *Mahan*, 342; Mahan, *Armaments and Arbitration*, 126, 153–154; "The Grand Illusion [a review of Norman Angell's book with that title]," *North American Review*, CXCV (March, 1912), 319–322; Angell, "The Grand Illusion: A Reply to Rear Admiral A. T. Mahan," *North American Review*, CXCV (June, 1912), 754–772, esp. 755. Huntington, *Soldier and State*, 65, 263, makes less of the military man's conviction that economic forces were the primary reasons for wars than my own evidence would appear to call for.

Surgeon J. F. Leys, U.S.N., "Mental and Moral Training for War," *PUSNI*, XXXVIII (1912), 1242, wanted Americans to be taught that war was "right, a moral idea."

89. Macartney, *Mr. Lincoln's Admirals*, 81; Mahan, *Admiral Farragut* (New York, 1892), 277, 325; Fiske, *War Time in Manila* (Boston, 1913); "Winslow, Cameron McRae," *Dictionary of American Biography*; McCalla, "Memoirs," Ch. XXVIII, 21. McCalla was quoting a letter he had written to his wife in 1900.

90. Mahan, *The Harvest Within*, 79, 277; and "Twentieth Century Christianity," *North American Review*, CXCIX (April, 1914), 593–598; 33rd Cong., 2nd Sess., *Senate Exec. Doc.*, No. 34 (Wash. 1855), 4–9; Stanton, "The Japan Expedition," Unpublished mss., Stanton Papers, Mystic; Bernadou to Foulk, March 6, 1887, Foulk Papers, N.Y.P.L.; Kelley, *Question of Ships*, 112; and *Our Navy*, 10; Belknap, "The Old Navy," in *Naval Actions and History, 1799–1898*, Vol. XII of the Papers of the Military History Society of Massachusetts (Boston, 1902), 62; Lafeber, *New Empire*, 211–213; Hobson, "America, Mistress of the Seas," *North American Review*, CLXXV (1902), 555; Mahan, *Retrospect and Prospect*, 16–17; Barker, *Everyday Life*, 396; Overstreet, "The Danger of Disarming America," *PUSNI*, L (1924), 1498. Cf. William Neumann, "Religion, Morality, and Freedom: The Ideological Background of the Perry Expedition," *Pacific Historical Review*, XXIII (Aug. 1954), 247–257. Cf. Drake, "Shufeldt," Ph.D. thesis, 217–218, 386. Even naval wives were "presumed without question" to "show loyalty to God." Johnson, *Welcome Aboard*, 240.

91. Sperry to his wife, September 4 & October 3, 1885, Sperry Papers; Porter, *United Service*, I (1879), 319; Henson, "U.S. Navy and China," Ph.D., 183; Sperry to Mark, April 21, 1885, Sperry Papers; Lovette, *School of Sea*, 123–124.

92. Fred Harvey Harrington, *God, Mammon, and the Japanese: Dr. Horace Allen and Korean-American Relations, 1884–1905* (2nd ed., Madison, Wis., 1961), 100n.

93. See, for example, Varg, *Missionaries*, 41, 128; Rodman, *Yarns of a Kentucky Admiral*, 194, 145, 154, 202–204; Goldsborough to his wife, June 1 & July 15, 1853, Goldsborough Papers, L. of C.; Hugh Dinsmore to George Foulk, July 31, 1887, Foulk Papers, N.Y.P.L. (first cited in Harrington, *op.cit.*, 99–100); Kirkland to the Secretary of the Navy, September 18, 1895, and accompanying documents in Syrian Folder, Box 7,

Subject File VP (Protection of Individuals and Property), R.G. 45; McCalla, "Memoirs," Ch. XXV, 11; Wiley, *Admiral from Texas*, 114; Arthur O. Brown, *The Mastery of the Far East: The Story of Korea's Transformation and Japan's Supremacy in the Orient* (New York, 1919), 322; Lieutenant Edwin Anderson to his wife, Jan. 11, March 7, and March 9, 1903, Anderson Papers, S.H.C. U. of N.C.L.

Commander Andrew Foote appears to have gotten along rather well with missionaries (*Africa*, 76, 208–210), but he was neither an Academy graduate nor an Episcopalian; he was a Connecticut Congregationalist, and an abolitionist to boot.

94. Mahan, "Prayer Book Revision," *The Churchman*, XC (1914), 465–466, 497–498.

95. See, for example, Mahan, *Armaments and Arbitration*, 117; Major General Smedley Butler, U.S.M.C., "On Missionaries," *Missionary Review of the World*, LIII (June, 1930), 419; Major Evans F. Carlson, U.S.M.C., *Twin Stars of China* (New York, 1941), 208; Sperry to his wife, December 6, 1879, Sperry Papers; Evans, *Admiral's Log*, 13; McCalla, "Memoirs," Ch. XXVI, 3; Washburn to C-in-C Asiatic Fleet, Nov. 8, 1911, R.G. 80, N.A. (I am indebted to Susan Kleinberg for this last citation.) Cf. Edmund S. Wehrle, *Britain, China, and the Antimissionary Riots* (Minneapolis, 1966); Drake, "Shufeldt," Ph.D. thesis, 180 (for Shufeldt's disapproval of missionaries who sought "a Gunboat in order to make the heathen understand them").

96. Assistant Surgeon Dudley Carpenter to his mother, May 3, 1898, Carpenter Papers, N.H.F.; Captain Wat Cluverius, *PUSNI*, LI (1925), 1919; Goldsborough to his wife, August 10, 1854, Louis Goldsborough Papers, L. of C.; Mahan to Ashe, March 23, 1859, October 29, 1858, and February 14, 1859, *Mahan–Ashe Letters*, ed. Chiles, 103–104, 86, 88, 11; Sperry to Helen, May 27, 1865 [misfiled in 1885 folder], Sperry Papers; Kimberly, "Reminiscences," p. xv, Louis Kimberly Papers, Chicago Hist. Soc.; Chaplain Fitch W. Taylor, *The Broad Pennant*, 134–136; Rear Admiral F. A. Roe to Rear Admiral G. E. Belknap, February 26, 1897, Box 424, R. R. Belknap Papers, N.H.F.; Sperry to "my dear cousin," August 1, 1865, Sperry Papers.

97. Mahan, *Interest of America in Sea Power*, 129; *Harvest Within*, 14, 50, 237–238; "Personality and Influence," Unpublished speech given at Dartmouth Royal Navy

Officer's Training School, Mahan Papers, L. of C.

98. Meade, "Suggestions of Professional Experience . . .," 17–19, Box II, R. W. Meade, 3rd, Papers, N.Y.H.S.

99. Kelley, *Our Navy*, 10; Staunton, *The War in Tong-King* [*Tonkin*]: *Why the French Are in Tong-King, and What They Are Doing There* (Boston, 1884), 13.

100. Goldsborough, *Reply to Coues*, 5–6; Fiske, *Navy as a Fighting Machine*, x; Mahan, *Lessons of the War with Spain and Other Essays*, 231, 235; *Interest of America in International Conditions*, 42, 168 (compare the logic of these two pages); *Harvest Within*, 112, 259, 180–181; and "The Apparent Decadence of the Church's Influence," *The Churchman*, XIII (April 25, 1903), 545.

101. Taylor, "The General Question of Isthmian Interest," *Nicaraguan Canal Discussion before the American Association for the Advancement of Science*, 36th Meeting (N.Y., August, 1887), 12–14; Taylor, "The Future of Our Navy" [1899], Rear Admiral Henry C. Taylor Collection, Box 319, Naval Historical Foundation, 4–5.

The emergence of the concepts of naval strategy generally attributed to Captain Mahan will be the subject of a later chapter, but we may note in passing here that they were all present in these 1887 remarks of Taylor, who later relieved Mahan as president of the War College, remarks which were made several years before the appearance of *The Influence of Sea Power upon History, 1660–1783* or any of Mahan's other essays on strategy.

102. Shufeldt, "The Future of Cuba," undated mss. in General Miscellany & undated Correspondence section, Box 20, Robert Shufeldt Papers, N.H.F.; *The Nation*, LVIII (April 19, 1894), 285 (see also Young, "*Boston*" at Hawaii, 190–215, which argues that Wiltse's intervention was temperate and neutral; but then see Barker, *Everyday Life*, 200–240, which indicates that it was not); Chadwick to Representative Hilary Herbert, November 12, 1887, & December 21, 1888, [copies] Chadwick letterbook, N.Y.H.S.; Davis, *Life of Davis*, 140.

103. Chambers, "The Reconstruction and Increase of the Navy," *PUSNI*, XL (1885), 5; Mahan, "The U.S. Looking Outward," *Atlantic Monthly* (1890), in *The Interest of the United States in Sea Power, Present and Future* (Boston, 1897), 18, 21–22; Wainwright, "Our Naval Power," *PUSNI*,

XXIV (1898), 42–43; Taylor, *PUSNI*, XXII (1896), 202. Cf. Richard Hofstadter, *Social Darwinism in American Thought* (2nd ed., N.Y., 1955), 184–85, 202. See also Captain Henry Taylor, "The Study of War," *North American Review*, CLXII (February, 1896), 183; *Life and Letters of Remey*, x, 943; and "Racism" earlier in this chapter.

104. McCalla, "Memoirs," Ch. XXIX, 19; Luce, "An Address Delivered at the U.S. Naval War College," *PUSNI*, XXIX (1903), 541; Hobson, "America, Mistress of the Seas," *North Am. Rev.*, CLXXV (1902), 557.

105. Rear Admiral W. T. Sampson, "Admiral Dewey as a National Hero," *The Century Magazine*, XXVI (1899), 928; *Life and Letters of Dewey*, 211–212; Dewey to W. P. Newberry, February 18, 1907, Dewey Papers, L. of C.; Mahan, *Some Neglected Aspects of War*, 74; *Lessons of the War with Spain*, 88; and *From Sail to Steam*, 86–87. Cf. "Man, Pacifism, and the Causes of War" on pp. 218–222 of this chapter. It may be that Julius Pratt, who was an instructor at the Naval Academy in the 1920s, was influenced by this naval interpretation of the causes of the Spanish-American War. His *Expansionists of 1898* clearly puts "humanitarianism" over commercial considerations.

106. Kimberly, "Our Navy," Manuscript [c. 1898] in Louis Kimberly Papers, Chicago Historical Society; Mahan, *The Problem of Asia* (Boston, 1900), 168; Mahan to Sydenham Clarke, mid-August, 1898, cited in Puleston, *Mahan*, 200; "The Relations of the United States to their New Dependencies," in *Lessons of the War with Spain and Other Essays*, 249. See also Mahan, *From Sail to Steam*, 325.

Morris Levy ("Alfred Thayer Mahan and U.S. Foreign Policy," Unpub. Ph.D. dissertation, N.Y.U., 1965, 165–180) has wisely pointed out that Mahan initially was not very enthusiastic about the annexation of the Philippines but that he changed tunes once the deed had been done.

107. Mahan, "War from the Christian Standpoint," a speech before the Episcopal Church Congress in Providence, Rhode Island, 1900, cited in Puleston, *Mahan*, 217; *The Problem of Asia*, 31, 32, 98, 171, 187; *From Sail to Steam*, 325; "Current Fallacies upon Naval Subjects," in *Lessons of the War with Spain & Other Essays*, 284;

Mahan to Sydenham Clarke, mid-August, 1898, cited in Puleston, 200.

108. Taylor, "Future of Our Navy," *loc. cit.*; U.S. Senate, *Affairs in the Philippines: Hearings before the Philippine Committee*, Sen. Doc. No. 331, 57th Cong., 1st Sess. [1903], 2928; William R. Braisted, *The United States Navy in the Pacific, 1897–1909* (Austin, Texas, 1958), 46; Barker, *Everyday Life*, 320–326.

109. Beach, "Manila Bay in 1898," *PUSNI*, XLVI (1920), 602.

110. For a similar critique of the Tagalog treatment of the Moslem Moro tribes in the southern islands, see the remarks of the fictional Ensign Woodbridge in Marcus Goodrich, *Delilah* (N.Y., 1941), 78–79.

111. Fiske, *War Time in Manila* (New York, 1913), 173–179.

112. Welles to his mother, June 14, 1898, Roger Welles Papers, N.H.F.; Barker, *Everyday Life*, iv; Kimball, in *The Navy*, VIII (1914), 22.

113. Colvocoresses, *Four Years in a Government Exploring Expedition* (N.Y., 1852), 166; Kelley, *Question of Ships*, 121; Wainwright, *PUSNI*, XXIV (1898), 46; Chadwick, *PUSNI*, XXVIII (1902), 267; Hobson, "America, Mistress of the Seas," *North American Review*, CLXXV (1902), 549, 552–553; Navy General Board to the Secretary of the Navy, September 26, 1912, cited in Stillson, "Naval Establishment," Ph.D. thesis, 96; Cooper to Secretary of the Navy (Div. of Ops.), Jan. 26, 1911, Honduranean Corr., 1910–1911, Entry 310, R.G. 45. See also the remarks of the Senior Member of the Navy General Board to the Secretary of the Navy, April 19, 1922: "We must not fail to avail ourselves of every opportunity to see that the doctrines of our country are spread." Cited in Braisted, *U.S. Navy in the Pacific, 1909–1922*, 660.

114. Twining to his brother Walter, January 3, 1917, Nathan Twining Papers, State Hist. Soc. of Wis.; Frost, "The People's Role in War," *PUSNI*, XLIV (1917), 1117; Brown, "Social Attitudes . . .," *op. cit.*, 373. Cf. Mahan, *America's Interest in International Conditions* (Boston, 1910), 141–142; Schilling Ph.D. thesis, 249; Vincent Davis, *Postwar Defense Policy and the U.S. Navy, 1943–1946* (Chapel Hill, N.C.), 17; Fred Greene, "The Military View of American National Policy, 1904–1940," *American Hist. Rev.*, LXVI, Pt. 1 (Jan., 1961), 354–357; Roskill, *Naval Policy*, 515.

THE INTERNAL WORLD

We know and feel our cause is just; for this we'll always fight.
Unity pervades our fleet, this, in itself, is might.
Your chains across the river, your booms and mighty sway,
Shall not prevent our navigating the river Paraguay.

A song written by Fred Mowbray, U.S.N., at Corientes on the American
Fleet destined for Paraguay, October, 1858, in Robert Neeser,
American Naval Songs and Ballads.

In order to understand how the naval officer saw his role in implementating U.S. policy it is necessary to know more of what motivated him than can be learned from studying his understanding of the nature of social, political, and international relations alone. Frequently he saw reality through "service eyes" as well.*

The officer's identification with his profession was total. Duty and Honor were sacred countersigns, but they implied something more than service to the State. An inner loyalty existed as well—to the Navy, and to one's self as a part of the Navy world. The officer's need for achievement and official sanction was acute. In a world where the dollar counted for little, words of praise were the coin of the realm.

The routine life of the naval officer was filled with drills and tests designed to keep keen the sword's edge. Thus it is hardly surprising that officers saw in combat the golden opportunity to secure recognition, honor, glory. And if the pursuit of glory tended to result at times in a pursuit and glorification of war itself, that was not altogether the fault of the naval officer. How, he might have asked, could it be honorable and glorious to perish at your post and dishonorable to long for, and seek, an opportunity to do so?

Dedication to the Navy

Henry Stimson came to the conclusion that a "peculiar psychology" pervaded the world of naval officers—a psychology in which "Neptune was God, Mahan his prophet, and the United States Navy the only true Church."[1] In the words of Rear Admiral Bradley Fiske, "Duty, in whatever form it came, was sacred."[2] The "concept of service" offered something "of

---

* Elting E. Morison once displayed unnecessary modesty when he apologized for what he feared was a limited degree of insight into the naval mind on his part. "A man who has never worn the uniform cannot hope to recognize and understand the professional spirit in all its manifestations," he wrote in the introduction to *Admiral Sims and the Modern American Navy* (Boston, 1942), vii. The statement is not necessarily true, as Morison's own efforts demonstrated. Similarly, the converse of the statement does not necessarily follow —those who do know the nature of the "professional spirit" firsthand are rarely able to convey that knowledge in a meaningful form to the uninitiated. The present author falls between the two stools. I have neither the professional style and grace of an Elting Morison nor the career longevity of a Bradley Fiske (one of the better autobiographers), but a smidgen of each. Before training as an historian, I was for three years a naval officer. While the combination is not necessarily essential to an evaluation of the "inner world" of the naval mind, Morison is probably correct: It may help.

permanent value" in years "of increasingly transient values." In what more
appropriate institution might one "serve" than "the Service?" And what
institution merited one's loyalties more than the Navy? Rear Admiral David
Farragut explained that his "great ambition" throughout life had been "to do
all in my power to elevate the Navy." Midshipman Charles Sperry told his
sister of his hope to be "of use" to the Navy. Ex-Captain and Assistant Navy
Secretary Gustavus Fox praised Commodore David D. Porter's successes in
Western waters, not in terms of their importance to the Union cause but in
terms of the prestige they had brought to the Navy. Similarly, Fox thanked
Farragut, not for having bruised the Confederacy but for having "rendered the
Navy secure in the hearts of the people." When Midshipman Alfred Mahan
volunteered to head an expedition to trap the Confederate commerce-raider,
Sumter, whose depredations of Union shipping Mahan considered disgraceful,
he offered but one argument in justification of his plan: "Look at the prestige
such an affair would give to the Service."[3]

Identification with the Navy was not something localized in the Civil War
era. For Mahan and his messmates the Navy was their career; given the intensity
of their loyalty to its interest, it often became something more, their very life-
blood and reason for being. Like many men, they wanted to merge with
something that transcended and transfigured their own "concrete existence"
and was "more central in the 'ultimate' structure of reality" than their routine
life. In the foreword to Rear Admiral Albert Barker's autobiography Captain
Dudley Knox claimed that Barker had written the book in order to be of service
to the Navy. "Devotion to the Navy," he explained, "was the mainspring of
his thoughts and actions." Captain Caspar Goodrich spoke of "that paramount
object, the good of the Service." Captain Mahan praised those who gave their
all, not simply for their country, but "for the Service."

Mahan thought highly of those who gave their lives for the State as well, of
course. The two were not *necessarily* contradictory. Thus Lieutenant Commander
Oscar Smith advised his messmates to labor "for the sake of the service and the
glory of our country." And Abel Bowen maintained that naval men were
devoted to their commander, "with whom in their minds, the country is often
identified." But the naval officer's statement of commitment to his professional
institution generally stood apart from, and often above, all other expressions of
loyalty.[4] Consider the remarks of Rear Admiral Edward Simpson, who in 1888
was the senior surviving graduate of the Academy and president of its Graduate
Association. Simpson told a reunion of officers of his lifelong "love of the Navy,"
and added that the Navy had been an "inspiration" in his life. Simpson identified totally with the institution "in which has been merged my whole identity,
for which I have worked, and *in* which I take my greatest pride, which has been
the mistress I tried to adorn, whose favors alone I coveted." One could never
do "too much," he concluded, for the Service.[5]

Simpson was thinking of the training and acculturation his Academy experience had provided, but he also had in mind the lifetime acculturation provided

252   by the close quarters and self-discipline of shipboard and navy yard living, and the self-denial of a career whose reward, in the words of Captain Charles Davis, Jr., was "generally only the fulfillment of a high ideal all its own." After six years of training and thinking of the life before them in the service of their country, it took a catastrophe or an enormous act of will for a newly-commissioned officer to resign his commission and embark upon a new occupation. As the wife of Rear Admiral Remey explained to her son, as time passed and other opportunities faded, the profession tended to become even "more attractive."[6]

One measure of the intensity of Service identification and loyalty is the naval officers' attitude towards critics and criticism of the Navy. Few officers had much patience with newsmen, whose reporting of the Navy's role they often found either inadequate or inaccurate. "If the Department would give an order that no reporter should be allowed on board our ships under any circumstances," Captain David D. Porter wrote to Assistant Navy Secretary Fox in 1862, "it would prevent many false impressions getting out and the public might get (through official reports) a true history of transactions." Nearly half a century later successive commanders of America's "Great White Fleet" globe-girdling cruise ruthlessly censored news releases.[7]

Naval officers saw nothing wrong in such treatment of the press, nor was their attitude limited to the protection of the Service's good name on board warships. Many objected to the very publication of all things critical of the Navy. When essays deemed by some injurious to the Navy were read before the U.S. Naval Institute and offered for publication in the *Proceedings*, there were bound to be objections. Such was the case in 1890, when Commander S. W. Terry moved that Lieutenant William Fullam's paper on naval training and discipline "be suppressed."[8] But the naval aristocracy was at least as anxious about non-Service authors, such as Commander William Cushing's biographer E. M. H. Edwards, who was told by Rear Admiral Lester A. Beardslee to place "only the bright episodes" of Cushing's life before the world. One officer advised Americans to "arise in their might" and "muzzle" the press, especially during wartime. Not all journalistic criticism of the federal officialdom drew naval fire, to be sure; few officers ever sought the suppression of non-naval news. But if the Navy was involved, it was likely to be another matter altogether. Thus Rear Admiral Albert Barker objected when British, French, Russians, and Japanese interfered with the civil liberties of Koreans and Chinese and then noted with obvious delight the suppression of a Chinese paper which had published an article critical of U.S. naval officers.[9] The key to this double standard was Barker's intense loyalty to the Navy "band of brothers."

Naval officers were devoted, then, to their Service. Their aim in life was epitomized in the expression "THE NAVY, FIRST, LAST, AND ALWAYS." And their "esprit de corps" was particularly vibrant. Rear Admiral Thomas O. Selfridge, Jr., who believed that "service utility" was "the very essence of the navy," also spoke of "the close unity of thought and action that binds our profession into

a great fraternity." Lieutenant Commander H. H. Frost, and many others, **253**
spoke of the process of daily contacts with Academy classmates, present and
former messmates, and the like by which the officer corps became a "band of
brothers."[10]

Little wonder that Mahan and his messmates despised advocates of pacifism
and arbitration—both of which threatened the growth of the Service. "A
military man," Mahan once wrote, "could scarcely . . . listen without a certain
repugnance and dissent to denunciations and prophecies which, if just, signified
the passing away of a profession with which his life had been identified." Any
threat, real or imagined, to the strength or prestige of the Navy was looked
upon as a threat to the "band of brothers" and one's own personal standing and
career, and the response to that threat was certain to be vigorous. When Vice
Admiral David D. Porter told Representative E. B. Washburne, "I want to see
the Navy preserved . . .," he spoke for his messmates as well.[11]

Inter-Service Relations

By believing in the superiority and importance of their own service
[officers] also provide themselves a degree of personal status, pride,
and self-confidence. . . . Parochial pride in Service, personal ambitions,
and old Army–Navy game rivalry stemming back to academy
loyalties can influence strategic planning far more than most civilians
would care to believe.

General David Shoup, U.S.M.C.(ret.), *Atlantic Monthly* (April 1969), 52–54

Commitment to the naval profession accounts for much of the
naval officer's behavior. For example, it explains his camaraderie with officers
of other navies such as the British Navy or the Brazilian naval forces of Admiral
Jose de Mello, whose revolt against the landlubber government of President
Floriano Peixoto in the fall and winter of 1893–94 was regarded with an
untoward and inapt degree of sympathy by ensigns such as Yates Stirling,
commanders such as Henry Picking, and the squadron commander himself,
Commodore Oscar F. Stanton.* It explains why Rear Admirals John Rodgers
and Daniel Ammen intervened with the Emperor of Japan in 1871 on behalf of
their professional counterpart, Admiral Enomoto Takeaki, leader of an abortive
revolt in 1869. It explains why Captain Clark Wells went to the aid of Spanish
royalist naval officers in the 1873 Spanish revolution. It explains why Lieutenant

---

* Stanton's salute to his Brazilian counterpart, Admiral Mello, whose blockade of Rio
had irritated U.S. Minister Thomas S. Thompson, Secretary of State Walter Q. Gresham,
and American businessmen in general, resulted in Stanton's recall and replacement by Rear
Admiral A. E. K. Benham, who understood his mission more clearly and broke the blockade.
For a good account of the incident see LaFeber, *loc. cit.*; for a more recent, but, I think, less
persuasive account, see Grenville & Young, *Politics, Strategy, and American Diplomacy*, 118.

Bernard Brodie offers another example of this international respect of military professionals for one another in *Sea Power in the Machine Age* (Princeton, 1949), 449. He relates
the story of the commanding officer of H.M.S. *Courageous*, who remarked, as a torpedo from
a German warship bore down on his ship: "That was a damned good shot!"

254   Commander Yates Stirling's fictional hero of *A U.S. Midshipman in Japan* (1911) was eager to team up with his Academy classmate, a Japanese midshipman, to scotch those seeking to precipitate a war between the U.S. and Japan. And it does explain why Rear Admiral Henry Mayo initially ordered his vessels to exchange salutes and friendly calls with elements of the Mexican Federal [Huerta] Navy, an act of virtual U.S. recognition of Huerta, in spite of the fact that the administration of President Woodrow Wilson was clearly unwilling to extend such recognition.[12]

Service loyalty also explains the traditional naval rivalry with the Army (and, eventually, with the Air Force) over such seemingly diverse matters as Congressional appropriations, football scores, and combat laurels. This is not to say that the military services cannot find common cause when confronted with civilian opposition or criticism. Thus one always applauded the successes of Army football teams over civilian opponents, in spite of the fact that the Army game was considered the climax of the Middy schedule.* And publicly one praised the Army, as David D. Porter praised General Grant at Vicksburg while writing privately of his chagrin that, "army-like," Grant had slipped in "ahead of us."

Naval officers were annoyed by the credit the Army received for the victory of Union arms in the War of the Rebellion, and throughout the late nineteenth century they encouraged one another to "keep hammering away" at the fame of their shorebound comrades-in-arms. In some cases this envy encompassed the political popularity that Army officers enjoyed. Naval officers complained of the number of Army officers who had become President. The soldier's was the only military voice truly "powerful in public councils." The sailor remained "an exile, often on distant seas," whose spokesmen, almost without exception, were "not of his own cloth."[13]

Army–Navy relations in the field were often strained. Whatever the Army officers may have thought of inter-service cooperation in these years, the naval aristocracy's views on the subject are quite clear. For example, in 1862 Captain David D. Porter assured Assistant Navy Secretary Fox:

> Don't be afraid of my raising a point with a soldier. . . . We get along with them first rate. I get all out of them I can, and give them nothing in return.

Rear Admiral S. F. DuPont and his staff found many of his Army colleagues to be "très communs," lacking "the slightest idea of civility." His friend Captain Percival Drayton tried to "convey to them now and then some of the proprieties of life." Lieutenant Commander Charles H. Davis, Jr., officer in charge of the Office of Naval Intelligence in 1890, told one of his agents that he suspected Army Lieutenant Zalinski of stealing the agent's copy books. "I generally . . . don't let them [U.S. Army officers] go into the file room at all," he wrote, and added the remark that Army officers were "of a lower order of intellect

---

* Perhaps this is the meaning of the old saw: "A messmate before a shipmate, a shipmate before a sailor, a sailor before a dog, a dog before a soldier, and a soldier before a civilian."

than the mule." Two months later Davis' superior, Commodore Francis Ramsay, Chief of the Bureau of Navigation, officially warned all U.S. naval attachés not to take U.S. Army attachés into their confidence or to "cooperate with them or give them any information in regard to [your] work." Similarly Captain Caspar Goodrich told Navy Secretary Long in July, 1898:

> I have found in my intercourse with Army officers that a most courteous "No" always worked well. It achieved its immediate purpose and was of educational value as well. They need more of the same kind.

In 1899 Commodore Dewey went so far as to warn General Otis, U.S. Army Commander in the Philippines, that he planned to *sink* the U.S. Army's three river gunboats operating on the Pasig River if they entered Dewey's zone of influence a second time![14]

The arguments of military men before Congressional appropriations committees on behalf of their particular branch of the Service may be perfectly sincere, but the inter-service rivalries they reflect are often at the heart of these different philosophies of strategy and reality. A questionnaire recently given to some 300 students at Annapolis and in Army, Air Force, and Navy ROTC units at Ohio State University and the University of Pittsburgh revealed that 71% of 157 Annapolis and Navy ROTC students felt that the Navy was the Service "most vital to the nation's defense," while only 2% of a comparable sample of Army and Air Force ROTC students would confess to such a heresy. Conversely, 72.5% of the Army and Air Force ROTC students were convinced that *their* Service was the one "most vital" to the nation, while only 9% of the Navy's officer candidates would grant that either the Army or the Air Force was more vital than the Navy. Only about one in every five indicated that the services were of equal worth. Service loyalty is a strangely powerful phenomenon, both then and now.*

Personal Honor

We are brought up to certain standards as gentlemen and officers; we can no more shake them off than a leopard can change his spots.
Rear Admiral S. F. DuPont to his wife, June 5, 1863, *DuPont Letters*, III, 162

[During my imprisonment] the thought that preyed on my mind was the embarrassment to my country because of the loss of one of its fine ships.
Commander Lloyd Bucher

Just as the officer protected the honor of the nation and the honor of the Navy, so also he acted in ways that ensured the security of his own

---

* Inter-service rivalries may have a few redeeming side-effects. As one member of the House Armed Services Committee recently put it, "What we need is more inter-service squabbling. When the military *falls* out, then and only then can the Congress *find* out." Lewis Dexter, "Congressmen and the Making of Military Policy," in Nelson Polsby, ed., *New Perspectives on the House of Representatives*, 187–188.

personal sense of honor. A bogus* quotation which stressed personal honor, attributed incorrectly to John Paul Jones, highest of all the naval heavenly hosts, was (and still is) afforded the highest rites in the cabins, wardrooms, staterooms, and homes of Mahan's messmates, "the first thing to greet our eyes in the morning, the last thing at night, a constant reminder of that perfect officer character which we should ever strive to emulate." The man-o'-warsman was looked upon as "the true knight-errant" of the age, and as late as 1950 a Navy wife could write of the "quiet pleasure" to be found in "those niceties of gentlemanly conduct that are so highly stressed in the Navy" as a contrast to "this present day of 'push-and-shove.'"[15]

The preservation of gentlemanly composure and honorable status was essential to the officer-and-gentleman's venerable, but volatile, self-image. In the first place, it was (and is) a criminal offense to "bring discredit" upon the naval service. But besides the threat of official censure there was the danger of quasi-official or even unofficial censure. Hazing, it will be recalled, bore no official public seal of approval, but it was an immensely effective means none the less of enforcing "the code." When one graduated into the fleet, the pressure from one's fellow-officers to remain within the pale was more diffuse, but no less effective. The officer learned to long for the respect of his fellow officers. Commodore Andrew Bryson, who looked upon the Navy as "one great family," told the House Naval Affairs Committee that "no one member of that family can disgrace himself without disgracing me." An officer's conduct was under constant scrutiny by all about him, or so the naval officer-and-gentleman believed. For example, during the Civil War, when George Dewey was a lieutenant, the ship of which he was Executive Officer came under heavy fire and was in imminent danger of sinking. He accompanied one of the ship's boats to shore, to insure its return, and then remembered that "the code" called upon him to be the second-to-last to leave the ship. "This was the most anxious moment in my career," he recalled. Rear Admiral S. F. DuPont, on the other hand, was reluctant to attack Charleston with his inadequate forces because the defeat that he was certain to suffer would "risk and possibly lose whatever of prestige pertained to a long and successful professional career." DuPont had "a national reputation to keep right for history." With the failure of the attack on Charleston, he commenced a life-long struggle to salvage that reputation.[16] Similarly, Captain Mahan, worried about a forthcoming inspection of his last command, was unable to "get rid of the fear that some censure will fall on me." When the Battleship *Hartford* went aground on her maiden voyage in 1907 her commanding officer was so upset at the disgrace that he fainted on

---

* The apocryphal passage reads: "It is by no means enough that an officer of the Navy should be a capable mariner. He must be that, of course, but also a great deal more. He should be as well a gentleman of liberal education, refined manners, punctilious courtesy, and the nicest sense of personal honor." Evidence of its fraudulence is offered in S. E. Morison, *John Paul Jones* (Boston 1959), 428; and Milton Hamilton, "Augustus C. Buell, Fraudulent Historian," *Penna. Mag. of Hist. and Biog.*, LXXX (1956), 478–492. See also Heinl, ed., *Dictionary*, 206.

the bridge. In late 1844 Commander W. D. Newman, Commanding Officer   **257**
of the *Bainbridge*, went further. He committed suicide when court-martialed
for failing to return the fire of a Buenos Aires schooner that had erroneously
fired on his ship. Commander William Cushing, whose Civil War exploits
had made him the paragon of naval virtue, cried out in a deathbed delirium of
"anger and disgust" for the conduct of others "which he deemed dishonorable." .
(The loss of Cushing's sanction must have been a terrible blow to a messmate.)
And though Captain Andrew Foote knew how unpopular duty with the
Africa squadron was, he considered it "a reflection on the chivalry of the service"
for anyone to suggest that the squadron "could not be well officered." When
Captain Edward H. Watson's destroyer squadron steamed in formation onto
the Honda reef off the California coast in 1923, he assumed total responsibility,
and wrote his father, retired Rear Admiral John C. Watson:[17]

> I have been distressed to cause you anxiety and to put a blot on our fair service record
> as a family. [I] Have done all I could to . . . prevent the Service from losing any
> prestige.

Relatively little impulse was required to stimulate an officer to feel that his
honor had been questioned. The mention of Pierre Loti's characterization of an
American naval lieutenant in his "Madame Crisantheme" (Puccini's "Madame
Butterfly") might arouse him; the suggestion that he had strayed from the
truth was sure to. He might feel outraged at the proposition that the Service
would be improved by such an act as the banning of the officers' wine mess.[18]
And once the officer's righteous wrath broke forth, restraints were hard to come
by. As late as 1898 a naval lieutenant could be commended by his commanding
officer for having challenged an enemy to a duel![19]

The Pursuit of Glory

> Be to the nation's standards true;
> To Britain, and to Europe shew,
> That you can fight and conquer too,
> . . .
> Beneath your feet let fear be cast,
> Remember deeds of valor past,
> And nail your colors to the mast.
>
> Philip Freneau, "To the Lake Squadrons," in Robert Neeser,
> *American Naval Songs and Ballads*

> . . . in democratic military institutions, the desire of advancement is
> almost universal; it is ardent, tenacious, perpetual; it is strengthened
> by all other desires, and only extinguished with life itself. But it is
> easy to see that, of all military institutions in the world, those in
> which advancement must be slowest in time of peace are the
> military institutions of democratic countries. As the number of

commissions is naturally limited, . . . none can make rapid progress—
many can make no progress at all. Thus, the desire of advancement
is greater, and the opportunities of advancement fewer there than
elsewhere. All the ambitious spirits of a democratic armed force are
consequently ardently desirous of war, because war makes vacancies
and warrants the violation of that law of seniority which is the sole
privilege natural to democracy.

Alexis de Tocqueville

To a bloody war and a sickly season.

Traditional British officer toast

Nothing was more gratifying to Mahan's messmates than praise
(unless it was rank). The autobiographies of the naval aristocracy reek of self-
praise. Each minute achievement, be it a Congressional vote of thanks or the
act of leaving port without a pilot, is described in detail.* The files of Lewis R.
Hamersly, who for many years published a quasi-official naval register, are
filled with letters from officers complaining of the omission of commendatory
data from Hamersly's account of their careers. When Navy Secretary James
Dobbin commended the work of Commander John Rodgers, Rodgers summed
up the feelings of his fellow officers in these words:

> An expression of Official Satisfaction is very dear to the heart of a Naval man. His
> Chief is to him the fountain of honor, and the hope of winning approbation cheers
> him in hours of difficulty or privation.
> It has been with a sentiment of . . . military pride that your encomium has been
> read at "General Muster."

Captain Percival Drayton went even further, when he wrote Alexander
Hamilton, Jr., "Good repute, not rank, is what I desire." In 1881 Lieutenant
Theodorus B. M. Mason argued for the extension of the eligibility requirements for the Congressional Medal of Honor to include officers as well as
enlisted men, and added the explanation: "There is a certain something in
human nature—call it vanity, if you will—which craves a reward for duty well
performed." Lieutenant Commander H. R. Snyder spoke of the "lump of
gratitude" that rose in his throat every time he received words of praise "in the
hearing of the big family." Admiral Dewey's last delirious deathbed words:

> The Navy shall always be indebted to you, sir, for your courage, and this nation
> shall always do you honor

are ascribed by his biographers to praise of such a man as Theodore Roosevelt,
which is possible. But it seems more likely to me that Dewey had himself in
mind.[20]

One might feel pride in a number of ways. The appointment to a prestigious

---

* Any autobiography will bear this out, but see especially those of McCalla and Steedman for the more excruciating examples.

command such as the Naval Academy, the Bureau of Navigation, or the North **259** Atlantic Squadron was certain to be "particularly gratifying" to one's "professional pride and ambition."[21] The success of one's invention or recommended reorganization might provide the "sense of gratification."[22] Or, like Rodgers and Snyder, one might simply feel pride in a job well done and well recognized. But there were other reasons for doing the job well.

Commander Goldsborough, who used the expression "professional pride and ambition" just cited, wasn't using the word "ambition" idly. In the age of Horatio Alger novels, when one's brothers and boyhood chums might appear to advance more rapidly, in some cases, in income and social standing, the naval officer plodded along, advancing at a rate proportional to the sum of the death and retirement rates of the upper service ranks. Before 1916 there were no conditions other than those of wartime under which an officer might "gain numbers" in the professional register. Ambitious junior officers, reflecting the "need for achievement" so characteristic of the age, reacted in a variety of ways to secure ends denied them by the stagnation in promotion, as we shall see. A widespread response was to attempt to excel in one's routine naval duties. "Ambition comes in many a form," wrote Rear Admiral Thomas H. Stevens, "and oft . . . assumes the garb of Duty."[23] But commendation in peacetime from one's superiors was insignificant compared to a vote of thanks for gallantry in combat, the very act of which might raise one 30 numbers or more on the active list. For both reasons—professional pride and personal ambition—war was a welcome relief to many officers.

Samuel P. Huntington has argued that the "love of violence, glory, and adventure" had "little appeal" for the "professional military man," who "raises the strongest voice against immediate involvement in war."* But while this may be true of some military orders, it was not true of U.S. naval officers in the nineteenth and early twentieth centuries. They "gladly welcome[d] and anxiously court[ed]" every opportunity to risk their lives and sacred honor "in the accomplishment of an achievement which should accord glory to their country and individual fame to themselves." The "love of glory," the "ardent desire for honorable distinction by honorable deeds," were primary "military motives."[24] Ensign Alfred A. McKethan's "ambition" was to have his "name go down in history." Commander John Worden, the *Monitor*'s Commanding Officer, confided that "the greatest hope of [his] existence" had always been to carve his niche in the hall of naval heroes. Lieutenant Commander Charles Flusser, the Marcus Aurelius Arnheiter of his day, dreamed of "future fame" and lived in dread that he would never "gain any." Commander D. M. Fairfax begged for a vessel, even if it were only a gunboat, to command in 1862, "in

---

* Huntington, *Soldier and State*, 69–70. Huntington goes so far as to argue that the military man is almost pacifistic in his reluctance to risk a war. He cites but one U.S. source to substantiate this view, but it is surely true, on occasion, of many U.S. naval officers. No officer ever feels he is *totally* prepared for war. But this is not the same thing as saying that the military is pacifistic. It would prefer to fight with a million men, but will generally settle for something less—say 600,000.

time to come in for some of the glory." "Think of what a fellow has to endure," he complained to a friend, "when so many are being killed with glory." Midshipman Mahan had asked for a vessel to trap the *Sumter* in order to boost the Navy's sagging "prestige," but his Academy letters to his friend Samuel Ashe indicate that he sought glory as well, like every good Annapolite. Lieutenant Commander William Grenville Temple told his friend Commander Henry Wise in 1862 that he "would naturally like a chance to jump over other people's head" and complained that as yet he had "not seen a single shot fired in anger." "My cussed luck has been against me," he fretted.[25]

When Panamanian revolutionaries seized the U.S.-owned Panama Railroad Company in 1885, the Navy Department prepared a military expedition, and Navy Secretary William A. Whitney was peppered with telegrams from eager young officers who longed for a piece of the action. Similarly, when the nation went to war with Spain in 1898, officers caught behind desks in Washington "pleaded with tears in their eyes for service afloat" in "the fighting line." Like Mahan, Lieutenant William Winder saw a chance to win laurels. Winder, Commodore Dewey's nephew, was serving aboard Dewey's flagship when it stood into Manila Bay. He approached his uncle and begged to be given command of the first vessel to enter the harbor channel. If the channel was mined, as was feared, Winder hoped he might clear a path at the sacrifice of his vessel. "Sir," he told Dewey, "this is the one chance I have to become famous." Dewey was sympathetic, but he doubted that there would be any mines to speak of. In any event, he told his nephew, "I am leading the squadron in myself."

Half way around the world Assistant Engineer Richmond Hobson was more fortunate than Winder. He was given command of a skeleton crew with orders to sink the *Merrimac* in the Santiago harbor channel in an effort to bottle up the Spanish fleet. But there were many of Hobson's messmates who were disappointed; when volunteers were called for "the junior officers' mess responded en masse," but Hobson was the only one to go.

After the victories at Manila Bay and Santiago, some officers still had not won laurels. But rumors of the preparation of a fleet to be dispatched to Spanish home waters left them with a spark of hope. Captain Caspar Goodrich implored Secretary Long for command of one of these battleships. "The heroes of the 3rd of July [Santiago] can well afford to give others a chance," he wrote. "I have worked faithfully and well . . . with the tools at hand—now put a weapon into them I pray you."[26]

Later, when the Boxers threatened to exterminate the foreign community in North China, Captain Bowman McCalla seized his opportunity to bring his family "joy and honor" and joined British Vice Admiral Edward Seymour's drive toward Peking. According to Seymour, McCalla's courage "amounted perhaps to rashness," so determined was that American to demonstrate his daring and to win renown.[27]

Not all those fortunate enough to see combat survived, of course. But one could achieve honor and fame in death as well as in life. In 1862 David Farragut **261** attained flag rank, something he had been "looking for" all his life, and "having attained it" he wrote:

> all that is necessary to complete the scene is victory. . . . He who dies in doing his duty . . . has played out the drama of life to the best advantage.

Similarly, Lieutenant George Perkins, who proudly instructed his sister in 1863 to "Tell Uncle Paul that I am the youngest officer at this time that has . . . command" of a regular Gulf gunboat, reminded his mother a year later, on the eve of Mobile Bay,[28]

> if I get killed it will be an honorable death, and the thought should partly take away your sorrow.

Neither Farragut nor Perkins rounded out his "drama" with a noble and glorious death. Lieutenant S. W. Preston was more fortunate. The description of his demise before the gates of Fort Fischer merits repetition here. "He was the courtly gentleman to the last," Preston's Boswell reported.[29]

> As I was told by a comrade who lay near him, when Preston found that he was dying he turned himself on his back on the beach, straightened out his handsome form to the full, reached up his arms, and with both hands carefully gathered under his head the soft sand and a tuft or two of the shore-grass, as a supporting pillow, then folded his arms, with his neatly-gloved hands across his chest, and deliberately composed himself to die.

I think Preston had a powerful sense of the behavior expected of him.

Not everyone obtained a Congressional vote of thanks or a glorious death. For many officers the pursuit of glory was either altogether futile or too competitive to prove fruitful. In some cases, solid achievements might even prove one's undoing, as in the case of Lieutenant Charles Hunter, who was given a General Court-Martial resulting in a stiff reprimand and was relieved of his command when he captured two fortified Mexican towns in advance of Commodore Matthew Perry's squadron. Perry was not about to allow a subordinate to preempt the glory of seizing towns "belonging to a Commander-in-Chief," as he duly advised Lieutenant Hunter.* Vice Admiral David D. Porter delighted in doing all he could "to make [Admiral] Farragut," his only naval senior, "feel bad." In Porter's eyes, Farragut had "stole[n] half of my thunder during the war," a measure that Porter always held against him. Lieutenant Preston, before his glorious death, complained that his exploits as

---

* Perry to Hunter, April 9, 1847, cited in Taylor, *Broad Pennant*, 390–391. Samuel E. Morison's biography of Perry takes Perry's side against Hunter ("*Old Bruin*," 223), but see Rear Admiral Caspar Goodrich, "Alvarado Hunter," *PUSNI*, XLIV (1918), 495–514, for a more balanced account of the incident.

Lieutenant George Perkins was more rank-conscious than Hunter. After battering the Confederate ram *Tennessee* into submission, he put his vessel aside and let a more senior officer, Commander Leroy, accept the rebel's surrender. *Letters of Perkins*, 100–140.

262   Executive Officer of the powder boat *Louisiana* should have earned him more
than the advance of ten numbers in the Navy Register that he had been awarded,
or at least as many as his commanding officer, Captain Alexander Rhind, had
received.

Personal ill-will, however, did not bar Porter from complaining that Farragut,
as a fellow naval officer, did not receive "half the credit he deserved" for his
successful running of the forts at New Orleans in 1862. An English officer who
had achieved as much, Porter declared, "would have been loaded by his
government with no ends of rewards." Similarly, Captain George Belknap
expressed chagrin over the lack of proper recognition for the feats of an old
messmate, Captain George Perkins, and insisted that an English officer would
have been knighted for deeds for which Perkins, "as an American . . . still wants
recognition." When the Congressional Medal of Honor was finally granted to
naval officers, there were many veterans of Civil War naval actions who deeply
resented the omission of their names from the lists of Medal recipients.[30]

The Spanish-American War posed a dilemma. The action was so brief that
many saw insufficient combat to qualify for laurels. Ensign Roger Welles, for
example, was furious with his superiors for having failed to provide him with
an adequate opportunity "to get any particular glory out of the war." And
Captain Goodrich, who had been given the *Newark* by Secretary Long in
response to his plea for a chance to match the exploits of the "heroes of the 3rd
of July," was crushed by news of peace and cease-fire in August 1898. The news
reached Goodrich after he had been shelling the Spanish batteries at Manzanillo,
Cuba, for several hours, and was preparing a final assault. "My disappointment,"
he reported to his chief, Rear Admiral William Sampson, "was, as may be
imagined, very great, for I had every reason to believe that the garrison was
entirely ready to surrender. I had hoped that the fleet under your command
might have won one more laurel and gained one more important victory
before the conclusion of peace."[31]

But even for those who saw action, there were not enough laurels to go
around. The competition between commanders, and between the staffs of
different commanders, was considerable. When Commodore Dewey heard of
Sampson's victory on July 3rd, his first thought was one of concern that "the
American people" might "put us behind those who were at Santiago." Captain
Albert Barker actually wept when he realized that the ship he commanded at
Santiago was smaller than a consort vessel, U.S.S. *Oregon*, whose command
Barker had surrendered only a few months before. Captain Charles Clark and
Captain Robley Evans vigorously disputed the distinction of having been the
first to signal the appearance of the Spanish fleet at the mouth of the channel.
The intense rivalry of Rear Admirals Sampson and Schley for the honors of the
day at Santiago—a rivalry, it must be said, waged more by their staffs than by
the flag officers themselves—is still another illustration of this scramble for
fame and renown.[32]

After the war with Spain one heard the same complaints: Captain A received insufficient recognition for his service at action B; Rear Admiral C was not **263** advanced as rapidly as Rear Admiral D. Thus, Captain Charles Clark, who commanded the *Oregon* on its run from California to Cuba in record time and participated in the Battle of Santiago, was outraged at having been advanced only 6 numbers on the officer's register, and told Secretary Long as much. Clark insisted that this trifling reward had "lowered or obscured" his prestige. Rear Admiral Robley Evans looked upon Congress's reluctance to elevate Rear Admiral Sampson to Vice Admiral as a slight to the Service itself. "We have not been justly treated," he complained in his autobiography. Other examples could be given, but perhaps the point has been made: Naval officers loved glory no less than honor itself; in fact, the two were often inseparable. As Chaplain Gleason of the *Missouri* put it in 1905: "Our motto is: The Navy and the flag; Our Mistress: Glory." The pursuit of glory was a constant in the naval officer's constitution. In the words of Lieutenant Thomas Stevens, naval bard:[33]

> With a mighty purpose fill'd, the Chosen,
> Striding swift through torrid zones or frozen,
> Come, god-like, in conscious pow'r;
> With far-reaching eye, see bright reward,
> And eager rush to meet the slow-paced hour,
> In which they carve their names with naked sword.

The Warmongers and the Military Spirit

Wars add to the military traditions the self-nourishment of heroic deeds, and provide a new crop of military leaders who become the rededicated disciples of the code of service and military action . . . .
[F]or far too many senior professional officers war and combat are an exciting adventure, a competitive game, and an escape from the dull routine of peacetime . . . . [M]any ambitious military professionals truly yearn for wars and the opportunity for glory and distinction afforded only in combat.

General David Shoup, U.S.M.C. (ret.), *Atlantic Monthly* (April 1969), 53–54, 56

I'm taking you where the action is!

Lieutenant Commander Marcus Aurelius Arnheiter to the crew of the U.S.S. *Vance*, enroute southeast Asian waters, 1967

Not every naval officer confused the pursuit of glory during wartime with the glorification of war itself, but there were many who did.* Pugnacity was virtually a custom. The heroes of the early days of the Navy had

---

* Enlisted personnel were not in decision-making positions, but they probably lusted for a "good fight" as much as their officers. See, for example, Connolly, *Navy Men*, 36–37; and Julius Pratt, ed., "Our First 'War' in China: The Diary of William Henry Powell, 1856," *Amer. Historical Review*, LIII (1948), 781–786.

264   set the mood. "What shall I do?" Captain Stephen Decatur brooded in 1818. "We have no war, nor sign of war, and I shall feel ashamed to die in my bed." Two years later Decatur found his war—a personal feud with Commodore Samuel Barron, who shot him to death in a duel. Decatur's professional descendants were just as insistent as he about dying with their boots on. The Annapolite hero of Academy Chaplain Henry Clark's *The Admiral's Aid* [sic] displayed the breeding befitting the fictional descendant of Commodore Robert Stockton. After hearing a particularly exciting tale of his ancestor's exploits, the young Stockton was represented as having bounded about the room squealing, "I'm goin' to be a nabal obbicer an'—an' kill people." A daring young officer-and-gentleman, Clark's hero was disappointed at "the mere spoonfuls of blood spilt in the revolutions" in Central America. He "wanted things done on a grand scale." Lieutenant John Rodgers found slave patrol duty off the Coast of Africa too tame for his taste in 1846. "This is a *d — — — l* of a coast for want of interest," he wrote his brother,

> and if Jimmy Polk and the Mexicans had not fallen out so that we have bloody wars to speculate upon I do not know what we should do.

When Commander Duncan Ingraham forced an Austrian warship to release a Hungarian colleague of Louis Kossuth in 1853, Passed Midshipman Ralph Chandler noted in his diary that all the officers of Ingraham's ship "seemed anxious for a fight." In 1854 Captain George Hollins was urged by the Navy Department to exercise restraint, but he waved that and the protest of the commander of a British schooner aside and razed an undefended town on the Mosquito Coast within 24 hours of his arrival on the scene. His colleague, Lieutenant Thomas Jefferson Page, used the same degree of restraint in 1855 when, guns primed, he sailed the *Water Witch* into closed Paraguayan waters in an unauthorized "exhibition of . . . force."

When a Japanese merchant refused to accept one officer's gold in payment for goods in 1857, the officer damned him and his Emperor and advised him that "Commodore Perry'll come back here some day and blow you sky-high." To these remarks Lieutenant Alexander Habersham added his own estimate of the situation:[34]

> In my opinion, a good filibuster's drubbing is the only thing that will ever introduce [the Japanese] to honesty.

The Civil War delighted men like Habersham, David D. Porter, and William Cushing. Listen, for example, to the way in which Cushing described to his mother a battle through which he had just passed:[35]

> Crash! go the bulkheads; a rifle shell has exploded on our deck, tearing flesh and woodwork. A crash like thunder is our reply—and our heavy shell makes music in the air and explodes among our traitor neighbors with a dull, sullen roar of defiance. Up goes the battle flag, the air is filled with the smoke of furious battle and the ear thrills with the unceasing shriek and whistle of all the shell and rifle bolts that sinful

man has devised to murder his fellow creatures. Crash! Crash! Splinters are flying in the air; great pools of blood are on the deck, and the first cry of wounded men in agony rises on the soft spring air. The dead men cannot speak; but there they lie, motionless and mangled, who, a moment ago, sailed under the old flag that floated over them, and fought for its honor and glory.

Just as Leo Marx found malignant expressions in the rhetoric of technological progress,[36] one can find ethical undertones in this exaltation of battle. The Christian in Cushing compels his attention to "sinful man" and the weapons he has "devised to murder his fellow creatures," but the navalist in him brushes these considerations aside easily in the excitement of describing the heated action. One senses that this passage, like that of Captain Mahan cited in an earlier chapter, glorifies the combat it describes.

There are other indications of a warmongering spirit in the naval officer's psyche. Lieutenant Cornelius Schoonmaker boasted to his mother in 1862 of the power of the blockading fleet and recorded a desire to see the Service take on "the combined nations of the earth." When Korean authorities put an end to the depredations of the American-owned merchantman *General Sherman* in 1866, Rear Admiral John Bell admitted that the *General Sherman* had violated numerous Korean laws, but he still argued for the "prompt punishment" of Korea. Several years later Rear Admiral John Rodgers led a punitive "surveying" expedition to Korea with wardrooms filled with young, post-Civil War officers "just spoiling for a brush." "Many of us were new to war," one Lieutenant later recalled, "and [we] wanted a taste of fire."[37] When Secretary of State Hamilton Fish negotiated a settlement of the *Virginius* affair with Spain, Captain Stephen Luce expressed his "disappointment" in "seeing the bottom knocked out of the Cuban Expedition so soon," in spite of the fact that Luce, like each and every one of his brother officers, knew of the pitiful condition of the Atlantic squadron. Lieutenant William Hunter actually took three months' leave in 1876 and joined the 5th Cavalry to fight Sioux in the Black Hills. Ensign Hugh Rodman, among others, positively *longed* for a chance to fight in Panama in 1885, glory or no glory. When the death of two *Baltimore* sailors in a street fight led Chile and the United States perilously close to war in 1891, Captain Robley Evans, Navy Secretary Benjamin F. Tracy's man-on-the spot in Valparaiso, confided to his journal: "I wish I could have a scrap with the [Chilean cruiser] *Errazuriz* for I feel confident we could take her." And Evans' old messmate, William Emory, wrote concurrently to Commander William Folger:

> O God! I pray for the time when my country will be so powerful afloat that she can wipe out of existence any country that has the audacity to . . . insult us.

Similarly, when Rear Admiral A. E. K. Benham gave the order to break de Mello's blockade of Rio de Janeiro in 1894, Captain John Philip displayed obvious satisfaction at the thought of "clean[ing] out those fellows." *Commander* Caspar Goodrich, addressing a civilian audience in 1895, admitted that most naval officers "would quickly profit" by war, but he insisted that few "would welcome war *because* of such opportunities." But as *Captain* Caspar Goodrich, addressing the "band of brothers" some two years later on the eve of the war with Spain, he spoke of how "unfortunate" it was that the service had been "denied . . . hostilities" for so long. Commander Fredrick Wise felt "a natural regret, shared no doubt by the officers," that the *Monocacy* had been denied the opportunity to participate in the 1900 shelling of the forts at the Taku Bar. Shortly after the battle of Manila Bay Commodore Dewey exploded at the German Admiral, whose actions Dewey deemed unfriendly: "You can have war right now!" And in 1906 Captain Nathan Sargent reported to Dewey that he was keeping naval forces ashore at Chinkiang for several weeks, "waiting and hoping for something to happen."[38] Some officers were not belligerent all the time, and all officers were quiescent at least some of the time, but many officers were warmongers much of the time; and consequently the warmonger label, if judiciously applied, may be a valid one to describe the behavior of an important group of Mahan's messmates.

The naval officer's belligerent nature is evident in the way he conceptualized and defended war and something he called "the military spirit." War tended to "quicken the pulse of the nation and send a brighter, stronger current to eliminate morbid germs from all the tissues of the body politic, offsetting tendencies toward commercialism and materialism." Some found an abstract "delight in war." Others found that it made them "superhuman." Captain Fiske conceived of war as "the acme of the endeavor of man" and urged his Naval Academy Alumni Association brethren to "keep alive our military spirit." Rear Admiral Mahan feared that the "decay of warlike habits" in America would aid the Oriental races and "communism." Just as he had praised Prussian political philosophy, so he praised Prussian militarism, for which "too great gratitude cannot be felt." After all, he asked, "Is militarism really more deadening to the spirit than commercialism? or legalism?" It wasn't even necessary to win. "An occasional beating" was "good for men and nations." War was imbued with spiritual power and endowed with the nobility of an "art." In short, naval officers were virtually as active in the defense of the fruits of their profession as they were of the profession itself.[39]

Not all warmongers were psychotic, blood-lust types. Many appeared to long for war primarily because it stimulated promotion, furnished opportunities for glory, and elevated the Navy to higher national prestige. Thus Lieutenant Albert Caldwell feared in 1868 that the Civil War "hump" of lieutenant commanders and commanders would prevent his advancement for many years unless, as he hoped, "something turns up in the way of blood and thunder." Concurrently, Vice Admiral Porter advised one of his old staff officers, John Barnes, "The Navy will be dead for many years to come unless we have another war. . . ." Commander George Dewey told a friend of his fear that there would be no war before he retired. "Without it there is little opportunity for a naval man to distinguish himself . . ., and I will simply join the great majority of naval men . . . 'who entered the Navy at a certain date and retired **267** as Rear Admiral at the age limit!'" After Chile was forced to apologize to the United States for the *Baltimore* incident, Commander Emory told a fellow officer of his "regret" at "the pacific turn that affairs have taken, as it relegates to the dim future any chance of active service." "Naval officers," as "Nauticus" announced at the time of the Sampson–Schley controversy, "get few chances to fight, and such chances they invariably embrace with eagerness." Naval officers had little use for either politicians or businessmen, but they were the arch-enemies of pacifists. After all, as Rear Admiral Yates Stirling explained to prospective Perrys, "[Y]ou can be dismissed neither by politics nor business conditions. World disarmament alone can affect you." Brutal as the charge may appear, the fact is that the record supports it: Naval officers often longed for and sought hot or cold war to insure the viability of their service and the development of their own careers. "Patriotism" alone does not account for Commander Lovette's discerning observation that morale at the Academy "has always been high when a national emergency was imminent."[40]

The actual effect of this warmongering trait on the daily behavior of naval officers is difficult to evaluate. It may have been a key factor in the decision of Captain George Hollins to destroy Greytown in 1854 or the decision of Rear Admiral Henry Mayo to press the Huerta government as relentlessly as he did for a full apology and 21-gun unreciprocated salute to the flag in response to the Tampico incident in 1914. Categorical statements are difficult or impossible to make about such instances when the officers involved have left incomplete personal records of their state of mind. But this much can be said: Samuel P. Huntington's description of irresolute officers with no taste for glory, violence, or adventure does not fit Mahan's many belligerent messmates.

SUMMARY: THE NAVAL OFFICER'S CONCEPT OF HIS ROLE

The naval officer paid tribute to the State, the Navy, and his own honor and status within the "band of brothers."

Externally, his fame of reference was national, but within this national framework he incorporated a Blessed Trinity—Commerce, Christianity, and Constitutional Republicanism. The tenets of the American way were interrelated, of course. Imperialism was the product of humanitarianism, mercantilism, and national Darwinism. If American trade grew, so would American power and prestige. And if American power grew, the world was bound to learn the blessings of Christianity and constitutionalism. Once "develop" a country and it was certain to become "civilized"; once "civilize" a country and it became easier to "develop" it. The orders officers received from Washington read: insure economic growth. But there was a common understanding that America wanted something more than the yen, that she was selling something more clinging than cotton underwear. The "American way of life"—complete with Law, Progress, Protestantism, and Industrialism—was also being sold. The cost was often high—the control of the customer's institutions and resources. But the Navy could be called on to try to insure that it was paid. And given the expansionistic nature of his Trinity, the naval officer looked upon the *Pax Americana* as the only proper millennium.

Internally, the stability of officer values and the conviction that officer duties and officer values were in harmony produced a dedicated corps, committed to the naval institution, its survival, and its growth.* Personal honor, ambition, and a consciousness of the importance of professional sanction all stimulated a pursuit of glory; in some instances, the militaristic pursuit of a "heroic" career led to warmongering.[41]

How naval officers conceptualized their role must have contributed in a significant way to the shaping of their official conduct—to the ways that they carried out their assignments. But nothing in this chapter should be read as a repudiation or negation of what was said in the preceding chapter. Naval officers might think what they liked about their duties, but the primary result of their labors was to aid American businessmen abroad. It is perfectly true that business interests and national interests were deemed identical by businessmen, policy-makers, and naval officers alike. But some businessmen may have been puzzled, or even tickled, by the solemn patriotism and moral platitudes of their naval colleagues.

* Cf. Allan Wheelis, *The Quest for Identity* (N.Y., 1958), 19, and Nevitt Stanford, "The Dynamics of Identification," *Psychological Review*, LXII (1955), 106.

Kurt Lang has argued that in today's military establishments "the new nature of military service drastically alters the significance of being an officer. For many it is less a professional commitment than a phase in a longer occupational career." ("Technology and Career Management in the Military Establishment," in *The New Military: Changing Patterns of Organization*, ed. Morris Janowitz [N.Y., 1965], 69.) While it is true that the modern officer embarks on a second career in mid-life, this does not necessarily mean that his commitment to the Service is significantly weaker, or that it dies out altogether when he takes the uniform off. It seems to me that many of the more vigorous navalists today are men who retired years ago.

Chapter 5 (The Internal World)

1. Henry Stimson & McGeorge Bundy, *On Active Service in Peace and War* (New York, 1948), 506, cited in Samuel P. Huntington, *The Soldier and the State: The Theory and Politics of Civil–Military Relations* (Cambridge, Mass. 1957), 303.

2. Fiske, *PUSNI*, XLI (1915), 2; *The Navy as a Fighting Machine*, 240; Roe, *Naval Duties and Discipline*, 192. See Huntington, 259, for similar views of an army officer: "Duty is the Army's highest law, and supercedes all other law."

For an early example of this sense of identification with the Navy, see Captain Charles Stewart's "Internal Rules and Regulations of the U.S.S. *Franklin*," [1822], Mss. Div., L. of C., where he wrote of midshipmen: "Having devoted themselves to a Service which will probably [!] be permanent as the Nation and will rapidly increase with its resources, it is confidently hoped that ' the Gentlemen Midshipmen will Studiously endeavor to maintain that character and acquire Such information as Shall not only enable them to maintain but to increase the present high reputation of the American Navy."

3. RADM James Calvert, *The Naval Profession* (New York, 1965), 163; Farragut to Captain Davis, Oct. 1, 1964, *Life of Davis*, 313; Sperry to Mary, December 17, 1865, Sperry Papers; Fox to Porter, February 6, 1863, and May 13, 1862, *Confidential Correspondence of Fox*, II, 156–157, 101; Mahan to Fox, Sept. 9, 1861, *Official Records of the Union and Confederate Navies in the War of the Rebellion*, I (Wash., G.P.O., 1894), 87–88.

4. Edward Shils, cited in Lee Benson, *Turner and Beard* (Free Press Paperback ed., 1965), 225; Barker, *Everyday Life*, iii; Elizabeth Leonard to Commodore Dudley Knox, October 24, 1938, Captain John Leonard Papers, Naval Historical Foundation; Goodrich, "Esprit de Corps . . .," *PUSNI*, XXIV (1898), 4; Mahan, *The Life of Nelson: The Embodiment of the Sea Power of Great Britain* (Boston, 1897), I, 240; Smith, *PUSNI*, L (1924), 1846; Bowen, *The Naval Monument* (Boston, 1816), 74; Rodman, *Yarns*, 311. See also U.S. Naval Academy Graduate Association, *4th Annual Reunion*, 1889 (Baltomore 1890), 20.

5. U.S. Naval Academy Graduates Association, *3rd Annual Reunion, 1888* (Baltimore, 1889), 27.

6. Davis, Jr., *Life of Davis*, 336–37; J. D. Jerrold Kelley, *Question of Ships*, 89; Mary Remey to Charles M. Remey, December 16, 1895, *Mary Remey's Letters*, IX. Ensign Winston Folk apparently reasoned that if "esprit de corps" grew stronger as one grew older, it would be stronger still if prospective officers were sent to Navy preparatory schools before Annapolis. Such schools would fill young minds with "thoughts of the Navy and its ideals until those thoughts become a part of them." Folk, "Basic Education of Officers," *PUSNI*, LI (1925), 275.

7. Porter to Fox, June 2, 1862, *Conf.*

Corr. of Fox, II, 113; Hart, *Great White Fleet*, 172.

8. *PUSNI*, XVI (1890), 528. The fact that Fullam's paper was printed, however, is evidence that Terry's views were not shared by his comrades-in-arms, at least on this particular issue.

9. Edwards, *Cushing*, 201; Commander Nathan Sargent to Cyrus E. Lothrop [a Detroit businessman], copy June 9, 1905, Sargent Papers, N.H.F.; Lieutenant H. H. Frost, "Criticism in Wartime," *PUSNI*, XLIV (1918), 1745–51; Barker, *Everyday Life*, 151, 162. Cf. James Mock, *Censorship*, 1917 (Princeton, 1941), 154–155. For a World War II example of naval censorship of a publication critical of naval policy, see William B. Huie, *The Case Against the Admirals* (N.Y. 1946), 126–131.

Enlisted personnel could be just as irritated by unfavorable publicity as their officers. In 1921 some 30 U.S. Marines destroyed the offices of *La Tribuna*, a Nicaraguan newspaper that had spoken critically of marines. Denny, *Dollars for Bullets*, 182.

10. Brokholst Livingston, "The Naval Publicist's Aim," *PUSNI*, L (1924), 1256; Selfridge, *Memoirs of Thomas O. Selfridge, Jr., Rear Admiral* (New York, 1924), 287; Frost, "The Naval Service," *PUSNI*, L (1924), 36; Lovette, *School of Sea*, 206.

Similarly, Captain William Grenville Temple hoped enlisted personnel could be encouraged to "spend their whole lives" in the Service and "look upon it as their home," thus becoming "identified with it." Temple before a House Naval Affairs Committee, 44th Cong., 1st Sess., *Investigation . . .*, House of Representatives Misc. Doc. No. 170, Pt. 6, (Wash., G.P.O., 1876), p. 24.

11. Mahan, *Armaments and Arbitration*, 37–38; Porter to Washburne, January 11, 1869, Letterbook, David D. Porter, Collection, N.H.F. Chapter 6 should illustrate the steps naval officers took in the defense of their institution.

12. Stirling, *Sea Duty*, 23–24; Field, *America*, 333; LaFeber, *New Empire*, 211–213; Stanton Papers, Mystic; Johnson, *Rodgers*, 334; Quirk, *Affair of Honor*, 14. Cf. Tuleja, *Statesmen*, 68, 168.

13. McCandless, *et al.*, *Service Etiquette*, 251; Porter to Foote, November 13, 1862, and Porter to Fox, circa 1863, cited in John D. Milligan, *Gunboats down the Mississippi* (Annapolis, 1965), 102–103; Rear Admiral George E. Belknap, in *Letters of Captain*

George Perkins, 254; Porter, *Incidents and Anecdotes to the Civil War* (N.Y., 1885), 212; Captain Caspar F. Goodrich to Rear Admiral George E. Belknap, November 15, 1894, Rear Admiral Reginald R. Belknap Papers, Box 424, Naval Historical Foundation; Lieutenant Commander J. H. Gibbons, "Navy Leagues," *North American Review*, CLXVI (1903), 760.

See also Rear Admiral Louis Goldsborough to Assistant Secretary Fox, June 16, 1862. He complained of the credit given to General Burnside for the Elizabeth City Expedition and argued that, "compared to army officers," naval officers were "treated as an inferior race of men, & they are getting very restive about it." *Confidential Correspondence of Gustavus Vasa Fox, Assistant Secretary of the Navy, 1861–1865,* ed. Robert M. Thompson & Richard Wainwright (2 vols., New York, 1918–1919), I, 291.

14. Porter to Fox, November 12, 1862, *Confidential Correspondence of Fox,* II, 151; *DuPont Letters,* II, 67, 199; Davis to Lieutenant Nathan Sargent, May 9, and June 25, 1890, Corr. of Sargent, Nav. Attaché to Rome, Vienna, and Berlin, 1888–1893, Letters Received, Vol. II & III, Entry 300, R.G. 45; Ramsay to Sargent, July 1, 1890, Letters Received, Vol. III, Entry 300, R.G. 45; Goodrich to Long, July ?, 1898, [copy] Caspar Goodrich Papers, New York Historical Society. Cf. Fox to DuPont, June 3, 1862, *DuPont Letters,* II, 96; Stirling, *U.S. Midshipmen in Philippines,* 102–125, *passim;* Rear Admiral A. Farenholt, "Some Yarns of the Old Navy," NL Box 274, Entry 464, R.G. 45.

The creation of the Joint Army-Navy Planning Board in 1903 may have improved inter-service relations, but see the discussions of inter-service rivalries in the 1930s in Fred Greene, "The Military View of American National Policy, 1904–1940," *American Historical Review,* LXVI (Jan. 1961), 354–377; and Louis Morton, "Army and Marines on the China Station: A Study in Military and Political Rivalry," *Pacific Historical Review,* XXIX (Feb. 1960). For a World War II example of inter-service rivalry see Huie, *Case Against the Admirals,* 130.

15. McCalla, "Memoirs," Ch. III, 41; Lieutenant Commander R. P. Builer, "Naval Mirrors," *PUSNI,* L (1924), 701–702; Roe, *Naval Duties,* 194; Florence Ridgely Johnson, *Welcome Aboard: A Service Manual for the Naval Officer's Wife* (Annapolis, 1951), 73.

16. Fiske, *Navy as a Fighting Machine,* 243; 44th Cong., 1st Sess., House of Representatives *Misc. Doc. No. 170, Pt. I, Investigation by the Committee on Naval Affairs* (Wash., G.P.O., 1876), 12; Clarence E. Macartney, *Mr. Lincoln's Admirals* (New York, 1956), 59; *DuPont Letters,* II, 527, 531; III, 120, 156, *passim.* The only crew member willing to row Dewey back to the sinking warship was a "contraband," which outraged the future hero of Manila Bay.

17. Mahan to his wife, February 1, 1895, Box 21, Mahan Papers, L. of C.; Stillson Ph.D., 146n; Foltz, *Surgeon,* 116–117; Rear Admiral Beardslee to E. M. H. Edwards, cited in Edwards, *Cushing,* 201; Foote, *Africa,* 360; Janowitz, *Professional Soldier,* 215–232; Irving McKee, "Captain Edward Howe Watson and the Honda Disaster," *Pacific Historical Review* (August 1960), 301; Rear Admiral John C. Watson Papers, N.H.F.

18. Sawyer, *Sons of Gunboats,* 7; Midshipmen Francis G. Dallas to Navy Secretary John Mason, June 21, 1848, *The Papers of Francis G. Dallas, U.S.N., Correspondence and Journal, 1837–1859,* ed. Gardner W. Allen (New York, Navy History Society, 1917), 38–39; Rear Admiral Thorton B. Jenkins to W. C. Whitthorne, Chairman, House Naval Affairs Committee, 44th Cong., 1st Sess., House of Representatives, *Misc. Doc. No. 170, Pt. 8, Investigation . . .* (Wash., G.P.O., 1876), 42; Rear Admiral Bradley Fiske to Navy Secretary Josephus Daniels, May 27, 1914, cited in Grenville & Young, *Politics, Strategy and American Diplomacy,* 324–325.

19. Capt. John Philip to his wife, July 19, 1898, Philip Papers, "ZB" File, Nav. Hist. Div., N.A.; McCalla, "Memoirs," Ch. XXII, 14–15; Pratt autobiog., 25–26.

Similarly, British naval officers had a high sense of honor and reacted violently when their gentlemanly nature was questioned. When someone suggested that British naval officers were "rough-mannered," young Lewis Bayly and another junior officer threatened the fellow with a beating! *Pull Together!: The Memoirs of Admiral Sir Lewis Bayly* (London, 1939), 51.

20. Hamersly's File Book of Naval Officer's Letters, 1870–1879, New York Historical Society; Rodgers to Dobbin, January 29, 1856, in *Yankee Surveyors in the Shogun's Seas,* ed. Cole, 159; Drayton to Hamilton, Jr., January 10, 1865 [typed copy—original not deposited], Drayton Papers, U.S. Navy Collection, Manuscript Division, New York

Public Library; Mason, "A Medal of Honor for Officers," *The United Service*, IV (January 1881), 10; Snyder, "If I Were to do my Service over again," *PUSNI*, LI (1925), 62; Kutner & Healy, *Admiral*, 310. See also Cadet-Midshipman Frank Bunts to his mother, Feb. 1, 1883, *Letters from the Asiatic Station*, ed. Bunts, 201; Connolly, *Navy Men*, 304; Lieutenant Edwin Anderson to his wife, Jan. 30, 1903, E. A. Anderson Papers, S.H.C., U. of N.C. Library.

Anyone who has served in the modern navy for any length of time will recognize the modernity of the views of Rodgers and Snyder. Encomia emanate with regularity.

21. Commander Louis Goldsborough to his wife, October 17, 1852, Goldsborough Papers, L. of C.

22. See, for example, the "pride" Bradley Fiske felt as he watched shells guided with the use of gun sights he had designed fall accurately on Filipino churches in 1899. Fiske, *From Midshipman to Rear Admiral*, 301, 314.

23. Stevens, "Ambition" [a poem], *United Service*, 3rd Series, IV (1903), 67. See also Fitzpatrick & Saphire, *Navy Maverick*, 69.

24. Reverend Fitch W. Taylor, U.S.N., *The Broad Pennant; or, a Cruise in the United States Flag Ship of the Gulf Squadron* (New York, 1848), 3; Mahan, *Life of Nelson*, I, 280. See also, Mahan, in William Laird Clowes, *The Royal Navy: A History* (Boston, 1898), III, 508–509. Tom Philips' research indicates that U.S. Army officers of the late nineteenth century were similarly motivated. They preferred assignment to cavalry, rather than infantry, regiments because of the higher combat duty cavalry personnel experienced, with attendant opportunities for glory and promotion. See his forthcoming study of the U.S. Army in the late nineteenth century.

25. McKethan to his mother, April 3, 1895, A. A. McKethan Papers, Perkins Library, Duke; Worden to Secretary of State of New York, December 20, 1862, Worden Papers, Lincoln Univ. Library, Harrogate, Tennessee; Flusser to his mother, Jan. 13, and Jan. 31, 1862, Flusser Papers, "ZB" File, Nav. History Sec., Nat. Archives; Fairfax to Wise, August 10, 1862; *Mahan–Ashe Letters*, *passim*; Samuel Ashe, "Memories of Annapolis," *South Atlantic Quarterly*, XVIII (1919), 203; Temple to Wise, August 27, 1862, Wise Papers, N.Y.H.S.; Drake, "Shufeldt," Ph.D., 90. Arnheiter is, of course, the recent Anna-

polite who is said to have jeopardized his vessel to draw enemy fire.

26. Telegrams for April 2 and 3, 1885, in "Correspondence relating to the Naval Expedition to the Isthmus of Panama, 1885," Item 13, Entry 25, Appendix A, R.G. 45; Rear Admiral J. C. Watson to Rear Admiral William T. Sampson, June 26, 1898, Entry 53, R.G. 313, and Watson to John Marshall Harlan, Jan. 17, 1899, Entry 2, R.G. 313; Long, *New American Navy*, I, 99; Kutner & Healy, *The Admiral*, 174–175; Goodrich to Long [copy], July ?, 1898, Goodrich Papers, N.Y.H.S.; R. Hobson, *The Sinking of the "Merrimac"* (N.Y., 1899), 43.

27. McCalla to his wife, June 13, 1900, cited in McCalla, "Memoirs," XXVIII, 21; Seymour to Admiral Dewey, August 16, 1900, also cited in "Memoirs," Ch. XXVIII, 23.

28. Albert B. Paine, *A Sailor of Fortune: Personal Memoirs of Captain B. S. Osbon* (New York, 1906), 177; Alden, *Perkins*, 160–175.

29. H. Clay Trumbull, "Four Naval Officers Whom I Knew," *United Service*, I (1879), 38.

30. Porter to his mother, December 16, 1867, Porter Papers, N.Y.H.S.; DuPont Letters, III, 425; Porter, *Incidents and Anecdotes of the Civil War* (New York, 1886), 56–57; Belknap, "Sketch of the Life of Captain George H. Perkins," in *Letters of Captain George Hamilton Perkins, U.S.N., 1858–1880*, ed. Susan Perkins (Concord, N.H., 1886), 243–244; Francis A. Roe to George E. Belknap, October 26, 1897, Rear Admiral R. R. Belknap Papers, Box 424, Naval Historical Foundation.

31. Welles to his mother, July 10, 1898, Welles Papers, Naval Historical Foundation; Goodrich to Sampson [copy], August 13, 1898, Goodrich Papers, N.Y.H.S.

32. Kutner & Healy, *The Admiral*, 226–227; Barker, *Everyday Life*, 292, 299. Apparently fleet actions were more prestigous than helping the Army quell the insurgent's independence movement in the Philippines, for neither Lieutenant Commander Sperry nor Rear Admiral Remey saw any "prospect of glory" in the latter. Sperry to his wife, May 4, 1899, Sperry Papers, L. of C.; Mrs. Remey to her son, July 22, 1901, *Mrs. Remey's Letters*, XII, 905.

33. Clark to Long, May 2, 1902, *The Papers of John Long*, 428–430; Clark to S. Weir Mitchell, March 9, 1905, S. Weir Mitchell Papers, N.Y.P.L.; Evans, *Admiral's*

272

Log, 6; Stevens, "Lines in an Autograph-Book," *The United Service*, VI (May 1882), 553.

34. Fletcher Pratt, *Preble's Boys: Commodore Preble and the Birth of American Sea Power* (N.Y., 1950), 110; Clark, *Admiral's Aid*, 12, 14; Johnson, *Rodgers*, 76; Andor Klay, *Daring Diplomacy*, 94; Beard, *Idea of National Interest*, 366–367; Wriston, *Executive Agents*, 665–670; Habersham, *North Pacific Surveying and Exploring Expedition*, 235–236. Cf. Billingsley, *Defense of Neutral Rights*, 102; K. Jack Bauer, "The Sancala Affair: Captain Voorhees Seizes an Argentine Squadron," *American Neptune*, XXIX (1969), 174–186.

35. Cushing to his mother, cited in McCartney, *Mr. Lincoln's Admirals*, 205. See also Leo Marx, "The Machine in the Garden," *New England Quarterly* (1956), 27–42; and Marx, Arnold Rose, and Bernard Bowron, "Literature and Covert Culture," *American Quarterly* (1957), 377–386.

36. See chapter 3, note 2.

37. Bell to Navy Dept., "Letters of the Commanders of the Asiatic Squadron . . .," pp. 89–93, Microcopy M–89, R.G. 45; H. A. Goswell, "The Navy in Korea, 1871," *American Neptune*, VII (1947), 112; Rodgers to his wife, June 19, 1871, John Rodgers Family Papers, N.H.F.; "Our Little Battle in Corean Waters," *Overland Monthly*, VIII, 2nd Series (Aug. 1886), 126, cited in Bernard Nalty and Freeman Strobridge, "Our First Korean War," *American History Illustrated*, II (Aug. 1967), 10ff.

Rodgers himself had mellowed, and "wanted to attain a treaty without fighting."

38. Schoonmaker, "Life of Schoonmaker," 50; Luce to John Barnes, December 29, 1873, N.Y.H.S.; Rodman, *Yarns of a Kentucky Admiral*, 215; Edwin A. Falk, *Fighting Bob Evans* (New York, 1934), 154; Emory to Folger, December 5, 1891, *Life of an American Sailor: Rear Admiral William Emory*, ed. Albert Gleaves (New York, 1923), 146; *The Life and Adventures of Jack Philip, Rear Admiral, U.S.N.*, ed. Edgar S. Maclay (New York, 1904), 214; Goodrich, "Naval Education," *Journal of Social Science*, XXXIII (November, 1895), 29; Goodrich, "Esprit de Corps—A Tract for the Times," *PUSNI*, XXIV (January, 1898), 5; Sperry to his wife, Feb. 25, 1899, Sperry Papers; R. E. Dupuy and Wm. H. Baumer, *The Little Wars of the United States* (N.Y., 1968), 112; Sargent to Dewey, Feb. 3, 1906, Sargent Papers, N.H.F. See also "A Naval Officer," "A Plea for Gunboats," *United Service*, 2nd Series, I (1899), 93; Clark, *Joe Bently*, 63; Ensign Roger Welles to his mother, January 16, 1896, Welles Papers, Naval Historical Foundation, for his paean to the new battleship *Indiana* ("What a death dealing machine she is!" etc.); and Drake, "Shufeldt," Ph.D. thesis, 213, for Shufeldt's wish that the Asiatic Squadron "might have a dash before I go . . . at some foe worthy of our steel."

39. Russell, *Diary North and South*, 30; Fullam, *PUSNI*, XVI (1890), 475; Taylor, *PUSNI*, CLXII (1896), 181–183; Lejeune, *Reminiscences*, 125; Hobson, *North Amer. Rev.*, CLXXV (1902), 555; Chambers, *PUSNI*, XI (1885), 343; Fiske, *Art of Fighting*, 367–368; *From Midshipman to Rear Admiral*, 490; and *Navy as a Fighting Machine*, 100; Mahan, *Interest of America in Sea Power*, 253; Luce, *The Navy*, V (Oct. 1911), 27; *PUSNI*, XIV (1888), 628; *PUSNI*, XXX (1906), 1367–1386; and "The Benefits of War," *North Amer. Rev.*, CLIII (Dec., 1891), 672–683; Gleaves, *Luce*, 174, 297; Mahan, *Armaments and Arbitration*, 10; *Harper's Monthly*, CXIV (Feb., 1907), 375; *From Sail to Steam*, 9–10; *Some Neglected Aspects of War* (Boston, 1907), 108; Nelson, I, 296; "The Moral Aspects of War," *North Amer. Rev.* (Oct., 1899). See Brown, "Social Attitudes of American Generals," 272, for some examples of similar Army officer glorification of war.

I found one clear dissent from this paean to war—the ambivalent Admiral David D. Porter's poem, "The Siege of Vicksburg," wherein appears the following passage: "In war man's a demon. His nature set free,/ His soul is a desert, parched as [can] be/ . . . Man, urged by his passions, without due restraints,/Will desecrate altars and martyrize saints."

40. Caldwell to his mother, July 27, 1868, Albert Caldwell Letters, John Caldwell Collection, Indiana Historical Society Library; Vice Admiral David D. Porter to John Barnes, February 25, 1869, David D. Porter Papers, N.Y.H.S.; J. Barnett, *Admiral George Dewey, A Sketch of the Man* (New York, 1899), 13–14; Emory to Lieutenant Mulligan, January 30, 1892, cited in *Life of an American Sailor*, ed. Gleaves, 148; "Nauticus," *The Truth about the Schley Case* [n.p., n.d. c. 1902] (copy in N.Y.P.L.), 7; Stirling, *How to be a Naval Officer*, 11; Lovette, *School of Sea*, 129.

Midshipman F. F. Foster was delighted by World War I; he was convinced that the Navy would gain prestige, ships, and manpower. "War's Benefits," *PUSNI*, XLIV (1918), 1447. But see also Fiske, *Navy as a Fighting Machine*, 31, who denies that naval officers are eager for war in order to gain promotion. Fiske intended his remark for publication; the officers cited herein to establish a contrary view did not. It would be interesting to know Fiske's private thoughts, circa 1895, on war and promotion, but unfortunately his private papers are unavailable or nonexistent. Commander Nathan Twining's papers are available, however. And on March 14, 1898, he *did* privately advise his brother that no one in the Navy "*hopes*" for war." But Twining did not say that wars were unwelcome. And in 1914 he inveighed against "the timorous, cowardly policy" of President Wilson in Mexico and hoped for "more decisive action." Twining to his brother, March 14, 1898, and to his father, May 29, 1914, Twining Papers, State Historical Society of Wisconsin. Lieutenant Commander Charles Flusser, who inveighed against war and adventurism in a January 13, 1862, letter to his mother also appears to have longed for fame; and he was killed two years later in a brave, but reckless, engagement. Flusser Papers, "ZB" File, Naval History Div., Nat. Archives.

None the less, there are a few officers who appear to have favored restraint. Commodore John C. Watson longed for action against the Spanish in 1898, but when the Spanish forces in Cuba surrendered, he was not disconsolate; the surrender would "save many lives," he told his sister. (Watson to Sarah Watson, July 14, 1898, Watson Papers, N.H.F.) Commanders Queen and Dewey had been willing to shell La Paz, Mexico, in 1875, but Rear Admiral Alexander Murray vacillated. When asked to repeat the threats of his "hard-line" colleagues, Murray first agreed. But he soon withdrew the threat after observing the "absolutely helpless" condition of the "thriving little town." Murray prefered to have the Triunfo Mine people appeal to the friendly auspices of the Mexican legal system. Murray's judgment was sound; the Triunfo Mine secured satisfaction. (Dewey, *Autobiography*, 146–149; Consul Turner to Assistant Secretary of State, Oct. 19, 1876, La Paz Consular Reports, N.A.)

41. In this sense I am close to the view of the military's role in the process of imperialism taken by William L. Langer in "A Critique of Imperialism," *Foreign Affairs*, XIV (Oct. 1935), 114, and the "heroic model" of the military man presented in Morris Janowitz, *The Professional Soldier*, 150ff.

part two

The Ideological Roots of Modern American Navalism

chapter 6

Career Anxiety and the "New Navy": The 1880s

Of all careers, the Navy is the one which offers the most frequent opportunities to junior officers to act on their own.

Napoleon, *Political Aphorisms*

What has a Lieutenant to show for his thirty years of service? Nothing, absolutely nothing . . . while his contemporaries in civil life have accumulated wealth or high position. *They have reached the goal they started for.*

Lieutenant "W.X.," *National Defense* (*circa* 1883)

Elting Morison has remarked that the U.S. Navy of the late nineteenth century "is a paradise for the historian or sociologist in search of evidence of a society's response to change."[1] Morison had in mind technological change, and that is important; but the Navy experienced other tensions as well in the late nineteenth century. An institution that believes its survival is threatened may respond to the menace in a host of ways. Individuals who feel that their professional lives are imperiled react vigorously. The late nineteenth century U.S. Navy brimmed with such tensions—tensions that kept the Service in a state of turmoil for nearly two decades and measurably altered the nature and complexion of both the naval aristocracy and the Navy itself.

The Background

In 1875 the U.S. Navy was a third-rate assemblage of wooden or thin-skinned iron-plated sailing ships with the capacity, but without the inclination, to burn coal. In an emergency, if becalmed, these vessels might hope

Numbered footnotes for Chapter 6 begin on page 317.

to develop enough power to rattle along at all of eight knots.[2] The Civil War blockade had demonstrated the merit of steam power, but steam-powered vessels burned too much coal to suit economy-minded administrators. In "showing the flag" on foreign stations sail power was more efficient and strategically feasible than the somewhat unpredictable, coal-dependent steamer with its small cruising radius. The 1870s were the days of the great clipper ships, the "last word" in sail. Such craft were aesthetically pleasing to both naval and public leaders, compared to the lumbering experimental steam and armor vessels. Men still thrilled to a broad expanse of canvas. Three new warships were authorized in 1872; all three were to be wooden.

The ships were a motley lot, in various states of disrepair. Admiral David D. Porter considered them "ancient Chinese forts on which dragons have been painted to frighten away the enemy." Representative John D. Long of Massachusetts spoke of them as "an alphabet of floating washtubs" regarded by the public as "marine Falstaffian burlesque." He noted that the running down of the U.S.S. *Tallapoosa* by a coal barge had become a discomforting national joke.[3] Moreover, training cycles were infrequent or nonexistent, and the gunnery, by contemporary European standards, was often exceptionable. The chiefs of the Navy bureaus were long-time appointees, "Coburgers," virtual fixtures on the Washington landscape. It was easy for an officer to lose touch, quite unintentionally, with affairs and needs of the fleet. There was little or no cooperation between bureaus, and, after 1869, the post of Assistant Secretary, till then ably filled by Gustavus Vasa Fox, was abolished. In one of Oscar Wilde's plays of the day, an American lady who bemoaned her country's lack of curiosities and ruins was told, "Well, you have your manners and your Navy."

In 1874 Commander Fredrick McNair reported on naval maneuvers in the Bay of Florida:

> The vessels before us were in no respect [those] of a great nation like our own, for what could be more lamentable—what more painful to one who loved his country and his profession—than to see a fleet armed with smooth-bore guns, requiring close quarters for their development, moving at a rate of $4\frac{1}{2}$ knots? What inferior force could it overtake, or what superior force escape from, of any of the great naval powers of the earth?

McNair's professional pride grievously wounded, he reacted by painting a grim scene of *Realpolitik*. Were ships of war to be "dispensed with" and left to "rot alongside of decaying wharves," the nation would run the risk of national insult and possible downfall. In his 1874 report to the Secretary of the Navy, Admiral D. D. Porter likened the nation's naval resources to a "foot-soldier armed with a pistol encountering a mounted man clad in armor and carrying a breech-loading rifle."[4]

Officers ordered to cruise on foreign stations in "old tubs" felt particularly the "wounds" to their "sense of professional pride." More than one Annapolite, mortified by the sneers of foreign-service counterparts, was convinced that the

U.S. Navy had become "the laughing stock of the Naval World." "I am disgusted with the whole business and mistified [sic] at the [*Pinta*'s] performance and appearance," Lieutenant Commander Albert Caldwell wrote his mother in 1884. "She is a beast. I want to be at rest on a farm and have done with all the harrassing things of the sea. . . . [W]e will never have a Navy."[5]

Younger officers, many experiencing their first naval cruises, were hardest hit. Older men had witnessed the slow decline over a long period of years and many had at least learned to live with it. But the striking differences between the American Navy, and the French, British, Italian, or Chilean navies made the idealistic officer fresh from the Academy "feel sort of insignificant and ashamed." Cadet Midshipman Frank Bunts complained of his ship, the *Richmond*, "a poor excuse for a tub, unarmored, with pop-guns for a battery and a crew composed of the refuse of all nations, three-fourths of whom cannot speak intelligible English." The Navy was "the laughing stock of the world," he told his brother Harry. "You can see what makes me disgusted with the whole thing sometimes." And Ensign George Foulk, stationed in Korea, wrote to a classmate, "So help me Bob if I can respectably do it I am not going to sea in a United States man of war, until one is built fit to be called such!"[6]

Many spoke of the need for a "new Navy," to be sure. In Europe the rate of technological advances in naval engineering, architecture, and gunnery was such that a ship but a month out of the slip might well be antiquated before it could be commissioned. This rapid rate of change was not entirely lost to Americans. In 1873 a group of progressive naval officers founded the Naval Institute, a semi-official organization "having for its object the advancement of professional and scientific knowledge in the Navy."[7] But in the 1870s the federal government offered little support for naval revitalization. American statesmen saw little need for expensive warships that would be obsolete in a matter of months. Three thousand miles of bounding main separated them from the evolving European arms race. The nation was expanding, but it was expanding primarily over land, not sea. The West still offered a "frontier," commercial vantage, and challenge.

Consequently, the Navy in 1882 was even less well off than it had been a decade before. Secretary William H. Hunt's annual report in 1881 spoke of 140 naval vessels "in commission," but of these all but 31 were unserviceable. An 1881 naval review for President James A. Garfield included the side-wheel steam boat *Powhatan* and, relic of relics, the pride of the War of 1812, the U.S.S. *Constitution*, nicknamed "Old Ironsides" but made of wood. In 1882 Secretary William E. Chandler's annual report noted that of 2,664 guns installed, 2,233 were smooth-bore, muzzle-loading cannon, and that of the remainder only 87 were worth retaining.[8]

Decaying ships and antique equipment were not the Navy's only woes: there were personnel problems as well. In contrast to the difficulty naval authorities had in recruiting an ample number of adaptable native American seamen, the service had an excess of officers. Consequently promotions were few and far between; the careers of many younger officers lay becalmed.

The Civil War had been a glorious period for junior officers. "[S]ecession has decimated the *Navy Register*," Lieutenant George Preble wrote his niece Lizzie in October 1861.

> [I]t has increased your venerable uncle's chances of promotion. After remaining at a standpoint between no. 65 and 70 on the list of Lieutenants for five years, I am carried up by this wave of rebellion to *no. 20.*

"In these times the promotion is very rapid," Midshipman Charles Sperry wrote to his sister in early 1863. But with the termination of hostilities in 1865 came a termination in career growth. Even after the departure of civilian volunteers and enlisted wartime appointees the ranks of the naval aristocracy remained swollen out of proportion to their obligations. Between 1861 and 1865 some 858 midshipmen had been admitted to the Academy. The graduates of the 1864, 1865, 1866, 1867, and 1868 classes filled and blocked the lower echelons of the naval officer hierarchy. The twelve top graduates of the class of 1868 remained lieutenants for twenty-one years. In 1867 there were many lieutenant commanders, like George Dewey and Alfred Mahan, with less than eight years of post-Annapolis service; in 1897 there were many ensigns, like Hugh Rodman, with over fifteen years of service in that grade. And with each succeeding class the number of years one was required to remain the same grade increased. Promotion was strictly linear;[9] there was no way, in peacetime, that one might advance any more rapidly than the sum of the deaths or retirements of senior officers. Every officer who had received a note of thanks from Congress during the Civil War (and there had been quite a few) could be retired only with his permission unless he had committed a felony or had compiled no less than fifty-five years of naval service. The rest of the Civil War breed were free to stay for forty years, or until age 62. "What is this but a life thrown away," one Lieutenant bemoaned in December, 1865, and his anxiety was echoed by others.[10]

The first response of the federal government to this Civil War "hump" in the *Navy Register* appears to have been the Act of July 15, 1870, which proposed to unsnarl the promotion pile-up in a curious way. The status of midshipmen at the Naval Academy was lowered by the creation of the grade "Cadet Midshipman," an interim position without legal rank in the Service. Upon graduation the prefix "Cadet" was dropped, and the graduate, now a full-fledged midshipman, began his service at the bottom of the list in this rank. In short, Congress had simply created a new bottom rung on the Navy promotion ladder. The number of years now required to reach substantial rank continued to climb, but now the junior officer was paid less than before in his first years with the fleet, and had the dubious satisfaction of being advanced to ensign anywhere from two to six years after graduation.[11]

Obviously, this artificial addition to the chain of command did nothing to relieve the stagnation in the lower ranks. Junior officers complained bitterly of the lack of stimuli. "As a general thing in the Navy it makes no difference whether one does his duty a little better or a little worse than another, save for **281** one's own satisfaction, as there is no incentive," wrote Passed Assistant Engineer J. P. Stuart Lawrence. "Promotion comes no sooner or later on that account." The "weary waiting" for automatic advancement dulled many an officer's ambition. Navy Lieutenants grew grey, "broken by the heart-sickening prospect of always being compelled to perform the same duty they did in their youth." "We are forced to inglorious idleness," one Lieutenant complained in 1879, while another, in 1881, sighed:[12]

> Individuality is crushed, no opportunity is given for the development of latent powers of command, and self-reliance dies a natural death.

In 1890 Lieutenant William F. Fullam recalled the stultifying years:

> Those who have passed through the junior grades during the past decade can bear testimony to the fact that their minds have been subjected to a smoothering, stunting process.

Zeal had been "discouraged"; ambition, "murdered."[13] Rear Admiral Fiske, who had been just such a junior officer in 1880, recalled the "crushing hopelessness" that officers his age had felt during the "doldrum" years. "The most aspiring years of our lives" had been spent in "the dullest, the most uninteresting, and the most useless duties. . . ." And to such junior officers the sense of futility was compounded whenever contact was made with a British warship, whose captain was often younger than the senior American lieutenant on board, and all of whose junior officers were significantly younger than their American counterparts.[14]

Consequently, many junior officers left the Service in the years after the Civil War. No less a figure than the senior U.S. naval officer himself, Admiral David D. Porter, told one of his former subordinates who had just resigned, "I think you were wise in leaving the Navy as there is little inducement for remaining in it." More than one junior officer, in submitting his resignation, gave as his reasons: "the slowness of promotion, the overcrowded conditions of the lower grades of the Service, and the low rate of pay for which I would have to serve for a number of years." "To one in my position," one cadet-midshipman explained to the Secretary of the Navy in May 1881, "the outlook is especially discouraging. It would be seven years before I would receive a commission." Fully twenty-six per cent of nineteenth century Academy graduates resigned within fifteen years of graduation, but classes of the 1860s and 1870s suffered ever greater rates of attrition.[15]

Those with "good connections on the outside," sons of bankers or merchants, appear to have fled the Navy first, whereas those from families oriented toward public service, sons of clergymen, educators, and officers and other government officials (as well as the sons of shopkeepers), were considerably less likely to resign (see Table 6-1). Only 26.5% (126 of 476) of my sample of Annapolites appointed between 1861 and 1875 from the Northeast or Midwest resigned

282   within a decade of graduation, while the figure was over 50% (35 of 65) for those appointed from the South or West where opportunities may have been more open to a man with a college degree in engineering. A stagnant navy was no place for many a man on the make.

Table 6-1 Percentage of a sample of 552 Naval Officers commissioned between 1865 and 1880 who resigned within 10 years of graduation, ranked by their father's occupation (plus widows)

Occupation of Graduate's Father (No.)	Percentage resigning within 10 years	(No.)
Banker (35)	52	(18)
Merchant (85)	40	(34)
Widow (52)	36.5	(19)
Farmer, Planter, Rancher (47)	34	(16)
Attorney, Judge (58)	32.7	(19)
Artisan, Clerk (19)	31	(6)
Average (552)	29.2	(162)
Physician, Druggist (53)	28.3	(18)
Manufacturer (35)	25.3	(9)
Shopkeeper (25)	20	(5)
Officer (76)	15.8	(12)
Government Official (39)	15.6	(6)
Clergyman, Educator (28)	10.3	(3)

None the less, many were reluctant to give up what little they had achieved. "There is nothing else for me but the Navy," Cadet-Midshipman Frank Bunts told his brother in July 1882. "I have spent nearly six of the best years of my life endeavoring to perfect myself in this profession and I feel totally unable to enter into any other profession with that zest, interest, and spirit necessary to insure success." "All the attractions of this life, which once existed for me, no longer exist," he wrote elsewhere. "Still I cannot see my way out of it very clearly. . . . Now that I have fairly gotten started, I cannot leave [the Navy]. I shall endeavor to make the best of a not exceedingly good bargain." Some, like John Crittenden Watson, Alfred Thayer Mahan, and John Grimes Walker, made at least token efforts to find attractive civilian employment, but failing to meet success, they returned to the "broad bosom of mother ocean." Many never bothered to try. "I expect that after all the Navy is the most comfortable place for me," Lieutenant Albert Caldwell wrote his aunt, "otherwise I might be tilling the soil. . . . " The security of a naval career, boring and stultifying as it was to the junior officer in the late nineteenth century, was, after all, more appealing to members of the naval aristocracy than tilling the soil! And if one were to survive the period of "weary waiting," the reward of rank was certain. "I am afraid you will have to live a good many years to see me an Admiral," young Charles O'Neil wrote to a friend in 1877, "as promotion is slow with us, but if I live *long enough* there is no reason why I shouldn't arrive at that dignity some day."[16]

Stagnation in the officer promotion stream, resulting in a "top-heavy navy," as one *Puck* cartoonist put it in this 1882 view of naval affairs.

Officers of the U.S.S. *Lancaster*, 1893. Note white-haired lieutenants (Naval Photographic Center).

The Crisis

The American Republic has no more need for its burlesque of a navy than a peaceable giant would have for a stuffed club or a tin sword. It is only maintained for the sake of the officers & the naval rings. In peace it is a source of expense and corruption; in war it would be useless. . . . If war should ever be forced upon us, we could safely rely upon science and invention, which are already superseding navies faster than they can be built. . . . The whole [naval] system is an insult to democracy and ought to be swept away.

Henry George, *Social Problems* (Garden City, N.Y., 1882),

In June, 1881, President Garfield told the graduating class of the Naval Academy:

The world is open to you, and if naval service does not bring you success then you are lazy or hopelessly incompetent. Gentlemen, as I stand here I almost experience a feeling of envy when I think of the possible future before you. . . . The very gods . . . look down with interest upon you. You have so much to mold, shape, and build up. . . . The profession to which you belong has made this nation.

There was some truth in the President's words, but they appeared the grossest hypocrisy to some members of his audience who knew the state of the Service they were entering.[17] By 1882 there was one naval officer for every four enlisted men, and the growing criticism of "this swarm" of officers had moved Congressmen and naval authorities alike to demand "radical change (see cartoon). The officer complement had to be decreased in numbers.

Several options were available: "Deadwood" could be pruned out of the upper ranks; provision could be made for more rapid rates of advance for meritorious officers; or the size of the graduating classes of the Academy could be reduced.

The second option—promotion on merit—had some defenders, but many critics. Officers and politicians alike were too conscious of the power of "political, social and personal influences" in such a method to press for its acceptance. When Navy Secretary George Bancroft argued for promotion on merit in 1846, senior officers sought his removal. In 1868 Rear Admiral Thomas Turner expressed "very serious fears" that Navy Secretary Gideon Welles was planning to institute "that system of scoundrelism—of *selecting* Officers for promotion." Turner may have had in mind the case of Lieutenant Ira Harris, who was alleged to have used political influence to secure premature promotion in 1866. Many officers protested this and other apparent instances of favoritism. A naval review board was convened in early 1872 to consider and adjust the claims of those passed over, and several petitioners were promoted or advanced in numbers in the *Navy Register*. In any event, few could see how such a provision would effect much change in the officer complement.[18] "Selection up or out" was not to come for several decades.

The first option—that of pruning out and retiring officers of the senior ranks—

was vigorously opposed by Admiral David D. Porter, the bureau chiefs, and **285** most of the senior officers, who inveighed against such *"total disregard & ignoring of Seniority."* "Stand by me and see that this injustice is not done me," Porter, fearing involuntary retirement, begged Representative William E. Robinson of the House Naval Affairs Committee. "Pruning" or "plucking" had an ample store of powerful, if hoary, foes.[19]

The post-Civil War era was not the first period of stagnation in the lower ranks of the naval aristocracy. Pre-Civil War years were just as sluggish. As early as 1839 the complaint had been voiced that, at the existing rate, a midshipman appointed in that year would not be advanced to lieutenant until 1870. "Young Turks"* such se Lieutenant Matthew Fountaine Maury and Passed Midshipman Edward Simpson complained of the lack of incentives for junior officers and argued for the forced retirement of senior officers. Such agitation for reform of the promotion system resulted in the 1855 retirement board of officers, who retired 152 and dismissed 49 of 800 comrades-in-arms, most of them senior officers, before adjourning.[20] Porter and his contemporaries wanted no recurrence in the early 1880s of such an attrition of the upper echelons of the Service.

That left only the proposal to reduce the number of Academy graduates. This plan, advanced by Rear Admiral C. K. Stribling and Commander A. T. Mahan ('59) as early as 1876 and pressed again in 1881 by Academy Superintendent C. R. P. Rodgers, drew attention to the fact that Academy graduates were without hope of advancement for years and called for a reduction in the sizes of Academy classes and an immediate cutback in the number of graduates commissioned.[21] This scheme was adopted by Congress and made law on August 5, 1882.

The Act of August 5, 1882, specified the exact number of officers intended for each rank, but the actual complement in 1882 included a surplus of at least 115 officers in the upper ranks. Under such conditions, the Act required the creation of two vacancies in each higher rank before anyone from a lower rank might be advanced, in order to arrive eventually at the stipulated allowances for each grade. Thus officers began to speak of "this curious legislative freak" as "the system of promotion which required the death or retirement of 64 Commodores or 128 Rear Admirals to promote one Ensign." One result was that for several years only a handful of Academy graduates—the top 25% of each class—were given commissions. Another was that the tenure of cadet midshipmen in "interim" pre-commissioned status was extended from four to six years. "After six years of study and service at the school, in competition with several hundred," one observer wrote in an 1891 pamphlet entitled *How to Become a Naval Cadet,* "the cadet frequently is disappointed by finding no

---

* Charles E. Neu (*An Uncertain Friendship: Theodore Roosevelt and Japan, 1906–1909* [Cambridge, Mass., 1967], 240–241) refers to the Navy's "Young Turks" as being active "since the turn of the century," but I would suggest that the "Young Turk" tradition in the Navy is a hardy perennial.

286   vacancy in the navy, and has to go off with an honorable discharge, and a year's pay [900 dollars], bitterly chagrined." Only 7% of those who entered the Academy in 1881 received commissions in 1887.*

The Response

The reaction of junior officers to this new impediment to their careers should have been predictable. The Academy erupted into its most violent period of fighting, hazing, and chaotic abuses of discipline. In the winter of 1882–1883 Superintendent Francis Ramsay faced a "virtual mutiny."[22] Elsewhere midshipmen, ensigns, lieutenants (junior grade), and lieutenants all made their discontent known. Ensign C. C. Marsh ('79) wrote to one classmate:

> You know, of course, long before this of the infernal bill that our sage law makers passed concerning the Navy. Prospects before dark are now blacker than damnation. What to do? is a question that flies through my brain every time I get my pipe and seat myself. . . . What is to come?

Cadet Bunts considered the Act "enough to dishearten and paralyze a young officer." "What am I to do?" he asked his mother, and himself. Lieutenant Charles Sperry ('66) told his wife of the rampant dissatisfaction with the state of affairs and spoke of following his classmates out of the Service. "Every now and then," he told his wife, "I feel as if the bottom had dropped out of everything and wish I had never heard of a ship." One anonymous officer, whose pamphlet, *National Defense*, appeared shortly after the passage of the August 5 Act, drew an analogy between the despondent junior naval officers and the junior members of another profession:[23]

> What would the gentlemen of the legal profession say and feel if an arbitrary law was in existence, to wit, that none shall be permitted to rise in their profession above that of an attorney, until regularly promoted through a vacancy, created by the death of a judge or counsellor, and that only by seniority.

The legal profession would be outraged, of course, as were the junior officers of the naval profession. The August 5 Act was a blow to their ambitions:

* The Act of August 5, 1882, fixed the levels of each rank at the following figures: 75 Ensigns, 75 Lieutenants (junior grade), 250 Lieutenants, 74 Lieutenant Commanders, 86 Commanders, 45 Captains, 10 Commodores, 6 Rear Admirals, 1 Vice Admiral, and 1 Admiral. 22 *U.S. Stat.* 391; Captain W. I. Chambers, *The Navy*, IX (March–April 1915), 98; 50th Cong., 1st Sess., Senate Report of Comm. on Naval Affairs, *No. 1377* [1887]; 49th Cong., 1st Sess., "Views of Senator Hale of Committee on Naval Affairs to Accompany Bill S. 371," Misc. Doc. 75 [1886]; Acad. Grad. Assoc., *Register of Grads.*; 66th Cong., 2nd Sess., Senate Naval Affairs Sub-Committee on Estimates, *Naval Investigation* [1920], I, 1621; Leon B. Richardson, *William E. Chandler* (N.Y., 1940), 305; Luis Senarens, *How to Become a Naval Cadet* (N.Y., 1891), 3; *PUSNI*, XXXI (1905), 426. James Calvert, *Naval Profession*, 110–128, provides a review of naval promotion legislation from the 1850s to the 1950s, yet omits all mention of the Act of August 5, 1882.

Marine officers suffered a similar reduction with the Act of January 30, 1885, designed to reduce their numbers progressively to 75. Their response would be worth attention and comparison to that of their naval brethren.

What has a Lieutenant to show for his thirty years of service? Nothing, absolutely nothing, . . . while his contemporaries in civil life have accumulated wealth or high position. *They have reached the goal they started for.*

The young naval aristocracy had read its Benjamin Franklin and Horatio Alger too, but neither virtuous behavior nor hard work had caused success to smile on the junior officers of the early 1880s.

Some chose to resign. Lieutenant Edward Very joined Benjamin Hotchkiss' arms company in France. Ensign Frank Sprague took a job with an electrical firm, giving low pay and the slow rate of promotion as his reasons for leaving the Navy. Over a dozen uncommissioned Annapolites, anxious to remain in some branch of Uncle Sam's service, changed uniforms to join the Coast Guard, the Revenue Cutter Service, or, all else failing, the Army! Others were more adventurous. Cadet Midshipman John Lejeune reported that three uncommissioned graduates of the class of '84 were advancing rapidly in the Chinese naval service, and, though he remained in the U.S. military service, Lejeune expressed himself to be of "half a mind" to join the Chinese Navy himself. Lieutenant (j.g.) George Foulk went to work for the American Trading Company in Japan and wrote a classmate of his new view of the U.S. Navy, "as I see it over here—in my new character of citizen abroad." It was "but a silly—empty face [farce?]—and I feel proud that I am out of it and a member of a body of [workers]." "I'd be a scallawag almost to the hum-drum *useless* life of the Navy," he wrote elsewhere. "The navy is, if changed at all—only *deader* than it was."[24]

But Act of August 5 or no, most junior officers *still* found it hard to give up their plans of a naval career. The recession of the mid-80s made the shift to civilian careers hard sledding for some. Even where one was offered a job at an attractive salary there was no guarantee it would be as permanent as the Service. "$1,700 a year and a sure thing is better than $5,000 [a year] for some months," Ensign John Bernadou warned Lieutenant (j.g.) George Foulk. One member of the class of 1881 who had left the Service advised his classmates not to follow his lead:

Chandler, Wm. E. [Secretary of the Navy, 1881–1885], intimated [at one of the Academy's graduation exercises] that those who had received their education at the U.S.N.A. could make a handsome living because of the training received at that institution. I am sorry to say that I must differ with that great statesman, and I am sure the majority of '81 will say that his views . . . are useless when put to the practical test of bread-winning.

The Service was not an avenue of golden opportunity to the junior officer in the 1880s, but after years of preparation for its Mysteries, it was still a desirable career to many. In 1883 the Academy cadet-midshipmen memorialized Congress for an exemption from the Act of August 5, 1882. "We entered the

Academy when we were at the age to have commenced a business or a professional training," they explained:

> Under the implied conditions of the papers we signed when entering the Naval Academy, we supposed we would be retained in the Service, gave up all thoughts of securing a business education, and applied ourselves to attaining a [naval] education. . . . If, at the end of six years of service, we are retired, in order to support ourselves we must learn either a business or a profession; we must start back at the point where we left off six years ago.

And what was perhaps more important, the cadet midshipmen had no *desire* to pursue any other profession. They were at home in the Navy. "A man's tastes," they observed, could not be "so easily transferred from one mode of living to another." With the "aptitude and liking for one profession comes the unfitness for any other."

Congress remained unsympathetic. Senator Benjamin Butler, long-standing foe of Admiral Porter, championed the cadets' cause; but Senator Eugene Hale, Chairman of the Naval Affairs Committee, and his House compeers, did not agree that entry into the Academy was a guarantee of life-long naval employment or that an Academy education was inadequate in the civilian world. Thus when he completed his six years of apprenticeship, Cadet-Midshipman Robert Coontz, one of the signers of the 1883 memorial and later Chief of Naval Operations, was compelled to race about Washington for days to convince Navy Department officials that enough officers had died or retired to allow for his commissioning.[25]

The junior officers, their professional careers threatened, drew analogies between their own condition and what they deemed to be the precarious state of the Navy itself. By 1883 the U.S. had no modern warships to speak of, and from the junior officer's perspective it was unclear as to when it would. Many were persuaded that the threat was not simply to their own careers, but to the entire Navy. Even Admiral D. D. Porter came to fear by 1883 that he might someday "wake up to find the Navy abolished. . . . " In any event, a decline in naval strength meant even fewer billets for junior officers and more attrition. The expression "Don't give up the ship" took on new meaning and urgency. Officers noted with alarm the arguments of the pacifists, arbitrationists, and other foes of a "big navy" policy and feared their strength. Henry George and a host of localistic Congressmen fought all efforts to increase naval expenditures. In the words of Representative William Oates of Alabama: "A large naval establishment is inconsistent with the spirit and genius of our Government, inconsistent with economy, and dangerous to the liberty of the people." These deadly foes of the Service, who continued "to clamor for its extinction," had to be countered. But even if their foes only managed to preserve the *status quo*, without actually abolishing the Service, such a standing-still amounted in reality to the gradual dismembering of what remained of the great Navy of Hull, Decatur, Bainbridge, Truxton, and Farragut. "Not to progress was to die," one officer observed. "We had reached a point when the very life of the Navy seemed at **289** stake," Caspar Goodrich later wrote of the 1880s.[26] The junior officers responded to the Act of August 5, 1882, and to what they conceived to be the threat to the Navy itself in three ways. First, they organized to fight for the repeal of the obnoxious promotion provisions of the 1882 law. Second, they made themselves as useful to the Navy as possible, and became instrumental in the creation of the "new Navy." And finally, as a part of the naval aristocracy itself, they and many of their more senior colleagues aggressively strove to change the attitude of Congress and the public regarding the part the Navy played in the national life. The stakes were high; each increase in naval expenditures meant more ships, more billets, and thus greater career security to Mahan's junior messmates. In a host of ways the Navy's "Young Turks"* sought to demonstrate the desirability of a "new Navy."†

The first response—that of organized opposition to the 1882 promotion system—was reflexive and immediate. The propensity to form pressure-groups was commonplace and natural for Americans in the 1880s.[27] Various Academy classes, among them 1881, 1882, and 1883, with personal, immediate anxieties, hired Washington attorneys and lobbied for repeal or exemption. Their first

* I isolated a total of 37 of these advocates of change (the most active 10% of their peer group), some 16 of their more senior "allies," and 11 of their "conservative" opponents, and I then examined the social backgrounds and Academy performance records of these three groups. Neither the size of the home towns, nor the regions of the country they were from, nor their fathers' occupations were in any sense exceptional. But 40% of the "Young Turk" group were from the top 10% of their Academy classes.

† Similarly, when naval opposition to the presence of marines on ships rose in these same years, marine officers feared their withdrawal would mean "the ultimate abolition of the Marine Corps." They responded by attempting to demonstrate to Congress and the public the Corps' "great usefulness," and to "enlarge" this "usefulness in every possible way" by seeking new missions and by pursuing "a regular campaign of entertainment" to "make themselves 'solid' with those who are in power." This, coupled with the fact that the father of one of their members, Captain Smedley Butler, was a member of the House Naval Affairs Committee, sufficed to hold the line until Cuba and the "gunboat diplomacy" of Taft and Wilson required the services of specialists in artillery, cavalry, infantry, field logistics, and the like within the Navy, and the Marines were preserved. Lejeune, *Reminiscences*, 115; Captain Henry Clay Cochrane, U.S.M.C., to Colonel Charles Heywood, U.S.M.C., Feb. 15, 1891, Cochrane Papers, M.C. Museum, Quantico, Va.; Commander P. F. Harrington to Lieutenant Commander Wm. F. Fullam, May 5, 1896, Box 1, Fullam Papers, N.H.F.; Commandant of the Marine Corps to Commander Henry Clay Taylor, Dec. 29, 1893, "Letters of the Presidents of the War College," Box 358, N.H.F.: Colonel R. D. Heinl, Jr., "An Association Was Formed," *Marine Corps Gazette*, XLVII (April 1963), 14–17.

General David Shoup, U.S.M.C. (Ret.), recently pointed out a case of Marine anxiety over survival in relation to Vietnam: "There was a growing concern [by 1965] that the Corps should get involved [in Vietnam] on a larger scale [which] would help justify the Corps' continued existence, which many Marines seem to consider to be in constant jeopardy." *Atlantic Monthly* (April 1969), 55.

For indications of another military institution's vigorous response to the threat of extinction, see Martha Derthick, "Militia Lobby in the Missile Age: The Politics of the National Guard," in *Changing Patterns of Military Politics*, ed. Samuel P. Huntington (N.Y., 1962), 190–234, esp. 220–221. And for more recent evidence of a similar naval response to the threat of the life of the Service see Vincent Davis, *Postwar Policy and the Navy, 1943–1946* (Chapel Hill, N.C. 1966), 149–201.

290   victory came with the passage of the Act of March 3, 1883, which reinstated
the rank of "Midshipman" upon graduation. But this was only a token. The
more substantial effort, to gain reinstatement for 145 midshipmen who had
been released upon graduation in the first three years after the passage of the
"obnoxious" clause of the Act of August 5, 1882, failed to receive a favorable
Senate committee report in 1886 and was lost. Emboldened by their solidarity
and the hope that those with "personal influence" with the Cleveland administration might "have our wrongs righted," the dispossessed Annapolites per-
severed. The class of 1881 published its own annual reports, and many a member
voiced his hope to meet his exiled classmates "again on the quarterdeck, or the
forecastle—Doesn't matter much which, just so we are wearing the 'blue and
gold." "I hope the fellows will not give up the fight until our last chance is
gone," another wrote with bitterness after the Senate's rejection of the reinstatement bill:[28]

> Let us keep at Congress and at the same time give our "great and glorious" country
> a showing in her own courts. Then if we lose at every point let us console ourselves
> with the fact that in case of conscription, we come in just ahead of the cripples.

The courts were no more sympathetic than the Congress, and the exiled
classmates remained beyond the pale. Those who survived the purge, however,
had learned one lesson; they had discovered that much of their opposition wore
"blue and gold" too. Senior officers such as Rear Admiral George Belknap still
vigorously opposed promotion reform such as "selection-up-or-out," or
"plucking." Selection was a "mild term for favoritism" to Belknap, "so evil
since political." Many senior officers regarded the promotion reform measures
introduced by the "Young Turks" to be the products of "a clique of ambitious
officers who want to get on top by whatever means they can bring to bear."
"A large majority of the older line officers openly and actively opposed us,"
one ensign-lobbyist wrote in late 1886. This opposition appeared to have
guaranteed their defeat. The ensign was not surprised. He reminded his classmates of the "selfishness" of that coterie of senior officers whose rank-conscious
scraps "remind one of the struggle of the Kilkenny cats." None the less, many
junior officers were furious at this "eager desire" on the part of the senior
members of the aristocracy "to prevent any of their fellow officers from securing
an advantage over them."
They reacted by arguing for the forced retirement of their elder adversaries.
In 1885 Navy Secretary William Whitney received a memorandum from one
of his junior aides arguing for "promotion by selection, in the form of special
advancement for the meritorious, an incentive at all times to application, zeal,
and good conduct." But others called for more drastic reform. *Old men and
old material must be got rid of at all hazards.* A "new life, a young life," must be
given to the Service "to prepare for the work so soon expected of it." Admiral
Porter had used the same argument in early 1862 when he tried to persuade the
Navy Department to recall and retire his rival, Flag Officer David Farragut.

"Men of his age in a seafaring life" were "not fit for the command of important **291** enterprises," Porter had advised Assistant Secretary Fox. They lacked "the vigor of youth." "To be successful we must have young men in command."[29] Porter was seventy-five in 1882.

One officer, Commander Joseph Coghlan, thought the whole business of the scramble for promotion was deplorable. He conveyed his perceptive thoughts on the matter to the editor of the *Vallejo Evening Chronicle*:

> The Line Officers are all mad and dissatisfied because they are not Admirals and Commodores. About all you hear aboard ship, is, "Well, Captain So and So is only so many years old. Now I am only two years younger, and yet, here I won't be a Captain for so many years, if I am at all. They (meaning the Government), ought to retire all men so old, or after so many years service," etc., etc., *ad nauseum*. . . . They seem to forget that the government never contracted to have wars or pestilences as common affairs, just for their benefit, for the purpose of killing off men who rank them.

Coghlan, extremely unpopular with junior officers, drew a general court-martial on charges of bringing discredit on the Service for making these observations public, but the court, composed entirely of rear admirals and captains, most of whom must have agreed with Coghlan's observations, speedily acquitted him.[30]

The intra-Service division was largely junior versus senior, but not all senior officers were unsympathetic. Morris Janowitz has postulated that "the lower the rank, the greater . . . the officer's sense of professional and service frustration." This certainly describes the situation with regard to the 1882 promotion law. But many greyhaired lieutenants, lieutenant commanders, and commanders, for whom the future held "no promise," also fought for promotion and materiel reform even if they, personally, could "derive no profit" from their labors. Just as Lee Benson's Anti-Federalists had in common an "agrarian-mindedness," so the naval aristocracy of the late nineteenth century must have seen many problems in a common light because of their Navy-mindedness. In spite of age and individual career interest, many a senior officer's life-long perspective led him to sympathize with the "young blood" striving to assert itself and to reinvest life in the Navy.*

Thus captains like William Sampson of the class of 1861, and commanders like Caspar Goodrich and Bowman McCalla, both of the class of '65, allied with "Young Turks" like Albert A. Ackerman ('80), William Fullam ('77), and Washington Irving Chambers ('76). In 1885 McCalla proposed promotion by selection, forced retirement, and the abolition of the practice of

---

* Thus in 1883 Commodore Robert W. Shufeldt (b. 1822) told Navy Secretary William E. Chandler of his hope that "the coming men" would "reform" the Service. (Cited in Fredrick Drake, ". . . Shufeldt . . .," Ph.D. thesis, 568.) Similarly, at least one senior Marine officer aided junior Marine officers in their struggle to "relieve the deplorable situation of the old officers as to promotion." Captain Henry Clay Cochrane to Colonel Charles Heywood, Oct. 22, 1891, Cochrane Papers, M.C. Museum, Quantico.

selecting paymasters from civilian life. Replacement of these supply officers by Academy graduates would create new billets for Annapolites. In 1888 Academy Superintendent Sampson argued before a Senate committee for an increase in the number of billets for Academy graduates in response to an appeal from the previous year's graduates who had found only 12 openings available for their class. "I wouldn't be too sure that promotion will be very slow [from now on]," Ensign John Bernadou wrote to Lieutenant (j.g.) George Foulk in the late '80s. "[T]he head of the Senior Lieutenants lists [sic] is being squeezed from both ends, and the cries of the selectionists are growing louder." Complaints of a weakening of the "feeling of comradeship and brotherhood among the officers," and of officers "watching one another to detect trivial errors" led to the creation of the Naval Academy Graduate Association in 1886. This organization sponsored regional and annual get-togethers to boost sagging morale during the "doldrum" years and was "a powerful means of keeping alive the feeling of devotion to the service" when many suffered from "slow promotion" and "a feeling of lack of appreciation."[31]

Many young line and staff officers went so far as to reject the logic of the perennial line-staff controversy and argued that the two branches should "combine for the general good." In 1890 three line ensigns and three assistant engineers actually collaborated to draft a bill that would guarantee both ranks promotion to lieutenant (j.g.) and its engineer equivalent upon the completion of ten years of service. "We cannot all be Nelson," one crusader remarked, "but we can and must be a band of brothers."[32]

The second response of junior officers to the 1882 promotion law and their perception of the state of the Service in the 1880s consisted of efforts to make their careers as functional and meaningful as possible. There was no inconsistency here; dissatisfaction with the promotion system and zealous attention to naval affairs were two sides of the same coin—a coin intended to buy naval reform and career security. With or without immediate promotion incentive, these sons of Horatio Alger and Horatio Nelson, filled with nineteenth-century American self-reliance and Annapolis-bred enthusiasm for the Navy, were possessed with what David McClelland calls a high "need for achievement." As early as 1868 junior officers sensed the significance to their careers of a "long peace." Lieutenant Commander Ira Harris assured Lieutenant Charles Mac-Gregor in that year the nation was not going to go to war for quite some time, "and the only chance for fellows like you and I, to get along, is to have a specialty and work hard at it." Alfred Mahan often maintained that "the only stimulus in peace to exertion beyond the simple line of duty" was one's interest in "matters professional for their own sake." This "sense of duty" or "professional enthusiasm" created initiative and sustained energy, "thus becoming a productive force for personal improvement, as well as for naval progress."*

---

* McClelland, *The Achieving Society* (Princeton, N.Y., 1961), 47; Harris to MacGregor, October 16, 1868, Folder 12, Box 209, N.H.F. Harris planned to become a naval constructor; MacGregor, a naval astronomer. Mahan, *Retrospect and Prospect.* 290; "Rear

In the 1880s, after the decommissioning of many of the old wooden vessels, none of which were allotted repair funds by 1883, many junior officers were forced ashore for periods of from three to five years. There, a more senior officer explained, they "naturally" became interested in "the absorbing question of rebuilding the Navy and providing the most improved armament" for the "new Navy." Key planning positions were not dished out to these ensigns and j.g.'s on a silver platter. Some, like Ensign Hiero Taylor of the Class of 1877, spent fifteen months in 1883–1884 on "waiting orders," at $66.66 per month. And once orders did come, they were seldom very exciting. Junior officers often found themselves in medial clerical positions in the innards of some bureau or yard, a status comparable at first appearance to their shipboard billets.[33]

But shore billets generally had more creative potential than ones at sea, where the Executive Officer or department head, armed with regulations, traditions, and prejudices, was never more than a few staterooms away. Ashore the younger men breathed more easily. Ensign Bernadou wrote Lieutenant (j.g.) Foulk in early 1887 of the "whole fields open" in the Service in a stateside shore billet. There was "a chance for a man like you to make a name. Look at your friend [W. I.] Chambers; he is fast going to the front." Foulk was advised to "go in for some professional specialty."[34] He resigned instead; but that did not alter Bernadou's argument. And for every George Foulk, who opted out, there was a Washington Irving Chambers ('76), a William F. Fullam ('77), a Bradley Fiske, ('74), or a William S. Sims, ('80) who stayed, "buoyed up by noble traditions" and "inspired by unsullied ideals," to build the "new Navy." And the senior officers who had damned the "Young Turks" for "launching out in a ruthless process of reconstructing [the naval] personnel [laws]," actively encouraged them to reconstruct the naval operating forces and support services.[35]

The contributions of junior officers to the creation of the "new Navy" in the 1880s were impressive. Assistant naval constructors such as Francis Bowles ('79),

---

Admiral William T. Sampson," *Fortnightly Review*, LXXVIII (1902), 232; *From Sail to Steam*, 103.

Morris Janowitz (*Professional Soldier*, 150–172) has found that there are a disproportionate number of officers with innovative, unorthodox career patterns in the elite nucleus of the military leadership in the recent past. Such "adaptive" career patterns are common among nineteenth and early twentieth century naval elite as well. It is my view that career anxieties are at the heart of these "adaptive" traits—anxieties not only for one's own career, but for the Service as a whole. "Young Turks" who "did their own thing" (even if it meant inventing it) were probably driven by the same forces that moved the more modern Hyman Rickovers—the Bradley Fiskes of the Atomic Age. Vincent Davis, describing recent naval innovators, maintains that the typical naval "innovation advocate" is "usually a man in the broad middle ranks . . . [who] has been in the organization (i.e., the Navy) long enough to have acquired an organization-wide perspective, and an affectionate concern for the welfare and the future of the whole organization." (Davis, *The Politics of Innovation: Patterns in Navy Cases* [Denver, 1967], 51–52.) See his *Postwar Defense Policy and the U.S. Navy*, and *The Admirals Lobby*, for the correlation in the modern age of career anxieties and naval innovation.

OUR NAVY.
Even Chili could warm U S.

By 1880 naval officers and some civilians were displaying considerable doubt about the ability of aging U.S. warships to stand against the more modern vessels of other nations (*Harper's Magazine*, 1881).

While Congress debated the merits of a "new navy" in the mid-1880s, Thomas Nast offered a plea for home-made American warships (*Harper's Magazine*, 1884).

The construction of the first four American-built steel warships in the mid-1880s **295**
was no guarantee that more were to follow, for there were several performance
deficiencies and "cost-overruns" with these vessels. This cartoon mocks the less
than successful July, 1885, trial run of the U.S.S. *Dolphin* (*Harper's Magazine*,
1885).

DOLPHIN. "Put me into a heavy sea, Secretary WHITNEY! Why, you'll want me to fire off a gun next!"

One key bastion of the Navy's "Young Turks" in the late nineteenth century was the Office of Naval Intelligence, created in 1882. Commander Charles H. Davis and his assistants are shown in this 1890 photo of the main office (Naval Photographic Center).

The first elements of the "new navy," forming the "Squadron of Evolution" in 1889. Left to right: *Chicago, Yorktown, Boston, Atlanta* (Detroit Collection, Library of Congress).

The Navy's "Young Turks" found Captain A. T. Mahan's Naval War College lectures on naval history and strategy to be moderately useful to their cause, but archaic and boring. "War gaming" they found more functional and up-to-date. Note the presence of Chinese stewards in the background of Rufus Fairchild Zobgaum's 1894 rendition of a naval war game problem at the War College (*Harper's Magazine*, 1895).

As a naval historian in the 1880s, as Assistant Navy Secretary in 1897–98, and as President, Theodore Roosevelt often sided with the Navy's "Young Turks." Here he is seen in the company of students and instructors at the Naval War College, *circa* 1902 (U.S. Naval Institute).

Richard Gatewood ('79), Washington L. Capps ('84), Lewis Nixon ('82), Homer Ferguson ('82), Ira N. Hollis ('78), and Holden Evans ('92) brought ideas home from the Royal Navy people at Glasgow and Greenwich and were assigned to shipyards all over the U.S. Capps was an ensign until he changed his designation to assistant constructor in 1888. By 1903 he was Chief of the Bureau of Construction and Repair, and thus head of the Construction Corps, a position that rated flag rank—all before he was forty-five.[36]

Ordnance inventors of the 1880s included Seaton Schroeder ('68), Frank Fletcher ('75), Francis Haeseler ('80), Robert Dashiell ('81), William Jaques ('67), C. A. Stone ('68), John B. Bernadou ('80), J. A. Barber ('71), Joseph Strauss ('85), and Bradley Fiske. Only one had risen to the rank of Lieutenant Commander by the '80s. Many studied British techniques. Lieutenant Jaques was made secretary to the gun-foundry board in 1883. Shortly thereafter he was sent to Britain to study Sir Joseph Whitworth's hydraulic forging press. He finally resigned in 1887, but his reports and recommendations were vital to the armor production processes established at Pittsburgh by 1890.[37]

Other "Young Turks," among them Fiske, Frank Sprague ('79), David Taylor ('85), William Emmet ('81), and Louis Duncan ('80), pioneered in electrical and hydroelectrical inventions and in important steam turbine modifications in these years. Fiske, whose *Electricity in Theory and Practice* appeared in 1883 while he was attached to the Bureau of Ordnance, patented no fewer than 17 key inventions—among them the battle-order telegraph, the hydroelectric turret train, the stadimeter, the telescopic sight, the first electric gun director system, and the first electric interior communications system. Academy Chronicler Park Benjamin, who scorned the "theoretical" or "philosophical" spirit, was more generous to the "useful" mind, the engineer. And the record indicates that the Academy produced more than its share of these "useful" scientists.[38]

Since the task of rebuilding the Navy involved frequent and often prolonged relationships with captains of industry, it was not surprising that some inventors and engineer-managers, when asked to take their "stand as a Naval officer or as an inventor," chose to leave the Navy. Their talents went to American industry, but their affections remained with their beloved Service.[39] Such future industrial leaders as Lewis Nixon ('82), J. W. Powell ('97), and Robert Thompson ('68) would also be founding fathers of the Navy League. And those who were assigned to billets at industrial sites and chose to remain in the Navy, men like Caspar Goodrich and Robley Evans, both of whom had learned managerial techniques from Fredrick Taylor himself, brought these skills to bear on naval problems.

It was these managerial experiences that provoked Lieutenant C. C. Rogers ('76) to call for administrative reform, and it was these same managerial skills that made possible the installation on the U.S.S. *Minnesota* in 1905 of the Sims-Scott continuous-aim fire control system. Consequently, the views of two civilian efficiency experts who inspected the *Minnesota* were predictable:[40]

The synchronization of gun operations, fire control, and engine room was a model exhibition of scientific management—stopwatch work, no waste effort, no lost motion, but every movement standardized and unified to the shortest possible time.

"The subject of naval reorganization seems now to be in the air and to occupy naval thought," one officer observed in 1886. Whether that subject was Navy yards, supply systems, enlisted personnel, war planning, or fleet maneuvers, every aspect of the naval establishment was subjected to the test of efficiency. Pork-barrel navy yard politics might be essential to the vitality of local political machines, but they clashed with the more functional objectives of the builders of the "new Navy" and were condemned. The shortcomings of the fragmented bureau system demonstrated the need for the "introduction of business methods into our system of naval administration." Managers trained to "think for the railroad," by correlating the various facets of the company and noting the activity of rival lines and local legislators, could "watch the future and prepare, their systems to draw all possible advantage from events . . . ." These skills long "employed by the great commercial companies," could be utilized by a trained Navy General Staff as well. Vital military resources, such as oil and steel, should be developed with "method and system" and an eye for the future. Discipline should be redesigned to breed coordination rather than the less efficient subordination. Efficiency ("E") awards should be granted to vessels with low rates of fuel consumption or high rates of target destruction. Sailors should receive national citizenship training. In short, every aspect of naval life was to be rationalized and put in harmony with the mission of the "new Navy" in the coming American Century.[41]

Invention and managerial reorganization were but two of the talents young officers exercised. Others included the writing of naval history; the drafting of fresh surveys of inlets, harbors, and seas; the publication of exploration and navigation treatises; and the analyses of foreign cultures, economies, and naval establishments.[42] The publications of U.S. naval officers gradually increased in number throughout the late nineteenth century, reaching a peak during the Spanish-American War, but the 1880s appear to have been a kind of "take-off" period, a decade in which all naval publications increased by 80% over those of the previous decade and the publications of junior officers nearly tripled. A certain measure of this steadily increasing output may be attributed to the concurrent growth of American publishing, but much of the high rate of growth is properly viewed as a function of the increased industry of the Navy's "Young Turks." Not surprisingly, by 1912 senior officers who had participated in the "naval revolution" of the late nineteenth century and had witnessed its results felt that "our profession demands that we should . . . heartily encourage every officer who is trying to *do something*. We need do-ers in the Navy," one veteran of the doldrums of the 1880s observed.[43]

Among the more active "Young Turks" were those attached to the Office of Naval Intelligence. Inspired by British views on naval intelligence, and possibly by Lorenz von Stein's *Lehre vom Heerwesen* (1872), a group of lieutenants, headed by Theodorus Mason ('68), persuaded Commodore John G. Walker, Chief of the Bureau of Navigation, to create the Office in 1882. Thereafter, young naval attachés were dispatched as overt spies to London, Berlin, Paris, Vienna, St. Petersburg, Rome, and other capitals. The list of officers so ordered in the '80s and '90s includes several of the leading naval activists of the day—Mason, Nathan Sargent ('70), French Chadwick ('65), William S. Sims ('80), Charles Vreeland ('70), and William Emory ('66). By 1914 the United States had more attachés abroad than any other nation. The O.N.I.'s many publications served as media through which activist naval strategy found expression. Thus in 1889 one O.N.I. volume, entitled *Naval Mobilization and Improvement in Materiel*, contained a piece by Lieutenant Sidney A. Staunton ('71) which called for formal war planning and a naval general staff and an essay by Lieutenant John Forsythe Meigs ('67) calling for a "gun control" system and more gunfire exercises.[44]

By 1880 a Torpedo School was operating at Newport, training future destroyer captains, and in 1893 M.I.T. initiated a Naval Architecture program that was to provide many of the designers of the Navy of the twentieth century. Activists at the Naval Academy were helping to provide "practical and progressive" courses in electricity, construction, photography, steam engineering, and modern gunnery.[45] Others argued for the creation of a naval postgraduate school to provide advanced training in math, mechanics, physics, chemistry, astronomy, metallurgy, torpedoes and ordnance, shiphandling, naval architecture, steam engineering, international law, naval history, strategy, and tactics. The plan of Commodore Stephen Luce ('48) for a naval war college that would focus on the last four subjects did not satisfy the more progressive of the younger officers, but when it became clear that the Navy Department and its senior naval advisors would approve of no more extensive a program of postgraduate training than Luce's scheme encompassed, the progressives accepted the Luce War College—and made the best of it.[46] After all, as Army Colonel Emory Upton had told Luce in 1878, a war college could "keep the officers occupied as one means of preventing reduction of the Navy."[47]

The Concept of Sea Power

Most historians fix 1882 as the date of the beginnings of the "new Navy," since the 1882 Naval Appropriations Act paved the way for the first U.S.-built armored cruisers. Such a date *seems* reasonable—from our twentieth century vantage. But it must be recalled that these first warships were created on an altogether experimental basis,* and that further expenditures were slow in coming. As late as 1886 legislators and junior officers alike were convinced that the U.S. Navy continued to decline in calibre and prestige relative to the navies of other nations.[48] "There is a good time coming—in the far distance—however," one young officer wrote his mother in 1886, "when we *hope* to have a

---

* See Nast's *Dolphin* cartoon, p. 295.

few vessels that we will not be afraid or ashamed to show to foreign powers, and **301** that will keep up the dignity of the great American Republic."⁴⁹ The "good time coming" was not the result of chance or unsolicited legislative generosity. Young officers could foresee increases in naval appropriations because they had a hand in the creation of the climate of opinion that nurtured this growth of the "new Navy" in the late 1880s and early 1890s.

As every young officer knew, an increase in the number and size of commissioned warships meant an increase in the number of officers required to man them, with a consequent increase in the rate of promotion. In 1859, after just such an increase in the number of commissioned vessels, Captain George Blake, Superintendent of the Academy, told a fresh graduate, "Mr. Mahan, you will [all] be lieutenants before you can turn around...." Thus it was natural to expect that the Navy's "Young Turks" of the 1880s would make every effort to increase the number of vessels on the lists or, at the very least, to retain the same number of vessels in commission. "Any reduction would stop promotion, already very slow, and would cause dissatisfaction and want of zeal," as Lieutenant R. M. G. Brown ('68) had put it in 1881.⁵⁰

The "Young Turks," therefore, constituted a body of amateur but aggressive Navy public relations men. They did what they could to improve the public image of the Service. "If you fellows want good appropriations," one class of 1881 Annapolite wrote his classmates, "prevent the spread of the idea that the Navy and the Army are 'aristocracies.'" In or out of the Service, every naval aristocrat was expected to "lose no opportunity" to "sell" the Navy to any prominent relation, friend, or member of Congress he might "happen to know." There was nothing new here. The Line Officers Association, a naval lobby organized shortly after the Civil War, had long urged officers to coordinate their efforts to influence Congress "on questions relating to naval subjects." The practice was a hoary and dignified one. But Mahan's messmates worked harder at lobbying than had their predecessors. They believed that the times demanded such effort. "The Nazareth of public opinion" was not overly responsive to "service needs" in the 1880s, as Lieutenant J. D. Jerrold Kelley put it in 1892, and "foolish critics" had begun "to clamor for [the Navy's] extinction."⁵¹

> And so it went from bad to worse, until in sheer desperation the remedy had, at last, to come from within the service. A number of officers... began a campaign of education.

The first, and perhaps most amenable,* targets of this campaign were the special industries affected by naval construction—shipbuilders, steel firms, and

---

* Dean Allard has indicated that it was naval officers who provoked the American Iron and Steel Association to agitate, in 1885 and 1886, for more warships (Allard, "The Influence of the U.S. Navy upon the American Steel Industry, 1880–1900," unpub. M.A. essay, Georgetown Univ., 1919, pp. 61–64). Concurrently, in Germany Kaiser Wilhelm urged naval officers to publish *Marine Rundschau* more frequently, and to try to involve "that part of private industry which profits directly" from naval development. (Jonathan Steinberg, *Yesterday's Deterrent: Tirpitz and the Birth of the German Battle Fleet* [London, 1965], 100.)

302 weapons manufacturers. These interest groups, Rear Admiral Thornton Jenkins told a Naval Institute audience in 1885, should be led to "recognize their opportunity, and find that their interests lie in supporting our efforts." From the Office of Naval Intelligence and other Bureau of Navigation retreats of "Young Turks" and their sympathizers came a steady stream of "Naval Professional Papers," distributed throughout the 1880s "to manufacturers who might be interested in their contents."[52]

The second target of this "campaign of education" was that group of businessmen and lobbyists affiliated with the U.S. merchant marine. U.S. merchantmen and naval officers had always enjoyed cordial relations in the various ports of call throughout the world. The camaraderie of nautical life and the merchantman's occasional reliance on naval power drew the two services together. The merchant marine had suffered considerable attrition during the Civil War. Whereas American-registered vessels carried 75% of all U.S. trade in 1856, they carried only 17.5% of that trade in 1880. Moreover, since 1836, naval officers,

Some "Young Turks" . . .

John Bernadou, '80
(*Harper's Magazine*).
See p. 293.

Francis Tiffany Bowles' '79
(J. D. Long, *The New
American Navy*). P. 293.

Washington Irving Chambers,
'76 (*National Cyclopedia of
Biography*). Pp. 293, 309.

Chambers of Commerce, Boards of Trade, shipowners, shipbuilders, shipmasters, underwriters, and ship commission merchants had been offering parallel arguments for the creation of government-supported schools for merchant seamen.

In 1873 New York City was authorized by the U.S. Congress to set up a Maritime Academy for young merchantmen at Fort Schyler under the direction of Captain Robert Phythian, U.S.N. Consequently, it is not surprising that naval officers thought of the merchant marine in their mutual hour of need. The interests of the two services, in the words of Lieutenant R. M. G. Brown, were "so closely bound together" that "when speaking of the rebuilding of one we must necessarily provide for the other." Ensign William David won the Institute's essay prize in 1882 with a paper on the state of the U.S. merchant marine, but he made the order of his loyalties quite clear. "It does not follow," he told his fellow officers, "that a strong navy will produce a merchant marine;

but the reverse does follow." Every blow dealt for the "revival" of the merchant marine was a blow dealt for the "new Navy." Commander N. H. Farquhar, who chaired the meeting at which David's paper was read, told the assemblage that, "as naval officers, we should keep the subject of the revival of the merchant marine before the public, for its revival will benefit the Navy." A year later Captain A. P. Cooke told a similar group of officers that closer relations between merchant mariners and the Navy "would very materially increase the

John M. Ellicott, '83 (Lewis Hamersly, *The Records of Living Officers of the U.S. Navy,* 1902 edition). See p. 387.

Bradley Fiske, '74 (Lewis Hamersly, *The Records of Living Officers of the U.S. Navy,* 1902 edition). See p. 298.

sphere of usefulness of navy officers." And in 1890 Ensign J. B. Bernadou repeated the point. The best way to "obtain a powerful navy" was to "build up a merchant service":[53]

> As soon as our flag floats over American merchantmen upon all seas of the world the great private interests at stake will develop a national character, and a need of adequate protection for investment will be felt—a protection only to be offered by numerous and powerful squadrons of vessels of war.

Naval officers consistently argued for federal legislation that might aid the U.S. merchant marine,[54] but fundamentally they had the interests of their own service in mind.[55]

A third target of the "campaign of education" was the American public, the most important and most difficult of the three. "The navy is not popular with the people at large," one officer confided to a colleague in 1874, "and our existence depends on our keeping up a high standard of usefulness." Lieutenant Theodorus B. M. Mason maintained in 1879 that the U.S. Naval Institute should serve as "the bureau of [public] information of the navy" and that all

William F. Fullam, '77, and fiancée (Naval Photographic Center). See pp. 89, 329.

papers, historical as well as current, should be related to "the questions of the day." In 1881 the junior editor of the Naval Institute's *Proceedings*, Lieutenant Charles Belknap ('67), solicited manuscripts from accomplished naval writers "upon points connected with the history of our Navy"; but Belknap insisted that these papers be drafted in such a manner as to illuminate the Navy's role in national affairs "as much as possible." In 1882 the Naval Institute offered a prize

J. D. J. Kelley, '68 (N. J. K. Cook, *J. D. J. Kelley, Commander, U.S.N.*). P. 308.

William Wirt Kimball, '69 (Naval Photographic Center). See pp. 167*n*, 329.

Theodorus B. M. Mason, '68 (Naval Photographic Center). See pp. 300, 303.

for the best essay on the subject "How May the Sphere of Usefulness of Naval Officers be Extended in Time of Peace with Advantage to the Country and the Naval Service." First place went to Lieutenant Carlos G. Calkins ('71), whose essay began by describing the effect of the Act of August 5, 1882, on officers of "the rising generation." Calkins doubted that he and his messmates could ever find "security" until the "usefulness of naval officers" were to become "a fact admitted by the organs and representatives of public opinion." He recommended an aggressive public relations effort designed to prove the value of the Service to the public at large. There could be no more "pre-scientific" or purely literary offerings from the pens of the naval aristocracy. All material prepared for publication now had to be polemical and tightly reasoned. Historical offerings had to illuminate the Navy's key function in national affairs.

Assistant Navy Secretary James Russell Soley (Naval Photographic Center). See pp. 307, 321.

Officers were told they would "escape from obscurity" by bearing this message of usefulness to the public. "Slowly but surely," Captain Henry Clay Taylor observed, "the naval mind, groping for something tangible to base itself upon in these thoroughly professional questions, settles upon the experience of past wars as the only foundation of knowledge, and realizes that in the study of naval history lies the key to the problem."[56] Most of the papers printed in the *Proceedings* throughout the '80s and '90s were not historical, but all—whether they dealt with history, tactics, administration, materiel, construction, national strategy, or naval planning—carried the same argument: The U.S. needs more warships.

At the heart of each argument lay one principle with which every one of the "band of brothers" was familiar—warships were invaluable aids to U.S. businessmen abroad. In the nineteenth century the foreign offices of many U.S.-owned commercial firms left "spare seats at the dinner table every day" which naval officers were expected to fill without formal invitation whenever they were ashore. These merchants knew the many uses of the Navy. It was the great mass of American businessmen, with local concerns far from these African, Asiatic, and Latin American marts, who were generally less conscious of the Navy's importance to their livelihoods and consequently less enthusiastic about new ships. "Our business men practically control our national expenditures,"

306   Lieutenant William Wirt Kimball observed. Those immersed in domestic pursuits simply had to be made aware of the Navy's role in facilitating the movement of cattle, grains, cotton goods, manufactured goods, and other raw and finished commodities to and from the "Great Middle Kingdom" and her foreign markets and sources of supply. The "history of trade" surely told one clear story: There was "no diplomatic sentence so short as *'justice* or *shells.'*"[57]

Men like Professor James Russell Soley, Ensigns W. I. Chambers ('76) and William David ('77), Lieutenant (junior grade) C. G. Calkins ('71), Lieutenants Theodorus Mason ('68), Charles Belknap ('67), Richard Wainwright ('68),

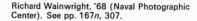

Richard Wainwright, '68 (Naval Photographic Center). See pp. 167*n*, 307.   French Ensor Chadwick, '65 (Naval Photographic Center). See p. 357.

J. D. J. Kelley ('68), R. M. G. Brown ('68), Fredrick Collins ('67), and C. C. Todd ('66), and Commanders William Bainbridge-Hoff ('64), Caspar Goodrich ('65), French Chadwick ('65), and Bowman McCalla ('65) outdid one another throughout the 1880s in their published efforts to persuade the public of the historical value of the Navy to commerce. "The voice of history" was clear, wrote Lieutenant Collins. "In all nations commercial supremacy and naval power have gone hand in hand." And he was echoed by Charles Belknap and a host of other members of the Navy's "rising generation" over the next decade. In appealing to the past to demonstrate the necessity of the Navy to protect one's commerce, Ensign David ranged back to the days of the Phoenicians, Carthaginians, and Romans and then up to the more recent Venetian, Spanish, Dutch, and British empires to prove the importance of sea power; while Lieutenant (j.g.) Calkins was satisfied in offering the English-Dutch naval struggles of the seventeenth century to establish that "[a]lmost every memorable epoch in the history of the nations has been connected more or less intimately with a battle on the sea."[58]

The importance of the "command of the sea," of fleet tactics, heavy guns and armor, concentrated forces, and available coaling stations were frequently underscored. "All naval strategists are agreed," Lieutenant Wainwright remarked, "that ... commerce destroyers ... will have little effect on the ultimate results of [a] War." "If we look upon the vessels of our Navy as 'commerce destroyers' we make a grievous mistake," young Academy professor James Russell Soley told an 1878 Naval Institute meeting chaired by a Commander Alfred Thayer Mahan.* And Lieutenant John Forsythe Meigs made the

Some of their "Allies" . . .

Robley Evans, '64 (Lewis Hamersly, *The Records of Living Officers of the U.S. Navy*). See p. 355.

Caspar Goodrich, '65 (Naval Photographic Center). See pp. 328, 358.

William Bainbridge-Hoff, '64 (Naval Photographic Center). See p. 353.

same point in an 1887 Naval War College lecture: "History positively stamps [the commerce-raiding strategy] as false. ... The control of the sea has ... powerfully contributed to deciding great wars and the fate of nations." Fleet actions with battleships were the only sensible ways of waging naval warfare.[59] The isthmian regions of Central America were cited as strategic objectives of the highest value. Virtually every article or book included the admonition that the day was not distant "when our increasing manufactures shall exceed the needs of our own people, and when our commerce shall be reaching out to the markets of the world."[60] In short, history, day-to-day observation, and common sense all established that the nation's health and growth required trade expansion and commercial security abroad, and that a strong Navy, capable of taking the offensive, was a prerequisite for such development.†

* Bowman McCalla remembered Soley's lectures at the Naval Academy in the early 1880s in the same glowing terms that others were to recall Mahan's at the War College in the late 1880s. "Memoirs," Ch. XI, 21.

† Thus Walter Herrick, Jr.'s recent remark that the articles written for the *Proceedings* in the 1880s reveal an isolationist, rather than a expansionist or imperialist, bent of mind is simply incorrect. Herrick, *The American Naval Revolution* (Baton Rouge, 1966), 24.

One officer, Lieutenant Commander H. H. Gorringe, took a different tack. He felt the best means of "gaining public sympathy and support" was to stress the Navy's role in exploration and surveying. *North Amer. Rev.*, CXXXIV (1882), 498. But such a position as Gorringe's was exceptional, and Gorringe was not an Annapolite but a gentleman explorer who joined the Service in the Civil War and resigned shortly after this essay was published.

308   Many young officers excelled in this task of persuasive essaying, but two
names deserve particular mention—Lieutenant J. D. Jerrold Kelley and Ensign
Washington Irving Chambers.

Kelley's ornate style and statistics-laden argument made him one of the
more popular* and successful naval publicists. In 1884 he obtained orders to duty
at James Gordon Bennett's New York *Herald*, where he could bring his "new
Navy" salesmanship directly to bear on the public's pulse.[61] Kelley called for a
host of subsidized merchant vessels as "essential instrumentalities" for the retention of new "foreign markets" for "our enormous productive surplus"—in
particular that of the agrarian sector of the economy. Americans were urged to

Bowman McCalla, '65 (Navy History Division,
Navy Department). See p. 291.

William Sampson, '61 (J. D. Long, *The New
American Navy*). Pp. 292, 327, 357.

assume their "place in the world" both in order to "assert the natural rights of
man wherever such may be assailed" and to bring prosperity to the "Great
Middle Kingdom." Commercial supremacy and naval power had gone "hand
in hand in all countries," Kelley wrote in 1884, borrowing Collins' 1879
phrase. Sea power determined "the fitness of a nation":

> Prosperity on land is the handmaiden of power at sea, and whose is the ocean, his also
> are the lands around and about it.

Coaling stations, an isthmian canal, and fleet tactics were vital, as, of course,
was "an efficient and powerful [naval] war machine." Congressmen were too
partisan and "political" to do the patriotic thing and unite to order the necessary

* A. F. Matthews, for example, wrote of "the ever-delightful Kelley, the *littérateur* of
the Navy—a pleasant breeze blowing through the rigging." *Harper's Weekly*, XXXVIII
(1894), 327.

appropriations. "Action, action, action is needed." Kelley appealed to "the **309** people" for aid in the great work that lay ahead.[62]

Ensign Washington Irving Chambers, whose essay, "The Reconstruction and Increase of the Navy," won the *Proceedings* prize in early 1885, was highly regarded by his classmates and messmates for his "many ideas of how things should be." "A prize essay published by so important a body as the Naval

... and Some of their "Conservative" Foes.

Silas Terry, '60 (*National Cyclopedia of Biography*). See p. 329.

Joseph Coghlan, '64 (Naval Photographic Center). See p. 291.

Charles Gridley, '64 (J. D. Long, *The New American Navy*). See p. 327.

Institute goes before the world stamped with a rare authority," or so Lieutenant Commander Caspar Goodrich vaunted in commenting on the Chambers essay. In any event, the essay gave Chambers considerable visibility and prestige within the naval aristocracy. "*You* are the man for the profession," one well-wishing friend advised him in 1886.

Like many of his friends, Chambers was humiliated by the "evil impotency" into which the Service had degenerated. Like his friend, Lieutenant Theodorus Mason, Chambers was tired of being considered a "useless member of the community and an unnecessary expense." He saw the "influence" Britain's Navy exerted as "insurance on the prosperity of its nation's industries." Like Kelley, he hoped to "arouse" the American voter to a more honorable and "patriotic" state of naval consciousness, though he was quick to point out that naval construction stimulated the economy. He designed a rocket-torpedo and a heavy cruiser and called for legislation that would provide a host of exciting dreams: battleships capable of eighteen knots with cruising radii of fifteen thousand miles, frequent tactical exercises stressing concentrated fire power, the acquisition of a number of "strategic" coaling stations, the use of "liquid fuel" (oil) instead of coal, "transports" and "supply ships" capable of sustaining offensive forces far from their bases, government subsidy of the U.S. merchant marine, and the naming of a professional naval officer to the vacant post of Assistant Navy Secretary. Only after all of these things had come to pass, Chambers concluded, would "the rising generation" hold its head high. "The country, secure against invasion, prosperous in all its branches," would then "have reached a state of perfect accord."[63] The Heavenly City, the millennium, was to be revealed by gunsight and sextant.

The officers of "the rising generation" were in the van of the movement to demonstrate the importance of naval power to the public in the 1880s, but on this score they met with very little opposition in the Service. "Young Turks" and "Old Salts" were all potential navalists. In early 1890 the Navy Policy Board, created by Secretary Benjamin Franklin Tracy and headed by Commodore W. P. McCann ('54), warned of the dependence of "the enormous home industries and inland transportation" upon seaborne trade routes, noted the steady increase in exports, and called for a greater Navy and the acquisition of strategic depots. And the Navy Policy Board officers had many predecessors, all active before the appearance of Captain Mahan's *Influence of Sea Power upon*

Benjamin Lamberton, '65 (*National Cyclopedia of Biography*). P. 358.

Stephen B. Luce, '49 (Naval Museum). Pp. 327, 356.

Alfred T. Mahan, '59 (Naval Museum). Pp. 285, 335, 342,

History. In 1889 Admiral Luce had given readers of the *North American Review* numerous historical examples of the role of foreign commerce in national prosperity and the dependence of commerce on powerful "offensive" fleets. In 1888 Admiral D. D. Porter had called for Pacific coaling stations and a greater Navy to compete with Britain for the Oriental markets. Captain A. P. Cooke had offered readers of the *Public Service Review* the same argument in 1887; and in 1884 Commodore Luce, Commander William Sampson, and Lieutenant Commander Caspar Goodrich, the "War College" Board, had recommended the study of the historical importance of sea power in order to improve the nation's ability to comprehend the uses of "the floating force of the country."[64]

These arguments might be deemed mere reflections of those of Kelley, Chambers, and company, were it not for the fact that prior to 1880 numerous officers had also pointed out the historical importance of sea power and argued for the creation of great navies. From 1865 to 1882 Rear Admirals Daniel Ammen and Francis Roe, Commodores George Ransom and Robert Shufeldt,

Captains Stephen Luce and Francis Ramsay, Commander R. W. Meade, 3rd, **311** and Admiral David Dixon Porter frequently noted "the influence exercised by ... naval power" in the creation of national prosperity and strength. "Whichever navy had the ascendancy, the commerce which it protected also gained the advantage," Admiral Porter wrote in 1882, adding, "What gives England her prestige as the leading nation of the world but her navy ... ?" Commodore Robert Shufeldt's 1878 essay on *The Relation of the Navy to the Commerce of the United States* styled the Navy and the merchant marine "joint apostles, destined to carry over the world the [American] creed. . . ." "The nation that controls the sea controls the world," Commander Meade told a House Naval Affairs Committee in 1876. The 1865 annual naval report stressed the interdependence of "commerce and the Navy," and insisted that "both are essential to national prosperity and strength." And Lieutenant Commander Roe told his readers of Salamis, Lepanto, the Armada, and Trafalgar, and linked them to the fates of Persia, Turkey, Spain, and Napoleon.[65]

Admiral David D. Porter, b. 1807 (Naval Photographic Center). See pp. 285, 291, 328.

George Remey, '59 (Naval Photographic Center). See p. 358.

Commerce raiding was a lively strategic precept in post–Civil War years, to be sure, but for good reason. Commerce raiders were difficult to detect in pre-air and pre-radar days. Nevertheless, the commerce-raiding, single-ship strategy alone was rarely regarded as sufficient. Concentrated force was deemed superior to single cruiser tactics. "We could not ... carry on a foreign war in our old-fashioned way of fighting single ships," Lieutenant Commander Roe insisted in 1865. "We must fight squadrons and fleets now. . . . " The command of the sea lanes was a fully respected strategic objective. "When we have a war," Vice-Admiral Porter wrote to Naval Constructor John Lenthall in 1867, "the question will be . . . who can longest keep the sea." Admiral Porter had to

312   consider commerce-raiding as an alternative strategy, to be sure, but it must be
kept in mind that these were years of internal development and naval parsimony.
Leaders of what Lance Buhl has aptly called "the smooth-water Navy" simply
had to make the best of the existing Congressional appropriation limits.
Post-Civil War Congresses couldn't be persuaded to build vast iron-clad fleets,
though they were willing to consider an occasional coast defense craft or commerce raider. Naval officers who called for such vessels, then, were not necessarily poor strategists; they were more often simply politically astute, and
practical. Similarly, sail or a combination of steam and sail was often compared
favorably to steam propulsion alone, not because Porter and his officers were
ignorant reactionaries, as some have claimed, but primarily because they knew
that the United States had an insufficient number of coaling stations to support
a coal-burning fleet far from home waters. Time and time again Porter and his
associates attempted to persuade their civilian superiors in Congress and the
Executive Department of the merits of acquisition of the Sandwich Islands,
Samoa, Samara Bay in Santo Domingo, or the Isthmus of Darien. Naval
officers of the post-Civil War era were thoroughly familiar with the concept of
sea power in all of its ramifications.[66]

But to say that members of the post-Civil War naval aristocracy understood
the concept of sea power is not to say that pre-Civil War American naval
officers were unfamiliar with this same concept, which Captain A. T. Mahan
was to popularize in the 1890s. They, no less than their postwar descendants,
sensed the historical function navies had played in the creation of empires.
Captain S. F. DuPont knew that the function of the Navy in 1852 was aggressive,
"to contend for the mastery of the seas. . . . " " On the ocean," wrote Chaplain
Walter Colton, U.S.N., in 1851, "thrones have been lost and won. On the fate
of Actium was suspended the empire of the world. In the Gulf of Salamis, the
pride of Persia found a grave. . . . " Concurrently Lieutenant George Emmons
pointed out that navies had determined "the supremacy of Empire six hundred
years before our Savior's advent upon earth."

Similarly, mid-nineteenth century members of the naval aristocracy sensed
the relationship of commerce, island outposts, navies, and national power.
The Navy consciously guarded commerce, "the great source of national wealth,"
in 1839 just as it did half a century later. Many a mid-nineteenth century naval
officer coveted the Sandwich Islands for their strategic value. And, of course, all
hoped for a larger navy. Merchantmen required "protection." The Navy
therefore required "augmentation." Thus argued such men as Lieutenant
Matthew Fontaine Maury and Commanders Andrew Foote and John Rodgers
in the 1840s and '50s.[67]

With these examples of "Mahanite" thought in mind, it seems clear that
(a) those who believe that "U.S. naval thought before Mahan had hardly
progressed beyond coastal defense and commerce raiding"[68] misunderstood
pre-Mahanite navalists; (b) those who claim that, prior to Mahan, "comparatively little was said about the Navy as an agency for promoting foreign trade"[69]

are mistaken; (c) those who believe that the naval aristocracy, young and old, was slow in accepting Mahan's philosophy of sea power[70] underestimate Mahan's messmates; and (d) those who attribute the naval expansion and strategy of the 1890s and thereafter largely to Mahan are like those who ascribe all black unrest in America today to H. Rap Brown.[71] To suggest that naval officers would have gone about their business for the greater part of their lives without sensing and articulating the concept of sea power is being rather hard on the officer corps. Yet this is what those who isolate and magnify Captain Mahan appear to be saying.

It would be equally unreasonable to suggest that the idea of sea power was something that could find life only in naval circles. As Admiral Porter himself wrote in 1870, "I do not . . . claim any originality for the views [on sea power] I have expressed, for they must be shared by thousands of our intelligent countrymen." Army officers such as Ulysses S. Grant and Captain Mahan's father, Dennis Hart Mahan, sensed them. And so did a host of nonmilitary essayists and statesmen. In 1881 Henry Hall's plea for a renovated merchant marine and Samuel McCall's "plea for a strong navy" were both laden with historical analogies and talk of commercial security. Scribners, the publishers of the three-volume *Navy in the Civil War* series, spoke in their advertisements of America's "powers at sea." A good many publicists and Congressmen in the 1880s, as Robert Seager and William A. Williams have pointed out, were conscious of the role that naval and mercantile strength played in the nation's economic life and were already calling for a fleet able to "protect us *en route* to new countries for the development of our commerce and for the sale or barter of the increasing surplus productions of our soil and factories."[72]

Some of this civilian consciousness in the 1880s of the role of sea power may be attributable to the efforts of young officers to rescue their profession from the "doldrums." It is difficult to determine the degree of "influence" that men like Kelley, Chambers, Chadwick, Luce, or Porter exercised with policy makers, just as it is difficult to evaluate the role of the works of Captain Mahan in the shaping of post-1890 naval policy. In any event, the concept was not something restricted to the 1880s in civilian circles. Throughout the nineteenth century writers like Charles Cowley, Henry Barnard, W. V. McKean, Francis Parkman, George Reynolds, and Samuel Eliot, as well as many Congressmen, were conscious of the commercial and naval value of "supremacy on the sea." They spoke of the need for "coal depots, and docks and machine-shops, established in ports easy of access" scattered at great distances "all over the commercial world," and of "well-chosen colonies." And they called for a strong Navy "to which the successes of [commercial] business undertakings are principally due."[73]

But the idea of "sea power" was not born in the nineteenth century. Langdon Cheves, James Monroe, Thomas Clark, David Humphreys, William Henry Drayton, John Adams, George Washington, Alexander Hamilton, Thomas Jefferson, Gouverneur Morris, Edmund Randolph, and James Madison, to name but a few of the "founding fathers" who held "Mahanite" views, all spoke of

314   the role navies and merchant marines played in the creation of empires. "[T]he maritime states," Drayton pointed out, had always had "the greatest influence upon the affairs of the universe." "The trident of Neptune is the scepter of the world," John Adams wrote in 1802. After noting the role of sea power for Greece, Rome, England, Holland, and France over the centuries, Adams observed that since "the great questions of commerce and power between nations and empires" were answerable only by naval force, and since all issues of "war and peace are determined at sea, all reasonable encouragement should be given to the Navy." Early American policy makers had understood the concept of sea power.[74]

The Founding Fathers had not been, any more than Porter, Chambers, or Mahan, the only ones to "discover" these principles. In spite of all the pomp and circumstance attending Captain Mahan's reception in Britain in 1894, the truths Englishmen claimed Mahan had revealed to them had been fully understood by generation after generation of Englishmen. The emergence of mid-Victorian island-defense strategy, sponsored by an economy-minded Gladstone government and a burgeoning British Army, imperiled naval professionalism in Britain in much the same way that the Act of August 5, 1882, imperiled it in America; and the British response was just as vigorous. Like the "Young Turks" across the sea, the "blue-water school" of Sir John Knox Laughton, William Laird Clowes, Admiral R. Vesey-Hamilton, Admiral Sir Astley Cooper-Key, Rear Admiral Philip H. Colomb, Captain Sir John C. R. Colomb, and their associates had waged a vigorous publicity campaign for a new British Navy in the 1880s, culminating in the Naval Defence Act of 1889. Indeed, the "blue-water" navalists were in some ways more sophisticated in their understanding of the role of sea power in history than their American counterparts.[75] Laughton's *Studies in Naval History*, published as articles throughout the 1870s and '80s, John Colomb's *Defence of Great and Greater Britain* (1880), Philip Colomb's "Great Britain's Maritime Power" (1878), and Laughton's "The Scientific Study of Naval History" (1874) are only the more strikingly "Mahanite" of British publications of the 1870s and '80s that deal with questions of the "command of the sea," coaling stations, naval-commercial interrelations, and naval appropriations. Laughton's "Scientific Study of Naval History," for example, provided the "blue-water school" with a ringing statement of naval usefulness. "Through many centuries," he wrote, the Royal Navy has been "our chief, almost our only claim to be considered as a powerful nation; and the commerce it has protected through long seasons of trouble and danger has been the main source of that wealth which has enabled us to develop our industry at home, or to extend our empire abroad."[76]

Mahan and his messmates clearly had not brought the idea of sea power to Britain. Indeed, a case might be made that Laughton's 1874 argument for a "scientific study of naval history" precipitated Stephen Luce's own campaign for just such a study at an American naval war college, or that the works of the Colomb brothers, which aroused the interest of men such as J. R. Soley,

French Chadwick, and Bowman McCalla, stimulated the navalist conceptualizations of American naval officers. One thing, in any event, is certain: Sir John Laughton's 1883 review of Commander A. T. Mahan's *The Gulf and Inland Waters* revealed a greater consciousness of the function of sea power than did Mahan's book itself.[77]

The "blue-water school" had many ancestors in Britain. In 1866 Charles Yonge offered the same analysis of the key role British sea power played in the nation's life, as did William P. O'Byrne in 1849, Henry Redhead Yorke and William Stevenson in 1817, Robert Beatson in 1804, John Charnock in 1794, William Blackstone in 1765, William Pitt in 1759, John Entick in 1757, John Campbell in 1744, Thomas Lediard in 1735, Joseph Addison in 1727, Josiah Burchett in 1720, George Savile, Marquis of Halifax, in 1694, John Locke in 1690, Algernon Sidney in 1680, Charles II in 1672, Sir Robert Slingsby in 1660, John Holland in 1658 and 1638, Sir Walter Raleigh in 1607, Francis Bacon in 1579, Richard Hakluyt in 1589, and Adam de Moleyns in 1436.* Not every

---

* O'Byrne claimed the Royal Navy was the central reason for England's "proud preeminence in the scale of nations." Campbell believed that "the great figure we make in the world, and the wide extent of our power and influence," were due to British "naval strength," to which Britishers stood indebted for their "flourishing plantations, the spreading of British fame, and . . . British freedom. . . ." Halifax felt sea power to be essential "to our very being" because of the protection it afforded the vital sea-borne English trade. "The Navy is of so great importance," he wrote, "that it would be disparaged by calling it less than the life and soul of government." Charles II, whose father's fateful struggle with the Commons had begun over the issue of a "ship-money" tax for the Royal Navy, maintained that the "wealth, safety, and strength of the kingdom" depended on sea power. Sir Walter Raleigh's maxim—"Whosoever commands the sea commands the trade; and whosoever commands the trade of the world commands the riches of the world and consequently the world itself"—is probably the most compact statement of the concept of sea power. But Adam de Moleyns had the same thought in mind in 1436 when he wrote "Cheryshe marchandyse, kepe thamyralte/That we bee maysteres of the narrow see." Yonge, *History of the British Navy* . . . (2nd ed., 3 vols., London, 1866), I, 1; O'Byrne, *A Naval Biographical Dictionary* (2 vols., London, 1849), I, v; *Lives of the British Admirals: Containing an Accurate Naval History from the Earliest Periods by Dr. John Campbell . . . Continued by Dr. Berkenhowt . . . revised . . . by . . . Henry Redhead Yorke, Esq., and further continued . . . by William Stevenson, Esq.* (8 vols., London, 1817), I, 1; Beaston, *Naval and Military Memoirs of Great Britain* (6 vols., London, 1804), I, ix; Charnock, *Biographia Navalis* (London, 1794), introduction; Clerk, *An Essay on Naval Tactics, Systematical and Historical* (3rd ed., Edinburgh, 1827), xxvi; Kent, *Biographia Nautica; or memoirs of those illustrious seamen to whose intrepidity and conduct the British are indebted for the victories of their fleets, the increase of their commerce, and the preeminence on the ocean* (3 vols., London, 1781), preface; Hervey, *The Naval History of Great Britain* (5 vols., London, 1779), *passim*; Entick, *A New Naval History, or, Complete View of the British Marine* (London, 1757), introduction; Lediard, *The Naval History of England* (2 vols. in 1, London, 1735), preface; Burchett, *A Complete History of . . . Transactions at Sea . . .* (London, 1720), *passim*; Halifax, *Rough Draught of a New Model at Sea* (London, 1694), *passim*; Locke, "Considerations on Money," in *The Works of John Locke in Nine Volumes* (12th ed., London, 1824), IV, 13–14, 21; *Dictionary*, ed. Heinl, 210, 288; The Navy Records Society (L.), *Two Discourses of the Navy, 1638 and 1659, by John Hollond also a Discourse of the Navy, 1660, by Sir Robert [Slingsby]*, ed. J. R. Tanner (London, 1896), 327, 5–6; Raleigh, cited in Josiah Strong, *Expansion* (N.Y., 1900), 194; de Moleyns, *Libelle of English Polycye* (London, 1436), *passim*.

According to Admiral Charles C. Taylor, R.N., Sir Edward Coke, William Shakespeare, and Alfred Lord Tennyson were also exponents of the role of sea power. *The Life of Admiral Mahan*, 41ff.

Englishman felt it necessary to spell out the concept of sea power, it being so much a part of their lives.* But a good many did, especially in moments of "crisis," and this list of names could probably be extended almost indefinitely.

The English-speaking world had no monopoly on the idea of sea power. Germans such as Karl Jacob, Swiss such as Jomini, and Frenchmen such as Baron Charles Dupin, Napoleon, Colbert, A. M. LeMierre, Henri Martin, and Father Paul Hoste all sensed it.[78] The Algerian Corsair Khair ad-Din (Barbarossa), Admiral of the Turkish fleet in the early sixteenth century, observed that "he who rules on the sea will very shortly rule on the land also." Archibald Lewis has suggested that the concept of sea power was alive in the Mediterranean region during the "dark ages"; and it appears that King Offa of Mercia, an eighth century Briton, also articulated "Mahanite" views. King Offa had predecessors, however. Alcibiades wrote of the Athenians that "their strength lay in the greatness of their navy, and by that and that alone they gained their empire." And an anonymous colleague of Alcibiades maintained:

> There is not a single community that can live without imports and exports, and these will be denied to any community that does not show itself submissive to the masters of the sea. . . . If a country happens to be rich in ship-timber, what market is there for it, if it fails to conciliate the masters of the sea?

And even Alcibiades had predecessors. The author of I Kings, x, 22–23, may have sensed the relationship between international trade, a navy, and national power, for he wrote, "King Solomon had a navy at sea . . . and he exceeded in riches all the kinds of the earth." And the "sea kings of Crete" clearly demonstrated "Mahanite" qualities.[79]

In Arthur O. Lovejoy's sense, then, the concept of sea power was a perennial bloomer. But it came sharply into focus in the 1880s because of the efforts of the Navy's "Young Turks." Charles Beard once sagely surmised that naval officers, rather than statesmen or industrialists, were at the heart of the drive for a "new Navy" in the 1880s,[80] and I think he was right.

This is not to say that groups like the Grange, the Merchant Marine League, the American Iron and Steel Association, the American Shipping and Industrial League, the New York Chamber of Commerce, pro-Navy journalists like James Gordon Bennett and Thomas Nast, and cosmopolitan elites in and out of Congress were uninterested or unimportant in the creation of the "new Navy." On the contrary, their conscious support was absolutely *essential* to the new navalists, who might have led such policy-making horses to water for decades without success had they not been so willing to drink. But the "Young Turks" were catalytic, an inseparable part of the expansionist movement.

Their success should not be surprising. After all, Americans *were* seeking to

---

* Thus John Hollond considered the idea of the preeminent role of sea power in British affairs to be so widely espoused that he saw no need of "useless apologies" or "rhetorical persuasions" to arouse "that honorable esteem" which "every man" in England already "easily ascribe[d] to." Hollond, 2nd Discourse, *op. cit.*, 113.

expand their markets overseas, and the "new Navy's" publicists spoke their 317 language.* Given the nature of America's capitalist socio-economic system, she might *well* need an effective, modern fleet. In a sense, navalism's day had simply dawned in America. But the creation of the "new Navy" relieved the career anxieties of the "Young Turks," and that was more than peripheral. Indeed, their career anxieties may properly be cited as one of the primary forces behind the growth of the "new Navy" and the emergence of modern American navalism.

* Some civilian navalists were quite capable of rationalizing naval expansion with little prompting from naval officers. For an example in the 1880s and '90s, see my article, "The Nature of 'Influence': Roosevelt, Mahan, and the Concept of Sea Power," *American Quarterly* (Winter, 1971–72).

Chapter 6

1. Elting E. Morison, "A Case Study of Innovation," *Engineering and Science Magazine* (April 1950), 7.

2. Sprout, *op. cit.*, 165–182. 1870 Navy Regulations required a Commanding Officer to enter his reason for burning coal in the log in red ink.

3. Seager, *op. cit.*, 497.

4. McNair, "Our Fleet Maneuvers in the Bay of Florida, and the Navy of the Future," *PUSNI*, I (1874), I (1874), 162–176: Porter to Navy Secretary George Robeson, Nov. 6, 1874, *Annual Report of the Secretary of the Navy* (Wash., G.P.O., 1874), 199.

5. Dewey, *Autobiography*, 158–159; Rear Admiral Edward Simpson, "The U.S. Navy in Transition," *Harper's New Monthly Magazine*, LXXXIII (1886), 3, 16; Thomas Hunt, *The Life of William H. Hunt* (privately printed, Brattleboro, Vt., 1922), 226ff; Charles Jones, *Address to Naval Academy*, 3; "Our Navy" Mss., p. 4, Rear Admiral Louis Kimberly Papers, Chicago Hist. Soc.; Passed Assistant Engineer Frank Bennett, *The Steam Navy of the United States* (N.Y., 1897), II, 772; Fiske, *From Midshipman to Rear Admiral*, 272; Theodore Roosevelt, *The Naval War of 1812* (New York, 1882), v, 136; *Autobiography* (New York, 1926), 205; Caldwell to his mother, January 16, 1884, Caldwell Papers, Indiana State Hist. Soc. Library.

6. *Letters from the Asiatic Station, 1881–1883: Cadet-Midshipman Frank Emory Bunts*, ed. Alexander T. Bunts (Cleveland, Ohio, 1938), 55, 78, 144, 201, 203; Foulk to Ensign W. I. Chambers, December 28, 1883, and Ensign C. C. Marsh to Chambers, August 18, 1883, Chambers Papers, N.H.F.; Passed Assistant Engineer J. P. Stuart Laurence to his mother, November 2, 1881, Laurence Papers, Naval Museum, Annapolis.

7. From the editorial notice in *Proceedings of the United States Naval Institute* during the first decade of its inception; Captain J. M. Ellicott, *PUSNI*, L (1924), 1615.

8. New York *Times* (6 July 1882), 3; *Nation*, XXXIV (22 June 1882), 511; XXXVII (1 November 1883), 371–372; Fiske, *From Midshipman to Rear Admiral*, 133; Sprout and Sprout, *Rise of Naval Power*, 174; G. R. Clark and others, *A Short History of the U.S. Navy* (Philadelphia, 1911), 406–408; *Report of the Secretary of the Navy* (Wash., G.P.O., 1882), 7.

9. Thus when C. Wright Mills remarked that the senior naval officers of 1900 "slowly rose by avoiding innovation," he was only partly correct. Many did avoid innovation, but not out of fear of reprisal. *Power Elite, 182.*

10. Preble to Lizzie, Oct. 17, 1861, Preble Papers, Mass. Hist. Soc.; Sperry to his sister, January 18, 1863, Sperry Papers, L. of C.; Benjamin, *U.S.N.A.*, 255; Rodman, *Yarns*, 44; 50th Cong., 1st Sess., *Senate Report of the Committee on Naval Affairs, No.*

318

485 [1888]; *passim Compilation of Laws Relating to the Navy* . . ., ed. John W. Hogg (Wash., G.P.O., 1883), 84–85; Harris, *Age of Battleship*, 33; Schroeder, *Half Century of Naval Service*, 65; Lieutenant Cornelius Schoonmaker to his family, December 5, 1865, Schoonmaker, "Life of Schoonmaker," p. 139, Box 152, N.H.F.; Master Albert Caldwell to his mother, July 27, 1868, Caldwell Papers, Indiana Hist. Soc. Lib.

11. *In re Grambs' Case*, 15 A.G.Op. 561, 635, *Notes on the Revised Statutes of the U.S.* . . ., ed. John Gould and George Tucker (Boston, 1889), 415; Benjamin, *U.S.N.A.*, 284–285.

12. Laurence to his aunt, July 29, 1877, Laurence Papers, Naval Museum; Mahan, *PUSNI*, V (1879), 360; Lieutenant J. D. J. Kelley, *United Service*, I (1879), 274; Lieutenant, "A. P. Mantus," "Wasted Energy in the Navy," *United Service*, V (Nov. 1881), 638. Cf. "A Naval Officer," *United Service*, III (Sept. 1880), 367; "W.X." *National Defense*, 3; "A Naval Officer," *United Service*, 2nd Series (January 1889), 98.

13. Fullam, *PUSNI*, XVI (1890), 481–482. Apparently commanders could be just as disgusted. "Promotion exclusively by seniority! Fudge!!" Commander Louis Goldsborough exclaimed to his wife, July 12, 1853, Goldsborough Papers, Perkins L., Duke U.

14. Fiske, *War Time in Manila*, 235; Lewis, *Social History of the Navy*, 162; William Leahy "Diary 1897–1931," p. 5, Fleet Admiral W. D. Leahy Papers, Division of Archives and Manuscripts, State Hist. Soc. of Wisc.

15. Porter to John Barnes, April 13, 1870, Porter Papers, N.Y.H.S.; "Letters of Resignation, 1878–1886," Vol. I, Entry 202, Record Group 24, National Archives; *Class of '71, U.S. Naval Academy, passim*; U.S. Naval Academy Graduates Association, *Register of Graduates* (Annapolis, 1916), *passim*; Park Benjamin, "The Unused Products of the Naval Academy," *The Independent*, L (Oct. 27, 1898), 1179–1183.

16. *Letters from the Asiatic Station*, ed. Bunts, 40–41, 108; Thomas, *Career of Walker*, 34, 50, 53, Caldwell to his aunt, September 23, 1870, Caldwell Papers, Ind. Hist. Soc. Lib.; O'Neil to Mrs. Smith, September 15, 1877, O'Neil Papers, Box 340, N.H.F.; McCalla, "Memoirs," Ch. XXX, 43.

17. Cited in 49th Cong., 1st Sess., House

of Rep., *Report of the Comm. on Naval Affairs, No. 1678* [1886].

18. John Betts, "The U.S. Navy in the Mexican War," unpublished Ph.D. dissertation, U. of Chicago, 1954, p. 54; Turner to Rear Admiral T. T. Craven, July 22, 1868, Craven Papers, Syracuse Univ. Library; Lieutenant Commander Charles Sigsbee to his brother-in-law, Jan. 27, 1872, Sigsbee Papers, N.Y. State Library, Albany, N.Y.; Commander P. F. Harrington to Lieutenant Commander William F. Fullam, May 5, 1896, Box 1, Fullam Papers, N.H.F.; Park Benjamin, "Promotion in the Navy," *Independent*, L (1898), 683–687.

19. U.S. Bureau of Census, *Historical Statistics*, 736; Davis, *Navy Second to None*, 469; Jewell, *Among Our Sailors*, 235, 252; Lieutenant Commander Caspar Goodrich, *PUSNI*, 327; Lieutenant C. C. Todd, *United Service*, VI (Mar. 1882), 263; McCalla, "Memoirs," Ch. XII, 10; Pay Director Thomas Looker, U.S.N., to Navy Secretary William E. Chandler, May 11, 1882, Vol. 53, Chandler Papers, L. of C.; Porter to Robinson, June 19, 1882, Porter Papers, N.Y.H.S.; Commodore Thornton A. Jenkins, *Rear Admiral Goldsborough and the Retiring Laws of the Navy* (Wash., 1868).

20. Langley, *Social Reform in the Navy*, 22–25, 34; "Naval Tables," George H. Preble Papers, Chicago Hist. Soc.; "Hibble Bubble," "Stand Still or Reform?" Folder 113, Thomas Butler King Papers, S.H.C., U. of N.C. Library; Maury to Navy Secretary Graham, Oct. 7, 1850, *Papers of Graham*, ed. Hamilton, III, 409–410, 427; Surgeon W. M. Wood, *A Shoulder to the Wheel*, 165; Passed Midshipman Edward Simpson and eleven others to (?), approx. early 1851, Commodore Somerville Nicholson Papers, N.H.F.; Calvert, *Naval Profession*, 114.

21. 44th Cong., 1st Sess., House Misc. Doc. No. 170, Pt. 8, *Investigation by the Committee on Naval Affairs* [1877], 12, 122; Mahan to Navy Secretary William Hunt, April 20, 1881, cited in William E. Livezey, *Mahan on Sea Power* (Norman, Okla., 1947), 207; "Education of American Naval Officers," *The Critic* [N.Y.], II (Feb. 25, 1882), 56; Rodgers to Navy Secretary Hunt, Nov. 10, 1881, Correspondence of the Superintendent of the Naval Academy, R.G. 24; *Puck* [N.Y.], VIII, No. 208 (Mar. 2, 1881), 432, 446.

22. Lovette, *School of Sea*, 107–108; Benjamin, *U.S.N.A.*, 323.

Cadet Midshipman Willie G. McMillan, for one, kept a wry sense of humor through it all. When the Academy discovered that some of its artillery practice ammunition was faulty, McMillan suggested that the Government was hoping to kill off "some surplus Naval Cadets." McMillan to his uncle Ed McKethan, Oct. 12, 1884, A. A. McKethan Papers, Perkins Library, Duke U.

23. Marsh to Ensign W. I. Chambers, October 30, 1882, Box 5, Chambers Papers, N.H.F.; *Letters from the Asiatic Station*, 121, 132; Sperry to his wife, July 18, 1884, June 29, and July 21, 1885, Sperry Papers, L. of C.; Rodman, *Yarns of a Kentucky Admiral*, 44; "W.X.," *National Defense* (n.p., circa 1883 [copy in St. Hist. Soc. of Wisc.]), 3 (his emphasis).

24. "Letters of Resignation, 1878–1886," Vol. I, Entry 202, Record Group 24, National Archives; Lejeune to his sister, Feb. 23, 1885, Box 16, Lejeune Papers, N.H.F.; Foulk to Lieutenant (j.g.) W. I. Chambers, March 13, 1886, and March 23 and April 17, 1888, Chambers Papers, N.H.F.

25. Bernadou to Foulk, March 6, 1887, Foulk Papers, N.Y.P.L.; Samuel Bryan to the class of '81, October, 1888, *5th Annual Report of the Class of '81*, 3; 48th Cong., 1st Sess., Senate Misc. Doc. No. 18, "Memorial of Cadets of the U. S. Navy"; Coontz, *From Mississippi to Sea*, 66, 105, 185. Cf. E. M. "Doc" Harmon to Ira McJunkin and the class of '81, Nov. 29, 1885, *2nd Annual Report of the Class of '81*, 21: "Civil life may suit some of you, but it does not suit me. I would give all my old clothes to get back...."

26. Mark D. Hirsch, *William C. Whitney: Modern Warwick* (N.Y., 1948), 262; Kelley, *Our Navy*, 7–8; Goodrich, *PUSNI*, XXIV (1898), 3, 7; *Letters from the Asiatic Station*, ed. Bunts, 168; Porter to Rear Admiral S. B. Luce, July 12, 1883, Box 1, Luce Papers, N.H.F.; *Cong. Record*, *49th Cong., 2nd Sess.*, 2344, first cited in Thomas Coode, "Southern Congressmen and the American Naval Revolution," *Alabama Historical Quarterly* (1968), 99. For a recent (1949) example of naval officers who feared that the Navy was being "nibbled to bits" see Paul Y. Hammond, "Supercarriers and B-36's: Appropriations, Strategy, and Politics," in Harold Stein, ed., *American Civil–Military Decisions* (U. of Alabama Press, 1963).

27. See, for example, Wallace E. Davies,

Patriotism on Parade (Cambridge, Mass., 1955), 28; and Jerry Israel, ed., *Building the Organizational Society* (Free Press, Spring, 1972).

28. *Letters from the Asiatic Station*, ed. Bunts, 164, 217; MacDonough Craven to the class of '81, December 8, 1885, *2nd Annual Report of the Class of '81* (Butler, Pa., 1886), 1, 10; 49th Cong., 1st Sess., "Views of Senator Hale of the Committee on Naval Affairs to Accompany Bill S. 371," *Misc. Doc. 75* [1886]; Harmon to class of '81, *2nd Ann. Rpt.*, 21; Samuel Bryan to class of '81, Nov. 15, 1886, *3rd Ann. Rpt.*, 8.

29. Belknap to Rear Admiral George Balch, Feb. 1, 1883, Balch Papers, U. of N.C. Library; *3rd Annual Report . . .*, 110; "W.X.," *National Defense*, 3; McCalla, "Memoirs," Ch. XII, 10; Porter to Fox, March 28, 1862, *Conf. Corr. of Fox*, II, 89, 91–92.

30. Coghlan to the editor, October 20, 1889, in Coghlan pamphlet, Box 4, *Monocacy* file, Albert Gleaves Papers, N.H.F. See Richmond Hobson's characterization of Coghlan, "Commander Cogwheel," in his novel *In Line of Duty*.

31. Janowitz, *Professional Soldier*, 368; Captain Caspar Goodrich, "Naval Education," *Journal of Social Science*, XXXIII (Nov. 1895), 48; Davis, *Life of Davis*, 187; U.S. Nav. Acad. Grad. Assoc., *Minutes of the 1st 4 Annual Reunions* (Annapolis & Baltimore, 1886–1890 [available in one volume at the Library of Congress]), *passim*; Lieutenant (j.g.) C. C. Marsh to Lieutenant (j.g.) W. I. Chambers, June 10, 1886, Chambers Papers, N.H.F.; McCalla, "The Training of Naval Officers," *Public Service Review*, I (1887), 53; and "Memoirs," Ch. XII, 10; XVI, 5; 50th Cong., 1st Sess., Senate, *Report of Committee on Naval Affairs*, No. 1377 [1888]; *6th Annual Report of Class of '81*, 122–124; Bernadou to Foulk, March 6, 1887, Foulk Papers, N.Y.P.L.; Benson, *Turner and Beard* (Glencoe, Ill., 1959), 216.

32. 51st Cong., 1st Sess., Senate Exec. Doc. 86, *Letter from the Secretary of the Navy transmitting . . . a report upon certain alleged organizations among naval officers not authorized by the Navy Department* [1890]; Captain Caspar Goodrich, "Esprit de Corps—A Tract for the Times," *PUSNI*, XXIV (1898), 12.

Richmond Hobson ('89) created a hero, "Ensign 'Buck' Jones," who managed very ably as a surrogate engineer in *In Line of*

320

Duty, a fact that Jones' Executive Officer, "Commander Cogwheel" ('64), found incomprehensible.

33. Commander S. W. Terry, *PUSNI*, XVI (1890), 523; Coontz, *From Mississippi to Sea*, 101; Paullin, *PUSNI, XXXIX* (1913), 1499–1500.

34. Bernadou to Foulk, March 6, 1887, Foulk Papers, N.Y.H.S.

35. Chambers, *The Navy*, IX (1915), 98–99; Belknap to Rear Admiral George Balch, Feb. 1, 1883, Balch Papers, U. of N.C. Library.

36. Lovette, *School of Sea*, 104, 295; entries for "naval constructors" in *D.A.B.*

37. Benjamin, *U.S.N.A.*, 424–425; Lovette, *School of Sea*, 305, 324–330; Strauss to Knox, n.d., NA "New Navy," Entry 464, R.G. 45; *Report of the [Senate] Select Committee on Ordnance and War Ships* (Wash., G.P.O., 1886), 147–212; *Hearings of an Investigation by the Committee on Naval Affairs of the U.S. Senate in Relation to Prices Paid for Armour for Vessels of the Navy* (Wash., G.P.O., 1896), 194, 346–353. Many published progress reports and argued their cases in the pages of the *Proceedings* . . . throughout these years.

38. Lovette, *School of Sea*, 323–330; Benjamin, *U.S.N.A.*, 362, 424–425; Fiske, *Electricity* . . . (N.Y., 1883). Fiske later topped his offerings off by planning the first torpedo plane.

Lieutenant J. D. J. Kelley was no inventor, but he was a staunch advocate of Marconi's wireless as a means of improving naval communications, and became a member of Marconi's Board of Directors upon retirement. Nathalie Cook, *J. D. J. Kelley, Commander, U.S. Navy* (n.p., 1942), 6.

Albert A. Michelson (1852–1931), an Academy product and an instructor at Annapolis in the early 1880s, may have been the exception that proves the rule. His experiments with light refraction and measurement, conducted on the banks of the Severn, were not conceived to satisfy the needs of the Service; but then Michelson left the Navy shortly thereafter. *PUSNI*, VII (1882), 495–499; R. A. Millikan, "Biographical Memoir of A. A. Michelson," *National Academy of Sciences* (Wash., 1938), 121–147.

39. For example, Michelson "resigned" but never retired from the Navy. He served in both the Spanish–American War and the First World War, and his devotion to the Navy was profound. See Dorothy Michelson Livingston, "Michelson in the Navy:

The Navy in Michelson," *PUSNI*, XCV (June 1969), 19.

40. Rear Admiral J. G. Walker to Lieutenant Martin E. Hall, April 23, 1889, Walker Papers, N.H.F., Box 595; *PUSNI*, XLVIII (1922), 1000; Lovette, *School of Sea*, 296, 298; Copley, *Taylor*, I, 379; II, 300–303; Captain A. P. Cooke, *PUSNI*, XII (1886), 491; *World's Work* (July 1917), 337.

41. Spector, 278–295; Rear Admiral Purnell Harrington to Rear Admiral Albert Gleaves, Sept. 27, 1924, Gleaves Papers, Perkins Library, Duke U.; Captain R. R. Belknap, "Military Character," *PUSNI*, XLIV (1918), 3; Commander H. O. Rittenhouse, "The Preparedness of the Future," *PUSNI*, XLIV (1918), 739, 743; and my Chapter 5, fns. 46, 50, and 52.

42. See, for example, Cummings, *Wainwright*, 38; Lieutenant Nathan Sargent, "The Quasi-War with France," *United Service*, IX (July 1883), 1–27; Lieutenant Charles Vreeland and Surgeon J. F. Bransford, *Antiquities at Pataleon, Guatemala* (Washington, 1884); O.N.I. [Lieutenant William Beehler], *A Study of Exposed Points on Our Frontier, Lines of Communication, and Possible Bases of Hostile Operation* . . . (Wash., 1885); Lieutenant Seaton Schroeder, *The Fall of Maximillian's Empire as Seen From a U.S. Gunboat* (N.Y., 1887); the many survey publications (within the naval establishment) of Lieutenant R. G. Davenport; Lieutenant Lucien Young, *Archeological Researches in Peru*, and *Simple Elements of Navigation* (N.Y., 1890); Ensign Albert P. Niblack, "The Coast Indians of Southern Alaska and Northern British Columbia," *Annual Report of the . . . Smithsonian Institution* . . . (Wash., G.P.O., 1890), 226–386; Engineer George H. Melville, *In the Lena Delta . . . and a Proposed Method of Reaching the North Pole* (Boston, 1885); Lieutenant J. F. Meigs, "The War in South America," *PUSNI*, V (1879), 461–479; 46th Cong., 2nd Sess., "Report on the Training Systems for the Navy . . . of England . . . by Lieutenant Commander French E. Chadwick," *Senate Exec. Doc. 52*, [1880]; and all of the Office of Naval Intelligence publications, be they the *Recent Naval Progress* series, the *Information from Abroad* series, or the *General Information on War* series. Cf. Navy Department, Bureau of Navigation, *Catalogue of Works by American Naval Authors, compiled by Lieutenant Lucien Young* (Wash., 1888).

43. Robert Neeser, *History of Navy*, I, 124–134; Captain Wm. Fullam to Captain

Wm. Sims, Jan. 11, 1912, Sims Papers, N.H.F.

44. McCalla, "Memoirs," Ch. X, 17–18; Alfred Vagts, *The Military Attaché* (Princeton, 1967), 31, 33–34; Rear Admiral Albert Niblack, *The O.N.I., Its History and Aims* (Wash., G.P.O., 1920), 2, *passim*; Lieutenant William L. Sachse, "Our Naval Attaché System; Its Origins and Development to 1917," *PUSNI*, LXXII (May 1946), 661–672; O.N.I., *Naval Mobilization . . .* (Wash., G.P.O., 1889), 2–3, 163–184. Meigs anticipated the view of W. S. Sims in insisting that what counted in naval gunfire was the number of hits per unit of time (O.N.I., *Naval Mobilization*, 176).

45. Rear Admiral Richard Wainwright, "The New Naval Academy," *World's Work*, IV (1902), 2275–2280; Lieutenant (j.g) E. E. Capehart to class of 81, Nov. 12, 1889, *6th Annual Rpt. of the Class of '81*, 25–26.

In 1881 young James Russell Soley, a Harvard graduate who had been appointed to the staff at the Naval Academy, was named Officer-in-Charge of the newly-created Office of Naval Records and Library (U.S. Navy Department Library, *Naval Library Conference . . .* [Wash., G.P.O., 1953], 1). Soley, a great popularizer of naval views, identified closely with the aristocracy's "Young Turks."

46. Thus it is exaggerating things to say, as Ronald Spector and Harry J. Sievers recently have said ("Professors of War . . .," 163, 165; *Journal of American History*, LIV [1968], 904), that the Luce–Mahan–Tracy War College curriculum "served to convince officers of the need for a stronger navy" and "inaugurated the navy's approach to professionalism." Luce, Mahan, and Navy Secretary B. F. Tracy invigorated the War College—not the "Young Turk" interest in a strong Navy or the Navy's approach to professionalism. See pp. 342–346 for more on Mahan, the "Young Turks," and the War College.

47. Goodrich, "Naval Education," *PUSNI*, V (1879), 331; McCalla, "The Training of Naval Officers," *Public Service Review*, I (1887), 52; Mason, "Naval Education," *United Service*, III (1881), 165, 180; Upton to Luce, August 26, 1878, Naval Museum Miscellaneous Mss.

Colonel Charles Heywood, Commandant of the Marine Corps, had the same objective as Luce and Upton in mind in 1893 when he sought a Marine billet at the War College. Heywood to Commander H. C. Taylor,

Dec. 29, 1893, Letters of the Presidents of the War College, Box, 358, N.H.F. For further discussion of the value of the War College see the following chapter.

48. This "decline" and "sad state" can easily be overdrawn, or misunderstood. In 1880 Captain John C. R. Colomb, an astute British observer, considered the United States to be "the second maritime power in the world." Colomb, *The Defense of Great and Greater Britain* (London, 1880), 178.

49. 49th Cong., 1st Sess., "Views of Senator Hale and Others of the Committee on Naval Affairs to Accompany Bill S. 371," *Misc. Doc. No. 75*, Pt. 1, p. 3 [1886]; Ensign Roger Welles to his mother, Feb. 4, 1886, Welles Papers, N.H.F.

50. Mahan to Ashe, Dec. 19, 1858, and Spring, 1859, *Letters*, ed. Chiles, 55, 98; Brown, *United Service*, IV (1881) 609.

For a similar account of the response of junior naval officers to a real or imagined threat to the life of the Service that also resulted in the creation by these junior officers of a reasoned strategic theory to support the Service, see Davis, *Postwar Defense Policy and the Navy*, 149–150.

51. Wm. G. Ford, Jr., to the class of '81, Mar. 5, 1890, *6th Annual Report*, p. 53; Admiral Porter to John Barnes, April 13, 1870, Porter Papers, N.Y.H.S.; Commodore Joseph Lannman, Vice President of the U.S.N. [Line] Association, to Vice Admiral D. D. Porter, Dec. 14, 1867, Porter Papers, Perkins Library, Duke U.; Captain A. P. Cooke, *PUSNI*, IX (1882), 220; Kelley, *Our Navy*, 8.

For good examples of the naval aristocracy's appeals to politicians for more ships in the 1880s see the correspondence of Captain George Dewey, Lieutenant Commander French E. Chadwick, and ex-Lieutenant John S. Barnes with Cleveland's Treasury Secretary Charles Fairchild, Fairchild Papers, Boxes 1–3, N.Y.H.S.; Rear Admiral Luce with Senator Nelson Aldrich in 1889, Luce Papers, N.H.F.; and Commander Chadwick with Representative Hilary Herbert, Chairman of the House Naval Affairs Committee, August 19, 1887, and October 29, 1888, and Chadwick to Captain J. G. Walker, October 8, 1887, Personal letters copybook, Chadwick Papers, N.Y.H.S.

52. Jenkins *PUSNI*, XII (1886), 25, 38: Captain A. P. Cooke, *PUSNI*, XIV (1888), 172; McCalla, "Memoirs," Ch. XII, 9.

I have said little of the views of Navy Department Secretaries or navalists in

322 Congress. For good accounts of these see George T. Davis, *A Navy Second to None: The Development of Modern American Naval Policy* (N.Y., 1940); Sprout and Sprout, *Rise of Sea Power*; Seager, "Ten Years before Mahan . . .," *op. cit.*

53. *Preble Diary*, ed. Szczesniak, 376–377; Brown, "The Commercial and Naval Policy of the U.S.," *United Service*, IV (1881), 604; Kelley, *Question of Ships*, 19; 24th Cong., 1st Sess., *Senate Doc. 327* [1836]; 33rd Cong. 1st Sess., *House Misc. Doc. No. 70* [1854]; 37th Cong., 1st Sess., *Senate Misc. Doc. No. 6* [1861]; Lieutenant Robert Wyman to Commander Louis Goldsborough, Nov. 25, 1854, Goldsborough Papers, L. of C.; Barnard, *Military Schools*, 940; *Memorial of Officers of . . . the Navy for an Increase of Their Pay . . .*, *passim*; Jewell, *Among Our Sailors*, 224; Luce to John Barnes, January 1874, Luce Papers, N.Y.H.S.; *35th Annual Report of the Board of Education of the City and County of New York* (N.Y., 1877), 251–257; Luce to the New York Board of Education (c. 1873), *Life and Letters of Luce*, ed. Gleaves, 139–140; David, "Our Merchant Marine: The Causes of its Decline, and the Means to be taken for its Revival," *PUSNI*, VIII (1882), 156; Farquhar, *loc. cit.*, 475–476; Cooke, *PUSNI*, IX (1883), 215; Bernadou, XVI (1890), 423. Cf. *PUSNI*, VIII (1882), 146; *United Service*, IV (1881), 603; and especially *PUSNI*, VIII (1882), 73.

54. See, for example, Commander F. E. Chadwick to Navy Secretary William C. Whitney, August 25 and September?, 1887, Chadwick to "General Hawley," August 31, 1887, Chadwick to Edward Phelps, U.S. Minister to the Court of St. James, October 4, 1887, Personal letters copybook, Chadwick Papers, N.Y.H.S.

Lieutenant R. M. G. Brown and other officers from time to time recommended the creation of a Department of Commerce, a proposal that may have endeared them to some U.S. merchants and investors. See, for example, Brown, "The Commercial and Naval Policy of the U.S.," *United Service*, IV (1881), 610; Captain Stephen Luce to John Barnes, Feb. 24, 1874, Luce Papers, N.Y.H.S.

55. Thirty-eight years ago Charles Beard sagely suggested that naval officers might have been calling for a merchant marine in order to obtain increases for the Navy. *Navy: Defense or Portent?*, 67.

56. Farquhar to Shufeldt, May 4, 1874, Box 11, Shufeldt Papers, N.H.F.; Calkins,

PUSNI, IX (1883), 155–194. See also Calkins, *PUSNI*, V (1879), 177, 179; Mason, "The United States Naval Institute," *United Service*, I (1879), 295; Belknap to Captain George Belknap (no relation), Jan. 24, 1881, R. R. Belknap Papers, N.H.F : Taylor, "The Study of War," *North American Review*, CLXII (1896), 188.

57. Morison, *Perry*, 296; Rear Admiral Samuel Franklin, *Memoirs of a Rear Admiral* (New York, 1898), 156; Lieutenant R. M. G. Brown, *United Service*, IV (1881), 603; Kelley, *Question of Ships*, 10, 109; Kimball, *Practical Prevention of War* (Wash., n.d. [c. 1899]), 3.

Diplomat Joseph Grew urged his colleagues to employ the same arguments before the U.S. Chamber of Commerce and the public-at-large to establish the importance of the Diplomatic Service to U.S. trade and commerce: "The public doesn't care about the political situation in Silesia . . . . The only element of the Foreign Service that appeals to the public is the ability of the Service to ensure business, better business, and bigger business. We must get it out of the mind of the public that the Consular Service is the only one that looks after that side." Cited in Ilchman, *Professional Diplomacy*, 152.

58. Collins, *PUSNI*, V (1879), 159–179; Belknap, *PUSNI*, VII, 375–391; "W.X.," *National Defense* [n.p., ca. 1882], 2; David, *PUSNI*, VIII (1882), 151–186; Kelley, *PUSNI*, VIII (1882), 64, 58. Kelley, Collins, and David argued the same point, using the American Civil War as their illustration. Kelley, *Question of Ships*, 108; Collins, *PUSNI*, V (1879), 162; David, *PUSNI*, VIII (1882), 166. Collins, one of the more promising junior officers in the Service, died suddenly in 1881, shortly after serving on the Rodgers Naval Advisory Board, which recommended the first American-made modern armored warships with rifled guns.

59. Wainwright, *PUSNI*, XVI (1890), 425; Soley, *PUSNI*, VI (1878), 129; Meigs, *PUSNI*, XIV (1888), cited in Spector, "Professors of War . . .," 91.

60. Taylor, "Battle tactics: the value of concentration," *PUSNI*, XII (1886), 141; McCalla, "Memoirs," Ch. XII, 13; Bainbridge-Hoff, *Modern Naval Tactics*, vol. III of the O.N.I., *Information from Abroad*, General Information Series (G.P.O., 1884), 11, 19–20, 82, 84, 89; Taylor, "The General Question of Isthmian Interest," *Nicaraguan Canal Discussion before the American Assoc.*

for the Advancement of Science, 36 Meeting (N.Y., 1887), 12; Jewell, *PUSNI*, XVI (1890), 410, 425, 428. Cf. Sampson, *PUSNI*, XV (1889), 169–232; 46th Cong. 2nd Sess., "Report on the Training Systems for the Navy . . . of England . . . by Lieutenant Commander French E. Chadwick," *Senate Ex. Doc. No. 52* [1880], 160; *Life of Emory*, ed. Gleaves, 115; J. R. Soley, "The Maritime Industries of America," in *The United States of America*, ed. Nathaniel Shaler (2 vols., N.Y., 1894), I, 518–530, 535, 561, 576–585; Soley, *The Boys of 1812 and Other Naval Heroes* (Boston, 1887), 262; Soley, *The Blockade and the Cruisers* (N.Y., 1883), 7–8, 10, 43–45, 234; Lieutenant C. C. Todd, "Some Needs of the Navy," *United Service*, VII (1882), 93; Kelley, "Free Ships and Subsidies," *United Service*, IV (1881), 519–523; "W.X.," *National Defense*, 5–6; "A Junior Officer," "Naval Reorganization," *United Service*, II (1880), 461–467.

In Britain there was a similar movement by R.N. officers in the '80s and '90s to persuade English policymakers and voters of the usefulness of the Navy, and there is some evidence that American naval Lieutenants learned from their R.N. counterparts of the value to their cause of intelligent appeals to business interests. See Marder, *Anatomy of British Sea Power*, 5–20, and his chapter entitled "The Naval Defense Act," and Lieutenant W. W. Kimball, U.S.N., *Practical Prevention of War*, 2. See Beard, *Navy: Defense or Portent?*, 17–18, for a similar argument about Germany in the 1890s.

61. *Navy Register*; Hirsch, *Whitney*, 265. Kelley dedicated *The Question of Ships* to Bennett for that man's "loyalty" to naval and merchant marine interests. Scribners, Kelley's publisher, also published the three-volume *Navy in the Civil War* series in the early 1880s.

62. See, for example, Kelley, *Question of Ships*, 4, 7, 10, 69, 108–109, 114, 122–123, 138–145, 184–185; and Kelley, Sir Edward J. Reed, and Rear Admiral Simpson, U.S.N., *Modern Ships of War* (N.Y., 1888), 148–215. Cf. J. Steinberg, *Yesterday's Deterrent*, 2.

63. Ensign George Foulk to Chambers, Sept. 11, 1884, and March 13, 1886, Chambers Papers, N.H.F.; Goodrich, *PUSNI*, XI (1885), 70; Chambers *PUSNI*, XI (1885), 5, 7, 9, 12, 57, 60, 72; Jan. 5, 1885, entry in Private Journal, Box 37, Chambers Papers, N.H.F.; Chambers to Navy Secretary Wm. E. Chandler, Jan. 9, 1885, Chandlers Papers, L. of C. (Chambers had

received orders from Chandler to go with the McCalla expedition into the Atlantic waters of the Isthmus of Darien to write confidential reports to Chandler concerning the isthmus.)

Apparently the Chambers essay was well received in some government circles. It was cited in the Senate's *Report of the Select Committee on Ordnance of War Ships* (Wash., G.P.O., 1886), 5.

64. *PUSNI*, XVI (1890), 202–207; Luce, "Our Future Navy," *North Amer. Rev.*, CXLIX (1889), 54–65; 50th Cong., 1st Sess., Senate Misc. Doc. 118, *Letters of Admiral David D. Porter . . . to Hon. John W. Mitchell*, *U.S. Senate, Relative to Site for Naval Station on the Pacific Coast, 15 March 1888* (Wash., G.P.O., 1888), 3–5; "An Indignant Briton" [Porter] to the editor of the New York *Herald*, Nov. 5, 1888 [with election day in mind], vol. VII, Porter Papers, L. of C.; Cooke *Public Service Review*, I (1887), 117–119; 48th Cong., 2nd Sess., Senate Ex. Doc. No. 68, *Letter from the Secretary of the Navy reporting . . . the steps taken by him to establish an advanced course of instruction of naval officers . . .*[1885], passim. Captain John Stapler, "The Naval War College, A Brief History," *PUSNI*, LVIII (1932), 1157–1158. See also Medical Director Edward Shippen U.S.N., *Naval Battles, Ancient and Modern* (Phil., 1883).

65. Ammen, *PUSNI*, V (1879), 111–112; Roe, *Reasons Why Our Navy Should not be Reduced!* (Wash., ca. 1880), 1–7; Ransom, "The Naval Policy of the United States," *United Service*, II (1880), 113; undated Mss [c. 1882] in Box 30. Porter Papers, L. of C., pp. 3, 11, 16, 27–28; Porter, "Our Navy," *United Service*, I (1879), 4; David Pletcher, *The Awkward Years* (Columbia, Mo., 1962), 120, 126; Porter, *Memoir of Commodore David Porter* (Albany, 1875), 148; 44th Cong., 1st Sess., House Misc. Doc. No. 170, Pt. 8, *Investigation by Naval Affairs Committee* [1876], 114, 123, and appendix 18, pp. 1, 24–25, and 29; Shufeldt, *The Relation of the Navy to the Commerce of the United States: A Letter Written by Request to the Honorable Leopold Morse, Member of the Naval Affairs Committee, House of Representatives* (Wash., 1878), 3–8; Chaplain Charles Boynton, U.S.N., *The History of the Navy During the Rebellion* (2 vols., N.Y., 1867), I, 5–6; Roe, *Naval Duties and Discipline*, 212–213.

66. Swann, *John Roach*, 166; Sloan, *Isherwood, passim*; Sprout and Sprout, *Rise of Naval Power*, 170ff; Roe, *Naval Duties*

and Discipline, 14, 16, 23; Porter to Lenthall, March 20, 1867, Porter Letterbook, N.H.F.; Porter, *Island of San Domingo*, 5–6. See also Kenneth J. Hagan, "Admiral David Dixon Porter: Strategist for a Navy in Transition," *PUSNI* (July, 1968).

For a different view of these post-Civil War strategic conservatives see Sprout and Sprout, *Rise of American Naval Power*, 174.

67. *U.S. Nautical Magazine and Naval Journal*, VI (N.Y., 1857), 58; *Ibid.*, III (1856), 401–404; *Ibid.*, I (1854), 31; DuPont, *Report on the National Defenses* (Wash., G.P.O., 1852), 4; Colton, *The Sea and the Sailor* (N.Y., 1851), 22; Emmons, *The Navy of the United States* (Wash., 1853), 207; Young, *"Boston" at Hawaii*, 290; McNally, *Evils and Abuses*, 17; Maury to Navy Secretary Graham, Oct. 7, 1850, *Papers of Graham*, ed. Hamilton, III, 420–423; Frances L. Williams, *Matthew Fontaine Maury: Scientist of the Sea* (New Brunswick, N.J., 1963), 130–141; Foote, *Africa*, 379; Commander John Rodgers to Navy Secretary James Dobbin, Jan. 29, 1856, in *Yankee Surveyors*, ed. Cole, 160–161.

68. Huntington, *Soldier and the State*, 237, 276; Zook and Higham, *A Short History of Warfare* (N.Y., 1966), 243; LaFeber, *New Empire*, 80; T. and H. Dupuy, *Military Heritage of the United States* (N.Y., 1955), 196; Herrick, *American Naval Revolution*, 51.

69. Sprout & Sprout, *Rise of American Naval Power*, 176.

70. Beard, *Idea of National Interest*, 340; Tuckman, *The Proud Tower* (Bantam paper ed., 1967), 151–512; Schilling, "Admirals and American Foreign Policy, 1913–1919," unpublished Ph.D. dissertation, Yale Univ., 1953, 3.

71. Puleston, *Mahan* (New Haven, 1939), *passim*; Ernest May, quoted in John Garraty, *Interpreting American History: Conversations with Historians* (N.Y., 1970), II, 76; C. C. Taylor, *The Life of Admiral Mahan* (N.Y., 1920), *passim*; Bryant, *Sea and States*, 348, 355; Davis, *The Admirals Lobby* (Chapel Hill, 1967), *passim*; Hacker, "Incendiary Mahan: A Biography," *Scribner's Magazine*, LXIV (November 1934), 263–268, 311–320; Fiske, *The Navy as a Fighting Machine*, 45; Janowitz, *Professional Soldier*, 158; Sprout and Sprout, *Rise of American Naval Power* (5th ed. Princeton, paper, 1966), introduction; George Kennan, *American Diplomacy, 1900–1950* (N.Y., 1951), 11–12; Robert E. Osgood, *Ideals and Self-Interest in America's Foreign Policy: The Great Transformation of the Twentieth Century*

(Chicago, 1953), 28; Leonard Krieger in John Highan, *et al.*, *History* (Englewood Cliffs, N.J. 1965), 252–253; Rolf N. B. Haugen, "The Setting of Internal Administrative Communication in the U.S. Naval Establishments, 1775–1920," unpublished Harvard Ph.D. thesis, 1953, p. 249; Harry Sievers, *Journal of American History*, LIV (1968), 904; Theodore Ropp, "The Rise of American Military Power," in *Institutions in Modern America*, ed. Stephen Ambrose (Baltimore, 1967), 109.

For example, consider the views of Albert C. Stillson: "It is difficult to overestimate Mahan's influence on his brother officers . . . It probably does not stretch the truth too far to say that Mahan was like a great religious leader, and most of his brother officers were his disciples. . . . Any understanding [of the] naval officer's image of world politics must begin with Alfred Thayer Mahan." "The Development and Maintenance of the American Naval Establishment, 1901–1909," unpublished Ph.D. thesis, Columbia, 1959, pp. 92, 93, 99.

72. *Correspondence between Governor [John W.] Geary of Pennsylvania and Vice Admiral Porter, Relating to the Foreign Commerce of the United States* (n.p., 1870), 3–4, 7–8; *The Personal Memoirs of U.S. Grant*, ed. Philip Van Doren Stern (Premium paper ed., 1962 [orig. pub. 1885]), 454; D. H. Mahan, *Advanced-Guard, Out-Post, and Detachment Service of Troops . . .* (N.Y., 1864 ed.), 7, 175, 217; Hall, "The Future of American Shipping," *Atlantic Monthly*, XLVII (1881), 174; McCall, "A Plea for a Strong Navy," *The Penn Monthly*, XII (Jan. 1881), 48–49; Daniel Ammen, *The Atlantic Coast* (N.Y., 1883), ad for 3 vol. *Navy in Civil War* series that appears at the back of Ammen's volume; Williams, *The Roots of the Modern American Empire* (N.Y., 1969), 236–270; Seager, "Ten Years before Mahan: The Unofficial Case for the New Navy, 1880–1890," *Mississippi Valley His. Rev.*, XL (1953), 491–512. Seager's and Williams' examples are numerous, but the passage I have used here happens to be a previously uncited one—that of Representative Samuel Cox, *The Navy—The Guardian of Commerce* (N.Y., 1884), 3, 6.

73. Cowley, *Leaves from a Lawyer's Life Afloat and Ashore* (Lowell, Mass., 1879), 9–10; 45th Cong., 2nd Sess., *House Report No. 432* [1878], 4; Barnard, *Military Schools* [1872], 919–920; McKean, *United States Service Magazine*, I (N.Y., 1865), 337–344; Puleston, *Influence of Force in Foreign*

Relations, 7n; Reynolds, "English Naval Power and English Colonies," *Atlantic Monthly*, XII (1863), 95, 97–98; Eliot, *Manual of U.S. History* [1856], 359; Foote, *Africa* [1854], 381–382.

74. *PUSNI*, XX (1894), 402–405; Clark, *Naval History of the United States* (Phil., 1813), 1–20; Humphreys, *Miscellaneous Works* (N.Y., 1804), 78–83; Charles Van Alstyne, *The Rising American Empire* (N.Y., 1960), 41; Hamilton, *The Federalist*, ed. Edward M. Earle (N.Y., 1938), 152, 67; George T. Davis, *A Navy Second to None: The Development of Modern American Naval Policy* (N.Y., 1940); William A. Williams, *The Contours of American History* (Cleveland, 1961), 118, 140, 142; Frederic H. Hayes, "John Adams and American Sea Power," *American Neptune*, XXV (1965), 35–45; A. T. Mahan, *Sea Power in its Relation to the War of 1812* (2 vols., Boston, 1905), I, 71; Adams to Franklin, Dec. 6, 1780, and Adams to Mr. Kalhoen, Oct. 17, 1780, *The Correspondence of John Adams* (Boston, 1809), 229–292; Washington to Lt. Colonel John Laurens, Jan. 15, 1781, *The Writings of George Washington* (40 vols., Wash., 1931–1944), XXI, 108; Marshall Smelser, *Congress Founds a Navy, 1787–1798* (Notre Dame, 1959), 11.

75. For example, Philip Colomb effectively pointed out something Mahan never sensed—that prior to the seventeenth century "raiding" was more effective a strategy than efforts to "sweep" or "command" the seas. *Naval Warfare: Its Ruling Principals and Practice Historically Treated* (London, 1891 [orig. pub. in a series of articles in *Illustrated Naval and Military Magazine* (London), 1890]), v.

76. Philip Colomb, *Naval Warfare*, 32–33, 43; Laughton, *Studies in Naval History* (London, 1880), 4, 20–22, 40, 61, 74, 81, 143, 149, 245–254; Philip Colomb, "Great Britain's Maritime Power," *Journal of the Royal United Service Institution*, XXII (1878), *passim*; Laughton, "Scientific Study," *Journal of the Royal United Service Inst.*, XVII (1874), 509–510, 523. See also Joseph Allen, *Battles of the British Navy* (Rev. ed., 2 vols., London 1878), I, v; Donald M. Schurman, *The Education of a Navy: The Development of British Naval Strategic Thought, 1867–1914* (Chicago, 1965), 2–3, 16, 53–55, 86–89; Vessey-Hamilton, "Discussion of J. C. R. Colomb's 'British Defence, 1800–1900,'" Royal Colonial Institute *Proceedings* (London, 1900), 26–27; Lieutenant Commander W. S. Cowles, U.S. Naval Attaché, London,

to Assistant Navy Secretary J. R. Soley, April 18, 1893, Cowles Letterbook, Entry 301, R.G. 45; C. J. Bartlett, "The Mid-Victorian Reappraisal of Naval Policy," in *Studies in International History*, ed. K. Bourne and D. C. Watt (London, 1967), 207, and *passim*.

77. Soley, "Maritime Industries," U.S.A., ed. Shaler, I, 567; Chadwick to McCalla Aug. 18, 1886, personal letters copybook, Chadwick Papers, N.Y.H.S.; Laughton, *Edinburgh Review*, CCCXXIV (1883), 281–302.

78. Jacob, "Does Germany Need a Navy?" *Army and Navy Quarterly: An Eclectic Magazine* (Phil., 1885), I, 381–384 [*reprinted from Colburn's United Service Magazine*]; Mahan, *Armaments and Arbitration*, 23; Williams, *Contours of American History*, 216; Mahan, *From Sail to Steam*, 281–282; Luce, *PUSNI*, II (1877), 5–24; *Dictionary*, ed. Heinl, 288; Gerald Graham, *The Politics of Naval Supremacy* (Cambridge, 1965), 97–98. But see Theodore Ropp, "Continental Doctrines of Sea Power," in *Makers of Modern Strategy*, ed. Edward M. Earle (Princeton, 1941), 446–456.

Early nineteenth century U.S. naval officers may have sharpened their perceptions of the role of sea power through a perusal of the works of some of these British and European predecessors. Mahan read Henri Martin, and we know that Hoste's *Naval Tactics*, Ledyards' *Travels*, Clark's *Naval Tactics*, and Charnock's *Works* were available in the libraries of U.S. warships in the 1820s, '30s and '40s. Burr, *Education in the Early Navy*, 173–175.

79. Lewis, *Naval Power and Trade in the Mediterranean, A.D., 500–1100* (Princeton, 1951), *passim*; Taylor, *Life of Mahan*, 41; Captain J. M. Scamnell, "Thucydides and Sea Power," *PUSNI*, XLVII (1921), 701–704; Sidney Gunn, "The Earliest Exponent of Sea Power [Homer]," *PUSNI*, XLIV (1918), 1031–1035; Alcibiades, *Of the Athenians*, *passim*; *Greek Historical Thought*, ed. Arnold J. Toynbee (N.Y., 1952), 162–163; Charles Brown, "The Heritage of Tyre," *Naval War College Review* (Feb., 1949), 33–46; Arthur M. Shepard, *Sea Power in Ancient History* (Boston, 1924); James Baikie, *The Sea-Kings of Crete* (London, 1910), 9–10; J. H. Thiel, *A History of Roman Sea-Power before the Second Punic War* (Amsterdam, 1954).

80. Arthur O. Lovejoy, *Essays in the History of Ideas* (Balt., 1948), 228–254; Beard, *Navy: Defense or Portent?*, 44–46.

chapter 7

Mahan Reconsidered

Captain Alfred Thayer Mahan may be the most familiar and most frequently studied of the naval aristocracy; but he has been regarded, variously, with such awe, veneration, or disapprobation that his role in the emergence of modern navalism has been overdrawn. Mahan, born in 1840, midway between the inclusive birthdates of the subjects of this study (1805–1875), possessed both "progressive" and "conservative" traits, but he found the "conservative" outlook more comfortable by 1890, largely because of his association with the world of sail, seniority, and naval history. In one respect, however, he was a thorough-going "progressive": his identification with his profession made him anxious about the state of the Navy and provoked him to seek sophisticated and effective ways of inducing Congress and the public to create a navy worthy of its noble missions, traditions, and officers. Endowed with no more originality or imagination than any other member of the naval aristocracy, Mahan was "chosen" only in the sense that he had been officially selected by his seniors to perform the formal acts of synthesizing the new navalist philosophy of his colleagues and his age. Far from being the atypical genius many have styled him, Mahan was a quite conventional member of his generation of the naval aristocracy.

From Sail to Steam

Despite the similarity of the arguments for naval expansion of men like Ensign W. I. Chambers and Commodore Stephen B. Luce, there were significant differences between the presentations of the "rising generation" and their seniors.* The unrealized expectations of the junior, and the guarded

---

* The average age of 37 identifiable "Young Turks" in 1885 was 31.5. Concurrently, 16 of their more senior "allies", and 11 of their "conservative" opponents, averaged 42 and 48 years of age, respectively, in spite of the fact that the "conservative" group included young Lieutenant Dennis Hart Mahan, Jr.

Numbered footnotes for Chapter 7 begin on page 348.

contentment of the senior, together with the speed of technological development in the late nineteenth century, made for "a sharply defined line where the
old and the new joined, instead of the former merging gradually into the latter,
as had been the case in other navies."¹ Lord Nelson's flagship, H.M.S. *Victory*
(100 guns), threw a broadside of metal that weighed less than a single shell from
one of the 1905 naval rifles; the newer rifles threw shells further and more
accurately; and the shells themselves carried more explosive and had greater
penetrating power. Tempered steel plate protected high-pressure boilers and
propulsion plants that were unknown on the sail and spar ships on which
Admiral Porter, Commodore Luce, and their peers had been reared. With the
blueprints of vessels authorized for the "new Navy" in the 1880s, there began a
tug of war between those who identified with the "old" Navy of sail—generally
senior officers—and those who identified with the "new ideas" and "new forms"
of construction, propulsion, and armament—generally junior officers.²

Officers whose careers predated the Civil War found positive delight and
value in sail-navy seamanship—in wind baffling, reefing, working to windward,
flying-moor anchoring, in all the mysteries of rope and canvas. They knew that
the return of the Navy to canvas after the Civil War had "kept the service and
the spirit of the service alive when it was an alternative between sail and
extinction." They knew the beauty of dazzling expanses of white sail and the
filth of coal-burning steamers. "Coaling a steamer," one wrote in the 1870s, "is
one of the most disagreeable tasks; the dirt penetrating every corner. For this
reason I would prefer to cruise in the old sailing ships as in the days gone by."
They believed that "the sailing of a ship, the handling of spars, the trimming of
sails, the hoisting of weights, the stowing of a hold" were all essential for the
proper character formation of midshipmen and apprentices. Rear Admiral
Thornton Jenkins, one of the more vigorous proponents of sail, carried the
logic of the "conservative's" argument to its natural conclusion in 1886 when
he argued that *since* there were very few sailing vessels remaining "in general
service," the Navy ought *therefore* to provide "more earnest training in this
branch before an officer or man is launched into the regular service." Spar and
canvas had become abstractions, worthy of attention in spite of their declining
function. When Captain William Sampson, one of the Academy's more progressive superintendents, went before a Congressional committee in 1888 to
argue that the Academy be given a steel vessel to replace the antique wooden
sailing vessel with its smooth-bore cannon that served the Academy as a practice
ship, Commodore Stephen B. Luce dispatched a round-robin letter to his
colleagues calling for their views on the matter and received a veritable broadside in defense of the sail training-vessel. One officer, Commander Charles
Vernon Gridley, later of Manila Bay fame, was particularly adamant.³

> I am on the sailing ship side of the question fully; so much so that I would not give
> any of [the midshipmen] a steam launch if I had my way. . . . I am sorry to see the old
> ships going. If I was going to sea tomorrow . . . I would rather have the *Constellation*
> than the *Omaha*.

328   Influential figures such as Admiral David D. Porter and William Conant Church, editor of the *Army and Navy Journal*, threw their support to Luce and "the magnificent sailing sloops that have done so much for the system." "The daring sailor" was extolled; the engineer and mechanic were scorned. As late as 1901 those who favored a sail training ship were still successfully combating those who hoped to shift to a more up-to-date training-vessel. Captain C. H. Davis, Jr., was frank about his opposition to a steam training-vessel; he favored sail "because I am by nature a conservative."[4] Forty-odd years of service on canvas-bearing vessels had given Davis and his fellow "conservatives"* their proclivity toward sail. Their ways were set; their "nature" formed. It took the younger generation two decades to overcome the inertia they represented.

The senior officers were not oblivious to technology. As early as 1861 men such as Academy Superintendent Commander Christopher Raymond Perry Rodgers sensed that the naval profession had become "a science, and while we cherish our love of seamanship, henceforward it must be considered only one of its elements." But even Rodgers was reluctant to dispense with canvas and the hearty pungency of pitch and tar. Bradley Fiske recalled that much of the midshipman's time in the late nineteenth century "was taken up with sails and spars."[5]

> We had sense enough to know that it was wrong, but we had to do it just the same. The whole life, the whole system, was damnable!

In the late 1870s a number of lieutenants and lieutenant commanders began to call for changes in the Academy curriculum and for greater acceptance of steam and the engineer. "The times have changed," Lieutenant Commander Caspar Goodrich told readers of the *Proceedings* in 1879. "More is demanded of the officer now than in by-gone days. . . . [T]he engineer is no longer the engine driver and mechanic, but an officer, like his colleague, of culture, science and reflection. The engine driving has passed into other hands." Lieutenant Commander Allan Brown, winner of the Institute's 1879 essay prize, argued for more engineering courses at the Academy and the merging of line and engineer corps:[6]

> The introduction of steam propulsion (much as we may regret its destruction of the romance of the sailing frigate) has made it necessary that the Naval Officer should not only know how to *sail* his vessel, but how to *steam* her. . . .

The advent of push-button, or trigger-and-throttle, warfare convinced many "progressive" officers that "the naval services of the future will have little of

---

* I do not mean to imply that each officer was either "conservative" or "progressive." Like C. H. Davis, Jr., or Henry Clay Taylor, he might be "conservative" on some issues (like the sail-stream controversy) and "progressive" on others (like promotion reform). And there were undoubtedly some officers who were indifferent to all intra-Service debates. But the "ideal type" labels do describe a great many of Mahan's messmates, and since they were sometimes used by the officers themselves to describe the different schools of thought, I see no harm in employing them here, with the foregoing *caveat*.

romance, but that it will be a cool, ready business—like the application of . . . modern science and research—with few, if any, opportunities for the display of personal prowess in boarding parties or cutting out expeditions." One officer told a Naval Academy Graduate Association gathering in 1888:

> The day has gone by for obsolete and obsolescent (Luce) seamanship. What we need most at the Naval Academy today is to teach the seamanship of the future. . . . To the devil, then, with topgallant and royal yards, their stupid and useless drills (even for gymnastic purposes), and the multitudinous and nonsensical questions that arise out of the practice of clinging to the dead corpse of obsolete methods. . . . We must cut loose from the dead past. . . . Shall we stick to the old practice because it is pleasant, poetical, romantic?

And another, a graduate of the class of 1881, wrote his classmates in 1890, "The old-time seaman is a thing of the past—out of place. . . . [The Navy should] do away with . . . fifteenth century notions. . . . [It should] drop off some of the idiotic rope block-strapping and bowsprit gammoning." That was essentially what "progressive" Captain Charles Sigsbee told Assistant Navy Secretary Theodore Roosevelt in 1897, and Roosevelt agreed that "sails" should go, "just as three centuries ago oars went."[7]

Perhaps Lieutenant William F. Fullam presented the strongest appeal for a shift from sail to steam in the Academy training curriculum. His 1890 *Proceedings* article drew comments from 19 officers. Fourteen officers, ten of them lieutenants or below, agreed with Fullam that sail was "as dead as Julius Caesar." Five disagreed, four being commanders or above. But the ayes did not necessarily have it, except in a purely academic sense. One of the "sail" men, Commander S. W. Terry, moved for the suppression of Fullam's article, and although his motion was defeated, Fullam's steam training vessel was too. As late as 1902, according to one ensign, many junior officers who favored a complete shift to steam training vessels were leary of airing their views. It was not until Fullam and his peers had physically displaced the advocates of sail in positions of authority—not, for example, until Rear Admiral Richard Wainwright sat in the chair Rear Admiral Luce had held throughout the 1880s and 1890s as president of the Naval Institute—that the "sails" were truly set and the "progressives" could claim that "the profession of naval officer" had "passed from the vocation of a partially educated sailor to that of a highly educated technical expert."[8]

"Wrapped Up in the Navy"

By the late 1880s Rear Admiral Luce was extolling the virtues of his successor at the War College, Captain Alfred Thayer Mahan. This man's name is familiar to tens of thousands who have never heard of Washington Chambers or William F. Fullam, but his significance, his place in history, is largely misunderstood.

Alfred Mahan was born at West Point in 1840. His father, Dennis Hart Mahan, was a professor of military engineering, tactics, and strategy at that institution.

The father "merged all personal aims" in the interest of West Point. As his son later recalled, "The spirit of the profession was strong in him." Professor Mahan firmly believed that history was "the source" of all military science. Alfred's uncle, Milo Mahan, was Professor of Ecclesiastical History at the General Theological Seminary (Episcopalian) in New York City. For two years, while in his teens, Alfred lived with the devout Milo and attended Columbia College before entering the Naval Academy. Like his brother Dennis Hart Mahan, Milo believed that history "explains and justifies itself" by a "living flow of events in their natural order." Mahan's father and his uncle were both dedicated to their professions and conscious of historical example.[9]

Midshipman Mahan was a typical Annapolite, wrapped up in his affection for the "band of brothers" and engaged in the familiar pastimes of most junior officers. "Yesterday was my [twentieth] birthday," he wrote an ex-classmate from his first foreign port, Rio de Janeiro, "and I . . . commemorated it by getting very drunk." Blockade duty during the Civil War was as boring for Lieutenant Mahan as it was for the rest of the naval aristocracy. His plan to bag Captain Rafael Semmes and the Confederate commerce raider *Sumpter* was rejected in spite of his case that such an "affair" would measurably lift the Navy's "prestige" (to say nothing of his own). Instead he was ordered to the wartime Academy at Newport where he was "universally hated" by the middies, but where he was able to serve as Lieutenant Commander Stephen Luce's Executive Officer in the *Macedonian* on a summer midshipman training cruise. Luce and Mahan risked an entire class of Annapolites looking for another rebel commerce raider, *Alabama*. When the war ended Lieutenant Commander Mahan was comfortably ensconced in a career that afforded "a pleasant chat with friends and a good cigar." In 1872 he married and was soon raising a family. But he was not altogether satisfied with this underachieving existence.

At 35 Commander Mahan's attitude toward life was simply a listless one. He complained of "an almost apathetic indolence and lack of interest" in nearly everything that once excited him. A few months after transiting the Suez he received two separate invitations to accompany surveying expeditions to Nicaragua "*a propos* of the ship canal business." But he declined. He later recalled that in 1875 he was "drifting on the lines of simple respectability as aimlessly as one very well could. My environment had been too much for me."[10]

In 1875 the Commander and his family returned to the States from duty on the South Atlantic Station and took up residence at the Boston Navy Yard. Within weeks Mahan was complaining of frauds and political jobbery. "There is little doubt that the Navy is rapidly getting into the most deplorable condition," he wrote his ex-classmate Sam Ashe, and asked Ashe to "stir up some people on our behalf." By 1876 Mahan was "very busy" writing to every one he could think of who would be "likely to feel an interest, or a duty" (he was not particular) in "seeing justice done by the Navy." [11] Increasingly, Mahan spoke of "we of the Navy," of "our Service," of "our behalf." Increasingly, the middle-aged Commander, dependent on his profession for income, social position, and personal sense of accomplishment, became identified with the Navy and its fortune. He bemoaned the Navy's "losing power and influence" in the community, and he unveiled an "intense and long hidden indignation" at the state of naval affairs. As he told Sam Ashe in 1876, his "interests" were "wrapped up in the Navy."[12]

In 1876 Commander Mahan was placed on temporary furlough pay, his salary cut in half. Today retirement on half-pay after twenty years of service is commonplace. In 1876 it was unheard of. The move was a department economy measure; Mahan considered it "most unjust," a "wholesale slaughter" of the critics of Navy Secretary George Robeson. Within a year he was back on the active list, but he now spoke of the "constant . . . uncertainty" of naval life. He feared that a Democratic capture of the national Executive would result in "many officers who left the service in 1861" being "placed over our heads." This did not materialize, but in November of 1880 another "economy drive" threatened to displace Mahan from the active list once more. "I was left hanging by the eyelids," he wrote Ashe. "I went to Washington to see if I could find some occupation."

By 1880 Mahan had taken a fresh interest in the proposed isthmian canal. Such a project would require the construction of "a Navy which will at least equal that of England when the canal shall have become a fact." Mahan was hopeful, but not optimistic. "A popular government will never dare to spend the money necessary," he told his alter ego, Sam Ashe. "Immersed as the people are in peaceful and material pursuits, the military establishment is necessarily one of our lesser interests."[13] An increase in naval power meant increased career security and renewed prestige. If the isthmian canal served to achieve these objectives, so much the better. This is not to say that Mahan's interest in the canal was dictated solely by personal or professional considerations. But these considerations do appear to have stimulated an interest in a project, which, five years before, had failed to excite the Commander in the least.

In 1882 Scribners invited Commodore James G. Walker to write the third volume of that firm's three-volume history of the Navy in the Civil War. Walker declined. Scribners then offered Commander George Dewey this opportunity to write of "The Gulf and Inland Waters." Dewey also turned the offer down. Finally, Scribners turned to Commander A. T. Mahan, who accepted. Mahan's first book was an unimaginative, factual account of the campaigns in the Gulf, on the Red River, and on the Mississippi. It ventured no suggestions of the significance of sea power. In fact, the Commander noted at one point that the naval investment of Island No. 10 had been unnecessary since the island would eventually have been taken "by the advance of the army through Tennessee." The author was essentially unimpressed with the Navy's role in that theatre of the war.[14] It was three years too soon.

In 1883 Mahan assumed command of the *Wachusett* on the west coast of South America. In July 1884, he observed the withdrawal of the Chilean Army of Occupation from Callao, Peru. Chile had governed Lima and Callao for over a year after winning the War of the Pacific, and a pro-Chilean administration had been installed. No sooner had the Chilean vessels vanished over the horizon, however, than the air was "rife with unexpected strife and revolution." Less than twenty years before Mahan had witnessed a similar upheaval as a result of the withdrawal of French power from Mexican waters. Neither incident evoked remarks reflecting a consciousness of the primary function "sea power" had played in the outcome.[15] It was still too early.

Mahan demonstrated no personal concern for American commercial interests in these years. On the contrary, he displayed a decided lack of sympathy for U.S. businessmen in Peru. They had taken the risks; they must now suffer the consequences. "Americans have opportunity enough in America." Mahan was somewhat reticent about landing marines and sailors "in a foreign country." The "very suspicion of an imperial policy"—by which he understood "outlying colonies, or interests"—he deemed "hateful."[16] That was in 1884.

The *Wachusett's* cruise brought home what Mahan considered to be "the sad state of the Navy" with particular poignancy. When a French Admiral paid a visit to Mahan's command, the French Chief of Staff eyed the *Wachusett's* antique smoothbore cannon and remarked, "Ah, Capitaine, les vieux canons. 'Ou sont les neiges d'antan?' Oui, oui, l'ancien système. Nous l'avons eu." Mahan raged: "We 'had' things which other nations 'had had.'" In March, 1885, he wrote to Ashe,

> If we are to be a laughing stock, knowing that we are, must be, laughed at behind our backs, . . . you cannot expect our pride and self respect to escape uninjured. . . . The Country cares nothing for the service.

Two months later he asked to be relieved of command of the *Wachusett*, "probably the worst commander's command in the service." He had been sufficiently mortified, and, as he "stood No. 2 on the list of Commanders," he hoped the Secretary would permit him to report to his next assignment a few months early.[17]

Mahan and Sea Power

His next assignment was the presidency of the U.S. Naval War College. This institution, the brainchild of Commodore Stephen Luce, was designed to serve as the medium for the discovery of universally effective "principles of strategy" through an analysis of "the great naval battles of ancient times." As early as 1862 Commodore John Marston's Board of Visitors Report had recommended the creation of a separate department at the Academy "of Naval History and Strategy." This never materialized. In 1874 Rear Admiral William Reynolds' Board of Visitors Report repeated the Marston Board recommendation and added that there were "several officers qualified to study and teach the evolution of strategic principles based on naval engagement of the past." Captain Stephen Luce was a member of this board, and in 1877 he went a step further. In a letter to the Secretary of the Navy, Luce recommended the creation of a graduate school for naval officers, independent of the Academy, for "instruction in the Art of War," the principles of strategy, and "naval history." No action was taken in the 1870s, but in the early 1880s Commodore Luce continued to solicit support for his dream from influential Congressmen, such as Senators Nelson Aldrich and John C. Spooner. In 1883 he called again for the "study of the science of war" via the "philosophic study of naval history." Only by examining "the great naval battles of the world with the cold eye of professional criticism" could one "recognize where the principles of science have been illustrated." Navy Secretary William Chandler responded favorably; he created an advisory board, consisting of Luce, Commander W. T. Sampson, and Lieutenant Commander Caspar Goodrich, which quickly recommended the acquisition of a discontinued poorhouse on Coaster Island, Newport, Rhode Island. Chandler agreed and the Navy had a War College.[18]

Early in 1884 Commodore Luce invited Lieutenant Commander Goodrich, a promising and level-headed Annapolite who had impressed the Commodore, to serve as the War College's first president. Goodrich had just moved his family to a new Navy yard home "at considerable expense" and was reluctant to move again in such a short period of time. He recommended Lieutenant Commander M. R. Slidell MacKenzie. Luce then approached MacKenzie. MacKenzie apparently declined also. When the War College opened in the fall, Luce was himself in charge.[19]

Service conditions did not permit the Commodore to remain at the War College for long, however, and he soon wrote to another, older officer, Commander A. T. Mahan, his old executive officer and Academy staff colleague, asking that he take the post. The fact that Mahan was soon due for transfer to a shore billet may have been a key factor in Luce's choice of him, but Mahan's special attention only the year before to Civil War naval history had been noted by the Commodore. Commander Mahan was pleased, but "surprised" by the offer. "I fear you give me credit for knowing more than I do," he told Luce. Mahan was aware, if Luce was not, that *The Gulf and Inland Waters* had been a mundane piece of work. None the less, Mahan accepted. Here was an opportunity to illustrate the usefulness of the Navy to the world. Mahan submitted to Luce that he may have "inherited" some "aptitude" for the study of military principles from his father, and he professed to have the "capacity" to discover and reveal these principles. As early as 1859 Mahan had dreamed of achieving "distinction" through "intellectual performance," of doing something to leave his name behind. In early 1884 "an old [*Iroquois*] shipmate and friend," Commander Nicholl Ludlow, had written Mahan to congratulate him for *The Gulf and Inland Waters*, and to encourage him to go on to write a more substantial, analytical work:

A *good history*, such as would find a place on the shelves of every good library public and private, is what we need very much. I hope you will think the matter over . . . and see your way to giving us what I have indicated.

334   On January 24, 1885, the Navy Department drafted his orders, and Mahan had his chance.[20]

Ever since Navy Secretary George Bancroft ordered "scientific instruction" for the naval aristocracy in order that they might "make themselves as distinguished for culture as they have been for gallant conduct," the profession had sanctioned intellectual attainment. Commodore Luce was not the only visionary. Admiral Porter also urged naval officers to "be great philosophers," and in 1881 Lieutenant Theodorus Mason looked forward to the day when a grand "naval history of passing events" would be "written by a naval man."[21] In the same year that Luce recruited Mahan, the Commodore also told an assemblage of his colleagues that naval theoreticians would "raise" the Service "from the empirical stage to the level of a science." Mahan read the address in the pages of the Naval Institute's *Proceedings* and immediately assured Luce that his research would show "the causes of failure and success" on the seas, "thus enforcing certain general principles."*

"There came from within," Mahan later recalled, "the suggestion that the control of the sea was a historic factor which had never been systematically appreciated and expounded." Why had this suggestion from within waited until 1885? The answer can be found in Mahan's remark to Sam Ashe in early 1886: "I want . . . to raise the profession in the eyes of its members"; in his remark to War College students: "Gentlemen of the Navy . . . we find our noble calling undervalued in this day"; and in his remark in *The Influence of Sea Power upon the French Revolution and Empire, 1793–1812* that his War College lectures were intended to "imbue" his students "with an exalted sense of the mission of their calling."[22] The War College lectures were to serve naval prestige and interests by building an image of naval usefulness.

Commander Mahan's first efforts were hardly revolutionary. In early 1885 he told Samuel Ashe that naval warfare was "unlikely," given the "geographical position" of the United States. If war was to come, Mahan's strategy would be defensive:[23]

> The surest deterrent will be a fleet of swift cruisers to prey on the enemy's commerce. . . . Running away is demoralizing. This threat will deter a possible enemy, particularly if coupled with adequate defense of our principal ports. My theory however is based on the supposition that we don't have interests out of our own borders.

Mahan was still far from the views that were later to bring him fame.

While dining at the English Club in Callao, Peru, Mahan read Theodore Mommsen's *History of Rome*. He later recalled that he had been "struck" with the notion of "how different things might have been could Hannibal have

---

* In addition to this Luce article, Mahan probably saw those of Mason, Chambers, Collins, and the rest of the naval activists. Mahan was a participating member of the U.S. Naval Institute and chaired at least one of its sessions prior to his assumption of the command of the *Wachusett*. And he avidly read all issues of the *Proceedings*. For example, see Mahan to T. E. Chandler, Oct. 2, 1875, and Mahan to his mother, Feb. 10, 1875, Mahan Papers, L. of C., and *PUSNI*, IV (1878), 127.

invaded Italy by sea, as the Romans often had Africa." In September 1885 he placed the *Wachusett* out of commission, was promoted to captain, and started several months of leave. After a brief reunion with his family, Captain Mahan retired to a carrel at the Astor Library in New York where he poured over files of the *Revue Maritime* and the British *United Service Institute*. He read Lieutenant Laperouse-Bonfils' short *History of the French Navy* and noted its "quiet philosophical way of summing up causes and effects in general history as connected with maritime affairs." In January 1886, Mahan wrote once again to Commodore Luce, describing his plans for the War College lectures. They would "begin with a general consideration of the sea, its uses to mankind and to nations, the effect which the control of it . . . has upon their peaceful development and their military strength;" they would include "a consideration of the sources of Sea Power,* whether commercial or military"; and they would discuss the significance of a country's "possession of military ports in various parts of the world, its colonies, etc."[24]

Mahan ('59) reported to the War College where he was greeted by Naval Academy Professor J. R. Soley, Lieutenants John Forsyth Meigs ('67), William McCarty Little ('75), and C. C. Rogers ('76), and Lieutenant Commander William Bainbridge-Hoff ('64), five "Young Turks" who had seen the possibilities of Newport. By September he had completed his lectures. They dealt almost exclusively with the naval wars of the English, French, and Dutch from 1660 to 1783. In October, 1886, Mahan told Samuel Ashe of how "surprised" he had been by his discovery of the importance of the French fleet at Yorktown. Within a week he was advising Navy Secretary Whitney that "a naval war" was "needed" to test new weapons such as the torpedo boat and the naval ram. It was "undoubted," Captain Mahan told Whitney, that "the ram will play a large part in the future."[25] Soley, Meigs, Rogers, Little, and Bainbridge-Hoff, immersed as they were in the problems of the creation of the "new Navy," may have puzzled at their superior's confidence in this short-range weapon, but Mahan was less concerned with such present-minded theories or technicalities to give much attention to questions of modern warfare; he was involved in the more weighty business of assessing the historical role of "Sea Power."

In later years Mahan was to claim that he had "thought" of sea power's historical role independently of any external aids. "The light first dawned on my inner consciousness; I owed it to no other man." Mahan willingly granted that other men, such as Sir Walter Raleigh, had earlier formed a notion of the role of sea power, but he maintained that he had been the first to place sea power in its historical context.[26] In his wide-ranging preparatory research, Mahan touched upon a number of notions that required only the slightest of restatement

---

* Note Mahan's use of capital letters here. In 1897 he told his British publisher, R. B. Marston, that "the term 'sea power' . . . was deliberately adopted by me to compel attention, and I hoped, to receive currency. I deliberately discarded the adjective, 'maritime,' being too smooth to arrest men's attention or stick in their minds." (Taylor, *Life of Admiral Mahan*, 42) From the first, Mahan planned his War College lectures with the public's pulse in mind.

/

336   to reappear as the concept of the influence of sea power upon history. The "light" that dawned upon Mahan's "inner consciousness" and which he "owed to no other man" emanated from the heat generated when the observations of Laperouse-Bonfils, Mommsen, Jomini, Collins, Chambers, Luce, and others underwent metamorphosis within Mahan's "inner consciousness" to re-emerge as the doctrine of Sea Power.

This metamorphosis did not take place independent of other factors. There had been plenty of opportunity for Mahan's "light" to dawn before 1885. He had witnessed a number of excellent demonstrations of the influence of sea power while blockading the Confederacy and while serving off the coast of Mexico in 1866 and off the coast of Peru in 1884. He had seen the might of the British Lion, in ports whitened by the sails of the Royal Navy. In fact, in March of 1885 the *Wachusett* had been on hand when elements of the British and American navies had landed troops in Panama City to help quell rioting in that isthmus. One scholar has claimed that Mahan's "naval career had furnished preparation for writing his sensational book by providing leisure and professional knowledge, and by giving him a wider look at the world than most Americans of his day had had."[27] But it is not these incidents that one must examine to discover the source of Mahan's "light." These events were reported in his letters without analysis or inference. In fact, in the only instance in which Mahan *did* offer any observation of his own—in the case of Peru—it was only to *object* to the notion that the United States might concern itself with "outlying colonies, or interests." One must look elsewhere to understand Mahan's behavior after 1884—to his concern for the state of the service, to his desire to strike a blow on its behalf, and to the satisfaction he must have felt upon receiving Luce's invitation to preside over the War College.*

Luce's dream of a War College that would elevate naval strategy in the public eye was matched by Mahan's own desire to lift naval history and strategy "to the dignity of a systematic, well-digested system." The Navy needed more "dignity" and prestige. Before long Luce was claiming that "Captain Mahan was doing for Naval Science what Jomini did for Military Science," all "to the credit of the American Navy."[28]

Mahan now expressed concern for the plight of "merchants" and respect for "the instinct of commerce." The United States, it was true, still offered "large openings to immigration and enterprise," he wrote in 1890, but these openings were "filling up rapidly," and Americans were now obliged to "look outward."

---

* Walter LaFeber (*The New Empire: An Interpretation of American Expansion: 1860–1898* [Ithaca, New York, 1963], 80) has argued that Mahan's writings "can be understood when separated from the personality of the author," "his soul," "his past." As a result of this assumption, LaFeber misses the mark and does not fully understand the Captain. No man's thought—I believe this to be a maxim of universal application—can really be understood divorced from the man's personality, "soul," or past. The reading of causality into the conceptualizing of a man is always risky business, but this is not to say that the motives are not there. The problem then, is one of locating, correctly identifying, and evaluating these motives. In the case of one like Mahan, who consistently spelled out his position in intense and personal lifelong correspondence, the task is made somewhat easier.

He spoke constantly of controlling "the markets of the world" and of acquiring the Sandwich Islands and the isthmus of Panama[29] (though he never lost his disdain for "materialistic civilization").

Mahan also made much of the spiritual value of sea power to his country. America, "in its evolution," was compelled to "carry its life" beyond its borders. The United States was "naturally indicated as the proper guardian" of the Sandwich Islands. Their annexation would be "first fruit" and "token" of the "steady pressure of a national instinct so powerful" that "no individuality" could resist or greatly modify it. History was "simply the exhibition of a Personal Will"; it was "a great mosaic" which the race was "gradually fashioning under the Divine overruling." The universe obeyed immutable laws—in this sense, Newtonian. Yet within the confines of these laws, nations struggled for survival. Expansion was the rule for this survival—in this sense, Darwinian. And above all of this ordered chaos, sat the Divine Weaver—in this sense, and *only* this sense, Christian. The mission of the United States was clear. The unfit required superintendence. For this a Navy was required. His uncle, Milo Mahan, would have argued that the destiny of the glorious Christian Republic was written in the stars or some infinitely distant place. The nephew maintained that it was written in the waves that lapped the shores. But whenever Mahan ticked off the areas where God and American civilization were needed most, they always turned out to be either strategic or commercial "outposts." And in every case he concluded his argument with a call for a "great extension of our naval power."[30]

Mahan spoke of "adjusting" his mind "continually to changing conditions."[31] What conditions? And what adjustments? Walter Millis has remarked that he found it "difficult to resist the impression that Mahan's major impulse was simply to produce an argument for naval building."[32] Others have either resisted this impression or have never given it a thought, and Mahan has come to us as a neo-mercantilist, a political "realist," a Christian idealist[33]—in fact, in virtually every guise but his own, a simple navalist first and everything else thereafter. Like his fellow Annapolites, Mahan hoped to "expand" the public's appreciation of his profession. He recognized the value in the "backing" of a "widely spread, deeply rooted, civil interest, such as merchant shipping would afford us." He recognized the role of lobbying among "those who affect legislation." And he believed in the value of taking his case before the public at large. "The age needs prophets to arouse the people [to the need of naval power]" he told his first editor, Horace Scudder. The form his writing took followed the function he hoped it would serve—the advancement of the Service. His first book, *The Influence of Sea Power Upon History, 1660–1783*, was an *apologia* for naval appropriations. As he put it therein:

This study has been undertaken . . . with the belief that the importance [of Sea Power] is vastly underrated, if not practically lost sight of, by . . . the people of the United States in our own day.

338   And later publications bore the same message. In 1892 Mahan advised Scudder:

> The Navy—and I may even say the country—needs a voice to speak constantly of . . .
> matters touching the Navy. . . . Except myself, I know of no one in the Navy better
> disposed to identify himself with such a career—and in the lack of a better, I should
> greatly like to do it. . . . I certainly believe I could be more useful in this way than by
> simply seagoing.

With "representative government" naval expenditures were only forthcoming,
Mahan was convinced, if there were "a strongly represented interest behind it,
convinced of its necessity."[34] Special-interest lobbies and public opinion were
such forces; Mahan's mission was to harness them. In 1869 Henry Varnum Poor
wrote a pamphlet entitled *The Influence of the Railroads in The United States on
the Creation of Its Commerce and Wealth*, which was intended to persuade
Congress and the public of the merit in a land grant to the Northern Pacific
railway.[35] Twenty years later Captain Mahan's lectures were accepted for
publication by Little, Brown, and Co., styled *The Influence of Sea Power Upon
History, 1660–1783*. The Secretary of the Naval Institute had sought to publish
the lectures in the Institute's *Proceedings*, but Mahan declined. The *Proceedings*
reached too limited an audience.[36]

Mahan's *Influence*, like Poor's, was intended to convince "strongly represented
interests" (exporters, manufacturers, farmers, shipbuilders, "expansionists"), as
well as the public at large, that his profession was vital to the nation's "commerce
and wealth." The good Captain sometimes appears to have used arguments
that were popular, if not particularly sound, to win adherents. For example,
he called for overseas bases as a support for a strategy of commerce raiding.
"Public opinion," he observed,[37]

> has great faith in war directed against an enemy's commerce; but it must be remem-
> bered that the Republic has no ports very near the great centres of trade abroad. Her
> geographical position is therefore singularly disadvantageous for carrying on successful
> commerce-destroying, unless she finds bases.

Conscious of the popularity of commerce raiding in some circles, Mahan used
this questionable strategy to justify foreign bases. Occasionally he gave public
indications that the effort to acquire Hawaii or the isthmian canal would result
in a "distinct advance" toward the creation of a more impressive Navy,[38] but
generally he was more discreet. It wouldn't do for a navalist to telegraph his
punches. And Mahan was, first and foremost, a navalist. Everything else
followed in the wake of his devotion to the Service. "Expansionists," shippers,
and businessmen could use a strong navy? Well, Mahan would argue for
expansionism and mercantile growth. In 1884 Mahan had "distrusted arguments
for manifest destiny" and was "traditionally an anti-imperialist."[39] Within a
few years he was hard at work shaping the ideology of expansionism.

To be sure, expansionist ideology was quite agreeable to Mahan. He believed
in "mission," "evolution," "righteousness," national honor. Navalism was in

no ways adverse to these. Many, in fact, were inextricably woven into Mahan's philosophy. But it was the Navy's growth and prosperity that was the first mover. It was the Navy for which he fought. And the Navy, for Mahan, needed no justification.

One historian has recently claimed that Mahan's concern for the future of American industrial growth was his primary concern:*

> Industrial efficiency led to the creation of a strong navy, but stating the problem this way reverses Mahan's priorities. He did not define a battleship navy as his ultimate objective,

(a move which would have been as foolhardy as it would have been disastrous to his real objective)

> nor did he want to create a navy merely for the sake of doing so. In the 1890s he did not see military power for military power's sake.

I disagree.

*   *   *

In 1893 two separate blows fell: The *Nation* attacked Mahan's "naval politics" and "armed evangelism," and the Captain was ordered to sea. The *Nation*'s incisive editorial barbs were relatively harmless, but Mahan was crushed by the thought of being taken from his writing. He begged for relief. "The contribution I may be expected to make to professional thought," he told Chief of the Bureau of Navigation Francis Ramsay, outweighed the two years at sea. He was too "useful to the navy" at his writing desk, he explained to Theodore Roosevelt. The Service would "receive more benefit by my work, which no one else is prepared to carry on," he modestly advised John M. Brown of Little, Brown, and Co. Authoring *The Influence of Sea Power Upon History* was "more useful

---

* Walter LaFeber, "A Note on the 'Mercantilistic Imperialism' of Alfred Thayer Mahan," *Mississippi Valley Historical Review*, XLVIII, No. 4 (March, 1962), 677; LaFeber, *New Empire*, 88. See Osgood, *op. cit.*, 40, for a similar statement.

LaFeber finds it "ironic" that Mahan should take an interest in the creation of a commercial empire at a time when America was without any sizable merchant marine (676). And both he and W. E. Livezey point out that Mahan's interest in the merchant marine dwindled over the years (LaFeber, 680; Livezey, *Mahan on Sea Power* [Norman, Oklahoma, 1947], 241–242). When looked at from the perspective that I have outlined, Mahan's "interest" in the merchant marine will be understood to have survived only so long as such an interest served to support his argument for a stronger navy. At first, the merchant marine seemed necessary to Mahan if commercial interests were ever to "look outward" and require increased naval services. But when it became clear that foreign bottoms served the same purpose and that arguments for a strong navy were no worse off with the elimination of the merchant marine, Mahan accordingly dropped it from his agenda. At one point Mahan's own patron, Luce, noted this preoccupation with the naval half of "sea power." Luce's review of Mahan's *Interest of America in Sea Power, Present and Future* (1897) pointed out that Mahan had allowed the views of a naval strategist to dominate those of a political economist: "There is a weak link in his reasoning. . . . Sea Power, in its military sense, is the offspring, not the parent, of commerce." Cited in *PUSNI*, XCI (1965), 28.

340   for the navy" than commanding the modern cruiser *Chicago*, he explained to Samuel Ashe.[40]

Moreover, there was the War College to consider. Mahan now believed the War College was "essential to the proper advance of the navy," and he felt that his publications had become "the chief cards of the college." Mahan remembered President Cleveland's Navy Secretary, Hilary Herbert, as the "pig-headed" Chairman of the House Naval Affairs Committee, who had doubted the War College's importance in 1893.

Appeals notwithstanding, Mahan was sent to sea. But when Secretary Herbert advised Mahan that he now had no intention of disbanding the War College and that he was planning to use Mahan's views to buttress his request for battleship appropriations from Congress, the Captain wept with joy.[41] His efforts were beginning to bear fruit.

Herbert was not the first to respond favorably to Mahan, of course. Theodore Roosevelt and William Conant Church, to name but two, were full of praise for Mahan's "enthusiasm for his profession." His writings, Church claimed, "have done much to restore our naval prestige," and, as such, had aided the Service "in a most effective way." In December 1891, Mahan wrote tongue-in-cheek to Luce of the "disposition grown up to consider my opinion of importance (a kind of special knowledge) due to the reputation *The Influence of Sea Power Upon History* gained me." Mahan's irony was understandable; he knew of the universality of the "special knowledge" some believed he possessed.[42] Yet here he was being summoned to Washington for strategy consultations when war with Chile appeared imminent.

And then there was 1894, Mahan's *annus mirabilis*. German and French officials sang his praise. Queen Victoria welcomed him to dinners at Buckingham Palace. Lord Rosebery, the Prime Minister, privately entertained the Captain. Cambridge and Oxford both conferred honorary degrees. The London *Times* acclaimed him as "the greatest living writer in naval history." The Kaiser and the British Admiralty outdid one another in ordering Mahan's books for their naval libraries. By 1897 Japanese naval authorities had translated Mahan's *magnum opus* for use in their Academy.[43]

Mahan, of course, was ecstatic. "The London *Times* has been calling me Copernicus again," he wrote his wife. "Shall I sue for libel? . . . 'In the philosophy of the subject we must all sit at the feet of the eminent writer'—my dear, do you know that it is your husband they are talking about?"[44] And Mahan was not alone in citing the *Times'* laudatory comments. The New York *Tribune* and *Herald* both carried the encomium. During the summer of 1894 the sale of Mahan's books quadrupled. English distributors began falling behind in their orders due to this increased American demand. *Fortnightly Review*, a British journal, sensed the change and reported that "Mahan has found listeners among his own countrymen . . . . They mean to be in all senses of the words a great nation." The next March Mahan returned to the States, delivered his "new Navy" cruiser over to the commandant of the Brooklyn Navy Yard, and settled into a comfortable armchair billet, free to write to his heart's **341** content.[45]

By 1897 Mahan had been elevated to the rank of prophet. The *Army and Navy Journal* reported that he "secures attention for whatever he may write." In November 1896, he retired after forty years of service, but his fame followed him. He succeeded in his goal of raising the prestige of the service. As a German naval officer put it, Mahan had "raised the general standard of the naval officer in all navies and had established the rule of science for the Navy in a manner unthought of hitherto." In June of 1897 ex-Secretary of State Richard Olney told a gathering of businessmen in Philadelphia:[46]

> Sea-power—as an officer in the United States Navy [Mahan] demonstrates in a recent treatise conferring almost equal lustre upon himself and his country—sea-power is an essential element both of national security and national greatness. The fact seems to be now thoroughly implanted in the popular mind and is largely responsible for the birth of our Navy.

It is difficult to say with Olney's degree of certainty that Mahan was responsible for any significant shift in public opinion in the 1880s. Mahan's impact is truly an immeasurable one. "Nobody was the father of the new Navy," wrote Rear Admiral Bradley Fiske. "The new Navy was the child of a public opinion created by navy officers."[47] Mahan was prominent among these officers, but he was by no means unique.

Perhaps his public fame is a function of the fact that his efforts were coincidental with the rise of the magazine and book publishing trade in America. In any event, each article he wrote in the 1890s "was elicited," he recalled, "by the request of the editors, whose perceptions were quickened by their need to watch the trend of events and provide the public with matters concerning which its interest was stirring." Scudder, Brown, and their colleagues were thus virtually as responsible for the content (if not the tone) of Mahan's arguments for naval expansion as was Mahan himself.[48]

Active groups tend to seek intellectual defenses for their views. In 1892 Edward Bellamy, author of *Looking Backward*, noted a general truth, that books produce "an effect precisely in proportion" to "what everybody was thinking of and about to say." In January 1889, shortly before Mahan sought a publisher for his War College lectures, a Mr. D. Lothrop wrote to Navy Secretary William C. Whitney. Lothrop had just read Elbridge Brooks' *The Story of the American Sailor* (Boston, 1888), and he was pleased with Brooks' presentation. Such works might "interest all classes of our citizens in the strengthening and development of America's maritime interests." The "whole story of the rise and progress of . . . maritime power"should be "placed before the people of the United States," Lothrop believed, "and in the most popular and presentable shape." This was essentially what Commander Nicholl Ludlow had told Mahan in 1884, and there were many Lothrops and Ludlows by 1890. When *The Influence of Sea Power Upon History* and Mahan's other books and articles

342   appeared in the 1890s, an active group of "expansionists," young Theodore
Roosevelt among them, avidly received the Captain into their midst, and proclaimed him their spokesman. They were clever. Who better than Mahan, a
distinguished-looking, mature (Mahan was 50 in 1890) naval historian, President
of the Naval War College, could rationalize and ennoble their case?[49] The
familiar adage of the man who led his horse to water might very well have
applied in Mahan's case, had there not been a vast number of horses already
drinking. The notion of the influence of sea power on history was not unique to
Mahan's braincap. Ideas do not spring from the ether, but they are "in the air."*

Reflecting the mood of a vigorous segment of his contemporaries, Mahan
found a receptive audience. He was not original, but he was eloquent. He was
not a great thinker, but he was an effective popularizer.[50] Talent is probably a
constant in society, and the social order probably defines how this talent is
exercised.[51] Had Mahan not been offered the position at the War College by
Luce it is entirely possible that he never would have written two lines of his
famed treatises. Perhaps another man of his age, asked by Luce to deliver the
same lectures, might have come up with the same thesis.

But a younger man probably would have given them a more modern tone.

"Progressives," "Conservatives," and Captain Mahan

Harold and Margaret Sprout recently offered the following
observations in an unpaginated introduction to a new paperback edition of
their *Rise of American Naval Power, 1776–1918*:

> Mahan's intellectual universe was deeply rooted in the seventeenth and eighteenth
> centuries. . . . Nearly all his generalizations reflected judgements as to what would
> have been possible or impossible on the day of Trafalgar. . . . Essentially a conserva-
> tive thinker, Mahan seems to have taken it for granted that the future would not be
> very different from the immediate past.

The Sprouts are to be praised for this re-evaluation of the officer that their
original study extolled in unqualified terms. They do not, however, offer an
explanation as to why Mahan was so "conservative" in outlook. This I am
going to try to provide.

Mahan's training and service experience were of, and his affections were with,
the age of sail.† He was not a great seaman, as were Luce and Porter, but he
identified with their art none the less. He had served on vessels with steam
capability, but he had little sympathy with engineers and other "staff gentlemen," "snoring away below" while his class, the line officers, guided their

---

* Thus Mahan found Navy Secretary Benjamin F. Tracy's support of the War College
"wholly unexpected." "He has reached an independent conviction," Mahan told Luce in
December, 1889. "I hope much from him." Mahan to Luce, Dec. 3, 1889, copy in Box 3,
Albert Gleaves, Papers, N.H.F.

† Consequently, Assistant Navy Secretary Theodore Roosevelt observed that "before
taking my present office, the captains with whom I had been thrown most intimately
[Mahan being the foremost of these] were ardent believers in the theory of sails." Roosevelt
to Captain Sigsbee, Dec. 24, 1897, Sigsbee Papers, Albany.

vessels with "the watchful eye" that protects against "storm and foe." He scoffed **343** at those whose faith in technology was strong:

> As if the subtlest and most comprehensive mind that ever wrought on this planet could devise a machine to meet the innumerable incidents of the sea and of naval war. The blind forces . . . buried deep in the bowels of the ship . . . do everything? . . . The steed is all, the rider naught?

Mahan submitted an essay in the Naval Institute's 1879 contest on "Naval Education" that Lieutenant Allan Brown won. Whereas Brown argued for *more* technical training and the merging of line and engineers, Mahan preferred "English studies" and foreign languages to the "materialistic character of mechanical science." Engineering tended toward "narrowness and low ideals,"* while literature developed "a devotion to lofty ideals, . . . heroism and grandeur." Engines could be run by "men of very little education." Topside seamanship, on the other hand, required "moral power," "self-reliance," "readiness of resource," and "magnificence." "Confinement" and "closet work," such as that in which the technologically-oriented younger officers were engaged, was dangerous, inasmuch as it impeded "the growth of the class of moral powers needed at sea." No amount of "mental calibre, far less any mere knowledge," could compensate for "the storm of battle."[52]

Less than a decade later, when he established himself at the War College, Mahan may have remembered with embarrassment his testy strictures on "closet work," but he was unbending in his criticism of "mechanical science." In August 1888, he told an assembled class of War College students of his fear that "the study of the art of war" might come into "too close contact with that mechanical and material advance upon which its modifications depend." Time after time thereafter he warned of the debilitating and corrupting effects of "too exclusive attention to mechanical advance, and too scanty attention to the noble art of war. . . . " He criticized younger line officers for their "preoccupation" with the design, testing, and production of new weapons, shipboard devices, and vessels. He defended what he called the "conservative" position, one with "the warrant of experience," against what he called the "progressive factor" in the Service, and the "impetuous advance" in naval technology. He feared that naval officers were paying too little attention to the past. His conservative outlook led him to assume that his "laws" of naval warfare were immutable. He fought those who hoped to place the War College under the control of Commander Caspar Goodrich's Torpedo Station at Newport. He appealed to fellow conservatives, Admiral Porter and Commodore Luce, who also believed that "[t]he Navy . . . wants to stop grubbing in the machine shops and get up somewhere where it can take a bird's eye view of military truths." And he won the support of William Conant Church, aging editor of the *Army and Navy Journal*, who also preferred "the daring sailor" to the engineer and machinist.[53]

The technological revolution had come upon these veterans of the days of

344   spar and sail with too much of a rush. They tended to equate technological change and moral decay. They feared the displacement of virtues they associated with the "old Navy." They focused their attention on the days before steam in order to establish these virtues as first principles. Mahan's five-volume *The Influence of Sea Power Upon History*[54] never brought him beyond 1815. This is not to say that Mahan was totally unattentive to the naval issues of his day. Of course he was, to an extent. People are rarely unidirectional in their outlooks, and Mahan looked at the present with something of the interest he displayed for the days of Blake, Jervis, and Nelson. But when he did look at the present, it was often with the eyes of his eighteenth-century heroes.

Walter Herrick and Samuel Huntington have claimed that "anti-intellectual senior officers" like Rear Admiral Francis Ramsay almost killed the War College in the late '80s and early '90s. This is a little misleading. Superintendent of the Naval Academy in the critical years 1881 to 1886, Ramsay was sensitized to the goals of the "Young Turks." "From a purely naval point of view . . . ," Ramsay told Captain Henry Clay Taylor, "I am strongly in favor of higher education of officers and am ready to assist it every way in my power, but I do think that the present War College system has very much the appearance of a farce. . . . " Ramsay saw the value of Mahan's books, but he couldn't understand why naval officers had to go to the War College "to have them read to them" by their author. It is true that Ramsay wanted Mahan, after some eight years at the War College, to see a little sea duty in one of the vessels of the "new Navy." But this does not make Ramsay an anti-intellectual boor. At the same time that he was trying to pry Mahan from his swivel-chair at the War College for a year's cruise on the *Chicago*, Ramsay was extending Lieutenant Nathan Sargent's tour of attaché duty. Sargent was engaged in gathering valuable new data, Ramsay may have reasoned, while Mahan was beginning to repeat himself and was getting out of touch with the issues and materiel of the "new Navy." Moreover, Ramsay or no Ramsay, there were a good many senior officers who defended the War College against Congressional budget trimmers. Admiral Porter from the very beginning wanted to give War College graduates special billet consideration in war-time as an inducement to officers to apply. Commander Caspar Goodrich, Commanding Officer of the Torpedo Station in 1889, helped Mahan's War College weather the storm, as did Captains Winfield Scott Schley, William Sampson, Francis Higginson, George Dewey, F. V. McNair, Rear Admiral Samuel Franklin, and many others. When in 1893 Ramsay insisted that Mahan try his sea legs, Mahan's younger brother, Lieutenant Dennis Hart Mahan, Jr., wrote him from Washington:

> I met Dewey this morning and he tells me that there has been a tremendous pressure brought to bear from naval officers themselves to keep you on shore.

Captain McNair, Dennis Mahan reported, had even volunteered to take Captain Mahan's place on the *Chicago*.[55]

Captain Mahan also had the attention of a number of commanders and lieutenant commanders, among them William Bainbridge-Hoff, Bowman McCalla, French Chadwick, Albert Barker, and Robley Evans.[56] And he won the respect of a number of junior officers, such as Lieutenants B. H. Buckingham, W. I. Chambers, Richard Wainwright, W. W. Kimball, and Nathan Sargent, Ensign Robert Coontz, and Professor James R. Soley.[57]

But there were also a good many junior, and some senior, officers who were distrustful of Mahan's new "art of naval war." For example, in the same breath that he damned "obsolescent (Luce) seamanship," Captain Richard Meade, 3rd, told the third annual Academy Association reunion body in 1888 that naval officers ought to study "modern war," not the "ancient" things being taught by "naval conservatism" at the "Department of Ancient Naval History" at Newport. And in 1892 Chief of Naval Engineers Charles Loring, President of the American Society of Mechanical Engineers, complained to that society's membership of "contemporary historians" like Mahan who had

> but scantily drawn attention to the immense influence upon modern history by the steam engine. They follow in the same well-worn ruts, giving dubious description of battles, names of monarchs . . . and the whole array of puppets who seem to push the car of time, while they are only flies upon its wheels.

Naval engineer Asa Mattice looked upon the War College as a line officer scheme to expand the number of shore billets for their kind.[58] Some younger officers appeared less interested in Mahan's histories than in target practice, maneuvering drills, engineering and architecture training, and the like in the early 90s,[59] while many of those who attended the War College between 1886 and 1916 were depressed by the "obsolescence" they discovered there. One junior officer felt that the college "appeared to point backward instead of forward." Maxims were being offered dogmatically "which a novice could see would never apply successfully to future problems." Strategy was presented, another recalled, as something "independent of mechanism," of limited value in an era of rapid technological change. Lieutenant William McCarty Little's war gaming, "more practical and progressive," was popular and successful, but the "Department of Ancient Naval History" was not. Captain Mahan, "the swivel-chair artist with the fountain pen," as Hugh Rodman remembered him, and even his successor, Captain Henry Clay Taylor, were too unflinching in their conviction that the only laws of naval warfare worth knowing could be deduced from a study of past battles, or so Lieutenant Bradley Fiske believed. In 1897 Fiske argued with Taylor in class over the mutability of strategy and tactics, which "must change in order to keep pace with the new appliances and mechanisms that are born."[60] Fiske and his colleague, Washington Irving Chambers, had in mind naval aviation, an arm of the Service that both had a hand in building. Fiske predicted that a study comparable to Mahan's on the "Influence of Air Power on History" might well be written one day, while Chambers looked forward to "future mastery in air." By 1899 W. W. Kimball and others looked to submarines as weapons that would alter the nature of naval warfare. Mahan was content with Lord and Lady Nelson, Copenhagen, and Trafalgar, with only an occasional "elicted" sortie into the world of the Russo-Japanese war and the fire-control system. Between 1895 and 1914 the Office of Naval Intelligence and the War College clashed over the planning and control of naval strategy, and the post-Mahan War College was slowly drawn into the modern world. After Mahan left the War College, the Chair of Professor of Naval History remained vacant for decades.[61]

With his belief that history was a "great mosaic," with his faith in immutable laws, Mahan was a Newtonian strategist. He left himself no room to maneuver and only faintly sensed the potentialities of submarines or aircraft.[62] When Lieutenant William Sims tried to persuade the Navy in 1901 to accept a continuous-aim gunnery system with redesigned mounts and sights that corrected themselves automatically with the pitch and roll of the ship, he could not impress the bureau chiefs or senior officers and won no support from Mahan. And later, in 1905, when the question of the size of guns for new vessels arose and Sims advocated guns capable of long-range, armor-piercing accuracy, retired Rear Admiral Mahan disagreed, insisting that existing weapons were adequate. President Roosevelt eventually resolved the ensuing debate in Sims' favor, and Sims received letters of congratulations from friends. "As for Captain Mahan," one read, "it would be an excellent thing for the service if he should confine his . . . ability to historical and literary questions." Another put Mahan down in words just as harsh: "Your article makes a back number of Mahan. Hope it has that effect—he's dangerous."[63]

In short, Captain Mahan was closer to the "old school" than he was to the new. And he knew it. Conscious of the criticism directed at him by younger men, he showed signs of wilting by 1895, when, at the age of 55, he wrote his wife: "Painfully do I feel the need of rest. I am too old—too old." By September of 1896 he promised to leave the naval questions of the day and the "new naval monsters" to "younger men," and though his roles in the gunnery controversy of 1905 indicates that he found it impossible to keep strictly to his promise, in 1907 he pledged once more to leave Service matters to younger men. "Perhaps I may lag behind," he confessed; he admitted to espousing "a growing conservatism." The younger "progressives" could call the shots. He would retire to the world of sail, a world that knew him well and accepted him completely. "I look increasingly to the changeless past as the quiet field for my future labors." He made an effort in his eastern Long Island retirement to keep informed of naval change, and he called his autobiography *From Sail to Steam*, but it is a mistake to identify him with naval progressivism or reform.[64] Mahan was ambivalent, but he stood closer to Luce, Porter, and Farragut than to Chambers Fiske, and Sims.

Retirement and Beyond

In retirement Mahan turned to new affairs, to Episcopal Church matters and to questions of international arbitration. He served as one of the

U.S. delegates to the first Hague Peace Conference, but he found the atmosphere of legalism stifling. He persuaded his colleagues to cast the sole national vote against the outlawing of poison gas projectiles and scuttled any hope of limitations of naval armaments. He opposed President Taft's arbitration treaties in 1911, and his associates later cited him to help defeat efforts to empower the League of Nations to compel arbitration. He urged Britain to "spare not" in its naval arms race with Germany, and he was extremely depressed in 1914 when President Woodrow Wilson forbade him to publish an article that referred to Germany as "evil" for its role in bringing about, and waging, the war then raging in Europe.[65]

In the fall of 1914 he accepted historian J. Franklin Jameson's offer to come to Washington to attend a research seminar, and he began a "history of American expansion." On November 14 he complained to his doctor, Captain F. J. Pleadwell, of "stomach trouble and attendant nervous restlessness." His sleep was "logy, heavy, and very irritable," but the next morning he "joined in all the singing" at the Episcopal Cathedral.[66] He died December 1, 1914, of a heart attack.

Mahan's usefulness to the Service outlived him. In 1922, William Gardiner, President of the Navy League and a Naval Institute official, suggested "a national campaign to raise an appropriate memorial to Admiral Mahan" that would involve the memberships of the Navy League, the Naval Institute, and the Naval History Society. Gardiner felt such a campaign could "be so conducted as to be of very material aid to the Navy." "Our famous Mahan" would strengthen the Navy's position at the disarmament tables.[67] Gardiner was only the first of a long line of friends of the Service who have helped to elevate Mahan to the historical pedestal he now occupies. Allan Wescott, Admiral C. C. Taylor, R.N., Captain William Puleston, U.S.N., Samuel Eliot Morison, Harold and Margaret Sprout, and recently Raymond Moley,[68] to name but a few, have all contributed to the creation of this "demigod" image, just as Louis Hacker and Charles Beard sought to give him notoriety by painting him as the archwarmonger villain.

None of these glorifications or defamations are very useful, but perhaps Allan Wescott's image of Mahan is the least tenable. According to this Naval Academy instructor, Mahan was "without the slightest trace of jingoism or sensation mongering." Only a "fanatic advocate of immediate disarmament and universal arbitration" would deny Mahan's "steadying and beneficent effect." The Captain was not Satan; but neither was he Saint Francis. And if Wescott didn't realize this, Mahan himself may have. In 1894, in a passing but insightful moment at the height of his career, he told his wife, "I can never feel sure that I am walking in the way God would have me even now."[69]

Chapter 7

1. Passed Assistant Engineer Frank Bennett, *The Steam Navy of the United States* (Pittsburgh, 1897), II, 771–772; "A Lieutenant, U.S.N.," "Style in the Navy," *The United Service*, IV (1881), 490–498.

2. Connolly, *Navy Men*, 11–12; Commander S. W. Terry, *PUSNI*, XVI (1890), 523; Long, *New American Navy*, I, 34; Lieutenant Dudley Knox, *PUSNI*, XXVIII (1902), 305–306. Cf. Charles O. Paullin, *Paullin's History of Naval Administration, 1775–1911* (Annapolis, 1968), 422–423.

Vincent Davis has documented a more recent clash of "old school" and "Young Turk" naval officers. After World War II many older officers continued to identify with surface vessel strategy, in spite of the role aviation and submarines had played in the war. Younger officers, whose careers were often identified with aviation or subs, seized the initiative and rewrote naval policy and strategy. Davis, *Postwar Defense Policy and the U.S. Navy, 1943–1946,* (Chapel Hill, 1966), 120–134.

3. Captain C. H. Davis, Jr., *PUSNI*, XXVII (1901), 276; *Life of Jack Philip, Rear Admiral*, ed. Maclay, 120–121; Jenkins, *PUSNI*, XII (1886), 17; Richard West, "The Superintendents of the Naval Academy," *PUSNI*, LXXII (1946), 62; Gridley to Luce, Jan. 19, 1888, Luce Papers, N.H.F. For more "old school" thought see Luce, *Text-book of Seamanship* (rev. ed., N.Y., 1884), *passim*; Benjamin, *U.S.N.A.*, 361–362; "An Ex-staff officer," *An Appeal in Behalf of the Navy and its Personnel, With Notes of Some Incidents in its History* (N.Y., 1886), 11; Herrick, *American Naval Revolution*, 14–15.

By 1905 enlisted "salts," like their officer counterparts, were complaining of the influx of younger mechanics who knew how to operate the new machinery but were without sea legs or a training in marlinspike seamanship. Connolly, *Navy Men*, 82.

4. Porter to Rep. Boutelle, June 12, 1888, Porter Papers, L. of C.; Donald N. Bigelow, *William Conant Church and the Army and Navy Journal* (N.Y., 1952), 198, 216; *Army and Navy Journal* (18 Oct., 1890);

PUSNI, XVI (1890), 385; Commander Charles Rockwell, "A Plea for Seamanship," *United Service*, 2nd S., VIII (1892), 516–517; Luce to Captain G. C. Hanus, Feb. 13, 1907, Luce Papers, L. of C.

5. Rodgers to Commander Wise, May 17, 1861, Wise Papers, N.Y.H.S.; Fiske, *War in Manilla*, 236.

6. McCalla, "Memoirs," Ch. IX, 23; Goodrich, *PUSNI*, V (1879), 323–344; Brown, *PUSNI*, V (1879), 306–307. Cf. Calvert, *Mechanical Engineer*, 258–259.

7. Commander Henry Glass, *PUSNI*, XII (1886), 44; Captain R. W. Meade, 3rd, in U.S. Naval Academy Association, *Third Annual Reunion, 1888* (Baltimore, 1889), 34–36; G. E. Perry to class of '81, Feb. 6, 1890, *6th Annual Report of the Class of '81*, 94–95; Roosevelt to Sigsbee, Dec. 24, 1897, Sigsbee Papers, Albany.

8. *PUSNI*, (1890), 505–531; Wainwright, "The New Naval Academy," *World's Work*, IV (1902), 2270–2271, 2280; Cf. "Nauticus," *The Truth About the Schley Case* (n.p., n.d., c. 1902 [copy in N.Y.P.L.]), 13; Rear Admiral French Chadwick, "The Great Need of the U.S. Navy," *Munsey's Magazine*, XXXII (1906), 559–561; Ensign T. C. Hart, *PUSNI*, XXVIII (1902), 298.

Joseph Schumpeter argues that the European professional soldiers of the mid-nineteenth century, representing an aristocracy often highly critical of industrialism and what it considered to be an attendant pacifism, vigorously opposed technological innovation and military reorganization along industrial lines. *The Sociology of Imperialism* (N.Y., 1955), *passim*. But this kind of military conservatism was thoroughly challenged within the naval aristocracy of the late nineteenth century in America.

9. Mahan, *From Sail to Steam*, v, ix, xiv, 89, 151; Henry I. Abbot, "Memoirs of Denis Hart Mahan," in *National Academy of Sciences Biographical Memoirs* (Wash., 1886), 31–37; Puleston, *Mahan*, 16; Milo Mahan to A. T. Mahan, Oct. 3, 1864, Box 21, Mahan Papers, L. of C.; A. T. Mahan to Samuel Ashe, Sept. 30, 1870, Ashe Papers, Duke U. Library; *The Collected*

Works of the Late Milo Mahan, D.D., ed. J. H. Hopkins (N.Y., 1875).

10. Mahan to Ashe, Sept. 21, 1869, July 11 and Sept. 30, 1870, Ashe Papers; Mahan *From Sail to Steam*, 274.

11. Mahan to Ashe, May 21, 1875, Dec. 27, 1875, Jan. 27, 1876, June 16, 1878, April 13, 1876, Ashe Papers.

12. Mahan to Ashe, Dec. 27, 1875, Feb. 1, 1876, Jan. 27, 1876, Jan. 10, 1881, Dec. 21, 1882, Ashe Papers. Cf. Mahan, "Our Navy Fifty Years Ago," *Harper's Magazine*, CXIV (Feb. 1907), 375–80; Mahan, *From Sail to Steam*, 8, 196–197.

13. Mahan to Ashe, July 23 and Aug. 19, 1876, Oct. 21, 1877, Nov. 13, 1880, May 9, 1879, March 12, 1880, Dec. 21, 1882, Ashe Papers.

14. Thomas, *Career of Walker*, 58; Scribers to Dewey, Sept. 12, 1882, Dewey Papers, L. of C.; Mahan, *The Gulf and Inland Waters* (N.Y., 1883), 31, *passim*.

15. Mahan to Ashe, July 26, 1884, Ashe Papers.

16. *Ibid.*

17. Mahan, *From Sail to Steam*, 197; Mahan to Ashe, March 1885, Ashe Papers; Navy Secretary William C. Whitney to Mahan, May 26, 1885, Letters to Officers Generally, 1884–1886, Vol. I, Entry 18, R.G. 45.

18. Barnard, *Military Schools*, 926; 43rd Cong., 2nd Sess., *House Exec. Doc. No. 1, Pt. III*, Vol. V, p. 39; Luce to Navy Secretary Robert Thompson, August 8, 1877, Box 1, Luce Papers, L. of C.; Luce, *PUSNI*, III (1877), 24; Luce to Lieutenant Boutelle Noyes, July 19, 1883, Box I, Luce Papers, and cited in *Life and Letters of Luce*, ed. Gleaves, 162–163; Gleaves, 82, 173–174; Rear Admiral Caspar Goodrich, *In Memoriam: Stephen Bleecker Luce* (N.Y., 1919), *passim*; Franklin, *Memories*, 273; Navy Dept. General Order No. 325, dated Oct. 6, 1884 (Chandler's order establishing the War College).
Concurrently (in 1883), West Point began teaching history as a separate subject for the first time. *Centennial of the U.S. Military Academy at West Point, New York, 1802–1902* (2 vols., Wash., 1904), I, 373–374.

19. Goodrich to Luce, Feb. 12, 1884, Letters of the Presidents of the U.S. Naval War College, Box 358, N.H.F.; Luce to Captain J. G. Walker, Aug. 29, 1884, Luce Papers, N.H.F.

20. Mahan to Luce, Sept. 4, 1884, Box 1, Luce Papers; Mahan, *From Sail to Steam*, 273; Samuel Ashe, "Memoirs of Annapolis," *South Atlantic Quarterly*, XVIII (1919), 203; *Mahan–Ashe Letters*, ed. Chiles, 47, 104; Ludlow to Mahan, Jan. 6, 1884, Mahan Papers, L. of C.; Secretary Chandler to Mahan, Jan. 24, 1884, Letters to Officers Generally, 1884–1886, Vol. I, Entry 18, R.G. 45.

21. Bancroft to Commander Franklin Buchanan, cited in Lovette, *School of Sea*, 59; Porter, *United Service*, I (1879), 476; Mason, *United Service*, III (1881), 180. Cf. Huntington, *Soldier and State*, 235–237, 241, 254–269.
Thus Commodore Francis Ramsay's alleged remark that "[it] is not the business of naval officers to write books" (Puleston, *Mahan*, 115) is not representative of all late nineteenth century naval officers.

22. Luce, "The U.S. Naval War College," *PUSNI*, XI (1885), 28; Mahan, *From Sail to Steam*, 274–275, 277; Mahan to Ashe, Feb. 2, 1886, Ashe Papers; Mahan, "Objects of the U.S. Naval War College" in *Naval Administration and Warfare*, 188; *Influence . . .* (2 vols., Boston, 1894), I, iv.

23. Mahan to Ashe, March 11, 1885, Ashe Papers.

24. Mahan, *From Sail to Steam*, 277, 281–283; Mahan to Luce, April 21, 1886 (copy), Box 3, Albert Gleaves Papers, N.H.F.; Mahan to Luce, Jan. 22, 1886, Box 1, Luce Papers, N.H.F. Theodor Mommsen (1817–1903) was a noted German historian of the Greco-Roman world.
Mahan also read Baron Antoine Henri Jomini's *History of the Campaigns of the Revolution and Empire* and *The Summary of the Art of War* in these years. Jomini argued for massive attacks on the enemy's main force—the army equivalent of battleship operations against an enemy's fleet. The extent of Mahan's indebtedness to Jomini (1779–1869) may at least in part be measured by the fact that, while at the War College, the Mahan's named their dog "Jomini." Puleston, *Mahan*, 85. See also Mahan to Luce, Jan. 22, 1886, Box 1, Luce Papers, N.H.F.

25. Mahan to Ashe, Oct. 31, 1886, Ashe Papers; Mahan, *From Sail to Steam*, 285; Navy Department, *Annual Report of the Secretary of the Navy* (1886), 153, 173–175. See also *Annual Report* (1887), 163.

26. Mahan, *From Sail to Steam*, 276. Mahan's introduction to the concept of sea power may have occurred at the Academy. As a midshipman, he had heard Academy Assistant Librarian Thomas Forde lecture on Sir Walter Raleigh. "It certainly

interested me, as very few lectures do," he told Samuel Ashe. Mahan to Ashe, Jan. 9, 1859, Ashe Papers.

27. Bates Gilliam, "The World of Captain Mahan," unpublished doctoral dissertation, Princeton Univ., 1961, 10.

28. Mahan, *Naval Administration and Warfare*, 188, 232; "The Navy as a Career," *Forum*, XX (1895), 283; Luce to Mahan, July 15, 1907, Mahan Papers; Mahan to Ashe, Sept. 8, 1887, Ashe Papers; Luce to Navy Secretary Benjamin F. Tracy, March 14, 1889, Luce to Captain J. S. Barnes, Aug. 5, 1889, and Luce to Lieutenant J. F. Meigs, Oct 27, 1888, Box 1, Luce Papers.

29. See, for example, Mahan, *The Influence of Sea Power Upon History, 1660–1783* (Hill and Wang paper ed., 1962, orig. pub. Boston 1890), 23, 25, 30, 34, 40, 42, 46, 50, 62, 287; *The Interest of America in Sea Power, Present and Future* (Boston, 1897), 8, 12.

30. *Interest of America in Sea Power*, 118, 239, 36–37, 50, 307–308, 325; *The Problem of Asia and its Effect upon International Policies* (Boston, 1900), 98; *From Sail to Steam*, 324; "Subordination in Historical Treatment," *American Historical Association Annual Report*, 1902 (Wash., 1903), I, 61; Mahan in the New York *Times*, Jan. 31, 1893.

31. *Interest of America in Sea Power*, v.

32. Millis, *Arms and Men* (Mentor Paper ed., 1958), 114.

33. See, for example, LaFeber, *New Empire*, 80; Kennan, *American Diplomacy*, 11–12; Osgood, *Ideals and Self-Interest*, 28, 40; Ralph Gabriel, *The Course of American Democratic Thought* (N.Y., 2nd ed., 1956), 372ff.

34. Mahan, *Naval Administration and Warfare*, 229; *Naval Strategy*, 447; Mahan to Scudder, Oct. 11, 1890, and Nov. 22, 1892, Mahan Papers; *Influence of Sea Power*, 76, 79; *From Sail to Steam*, 2–3. Captain William Puleston cited this passage from Mahan's 1892 letter to Scudder without comment (*Mahan*, 133). Autobiographies are, by their very nature, somewhat suspect documents, but often biographies must undergo the same scrutiny. Puleston was an apologist and glorifier of Mahan, less concerned with critical analysis of the biographical materials at his disposal than with their proper chronological arrangement. He traced the development of Mahan's ideas on the plane of naval strategy, but avoided the admittedly more tricky extra-dimensional problem of motivation by

accepting Mahan's own explanations regarding each transition and position. Captain Puleston "undertook this task" of writing a biography of Mahan, as he told Mahan's son, Lyle, in 1934, "because of my almost reverence for your father," and in order to "reply to [Louis] Hacker," a "contemptible person." Hacker had accused Mahan of spurring the arms race prior to World War I. "I would enjoy nothing so much as horsewhipping him," Puleston assured Captain Mahan's son. (Puleston to Lyle Mahan, March 2, 1935, Puleston to "Miss Mahan," Dec. 13, 193(?), Puleston to C. Parker Connolly, September 28, 1936, and Lyle Mahan to Puleston, June 10, 1935, Puleston Papers, L. of C.).

35. Alfred Chandler, Jr., *Henry Varnum Poor* (Cambridge, Massachusetts, 1956), 271. Poor was paid five hundred dollars by Northern Pacific men for the pamphlet.

36. Mahan to Luce, October 16, 1889, and Mahan to the Secretary of the U.S. Naval Institute, November 27, 1888, Mahan Papers, L. of C.

37. *Influence of Sea Power*, 116–121, 404, 27–28.

38. *Interest of America in Sea Power*, 102–103.

39. Mahan, *From Sail to Steam*, 295–296.

40. Mahan to Ramsay, March 17, 1893, Mahan to Roosevelt, March 1, 1893, Mahan to John M. Brown, May 31, 1893, Box 15, Mahan Papers; Mahan to Ashe, Nov. 24, 1893, Ashe Papers.

41. Mahan to his wife, Jan. 14, 1894 (or 1895), Mahan Papers; Mahan to Lieutenant W. L. Chambers, June 1, 1893, Box 5, Chambers Papers; Mahan to J. C. Roper, Feb. 28, 1888, Mahan Papers; Herbert to Mahan, Oct. 4, 1893, Mahan Papers.

42. Roosevelt to Mahan, May 12, 1890, Mahan Papers; *Atlantic Monthly*, LXVI (1890), 564; Bigelow, *Church*, 218; *Army and Navy Journal*, XXX (May 24, 1890), 532; Mahan to Luce, Dec. 26, 1891, Luce Papers.

43. Puleston, *Mahan*, 156–157, 159, 164; Warren Livezey, *Mahan on Sea Power* (Norman, Okla. 1947), 55–76; Louis Hacker, "Incendiary Mahan," *Scribner's*, XCV (1934), 263–268, 311–320; C. C. Taylor, *Mahan*, 60.

44. Mahan to his wife, June 23, 1894, Mahan Papers, cited in Puleston, *Mahan*, 157.

45. New York *Tribune*, 23 & 25 May, 1894, 1; 3 & 19, June, 1894, 1–2; 29 January, 1895, 2; 30 March, 1895, 2; 27

June, 1895, 5; New York *Herald*, 19 June, 1894, 9; Puleston, *Mahan*, 161–62; *Army and Navy Journal*, XXXI (1894), 824.

46. *Army and Navy Journal*, XXXV (1897), 54; Mahan to Ashe, 3 January, 1897, Ashe Papers; Acting Director of the German Naval War College to Mahan in 1910, cited in Dupuy & Dupuy, *op. cit.*, 196; Olney, 2 June, 1897, cited in LaFeber, *New Empire*, 240.

47. Fiske, *From Midshipman to Rear Admiral*, 88.

48. Richard Hofstadter, *Anti-Intellectualism in American Life* (New York, 1964), 409; Mahan, *Retrospect and Prospect*, 23; Robert Bridges (editor of *Scribners*) to Lieutenant W. I. Chambers, Nov. 14, 1891, Box 5, Chambers Papers, N.H.F.

49. Edward Bellamy, "The Progress of Nationalism in the United States," *North American Review*, CLIV (June 1892), 746; Lothrop to Whitney, Jan. 12, 1889, Vol. 58, Whitney Papers, L. of C. Cf. Peter Karsten, "Roosevelt, Mahan, and the Navy," unpublished M.A. essay, U. of Winconsin, 1965, *passim*.

50. For some conflicting views on the uniqueness and importance of Mahan see Millis, *Arms and Men*, 147; Grenville and Young, *op. cit.*, 11; Spector, "Professors of War . . .," Ph.D., 80.

51. Jack Ladinsky and Lawrence Friedman in the *Columbia Law Review*, LXVII (1967), 82.

52. Mahan to Ashe, Jan. 27, 1876, Ashe Papers; Mahan to William C. Church, Nov. 25, and Nov. 29, 1876, Church Papers, L. of C., cited in Donald N. Bigelow, *William Conant Church and the Army and Navy Journal* (New York, 1952), 218; Mahan, *PUSNI*, XIV (1888), 626–627; Mahan, "Naval Education," *PUSNI*, V (1879), 350, 352.

It was the pace-setting President Eliot of Harvard who headed the prize committee that picked Brown's essay over Mahan's.

53. Mahan, *PUSNI*, XIV (1888), 625ff.; and *Naval Administration and Warfare*, 188, 202; H. W. Wilson, *Ironclads in Action*, introduction by A. T. Mahan (London, 1896), I, ix–xiv; Captain D. W. Knox, *PUSNI*, XLVI (1920), 335; *Life and Letters of Luce*, ed. Gleaves, 325; Luce, "On the Relation between the U.S. Naval War College and the Line Officers of the U.S. Navy," *PUSNI*, XXVII (1911), 788, 790; Bigelow, *Church*, 198, 211–216, 220.

Similarly, British Rear Admiral Phillip H. Colomb, Mahan's British alter ego, expressed the hope that the "laws" of naval warfare he and his colleagues were revealing would prove that all had not been "entirely swept away and destroyed by the advent of steam. . . ." Colomb, *Naval Warfare: Its Ruling Principles and Practice Historically Treated* (London, 1891), v.

54. *The Influence of Sea Power upon History, 1660–1783* (Boston, 1890); *The Influence of Sea Power upon the French Revolution and Empire, 1793–1812* (2 vols., Boston, 1892); and *Sea Power in its Relation to the War of 1812* (2 vols., Boston 1905). Cf. Commodore Foxhall Parker, *The Fleets of the World: The Galley Period* (N.Y., 1876).

55. Herrick, *American Naval Revolution*, 10; Huntington, *Soldier and the State*, 241; Lieutenant Commander C. H. Davis, Jr., to Lieutenant Sargent, March 12, 1891, Vol. IV, Letters to Sargent, Entry 300, R.G. 45; "An Ex-Staff Officer," *An Appeal in Behalf of the Navy . . .*, 11, addendum; *Sec. Nav. Annual Report* (1885), I, 277–278; Ramsay to Taylor, Sept. 13, 1893, cited in Ronald Spector, "Professors of War . . .," a fine unpublished Ph.D. thesis, Yale, 1967; Goodrich to Captain Charles Sperry, March 5, 1906, Luce Papers, N.H.F.; Franklin, *Memories of a Rear Admiral*, 271–272; Dennis H. Mahan, Jr., to A. T. Mahan, May 3, 1893, Mahan Papers, L. of C.; Goodrich to Mahan and Schley to Mahan, *circa* 1890–1891, Mahan Papers; Mahan to his wife, Jan. 23, 1894, Mahan Papers; Captain Higginson to Lieutenant W. I. Chambers, Oct. 4, 1892, Chambers Papers, N.H.F.

56. Bainbridge-Hoff, *PUSNI*, XII (1886), 123, 125; Chadwick to McCalla, July 24, 1886, Personal letters copybook, Chadwick Papers, N.Y.H.S.; Barker, *Everyday Life in the Navy*, 380; McCalla, "Memoirs," Ch. XII, pp. 6–7; Mahan to his wife, Jan. 23, 1894, Mahan Papers.

57. Coontz, *From the Mississippi to the Sea*, 297; Wainwright, *United Service*, 2nd Series, III (1890), 20–21; Chambers, *PUSNI*, August 10, 1893, entry page, and in "excerpts" in black Ledger in Box 149, Nathan Sargent Papers, N.H.F.; Kimball, *Practical Prevention of War* (Washington, 1899), 4; Mahan to Chambers, June 1, 1893, Box 5, Chambers Papers, N.H.F.

In fact, Soley was instrumental in finding a publisher for Mahan's *Influence of Sea Power Upon History*. (Puleston, *Mahan*, 90.)

58. U.S. Naval Academy Association, *3rd Annual Reunion, 1888* (Baltimore, 1889),

352 34; Loring, cited in Calvert, *Mechanical Engineer*, 159; Mattice, *Queer Doings in the Navy*, 31.

59. See, for example, the correspondence of Lieutenant Commander Charles Davis with Lieutenant Nathan Sargent, Vol. IV, Letters to Sargent, Entry 300, R.G. 45; the torrent of letters Lieutenant William Fullam received in response to his article, "The System of Naval Training and Discipline Required to Promote Efficiency and Attract Americans," *PUSNI*, XVI (1890), 473–536, in Fullam Papers, N.H.F.; and Commander Bowman McCalla's "system of Naval Tactics," which he compared to Colonel Emory Upton's "Military Policy of the United States." McCalla, Ch. XVIII, 23–24; McCalla, "The Training of Naval Officers," *Public Service Review*, I (1887), 53.

60. Smith, *Coral and Brass*, 55–57; Captain W. S. Sims in *Hearings before the House Naval Affairs Committee on Estimates Submitted by the Secretary of the Navy, 1916*, II, 2609; Lieutenant L. C. Farley, "The Seagoing Officer and the War College," *PUSNI*, XLII (1916), 211–213; Fiske, *From Midshipman to Rear Admiral*, 221–222; Rodman, *Yarns of a Kentucky Admiral*, 31. Cf. Soley, "Our Naval Policy," *Scribner's*, I (1887), 228.

For a good account of the war-gaming efforts of Lieutenant Little (who had retired briefly in the 1884 doldrums) see Ronald Spector, "Professors of War: The U.S. War College and the Modern American Navy, 1885–1915," Ph.D. thesis, 130–136.

61. Fiske, "Air Power," *PUSNI*, XLIII (1917), 1704; Chambers, "The New Year, 1919," Box 48, Chambers Papers, N.H.F., Kimball, *Practical Prevention of War*, 6; Spector, "Professors of War . . .", 240–244, 261.

62. Mahan, "Subordination in Historical Treatment," *American Historical Association Annual Report, 1902* (Washington, 1903) I, 61. Cf. Livezey, *Mahan on Sea Power*, 250ff.; Gerald S. Graham, *The Politics of Naval Supremacy: Studies in British Maritime Ascendancy* (Cambridge, 1965), 28.

63. E. E. Morison, *Admiral Sims and the Modern American Navy*, 171; W. S. Sims, "Theodore Roosevelt at Work," *McClure's* (Jan. 1923), 98ff.

64. Mahan to his wife, March 4, 1895, Box 21, Mahan Papers, L. of C.; Mahan to Ashe, September 7, 1896, Ashe Papers, Duke U. Library; Mahan, *From Sail to Steam* (1907), 325; Mahan to Rear Admiral George Balch (Ret.), March 4, 1908, Balch Papers, U. of N.C. Library.

65. Mahan to Ashe, Sept. 7, 1896; Mahan, *The Harvest Within*, passim; *Armaments and Arbitration*; Beard, *Idea of National Interest*, 390; Puleston, *Mahan*, 318, 333, 342; Mahan to Josephus Daniels, August 15, 1914, cited in Taylor, *Mahan*, 275–276; F. A. Mahan to Theodore Roosevelt, February 11, 1915, Mahan Papers. Barbara Tuchman's account of Mahan's role in the Peace Conference (*Proud Tower*, 302–312) is exquisite. See also Livezey, *Mahan on Sea Power*, 19–20, 247.

66. Mahan to Captain Pleadwell, Nov. 14, 1914, Mahan Papers; Fiske, *From Midshipman to Rear Admiral*, 561.

67. *Annual of the Naval History Society* (Wash. 1922), 32–33.

68. See, for example, Moley's "Mahan's Long Shadow," *Newsweek* (July 18, 1966), 100; and "Meeting to Commemorate the Centenary of the Birth of Admiral A. T. Mahan, U.S.N.," *Journal of the Royal United Service Institution*, LXXXV (Nov. 1940), 617–629.

69. *Mahan on Naval Warfare*, ed. Allan Westcott (Boston, 1918), xvii; Mahan to his wife, Nov. 21, 1894, Mahan Papers.

chapter 8

Victory: The New Navalism

> Nothing is gained by increasing the armed forces amongst a democratic people, because the number of aspirants always rises in exactly the same ratio as the armed forces itself. Those whose claims have been satisfied by the creation of new commissions are instantly succeeded by a fresh multitude beyond all power of satisfaction; and even those who were but now satisfied began to crave more advancement, for the same excitement prevails in the ranks of the armed forces as in the civil classes of democratic society, and what men want is, not to reach a certain grade, but to have constant promotion. Though these wants may not be very vast, they are perpetually recurring. Thus a democratic nation, by augmenting its armed forces, only allays for a time the ambition of the military profession, which soon becomes even more formidable, because the number of those who feel it is increased.
>
> Alexis de Tocqueville

The concept of sea power, be it that of W. I. Chambers or A. T. Mahan, proved to be an effective ideological weapon in the appropriations battles of the fin de siècle. And eventually the new ships, a "splendid little war," and Congressional legislation broke up the promotion log-jam. The lessons learned in the anxious years were recalled by the exponents of sea power time and time again in the twentieth century, and navalism steadily gained ground on its foes until, by mid-century, the U.S. Navy was more powerful by far at sea than the combined naval forces of the rest of the world and was holding its own with the U.S. Air Force in strategy debates. The growth of the "new Navy" eventually outran the capacity of Annapolis to produce enough officers for all the new warships, which resulted in the commissioning of enlisted personnel and non-Academy college reservists. But navalism survived the growing pains. The

Numbered footnotes for Chapter 8 begin on page 379.

353

354   modern naval officer is less aristocratic than his naval ancestor, but he has basically the same navalist mores.

The Ships

The naval aristocracy's efforts on behalf of the merchant marine
may have facilitated the passage of the Ocean Mail Act of 1891 and a similar Act
of May 10, 1892, both of which were designed to encourage the construction of
U.S.-owned and operated merchantmen. But neither act stemmed the flow of
trade to foreign-registered bottoms. While 12.5% of the nation's overseas
trade had been carried by U.S. ships in 1891, only 8.2% of it was so carried by
1901.[1]

Naval officers could not have been *too* upset. After all, merchant marine
expansion had been fundamentally a means of securing naval expansion to
them. And if merchant marine growth was slow, *naval* tonnage grew at a better
pace. A Treasury surplus in the 1880s provided a rationale for initial expenditures, while, conversely, policy elites in business and government promoted
naval construction during the depression of the 1890s to protect fabled overseas
markets that were to absorb American overproduction. Four ships were
authorized in 1883, and four more in 1885. Between 1885 and 1889, 30 more
vessels were allowed, including two armored battle cruisers, *Texas* and *Maine*,
and a light cruiser, *Olympia*. Four battleships were authorized between 1890
and 1894; and in April 1895, in the same week that one of the battleships, *Iowa*,
and several torpedo-boat destroyers were completed, two more battleships,
Kentucky and *Kearsarge*, were authorized. It had been "a *grand* week for the
naval service," one junior officer remarked. Locally-oriented anti-navalists like
Jerry Simpson of Kansas and Oscar Callaway of Texas fought every naval
appropriations bill tooth and nail, but cosmopolitan congressional leaders
such as Henry Cabot Lodge of Massachusetts, Benjamin F. Tracy and
William Whitney of New York, and William E. Chandler of New Hampshire steadily added more and more expensive warships to the emerging "new
Navy."[2]

As Congressional appropriations flowed more easily, and foreign navies
burgeoned, naval officers constantly revised their estimates of a minimal rate
of naval construction. In August 1888, Commander French Chadwick set his
sights on "nothing less than 150 ships." Three months later the figure had risen
to "nothing less than 200 ships as a minimum." Concurrently Rear Admiral
Luce was calling for "at least" 20 battleships. By 1903 the Navy General Board
wanted first 40, and then 48, battlewagons—one for every state or territory.
The number 48 had less strategical significance than it had political potential.
As ex-Navy Secretary John Long recalled,[3]

> Every State, of course, desired to have its name given to a man-of-war. No State was
> content with anything less than the biggest battleship. One senator came to me in
> great distress fearing that he would lose his reelection because a ship of not quite that
> size had been named for his state.

With the Anglo-German naval arms race and World War I, naval officers revised their goals again. Rear Admiral Bradley Fiske now spoke of the need for "superadequateness," and Rear Admiral Bowman McCalla began to talk of 75 battleships as a minimum. Consequently, when Rear Admiral Josiah McKean was asked to express a view on several alternative appropriation proposals in 1916, he told the House Naval Affairs Committee: 'Whichever [program] would call for the biggest appropriations is the one we need, and we need it as soon as possible."[4] By 1920 the "Navy second to none" had arrived.

The Line

As Naval appropriations grew in the 1890s, so did pressures for resolution of professional tensions. "Our types of ship and armament are undergoing radical change, and it is not unnatural to anticipate the need of change in other directions," Lieutenant Commander Harry Knox reasoned in 1890. In that year Navy Secretary Benjamin F. Tracy advised the Senate Naval Affairs Committee of several "organizations among naval officers not authorized by the Navy Department" that were "designed to advance the interests" of certain types of officers by "influencing Congressional legislation." These were the Line Officers Association, a similar association of naval engineers, an association of medical and disbursing officers, and an Ensigns Association.[5] By 1900, only one remained.

*　　　*　　　*

As early as 1868, Navy Secretary Gideon Welles had realized that the line-engineer controversy could be "prevented in only one way." "The officers must themselves become engineers as well as sailors." Welles failed to persuade either branch of the merits of merging. "A younger man than myself must embark in this conflict," he noted. Thirty years later Captains Bowman McCalla and Robley Evans proposed, and young Assistant Navy Secretary Theodore Roosevelt approved, the same "amalgamation" principle that Welles and his Chief of Engineers, Benjamin Isherwood, had advanced in 1867. The situation was different. "The engineering profession throughout the country had become a party to the issue," Navy Secretary John Long recalled, "and was demanding that its representatives in the navy should receive that measure of official recognition (absolute rank) which the high character of the calling requires."[6]

Not all officers felt that amalgamation was the answer, of course. Rear Admiral Thomas Selfridge, Jr., on the verge of retirement, warned Navy Secretary Long that any "mixing" of the two corps "would be fraught with great injury to the service." Line officers should not have to work with engines, he insisted. Selfridge's advice was not taken, and the 1899 Naval Personnel Act amalgamated the two corps. Younger line and engineering officers who had joined forces to lobby for promotion reform in 1890 were delighted; older ones were often less enthusiastic. Typical of this breed was ex-Chief Engineer G. W. Baird, who was offended by the move that made him a Rear Admiral but destroyed his corps. He had come from a family of engineers and was "not only satisfied with his title of chief engineer, but was proud of it." By the amalgamation, he "lost his identity," as he put it himself.[7]

The passing of the engineers presaged more than one propulsion-plant failure, as green ensigns unfamiliar with boiler tubes and shaft bearings found themselves doing the job of the old Passed Assistant Engineer. With the 1905 *Bennington* disaster, a young line officer in charge of that ship's engineering plant was initially saddled with the blame, and the foes of amalgamation spoke out once again. Charging that the amalgamated line-engineer officer was a "sterile hybrid" and that both line and engineering duties were suffering as a result of the merger, retired Rear Admiral Luce issued "a plea for an Engineer Corps in the Navy" in the *North American Review*. In time, however, the number of breakdowns declined. In 1901 the Navy Department had created a post-graduate engineering school at the Academy to teach young Annapolites what their warrant machinists were doing down below. By 1915 the Service required 223 of these surrogate engineers.[8] A high price had been paid—all naval aristocrats would have to learn the engineer's trade—but the line-engineer controversy was resolved.

The most urgent professional tension, the promotion bottleneck, was also relieved in these years, but this was not as simple a business as the resolution of the line-engineer controversy. The Naval Personnel Act of 1899, which provided for the amalgamation of the two feuding officer corps, also provided for a radically different system of promotion.

By 1891, the dissatisfaction among junior officers with the Act of August 5, 1882, had reached such proportions that the Navy Department convened a special board, chaired by Academy Superintendent Captain R. L. Phythian ('56) "to report upon the present stagnation of officers in the line of the Navy." This board argued for the restoration of 29 senior billets that had been cycled out of existence in accordance with the provisions of the 1882 Act. The "new Navy" had created a need for more of these senior billets, and the Phythian board saw their resurrection as a means of temporarily accelerating promotion. The board also recommended a voluntary retirement plan for captains and, in a radical gesture, suggested a system of forced retirement ("plucking") for captains who had not demonstrated sufficient ability to be awarded flag rank. The impetus for this final recommendation may have come from the board's "progressive" members, one of whom wrote to Lieutenant Nathan Sargent ('70) in the month the report was submitted of his pleasure with its form. Promotion law revision was "inevitable," Sargent was told, "and must come in spite of the open or secret resistance of those who are in a position to profit by the present preposterous state of affairs."[9]

Initially nothing came of the report's ambitious "plucking" recommendation,[10] but the junior officers persisted. In 1894, a joint Congressional Naval Committee heard testimony on naval promotion problems. Senior officers suggested a merit system by which a few exceptional junior officers might experience an accelerated promotion rate; junior officers countered with an appeal for sufficient "plucking" of senior officers to guarantee enough vacancies to provide for a proper promotion flow. Lieutenant Commander William Cowles ('67), Theodore Roosevelt's brother-in-law, wrote from his post as Naval Attaché, London, to Assistant Navy Secretary McAdoo, urging promotion law reform that would "avoid the necessity of having gray haired men in the Ward Room." British journalists were not being very "polite" in their treatment of U.S. naval promotion laws, Cowles advised McAdoo, but their criticism "certainly could not have been more true."[11]

The result of Congress' investigation of naval officers promotion problems was the drafting of the so-called Meyer Bill which proposed to "pluck" officers from "the hump"—that is, from thoses classes that entered the Academy between 1861 and 1865. The Line Officers Association, controlled by "conservative" senior officers, fought this bill tooth and nail. Younger "radicals,"* in turn, sought support for the Meyer Bill. "We cannot stand this stagnation in promotion any longer," Ensign Roger Welles ('84) dramatically confided to his father, in October 1895:[12]

> and we (the junior officers particularly) are doing all we can to relieve it. The Junior Officers are a large majority of the whole Navy and I think will accomplish something; but it will only be done by our work and by the work of those interested in us, principally the latter. . . . [U]nless something is done this Congress your son will spend the best days of his life in subordinate grades.

A month after Welles wrote this letter, he and his fellow junior officers overthrew the leadership of the Line Officers Association. On November 23, 1895, an unusually large number of junior officers attended the scheduled annual business meeting of the Association. Some 65 officers in all were present, the majority being lieutenants, lieutenants (junior grade), and ensigns. Lieutenant W. H. Schuetze ('73,) a Phythian board veteran, and "one or two others" held proxies of 297 junior officers. After defeating a senior officer motion to elect new officers by rank, Lieutenant David Peacock ('74) nominated an entire slate of junior officers; and with the support of a few senior officers such as Captain William Sampson and Commander French Chadwick the junior officer majority elected their own kind to take the helm of their profession's primary lobbying organization.[13]

Within a week, senior line officers were hard at work organizing a group of their own, "The Naval Association." Mrs. Captain George Remey reported to her son on November 29 that her husband had "gone to a meeting" of senior officers the previous evening "in regard to matters of the Navy which are to be brought before the Congress this session." There were "many younger officers

---

* The "conservative" and "radical" labels in this case were given to the two factions by Marine Commandant Colonel Charles Heywood, in a Dec. 29, 1893, letter to Captain H. C. Taylor (Class of '64), whom he calls "conservative" (in Letters of the Presidents of the War College, Box 358, N.H.F.).

working against the older ones. . . . I think there is a danger of injustice to many of your father's grade and higher."

The Naval Association proposed to fight "the essential features of the Meyer Bill" and to "substitute" one of its own, drafted "upon conservative lines." All officers with the rank of lieutenant or above were invited to join. Membership was to be confined, a Naval Association circular explained, "to Line Officers of experience." The key organizers were Commodore Edmund O. Matthews ('55), the ousted head of the Line Officers Association, Captain George Remey ('59), Commander Charles Sigsbee ('64), Commander Benjamin Lamberton ('65), and Lieutenant Dennis Hart Mahan, Jr. ('69), Captain A. T. Mahan's younger brother. The Naval Association conceived of its parent, the Line Officers Association, now in the hands of junior line officers, as "an instrument for promoting Class legislation, most injurious to the Navy." Naval Association leadership sought to persuade Congressmen and senior members of the naval aristocracy who had not yet thrown in their lot with either group that the Line Officers Association was no longer representative of the line and that the Navy ought to "repress" its publications and directives.

The Naval Association gambit was bold, but it failed to crush the revolt. Two days before the senior group's circular was dispatched, the new officers of the Line Officers Association were already in communication with uncommitted officers. They were fully aware of the "bitter feeling" among "many senior officers," and they advised the profession of the resignation of 10 disaffected senior men, all known opponents of the Meyer Bill. The new leaders of the Line Officers Association accurately advised uncommitted personnel that a number of senior officers sided with them and favored the Meyer Bill as a means of relieving stagnation. "In unity of action alone, can success of any kind be secured," Ensign Thomas Magruder ('89), the new Secretary of the Line Officers Association, wrote to one key Captain, Caspar Goodrich ('65). Magruder asked for Goodrich's support.

Goodrich was not altogether satisfied with the Meyer Bill. He preferred a "more conservative" measure. But he was willing to accept the "Young Turk" coup as a *fait accompli* and to lobby for the Meyer Bill until something more viable was offered. "Our condition is such that any change is better than nothing," he told Commander "Ben" Lamberton of the Naval Association faction on December 8.

It took three and a half more years for the junior officers to persuade the Navy Department (represented in 1897–1898 by Lieutenant Commander Cowles' brother-in-law, Assistant Navy Secretary Theodore Roosevelt) and the Congress to "weed out" the chaff among the senior officers and thus spur promotion. Some, like Joel Barber, Allan Brown, and Theodorus Mason, lost hope and resigned (Mason only a few years before the "splendid little" Spanish-American War would have made him an admiral in nothing flat). But for those "Young Turks" who kept the faith, the 1899 Naval Personnel Act was, at least vicariously, a triumph.[14]

The passage of this Act, with its provision for the "plucking" of unsatisfactory captains, capped a string of victories for the younger officers. A "new Navy" had been built, the Service had covered itself with glory during the war with Spain, a new enlisted recruitment policy designed to attract "native Americans" had been initiated, the line-engineer controversy had been resolved, and now the promotion bottleneck had been eliminated. The naval aristocracy had dwindled from 1,866 officers in 1881 to 1,399 officers in 1897, and career anxiety had been high. But by 1899, the Annapolites had won their "struggle, against bigotry and caprice, for a mere continued existence." In 1903 Congress increased the pay and allowed complement of each level of the line officer corps and doubled the number of Academy appointments allowed each Congressman. By 1904, there were 2,014 active duty naval officers, and by 1925, the figure had burgeoned to 8,918, over six times the 1897 complement. In the 1880s and '90s the Academy graduated an average of 41 Annapolites per year. By 1905 the figure had risen to 114, and it continued to grow thereafter until the 1920s. Rear Admiral Luce ('48) had served as president of the Naval Institute throughout the late 1880s and the '90s. He had opposed amalgamation, the shift to an all-steam fleet, and the 1899 Personnel Act. By 1900, "progressive" Rear Admiral William Sampson ('61) had relieved him, to be succeeded by Rear Admirals Caspar Goodrich ('65), Richard Wainwright ('68), and Bradley Fiske ('74).[15] The "Young Turks" of the 1880s had slowly risen to the top by the first decade of the twentieth century, and found themselves in control of their profession (albeit by attrition and by-the-numbers promotion).

Paradoxically, the "Young Turks" of the 1880s became the "Old Guard" of the early twentieth century. Thus the rise of a new generation of naval leaders was not the panacea some may have imagined it would be. Organizational reforms, coordinating the Office of Naval Intelligence, the War College, the General Board, the Bureau of Navigation, and the Board of Inspection, produced a reasonably effective jury-rig of a naval general staff by 1902, but it would be another two decades before the decentralized bureau system would give way to a more centralized organization under a Chief of Naval Operations. The creation of the office of C.N.O. represented a victory for the "progressive" proponents of managerial reorganization, but World War II clearly demonstrated that the bureau system was virtually as vital as its fin de siècle defenders had claimed.[16]

When aviation attracted a number of young officers during and after World War I, they met with opposition from battleship-oriented veterans of the appropriations battles of the late nineteenth century such as Josiah McKean ('84); Robert Coontz ('85), C.N.O. from 1921 to 1923; Edward Eberle ('85), C.N.O. from 1923 to 1927; and S. S. Robison ('88), Commander of the U.S. Fleet in 1926. Thus the request of Lieutenant J. J. ("Jocko") Clark ('18) for flight school training in 1923 was disapproved by his superior, Admiral Henry B. Wilson ('81), who could see no benefit in it to Clark's career or the Navy's interest. Wilson, "fighting a losing battle against progress,"[17] prevented the adoption of a course at the Naval Academy on "the science and theory of aviation" until his retirement from the superintendency in 1925. And it was not until the late 1940s that carrier-oriented commanders were able to wrest the strategy-planning initiative from battleship-oriented admirals, and not until the mid-1960s that advocates of naval ballistic missiles (Regulus, Polaris, Poseidon) found a secure berth in the naval appropriations ledger. Apparently the "progressive" junior officers only remained "progressive" as long as they were junior officers. With seniority and rank came a decline in career anxieties—and, generally speaking, a concurrent decline in innovative propensities.[18]

Another paradox: The new promotion rules were neither immediately useful to, nor terribly popular with, much of the Chambers–Fullam generation of the naval aristocracy. In 1906, the youngest captain in the U.S. Navy was still some 20 years older than his British or European counterpart. The U.S. officer still spent, on the average, only about two years as a Rear Admiral before retiring, while in other navies officers enjoyed six or more years in flag rank. The men who had suffered from "the hump" and the Act of August 5, 1882, obtained little relief from the 1899 Naval Personnel Act; on the contrary, a good many of them suffered from it. In 1897, newly-elevated Captain McCalla ('65), long an advocate of promotion law reform, sent Assistant Navy Secretary Theodore Roosevelt a memorandum protesting the proposed Personnel Bill. Under its terms McCalla and his classmates would be singled out for "plucking," whereas they were the only officers sufficiently "experienced" to assume leadership of the "new Navy." McCalla's protest was ignored; Roosevelt, born in 1858, probably identified with younger "progressives"—with the generation of Sims and Welles. In any event, McCalla, dissatisfied with the consideration now shown to junior officers, complained of the "growing tendency in our naval service to give exclusive praise to subordinates, and none to the captains." Captain Washington I. Chambers ('76), another early advocate of promotion reform, took a different view of things after having been "plucked" himself in 1913 by the "star chamber" of officers assigned the task of retiring the deadwood from the ranks of captains. Retired Captain Chambers had only harsh words for "the evil tendency," the "insidious enemy," that had "crept into our organization"—"the selfish scramble for promotion." When Captain Rufus Johnston ('95) was "plucked," he received letters critical of the system of promotion by selection which, in the words of one of Johnston's "plucked" comrades, "had turned out just as I predicted it would." Even Admiral W. S. Sims was eventually disappointed by the selection board system.[19] The tables were now turned.

Some officers had foreseen this situation, of course. As early as 1895 Captain Caspar Goodrich saw that the "selection out" or "plucking" system "puts selection at the wrong end"—that is, Goodrich favored a selection process that weeded out the unfit while they were still junior officers. Rear Admiral McCalla argued for promotion for merit. Lieutenant Commander Lyman A. Cotten favored promotion by competitive process. Others favored the creation of selection or "screening" boards for each rank. It was this plan, which provided

for "plucking" at all levels, that became law in the Act of August 29, 1916, and **361**
it is essentially this system which is still in operation today.[20]

The Reserve

The "progressives" had succeeded in securing amalgamation and
promotion reform, but the concurrent growth of the "new Navy" took them
by surprise on their flank and created a new "enemy" that has slowly infiltrated
their ranks and weakened the Annapolite's control of the Service and its
codes.

As more and more new steel vessels were added to the Navy in the 1880s and
'90s, Congress and the Navy Department began to give consideration to the
need for naval militia or reserve forces to back up the fleet. If sea power *were*
essential and numerous warships of all sorts *were* necessary, then there might
come a day when Annapolis would not by itself be able to supply enough fresh
officers to the fleet.

State naval militia units were utilized in 1898, as they had been in the Civil
War, but these units had often been little more than a training ground for
wartime replacements for the fleet. Naval militia units were rarely deployed
intact. Moreover, since they were state troops, under the control of state
governors, they were not deemed to be the most effective of naval forces from
the national point of view of the more cosmopolitan naval aristocracy engaged
in planning a war fleet for the twentieth century.

Some officers recommended the creation of additional naval academies, but
this was rejected by Congress as too expensive. A national naval reserve was the
final choice of the Navy and the lawmakers.

The first naval reserve legislation in 1900 showed the stamp of the Annapolites.
Reserve officers were clearly subordinated to Academy graduates.[21] Reserve
officers found promotion and tenure difficult to obtain. World War I legislation,
designed to flesh-out the burgeoning fleet with reserves, also contained a
built-in safeguard for Annapolites which prevented reserve officers from rising
above the rank of lieutenant commander in peacetime. The Act of June 4,
1920, encouraged the 1,200 best reserve officers to enter the regular officer
corps, but reserve promotions were brought to a standstill. No less than 25,000
reserve officers were dropped from the reserve rolls by September 1921.
Reserve officer corps morale sank, and career anxieties rose among naval
reservists. In 1922 a group of naval reserve officers formed the Naval Reserve
Officers Association (NROA) and began lobbying for reserve officer permanence
and prerogatives. By late 1924 these reservist "Young Turks" had secured their
first breakthrough—448 reserve officers were finally given long-overdue
promotions. In 1925 the NROA and their allies persuaded Congress to create
the first peacetime Naval Reserve Officer Training Corps. As many as 1,200
students at selected colleges would take approved courses and receive a reserve
commission upon graduation. Status-conscious children of an upwardly-mobile
middle class were sorely needed to manage the growing, increasingly technical

362   Navy. By 1928, the reserve officer corps had been integrated with the Annapolites on a reasonably equitable basis, with one reserve commodore and eight
reserve captains; reserve morale was good.

The depression destabilized everything. Appropriations for the Navy
declined in the early thirties, halting promotions and reducing pay by 15%.
When it became clear that Annapolites, who still held all the top posts in the
naval establishment, were cutting reserve budgets to the bone, the NROA
went into action once again, infuriating many of the "band of brothers."
Admiral William Standley ('95), Chief of Naval Operations, rebuked the
NROA in don't-rock-the-boat language reminiscent of the senior–junior
promotion struggle of the 1880s and '90s. The NROA's lobbying, Standley
charged, would only "harm the Navy and cause uncertainty and confusion in
the minds of the [Naval Affairs] Committee, which is always harmful." But
reservists countered by charging that the "band of brothers" continually
refused to consult them on appropriation or policy matters. They demanded
an end to Annapolite opposition to the reserve officer aviation program. They
demanded an end to the ban on flag rank for reservists. They demanded the
"running mate" system of reserve promotion. And by 1938 they had won on
all three counts.

The naval reserve officer corps continued to grow during and after World
War II, and the non-Annapolites now make up the backbone of the Service,
vastly outnumbering their Annapolis counterparts. But Annapolis graduates
continue to hold disproportionate numbers of key posts in the naval establishment, and the coopted "citizen officers" seem virtually as orthodox navalists as
their Annapolis counterparts.*

"La Propaganda"

By the 1890s, all naval officers, young and old, were becoming
adept at the art of lobbying. "I am trying to sow the seed all over the country,"
Captain Henry Clay Taylor wrote to Rear Admiral Luce in 1894. "The more
you can stir up your friends the better it will be. I am beginning to work up
Boards of Trade, Chambers of Commerce and other commercial bodies all
along our coast and lake frontiers. . . ." The Navy's exhibit at the 1893 Chicago
Fair was a great success. Whether the issue was the future of the Naval War
College, promotion reform, or, as was more frequent, naval appropriations,
it was certain that officers would seize every opportunity to tell interest groups
of the importance of the Navy to each special interest.[22] By 1900, this propagan-

---

* However, it appears to have been *reserve* officers who first blew the whistle on Lieutenant Commander Arnheiter ('52). (Neil Sheehan, "The 99 Days of Captain Arnheiter,"
New York Times Magazine [Aug. 11, 1968], 7–9, 69–75.) There are indications that non-
Annapolis junior officers, from NROTC and OCS programs, are less absolutistic, less
authoritarian, and less belligerent than their Academy counterparts. See Ed Berger, *et al.*,
"ROTC, My Lai, and the Volunteer Army," *Foreign Policy* (Spring, 1971), 135–160. The
attitudes and values of non-Annapolis officers should be compared to those of Annapolis
graduates at successive stages in their respective careers before we can say anything definite
about Annapolite cooption of reservists.

The thrill of conquest. Officers and men of the U.S.S. *Oregon* cheer as the Spanish warship *Cristobal Colon* hauls down her colors off Santiago de Cuba, July, 1898 (Naval History Division, Navy Department).

War with Spain, and the "new navy" had established itself. *Puck* greets "the American battleship, no longer an unknown quantity," June 1, 1898.

Dewey's moment of glory. President McKinley rides with the Admiral in an 1899 "Dewey Day" victory parade in New York city (Naval Photographic Center).

One of several new battleships for "the great white fleet." Trial run of U.S.S. *Connecticut*, 1907. Photo by Enrique Muller (Prints & Photos, Library of Congress).

"New Navy" recruiting posters:
1. 1905 (U.S. Naval Institute)
2. 1919 (Naval Photographic Center)
3. 1917 (Naval Photographic Center)
4. 1930 (Naval Photographic Center).

1.

2.

3.

ONLY THE NAVY CAN STOP THIS

4.

"The naval aristocracy" queuing before a Presidential reception, 1930 (Bu Ships 13390, National Archives).

dizing, crowned as it was by Manila and Santiago, had achieved a measure of success. "Our Navy has never been intrenched more firmly in the popular heart than at this very hour," Assistant Navy Secretary Frank Hackett rightly told a group of Annapolites in that year.[23]

But Mahan's messmates didn't rest on their laurels. As one officer put it in 1902,

> We naval officers as a class can each do a little toward advancing the good of the service by judicious missionary work at times when some effect is likely to be produced.

In 1909, ex-Annapolites John Sanford Barnes and John Forsythe Meigs and Rear Admirals Luce, Chadwick, and Davis created a Naval History Society designed to "affect public opinion and public interest in the Navy." Barnes sought to found a Society repository for naval memorabilia in order to exercise "an inspiring influence upon the people."[24] This willingness to "sell the Navy" reflected the Annapolite's rejection of strictly apolitical behavior. Retired Rear Admiral Mahan assured his active brethren that politics were the proper concern of all the naval aristocracy:

> I cannot too entirely repudiate any casual word of mine reflecting the tone which once was so traditional in the navy that it might be called professional—that "political questions belong rather to the statesman than to the military man." I find these words in my old lectures, but I very soon learned better. . . .

368   Mahan sought, "by sustained apprehension, communicated to the nation, to maintain a pressure which shall constantly ensure a navy. . . ."[25] The Navy League, surely the most friendly pressure group the Navy was to experience in the twentieth century,* was born in the same year that Mahan's words were set in print.

The Navy League was not Mahan's idea, of course. But it was fundamentally the invention of naval officers. Lieutenant Commander R. C. Smith ('78) argued for the creation of such a lobby, as did "progressive" Rear Admirals Robley Evans ('64), Charles Sperry ('66), Richard Wainwright ('68), and William Wirt Kimball ('69), and ex-officers J. D. J. Kelley ('68) and Robert Thompson ('68). Lieutenant Commander J. H. Gibbons ('79) regarded the Navy League as central to the "important missionary work of spreading the naval propaganda among the people at large." Gibbons favored conferences with superintendents of public schools "and other educators" in order to spur instruction in naval history and customs, "beginning with toys of the kindergarten, fashioned after naval models, and working up through the stages of sea stories and nautical adventures to that of comparative history and the influence of sea power." He also sought a series of lectures and pamphlets, prepared in collaboration with "chambers of commerce, shipbuilding interests, marine underwriters and other organizations. . . ."[26]

It wouldn't be exaggerating to say that Gibbons and many of his colleagues had become skilled in public relations and lobbying.[27] As Captain Marbury Johnston put it, "The Navy is a fierce business proposition, and to get results we must use business methods." The remarks of Commander C. B. T. Moore ('73) at a San Francisco banquet, to the effect that the Navy advanced business

---

* Armin Rappaport feels that the munitions men and shipping magnates associated with the Navy League "might have been motivated by economic interest," but that it is "just as likely" that their motive was "patriotism" (22). He quotes approvingly Navy League denials that the steel, nickel, shipping, financial, and munitions interests of such League founders as J. P. Morgan, H. L. Satterlee, Henry Clay Frick, J. H. Schiff, C. H. Dodge, J. P. Grace, T. C. DuPont, John Jacob Astor, R. W. Thompson, H. P. Whitney, or Charles Schwab were of any significance (54). But surely men whose profession it is to make ships or weapons can easily persuade themselves that what is good for their industry is good for the country. Consider, for example, the remarks of Clement Griscom, president of a forerunner of the Navy League, the Society of Naval Architects and Marine Engineers: "A technical society of this kind has no *raison d'être* if there are no ships to build; and if its labors . . . result in reawakening general interest in the development of our great marine resources, there will be little doubt that the inception and growth of [this] society . . . is a national blessing (Prolonged applause)." *Transactions of the Society of N.A. and M.E.*, I (1893), xxii. See also *Transactions*, III (1895), xxvi–xxvii.

Rappaport is on more solid ground in claiming that the Navy League was considerably less effective than its German counterpart. But if the Navy League was a "paper tiger," its many co-navalists in the U.S. Chamber of Commerce, the National Security League, and the National Civic Federation were not. Furthermore, the nation's newspaper editors favored a big-navy policy by a nearly 3 to 1 margin in 1914, and as Mike Lutzker has demonstrated, the major peace societies were themselves big-navy! (*Literary Digest* [23 Jan. 1915], 137; Lutzker, "The Formation of the Carnegie Endowment for International Peace: A Study of the Establishment-centered Peace Movement, 1910–1914," in Jerry Israel, ed., *Building the Organizational Society* [Free Press, Spring, 1972].)

interests "by spreading over the world knowledge of this country's products," were typical. Warships, he told the assemblage, were worthwhile "to pay for the mere advertising your Navy does for you. . . ." Rear Admiral Bradley Fiske's maxim—"The importance to a country of her navy varies as the square of the value of her foreign trade"—with its cost-accounting tone, was a perfect example of the naval aristocracy's appeal to the "mere dollars and cents point of view."[28]

The creation of the "Navy second to none" didn't spell the end to "the naval propaganda." "The Navy has much ado to hold its own," an Academy professor wrote in 1916. World War I naval appropriations were still piling up when the armistice was signed; but when the U.S. appeared likely to enter the League of Nations, Rear Admiral Charles Badger ('73) of the General Board argued for further appropriations to enable the U.S. to "contribute a very large share of the international police force to render [the League] effective." With the rejection of such internationalism by the Senate, navalists returned to more familiar tactics, and in 1919 Annapolites were to be heard arguing that the war had "greatly intensified" the competition for the world's markets. A post-war naval arms limitation conference appeared imminent, and officers such as Bradley Fiske felt that the U.S. should "enter the conference with as large a navy as possible." Between 1919 and 1921 four new battleships were commissioned and a fifth was launched. In 1921, Academy professor William Stevens recommended a renewed and vigorous publicity "campaign, or at least a policy of public enlightenment." The Navy's mission, Stevens suggested, should be "to 'sell' the Navy to the American people."[29]

The Washington Naval Conference and the slight reduction in naval appropriations in the postwar decade was regarded as a serious setback to the profession of the naval aristocracy. Much of the reduction was due simply to "a universal desire for economy" and was not intended to imply a rejection of navalism. As Representative Fredrick Hicks of the House Naval Affairs Committee put it, the reductions were only temporary. "On the approach to normal of our economic and financial conditions, we can gather our resources and 'shove off' on the wider field of [naval] expansion." But few Annapolites were satisfied by such language. Rear Admiral D. W. Taylor feared the beginning of a new cycle of promotion difficulties if naval materiel was cut back once more. Captain W. I. Chambers paraphrased Oliver Wendell Holmes, Sr.,[30]

> Ay, tear their drooping ensigns down;
> Go bury them at sea.
> They [the Navy] won the war! But what of that?
> From sea power we would flee.

Naval officers were depressed by the turn of events. But most kept the faith. Lieutenant Commander H. H. Frost ('10) reminded his colleagues in 1924 of their duty to develop "the popularity of the service among the people," as did Lieutenants Wallace Wharton and R. E. Daniels and Lieutenant Commander G. E. Brandt. Brandt ('08) believed it to be "essential" that officers "take an

370   active part in publicity" in order to inspire future naval growth. But it was retired Captain Dudley Knox ('96) who offered the most complete case for the Annapolite's proper role in "public indoctrination." Knox advocated the use of the D.A.R., the American Legion, the Navy League, and the various chambers of commerce to cultivate public support.* "A navy for 'trade defense' should be the keynote. The function of defense against invasion" was to be "secondary." Americans were basically materialistic, Knox explained:

> Material welfare is a matter of such deep and continuous public interest that anything which can be shown to promote it meets with ready support.

And finally Knox advised his colleagues that "to successfully indoctrinate the country along sound naval lines" it was necessary to "give the impression that one stands for the promotion of 'world peace.'"[31]

Thus, throughout the 1920s, the naval aristocracy accelerated its efforts to persuade the public of the usefulness of the Navy. October 27, Theodore Roosevelt's birthday, became "Navy Day" in 1922. Americans visited warships on "Navy Day" in 1924, and each year thereafter has seen an increasing amount of Navy public relations to-do on that day. One bureau after another produced pamphlets and speeches in the 1920s designed to establish the cardinal role the Navy played in the development of the American economy. One officer after another told of the Navy's protection of foreign trade, of the Navy's "stabilizing" effect on investments, and of its role in the discovery of new "profitable outlets for our surplus products abroad." For example, Rear Admiral Mark Bristol ('87) warned the Senate Foreign Relations Committee in 1923 of the need for "stability in the foreign demands for our products. . . . When foreign markets close to us American prosperity ends." When the economy became depressed in 1930 his remarks were recalled. Thus it is not surprising that naval "disarmament" conferences in the late 1920s and early 1930s actually resulted in *increases* in tonnages, armaments, and appropriations. As Representative Fiorello H. LaGuardia put it in 1933:[32]

> The Navy had an effective lobby long before the Army ever attempted to start into its own about 1920. . . . [Naval officers] invoke every possible influence to prevent legislation they consider inimical to their own interests. At creating public opinion by the subtle use of propaganda, the Navy is a past master.

These efforts continued in the 1930s, of course. Pay cuts, promotion halts, and assaults by anti-navalists in such works as Charles Beard's *The Navy: Defense or Portent?* provoked another "career anxiety" crisis.[33] Rear Admiral Hugh Rodman ('80) warned that the key to future prosperity lay in "the sale of surplus products abroad" and then argued that this commerce was dependent upon the existence of a strong navy. Captain William Puleston ('02), O.N.I. Chief, maintained that the U.S. had been "designed" to be "a great sea-power" and charged that anyone "who would convince our people to the contrary,

---

* Loyal civilian navalists responded with élan, of course. In what may be the first use of that expression, the *Chicago Tribune* editorialized on February 17, 1928, that "the silent majority wants a navy as big and fit as the administration thinks it ought to be."

knowingly or unknowingly," lent a traitorous "aid and comfort to possible competitors." The 1925 warning of *Captain* Yates Stirling ('92) that a "commercial nation should buy foreign goods as well as sell to foreign consumers" was not repeated to a depression generation which sought relief via exports and reciprocal trade agreements. Rather, in 1935, *Rear Admiral* Stirling stressed the need for naval force to protect American exports and imports. The U.S., Stirling explained, was finally "realizing the great potential value of the China market." "The course of economic empire evidently lies to the westward," he observed, and only Japan imperilled the open door to those Asiatic riches. The Army was counselling withdrawal from China; the Navy, incapable of justifying much of its Pacific fleet budget without such a neo-mercantilist Asian policy, staunchly defended the open door in China. In 1941 Puleston argued that the U.S. had no reasonable choice but to meet head-on a Japanese commercial-territorial expansion that was closing the door to U.S. markets in the Far East.[34]

By the late 1930s, however, a subtle change in strategy was taking place. The Navy's role in the protection of American commerce began to yield the spotlight to another issue—the Navy's physical defense of the American homeland. Generations of Annapolites had argued that the mission of the Navy was "more than merely to defend the coasts of the U.S." Its "chief purpose," in the 1928 words of Rear Admiral W. L. Rodgers, was to support and maintain the "chiefly economic" policies of the U.S. abroad. Appropriately, it was a young reservist, Lieutenant Commander Frank Harris who, in a 1936 prize-winning essay in the Naval Institute *Proceedings*, elevated the Navy's role in the physical defense of America to primacy over that of the defense of the open door abroad.[35] The Navy had always been perceived of as the nation's first line of defense, of course, but it was not until the late 1930s that Americans *really* began to fear not only for their trade and investments in China, Nicaragua, and Turkey, but also for their own cities and industries. Pearl Harbor and the Battle of Britain reinforced these anxieties and accelerated the shift in emphasis. The advent of the aircraft carrier, the long-range bomber, and the V-2 rocket brought home the new dangers of intercontinental warfare. Simultaneously, the Navy ceased to be the nation's only first line of defense. Air power, and the Strategic Air Command, would now vie for leadership.*

Post-World War II navalists have had less to say of overseas trade or investments than they have of the "strategic" importance of such regions as the Middle East and the undersea continental shelf, whose oil resources are important to naval planners as well as industries and motorists. The continental shelf

---

* When the advocates of strategic bombing appeared likely to capture the lion's share of the appropriations pie in the late 1940s, a number of carrier pilot captains and commanders seized the initiative from battleship-oriented admirals and shifted the Navy's strategy outlook from surface ships to a mixed surface-air capability. They managed to claim a piece of the nuclear take, as Vincent Davis tells it, by flying a group of VIPs in a *P2V* off of a carrier (!) in order to impress them with the Navy's capacity to deliver a nuclear warhead. Only Dame Fortune and a strong headwind saved the Navy and its VIP guests from another *Princeton* disaster. Davis, *Postwar Defense Policy, passim.*

372   possesses other resources, however. Numerous minerals, as well as oil, can be exploited. Seafood could be farmed as well as hunted, and today's navalists recognize the value in discussing these factors. Admiral David McDonald, a recent Chief of Naval Operations, compared "the potential wealth of the sea" to the fabled "wealth of India." Navalists speak of underseas laboratories and cities and a kind of open door policy to the seabed. And, of course, they stress the need for undersea (naval) defenses of this undersea empire. But, as Seymour Hersh has pointed out, today's navalists, who virtually monopolize federal oceanography research, are less concerned in practice with the non-military schemes than they are with designs for undersea naval depots. As ever, navalists find that potentially non-military projects merit federal support for essentially navalist reasons.[36]

Navalist public relations are now more sophisticated and full-scale than they were in the past, but the same sort of ground rules apply. The Naval Office of the Chief of Information (CHINFO) controls the Naval Photographic Center, 31 Naval Reserve Public Affairs units (which seek, among other things, according to CHINFO, to "promote the playing and singing of the Navy Hymn in local churches"), and a "Speech Bureau," with a "Speech Evolution's Laboratory." CHINFO generates thousands of publicity photos, circulates as many "news" releases, edits the *Navy Speakers Guide*, and publishes annual editions of *Outstanding Navy Speeches* and *Quotable Navy Quotes*. Some officers want more. "Opinion makers should be cultivated," one Rear Admiral recently advised his colleagues. "Every senior naval officer should know his own Congressman and Senator" and should "stand up to be counted and to be heard." Every commanding officer should "not only be encouraged, but also required to make speeches—frequently—to every Garden Club, Kiwanis, PTA, and fraternity house that will hear him on the subject of U.S. seapower."[37] (Navalists have an uncanny sense for locating the secret storm centers of political power in America.)

Navalists have come to espouse, and believe in, missions such as "national security," "good will," and sea-borne anticommunism in the age of the hot peace, but they have also continued to call for the creation of a powerful merchant marine. Strong merchant fleets are deemed vital to the "control" of raw materials that play "an essential part" in the economic capability of the great "industrial island" and the process of exporting "the products of that greatness in both military and economic form.* Naval officers continue to urge "a closer working relationship" between naval and merchant marine officers. "Their problems are, in part, our problems," one has observed.[38]

---

* American warships are rarely called upon to defend American commerce now. The Navy's present *raison d'être* is to support counter-revolutionary "brush-fire" wars and to deter nuclear war. Neither mission offers *immediate* aid to commerce (though the former is *ultimately* keyed to the "open door" ideology). But the Navy reminds American industry that America now imports more raw materials than it exports. See the 1966 C.N.O. pamphlet, *United States Life Lines: Imports of Essential Materials . . . and the Impact of Waterborne Commerce on American Industrial Productivity*.

Rear Admiral John D. Hayes, at once the most articulate and the most **373** thoughtful of these recent naval propagandists for the merchant marine, regrets that the moribund American shipping industry no longer serves "to assure a significant economic presence of the United States around the world." Direct and portfolio investments, loans, grants apparently fail to qualify; they are not directly linked to "sea power." Hayes is convinced that "sea power" will "never get the full attention it merits" until a Cabinet-level Department of Maritime Affairs is created "with the Navy Department being transferred to it from the Department of Defense." How much of Hayes' proposal is a function of naval irritation at the control exercised over the Annapolites by the Defense Department and how much of it is objective and disinterested is hard to say. But it is worth noting that a recent merchant marine-sponsored study of "the economic value of the U.S. merchant marine" concluded that there was "little net economic contribution to the United States by the (existing) subsidized liner firms or deriving from the subsidy program." Control of merchant traffic is *facilitated* if that traffic is U.S.-owned and operated, but, as Rear Admiral Hayes says himself, all vessels can ultimately be controlled by U.S. naval power —that is, they can be made either to "withdraw from the sea or [to] submit to [U.S. naval] direction." Thus the Navy's role in the protection of trade, foreign investment, and the merchant marine are no longer very useful tenets in the ideology of navalism, but are now subordinate to the more ingenuous argument that a navy is essential if the United States is to control the seven seas at all times, for whatever reason. "The final adjudicator of all things maritime in peace and war," Hayes concludes, "must be the U.S. Navy."[39]

Strategists like Robert McClintock, and some Congressional liberals, appear to favor an essentially defensive ("deterrent") force of surface vessels, armed with ship-to-ship missiles, and ballistic subs as the Navy's foremost contribution to national security.[40] But most others prefer larger, more expensive,* potentially aggressive, fast carrier task forces. The latter argue that retaliatory capacity is not enough; traditional command of the seas, as *well* as retaliatory capacity, is necessary. Just as the manned bomber threatened the Navy's mission in the late 1940s, so the arrival of the ICBM caused many carried admirals to fear that

---

* Steve d'Arazien recently argued that the first option (ballistic subs *et al.*) could be prohibitively expensive too. Congress may give the Navy the green light on the Navy's newest "building blocks to peace," the Undersea Longrange Missile System (ULMS), a modification of the Poseidon missile submarine. The Navy is asking for 20 ULMS subs, each with a capacity for 24 missiles capable of spewing forth 17 independently directed warheads. D'Arazien estimates the cost of this bundle of 8,160 seaborne "building blocks to peace" to be about 20 billion dollars. And, as he points out, the acquisition of ULMS will not necessarily mean that there will be any coincidental cutback in funds for Air Force nuclear delivery systems. ULMS does have advantages over Air Force ICBM silos and the fabulously expensive manned bomber (B-1) proposal, and is thus tempting to those who fear that an overkill factor of 28 (the estimate for 1975) will not suffice, or that ULMS is "cheaper" than what we already have. (d'Arazien, "Blue Water Boondoggle," *Nation* [Nov. 16, 1970], 498–500.)

In short, "blue water" deterrence may be an appropriate naval mission, but it can swallow up as many resources as carrier strategies have if we let it.

Some modern American navalists:
Top, left—William D. Puleston, '02 (Naval Photographic Center); Above—Hyman Rickover, '22, on U.S.S. *Nautilus* (Office of Information, Navy Department); Top, right—John D. Hayes, '24 (Robert de Gast).

Modern gunboats in Asia. U.S. naval patrol craft in Vietnamese waters, 1969 (Office of Information, Navy Department).

Chiang Kai-shek and a State Department official on a visit to Chiang's guardian, the U.S. Seventh Fleet, are greeted by Captain S. W. Vejtasa on the U.S.S. *Constellation* in the 1960s, with Admiral Thomas Moorer, (presently Chairman of the JCS) standing by (Naval Photographic Center).

Soviet Navalism to the Rescue? Unchallenged for decades, the U.S. Navy is now warning of the emerging and ambitious Soviet Navy to justify appropriations. Elements of the Sixth Fleet in the Mediterranean, as seen from the U.S.S. *Enterprise* (Office of Information, Navy Department).

Right—Soviet navalism possesses limited capabilities, but the Soviet Navy's new visibility alarms many nevertheless. A recent photo of Russian frigates and sub tenders in the Mediterranean (Office of Information, Navy Department).

Below—A modern Soviet navalist, Admiral Sergei Gorshkov (Sovfoto).

their favorite warship was in imminent danger of extinction in the 1960s. Marcus Raskin maintains that in the Kennedy era naval officers sensed a "need for an expanded role for the Navy" and consequently "supported a new view of geopolitics, which required that the Navy be able to involve itself in many little wars simultaneously." Thus Admiral John J. McCain told a House Defense Appropriations Subcommittee of the "cancerous growth" of communism throughout the world, and added that the Navy

> must be prepared to move to any spot in a dozen different directions in order to be in a position to "nip in the bud" any possible trouble in its inception. . . . Seaborne striking forces . . . are the ideal instrument of this [graduated deterrence] policy.

Congress was initially impressed, but when later in the '60s Senator Clifford Case discovered that these carrier forces had been deployed 42 times in the 15 years since the Korean War on just such missions as these, that the State Department had been involved in only 29 of this deployments, and that in many instances the show of force had been grossly out of proportion to American interests in the area, Case was understandably chagrined. As John Wieklein recently put it, "The availability of carriers suggests their use." No less than 40% of the typical annual Navy budget goes to the carriers. Such funds could be spent more wisely, on defensive-oriented weapons, or on domestic needs.

The Navy's dream of a counter-insurgency fleet of Fast Deployment Logistics ships (FDLs) was on the ropes in 1969, but it may find new life now that naval and merchant marine forces are agreed that such support ships will be owned by the private sector but available to the Navy for "any contingency." In 1970 President Nixon proposed funds to build 15 FDLs over the next ten years. Who needs them?

The answer is, of course, the Navy and the merchant marine. These old allies remind us that, even if America should never use FDLs to police the world, the merchant marine can still use the ships, for "the merchant marine is essential to the national security." Our competitor in the field of ocean-bound traffic is the Soviet Union, and control of this traffic is a job only the Navy can properly perform. If the Navy were to be liberated from Defense Department restraints, and a U.S. merchant marine were to emerge that would be worthy of its defenders, then the Golden Age of navalism would surely arrive. But only with a monumentally expensive merchant marine would such a Golden Age be possible, for only with such a mercantile fleet would it make any sense. American businessmen, with their Liberian and Panamanian fleets, seem to be managing quite well. And the Soviet Navy, the only one in any way comparable to the U.S. Navy is (according to retired* Commander Robert W. Herrick, one of the Navy's top students of Soviet naval power) a defensive navy, posing no real threat to our command of the seas.

Herrick's view is not the view of all of the modern naval aristocracy, of course. Many would echo Commander James McNulty, whose essay on

* Herrick's future in the Navy became somewhat uncertain shortly after the Naval Institute, after some delay and misgiving, finally published his *Soviet Naval Strategy* in 1968.

378 "Soviet Seapower," subtitled "Ripple or Tidal Wave?," concludes that we are in peril of being engulfed:

> The Soviet maritime strategy now revealed to the West constitutes the most significant single threat to the peace and stability of the world since the establishment of the Iron Curtain around Eastern Europe.

Commander McNulty exaggerates the danger. Most American navalists privately opine that the existing American fleets are quite capable of handling any action of the Soviet's surface fleet and will remain so capable for some time. If Soviet submarines are more elusive, they constitute no serious menace to a *defensive* naval force. McNulty fears that we are on the verge of "forfeiting our position as the predominant naval power in the world." *Newsweek* reported in October 1970, three months after McNulty's essay appeared, that the Sixth Fleet "is rated five to ten times more powerful than the Russian fleet," and a clearly favorable ratio still prevails. In any event, we have become so accustomed to our own oceanic supremacy in the past few decades that we seem to have forgotten that rival navies *can*, and in the past *have*, shared the seas. Commander McNulty feels that "in a two-horse race there can be only one winner . . ." One hopes that the Navy is not planning a "horse race" or "shoot-out" with the Soviets. A regatta would be safer, and a lot more fun.

The Soviet Navy is a "paper tiger." Unless the Soviets can be persuaded to depart from their defense-oriented naval posture to embark on a massive carrier-building program (a possibility, of course, since the Soviet Union has navalists too*), the U.S. Navy's own building program may eventually strike Congress as making very little sense.[41] Today's navalists are getting perilously close to the rocks of anachronism, and some seem aware of it. In the words of Captain William Chapman, the command of the seas in peacetime "may be somewhat irrelevant."[42]

But if the rationale for a super-fleet is somewhat deficient, this does not necessarily mean that the super-fleet will not emerge. As inflation and Vietnam cut into naval appropriations, some of the same career anxieties that plagued the junior officers of the 1880s are becoming visible. "Today," Commander James Nesworthy wrote in December 1969, "the spirit and vigor is being eroded by

---

* Commander Herrick identifies a number of recent Soviet navalists: Admirals V. A. Alafuzov, N. G. Kuznetzov, and S. G. Gorshkov (see photo), who have been urging the land- and missile-force dominated Soviet leadership (so far without success) to construct attack carriers in order to defend the Soviet merchant marine and to contest U.S. control of the seas. (*Soviet Naval Strategy* [Annapolis, 1968], 102–103, *passim.*) Soviet navalism appears to be at the same "stage" that American navalism had reached in the late nineteenth century. Given the Soviet concern for its overseas markets and merchant marine and given the determination of its navalists, it is *possible* that the Soviet leadership might in the future be led into the enormously expensive business of abandoning its defensive posture and seeking to build a "navy second to none." Any U.S. denial of the "freedom of the seas" to Soviet shipping might be the signal for a Soviet version of the U.S. reaction to the 1917 U-boat campaign. Neither nation needs a naval arms race. But if Soviet navalism *does* threaten the peace, American navalists will not have been entirely blameless. As Commander F. C. Collins recently put it, "Perhaps we have done our job too well, and have created a threat to which the Soviets have reacted vigorously." *PUSNI* (June 1971), 81.

frustration and a sense of helplessness on the middle and lower strata of officers." **379**
The Navy's share of the budget is "inadequate." "We of the Navy are concerned for the future of our country . . . and the future role of our Navy."
Others speak of "agonizing—almost fearful—frustration" over recent appropriations struggles. "Turbulence" is being reported among junior officers
"bitter" about the possibility of a 20-25% cutback in naval tonnage in the early
1970s. Obviously there are many who honestly (if unnecessarily) fear for the
security of the nation; but there are others who are primarily concerned with
the future of their profession. Their response is similar to that of the "Young
Turks" of the 1880s. Thus Lieutennat Commander Richard C. Davis recently
invoked "a modern Mahan"and, referring explicitly to the 1880s and '90s, called
for "a second renaissance," while Lieutenant Commander H. J. F. Korrell an-
ticipates "a long-needed and . . . fierce competition for survival within the
[naval] organization."

Some officers cannot understand why the government has been unwilling to
blockade North Vietnam. They see "the powerful U.S. Navy . . . relegated to
being an adjunct to the Army in an overseas war" and a mere "partner with the
Air Force in a nuclear strategy." Naval prestige is "flagging" in many eyes in the
wake of the *Pueblo* incident. "How can a man cut a pretigious figure when he
is unable to market his product . . . or to practice the trade he has learned! How
can he hope to command respect in his community when he realizes that the
news media carry only embarrassing accounts of Navy mishaps. . . !" Commander R. T. E. Bowler (Ret.), the publisher of the *Proceedings of the U.S.
Naval Institute*, warned in January 1970 that the Navy was about to "experience
big changes in its size and in its composition," and urged "the naval profession"
to "influence" military appropriations by creating some imaginative new
navalist arguments. Vice Admiral James Calvert, the Academy's present Superintendent, suggested recently that, since the Navy was "entering a period of
declining support," one could expect "unusual professionalism and productivity" at Annapolis and elsewhere.[43] Such productivity may be too awesome
to allow for a serious public reconsideration of naval policy. It may be too late
for statesmen to overcome the momentum created by the architects of navalism in the American Century. Only time will tell if what is past is prologue.

Chapter 8

1. Samuel W. Bryant, *The Sea and the
States* (N.Y., 1947), 343-345; Luce, "How
Shall We Man Our Ships?" *North American
Review*, CLII (1891), 69.

In April 1893, Captain William Sampson,
Naval Constructor Francis Bowles, Charles
Cramp, W. H. Webb, and several others
formed the Society of Naval Architects
and Marine Engineers, the object of which
was to be the promotion of naval and

commercial shipbuilding. See *Transactions
of the Society of Naval Architects and Marine
Engineers*. I (1893), xxii; II (1894), xxvi;
and III (1895), xxvi.

2. *Messages and Papers of the Presidents,*
ed. James Richardson (Wash., 1899–1912),
IX, 200–202; Sprout and Sprout, *Rise of
American Naval Power*, final five chapters;
Ensign A. A. McKethan to his mother,
April 3, 1895, McKethan Papers, Perkins

Library, Duke U.; Davis, *Navy Second to None*, passim. Cf. Walter LaFeber, "A Note on the 'Mercantilistic Imperialism' of A. T. Mahan," *Mississippi Valley Hist. Rev.*, XLTIII (1962), 674–685.

For more on anti-navalist "locals" see Thomas Coode, "Southern Congressmen and the American Naval Revolution, 1880–1898," *Alabama Historical Review* (1968), 89–110; and John M. Cooper, "Progressivism and American Foreign Policy," *Mid-America*, LI (1969), 265. Coode notes (109) that the personal papers of anti-navalist Congressmen are filled with correspondence from constituents concerning entirely local matters, while my own examination of the correspondence of several Congressmen favorable to the Navy revealed a substantial constituent interest in foreign affairs.

3. Chadwick to Lieutenant Fredrick Rodgers, August 1, 1888, Chadwick to Lieutenant Royall Bradford, November 3, 1888, Chadwick to Rodgers, November 3, 1888. Chadwick letter copybook, N.Y.H.S.; Luce, "Our Future Navy," *North American Review*, CXLIX (1889), 65; U.S. Navy Department, *Annual Report of the Secretary of the Navy, 1913* (Wash., G.P.O., 1914), 31; Long, *New American Navy*, II, 163–164. Cf. Schilling, "Admirals and Foreign Policy" Ph.D. thesis, 40; Stillson, "Naval Establishment", Ph.D. thesis, 411–415.

4. Fiske, *Navy as a Fighting Machine*, 283–290; McCalla, "Memoirs," Ch. XII, 29; *Hearings before the Committee on Naval Affairs, House of Rep., 64th Cong., 1st Sess., on Estimates Submitted by the Secretary of the Navy, 1916*, 1735. Cf. L cdr. John W. Adams, "The Influences Affecting Naval Shipbuilding Legislation, 1910–1916," *Naval War College Review* (Dec. 1969), 41–63.

5. Knox, *PUSNI*, XVI (1890), 536; 51st Cong., 1st Sess., *Letter from the Secretary of the Navy transmitting . . . a report upon certain alleged organizations among naval officers not authorized by the Navy Department* (Senate Exec. Doc. 86).

6. *Diary of Welles*, ed. Beale, II, 253; *Argument of the Naval [Line Officers] Association in Relation to [House] Bill No. 3618* (Wash., 1896); McCalla, "Memoirs," Ch. XVIII, 19; Calvert, *Mechanical Engineer*, 258; Long, *New American Navy*, I, 84.

7. Selfridge to Long, Nov. 19, 1897, *Papers of Long*, ed. Allen, 35; McCalla, "Memoirs," Ch. XVIII, 20; Baird, *PUSNI*, XXXII (1906), 315. Baird referrred to himself in the third person in his remarks

on amalgamation; hence the form of the citation. Cf. Lieutenant John Hood, *PUSNI*, XXVII (1901), 1–27; and "The Line-Staff Controversy" in Chapter 3, pp. 65–69.

Marines secured their own line-staff consolidation in the early twentieth century. See the remarks of Colonel John Lejeune in *Hearings before the House Naval Affairs Committee on Estimates Submitted by the Secretary of the Navy*, 1916, II, 2253. The Construction Corps, on the other hand, waged a successful campaign to avoid amalgamation with the line in the early twentieth century. See, for example, Lieutenant Commander S. J. Zeigler, Jr. (C.C.), "Specialization versus Amalgamation," *PUSNI*, XLVIII (1912), 1073–1083.

8. Long, *New American Navy*, I, 77; Evans, *One Man's Fight*, 200–300; Luce, "Plea . . .," *North American Review*, CLXXXII (1906), 74–83; Earle, *Life at the Academy*, 277. Cf. Passed Assistant Engineer F. C. Bieg, "On the Necessity and Value of Scientific Research in Naval Engineering Matters as related to the U.S. Navy, and the Necessity of an Engineer Training for the Young Members of the Engineer Corps of the U.S. Navy," *Journal of the American Society of Naval Engineers*, VII (1895), 449–485. In the Act of March 3, 1899 (30 *U.S. Stat.* 1007), Congress sagely created the rank of warrant machinist to insure that there would always be men available to the naval aristocracy who know how to drive the ship through the water.

9. 52nd Cong., 1st Sess., *House Exec. Doc. 1, Pt. 3: Report of the Secretary of the Navy*, 39–42; "Report of a Board . . . to report upon . . . stagnation . . ., Sept., 1891," Entry 464 (Subject File). NI, R.G. 45; Davis to Sargent, Sept. 1, 1891, Vol. V, "Letters to Sargent," Entry 300, R.G. 45.

10. Thus Armin Rappaport is incorrect in stating that Secretary B. F. Tracy introduced "a new system of officer promotion by merit rather than by seniority." (*PUSNI*, XCIII [1967], 129). Cf. Rappaport, *Navy League*, 8, 12, 35.

11. *PUSNI*, XX (1894), 747 ff.; Cowles to McAdoo, Dec. 5, 1894, "Cowles Letterbook," Entry 301, R.G. 45, referring to an editorial in the London *Graphic* (Oct. 5, 1894). Cf. Ensign Archibald Scales to RepresentativeThomas Settle, July 4, 1894, writing "as a young officer of the Navy" on behalf of promotion reform legislation, Thomas Settle Papers, U. of N.C. Library.

12. Welles to his father, Oct. 19, 1895, Welles Papers, N.H.F.

13. "First circular of the Naval Association," Dec. 5, 1895, copy in official correspondence files of the Caspar Goodrich Papers, N.Y.H.S.

Admiral Robert Coontz, who had participated in the November 23, 1895, *coup d'état* while an ensign, recalled that Commander Royal Bradford and Lieutenant Commanders Richard Wainwright and Seaton Schroeder, as well as Sampson and Chadwick, had been prominent supporters of the junior line officers. Coontz, *From the Mississippi to the Sea*, 177–178.

14. *Life and Letters of Mary Remey*, IX, 437; "First circular . . .," Ensign T. Magruder to Goodrich, Dec. 3, 1895, Goodrich to Lamberton, Dec. 8, 1895, Official Corr. files, Goodrich Papers, N.Y.H.S.; *Proposed Personnel Bill with a Letter of Transmittal by the Assistant Secretary of the Navy* (Wash., 1897), 3–4, 9. Cf. Congressman Francis H. Wilson, "The Reorganization of the Naval Personnel," *North American Rev.* CLXVII (1898), 641–649. For more recent examples of efforts to provide for the promotion of junior officers after a war to avoid stagnation see Davis, *Postwar Defense Policy and the Navy*, 30; and Vice Admiral L. S. Sabin, "Deep Selections," *PUSNI*, LXXXVI (1960), 46 ff.

Brown was ordained into the Episcopal ministry upon resigning from the naval service; he went on to become the president of Norwich University. *National Cyclopedia of Biography* (N.Y., 1922), XVIII, 327.

15. Census Bureau, *Historical Statistics*, 736; Davis, *Davis*, 337; 32 *U.S. Stat.*, Pt. I, 1197 (Act of March 3, 1903); U.S. Naval Academy Graduate Association, *Register of Graduates* (Annapolis, 1916); Luce, "Notes on the Naval Personnel Act," Box 19, Luce Papers, N.H.F.

16. Paul Y. Hammond, *Organizing for Defense* (Princeton, 1961), 49–84; Huntington, *Soldier and State*, 301–303.

17. Adm. J. J. Clark, *Carrier Admiral* (N.Y., 1967), 6–7.

18. Zogbaum, *From Sail to "Saratoga,"* 359; Archibald Turnbull and Clifford Lord, *History of U.S. Naval Aviation* (New Haven, 1949), 59; Roskill, *Naval Policy*, 58n, 398–399; Clark, *Carrier Admiral*, 6–7. Cf. L.Cdr. Frank Hetrel, "The Naval Academy and Naval Aviation," *PUSNI*, LXXIV (1948), 37–41; Adm. Yates Stirling, Jr., *Warriors of the Sea* (Evanston, Ill., 1942), 35; V. Davis, *Postwar Defense Policy, passim*; Cpt. Dominic Paolucci, "The Development of Navy Strategic Offensive and Defensive Systems," *PUSNI*, XCVI (May 1970), 205–223.

Exceptional "progressives," whose innovative qualities survived the aging process, would include Chambers, Fiske, Sims, Vice Admiral Hyman Rickover, and Admiral William Raborn.

19. Lieutenant John Hood, "Naval Administration and Organization," *PUSNI*, XXVII (1901), 1–27; G. C. O'Gara, *Theodore Roosevelt and the Rise of the Modern American Navy* (Princeton, 1943), 102; *Mrs. Remey's Letters*, XI, 810; McCalla, "Memoirs," Ch. XVIII, 18; Ch. XXX, 3; Chambers, "Love, War and Efficiency or Naval Doctrine and National Character," Mss. dated Dec. 24, 1914, Box 48, Chambers Papers; Chambers, "Universal Peace, Naval Efficiency and the 'Plucking' System," *The Navy*, IX (1915), 99–100; Paul Heffron, "Secretary Moody and Naval Administration Reform: 1902–1904," *American Neptune*, XXIX (Jan. 1969), 30–53; ? to Captain Rufus Johnston, August 3, 1930, Johnston Papers, S.H.C., U. of N.C. Library; Zogbaum, *From Sail to "Saratoga,"* 386.

20. See, for example, Goodrich to Commander "Ben" Lamberton, December 8, 1895, Official Corr. files, Goodrich Papers, N.Y.H.S.; McCalla, "Memoirs," Ch. XXVIII, 65, Ch. XXXI; Cotten, *PUSNI*, XLII (1916), 1855–1869; 39 *U.S. Stat.* 556 (at 578).

21. Most of the information in the next few paragraphs is drawn from Harold Wieand's fine unpublished dissertation, "The History of the Development of the U.S. Naval Reserve, 1889–1941," Univ. of Pittsburgh, 1953, pp. 68, 153, 160–161, 172, 183, 207–208, 215, 323–337, 256–282. See also Gerald Wheeler, "Origins of the NROTC," *Military Affairs*, XX (1956), 170–174; Eugene Lyons and John Masland, *Education and Military Leadership: A Study of the ROTC* (Princeton, 1959), 51.

22. Taylor to Luce, February 9, 1894, Luce Papers, N.H.F. Cf. Luce to Senator Nelson Aldrich, Mar. 15, 1889, cited in Spector, "Professors of War . . .," Ph.D. thesis, 98: "The interest of the Navy and the people of Newport running in the same direction we can pull together for our mutual advantage."

For good examples of naval officer lobbying before chambers of commerce, etc., see the diary of Captain John W. Philip, Philip Papers, "ZB" File, Navy History Division, Nat. Archives; Barker, *Everyday Life*, 360; 55th Cong., 2nd Sess.,

382

Senate Doc. 26: Views of Commodore George Melville . . . (1898), 188; Melville, "Our Future on the Pacific—What We Have There to Hold and Win," *North American Review,* CLXVI (1898), 281–296.

23. Hackett, *Deck and Field,* 7. See also LaFeber, *New Empire,* 235.

24. Lieutenant Commander Roy Smith, *PUSNI,* XXVIII (1902), 44; *Annuals of the Naval History Society* (N.Y., 1913–1924), 20; *Catalogue of the Books, Manuscripts, and Prints and Other Memorabilia in the John S. Barnes Memorial Library of the Naval History Society* (N.Y., 1912); Barnes, "Naval Literature," *PUSNI,* XXIX (1903), 333–355.

25. Mahan, cited in Huntington, *Soldier and the State,* 277; Mahan, *Naval Administration and Warfare,* 7, 77. For an excellent account of similar efforts of Admiral Tirpitz to insure a German Navy see J. Steinberg, *Yesterday's Deterrent, passim.*

26. Smith, "The Navy's Greatest Need," *North American Review,* CLXXV (1902), 388–398; Rappaport, *Navy League of U.S.,* 3–4, 18–19, 22; Gibbons, "Navy Leagues," *North American Review,* CLXXVI (1903), 763–764.

27. Thus Vincent Davis writes incorrectly that the Navy never made "a thorough-going, overt, and continuing effort" to mobilize "grass-roots" support (*Admirals Lobby,* 6), and he is on faulty ground when he offers a single citation to support his claim that "competing for public favor was not thought by naval officers to be in keeping with the dignity of the service. . . . The new public relations techniques used by politically active interest groups were wholly alien to them because they considered themselves dedicated public servants taking no part in the political process." (*Postwar Defense Policy and the Navy,* 80–82, 334–335; *Admirals Lobby,* 98–100, 268–269).

28. Johnston, *PUSNI,* XXXVIII (1912), 852; Moore, cited in *Army and Navy Journal,* XLI (May 14, 1904), 985; Fiske, *Navy as a Fighting Machine,* 37–38, 67–68, 81. See also Lieutenant Commander Nathan C. Twining to his father, Aug. 3, 1908, Twining Papers, State Hist. Soc. of Wisc.

29. *PUSNI,* XLII (1916), 55; Hobson, *Alcohol and the Human Race,* 155; Fiske, *Navy as a Fighting Machine,* 89; Stevens, "The Naval Officer and the Civilian," *PUSNI,* XLVII (1921), 1732–1733, 1736; Ernest Andrade, Jr., "U.S. Naval Policy in

the Disarmament Era, 1921–1937," unpublished Michigan State Ph.D., 1966, pp. 1, 16.

One reason for these efforts on the part of naval officers to improve their profession's prestige and position in these years may be revealed in Academy instructor W. B. Norris' feeling that naval officers stood lower in status by 1916 than lawyers and big businessmen, and on a par with engineers. (*PUSNI,* XLII (1916), 55.) But this was the only indication of any loss of status that I was able to uncover in these years, and Norris was not himself an Academy graduate.

30. *A Hearing on Bill H.R. 13706 before the Committee on Naval Affairs* (Wash., G.P.O., 1921), 216–217; Knox, *The Eclipse of American Sea Power* (N.Y., 1922), 137–139, *passim;* Taylor (C. C.), "Some Reflections upon Commissioned Naval Personnel Problems," *PUSNI,* L (1924), 1774–1775; Box 48, Chambers Papers, N.H.F.

31. Frost, *PUSNI,* L (1924), 38–39; Wharton, "The Navy—A National Investment," *ibid.,* 1836–1838; Daniels, "Indoctrinating Civilians," *ibid.,* 1858; Brandt, "Newspaper Publicity for the Navy," *ibid.,* 916–930; Knox, "The Navy and Public Indoctrination," *PUSNI,* LV (1929), 488–489. Cf. Lieutenant Arthur J. Burks, U.S.M.C., "Selling the Corps," *Marine Corps Gazette,* IX (1924), 109–115; Robert G. Lindsay, *This High Name: Public Relations and the U.S. Marine Corps* (Madison, Wisc., 1956).

In 1945 naval officers, supported by Navy Secretary James Forrestal, launched a similar publicity campaign to protect against reductions in naval appropriations. Davis, *Postwar Policy and the Navy,* 82–86.

32. See, for example, Roskill, *Naval Policy,* 515; Rappaport, *Navy League,* 100; (anon.), *A Peacetime Navy* (n.p., n.d. [copy in State Hist. Soc. of Wisc.]), 1–3; U.S. Office of Naval Intelligence, *The U.S. Navy as an Industrial Asset: What the Navy has done for Industry and Commerce* (Wash., G.P.O., 1923 [republished in 1924 and 1931]), 1–3, 8; John Meigs, *The Story of the Seaman* (2 vols., Philadelphia, 1924), introduction by Rear Admiral William Rodgers, I, vi; Admiral Edward Eberle, "A Few Reflections on our Navy and some of its needs," (mimeo, n.p., n.d., circa 1925), 1–2; Lieutenant Commander Fitzhugh Green, *PUSNI,* XLVIII (1922), 1703–06; Captain Frank Schofield, "The Aims and Present Status of the Navy," (mimeo. o f remarks to

the press, February 1924, n.p. [copy at State Hist. Soc. of Wisc.]), 4–5; Bristol, cited in U.S. Cong., Senate Committee on Foreign Relations, *Hearings on Treaty on the Limitations of Naval Armaments* (Wash., G.P.O., 1930), 106–107; O'Connor, *Perilous Equilibrium*, 40–45, 111; LaGuardia, "Congress—the Nation's Scapegoat," *Scribner's Mag.* (June, 1933).

33. Tuleja, *Statesmen and Admirals*, 86.

34. Rodman, *Yarns of a Kentucky Admiral*, 303, 309; Stirling, "Sea Power: The Foundation of Successful World Trade," *PUSNI*, LXI (1953), 777; Stirling, "Some Fundamentals of Sea Power," *PUSNI*, LI (1925), 889; Puleston, "John Hay and Alfred Mahan versus Tyler Dennett, Charles Beard, et al." A manuscript (submitted to *Harpers*, May 7, 1935), p. 19, Puleston Papers, L. of C.; Puleston, *The Armed Forces of the Pacific* (New Haven, 1941), 252–253. Cf. *Fortune* (March 1938), 58; and Fred Greene, "The Military View of American National Policy, 1904–1940," *American Historical Review*, LXVI (1961), 354–377; Lloyd Gardner, *Economic Aspects of New Deal Diplomacy* (Madison, 1964), 138.

35. Rodgers, *PUSNI*, LIV (1928), 572; Knox, *PUSNI*, LX (1934), 774–785; Harris, "The Navy and the Diplomatic Frontier," *PUSNI*, LXII (1936), 480–485.

36. See, for example, Rear Admiral Ernest Eller, "U.S. Destiny in the Middle East," *PUSNI*, LXXXII (1956), 1161–1169; Captain Sherman Naymark (Ret.), "Power in the Sea," *PUSNI*, XCIV (1968), 19–27; Robert McClintock, "An American Oceanic Doctrine," *PUSNI*, XCVI (Feb. 1970), 56; Sam Brewer, "U.N. Gets U.S. Aims for Seabed Pact," *N.Y. Times*, Mar. 8, 1970; Seymour Hersh, "20,000 Guns Under the Sea," *Ramparts* (Sept. 1969), 41–44; Cf. Sam Baker & Kerry Gruson, "The Coming Arms Race under the Sea," in Leonard Rodberg & Derek Shearer, eds., *The Pentagon Watchers* (N.Y., 1970), 335–369.

37. Derek Shearer, "The Brass Image," *The Nation*, CCX (April 20, 1970), 460–461; Rear Admiral Malcolm Nagle, "The Most Silent Service," *PUSNI*, XCV (1969), 38–41; Fullbright, *Pentagon Propaganda Machine*, 49–66.

38. See, for example, the shipboard magazine for the U.S.S. *Utah*: The *"Big U,"* I (Jan. 5, 1929), 2; Peter Karsten, *Guns and Good Will: The Cruise of the "Canberra," 1943–1963* (N.Y. 1963), *passim*; Captain Ira Dye, "Flags of Convenience:

Maritime Dilemma," *PUSNI*, LXXXVIII (1962), 76–87; Calvert, *Naval Profession*, 11; Hanson Baldwin, "Red Flag over the Seven Seas," *Atlantic Monthly*, CCXIV (1964), 37–43; Raymond Moley's columns in *Newsweek* for Jan. 3, 1966, Aug. 22, 1966, and July 24, 1967; Noel Mostert, "Russia Bids for Ocean Supremacy," *The Reporter* (Feb. 10, 1966), 24–28; Captain Arnold Schade, "The Merchant Marine and National Security," *PUSNI*, LXXXVII (Jan. 1961), 84–89; Rahill, *PUSNI*, XCVI (Feb. 1970), 89.

39. Hayes, *"Sine Qua Non* of U.S. Sea Power: The Merchant Ship," *PUSNI*, XCI (1965), 26–33; *The Economic Value of the U.S. Merchant Marine*, ed. Allen Ferguson, et al. (Evanston, Ill., 1961), 470. Cf. Samuel A. Lawrence, *United States Merchant Shipping: Policies and Politics* (Wash., 1966 [a Brookings Institution publication]); and 83rd Cong., 1st Sess., *Merchant Marine Studies; Hearings before the Senate Committee on Interstate and Foreign Commerce* (Wash., G.P.O., 1953.)

40. McClintock, *PUSNI* (Feb. 1970), 57.

41. The systems analysts in the Department of Defense are already expressing considerable doubt about the Navy's annual insistence on a level of 15 operational supercarriers. Arthur Herrington, "U.S. Naval Policy," *Naval War College Review* (Sept., 1969), 9.

42. See Herrick (class of '45), *Soviet Naval Strategy*; and Lieutenant Commander David Cox, "Sea Power and Soviet Foreign Policy," *PUSNI*, XCV (June 1969), 32–44; Chapman, *PUSNI*, XCV (July 1969), 116; Raskin, "The Kennedy Hawks . . .," in Rodberg & Shearer, *op. cit.*, 95; Wicklein, "The Oldest Established Permanent Floating Anachronism on the Sea," *The Washington Monthly* (Feb. 1970), 10–23; *Newsweek* (Oct. 19, 1970), 27; Tom Klein, "The Capacity to Intervene," *Pentagon Watchers*, 214. For disagreement with Commander Herrick's assessment see *PUSNI*, XCV (May 1969), 19, and (June 1969), 151–152; McNulty, *PUSNI* (July 1970), 20, 25, *passim*; and *Naval War College Review* (Feb. 1969), 13–30, and the June 1969 issue.

43. Nesworthy, *PUSNI*, XCV (Dec. 1969), 114; S. A. Swarztrauber, *PUSNI*, XCVI (Feb. 1970), 99; Hayes, *PUSNI*, XCVI (May 1970), 350; Bowler, *PUSNI*, XCVI (Jan. 1970), 17; Juan Cameron, "The Armed Forces' Reluctant Retrenchment," *Fortune* (Nov. 1970), 68–69, 173; Lieutenant

384   Leon Brooks, *PUSNI* (Jan. 1971), 22; Calvert, *PUSNI* (Oct. 1970), 64. Cf. Arthur Herrington (Director of Naval Forces, Office of the Assistant Secretary of Defense for Systems Analysis), "U.S. Naval Policy," *Naval War College Review* (Sept. 1969), 9: "The Navy [of late] has felt pressed. At times it has even felt that its existence was threatened." Cf. Davis, *PUSNI* (June 1971), 85–86; Korrell, *PUSNI* (Sept. 1971), 97.

A Summing-up and Some Final Observations

> Senator Guy Gillette (Iowa): . . . [H]ow can we get back trade and reestablish trade routes if we leave them unprotected in any way?
> General Smedley Butler, U.S.M.C. (ret.): . . . We do not have to go out and sell them goods with a battleship. If you have something that they want, and it is cheap enough, they will buy it. . . . [Traders] can be insured. . . .
> Gillette: [Traders] are trading at their own risk?
> Butler: They are trading at their own risk.
>
> *Hearings before the (Senate) Committee on Naval Affairs— on H.R. 9218: Naval Expansion Program* (1938)

> We are what we pretend to be;
> so we must be careful what we pretend to be.
>
> Kurt Vonnegut, *Mother Night*

The naval officer candidate of the Golden Age of Annapolis was of the upper echelon of the American social order. His parents were Episcopal, well-to-do, Anglo-Americans with political influence. At the Naval Academy and later on board ship the Annapolite was trained to show ascetic fidelity to the Navy and its customs and to the State. As a junior officer he learned the meaning of rank, discipline, and boredom. The whole weight of his training and daily routine made him a conservative—politically, socially, and professionally. His respect for order was not confined to his ship or station. He chose a wife and raised a family by service standards. His sons often followed in his footsteps; his daughters often married their brothers' colleagues. When he retired, the naval officer continued to display devotion to his profession.

The naval officer's duties primarily involved the protection of U.S. business interests abroad, interests he identified with the State rather than with the individuals engaged therein. Only secondarily was he concerned with protecting missionaries or surveying the seas. He got along extremely well with his British comrades-in-arms and looked forward to the day when Anglo-American institutions would be established (under their auspices) all over the world. He earnestly sought an opportunity to demonstrate his valor and abilities in combat, an aim which appears to have led him to offer force in dubious situations.

Numbered footnotes for this section begin on page 395.

386   He had learned his role as the descendant of the glorious Jones and Decatur well; he had become what he pretended to be.

Naval appropriations failed to keep pace with technological change in the 1870s, and the U.S. Navy was not given the kinds of new vessels and weapons that other navies were sporting. A promotion bottleneck, created by Civil War officer recruitment measures, gravely troubled officers commissioned in the late 1860s and thereafter. In 1882 Congress acted to solve this promotion problem by reducing the number of Academy graduates eligible for commissions while declining to provide for more rapid advancement of the existing swarm of junior officers. These junior officers reacted to this additional threat to their careers by waging a campaign to revamp the promotion system and to secure more and more modern warships. In the latter case they were joined by senior officers in a comprehensive front of publicity and lobbying.

These publicists stressed the role of naval power in the economic and political life of states, as their navalist predecessors had for over two thousand years. And they fought to alleviate promotion anxieties and other intraservice tensions, such as the line-staff controversy. Captain Alfred Thayer Mahan, an effective naval publicist, differed from his younger colleagues on several scores and stood with the older officers and their ideological proclivities more often than he did with the "progressive elements." But he, like his younger predecessors, used the merchant marine-trade protection arguments to advance the interests of his Service.

By the twentieth century navalists had achieved a real measure of success (though some of the "progressives" of the 1880s and '90s were to become the "old guard" of the 1920s and '30s). Naval officers had learned public relations techniques which they have not forgotten since. Over the past eighty years they have offered many reasons for naval growth and are convinced of the reasonableness of their case, but their primary motive has always been their desire to see their profession thrive.

*   *   *

The navalist seeks to "sell" a Navy to his country fundamentally because of his identification with the naval profession, not simply because of his desire to serve the nation's best interests. He frequently equates the Navy and the national interest, to be sure, but that does not *make* them identical. Admiral W. S. Benson once told a convention of the National Rivers and Harbors Congress,

> Anything that helps commerce helps the Navy; anything that helps the Navy helps commerce; and whatever helps both helps the country (Applause).

But Benson and his messmates were only peripherally concerned with commerce. The exchange between Admiral Ernest King and Senator Lister Hill provides a better insight into the navalist's philosophy. Hill once asked King if it were not possible that the unification of the armed forces might be in the national interest in spite of King's claim that unification was not in the Navy's best interest. "Any step that is not good for the Navy, Senator, is not good for **387** the country!" King replied. While such narrow-mindedness is uncommon among thoughtful naval officers, King spoke for the vast majority of the naval aristocracy in assigning top priority to naval affairs.[1]

Now and then Congressmen sensed this *myopia navalisma*—sensed that the naval aristocracy had created a body of propaganda and rationalizations designed primarily to serve its own interests. When the Navy General Board warned of German maritime ambitions one year and Japanese the next, in appealing for more battleships, one House Naval Affairs Committee member criticized their reports as "an insult to the intelligence of the Committee" and "a fraud upon Congress and the American people." When Rear Admiral Austin Knight, a member of the Navy General Board and President of the Naval War College, once went before the House Naval Affairs Committee to argue for significant increases in naval construction, the following exchange took place between Knight and Representative Oscar Callaway of Texas:

> Callaway: Do you know of any [naval] threat [to the United States]?
> Knight: Nothing . . . that is specific enough so that I would be justified in mentioning it. . . .
> Callaway: Your doctrine, then, boiled down simply means that you think we are wealthy enough to build a navy that the other nations are not financially able to cope with, with their building?
> Knight: That is one way of putting it . . . but I think we need this navy whether we are rich or poor.

In 1884 Senator Eugene Hale came to the aid of the naval aristocracy, offering the hope that the Navy would become "the pet of the American people." Some thirty years later he was to recall that "the more we have done" for the Navy, "the more they have claimed." Hale came to the conclusion that the Army and the Navy believed "the Government is run for the benefit of those establishments."[2]

Hale's reasoning was understandable. As ex-naval constructor Holden Evans once put it, "Did you ever hear a naval officer suggest that naval expenditures should be reduced? Can you ever interest the average officer in naval economy?" Occasionally Evans may be answered affirmatively, but such instances are exceptional. Only once did I find a member of the naval aristocracy challenging a colleague's "demand for a colossal fleet." This was in 1896, when, after three decades of piping peace, Commander Caspar Goodrich heard Lieutenant John M. Ellicott warn his colleagues of the "daily jeopardy" the nation faced without massive naval growth. "If he be correct," Goodrich wryly observed, "then the wonder arises as to how we have managed to escape a direful fate during the twenty-five to thirty years following the late war when our navy was a negligible quantity." But for every Goodrich there were hundreds of Ellicotts. More recently Captain Robert H. Smith has had harsh words for both "the contractors who have let us down" and the officers who had swallowed their

388 pitches. Smith, a gadfly, worthy of the mantle of Goodrich and Hyman Rickover, urges his colleagues to "assess skeptically the promises of [industry weapons merchants] with their pointers and slides." Specifically he has called for an end to all production plans on the Navy's next generation of destroyers, the 963-class. Captain Smith, Admiral Rickover, and Admiral Eli T. Reich (one of the first to expose the shortcomings of the Terrier missile system), straight-talking men who don't jump at every new naval boondoggle to grace a drawing board, offer the kind of naval leadership we need (even if we may not need all the ships they would *like* us to have).[3]

*   *   *

Mahan's messmates were tragic examples of professional men whose every thought and action tended to reinforce, rather than to challenge, their attitude toward life. They grew in only one direction, while the world was growing in many. They believed and vicariously enjoyed the mystique of the State. They were fully aware of the race for empire, of those nations in the lead and those falling behind. They had seen this struggle first-hand. They felt they had discovered immutable laws of human behavior and international relations applicable to all ages. They "knew" that man was still a savage beast and that each "race" was a slightly different species of the beast. Foremost was the Anglo-Saxon "race," and foremost in its history had been the sea and the Navy. *Ipso facto*, a strong navy was essential to the future of Anglo-Americanism.

How unfortunate that Mahan and his messmates did not choose to argue for a truly *defensive* naval force. How unfortunate that they did not hold out some hope for the success of international arbitration, for the arrival of a peaceful "millennium." They did not argue for such a millennium, but then they could not reasonably have expected to. They were inseparably bound to their convictions.* In their world power was always a virtue, impotence always a vice, and the task of the virtuous was always to battle with the vicious. And if their views and actions offended some, it must be said that they were not wholly responsible. In 1867 Navy Chaplain Charles Boynton claimed that "from the beginning, the Navy has been the embodying of truly American ideas. . . . [M]ore than anything else, the Navy has been . . . a true outgrowth of distinctive American thought." And while Boynton's enthusiasm for the Service may have distracted him from the many "old world" ways of American naval life, he nevertheless did see that the Navy did not grow or exist in a vacuum. As Rear Admiral James Calvert put it recently, "The Navy is shaped by the society it exists to defend."[4] If the naval officer occasionally offered to

---

* Some had moments of liberation, to be sure. On several occasions David D. Porter, Bradley Fiske, John Rodgers, John Crittenden Watson, Alexander Murray, Caspar Goodrich, Percival Drayton, William Sampson, Washington I. Chambers, Joseph Coghlan, William F. Fullam, and Hoover's "chief of anti-naval operations" (editor of N.Y. *Tribune* to Cpt. R. Z. Johnston, Feb. 4, 1931, Johnston Papers, S.H.C., U. of N.C. Library), William V. Pratt, displayed remarkable insight, frankness, or self-restraint.

put the force at his disposal to use on behalf of dubious causes, he was only **389**
doing what he felt was expected of him by a vigorous, expansionistic nation.

This aggressive spirit was not always looking for a fight. It could be, and
often was, rechanneled. But it was always there. "What we need first is power,"
Theodore Roosevelt once said.[5] And his naval friends, keepers of the "Big
Stick," concurred. In August 1897, Rear Admiral William Sampson, Commander-in-Chief of the North Atlantic Fleet, was authorized by Assistant Navy
Secretary Roosevelt to conduct target practice "without regard to allowance"
in anticipation of war with Spain. In 1955, Captain William Puleston, one
of the Navy's more articulate recent spokesmen, reiterated the fin-de-siècle
view that war was good for mankind, that it was "the instrument" of progress,
and that the era of universal peace, such as was threatened by the machinations
of the United Nations, would "sap the spirit" of man. To the extent that
Puleston was characteristic, little had changed.[6]

To some extent Puleston probably was characteristic of the naval aristocracy
of the McCarthy era. But he was characteristic of a great many other Americans
as well. By 1955 a great many civilian leaders were just as interested as he in
military solutions. If we were able to interview military and civilian officials in
the Pentagon we *might* find that civilians in Defense are more belligerent than
their military counterparts. "Civilian control" is not enough. Someone must
control the civilian militarists too. As Gabriel Kolko has written,

> . . . [T]he notion of an independent military sector, with its own codes and objectives,
> saves critical observers the trouble of viewing the nature of American power as a much
> larger integrated phenomenon.

It is clear that today's policymakers are more willing to deploy force than were
their predecessors. And the works of William A. Williams, Lloyd Gardner,
Walter LaFeber, David Horowitz, Kolko himself, and a growing number of
other cold war revisionists all relate the policies of the civilian elite to the
earlier "open door" policy; all reject any notion of military dominance. I want
to make clear that I agree with most, but not all, of their analyses. The naval
officer is not responsible for the shaping of American foreign policy in the past
few decades any more than he was for its shaping in the nineteenth century.
But if the military does not *shape* foreign policy, it certainly influences its outcome. Adam Yarmolinsky has recently shown us how military options came
to displace diplomatic ones in the Kennedy years, largely because the military
was prepared to offer decision-makers with a number of specific, neatly
graduated alternatives. One of those options put us in Vietnam with both feet.
The "open door" ideology still designs the set, but the military is no docile
supporting player. It is stage front and wants to stay there.*

*   *   *

* Lloyd Jensen, "American Foreign Policy Elites and the Prediction of International
Events," *Peace Research Society Journal*, V (1966), 199–209; Kolko, *The Roots of American*

390   The naval aristocracy has consistently argued that "a powerful navy" posed no threat to "civil liberty." Indeed, as Lieutenant R. M. G. Brown put it in 1881, the Service was extremely fortunate in that "an increase of the navy is not considered by either political party as dangerous to the institutions of the country. The arguments against a large standing army do not apply to the naval service."[7]

'But though the U.S. Navy posed few direct threats to domestic U.S. freedoms, it could be and often was used to ride roughshod over the rights of foreign peoples. Naval officers were reluctant to admit this, of course. Indeed, they often took the opposite position. Captain William S. Sims once told a House Naval Affairs that it was

> particularly well known from all our recent [circa 1915] history, anyway, that . . . we want to be left alone, and that is all. . . . I can not quite imagine this country becoming ambitious for territorial expansion and world power and that sort of thing. Really, I cannot.

General Lemuel Shepherd, Marine Corps Commandant in 1956, and retired Marine Corps Major Vinson McNeill have recently offered similar words of praise for naval-marine interventions in Nicaragua and even Haiti, which the marines had made into "a solvent, responsible democracy, a bulwark to the peace and security of the Western Hemisphere."[8]

But one can also find criticisms of naval diplomacy in the words of naval officers themselves. In 1882, for example, mustang Lieutenant Commander Henry Gorringe saw "the seed of discord that may ripen into war" being sowed in Mexico by the use of naval power to protect U.S. investors ("the most prominent political and commercial 'bosses' in this country"). In 1916, Captain Washington I. Chambers criticized efforts to "command the markets" by "stealth" and force. And in 1924, Captain Frank H. Schofield, somewhat

---

Foreign Policy (Boston, 1969); Yarmolinsky, "The Military Establishment (or How Political Problems become Military Problems)," *Foreign Policy*, No. 1, Winter 1970–71, 78–97.

I think Kolko overstates his case when he writes: ". . . [No]t since Alfred T. Mahan has a professional officer penned a respectable rationale for the enlargement of American might that reflected distinctive ideological assumptions. . . . The failure of any significant sector of the military openly to rally to such theories of the positive and predatory state at any time reveals mainly that the American military is nonideological, even when civilians formulate a seemingly appropriate frame of reference for it." Compared to many foreign military officers and many civilian militarists, the American officer is less ideological, more detached, professional. But, as two separate studies have recently demonstrated, there is no statistical difference between "heroic" and "managerial" officer candidates at West Point, Annapolis, or ROTC units representing all three services; both types demonstrated uncommonly high levels of absolutism. (John Lovell, "The Professional Socialization of the West Point Cadet," in Morris Janowitz, ed., *The New Military* [N.Y., 1964]; E. Berger *et al.*, "ROTC, My Lai, and the Volunteer Army," *Foreign Policy*, No. 2, Spring 1971, 144.) Kolko is certainly right in pointing out that it has been the civilian leadership that has planned the "American century," but he goes too far when he writes the military out of ideology formation altogether. C. Wright Mills wisely spoke of a "coincidence of interests and a co-ordination of aims among economic and political as well as military actors," something he then "more accurately termed the power elite." (*Power Elite*, 224.)

accidentally, offered a fairly complete inditement of the dangers the U.S. Navy posed to the sovereignty of other nations.

Schofield was trying to describe the ruin the United States would face without a navy; to do so he drew numerous analogies to the role navies played in the affairs of other peoples. The ports of Norfolk and San Francisco might be "leased to any foreign power for 99 years" as we had "leased" Pago Pago, Guantanamo, and other foreign ports. Tariff funds might be "set aside by a collective foreign treaty that tells America she shall not collect more than 5% import duty," as had happened in China. Foreign troops might be quartered near Washington, as they were at Tientsin, "guarding foreign legations." Foreign gunboats might control the Mississippi, Hudson, and Chesapeake waterways, as they controlled the Yangtze, the Ozama, the Panama Canal, and the seven seas. Schofield painted a grim scene.

None the less, Rear Admiral John Hayes recently argued that the Navy should have been allowed to retain the North China ports of Chefoo and Tsingtao and the South China Sea island of Hainan in 1949, and Captain Edward L. Beach frankly boasts that naval power permits the U.S. to "project" its "influence for stability and national probity to the far reaches of the world." Beach cites Lebanon, Santo Domingo, and Vietnam to prove his point.[9] The landing of marines in these countries and the domination of the Tonkin Gulf only peripherally effect civil liberties in the U.S. (though it can be argued that efforts to control foreign peoples eventually result in the restriction of domestic liberties), but it strikes me that such force deployments have had an adverse effect on the independence and freedom of Dominicans and Vietnamese.*

We rule the seas chiefly because we have the ability to do so, but *must* we? *Must* we have every new naval, or army, or air force weapon that the weapons merchants create? We have plenty of U.S.S. *Enterprises* (indeed, no one else has any); couldn't we use a few more S.S. *Hopes*? *Must* we expand into post-colonial "vacuums" with such regularity? We would never have become involved in Southeast Asia had it not been for our naval potential to reach out across the full length of the Pacific in support of a 600,000-man Crusade. *Must* we take over from the British the control of Mauritius and the "defense" of the Indian Ocean? *Must* we "defend" an "open door" policy for the seabed?

It is not necessary to revert to a pre-industrial social order to provide for ecological balance. It is not necessary to experience economic depression at home in order to guarantee that American trade and investment abroad do not operate to enslave the economies and cultures of others. It is not necessary to disarm unilaterally to attain a more sensible naval posture. Expensive guided missile cruisers whose missiles are guided anywhere but toward their targets and fabulous nuclear super-carriers whose cost cannot presently be justified by any impartial cost analysis express a globe-girdling, world-policeman naval mission. Mine sweepers, submarines, destroyers, ASW carriers—comparatively

* See, for example, George Kahin and John Lewis, *The United States in Vietnam* (rev. ed., N.Y., 1969); and Richard Barnett, *Intervention and Revolution* (N.Y., 1969).

392 less costly—express an essentially defensive posture, such as that held by the Soviets. Most of the critics of navalism have always favored the creation of such a defense-oriented force and for some very sound reasons have opposed the creation of today's world-police force. In the final analysis, the "anti-navalists," men like Oscar Callaway and Charles Beard, believers in self-determination and the "open door at home," appear to have offered critiques of navalism[10] that have stood the test of time.

*   *   *

And what of the new naval aristocracy of merit? Morris Janowitz argues that the post-World War II world has seen the creation of a new, "civilianized" officer corps. Division of labor in an increasingly complex and technological military has resulted in a breakdown of traditional loyalties and values, and a greater emphasis on psychological manipulation, rather than "by-the-book" disciplining, of enlisted personnel. Janowitz understandably focuses on the recent acceleration of the process, but its origins are in the early twentieth century.[11] Business psychology concepts and reward-discipline methods were popular with the "Young Turks" of William Fullam's generation. Rear Admiral Henry Clay Taylor was just as "managerial" for his day as George Marshall or Maxwell Taylor would be half a century later. And Bradley Fiske was well aware, in 1921, of the fact that the technological revolution had made naval officers "but tiny parts" that seemed "to be growing smaller and smaller," as the "Modern Military Machine" grew larger and more complex.

The drift from "heroes" to "managers" in the modern military has not occurred in a vacuum, without resistance from those who prefer the earlier "hero" model so common among the naval aristocracy in the Golden Age of Annapolis. Coincidental with each managerial innovation is a widespread reaction in the officer corps to what is perceived to be the "alarming erosion of the status, privilege, and confidence heretofore reposed in the officer corps" attendant upon this alleged "civilianization." Marine Corps Colonel Robert Heinl, Jr., has maintained that this "erosion" awakened "widespread complaint, frustration, and even bitterness, among career officers" by "leveling out distinctions between officers and enlisted men. . . ." Navy Captain W. J. Maddocks is angered by the "constant whittling away of long-standing military 'privileges'." And a recent poll of Annapolites indicated that officers feel their professional status to be sinking in comparison with other professionals. This reaction may explain why Captain Richard Alexander was outraged, rather than pleased, by the Navy Department's recent removal of Lieutenant Commander Marcus Aurelius Arnheiter from command. Arnheiter apparently sought to draw enemy fire by approaching the North Vietnamese coast at unauthorized close range. Captain Alexander was less disturbed by this behavior than he was by Arnheiter's removal. Where was the "special trust and confidence?" "What all your officers will demand to know," he informed Navy

Secretary Paul Ignatius, "is just how in hell could this happen in the United **393** States Navy?"[12]

The struggle to repeal or "beef-up" the Uniform Code of Military Justice and to restore "special trust and confidence" in the officer corps won its first battle in 1963 with the toughening-up of Non-Judicial Punishment (Article 15 of the UCMJ). And there will be more struggles to check the "leveling" process that George Saville, Lord Halifax, first warned against nearly 300 years ago. Thus many career officers are worried, and some outraged, by the liberalizing "Z-grams" of Admiral Elmo Zumwalt, the new Chief of Naval Operations. Admiral Zumwalt is concerned with the low retention rates in ratings requiring highly technical skill levels and high initial training costs. He is also worried about the effect of President Nixon's "zero-draft volunteer army" on the Navy's recruiting figures. But many of Zumwalt's subordinates see only "new laxity" and "soda fountain morale."

My own view is that the "leveling" process has not gone far enough. With the influx of reserve officers and the rapid expansion of the Service, the term "naval aristocracy" is a misnomer; the modern naval officer corps now constitutes a coopted, upper-middle and middle class meritocracy. But many of the old features remain. For example, the Navy continues to provide Filipino and black stewards for its officer corps, a kind of racial subordination more suited to the days of Mahan than the age of Rickover. Why, for that matter, do officers need stewards at all? Moreover, though annual competitive entrance exams are held for Academy admission, no less than 70% of post-World War II Academy openings were filled by Congressional appointment, and politics still counts for much in the selection.

Many years ago someone proposed that admission to the service academies be restricted to college graduates, that the academies should become postgraduate schools. The 1944 Pye Board rejected the idea. Only Annapolis, Rear Admiral Pye argued, could instill the "discipline and indoctrination and character building." In rejecting a similar proposal for West Point in 1946, General Maxwell Taylor observed, "We must have these young men in their formative years if we are to implant the principles in them which we try to implant." But this is precisely why a proposal to make the service academies into graduate schools (or to abolish them altogether) merits reconsideration. A four-year "liberal arts" requirement might check the less desirable facets of service academy inculcation of values and mores. In any event the service academies, plagued as they are with unstable academic standards and high resignation rates, are not functioning as the professional institutions they were designed to be. The Academic Board at Annapolis today is composed entirely of officers. The civilian faculty are virtually powerless in the fixing of those very matters of academic policy that they should entirely control. J. Arthur Heise has recently called for a thorough study of the service academies. I add the hope that such a study would observe a healthy distrust for mindless traditionalism and military control of the wholly academic aspects of the curriculum. Samuel

394   P. Huntington unsportingly juxtaposes the "commonplace" town of Highland Falls, N.Y., and its neighbor, the extraordinary, nationally-endowed community of West Point, and then asks if it is "possible to deny that the military values— loyalty, duty, restraint, dedication—are the ones America most needs today? That the disciplined order of West Point has more to offer than the garish individualism of Main Street?" He answers himself:

> Today America can learn more from West Point than West Point from America. . . . If the civilians permit the soldiers to adhere to the military standard, the nation may eventually find redemption and security in making that standard their own.

Unless West Point were radically different from the Naval Academy (and it is not), I would find it difficult to agree with Huntington. The order and serenity he so admires at West Point are deceptive, unnatural, enforced. The Academy produces "loyal servants of a democratic society," as John Masland and Laurence Radway put it, servants who do not presently threaten to seize the reins of government by force.[13] But there is no point in *tempting* them. We sought the expertise of the professional soldier, but we needn't *emulate* him in civil affairs, and we shouldn't *isolate* him in military affairs. As I have argued elsewhere, we need non-Academy, liberal arts college officers with "civilian" values as a counter-balance to the Annapolite. The "redemption and security" Huntington proposes is the "redemption and security" of the garrison (or police) state. We may never have been a thoroughly military people, but then, happily, we have never had a thoroughly military state. The price of the former might well be the latter; we are better off without either.

Clemenceau felt that war was "too important" a business to be left to the generals. Similarly, naval power and its disposition are too serious to be left to the admirals (or to their civilian supernavalist cohorts). If this account of "the naval aristocracy" has any lesson for today, it is that we must always be suspicious of men in blue double-breasted suits with gold on their sleeves who want us to buy them big boats and things that go bang in order to save us all from evil. A people with wealth, ambition, and a fine impression of themselves want a modern, professional military. And I regret to say that I cannot as yet imagine a believeable scenario in which wealthy, proud America would realistically do without its fleets, missiles, or armies. But there is a wide range of possibilities between total disarmament and a multi-billion dollar post-overkill weapons innovation race. Such a race may be more than Americans bargain for, but it's theirs if they cease to believe that they have the ability to differ intelligently with the military elite or their Defense Department civilian counter-parts. Admiral Yates Stirling longed for the day when the naval leadership would "command such prestige that its say on naval matters would become the last word to the American People. Civilian interference then . . . would be eliminated."[14] It should be clear that such interested parties as Mahan's messmates should never be granted "the last word" on naval matters. It is not that there is anything intrinsically untrustworthy in naval officers; they are like all institutional spokesmen in their commitment to their profession. The point is that it is unwise to accept *uncritically* what *any* professional spokesmen have to say about the needs of their profession.*

We look to the military to see that we aren't pushed around. But we've got to remember to look behind us now and then to see who's doing the pushing. Once upon a time it was the "band of brothers" from Annapolis with their merchant marine caps and international trade jackets. They seemed quite selfless. But now and then, if you looked closely enough, your eye could catch a trace of navy blue or a glint of gold braid hidden deep beneath the seductive facade of "national interests."

* Thus I am at *least* as suspicious of the pleas of air and missile force advocates, AMA views on "socialized medicine," and Advertising Council "public service messages" as I am of navalists.

Notes
A Summing-up and Some
Final Observations

1. Benson, *The Relation of Inland Waterways to Naval Efficiency*, 4, cited in Beard, *Idea of National Interest*, 351; King, cited in William B. Huie, *The Case Against the Admirals* (N.Y., 1946), 171. See also Admiral Louis Denfield to Navy Secretary Francis Matthews, 28 Sept. 1949: (". . . any step that is not good for the Navy is not good for the nation") in Paul Y. Hammond, "Super Carriers and B-36 Bombers: Appropriations, Strategy, and Politics," in Harold Stein, ed., *American Civil–Military Decisions* (Huntsville, Ala., 1963).

2. Stillson Ph.D. thesis, 185; 64th Cong., 1st Sess., *Hearings before the House Committee on Naval Affairs on Estimates Submitted by the Secretary of the Navy, 1916* (3 vols., Wash., G.P.O., 1916), II, 2082; E. E. Morison, *Admiral Sims and the Modern American Navy*, 181; "Hale, Eugene," *D.A.B.*

3. H. Evans, *One Man's Fight for a Better Navy*, 141; Goodrich, *PUSNI*, XXII (1896), 553; Smith, *PUSNI* (Mar. 1971), 23.

While criticizing the Hungarian rebels of 1848, Commodore Matthew Calbraith Perry once remarked that Americans should "let our neighbors affairs alone and look out for our own" (Morison, "*Old Bruin*," 273), but it isn't clear what kind of self-restraint Perry had in mind; three years later he was forcing the door of Japan open at gunpoint.

4. Boynton, *History of the Navy During the Rebellion*. I, 14; Calvert, *Naval Profession*, 89.

5. Roosevelt, "An Address at Wheeling, West Virginia, 6 Sept. 1902," 81, Roosevelt Collection, Harvard University Library.

6. Roosevelt to Captain Charles O'Neil, Dec. 27, 1898, O'Neil Papers, R. B. Hayes Library, Fremont, Ohio; Puleston, *Influence of Force in Foreign Relations*, 232–237. Cf. Rear Admiral Henry Eccles, *Military Concepts and Philosophy* (New Brunswick, N.J., 1965), 271.

7. Brown, *United Service*, IV (1881), 610. See also Captain Stephen Luce, "A Powerful Navy not Dangerous to Civil Liberties," *United Service*, IV, 109 ff.; Captain William Puleston, *The Influence of Sea Power in World War II* (New Haven, 1947), 300; Captain William B. Prendergest, "The Navy and Civil Liberty," *PUSNI*, LXXIV (1948), 1263–1267; Rear Admiral Ernest

396

Eller, "Sea Power and Peace," *PUSNI*, LXXIII (1947), 1168–1169.

8. *House Naval Affairs Hearings, 1916*, II, 2743; Shepherd, in a foreword to James H. McCrocklin, comp., *Garde D'Haiti* (Annapolis, 1965); McNeil, "Nicaraguan Elections of 1928," *Marine Corps Gazette* (Sept. 1966), 32.

9. Gorringe, "The Navy," *North American Review*, CXXXIV (1882), 487; Chambers, "Preparedness, Feb. 22, 1916, a.d.," and "A Plan by Which the United States may Cooperate with Other Nations to Achieve and Preserve the Peace of the World," p. 8, Box 48, Chambers Papers, N.H.F.; Schofield, "The Aims and Present Status of the Navy" (mimeo. of a speech, dated February 1924 [copy in State Hist. Soc. of Wisc.]); Hayes, *PUSNI*, XCVI (May 1970), 346–347; Beach, *The Wreck of the "Memphis"* (N.Y., 1966), 8.

10. See, for example, Beard, *The Idea of National Interest*, and *The Navy: Defense or Portent?*

11. Janowitz, *Professional Soldier, passim*; Janowitz, *Sociology and the Military Establishment* (New York, rev. ed., 1965), 107, 116. Janowitz and his colleagues appear well aware that managerial techniques were introduced in the Navy long before World War II. See Maury Feld, "The Military Self-Image in a Technological Environment," in Janowitz, ed., *The New Military*

(N.Y., 1964), 188, and Janowitz, *ibid.*, 116.

12. Janowitz, "Changing Patterns of Organizational Authority: The Military Establishment," *Administrative Science Quarterly*, III (1959), 473–493; Captain R. R. Belknap, "Military Character," *PUSNI*, XLIV (1918), 3; Taylor to Navy Secretary John Long, cited in Spector, "Professors of War . . .," 291; Fiske, *Invention: The Master-Key to Progress* (N.Y. 1929), 300; Heinl, "Special Trust and Confidence," *PUSNI* (1956), 463; Maddocks, *PUSNI*, XCVI (Mar. 1970), 95; *PUSNI*, XCV (August 1969), 64; *Esquire* (July 1969), 87; Janowitz, "Armed Forces and Society: A World Perspective," in Jacques Van Doorn, ed., *Armed Forces and Society* (The Hague, 1968), 24. For the best account of the zany antics of Arnheiter see Neil Sheehan, "The 99 Days of Captain Arnheiter," *N.Y. Times Magazine* (Aug. 11, 1968), 7–9, 68–75.

13. Heise, *Brass Factories*, 176; Huntington, "Power, Expertise, and the Military Profession," *Daedalus* (Fall, 1963), 789–790, and *Soldier and State*, 465–466; Masland and Radway, *Soldiers and Scholars* (Princeton, 1957), 107–108, 175, 192, 196, 233.

Huntington wrote his praise of the values of West Point over a decade ago and may not feel the same today; I differ with the Huntington of the 1950s.

14. Stirling, *Sea Duty*, 135–136.

Acknowledgments

A number of people gave all or part of this essay a thoughtful reading at one stage or another. I particularly want to thank Merle Curti, Edward Coffman, Kenneth Hagan, Jerry Israel, William A. Williams, Jim Sens, Stephen Ambrose, Robert F. Smith, Lance Buhl, Allan Millet, Charles Brand, William Stanton, Samuel P. Hays, and Thomas McCormick. Professor Curti, my mentor and friend, was inspiring in every sense of that word, and I am most grateful to him.

Some of these readers disagreed with various aspects of the drafts they saw. They may be pleased to see that I have taken some of their wise suggestions and displeased to see that I have not taken others. In any event, I offer the usual declaration of independence and general absolution: The readers are not responsible for my judgments or attendant errors. Neither are the American Philosophical Society or the University of Pittsburgh's Center for International Studies, but these two institutions did help to finance some of the research trips that resulted in this essay. Ms. Michelle LaPrade, Ms. Sheila Rettger, and Ms. Marion Jefferson typed with care a difficult final draft; I appreciate that care. My wife, Bonnie, likes to investigate and question the established social order and its institutions too; she was a good critic.

Several nice people made my research trips more fruitful and pleasant than they might have been, and I want to acknowledge their assistance. Rear Admiral John McElroy and his assistant, Mr. Andrew Dixon, of the Library of Congress Manuscripts Division branch of the Naval Historical Foundation were quite helpful. Neither is still in the Manuscript Division, but Admiral McElroy is still with the Naval Historical Foundation; and along with Dr. William Morgan of the Naval History Division, and Mr. Richard von Doenhoff, Archivist of the Division of Naval History at the National Archives, he might be approached by one contemplating a study of the Navy. Ms. Mary M. Johnson, Mr. Joseph Ross, Ms. Elaine Everly, Mr. Harry Schwartz, and Dr. Milton Gustafson were particularly helpful when it came to dealing with complexities of the Navy and State Department records at the National Archives. Rear Admiral Ernest Eller, of Naval History, his secretary, Ms. Thelma Mertz, and his photo librarian, Ms. Agnes Hoover, were most thoughtful in helping me deal with those incidentals that can make or break one's research day. Dan Walker, Carl Copeland, and many more of my fellow students of the military in History 159

398   over the past several years were good critics, as were several members of the Free Press, among them James M. Cron, Wilbur E. Mangas, Linda Mattison, and Robert Harrington. Al Shane and Jerry McCavitt of the University of Pittsburgh helped me to reproduce a number of the illustrations appearing in this book; they are not responsible for any lack of detail or clarity in the originals.

At Annapolis, the home port of naval gentility, the hospitable tradition is very much alive in such generous folk as Doris M. Maguire, the ex-Naval Academy Librarian; Captain Richard Derickson of the Naval Academy Alumni Association; Ms. C. G. Halpine; Mr. H. G. Williams, Ms. Patty Maddocks, and Mr. Ed Holm, all of the U.S. Naval Institute; and Captain Dale Mayberry and Mr. L. B. Brown, both of the Naval Museum, Mr. Arthur Breton, Assistant Curator of Manuscripts at the New York Historical Society; Mr. Anthony Nicolosi, Archivist of the United States Naval War College, Newport, Rhode Island; Ms. Mattie Russell, Curator of Manuscripts at the George Perkins Library, Duke University; Ms. Wesley Wallace, Assistant Curator of Manuscripts of the Southern Historical Collection at the University of North Carolina Library; Mr. Jack T. Ericson, Head of the Syracuse University Library's Manuscript Division; Ms. Ruth Davis of the State Historical Society of Wisconsin; and Pamela Palm, Lee Spanos, Sarah Powers, and Carl Reed of the University of Pittsburgh Library were some of the archivists and librarians who were particularly helpful to me in locating a number of the sources that follow.

Bibliography

A. BIBLIOGRAPHIES

1. Non-Government Bibliographical Publications

Albion, Robert G., *Naval and Maritime History: An Annotated Bibliography* (3rd ed. Mystic, Conn., 1963).

Buggert, Elizabeth C., *Guide to the Manuscript Collections in the Library of the Ohio State Archives and Historical Society* (Columbus, Ohio, 1953).

Bolander, Louis, *Bibliography of Naval Literature in the U.S. Naval Academy Library* (Annapolis, 1928 [Library of Congress has a mimeograph copy]).

Carman, Harry J. and Arthur Thompson, *A Guide to the Principal Sources for American Civilization, 1800–1900, in the City of New York: Manuscripts* (New York, 1960).

Catalogue of the Books, Manuscripts, and Prints and Other Memorabilia in the John S. Barnes Memorial Library of the Naval History Society (New York, 1912).

Harrison, Curtis W., *The United States, 1865–1900* (3 vols., Fremont, Ohio, 1943–1945).

Hamer, Philip, ed., *A Guide to Archives and Manuscripts in the U.S.* (New Haven, 1961).

Harbeck, Charles, *A Contribution to the Bibliography of the History of the United States Navy* (Cambridge, Mass., 1906).

Hayes, John D., "The Writings of Stephen B. Luce," *Military Affairs*, XIX (1955), 187–96.

——, "The Papers of Naval Officers: Where Are They?" *Military Affairs*, XX (1956), 102–103.

Kirkham, George K., *The Books and Articles of Rear Admiral A. T. Mahan, U.S.N.* (New York, n.d. [circa 1928]).

Kuehl, Warren F., *Dissertations in History* (Lexington, Ky., 1965).

Lang, Kurt, "Military Sociology: A Trend Report & Bibliography," *Current Sociology* (Oxford, 1965), XIII, No. 1.

Merrill, James M., "Successors to Mahan: A Survey of Writings on American Naval History, 1914–1960," *Journal of American History*, L (1963), 79–99.

——, "The Naval Historian and His Sources," *American Archivist*, XXXII (1969), 261–268.

Neeser, Robert W., *Statistical and Chronological History of the U.S. Navy, 1775–1907* (2 vols., New York, 1909).

The Sea: Books and Manuscripts on . . . Naval History . . . (The Rosenbach Co., Philadelphia and New York, 1938).

Tilley, Nannie, *Guide to the Manuscript Collections in the Duke University Library* (Durham, 1947).

400   2. Government Bibliographical Publications

Library of Congress, *National Union Catalogue of Manuscripts* (Ann Arbor, 1962–1968).

National Archives, *Guide to Genealogical Records in the National Archives*, ed. Meredith Colket, Jr., and Frank Bridgers (Wash., G.P.O., 1964).

National Archives, *Preliminary Checklist of the Naval Records Collection of the Office of Naval Records and Library, 1775–1910* (Wash., G.P.O., 1943).

National Archives, *Preliminary Inventory of the Records of the Bureau of Naval Personnel* (Wash., G.P.O., 1960).

National Union Catalogue of Manuscript Collections (Wash., 1959–1968).

Naval Academy Museum, *Catalogue of Manuscripts* (Annapolis, 1957).

Naval Academy Museum, *Catalogue of the Rosenbach Collection of Manuscripts* (Annapolis, 1956).

Naval Academy Museum, *The Catalogue of the Christian A. Zabriskie Manuscript Collection* (Annapolis, 1956).

Navy Department, Bureau of Navigation, *Catalogue of Works by American Naval Authors*, compiled by Lieutenant Lucien Young (Wash., G.P.O., 1888).

Navy Department, Naval History Division, *U.S. Naval History Sources in the Washington, D.C., Area and Suggested Research Subjects* (Wash., 1965).

Navy Department, Naval History Division, *U.S. Naval History, Naval Biography, Naval Strategy and Tactics* (Wash., 1962).

Navy Department Library, *Bibliographical Catalogue of Periodicals* (Wash., 1897).

Navy Department Library, *Naval Library Conference, 18 and 19 June 1953, Proceedings* (Wash., 1953).

B. PRIMARY SOURCES

1. Manuscript Collections
(listed alphabetically by repository)

Some of the following manuscript collections have limited research value; all are brimming with calling cards, invitations, commissions, official orders and commendations, and the like, but some are short of much personal correspondence. Exceptionally rich collections are: the George H. Preble Papers at the Massachusetts Historical Society; the Samuel A'Court Ashe Papers, Duke; the Louis Goldsborough Papers, David D. Porter Papers, and Charles S. Sperry Papers, Mss. Div., L. of C.; Record Group 45, National Archives; the Stephen B. Luce Papers, Washington I. Chambers Papers, John A. Lejeune Papers, and Robert Shufeldt Papers, N.H.F.; the Henry Wise Papers, N.Y.H.S.; and the Edwin Anderson Papers, S.H.C., U. of N.C. Library.

G. W. Blunt White Library, Mystic Seaport, Mystic, Connecticut:
Rear Admiral Oscar F. Stanton Papers.
Chicago Historical Society, Manuscript Division:
"Navy Officers" File, George W. Childs Papers.
Waldo Healy Papers.
Rear Admiral Louis A. Kimberly Papers.
Lieutenant Hugh McKee Papers.
George H. Preble Papers.
Oral History Research Office, Columbia Univ.:
Reminiscences of Admiral Thomas Hart.

Reminiscences of Admiral Samuel M. Robinson.
Reminiscences of Commander E. E. Wilson.
Duke University, William Perkins Library Manuscript Division:
Samuel A'Court Ashe Papers, Flowers Collection [for A. T. Mahan letters].
Samuel L. Breeze Papers.
William P. S. Duncan Papers.
John McIntosh Kell Papers.
Commodore E. A. F. LaVallette Papers.
Alfred A. McKethan Papers.
John O'Neil Papers.
David D. Porter Papers.
Raymond P. Rodgers Papers.
Hilary H. Rhodes Papers.
Rear Admiral Charles Steedman Papers.
Rear Admiral Thomas H. Stevens, II, Papers.
Rear Admiral Thomas H. Stevens, III, Papers.
Mrs. C. G. Halpine, Annapolis, Md.:
Captain Edward Dorn Papers.
Rutherford B. Hayes Library, Fremont, Ohio:
Rear Admiral Charles O'Neil Papers.
Indiana Historical Society Library, Manuscript Division:
Letters of Albert G. Caldwell, John Caldwell Collection.
Library of Congress, Manuscript Division:
Admiral Mark Bristol Papers.
William E. Chandler Papers.
Rear Admiral Andrew Foote Papers.
Lieutenant (j.g.) George Foulk Papers.
Rear Admiral Louis Goldsborough Papers.
Alfred Thayer Mahan Papers.
Admiral David D. Porter Papers.
Letters, Papers, and Fragments of Theodore Roosevelt Collection.
Charles S. Sperry Papers.
Captain Charles Stewart, "Internal Rules and Regulations of the U.S.S. *Franklin*," 1822.
U.S. Navy, "Miscellaneous Manuscripts, 1775–1909."
U.S. Navy, "U.S.S. *Bainbridge* Letterbook, 1859–60."
U.S. Navy, "Lieutenant M. H. Bixby Papers."
William C. Whitney Papers.
Lincoln University Library, Harrogate, Tennessee:
Captain John L. Worden Papers.
Massachusetts Historical Society, Manuscript Division:
Captain's Clerk John E. Parkman Papers.
Captain George H. Preble Papers.
John D. Long Papers.
National Archives:
Microcopy T43, Roll 4, Vol. 5, Department of State Dispatches from U.S. Consuls in Manila, 1864–1874.
Microcopy 77, Roll 104, Diplomatic Instructions of the Department of State, Japan, Vol. I, 1855–1872.

Microcopy 89, Roll 53, Letters Received by the Secretary of the Navy from Commanding Officers of Squadrons, Pacific Squadron, 1871–1875.

Microcopy 89, Roll 270, Letters of the Asiatic Squadron, 1880–1885.

Microcopy 625, Roll 290, Geographical Area 9, Area Files of the Naval Records Collection, Jan. 1867–Dec. 1887.

Papers of Vice Admiral Stephen C. Rowan, Microfilm No. 180.

Record Group 24 (Bureau of Navigation):

Entry 1, Vols. 1–10, "Letters Sent 1885–1886."

Entry 21, Vol. 2, "Letters to Secretary of the Navy, 1881–1884."

Entry 6, Vols, 6–10, "Misc. Letters Sent, 1875–1884."

Entry 202, Vol. 1, "Letters of Resignation, 1878–86."

Correspondence of the Supt. of the Naval Academy to the Secretary of the Navy, 1850–1915.

Quarterly Returns on Enlistments on Vessels, and Weekly Returns of Enlistments at Naval Rendezvous, 1845–1900.

Record Group 38 (Office of Naval Intelligence):

Entry 68, Vols. 1 and 2, "General Correspondence, 1882–86."

Record Group 45:

Entry 18, "Letters to Officers Generally."

Entry 19, "Cipher Messages Sent, (deciphered) 1888–1906."

Entry 22, Vols. for 1875–90, "Officers Letters to the Secretary of the Navy."

Entry 23, "Letters from Commanders."

Entry 24, "Letters from Captains."

Entry 25 (14), "Letters from Commander P. F. Harrington of *Juanita* on disturbances on the Island of Johanna, East Africa, 1885."

Entry 30, "Copybooks of Rear Admiral Thornton Jenkins and others, Commanders of Asiatic Squadron, 1871–1872, and of Rear Admiral Earl English, Commander South Atlantic Squadron, 1885."

Entry 65, Vol. for 1866–77, "Resignations of Officers."

Entry 85, "Letters of Resignation of Volunteer Officers, 1866–1875."

Entry 90, Muster Rolls of *Kearsarge*, 1876, and *Ohio*, 1845.

Entry 300, Letters to Naval Attaché, Rome, Lieutenant Nathan Sargent.

Entry 301, William L. Cowles, Naval Attaché, London, Letterbook.

Entry 302, "Letters Sent by Lieutenant Albert P. Niblack, Naval Attaché of the U.S. in Berlin, 1896–1898," 2 Vols.

Entry 309, Nicaragua Correspondence, 1909–1910.

Entry 310, "Honduranean Correspondence, 1910–1911."

Entry 392, (99), Vol. II, "Civil War Journal of William B. Cushing."

Entry 392, (157), "Journal of Ensign Dudley Knox, Commanding Gunboat *Albany*, 1900."

Entry 395, (30), "Letterbook of Commander Guert Gansevoort [Herman Melville's cousin], Commanding U.S.S. *Decatur*, 1855–1856, Pacific Squadron."

Entry 395, (110), "Letters of Lieutenant George Rockwell, Commanding U.S.S. *Palos* to Rear Admiral John Rodgers, Commanding Asiatic Station, 1870–1872 Copybook."

Entry 395, (111), "Letters Received by Rear Admiral Charles Gove, 1871–1919."

Entry 395, (115), Vols. 2–5, "Copybook of Rear Admiral William Reynolds, Commanding Asiatic Station 1876–1877."

Entry 395, (119), "Letterbook of Rear Admiral C. R. P. Rodgers."   **403**

Entry 395, (128), "Press Copybook of Lieutenant Commander Richard Wainwright, Commanding Officer, U.S.S. *Gloucester*, 1898."

Entry 395, (132), Vol. 2, "Letterbooks of Caribbean Squadron, 1904–1907."

Entry 464, (Subject File), NA—Surveys of various isthmian routes.

——, NA—New Navy.

——, NI—Report of a Board convened by Secretary of the Navy . . . to report upon the present stagnation of officers in the line of the Navy, Sept. 1891.

——, NI—Naval Personnel, "Promotion and Privileges, Rank, Retirement, and Reinstatement."

——, NJ—Naval Discipline, Boxes 7–16.

——, NL—Living Conditions of Naval Personnel, 1860–1910.

——, NL—"The Idaho *Idler*," Box 274.

——, NL—"And There Were Giants in the Earth in Those Days: Some Yarns of the Old Navy," by Rear Admiral Oscar Farenholt, Box 274.

——, OY—Asiatic Fleet Reports, 1911–1927, Boxes 358–360.

——, NL—Mrs. Henry A. Wise, "Our Home Abroad," Manuscript in Box 274.

——, NO—Naval Personnel—Courts-Martial, 1860–1910.

——, SS—Naval Assistance to Merchant Ships.

——, VC—National Policy.

——, VI—Governmental Relationships.

Entry 473, "Letters of Naval Officers sent to the Library and Naval War Records Office in reply to Circular of December 1, 1904."

Ciphers Received, 1888–1910.

Record Group 80:

Chinese Theatre Reports, Office of the Secretary of the Navy and the Chief of Naval Operations, Secret Correspondence (Declassified), 1917–1926, Boxes 18, 19, and 29.

Record Group 84:

Hawaii, U.S. Legation Letters Sent, 1865–1897, Box 30–18.

Record Group 405:

Register of Candidates, U.S. Naval Academy, 1849–1929.

"ZB" File, Naval History Division:

Captain William J. Barnette Papers.

Commodore Franklin Buchanan Papers.

Captain Richard C. Davenport Papers.

Lieutenant Charles Flusser Papers.

Rear Admiral Andrew Foote Papers.

Rear Admiral A. T. Mahan Folder.

Captain John W. Philip Papers.

Naval Academy Library, Manuscript Division:

Lloyd Phoenix [Class of '61] "Fragments of a Private Journal."

Naval Historical Foundation, Washington, D.C.:

Rear Admiral Lester Beardslee Papers.

Rear Admiral Reginald R. Belknap Papers.

Journal of Charles F. Blake, 1862–1864.

Rear Admiral Frank Braisted Papers [including the autobiography of Rear Admiral H. D. Cooke].

404 Assistant Surgeon Dudley Carpenter Papers.
Rear Admiral Silas Casey Papers.
Captain Washington Irving Chambers Papers.
Rear Admiral Edmund Rose Colhoun Collection.
Rear Admiral Charles Cotton Papers.
Commodore William W. Dungan Papers.
Captain W. A. Egerton, R.N.–Commodore D. C. Bingham, U.S.N. Correspondence 1917–1919, Box 493.
Rear Admiral Robley D. Evans Collection.
Rear Admiral Julius A. Furer Papers.
Admiral William Freeland Fullam Papers.
Lieutenant S. P. Gillett Correspondence.
Admiral Albert Gleaves Papers.
Rear Admiral Hillary P. Jones Papers.
Commander Edward Kellogg Collection.
Commodore Dudley Knox Papers.
Rear Admiral Lewis A. Kimberly Papers.
Major General John A. Lejeune Papers.
Captain John Leonard Papers.
Rear Admiral Stephen B. Luce Papers [Building 210, Washington Navy Yard].
Captain John Marston Papers.
Surgeon Arthur Matthewson Papers.
Captain C. C. Marsh Collection [World War I Scrapbook].
Journal of Naval Cadet Edward Moale, Jr. [1887–1889].
Commodore Somerville Nicholson Papers.
Rear Admiral Charles F. O'Neil Papers.
Rear Admiral Hiram Paulding, Papers [Building 210, Washington Navy Yard].
Surgeon Ninian Pinkney, U.S.N., Papers.
Admiral David D. Porter Collection.
Admiral William V. Pratt Papers [Bldg. 210, Washington Navy Yard].
Letters of the Presidents of the War College.
Rear Admiral William Radford Collection.
Frank E. Ridgley Collection.
Rear Admiral John Rodgers Family Papers.
Rear Admiral Francis A. Roe Collection.
Captain Cornelius M. Schoonmaker Collection.
Rear Admiral Montgomery Sicard Papers.
Captain Nathan Sargent Papers.
Commodore Robert Shufeldt Papers.
Rear Admiral T. O. Selfridge Collection.
Charles Sperry Papers.
Rear Admiral Thomas Holdup Stevens, III, Collection.
Rear Admiral David F. Sellers Papers.
John F. Tarbell, Paymaster, U.S.N., Journal of the *Gettysburg*, 1876–77.
Rear Admiral Henry Clay Taylor Collection.
Admiral Montgomery Meigs Taylor Papers.
Thomas-Yarnell Papers [Building 210, Washington Navy Yard].
Rear Admiral Richard Wainwright Papers.

Rear Admiral John G. Walker Papers.   **405**
Rear Admiral John C. Watson Papers.
Admiral Roger Welles Papers.
Henry Williams Papers.
Lieutenant Samuel L. Wilson Correspondence.
Wood Collection [Chief Engineer William W. W. Wood and Lieutenant Thomas
    Wood, U.S.M.C.].
Naval Museum, Annapolis, Md.:
Miscellaneous Manuscript Collection.
Papers of Rear Admiral J. P. Stuart Lawrence.
Naval War College Archives, Newport, R.I. :
Early Records, 1884–1895
"An Admiral's Log" (autobiog. of Adm. Harris Lanning).
Captain William McC. Little Papers.
Navy Department Library, Washington, D.C.:
Rear Admiral Bowman H. McCalla, "Memoirs of a Naval Career," Copy of un-
    published autobiog. (original in possession of Dudley Knox, Jr., Wash., D.C.).
New York Historical Society, Manuscript Division:
John Sanford Barnes Papers.
Rear Admiral French Ensor Chadwick Papers.
Rear Admiral William S. Cowles Papers.
Admiral George Dewey Papers.
Charles Fairchild Papers.
G. V. Fox Papers [samplings].
"Journal of Admiral S. R. Franklin, kept on board U.S.S. *Pensacola*, 1885-1887."
Rear Admiral Caspar F. Goodrich Papers.
Captain Theodore P. Greene "Letterbook," 1863–1864.
Samuel Dana Greene Collection.
Lewis R. Hamersly's File Book of Naval Officer's Letters, 1870–1878.
Alexander Hamilton, Jr., Letters and Papers.
Stephen Luce Papers.
Captain Edward McCauley Papers.
A. T. Mahan Correspondence.
Rear Admiral Richard W. Meade, 2nd, Collection.
Rear Admiral Richard W. Meade, 3rd, Collection.
Ensign Denis W. Mullan "Private Journal, 1864–1865."
Admiral David D. Porter Papers.
Rear Admiral B. F. Sands Papers.
Rear Admiral Cameron McRae Winslow Papers.
Henry A. Wise Papers.
New York Public Library, Manuscript Division:
Journal of Commander John Almy, 1857–1864, U.S. Navy Collection.
Commodore Homer C. Blake Papers.
Captain Richard S. Collum, U.S.M.C., "The Expedition to Panama, 1885."
Seaman Bartholemew Diggins, "Recollection of the Cruise of the ... *Hartford* ...
    1862–1864."
Captain Percival Drayton Papers, U.S. Navy Collection.
George Foulk Papers.

406   Mrs. Louis Wirt Goldsborough Letters, 1830–1873.
Letterbooks of Rear Admiral A. K. Hughes, 1874–1884, U.S. Navy Collection.
S. Weir Mitchell Papers [24 letters from Rear Admiral Charles Clark].
Journal of Midshipman H. C. T. Nye, 1872–1873, on the *Kansas* and the *Richmond*, U.S. Navy Collection.
Letters to Captain Robert W. Shufeldt, 1871–1873, U.S. Navy Collection.
Rear Admiral Thomas Turner Papers.
Commodore Aaron Weaver Papers.
State Maritime College of New York at Fort Schuyler College Archives.
New York State Library, Albany, N.Y.:
Rear Admiral Charles Sigsbee Papers.
Southern Historical Collection, University of North Carolina Library, Chapel Hill:
Admiral Edwin Anderson Papers.
Bagley Family Papers [for correspondence of Ensign Worth Bagley].
Rear Admiral George Balch Papers.
Rear Admiral Victor Blue Papers.
Hamilton Brown Papers.
Francis T. Chew Papers.
Charles I. Graves Papers.
Hilary A. Herbert Papers.
Rear Admiral Rufus G. Johnston Papers.
Rear Admiral Andrew T. Long Papers.
Rear Admiral Edward Middleton Papers.
Rear Admiral Archibald Scales Papers.
Thomas Settle Papers.
George T. Winston Papers.
Lieutenant John Taylor Wood Diary.
Benjamin C. Yancey Papers.
Syracuse University, Carnegie and Arents Library Manuscript Collections:
Rear Admiral John A. Dahlgren File.
Admiral George Dewey File.
Admiral David Farragut File.
Captain Purnell F. Harrington Papers.
Rear Admiral Henry K. Thatcher Letterbook.
State Historical Society of Wisconsin, Division of Archives and Manuscripts:
Timothy Brown Papers.
Acting Volunteer Lieutenant James C. Gipson Papers.
Rear Admiral Albert W. Grant Papers.
Diary of Midshipman Sidney Harrington, 1837–1839.
Assistant Engineer John S. Hill Papers.
Fleet Admiral William D. Leahy Papers.
Admiral Nathan C. Twining Papers.

2. Congressional Reports

23rd Cong., 1st Sess., "Memorial of sundry citizens praying an academy be instituted for the instruction of mariners." *Senate Doc. No. 403* (1834).
24th Cong., 1st Sess., [similar petition] *Senate Doc. No. 327* (1836).
33rd Cong., 1st Sess., [similar petition] *House Misc. Doc. No. 70* (1854).

33rd Cong., 1st Sess., *House Exec. Doc. No. 53, Exploration of the Valley of the Amazon . . . by W. R. L. Herndon and Lardner Gibbon, Lieutenants, U.S. Navy* (2 vols., 1854).

33rd Cong., 1st Sess., *Senate Exec. Doc. No. 59, Report and Charts of the Cruise of the Brig "Dolphin" by Lieutenant S. P. Lee,. U.S. Navy* (1854).

37th Cong., 1st Sess., *Senate Misc. Doc. No. 6* (1861).

39th Cong., 1st Sess., *Senate Ex. Doc. No. 62: Letter of the Secretary of the Navy communicating . . . a report of Rear Admiral Charles H. Davis . . . in relation to the various proposed lines for interoceanic canals and railroads between the waters of the Atlantic and Pacific oceans* (1866).

41st Cong., 2nd Sess., *House Ex. Doc. No. 99: Assimilated Rank in the Navy: Letter to the Secretary of the Navy* (1869).

42nd Cong., 2nd Sess., *Senate Misc. Doc. No. 77: Letter from the Superintendent of the Navy Academy* (1872).

43rd Cong., 2nd Sess., *House Ex. Doc. 1, Pt. 3: 1874, Report of the Secretary of the Navy* (1875) and all ensuing Sec. Nav. *Reports to* 1915].

43rd Cong., 2nd Sess., *House Report No. 124: Alleged Sale of a Naval Cadetship* (1875).

44th Cong., 1st Sess., *Ex. Doc., No. 170: Protection of American Citizens in the Ottoman Empire* (1876).

44th Cong., 1st Sess., *House Misc. Doc. No. 170: Investigation by the Naval Affairs Committee* (1876).

45th Cong., 2nd Sess., *House Report No. 432: Enlistments in the Navy* (1878).

46th Cong., 2nd Sess., *Senate Ex. Doc. No. 51: Report on Foreign Systems of Naval Education by Prof. James R. Soley, U.S.N.* (1880).

46th Cong., 2nd Sess., *Senate Ex. Doc. No. 52: Report on the Training Systems for the Navy . . . of England . . . by Lieutenant Commander French E. Chadwick* (1880).

48th Cong., 1st Sess., *Senate Misc. Doc. No. 18: Memorial of Cadets of the U.S. Navy* (1883)

48th Cong., 1st Sess., *House Exec. Doc. No. 77: Report of the Gun Foundry Board* (1885).

48th Cong., 2nd Sess., *Senate Exec. Doc. No. 68: Letter from Sec. of Navy reporting . . . the steps taken by him to establish an advanced course of instruction of naval officers . . .* (1885).

49th Cong., 1st Sess., *Report of the [U.S. Senate] Select Committee on Ordnance and War Ships* (1886).

49th Cong., 1st Sess., *Misc. Doc. No. 75: Views of Senator Hale of Committee on Naval Affairs to Accompany Bill S. 371* (1886).

49th Cong., 1st Sess., *Report of House Committee on Naval Affairs, No. 1678* (1886).

50th Cong., 1st Sess., *Report of Senate Committee on Naval Affairs, No. 1377* (1888).

50th Cong., 1st Sess., *Senate Report of Committee on Naval Affairs, No. 485* (1888).

50th Cong., 1st Sess., *Sen. Misc. Doc. No. 118: Letter of Admiral David D. Porter, U.S.N. . . . to Honorable John H. Mitchell, U.S. Senate, Relative to Site for Naval Station on the Pacific Coast, 15 March 1888.*

51st Cong., 1st Sess., *Senate Ex. Doc. No. 86: Letter from the Secretary of the Navy transmitting . . . a report upon certain alleged organizations among naval officers not authorized by the Navy Department* (1890).

51st Cong., 1st Sess., *House Committee on Naval Affairs Report No. 1255* (1890).

53rd Cong., 3rd Sess., *Senate Exec. Doc. No. 16: Letter from Secretary of the Navy . . . transmitting . . . letters sent to the Department by Rear Admiral J. G. Walker relating to the Sandwich Islands* (1894).

54th Cong., 2nd Sess., *Hearings of an Investigation by the Committee on Naval Affairs of the U.S. Senate in Relation to Prices Paid for Armour for Vessels of the Navy* (1896).

55th Cong., 2nd Sess., *Senate of U.S. Public Doc. No. 188: Views of Commodore George W. Melville, Chief Engineer as to the . . . Nicaraguan Canal, the Future Control of the Pacific . . . [&] Hawaii . . .* (1898).

55th Cong., 2nd Sess., *Senate Doc. No. 116, Line and Engineer Corps of the Navy* (1898).

Hearings before a Subcommittee of the [House] Committee on Naval Affairs . . . on the Subject of Hazing at the Navy Academy (1906).

Hearings before the Senate Committee on Naval Affairs on the Bill (S. 3335) to Increase the Efficiency of the Personnel of the Navy and Marine Corps (1908).

64th Cong., 1st Sess., *Hearings before the House Naval Affairs Committee on Estimates Submitted by the Secretary of the Navy* (1916).

65th Cong., 1st Sess., *Hearings before Committee on Naval Affairs of the House of Representatives on Estimates Submitted by the Secretary of the Navy* (1917).

66th Cong., 1st Sess., *Hearings before the Committee on Naval Affairs, U.S. Senate* (1919).

66th Cong., 1st Sess., *Hearings before Committee on Naval Affairs of the House of Representatives on Estimates Submitted by the Secretary of the Navy* (1919).

66th Cong., 2nd Sess., *A Hearing on Bill H.R. 13706 on Relief of Contractors before the Council on Naval Affairs, House of Representatives* (1920).

66th Cong., 2nd Sess., *Hearings before the Subcommittee of the Committee on Naval Affairs, U.S. Senate* (1921).

66th Cong., 3rd Sess., *Hearings before the Committee on Naval Affairs, House of Representatives, on Disarmament in its Relation to the Naval Policy & the Naval Building Program of the U.S. in Estimates Submitted by the Secretary of the Navy, 1920–1921* (1921).

67th Cong., 4th Sess., *Hearings before Subcommittee of House Committee on Naval Affairs . . . in Charge of the Navy Department Appropriations Bill for 1924* (1924).

75th Cong., 1st Sess., *Hearings before the Senate Committee on Naval Affairs on H.R. 9218: Naval Expansion Program* (1938).

3. Other Government Publications

U.S. Navy Dept., *Compilation of Laws Relating to the Navy . . .,* ed. John W. Hogg (Wash., G.P.O., 1883).

——, *Historical Sketch of the United States Naval Academy by Professor James R. Soley* (Wash., G.P.O., 1876).

——, *History of the U.S. Navy Yard, Portsmouth, N.H. . . .* (Wash., G.P.O., 1892).

——, *Memorandum in Case of Captain James E. Jouett* (Wash., G.P.O., 1880).

——, *The History of the Chaplain Corps, U.S.N., by Chaplain Clifford Drury,* Vol. I, 1778–1939 (Bureau of Navy Personnel, 1948).

——, *Naval Courts and Boards* (Wash., G.P.O., 1917).

——, Office of Naval Intelligence, *Recent Naval Progress, Information from Abroad* (War and General Information Series) (Wash., G.P.O., 1882–1890).

——, Office of Naval Intelligence, *Naval Mobilization and Improvement in Materiel* (Wash., G.P.O., 1889).

——, Office of Naval Intelligence *A Study of Exposed Points on Our Frontier, Lines of Communication, and Possible Bases of Hostile Operation, Prepared for the Board on Fortifications by Lieutenant William Beehler* (Wash., G.P.O., 1885).

——, Office of Naval Intelligence, *The U.S. Navy as an Industrial Asset: What the Navy has done for Industry and Commerce* (Wash., G.P.O., 1923).

——, Office of Records Administration, *The American Naval Mission in the Adriatic, 1918–1921, by A. C. Davidonis* (1943).

——, Office of Records Admin., *U.S. Naval Forces in Northern Russia (Archangel and Murmansk), 1918–1919, by Henry P. Beers* (1943).

——, Office of Records Admin., *U.S. Naval Detachment in Turkish Waters, 1914–1924, by Henry P. Beers* (1943).

——, *Proposed Personnel Bill with A Letter of Transmittal by the Assistant Secretary of the Navy* (Washington, G.P.O., 1897).

——, *Regulations for the Government of the Naval Academy* (Wash., G.P.O., 1851).

——, *Record of Proceedings of a Court of Inquiry in the Case of Rear Admiral W. S. Schley, U.S.N.* (Wash., G.P.O., 1902).

——, *Register of the United States Navy* (Wash., G.P.O., 1871–1923).

——, *Register of the U.S. Naval Academy*, Vols. XVI–XLV (Wash., G.P.O., 1865–1895).

Bureau of Navy Personnel, "U.S. Naval Administration in World War II: The Negro in the Navy" (copy in possession of Prof. Richard Dalfiume, S.U.N.Y., Binghamton).

U.S. War Department, *Centennial of the U.S. Military Academy at West Point, New York, 1802–1902* (2 Vols., Wash., G.P.O., 1904).

American State Papers: Naval Affairs, IV (Wash., G.P.O., 1861).

Revised Statutes of the United States . . . (Wash., G.P.O., 1875).

The Statutes at Large of the United States of America [U.S. Stat.] (Wash., G.P.O., 1850–1925).

Paul Jones Commemoration at Annapolis, April 24, 1906, ed. Charles W. Stewart (Wash., G.P.O., 1906).

Official Records of the Union and Confederate Navies in the War of the Rebellion, ed. Richard Rush, *et. al.* (30 vols., Wash., D.C., 1894–1914).

4. Magazines, Journals, etc.

American Neptune.

Annals of the Naval History Society (New York, 1913–1924).

Army and Navy Journal, 1865–1910.

Army and Navy Life, 1905–1908.

Army and Navy Register, 1879–1910.

Congressional Record.

Great Lakes Bulletin, 1916–1920.

Hispanic-American Historical Review.

Journal of the American Society of Naval Engineers, 1889.

The Monthly Nautical Magazine and Quarterly Review, 1854–1855,

Naval War College Review, XVI–XXIII (1963–1970).

The Navy, 1906–1915.

The Navy League Journal, 1903–1906.

Pacific Historical Review.

The Marine Corps Gazette, 1917–1925.

The [Marine] Recruiter's Bulletin, Vols. I & II (New York, 1914–1916).

The Navy Chronicle (1899).

Proceedings of the United States Naval Institute, 1874–1970.

The Public Service Review, Vol. I (1887).

The Sailor's Magazine and Seaman's Friend, 1880, 1885, 1890, 1895, 1900, 1905.

Shipmate, 1939–1970.

Transactions of the Society of Naval Architects and Marine Engineers, 1893–1910

Uncle Sam's Magazine, 1909.

The United Service (all 3 Series).

410   The U.S. Nautical Magazine and Naval Journal, 1855–1857.
U.S. Naval War College Review.
U.S. Service Magazine, 1864–1866.

5. Some Important Articles from the Proceedings of the U.S. Naval Institute

Adams, Brooks, "War as the Ultimate Form of Economic Competition, *PUSNI*, XXIX, (1903), 829–881.

Ammen, Rear Admiral Daniel, "The Purposes of a Navy, and the Best Method of Rendering it Efficient," *PUSNI*, V (1879), 119–132.

Bainbridge-Hoff, Commander William, "A View of Our Naval Policy and a Discussion of its Factors," *PUSNI*, XII (1886), 121–139.

Brandt, Lieutenant Commander G. E., "Newspaper Publicity for the Navy," *PUSNI*, L (1924), 916–930.

Brown, Lieutenant Commander Allan D., "Naval Education," *PUSNI*, V (1879), 305–321.

Brown, Lieutenant R. M. G., "The Commercial and Naval Policy of the United States," *PUSNI*, IV (1881), 610 ff.

Calkins, Lieutenant Carlos G., "How May the Sphere of Usefulness of Naval Officers be Extended in Time of Peace with Advantage to the Country and the Naval Service?," *PUSNI*, IX (1883), 155–194.

Chambers, Ensign Washington Irving, "The Reconstruction and Increase of the Navy," *PUSNI*, XI (1885), 3–50.

Chandler, Lieutenant Commander L. H., "An Answer to Criticisms of 'Is Amalgamation a Failure?,'" *PUSNI*, XXXII (1906), 555–561.

Cluverius, Captain Wat, "The Array Against Sovereignty," *PUSNI*, LI (1925), 1916–1923.

Collins, Lieutenant Fredrick, "Naval Affairs," *PUSNI*, V (1879), 159–179.

Coontz, Admiral Robert, "The Navy and Business," *PUSNI*, XLVIII (1922), 987–1004.

Daniels, Lieutenant R. E., "Indoctrinating Civilians," *PUSNI*, L (1924), 1857 ff.

David, Ensign William G., "Our Merchant Marine: The Causes of its Decline, and the Means to be Taken for its Revival," *PUSNI*, VIII (1882), 151–186.

Farquhar, Commander N. H., "How May the Sphere of Usefulness of Naval Officers be Extended in Time of Peace with Advantage to the Country and the Naval Service?," *PUSNI*, IX (1883), 195–202.

Fullam, Lieutenant William F., "The System of Naval Training and Discipline Required to Promote Efficiency and Attract Americans," *PUSNI*, XVI (1890), 473–536.

Glass, Commander Henry, "Some Suggestions for Manning Our Future Naval Vessels," *PUSNI*, XII (1886), 44 ff.

Goodrich, Lieutenant Commander Caspar, "Naval Education," *PUSNI*, V (1879), 323–344.

——, "Esprit de Corps," *PUSNI*, XXIV (1898), 8 ff.

Green, Lieutenant Commander Fitzhugh, "Science and the Navy," *PUSNI*, XLVIII (1922), 1706 ff.

Harris, Lieutenant Commander Frank (USNR), "The Navy and the Diplomatic Frontier," *PUSNI*, LXII (1936), 470–485.

Jenkins, Rear Admiral Thornton A., "The Navy and its Prospects of Rehabilitation," *PUSNI*, XII (1886), 2 ff.

Kelley, Lieutenant J. D. Jerrold, "Our Merchant Marine: The Causes of its Decline, and **411** the Means to be Taken for its Revival," *PUSNI*, VIII (1882), 3–34.

Knox, Captain Dudley W. [Ret.], "The Navy and Public Indoctrination," *PUSNI*, LV (1929), 479–490.

Moses, Commander S. E., "The Orient in 1916: Its Interest to the United States," *PUSNI*, XLIII (1917), 78 ff.

Phelps, Commander W. W., "Naval Industrialism, Naval Commercialism, and Naval Discipline," *PUSNI*, XXXIX (1913), 509–550.

Sampson, Captain William T., "Outline of a Scheme for the Naval Defense of the Coast," *PUSNI*, XXV (1899), 169–232.

Stevens, Professor William, "The Naval Officer and the Civilian," *PUSNI*, XLVII (1921), 1732–1733.

Stirling, Captain Yates, "Some Fundamentals of Sea Power," *PUSNI*, LI (1925), 889 ff.

Wainwright, Lieutenant Commander Richard, "Our Naval Power," *PUSNI*, XXIV (1898), 43 ff.

Wharton, Lieutenant Wallace, "The Navy—A National Investment," *PUSNI*, L (1924), 1836–1838.

Zeigler, Lieutenant Commander S. J., "Specialization *versus* Amalgamation," *PUSNI*, XLVII (1921), 1073–1082.

6. Published Autobiographies of Naval Officers

The published autobiographies of Bradley Fiske, Hugh Rodman, Robert Coontz, Alfred Mahan, and Albert Barker are perhaps the most valuable, though virtually all were useful. The unpublished autobiographies of Bowman McCalla and William V. Pratt, and the oral history of Thomas Hart, are also worth consulting.

Ammen, Daniel, *The Old Navy and the New* (Philadelphia, 1891).

Barker, Albert S., *Everyday Life in the Navy* (Boston, 1928).

Batten, John M., *Reminiscences of Two Years in the U.S. Navy* (Lancaster, Pa., 1881).

Bowen, Harold, *Ships, Machinery, and Mossbacks: The Autobiography of a Naval Engineer* (Princeton, 1954).

Brady, Cyrus T., *Under Tops'ls and Tents* (New York, 1901).

Clark, Charles E., *My Fifty Years in the Navy* (Boston, 1917).

Clark, J. J. ("Jocko"), *Carrier Admiral* (New York, 1967).

Clements, A. B., "Forty Years After," *PUSNI*, XLVI (1920), 88 ff.

Coontz, Robert, *From the Mississippi to the Sea* (Phil., 1930).

Davenport, Francis O., *On A Man-of-War: A Series of Naval Sketches* (Detroit, 1878).

Dewey, George [with Frederick Palmer], *Autobiography of George Dewey* (N.Y., 1913).

Evans, Holden A., *One Man's Fight for a Better Navy* (N.Y., 1940).

Evans, Robley D. ("Fighting Bob"), *A Sailor's Log: Recollections of Forty Years of Naval Life* (N.Y., 1901).

——, *An Admiral's Log* (N.Y., 1910).

Farenholt, Oscar A., "From Ordinary Seaman to Rear Admiral," *War Paper No. 22* [*California*] *Commandery . . . of the Loyal Legion* (San Francisco, 1910).

Fiske, Bradley A., *From Midshipman to Rear Admiral* (N.Y., 1919).

Ford, John D., *An American Cruiser in the East: Travels and Studies in the Far East* (N.Y., 1905).

Franklin, Samuel R., *Memories of a Rear Admiral* (N.Y., 1898).

412   Goodrich, Caspar F., *Rope Yarns From the Old Navy* (N.Y., 1931).

Halsey, William F., *Admiral Halsey's Story* (N.Y., 1947).

Jones, Harry W., *A Chaplain's Experience Afloat and Ashore* (N.Y., 1901).

Kell, John McIntosh, *Recollections of A Naval Life* (Washington, 1900).

Kimmel, Husband E., *Admiral Kimmel's Story* (Chicago, 1955).

King, Ernest J., and Walter Whitehill, *Fleet Admiral King: A Naval Record* (N.Y., 1952).

Lejeune, John A., *The Reminiscences of a Marine* (Phil., 1930).

Mahan, Alfred T., *From Sail to Steam* (N.Y., 1907).

Morris, Charles, *The Autobiography of Commodore Charles Morris, U.S. Navy* (Annapolis, 1880).

Parker, William H., *Recollections of a Naval Officer, 1841–1865* (New York, 1883).

Potter, David, *Sailing the Sulu Sea* (N.Y., 1940).

Pugh, Herbert Lamont, *Navy Surgeon* (Phila. and N.Y., 1959).

[Rixey, P. M.], *The Life Story of Presley Marion Rixey, Surgeon General, U.S. Navy, 1902–1910: Biography and Autobiography* (Strasburg, Va., 1930).

Rodman, Hugh, *Yarns of a Kentucky Admiral* (Indianapolis, 1928).

Sands, Benjamin F., *From Reefer to Rear Admiral* (N.Y., 1899).

Sawyer, Fredrick L., *Sons of Gunboats* (Annapolis, 1946).

Schroeder, Seaton, *A Half Century of Naval Service* (N.Y., 1922).

Schley, Winfield Scott, *Forty-Five Years under the Flag* (N.Y., 1904).

Semmes, Raphael, *Service Afloat and Ashore During the Mexican War* (Cincinnati, 1851).

Selfridge, Thomas O., *Memoirs of Thomas O. Selfridge, Jr.* (N.Y., 1924).

Smith, Holland M. ("Howlin' Mad"), *Coral and Brass* (N.Y., 1948).

Standley, William H. [with Rear Admiral Arthur A. Ageton], *Admiral Ambassador to Russia* (Chicago, Regnery, 1955).

Steedman, Charles, *Memoir and Correspondence of Charles Steedman, Rear Admiral, U.S. Navy, with his autobiography and private Journals, 1811–1890*, ed. Amos L. Mason (Cambridge, Mass., 1912).

Stirling, Yates, *Sea Duty: The Memoirs of a Fighting Admiral* (New York, 1939).

Walke, Henry, *Naval Scenes and Reminiscences of the Civil War . . .* (New York, 1877).

Wiley, Henry A., *An Admiral from Texas* (Garden City, N.Y., 1934).

Zogbaum, Rufus, *From Sail to "Saratoga": A Naval Autobiography* (Rome, 1961).

(See also manuscript autobiographies of Bowman McCalla, Andrew T. Long, Cornelius Schoonmaker, Harris Lanning, and Charles McVay, cited above.)

7. Shipboard Recollections of Enlisted Men

Blackford, Charles, *Torpedoboat Sailor* (Annapolis, 1968).

Blanding, Stephen F., *Recollections of a Sailor Boy* (Providence, R.I., 1886).

Bruell, James, *Sea Memories; or, Personal Experiences in the U.S. Navy in Peace and War* (Biddeford Pool, Me., 1886).

Bullen, Frank T., *With Christ at Sea: Religious Life in the Fo'c's'le* (N.Y., 1900).

Buenzle, Fred J., *Bluejacket: An Autobiography* (N.Y., 1939).

Cobb, Josiah, *A Green Hand's First Cruise* (Boston, 1841, 2 vols.).

Cowley, Charles, *Leaves from a Lawyer's Life Afloat and Ashore* (Lowell, Mass., 1879).

Dana, Jr., Richard Henry, *Two Years before the Mast, and Twenty-Four Years After* (N.Y., 1909).

——, *Two Years before the Mast, with Journals and Letters . . .*, ed. J. H. Kemble (Los Angeles, 1964).

[Durand, James], *James Durand: An Able Seaman of 1812,* ed. George S. Brooks (New Haven, 1926).

Hazen, Jacob, *Five Years before the Mast* (2nd ed., Phil., 1856).

Hill, Fredric Stanhope, *Twenty Years at Sea* (Boston, 1893).

King, Stanton H., *Dog Watches at Sea* (Boston, 1901).

Leech, Samuel, *Thirty Years from Home; or, A Voice from the Main Deck* (Boston, 1843).

McKenna, Richard, *The Sand Pebbles* (New York, 1962).

McNally, William, *Evils and Abuses in the Naval and Merchant Services Exposed* (Boston, 1839).

Marshall, W. P., *Afloat on the Pacific; or, Notes of Three Years' Life at Sea* (Zanesville, Ohio, 1876).

Mayer, R. H., and A. H. Bischof, *Reminiscences of the Cruise of the U.S.S. "Brooklyn"* (Hong Kong, 1888).

Melville, Herman, *White-Jacket; or, the World in a Man-of-War* (Boston, 1892 [orig. pub. 1850]).

Montgomery, James E., *Our Admiral's Flag Abroad: The Cruise of Admiral D. G. Farragut . . . 1867–68 . . .* (New York, 1869).

Nordhoff, Charles, *Life on the Ocean* (Cincinnati, 1874).

Paine, Albert B., *A Sailor of Fortune: Personal Memoirs of Captain B. S. Osbon* [1827–1912] (New York, 1906).

Paynter, John H., *Joining the Navy* (Wash., 1911).

Sellstedt, Lars G., *From Forecastle to [National] Academy [of Design]* (Buffalo, 1904).

Vail, Israel E., *Three Years on the Blockade* (New York, 1902).

"Williams, Frederick Benton" [Herbert E. Hamblen], *On Many Seas: The Life and Exploits of a Yankee Sailor* (N.Y., 1897).

Willis, N. Parker, *Summer Cruise in the Mediterranean on Board an American Frigate* (Auburn & Rochester, N.Y., 1856).

8. Novels, Poems, and Stories by Naval Officers

Bassett, Lieutenant F. S., "The Spectral Sealer," *United Service,* 2nd. S., II (1889), 31–36.

Beach, Lieutenant Commander Edward L., *An Annapolis Plebe* (Chicago, 1907).

——, *An Annapolis Second Classman* (Phila., 1908).

——, *Ralph Osborn, Midshipman at Annapolis* (Boston and Chicago, 1909).

——, *An Annapolis First Classman* (Phil., 1910).

Brady, Cyrus T., *A Midshipman in the Pacific* (N.Y., 1904).

——, "A Hazing Interregnum: Some Doings at Annapolis," Lippincott's *Magazine,* LXVII (Apr. 1901), 485–492.

Brown, Commander Allan D., "Jack Haultaut, Midshipman, U.S.N.; or, Life at the Naval Academy," *United Service,* XII (1882), 32–45, 172–185, 328–334, 430–436, 555–563, 715–723; XII (1883), 101–110, 234–240, 361–369, 490–496.

Bunts, Frank E., *The Soul of Henry Harrington and Other Stories* (Cleveland, 1916).

Clark, Academy Chaplain H. H., *Boy Life in the U.S. Navy* (Boston, 1885).

——, *Joe Bently, Naval Cadet* (Boston, 1889).

——, *The Admiral's Aid: A Story of Life in the New Navy* (Boston, 1902).

Gibson, Commander William, *Poems of Many Years and Many Places* (Boston, 1881).

——, "Faith Militant," *United States Service Magazine,* I (N.Y. & London, 1864).

——, *United Service,* II (1880), 326.

Hobson, Richmond P., *Buck Jones at Annapolis* (N.Y., 1907).

414   Hobson, Richmond P., *In Line of Duty* (N.Y., 1910).

Kelley, Lieutenant, J. D. J., *A Desperate Chance* (N.Y. 1886).

Porter, Admiral David D., *Arthur Merton* (N.Y., 1889).

——, *Allan Dare and Robert le Diable* (N.Y., 1884).

——, *The Adventures of Harry Marline; or, Notes from an American Midshipman's Lucky Bag* (N.Y., 1885 [copy in N.Y. Public Library]).

Preble, Captain George H., *A Mixture of Prose and Verse* (Phila., 1884).

Rockwell, Commander Charles H., "The Captain's Story," *United Service*, 2nd S., VII (1892), 494–503.

——, "The Boatswain's Call," *United Service*, 2nd S., VIII (1893), 65–66.

——, "Recollection," *United Service*, 2nd S., IX (1893), 38–39.

Schenck, Paymaster Caspar, "A Story of Love and Faith," *United Service*, 2nd S., VII (1892), 550–561.

——, "Sweethearts and Wives," *United Service*, V (1881), 642–643.

Shippen, Medical Director Edward, *A Christmas at Sea* (Phila., 1892).

——, *Thirty Years at Sea: The Story of a Sailor's Life* (Phila., 1879).

Simpson, Rear Admiral Edward, Jr., *Yarnlets: The Human Side of the Navy* (N.Y., 1934).

Stevens, Lieutenant Thomas H., "Lines in an Autograph-Book," *United Service*, VI (1882), 553.

——, Rear Admiral Thomas H., "Ambition," *United Service*, 3rd Series, IV (1903), 67.

——, Lieutenant Commander Thomas, "Faith, Hope, and Charity," *United Service*, 2nd S., I (1889), 190.

Stirling, Lieutenant Commander Yates, *A U.S. Midshipman in Japan* (Phila., 1911).

——, *A U.S. Midshipman Afloat* (Phila., 1908).

——, *A U.S. Midshipman in China* (Phila., 1909).

——, *A U.S. Midshipman in the Philippines* (Phila., 1910).

——, *A U.S. Midshipman in the South Seas* (Phila., 1913).

Thomason, Colonel John W., Jr., U.S.M.C., *—And a Few Marines* (N.Y., 1945 [first published 1926]).

Wise, Lieutenant Henry, *Story of the Gray African Parrot* (N.Y., 1859).

——, *Captain Brand of the "Centipede"* (2nd ed., N.Y., 1887).

(See also manuscript novels in the George Balch Papers, S.H.C., U. of N.C.L., and the David D. Porter Papers, N.H.F.)

9. Other Primary Sources

"A Junior Officer," "Naval Reorganization," *United Service*, II (1880), 460–467.

"A Lieutenant, U.S.N.," "Style in the Navy," *United Service*, IV (1881), 490–498.

"A Midshipman's Views of Marriage in the Navy," *United Service*, VII (1882), 278–282.

"A Naval Officer," "The Navy, and How to Improve It," *United Service*, III (1880), 367 ff.

——, "A Plea for Gunboats," *United Service*, 2nd Series, I (1889), 93–100.

"An Unpensioned Volunteer," "Our Little Navy," *United Service*, XI (1884), 304 ff.

Acts for the Government of the U.S. Navy Together with an Outline of the Course of Study in Political Science (Newport, 1865).

Adams, Francis Colbourn, *High Old Salts* (Washington, 1876).

Alcock, Sir Rutherford, *The Capital of the Tycoon* (2 vols., New York, 1863), I, 42, 156.

American Activities in the Central Pacific, 1790–1870, ed. R. G. Ward (7 vols., Ridgewood, N.J., 1967).

Ammen, Daniel, "A Naval Hero [Cushing]," *Chicago Inter-Ocean*, 20 June 1886.
——, *The Atlantic Coast* (New York, 1883).
——, *Country Homes and Their Improvement* (Washington, 1885).
Angell, Norman, "The Grand Illusion: A Reply to Rear Admiral A. T. Mahan," *North American Review*, CXCV (1912), 754–772.
[Anonymous], *A Few Thoughts upon Rank in the Navy* (Phila., 1850).
[Anonymous], *A Peacetime Navy* (n.p., n.d., circa 1922 [copy in State Historical Society of Wisconsin]).
Argument of the Naval Association in Relation to [House] Bill No. 3618 (Washington, 1896).
Ashe, Samuel A., "Memories of Annapolis," *South Atlantic Quarterly*, XVIII (April 1919), 197–210.
Assimilated Rank in the Navy: Its Injurious Operation upon the Discipline, Harmony, and General Good of the Naval Service (Washington, 1850).
Assimilated Rank in the Navy: Its Injurious Operation upon the Discipline, Harmony, and General Good of the Naval Service (Philadelphia, 1860).
At 'Em "Arizona," Vols. I & II (1922–23).
The Badger, I (1904).
Barber, Lieutenant Francis M., *Lecture on Submarine boats and their application to torpedo operations* (Newport, R.I. [torpedo station], 1875).
Barnard, Henry, *Military Schools and Courses of Instruction in the Science and Art of War* (New York, 1872).
Bassett, Lieutenant Francis M., "America's First Admiral," [on Farragut], *Chicago Inter-Ocean*, 4 July 1886.
Bayly, Admiral Sir Lewis, *Pull Together!: The Memoirs of Admiral Sir Lewis Bayly* (London, 1939).
Beach, Captain Edward L., Jr., *The Wreck of the "Memphis"* (New York, 1966).
Beehler, Lieutenant William H., *The Cruise of the U.S.S. "Brooklyn"* (Philadelphia, 1885).
——, "The Needs of the Navy," *Annals of the American Academy of Political and Social Science*, XXVI (1905), 161–169.
Belknap, Rear Admiral George, "The Old Navy," *Naval Actions and History, 1799–1898*, Vol. XII of the *Papers* of the Military Historical Society of Massachusetts (Boston, 1902).
Belknap, Captain Reginald R., *The Yankee Mining Squadron* (Annapolis, 1920).
Bell, Surgeon A. N., "The Ship and the Sailor," *U.S. Nautical Magazine and Naval Journal*, III (1856), 194–198.
Benjamin, Park, "The Trouble at the Naval Academy," *The Independent* (1906), 154–158.
——, "Promotion in the Navy," *The Independent* (1898), 683–687.
——, *The United States Navy Academy* (New York, 1900).
——, "The Unused Products of the Naval Academy," *The Independent* (1898), 1179–1183.
Bennett, Passed Assistant Engineer Frank, "American Men for the Navy," *United Service*, 2nd Series, XI (1894), 102–105.
——, *The Steam Navy of the U.S.* (Pittsburgh, 2 Vols., 1897).
Bennett, Lieutenant Frank M., *The Monitor and the Navy under Steam* (Boston and New York, 1900).
Beresford, Admiral Lord Charles, "Possibilities of an Anglo-American Reunion," *North American Review*, CLIX (1894), 564–573.
——, "The Future of the Anglo-Saxon Race," *North American Review*, CLXXI (1900).

416   Beston, Henry B., *Full Speed Ahead: Tales from the Log of a Correspondent with Our Navy* (Garden City, New York, 1919).

Big "U" [Battleship "Utah"], Vol. I (n.p., 1928).

Blackwell, Commander Edward M., *Blackwell Genealogy* (Richmond, 1948).

Blake, Captain Robert, U.S.M.C., "The Marine at Sea," *The Marine Corps Gazette*, X (1925), 1–14.

Bowen, Abel, *The Naval Monument* (Boston, 1816).

Barnes, Elinor and James, eds., *Naval Surgeon: Blockading the South, 1862–1866: The Diary of Samuel P. Boyer* (Bloomington, Ind., 1963).

——, eds., *Naval Surgeon: Revolt in Japan, 1868–1869: The Diary of Dr. Samuel P. Boyer* (Bloomington, Ind., 1963).

Boynton, Chaplain Charles B., *The History of the Navy During the Rebellion* (2 vols., New York, 1867), I.

Bradford, Commander Royal R., "Coaling Stations for the Navy," *Forum*, XXVI (1899), 732–747.

Brown, Lieutenant R. M. G., "The Commercial and Naval Policy of the United States," *The United Service*, IV (1881), 603–610.

Bryce, James, "The Essential Unity of Britain and America," *Atlantic Monthly*, LXXXII (July 1898), 22–29.

Bunts, Alexander T., ed., *Letters from the Asiatic Station, 1881–1883: Cadet-Midshipman Frank Emory Bunts* (Cleveland, Ohio, 1938).

Burks, Lieutenant Arthur J., U.S.M.C., "Selling the Corps," *The Marine Corps Gazette*, IX (1924), 109–115.

Butler, Smedley, "On Missionaries," *Missionary Review of the World* (1930), 419.

Calvert, Rear Admiral James, *The Naval Profession* (New York, 1965).

Cassard, William, *The Battleship "Indiana"* (New York, 1899).

Catalogue of the Library of the U.S. Naval Academy (Annapolis, 1860).

Catalogue Sale of the Library of Admiral Thornton A. Jenkins (1872 [L. of C. has copy]).

Chadwick, French E., *Temperament, Disease and Health* (New York and London, 1892).

——, *Causes of the Civil War, 1859–61* [in *The American Nation* series] (New York, 1907).

——, *The Relations of the U.S. and Spain* (New York, 1911, 2 vols.).

——, *The American Navy* (New York, 1915).

——, "The Great Need of the U.S. Navy," *Munsey's Mag.*, XXXIII (1905), 643–645.

Chambers, W. I., "Universal Peace, Naval Efficiency and the 'Plucking' System," *The Navy*, IX (March–April, 1915), 74–79, 96–102.

Chauvenet, William, *A Treatise on Plane and Spherical Geometry* (11th ed., Philadelphia, 1854).

——, *History of the Origin of the U.S. Naval Academy* (St. Louis, 1860).

Clarke, Major Sir George Sydenham, "A Naval Union with Great Britain," *North American Review*, CLVIII (1894), 360 ff.

Class of '71, U.S. Naval Academy (privately printed, New York, 1902).

Annual Reports of the Class of 1881, U.S. Naval Academy, 2nd–6th (Butler, Pa., 1886–1890 [copies in New York Public Library]).

Cochrane, Captain H. C., U.S.M.C., "The Navy in the Labor Strikes of 1877," *United Service*, I (1879), 115–129, 616–634.

Clowes, William Laird, *The Royal Navy: A History*, Vol. III (Boston, 1898).

Collum, Captain Richard, U.S.M.C., *History of the United States Marine Corps* (Philadelphia, 1890).

Colomb, Captain John C. R., *The Defence of Great and Greater Britain* (London, 1880).

Colomb, Captain Phillip H., R.N., "Great Britain's Maritime Power," *Journal of the Royal United Service Institution*, XXII (1878).

Colomb, Admiral Sir Philip H., "The U.S. Navy under New Conditions of National Life," *North American Review*, CLXVIII (1898), 434–444.

Colomb, Rear Admiral Phillip H., *Naval Warfare: Its Ruling Principles and Practice Historically Treated* (London, 1891) [orig. pub. in series of articles in *Illustrated Naval and Military Magazine*].

Colton, Rev. Walter, *The Sea and the Sailor* (New York, 1851).

Colvocoresses, Lieutenant George M., *Four Years in a Government Exploring Expedition* (New York, 1852).

Cooke, Commander Augustus P., *A Text-book of Naval Ordnance & Gunnery prepared for the Use of the Cadet Midshipmen at the United States Naval Academy* (2 vols., rev. ed., New York, 1880).

Coontz, Robert, *True Anecdotes of an Admiral* (Phila., 1935).

Proceedings of the Naval Court Martial in the Case of Alex. S. MacKenzie, Commander, U.S. Navy, . . . to which is annexed an elaborate review by James Fenimore Cooper (New York, 1844).

Cooper, J. F., *Lives of Distinguished American Naval Officers* (Philadelphia, 1846).

Corbesier, Antoine, *Theory of Fencing* (New York, 1873).

Cox, Hon. Samuel S., *The Navy—The Guardian of Commerce* (New York, 1884).

Cunning, Duncan, "Promotion in the U.S. Navy," *Chambers's Journal*, 6th Series, LXXV (1898), 641–643.

Dahlgren, Commander John A., *Boat Armament of the U.S. Navy* (2nd ed., Philadelphia, 1856).

Dahlgren, Mrs. Madeline Vinton, *South Sea Sketches* (Boston, 1880).

——, *Thoughts on Female Suffrage and in Vindication of Woman's True Rights* (Wash., 1871).

The Papers of Francis G. Dallas, U.S.N., Correspondence and Journal, 1837–59, ed., Gardner W. Allen (New York, Naval Historical Society, 1917).

The Cabinet Diaries of Josephus Daniels, 1913–1921, ed. E. David Cronon (Lincoln Nebraska, 1963).

Daniels, Josephus, *Our Navy at War* (New York, 1922).

——, *The Wilson Era: Years of Peace—1910–1917* (Chapel Hill, 1944).

Davis, Major Henry C., U.S.M.C., "Self-Discipline," *The Marine Corps Gazette*, I (1917).

Danenhower, Lieutenant John W., *Narrative of the "Jeanette"* (Boston, 1882).

Davis, Rear Admiral C. H., ed., *Narrative of the North Polar Expedition* (Wash., G.P.O., 1876).

D'Egville, Howard, *Imperial Defence and Closer Union* (London, 1913).

DeLong, Emma, ed., *The Voyage of the "Jeanette": The Ship and Journals of [Lieutenant Commander] George W. DeLong* (2 vols., Boston, 1883).

DeLong, Emma W., *Explorer's Wife* (New York, 1938).

Dorn, E. K. and others, *The Island of Guam* (Wash., G.P.O., 1926).

A Navy Surgeon in California, 1845–1847: The Journal of Marius Duvall [1818–1891], ed. Fred. B. Rogers (San Francisco, 1957).

Earle, Commander Ralph, *Life at the U.S. Naval Academy: The Making of the American Naval Officer* (New York and London, 1917).

Eberle, Admiral Edward W., "A Few Reflections on our Navy and some of its Needs" [mimeograph, n.p., c. 1925, copy in St. Hist. Soc. of Wis.].

418   Eccles, Ret. Rear Admiral Henry E., *Military Concepts and Philosophy* (New Brunswick, N.J., 1965).

"Education of American Naval Officers" [an editorial], *The Critic* [N.Y.], II (Feb. 25, 1882), 56.

Eliot, Samuel, *Manual of United States History* (Boston, 1861) [orig. pub. 1856].

Emmons, Lieutenant George F., *The Navy of the United States* (Wash., 1853).

"An Ex-Staff Officer," *An Appeal in Behalf of the Navy and its Personnel, with Notes of Some Incidents in its History* (New York, 1886).

Fag-Ends from the Naval Academy (New York, 1878).

Farenholt, Rear Admiral Oscar W., "The Monitor 'Catskill,'" *War Paper No. 23, Commandery . . . of the Loyal Legion* (San Francisco, 1912).

Fiske, Lieutenant Bradley A., *Electricity in Theory and Practice* (New York, 1883).

Fiske, Rear Admiral Bradley, *War Time in Manila* (Boston, 1913).

——, *The Navy as a Fighting Machine* (2nd ed., New York, 1918).

——, and Enrique Muller, Jr., *The U.S. Navy* (Chicago and New York, 1917).

——, *The Art of Fighting* (New York, 1920).

——, *Invention: The Master-Key to Progress* (New York, 1921).

Foote, Commander A. H., *Africa and the American Flag* (New York and London, 1854).

Confidential Correspondence of Gustavus Vasa Fox, Assistant Secretary of the Navy, 1861–1865, Robert M. Thompson and Richard Wainwright, eds. (2 vols., New York, 1918–1919), I.

Freeman, Edward A., *General Sketch of European History* (3rd ed., London, 1873).

Frothingham, Captain T. G., *Naval History of the World War* (3 vols., New York, 1924–1927).

Fullam, Lieutenant William, "The American Navy of Today," *The American Magazine* [Brooklyn], VIII (Sept., 1888), 515–532.

Gibbons, Lieutenant Commander J. H., "Navy Leagues," *North American Review*, CLXXVI (1903), 758–764.

Goode, W. A. M., *With Sampson Through the War* (New York, 1899) [with chapters by Sampson, Captain Robley Evans, and Commander C. C. Todd].

Goodrich, "Naval Education," *Journal of Social Science*, XXXIII (Nov., 1895), 29–48.

Gorringe, Lieutenant Commander Henry H., "The Navy," *North American Review*, CXXXIV (1882), 486–506.

Greene, Duane M., *Ladies and Officers of the U.S. Army: American Aristocracy* (1880).

Habersham, Lieutenant Alexander, *The North Pacific Survey and Exploring Expedition* (Philadelphia and London, 1857).

Hackett, Frank Warren, *Deck and Field* (Washington, 1909).

Hall, Henry, "The Future of American Shipping," *Atlantic Monthly*, XLVII (1881), 166–174.

Hamersly, Thomas, ed., *Guide to Officers of the U.S. Navy* (4th ed., Philadelphia, 1890).

——, ed., *Complete Army and Navy Register of the U.S.A. from 1776 to 1887* (New York, 1888).

——, *The Records of Living Officers of the U.S. Navy . . .* (7th ed., N.Y., 1902).

Hanford, Rear Admiral Franklin, *How I Entered the Navy* (Walton, New York, n.d. [in Rare Book Room of Navy Department Library]).

Harrison, John and George McCune, eds., *Korean–American Relations*, Vol. I (Berkeley, 1951).

Henderson, W. J., "War-ship Community," *Scribner's Magazine*, XXIV (1898), 285–295.

Higginson, Rear Admiral Francis, *Naval Battles of the Century* (Edinburgh, 1906).

Hitchcock, Mary E. [wife of Commander Roswell Hitchcock], *Tales out of School About Naval Officers* (N.Y., 1908).

Hobson, Richmond P., "American Mistress of the Seas," *North American Review*, 175 (1902), 553 ff.

——, *An Adequate Navy and the Open-Door Policy* (Washington, 1915).

——, *Alcohol and the Human Race* (New York, 1919).

——, *The Sinking of the "Merrimac"* (N.Y., 1899).

Hollis, Ira N., "The Navy in the War with Spain," *Atlantic Monthly*, LXXXII (1898), 605–616.

Jenkins, Commodore Thornton A., *Rear Admiral Goldsborough and the Retiring Laws of the Navy* (Washington, 1868).

"The Journals of Daniel Noble Johnson, United States Navy," ed. Mendel L. Peterson, *Smithsonian Miscellaneous Collections*, CXXXVI, No. 2 (1959).

Johnson, Florence Ridgely, *Welcome Aboard: A Service Manual for the Naval Officer's Wife* (Annapolis, 1951).

Jomini, General Baron Antoine Henri, *Summary of the Art of War*, trans. Captain G. H. Mendell & Captain W. P. Craighill (Philadelphia, 1863).

——, *The Political and Military History of the Campaign of Waterloo*, trans. Stephen Vincent Benét (New York, 1853).

Jones, Charles W., *Address to Naval Academy* (1882).

Journal of a Cruise to the Pacific Ocean, 1842–1844, in the Frigate "United States," ed. Charles R. Anderson (Durham, 1937).

Junk: A Collection of songs and poems by Cadets at the U.S. Naval Academy, ed. George F. Gibbs (Wash., 1889).

Jurien de la Graviere, Vice Admiral Charles, "Le Drame Macedonien," *Revue de Deux Mondes*, XLI (Sept.–Oct. 1880), 124–146, 783–801; XLII (Nov.–Dec. 1880), 394–412; XLIII (Jan.–Feb. 1881), 599–624.

——, "Les Héros de Grand-Port," *Revue de Deux Mondes*, LXXXIV (Nov., 1887), 101–123.

Aboard the U.S.S. "Florida": 1863–1865: The Letters of Paymaster W. F. Keeler . . . Daly, Robert M., ed., (Annapolis, 1968).

Kelley, J. D. Jerrold, *The Question of Ships: The Navy and the Merchant Marine* (New York, 1884).

——, *Our Navy: Its Growth and Achievements* (Hartford, Conn., 1897) [orig. pub. 1892].

——, *The Ship's Company* (New York, 1897).

——, in *The United Service*, V (Sept. 1881), 285–286.

——, "Free Ships and Subsidies," *The United Service*, IV (May 1881), 519–523.

——, "A Lay Sermon—Armored Vessels," *United Service*, I (1879), 263–274.

Kimball, W. W., *Practical Prevention of War* (Wash., 1899) [reprinted from *The Forum*].

King, Chief-Engineer James W., *The Warships and Navies of the World* (Boston, 1881).

Knapp, Rear Admiral Harry S., "The Naval Officer in Diplomacy," *PUSNI*, LIII (May 1927), 309–317.

Knox, Captain Dudley, *The Eclipse of American Sea Power* (New York, 1922).

——, *The Naval Genius of George Washington* (Boston, 1932).

Laughton, J. K., "The Scientific Study of Naval History," *Journal of the Royal United Service Institution*, XVIII (1874), 508–527.

——, *Studies in Naval History* (London, 1887).

420 *Letters from Naval Officers in Reference to the United States Marine Corps.*, ed. Colonel John Harris, U.S.M.C. (Wash., 1864).

Line and Staff (n.p., n.d., circa 1871).

Papers of John Davis Long, 1897–1904, ed. Gardner W. Allen (Mass. Historical Society Collection, Vol. 78, 1939).

The Journal of John D. Long, ed. Margaret Long (Rindge, N.H., 1956).

America of Yesterday as Reflected in the Journal of John Davis Long, ed. L. E. Mayo (Boston, 1923).

Long, John D., *The New American Navy* (2 vols., New York, 1903).

Lovette, Commander Leland P., *School of the Sea: The Annapolis Tradition in American Life* (New York, 1941).

Luce, Stephen B., "My First Ship," *Youth's Companion*, LXV, No. 2 (22 Dec., 1892), 673–674.

— –, "Naval Administration," *PUSNI*, XIV, No. 3 (Fall, 1888), 559–565.

——, "The Benefits of War," *North American Review*, CLIII (1891), 673–679.

— ·, "The Department of the Navy," *PUSNI*, XXXI (March 1905), 81–96.

The Life and Letters of Rear Admiral Stephen B. Luce, ed. Albert Gleaves (New York, 1925).

——, "The Manning of Our Navy and Merchant Marine," *PUSNI*, I (1874).

——, "The United States War College," *PUSNI*, XI, No. 1 (Jan. 1885), 13–34.

——, "War Schools," *PUSNI*, IX (1883), 663–667.

——, "The U.S. Naval War College," *The United Service*, XII (1885), 79–90.

——, "A Plea for An Engineer Corps in the Navy," *North American Review*, CLXXXII (1906), 74–83.

——, ed., *Naval Songs* (3 eds., New York, 1883, 1889, 1902), [Music Collection at New York Public Library at Lincoln Center].

——, *Squadron Evolutions* (New York, 1887 [New York Public Library call card reads: VYE: Hart, *Squadron Evolutions*]).

——, *Text-book of Seamanship* (New York, 1884).

——, "On the Relation between the U.S. Naval War College and the Line Officers of the U.S. Navy," *The Navy*, V (Oct. 1911), 25–30.

——, "How Shall We Man Our Ships,?" *North American Review*, CLII (1891), 64–69.

——, "Christian Ethics as an Element in Military Education," *The United Service*, VIII (1883), 1–16.

——, "Our Future Navy," *PUSNI*, XV (1889), 542–552.

——, "On the Study of Naval History," *PUSNI*, XIII (1887), 175–201.

——, "On the Study of Naval Warfare As a Service," *PUSNI*, XII (1886), 527–546.

The Lucky Bag (Annapolis, 1887 [and 1894 and 1895]).

Lynch, William F., *Naval Life; or Observations Afloat and on Shore: The Midshipman* (New York, 1851).

McCall, Samuel, "A Plea for a Strong Navy," *The Penn Monthly*, XII (Jan. 1881), 45–52.

McCalla, Commander Bowman, "The Training of Naval Officers," *Public Service Review*, I (1887), 53 ff.

McCandless, Rear Admiral Bruce, *et al.*, *Service Etiquette* (Annapolis, 1959).

McKean, W. V., "What the Navy Has Done During the War," *The U.S. Service Magazine*, I (New York, 1965), 337–344.

Mackenzie, Lieutenant A. S., *The American in England* (2 vols., New York, 1835).

McLean, Lieutenant Ridley, *The Bluejacket's Manual* (Annapolis, 1902).

Mahan, Alfred Thayer, "An Old-Time Frigate: The *Congress*," *Youth's Companion*, LXXII, No. 2 (22 Sept. 1898), 436–437.

——, *Armaments and Arbitration: or The Place of Force in the International Relations of States* (New York, 1912).

——, "Current Fallacies upon Naval Subjects," *Harper's Monthly*, XCVIII (June 1898), 42–53.

——, *The Harvest Within* (Boston, 1909).

——, "Misrepresenting Mr. Roosevelt," *Outlook*, XCVIII (17 June 1911), 357–358.

——, "Naval Education," *PUSNI*, V (1897), 345–376.

——, *Sea Power in Relation to the War of 1812* (2 vols., Boston, 1905).

——, "Subordination in Historical Treatment," *American Historical Association Annual Report: 1902* (Washington, 1903), I, 49–63.

——, *The Gulf and Inland Waters* (New York, 1883).

——, *The Influence of Sea Power Upon History: 1660–1783* (Hill and Wang edition, New York, 1957).

——, *The Influence of Sea Power Upon the French Revolution and Empire: 1793–1812* (2 vols., Boston, 1894).

——, *The Interests of America in Sea Power* (Cambridge, 1897).

——, intro. to H. W. Wilson, *Ironclads in Action* (2 vols., London, 1896).

——, "The Naval War College," *North American Review*, CXCVI (July 1912), 72–84.

——, *The Problem of Asia and Its Effect Upon International Policies* (Boston, 1900).

——, "Twentieth Century Christianity," *North American Review*, CXCIX (April 1914), 589–598.

——, "When Newport was Annapolis," *Harper's Weekly*, LI, No. 2 (16 Nov. 1907).

——, *Some Neglected Aspects of War* (Boston, 1907).

——, *America's Interest in International Conditions* (Boston, 1910).

——, *The Life of Nelson: The Embodiment of the Sea Power of Great Britain* (Boston, 2 vols., 1897).

——, *Naval Strategy, Compared and Contrasted with Principles and Practice of Military Operations on Land* (Boston, 1911).

——, *The War in South Africa* (New York, 1900).

——, "The Navy as a Career," *The Forum*, XX (Nov. 1895), 277–283.

——, *Retrospect and Prospect* (Boston, 1902).

——, "Rear Admiral William T. Sampson," *Fortnightly Review*, 78 (1902), 234.

——, "Why We Must Have a Greater Navy," *Leslie's Weekly*, 95 (Oct. 2, 1902), 318.

——, Review of M. Oppenheim, *A History of the Administration of the Royal Navy and of Merchant Shipping* . . . in *American Historical Review*, II (July 1897), 719–722.

——, Review of M. Eyre Matcham, *The Nelsons of Burnham Thorpe: A Record of a Norfolk Family* in *American Historical Review*, XVII (Oct. 1911), 131 ff.

——, Review of James Barnes, *Naval Actions of the War of 1812*, in *American Historical Review*, II, No. 3 (April 1897), 574.

——, *Types of Naval Officers* (Boston, 1901).

——, "Prayer Book Revision," *The Churchman*, 110 (Oct. 10 and Oct. 17, 1914), 465–466, 497–498.

——, "The Apparent Decadence of the Church's Influence," *The Churchman*, 13 (April 1903), 545.

——, "Letters of Alfred Thayer Mahan to Samuel A'Court Ashe (1858–59)," ed., Ross P. Chiles, *Duke University Library Bulletin*, No. 4 (Durham, N.C., 1931).

422   Mahan, Alfred Thayer, *Admiral Farragut* (New York, 1892).

——, "The Neopolitan Republicans and Nelson's Accusers," *English Historical Review*, XIV (1899), 471–501.

——, "Sailing Home to War," *Harper's Weekly*, LI, No. 2 (5 Oct. 1907), 1453 ff.

——, *Lessons of the War with Spain and other Essays* (Boston, 1899).

——, "The Submarine and its Enemies," *Collier's Weekly*, XXXIX (6 April 1907), 17–21.

——, "The Panama Canal and the Distribution of the Fleet," *North American Review*, CC (Sept. 1914), 406–417.

——, "Germany's Naval Ambitions," *Collier's Weekly*, XLIV (24 April 1909), 13–17.

——, "The Great Illusion [review of N. Angell's 1911 book of same name]," *North American Review*, CXCV (March 1912), 319–332.

Mahan, Denis Hart, *Advanced-Guard, Out-Post, and Detachment Service of Troops . . .* (New York, 1864).

The Rev. Milo Mahan, D.D., on Confession: An Introduction to the Rev. C. N. Gray's Statement on Confession (New York, 1872).

Mahan, Milo, *A Church History of the 1st Seven Centuries to the Close of the 6th General Council* (New York, 1873).

——, *An Essay on Slavery* (Philadelphia, 1862).

——, *The Exercise of Faith in its Relation to Authority and Private Judgement* (Philadelphia, 1851).

The Collected Works of the Late Milo Mahan, D.D., ed. J. H. Hopkins (New York, 1875).

"Mantus, Lieutenant A. P.," "Duty in the Navy," *United Service*, V (July 1881), 52–61.

——, "Gentility in the Navy," *United Service*, V (Sept. 1881), 345.

——, "Marriage in the Navy," *United Service*, VI (Feb. 1882), 207.

——, "Uniformity in the Navy," *United Service*, V (Aug. 1881), 144–156.

——, "Wasted Energy in the Navy," *United Service*, V (Nov. 1881), 637 ff.

Marryat, Captain Frederick, *Mr. Midshipman Easy* (London, 1836).

Marshall, Edward C., *History of the U.S. Naval Academy* (New York, 1862).

Mason, Lieutenant T. B. M., "A Medal of Honor for Officers," *The United Service*, IV (Jan. 1881), 10–19.

——, "Naval Education," *United Service*, III (1881), 165 ff.

——, "Desertion in the Navy," *United Service*, V (Sept. 1881), 259–270.

——, "The United States Naval Institute," *United Service*, I (1879), 290–296.

Mattice, Asa M., *Queer Doings in the Navy* (n.p., circa 1896).

Meigs, John F., *The Story of the Seaman* (2 vols., Philadelphia & London, 1924).

Melville, George H., *In the Lena Delta . . . and a Proposed Method of Reaching the North Pole* (Boston, 1885).

——, "The Important Elements in Naval Conflicts," *Annals of the American Academy of Political and Social Science*, XXVI (1905), 121–136.

——, "Our Future on the Pacific—What We Have There to Hold and Win," *North American Review*, CLXVI (March 1898), 281–296.

The Memorial of the Officers of the U.S. Navy for an Increase of Their Pay with Documents Setting Forth and Sustaining the Same (New York, 1866).

Memoranda showing why Captain J. E. Jouett should not be promoted over [our] heads (Wash., 1880).

Miller, Lieutenant Fredrick A., *The Advantages of Entering the U.S. Naval Service . . .* (Wash., Bureau of Equip. and Recruiting, Navy Dept., 1875).

Miscellaneous Addresses to the Graduating Class at the Naval Academy (Wash., G.P.O., 1862– **423**
1882).
Moeller, P. W., *The Naval Academy at Annapolis and Hazing* ... (New York, 1884).
Moore, John Bassett, *Personal Recollections of Admiral Mahan* (privately printed, 1940 [copy in Yale University Library]).
Morton, Paul [Secretary of the Navy], "An Anglo-American Navy," *The Independent*, 59 (1905), 20–22.
A Naval Encyclopedia, ed. Hamersly and Co. (Philadelphia, 1881).
Naval Personnel, Line and Staff, Memorial to the Secretary of the Navy (Wash., 1878).
"The Navy at Newport: A British View, 1864," ed. Frank Merli, *Rhode Is. History*, XXV (Oct. 1966), 110–116.
"Nauticus," *The Truth About the Schley Case* [n.p. 1902?] [copy in New York Public Library].
Neeser, Robert W., ed., *American Naval Songs and Ballads* (New Haven, 1938).
Niblack, Ensign Albert P., U.S.N., "The Coast Indians of Southern Alaska and Northern British Columbia," *Annual Report of the* ... *Smithsonian Institution* ... (Wash., G.P.O., 1890), 226–386.
——, *Why Wars Come* (Boston, 1922).
"Olimgus," *Naval Rank* (n.p., n.d.).
O'Byrne, William P., *A Naval Biographical Dictionary* (2 vols., London, 1849).
Parker, Captain Foxhall, *The Battle of Mobile Bay* (Boston, 1878).
——, *The Fleets of the World: The Galley Period* (New York, 1876).
"Passed Midshipman," *Assimilated Rank in the Navy* ... [Wash., 1850].
Pegram, John C., "Recollections of the U.S. Naval Academy," Soldiers and Sailors Historical Society of R.I., *Personal Narratives*, 4th Series, No. 14 (Providence, 1891).
Porter, David D., *The Island of San Domingo* [n.p., n.d., c. 1870].
——, "Naval Education and Organization," *United Service*, I (1879), 470–482.
——, "The Chinese in America," *United Service*, I (1879), 301–325.
——, *Incidents and Anecdotes of the Civil War* (New York, 1886).
——, *Memoir of Commodore David Porter* (1875).
——, *The Naval History of the Civil War* (New York, 1886).
Correspondence between Gov.[John W.] Geary of Pa. and Vice Admiral Porter, relating to the Foreign Commerce of the U.S. (c. 1870).
Pratt, Julius, ed., "Our First 'War' in China: The Diary of William Henry Powell, 1856," *American Historical Review*, LIII (1948), 776–786.
The Opening of Japan: A Diary of [George H. Preble] U.S.N. in the Far East, 1853–1856, Boleslaw Szczesniak, ed. (Norman, Okla., 1962).
Preble, Captain George H., *Naval Uniforms* [n.p., c. 1879].
——, *Our Flag* (Albany, 1872), 504–505.
Puleston, Captain William D., *The Armed Forces of the Pacific* (New Haven, 1941).
——, *The Influence of Sea Power in World War II* (New Haven, 1947).
——, *Influence of Force in Foreign Relations* (New York, 1955).
Pye, Anne B., and Nancy Shea, *The Navy Wife* (New York, 1942).
Ransom, Commodore George, "The Naval Policy of the U.S.," *United Service*, II (Feb. 1880), 206–210.
Reed, Sir Edward J., Edward Simpson, and J. D. Jerrold Kelley, *Modern Ships of War* (New York, 1888).

424   Remey, Charles Mason, *Reminiscences of His Childhood* (privately printed in 4 typed vols. [copy at State Hist. Society of Wis.]).

——, ed., *The Life and Letters of Mary J. M. Remey* . . . (privately pub. 12 vols., Wash., 1939 [copy in St. Hist. Soc. of Wis. Library]).

Revere, Lieutenant Joseph W., *Naval Duty in California* (Oakland, Calif., 1947).

Rieman, George, *Papalangee; or, Uncle Sam in Samoa: A Narrative of the U.S.S. "Narragansett" Among the Samoan Islands* (Oakland, Calif., 1874).

Rockwell, Commander Charles H., "A Plea for Seamanship," *United Service*, 2nd Series, VIII (Dec. 1892), 513–518.

——, "The Lessons of the Naval Review," *United Service*, 2nd Series, X (July 1893), 14–16.

Roden, Ernest K., *The Navy League and the Peace Movement* (Navy League, Wash., 1913?).

Rodgers, Rear Admiral W. L., "The Diplomatic Side of the Naval Officer's Profession," *Marine Corps Gazette*, II (March 1924).

Roe, Lieutenant Commander F. A., *Naval Duties and Discipline* (New York, 1865).

——, *Reasons Why Our Navy Should Not Be Reduced!* (Wash., 1880).

Roosevelt, Theodore, *The Letters of Theodore Roosevelt*, ed. Elting Morison and others (8 vols., Cambridge, 1951).

——, *The Letters of Theodore Roosevelt to Anna Roosevelt Cowles* (New York, 1924).

——, "The Naval Policy of America as Outlined in Messages of the Presidents of the United States from the Beginning to the Present Day," *PUSNI*, XXIII (1897), 509–521.

——, *The Naval War of 1812* (New York, 1882).

——, "The Need of the Navy," *Gunton's Magazine*, XIV (January 1898).

——, *Remarks of Theodore Roosevelt to the crew of the U.S.S. "Louisiana,"* 26 Nov. 1906 (Wash., n.d.), Harvard University Library.

——, Review of *The Influence of Sea Power Upon History: 1660–1783* in *Atlantic Monthly*, LXVI (Oct. 1890), 563–567.

——, Review of *The Influence of Sea Power Upon History: 1660–1783* and *The Influence of Sea Power Upon the French Revolution and Empire: 1789–1812* in *Political Science Quarterly*, IX, (March 1894), 171–172.

Russell, William Howard, *My Diary North and South*, ed. Fletcher Pratt (New York, Harper Colophon ed., 1965).

Sampson, Rear Admiral William T., "Admiral Dewey as a National Hero," *The Century Magazine*, XXXVI (1899), 928 ff.

Sargent, Commander Nathan, *Admiral Dewey and the Manila Campaign* [written in 1903] (Wash., D.C., 1947).

——, "The Quasi-War with France," *The United Service*, IX (July 1883), 1–27.

Schley, Commander W. S., and Professor J. R. Soley, *The Rescue of Greely* (New York, 1886).

Schofield, Captain Frank H., "Incidents and Present Day Aspects of Naval Strategy," (mimeograph, 1923).

——, "The Aims and Present Status of the Navy" (mimeograph to Press, Feb. 1924 [State Hist. Society of Wis.]).

Schroeder, Lieutenant Seaton, *Fall of Maximillian's Empire* (New York and London, 1887).

Senareus, Luiz, *How to become a Naval Cadet* (New York, 1891).

Shakings from the Naval Academy (Boston, 1867).

Shippen, Medical Director Edward, *Naval Battles, Ancient and Modern* (Philadelphia, 1883).

Shufeldt, R. W. [Commodore], *The Relation of the Navy to the Commerce of the United States: A Letter Written by Request to Hon. Leopold Morse, Member of Naval Committee, H. of Rep.* (Wash. [privately printed], 1878).

Sigsbee, Captain Charles D., *The "Maine"* (New York, 1899).

Simpson, Rear Admiral Edward, "The U.S. Navy in Transition," *Harper's New Monthly Magazine*, LXIII (June 1886), 3–26.

Sims, Admiral William S., *The Victory at Sea* (New York, 1920).

——, "Roosevelt and the Navy," *McClure's Magazine*, LIV, Pt. 2 (Nov. 1922), 32–41; (Dec. 1922), 56–62, 78; (Jan. 1923), 61–66, 95–101.

Smith, Rear Admiral Joseph A., *An Address Delivered before the Union League of Philadelphia . . . Jan. 20, 1906 . . .* (Philadelphia, 1906).

Society of Sponsors of the U.S.N. (n.p., 1915).

Soley, James R., *The Boys of 1812 and Other Naval Heroes* (Boston, 1887).

——, *The Sailor Boys of '61* (Boston, 1888).

——, "The Maritime Industries of America," in *The United States of America*, ed. Nathaniel S. Shaler (2 vols., New York, 1899).

——, *The Blockade and the Cruisers* (New York, 1883).

——, "Our Naval Policy—A Lesson from 1861," *Scribner's Magazine*, I (Feb. 1887), 223–235.

Spaulding, Lieutenant J. W., *Japan and Around the World . . .* (New York, 1855).

Staunton, Lieutenant Sidney A., *The War in Tong-King: Why the French Are in Tong-King, and What They are Doing There* (Boston, 1884).

——, "A Battle-ship in Action," *Harper's New Monthly Magazine*, LXXXVIII (April 1894), 653–668.

Steunsenberg, Lieutenant George (U.S.A.), "Negroes in the Navy," *Army and Navy Journal*, XLIV (19 Jan., 1907), 563.

Stewart, Chaplain C. S., *A Visit to the South Seas in the U.S.S. "Vincennes" during the Years 1829 and 1830* (2 vols., New York, 1831).

Stirling, Rear Admiral Yates, *How to be a Naval Officer* (New York, 1940).

——, *Warriors of the Sea: The Way of Life in the U.S. Navy* (Evanston, Ill., 1942).

Storey, Moorfield, *A Civilian's View of the Navy, a Lecture Delivered before the Naval War College, 6 September 1897* (Wash., G.P.O., 1897).

Strain, Lieutenant I. G., *A Paper on the History and Prospects of Interoceanic Communication by the American Isthmus* (New York, 1856).

——, *Sketches of a Journey: Chili and the Argentine Pampas* (New York, 1853).

Strictly Private and Confidential! [n.p., n.d., circa 1881].

Taunt, Lieutenant Emory H., *Young Sailor's Assistant in Practical Seamanship* (Wash., 1883).

Taylor, Bayard, *A Visit to India, China, and Japan in the Year 1853* (New York and London, 1855).

Taylor, Rev. Fitch W., U.S.N., *The Broad Pennant; or, a Cruise in the United States Flag Ship of the Gulf Squadron* (New York, 1848).

Taylor, Captain Henry C., "The Future of Our Navy," *The Forum* (March 1899).

——, "American Maritime Development," *Transactions of the Society of Naval Architects and Marine Engineers*, III (1895), 2–18.

——, "The Study of War," *North American Review*, CLXII (Feb. 1896), 181–189.

——, "The General Question of Isthmian Interest," *Nicaragua Canal Discussion before the*

American Association for the Advancement of Science, 36th Meeting (New York, Aug, 1887).

Taylor, Captain Henry C., "The Control of the Pacific," *Forum*, III (1887), 407–416.

Todd, Lieutenant C. C., "The Personnel of Our Ship's Companies," *United Service*, VI (March 1882).

——, "Some Needs of the Navy," *United Service*, VIII (July 1882), 87–93.

Totten, Commander Benjamin J., *Naval Text-Book . . . for the Use of the Midshipmen of the U.S. Navy* (2nd ed., New York, 1862).

Tracy, Benjamin, "Our New Warships," *North American Review*, CLII (1891), 641–655.

Trumbull, H. Clay, "Four Naval Officers Whom I Knew," *United Service*, I (1879), 38.

U.S. Bureau of the Census, *Historical Statistics of the U.S.: Colonial Times to 1957* (Wash., D.C., 1960).

U.S. Naval Academy Graduates' Association, *Minutes of the 1st Four Annual Reunions* (Annapolis and Baltimore, 1886–90 [available at Library of Congress in 1 volume]).

U.S. Naval Academy Graduates' Association, *Register of Graduates* (1886–1916).

VanDeuburge, Elizabeth D., *My Voyage in the U.S. Frigate "Congress"* (New York, 1913).

Very, Lieutenant Edward W., *Navies of the World* (New York, 1880).

Vesey-Hamilton, Admiral R., "Discussion of J. C. R. Colomb's 'British Defense, 1800–1900,'" Royal Colonial Institute *Proceedings* (London, 1900), 26–27.

Vreeland, Lieutenant Charles E., and Surgeon J. F. Bransford, *Antiquities at Pataleon, Guatemala* (Wash., 1884).

Wainwright, Lieutenant Richard, "Our Naval Policy," *United Service*, 2nd Series, II (Sept. 1889), 234–239.

——, "The New Naval Academy," *World's Work*, IV (1902), 2269–2285.

——, "Modern Naval Education," *United Service*, 2nd Series, III (Jan. 1890), 20–21.

Wakeman, Edgar, *The Log of an Ancient Mariner* (San Francisco, 1878).

Walker, W. D., *What is Wrong with the Navy? An Answer Written for the Businessman* (Wash., 1908?).

Ward, Aaron, "Naval Apprentices," *United Service*, III (Dec. 1880), 740–755.

Ward, Commander James, *A Manual of Naval Tactics* (N.Y., 1867).

Wayland, Francis, *The Elements of Moral Science*, ed. Joseph L. Blau (Cambridge, Mass., 1963).

Diary of Gideon Welles, ed. Howard K. Beale (3 vols., New York, 1960).

Werntz, R. L., *Entrance Examination Papers of the Naval Academy for 1888* (Baltimore, 1889).

White, Andrew P., *Autobiography of Andrew D. White* (2 vols., New York, 1904–05).

Wilson, Francis H., "The Reorganization of the Naval Personnel," *North American Review*, CLXVII (1898), 641–649.

Wright, *Sea Rhymes* (New York, 1894).

Wyatt, Harold F., *God's Test By War* (Navy League, Wash., 1911?).

"W.X." *National Defence* [n.p., c. 1882].

Yankee Surveyors in the Shogun's Sea, ed. Allan B. Cole (Princeton, 1947).

Young, Lieutenant Lucien, *Archaeological Researches in Peru* (n.p., n.d., circa 1880).

——, *Simple Elements of Navigation* (New York, 1890).

——, *The "Boston" at Hawaii; or, The Observations and Impressions of a Navigation Officer During a Stay of 14 Months in Those Islands on a Man-of-War* (Wash., 1898).

Zogbaum, Rufus F., *The Junior Officer of the Watch* (New York, 1908).

——, *"All Hands"* (New York, 1897).

C. SECONDARY SOURCES

Many of my thoughts on the secondary literature are contained in footnotes throughout this essay, but a few separate paragraphs on the most important of these secondary sources may be of use to some readers.

Two noteworthy efforts at collective biography of naval officers are those of Fletcher Pratt, *Preble's Boys: Commodore Preble and the Birth of American Sea Power* (N.Y., 1950), and Richard S. West, Jr., *Admirals of American Empire* (Indianapolis, 1948). Neither goes much beyond vignettes of a small number of selected naval leaders. The material dealing with naval engineering officers in Monte Calvert, *The Mechanical Engineer in America, 1830–1910* (Baltimore, 1967), is far more analytical and quantitative in nature (see my review of Calvert in *Western Pa. Historical Magazine*, LI [1968], 180–182). Though I can't appreciate the author's affection toward his subjects, there is no denying the high quality of E. Digby Baltzell's collective biography of a group of Americans who were the contemporaries and compeers of the naval aristocracy, *Philadelphia Gentlemen: The Making of a National Upper Class* (Glencoe, 1958). Michael A. Lewis, *England's Sea-Officers: The Story of the Naval Profession* (London, 1939), *A Social History of the Navy, 1793–1815* (London, 1960), and *The Navy in Transition, 1814–1864* (London, 1965), are notable models for military historians, as are Morris Janowitz, *The Professional Soldier: A Social and Political Portrait* (Glencoe, 1960), and Samuel P. Huntington, *The Soldier and the State: The Theory and Politics of Civil-Military Relations* (Cambridge, Mass., 1957).

There are two exceptionally good biographical studies of naval officers: Edward W. Sloan, III, *Benjamin Franklin Isherwood: Naval Engineer* (Annapolis, 1965); and Elting E. Morison, *Admiral Sims and the Modern American Navy* (Boston, 1942). Also competent are Laurin Healy and Luiz Kutner, *The Admiral* [on George Dewey] (Chicago, 1944); Robert E. Johnson, *Rear Admiral John Rodgers, 1812–1882* (Annapolis, 1967); and Samuel E. Morison, *"Old Bruin": Commodore Matthew C. Perry* (Boston, 1967). But it is worth noting that with the exception of Louis Hacker's 1935 sketch of "Incendiary Mahan" (*Scribner's Magazine*, LXIV, 263 ff.) and Fredrick Drake's recent unpublished biography of Robert Shufeldt (" 'The Empire of the Seas' . . .," Cornell Univ., 1970) there are no biographies or composite biographies written about American naval officers in a critical, or even detached, tone; all have applauded their subjects.

Naval diplomacy is a research area that historians are rediscovering of late. Edward Billingsley, *In Defense of Neutral Rights: The United States Navy and the Wars of Independence of Chile and Peru* (Chapel Hill, 1967), is an example of one such sortie into the Navy's role in early nineteenth century diplomacy; William R. Braisted, *The U.S. Navy in the Pacific, 1897–1909* (Austin, 1958), and *The U.S. Navy in the Pacific, 1909–1922* (Austin, 1971) are definitive accounts of naval diplomacy for a later era. Kenneth Hagan's forthcoming study of naval diplomacy from Hayes to Harrison will tell us much that is new about a virtually unexplored diplomatic era, and I eagerly await the appearance of the Navy Department's proposed multi-volume study of the Navy in the Far East, under the editorship of Richard von Doenhoff. Robert A. Hart, *The Great White Fleet* (Boston, 1965), is a readable account of the Round-the-World cruise. An older but still powerful work is Charles Beard, *The Idea of National Interest* (N.Y., 1934), recently reprinted in paper by Quadrangle. Older still, and more dated, is Charles O. Paullin's *Diplomatic Negotiations of American Naval Officers, 1778–1883* (1912). See also Seward Livermore, "The American Navy as a Factor in World Politics," *American Historical Review*, LXIII (1958), 863–879.

There are several good histories of naval administration and institutional growth. among them Charles O. Paullin, *History of Naval Administration, 1715–1911* (a series of early twentieth century essays reprinted in 1968 by the U.S. Naval Institute); Harold and Margaret Sprout, *The Rise of American Naval Power, 1776–1918* (2nd ed., Princeton, 1966); George T. Davis, *A Navy Second to None: The Development of the Modern American Navy* (N.Y., 1940); and Donald Mitchell, *History of the American Navy from 1883 to Pearl Harbor* (N.Y., 1946). None the less, Raymond O'Connor's planned history of the U.S. Navy will be a welcome updating of these surveys, all of which were written over 24 years ago. Walter Herrick, Jr., *The American Naval Revolution* (Baton Rouge, 1966), is a useful study of naval administration and diplomacy in the 1880s and '90s, but I have differences with Herrick's interpretation, which I have expressed elsewhere (*The Historian*, XXX [1967], 138–139). Lance Buhl's recent dissertation on naval affairs in the era of reconstruction has surely silenced the hind-sight school of criticism (that virtually all naval historians have offered of the post-Civil War years) with a sensible rendering of the contemporary case for the "smooth-water navy."

Vincent Davis, *The Admirals' Lobby* (Chapel Hill, 1967), is the best account of recent navalism, reviewed by the present author in *The Journal of American History*, LIV (1968), 927–928. Robert Seager, II, "Ten Years before Mahan: The Unofficial Case for the New Navy, 1880–1890," *Mississippi Valley Historical Review*, XL (1953), 491–512, is good on the navalism of Congress in the 1880s. Also of interest is Beard, *The Navy: Defense or Portent?* (N.Y., 1932). (By this time the reader has, I hope, gathered that I find Beard's views on naval diplomacy and navalism to be basically sound and wise.) On understanding Mahan, see William E. Livezey, *Mahan on Sea Power* (Norman, Okla., 1947), and Walter LaFeber, "A Note on the 'Mercantilistic Imperialism' of Alfred Thayer Mahan," *Mississippi Valley Historical Review*, XLVIII (1962), 674–685. (I have expressed my minor difference with the latter analysis in Chapter 7.)

See Donald Schurman, *The Education of a Navy: The Development of British Strategic Thought, 1867–1914* (Chicago, 1965), and Arthur Marder, *The Anatomy of British Sea Power* (Hamden, Conn., 1964 [orig. pub. 1940]), for good accounts of British navalism and navalists, and Jonathan Steinberg, *Yesterday's Deterrent: Tirpitz and the Birth of the German Battle Fleet* (London, 1965), for a similar analysis of German navalists.

1. Dissertations and Masters Essays

Allard, Dean, "The Influence of the U.S. Navy upon the American Steel Industry, 1880–1900," unpub. Masters Essay, Georgetown Univ., 1959.

Andrade, Ernest, "U.S. Naval Policy in the Disarmament Era, 1921–1937," unpub. dissertation, Michigan State Univ., 1966.

Armistead, Paul, "Retired Military Leaders in American Business," unpub. dissertation, Univ. of Texas, 1967.

Betts, John L., "The U.S. Navy in the Mexican War," unpub. dissertation, Univ. of Chicago, 1954.

Brandt, Walter I., "Steel and the New Navy, 1882–1895," unpub. dissertation, Univ. of Wisconsin, 1920.

Brown, Richard C., "Social Attitudes of American Generals, 1898–1940," unpub. dissertation, Univ. of Wisconsin, 1951.

Drake, Fredrick C., " 'The Empire of the Seas': A Biography of Robert W. Shufeldt, U.S.N.," unpub. dissertation, Cornell Univ., 1970.

Gilbert, Benjamin F., "U.S. Naval Operations in the Pacific, 1861–1866," unpub. dissertation, Univ. of California at Berkeley, 1951.

Gilliam, Bates M., "The World of Captain Mahan," unpub. dissertation, Princeton Univ., 1961.

Haugen, Rolf N. B., "The Setting of Internal Administrative Communication in the U.S. Naval Establishment, 1775–1920," unpub. dissertation, Harvard Univ., 1953.

Henson, Curtis T., "The U.S. Navy and China, 1839–1861," unpub. dissertation, Tulane Univ., 1965.

Jenkins, Innis LaRoche, "Josephus Daniels and the Navy Department, 1913–1916: A Study in Military Administration," unpub. dissertation, Univ. of Maryland, 1960.

Karsten, Peter, "Roosevelt, Mahan, and the Navy," unpub. Masters Essay, Univ. of Wisconsin, 1965.

Levy, Morris, "Alfred Thayer Mahan and U.S. Foreign Policy," unpub. dissertation, New York Univ., 1965.

Rasmussen, John Peter, "The American Imperialist Elite: A Study in the Concept of National Efficiency," unpub. dissertation, Stanford Univ., 1962.

Schilling, Warner R., "Admirals and American Foreign Policy, 1913–1919," unpub. dissertation, Yale Univ., 1953.

Sens, James F., "United States Relations with Turkey, 1831–1843," unpub. Masters Essay, Ohio Univ., 1964.

Spector, Ronald, "Professors of War: The U.S. Naval War College and the Modern American Navy," unpub. dissertation, Yale Univ., 1967.

Stillson, Albert C., "The Development and Maintenance of the American Naval Establishment, 1901–1909," unpub. dissertation, Columbia Univ., 1959.

Wieand, Harold T., "The History of the Development of the U.S. Naval Reserve, 1889–1941," unpub. dissertation, Univ. of Pittsburgh, 1953.

2. Biographies and Composite Biographies of Naval Officers

Alden, Carroll S., *George H. Perkins, Commodore, U.S.N.* (Boston, 1914).

Arpee, Edward, *From Frigates to Flat-Tops* [on Rear Admiral William Moffett] (privately printed, Lake Forest, Ill., 1953).

Barrett, J., *Admiral George Dewey, A Sketch of the Man* (N.Y., 1899).

Bayard, Samuel, *A Sketch of the Life of Commodore Robert F. Stockton* (N.Y., 1856).

Belknap, George E., "A Sketch of the Life of Captain George H. Perkins," in *Letters of Captain George Hamilton Perkins, U.S.N., 1858–1880*, ed. Susan Perkins (Concord, N.H., 1886).

Benjamin, Marcus, *Francis A. Roe*, in *Memorial Papers of the Society of Colonial Wars in the District of Columbia* (Nov. 1903).

Blockman, Laurence G., *Doctor Squibb: The Life and Times of a Rugged Idealist* (N.Y., 1958).

Conner, Philip S. P., *The Home Squadron under Commodore Conner in the Mexican War* (Phil., 1896).

Cook, Nathalie J. K., *J. D. J. Kelley, Commander, U.S.N.* (n.p., 1942).

Cummings, Damon E., *Rear Admiral Richard Wainwright and the U.S. Fleet* (Wash., 1962).

Dahlgren, Madeline, *Memoir of John A. Dahlgren* (Boston, 1882).

Davis, Charles H., Jr., *Life of Charles Henry Davis, Rear Admiral, 1807–1877* (N.Y., 1899).

De Meissner, Sophie R., *Old Naval Days: Sketches from the Life of Rear Admiral William Radford, U.S.N.* (N.Y., 1920).

430 *Life and Letters of Admiral Dewey*, ed. Adelbert M. Dewey (Akron, Ohio, 1899).

Dictionary of American Biography, ed. Allen Johnson, Dumas Malone, *et al.* (32 vols., N.Y., 1937–1958).

Edwards, E. M. H., *Commander William B. Cushing of the U.S. Navy* (N.Y., 1898).

Ellis, Edward S., *Dewey and Other Naval Commanders* (N.Y., 1899).

Elliot, John M., *The Life of John A. Winslow, Rear Admiral, U.S.N.* (N.Y., 1902).

Falk, Edwin A., *Fighting Bob Evans* (N.Y., 1931).

Fitzpatrick, Donovan, and Saul Saphire, *Navy Maverick: Uriah Phillips Levy* (Garden City, N.Y., 1963).

Foltz, Charles S., *Surgeon of the Seas: The Adventurous Life of Surgeon General Jonathan M. Foltz in the Days of Wooden Ships* (Indianapolis, 1931).

The Life of an American Sailor: Rear Admiral William H. Emory, U.S.N., ed. Albert Gleaves (N.Y., 1923).

Goodrich, Caspar, *In Memoriam: Stephen Bleecker Luce* (N.Y., 1919).

Hacker, Louis M., "Incendiary Mahan: A Biography," *Scribner's Magazine*, LXIV (Nov., 1934), 263–268, 311–320.

Headley, J. T., *Farragut and our Naval Commanders* (N.Y., 1867).

Healy, Laurin H., and Luiz Kutner, *The Admiral* [on Dewey] (Chicago, 1944).

Henderson, Daniel, *The Hidden Coasts: A Biography of Admiral Charles Wilkes* (N.Y., 1953).

Hill, Jim Dan, *Sea Dogs of the Sixties* (Minneapolis, 1935).

Hoppin, James M., *Life of Andrew H. Foote, Rear Admiral, U.S.N.* (N.Y., 1874).

Johnson, Robert E., *Rear Admiral John Rodgers, 1812–1882* (Annapolis, 1967).

Lewis, Charles L., *David Glasgow Farragut: Our First Admiral* (2 vols., Annapolis, 1943).

The Life and Adventures of Jack Philip, Rear Admiral, U.S.N., ed. Edgar S. Maclay (N.Y., 1904).

Maffitt, Emma M., *The Life and Services of John Newland Maffitt* (N.Y. and Wash., 1906).

Morison, Elting E., *Admiral Sims and the Modern American Navy* (Boston, 1942).

Morison, Samuel E., *"Old Bruin": Commodore Matthew C. Perry* (Boston, 1967).

National Cyclopedia of Biography (30 vols., N.Y., 1920–1922).

Parsons, Charles W., *Memoir of Usher Parsons* [Naval Surgeon] (Providence, 1870).

Paullin, Charles O., *Commodore John Rodgers, 1773–1838* (Cleveland, 1910).

Pirtle, Alfred, *Life of James E. Jouett, Rear Admiral, U.S.N.* (Louisville, 1896).

Pratt, Fletcher, *Preble's Boys: Commodore Preble and the Birth of American Sea Power* (N.Y., 1950).

Preble, George H., *Rear Admiral Henry K. Thatcher* (Boston, 1882).

Remey, Charles Mason, *Reminiscent* [sic] *of Colonel William B. Remey, U.S.M.C., 1842–1894 . . . and Lieutenant Edward W. Remey* (typescript copy, n.p., 1955 [St. Hist. Soc. of Wisconsin has a copy]).

Life and Letters of Rear Admiral George Collier Remey, U.S.N., 1841–1928, ed. Charles Mason Remey (10 vols., typescript copy, Wash., 1939 [St. Hist. Soc. of Wisconsin has a copy]).

Rochelle, James H., *Life of Rear Admiral John R. Tucker* (Wash., 1903).

Rosengarten, J. G., *William Reynolds, Rear Admiral, U.S.N. . . . . A Memoir* (Philadelphia, 1880 [reprinted from *United Service Magazine*, May 1880]).

Schuon, Karl, *U.S. Navy: Biographical Dictionary* (New York, 1964).

Sloan, Edward W., III, *Benjamin Franklin Isherwood: Naval Engineer* (Annapolis, 1965).

Soley, J. R., "Rear Admiral John Rodgers," *PUSNI*, VIII (1882), 251–267.

——, *Admiral Porter* (New York, 1903).

Stevens, William O., *Boyhoods of Our Naval Heroes* (New York, 1924).

Taylor, Charles Carlisle, *The Life of Admiral Mahan: Naval Philosopher* (New York and London, 1920).

Thomas, Frances P., *Career of John Grimes Walker, U.S.N., 1835–1907* (Boston, 1959) [available Library of Congress].

Thomas, Lowell, *Old Gimlet Eye: The Adventures of Smedley Butler* (New York, 1933).

Wainwright, Nicholas B., "Commodore James Biddle and his Sketch Book," *Pennsylvania Magazine of History and Biography*, XC (Jan. 1966), 1–50.

Warfield, Ethelbert D., *Joseph Cabell Breckenridge, Jr., Ensign, U.S.N.* (New York, 1898).

West, Richard S., Jr., *The Second Admiral: A Life of David Dixon Porter, 1813–1891* (N.Y., 1937).

——, *Admirals of American Empire* (Indianapolis, 1948).

Williams, Frances Leigh, *Matthew Fontaine Maury: Scientist of the Sea* (New Brunswick, 1963).

3. Secondary Sources : Articles and Chapters

Abbot, Henry L., "Memoirs of Dennis Hart Mahan," in *National Academy of Sciences Biographical Memoirs* (Wash., 1886), 31–37.

Adams, L.Cdr. John W., "The Influences Affecting Naval Shipbuilding Legislation, 1910–1916," *Naval War College Review* (Dec. 1969), 41–63.

Albion, Robert G., "The Naval Affairs Committees, 1816–1947," *PUSNI*, LXXXVIII (1952), 1227–1237.

Andrade, Ernest, "The U.S. Navy and the Washington Naval Conference," *The Historian*, XXXI (1969), 345–363.

Aptheker, Herbert, "The Negro in the Union Navy," *Journal of Negro History*, XXXII (1947), 169–200.

Bartlett, C. J., "The Mid-Victorian Reappraisal of Naval Policy," in *Studies in International History*, ed. Kenneth Bourne and D. C. Watt (London, 1967), 207 ff.

Bauer, K. Jack, "The *Sancala* Affair: Captain Voorhees Seizes an Argentine Squadron," *American Neptune*, XXIX (1969), 174–186.

——, "The U.S. Navy and Texas Independence," *Military Affairs*, XXXIV (1970), 44–48.

Brandt, John, "The Navy as an Indian Fighter," *PUSNI*, LVI (1930), 691.

Brown, Richard C., "General Emory Upton—The Army's Mahan," *Military Affairs*, XVI, No. 1 (Spring, 1952), 125–131.

Buell, Raymond F., "Anglo-American Naval Understanding," *Foreign Policy Reports*, V (1929), 175–192.

Cullen, L.Cdr. Charles, "From the *Kriegsacademie* to the Naval War College," *Naval War College Review* (Jan. 1970), 6–18.

Cumming, Duncan, "Promotion in the Navy," *Chambers's Journal*, 6th Series, LXXV (1898), 643.

Davis, Arthur K., "Bureaucratic Patterns in the Navy Officer Corps," *Social Forces*, XXVII (1948), 143–153.

Dennett, Tyler, "Early American Policy in Korea, 1883–1887: The Services of Lieutenant George C. Foulk," *Political Science Affairs*, XXXVIII (1923), 82–103.

Dornbusch, Sanford M., "The Military Academy as an Assimilating Institution," *Social Forces*, XXXIII (May, 1955), 316–321.

432   Earle, Edward M., "The Navy's Influence on our Foreign Relations," *Current History*, XXIII (1926), 648–655.

Elias, Norbert, "Studies in the Genesis of the Naval Profession," *British Journal of Sociology*, I (1950), 291–309.

Gallagher, John, and Ronald Robinson, "The Imperialism of Free Trade," *The Economic History Review*, 2nd Series, VI (1953), 1–15.

Giffin, Donald W., "The American Navy at Work on the Brazil Station, 1827–1860," *American Neptune*, XIX (1959), 239–256.

Gosnell, H. A., "The Navy in Korea, 1871," *American Neptune*, VII (1947), 107–114.

Greene, Fred, "The Military View of American National Policy, 1904–1940," *American Historical Review*, LXVI (1961), 354–377.

Gregory, Frances, and Irene D. Neu, "The American Industrial Elite in the 1870s: Their Social Origins," in *Men in Business*, ed. William Miller (Harper Torchbook, ed., 1962), 194–211.

Grenville, John A. S., "American Naval Preparations for War with Spain, 1896–1898," *Journal of American Studies*, II (April 1968), 33–48.

Griswold, A. Whitney, "The Influence of History upon Sea Power," *Journal of the American Military Institute*, IV (1940), 1–7.

Guttman, Allen, "Political Ideals and the Military Ethic," *American Scholar*, XXXVII (Spring, 1965), 221–237.

Harris, P. M. G., "The Social Origins of American Leaders . . .," *Perspectives in American History*, III (1969).

Hayes, Fredric, H., "John Adams and American Sea Power," *American Neptune*, XXV (1965), 35–45.

Heffron, Paul T., "Secretary Moody and Naval Administration Reform, 1902–1904," *American Neptune*, XXIX (January 1969), 30–53.

Hirsch, Charles B., "Gunboat Personnel on the Western Waters," *Mid-America*, XXXIV (April 1952), 75–86.

Hofstader, Richard, "Manifest Destiny and the Philippines," in Daniel Aaron, ed., *America in Crisis* (New York, 1952), 173–200.

Hurd, Archibald, "The Kaiser's Dreams of Sea Power," *Fortnightly Review* (August 1906).

Ives, C. B., "*Billy Budd* and the Articles of War," *American Literature*, XXXIV (March 1962), 31–39.

Janowitz, Morris, "Military Elites and the Study of War," *Journal of Conflict Resolution*, I (1957), 9–18.

——, "Changing Patterns of Organizational Authority: The Military Establishment," *Administrative Science Quarterly*, III (1959), 473–493.

Johnson, Arthur M., "Theodore Roosevelt and the Navy," *PUSNI*, LXXXIV (October 1958), 76–82.

Lammers, C. J., "Midshipmen and Candidate Reserve Officers at the Royal Netherlands Naval College: A Comparative Study of a Socialization Process," *Sociologia Neerlandica*, II (1965), 98–122.

Lang, Kurt, "Technology and Career Management in the Military Establishment," in Morris Janowitz, ed., *The New Military: Changing Patterns of Organization* (New York, 1965), 69.

LaFeber, Walter, "A Note on the 'Mercantilistic Imperialism' of Alfred Thayer Mahan," *Mississippi Valley Historical Review*, XLVIII, No. 4 (March 1962), 674–685.

Livermore, Seward W., "The American Navy as a Factor in World Politics," *American Historical Review*, LXIII, No. 4 (July 1958), 863–879.

——, "Theodore Roosevelt, the American Navy, and the Venezualan Crisis of 1902–03," *American Historical Review*, LI (April 1946), 452–471.

——, "American Naval-Base Policy in the Far East, 1850–1914," *Pacific Historical Review*, 13 (1944), 113–135.

McCormick, Thomas, "Insular Imperialism and the Open Door: The China Market and the Spanish-American War," *Pacific Historical Review*, 32 (1963), 155–169.

Mallan, J. P., "Roosevelt, Brooks Adams, and Lea: The Warrior Critique of the Business Civilization," *American Quarterly*, VIII, No. 3 (Fall, 1956), 216–230.

Meadows, M., "Eugene Hale and the Navy," *American Neptune* (July 1962), 187 ff.

Merrill, James M., "Men, Monotony, and Mouldy Beans—Life on Board Civil War Blockaders," *American Neptune*, XVI (1956), 49–65.

——, "The Asiatic Squadron, 1835–1907," *American Neptune*, XXIX (1969), 106–117.

Miller, William, "Historians and the Business Elite," in *Men in Business*, ed. William Miller (Harper Torch, ed., 1962), 322–328.

——, "The Recruitment of the American Business Elite," in *Men in Business*, ed. William Miller (Harper Torch, ed., 1962), 333–336.

Moll, Kenneth L., "A. T. Mahan, American Historian," *Military Affairs*, XXVIII, No. 3 (Fall, 1963), 131–140.

Morison, Elting E., "Incomparable Teddy," in Earl S. Miers, ed., *American Story* (New York, 1956), 265–269.

——, "A Case Study of Innovation," *Engineering and Science Magazine* (April 1950).

Mueller, Lieutenant William R., "The Negro in the Navy," *Social Forces*, XXIV (1945), 110–115.

Mullan, Hugh, "The Regular Service Myth," *American Journal of Sociology*, LIII (Jan. 1948).

Neumann, William L., "Religion, Morality, and Freedom: The Ideological Background of the Perry Expedition," *Pacific Historical Review*, XXIII (1954), 247–257.

Paullin, Charles O., "Early Voyages of American Naval Vessels to the Orient: The East India Squadron in the Waters of China and Japan, 1854–1865," *PUSNI*, 37 (1911), 387–417.

——, "The U.S. Navy in Mexico," *PUSNI*, 175 ff.

——, "Dueling in the Old Navy," *PUSNI*, 35 (1909), 1155–1197.

Pratt, Julius W., "Alfred Thayer Mahan," in *The Marcus Jernegan Essays in American Historiography* (Chicago, 1937).

——, Review of Walter LaFeber, *The New Empire*, in *Pacific Historical Review*, XXXIII, No. 3 (August, 1964), 360–361.

——, "The Ideology of American Expansion," in *Essays in Honor of William E. Dodd*, ed. Avery Craven (Chicago, 1935).

Ropp, Theodore, "The Rise of American Military Power," in Stephen Ambrose, ed., *Institutions in Modern America: Innovation in Structure and Process* (Baltimore, 1967).

Ryan, Captain Paul B., "The Old Navy and Santo Domingo: Pacification Patrols in the Nineteenth Century," *Shipmate* (Feb. 1967), 4 ff.

Sachse, Lieutenant William L., "Our Naval Attaché System: Its Origins and Development to 1917," *PUSNI*, LXXII (May 1946), 661–672.

Schilling, Warner, "Civil-Naval Relations in World War I," *World Politics*, VII (1955), 572–591.

434   Seager, Robert, II, "Ten Years before Mahan; The Unofficial Case for the New Navy, 1880–1890," *Mississippi Valley Historical Review*, XL, No. 3 (Dec. 1953), 491–512.

Stapler, Captain John, "The Naval War College, A Brief History," *PUSNI*, LVIII (1932), 1157–1163.

Stevens, Professor William O., "The Naval Officer and the Civilian," *PUSNI*, 47 (1921), 1727.

Stillson, A. C., "Military Policy without Political Guidance: Theodore Roosevelt's Navy," *Military Affairs*, XXV, No. 1 (Spring, 1961).

Tate, E. Mowry, "U.S. Gunboats on the Yangtze: History and Political Aspects, 1842–1922," Paper read at Midwest Conference on Asian Affairs, Boulder, Colo., Oct. 22, 1965.

Tuchman, Barbara W., "Perdicaris alive or Rasculi dead," *American Heritage*, X (August, 1959), 18–21 ff.

Uhlig, Frank, Jr., "The Great White Fleet," *American Heritage*, XV (Feb. 1964), 30–43 ff.

Vagts, Alfred, "Hopes and Fears of an American-German War, 1870–1915," *Political Science Quarterly*, LIV (1939), 514–535; LV (1940), 53–76.

West, Richard, Jr., "The Superintendents of the Naval Academy," *PUSNI*, LXXII (April 1946), 59–67.

Wheeler, Gerald E., "Origins of the Naval Reserve Officer Training Corps," *Military Affairs*, XX (1956), 170–174.

Willock, Roger, "Gunboat Diplomacy: Operations of the [British] North America and West Indies Squadron, 1875–1915, Pt. 2," *American Neptune*, XXVIII (1968), 85–112.

Zurcher, Louis, "The Sailor Aboard Ship," *Social Forces*, XLIII (1965), 389–400.

4. Secondary Sources : Books

Albion, Robert G., *The Rise of New York Port, 1815–1860* (N.Y., 1939).

Alden, Carroll S., and Ralphe Earle, *Makers of Naval Tradition* (Boston, 1942 [orig. pub. 1925]).

Ambrose, Stephen E., *Duty, Honor, Country: A History of West Point* (Baltimore, 1966).

——, *Upton and the Army* (Baton Rouge, 1964).

Aronson, Sidney, *Status and Kinship in the Higher Civil Service* (Cambridge, Mass., 1964).

Baltzell, E. Digby, *The Protestant Establishment* (N.Y., 1964).

——, *Philadelphia Gentlemen: The Making of a National Upper Class* (Glencoe, Ill., 1958).

Bartlett, C. J., *Great Britain and Sea Power, 1815–1853* (Oxford, 1963).

Beard, Charles, *A Foreign Policy for America* (N.Y., 1940).

——, *The Idea of National Interest* (N.Y., 1934).

——, *The Navy: Defense or Portent?* (N.Y., 1932).

Bigelow, Donald N., *William Conant Church and the "Army and Navy Journal"* (N.Y., 1952).

Billingsley, Edward, *In Defense of Neutral Rights: The United States Navy and the Wars of Independence of Chile and Peru* (Chapel Hill, 1967).

Historians and American Far Eastern Policy, ed. Dorothy Borg (N.Y., 1966).

Bourne, Kenneth, *Britain and the Balance of Power in North America, 1815–1908* (Berkeley, 1967).

Braisted, William R., *The United States Navy in the Pacific, 1897–1909* (Austin, 1958).

——, *The U.S. Navy in the Pacific, 1909–1922* (Austin, 1971).

Brodie, Bernard, *A Guide to Naval Strategy* (2nd ed., Princeton, 1959).

——, *Sea Power in the Machine Age* (Princeton, 1951).

Bryant, Samuel W., *The Sea and the States* (N.Y., 1947).

Burr, Henry L., *Education in the Early Navy* (Phil., 1939).

Calhoun, Daniel H., *Professional Lives in America: Structure and Aspiration, 1750–1850* (Cambridge, Mass., 1965).

Calvert, Monte, *The Mechanical Engineer in America, 1830–1910: Professional Cultures in Conflict* (Baltimore, 1967).

Campbell, Charles S., Jr., *Special Business Interests and the Open Door Policy* (New Haven, 1951).

——, *Anglo-American Understanding, 1898–1903* (Baltimore, 1957).

Carrison, Daniel J., *The Navy from Wood to Steel, 1860–1890* (N.Y., 1965).

Church, William Conant, *The Life of John Ericsson* (2 vols., N.Y., 1890).

Clendenen, Clarence, *et al.*, *Americans in Africa, 1865–1890* (Hoover Institute, 1966).

Clinard, Outten J., *Japan's Influence on American Naval Power, 1897–1917* (Berkeley and Los Angeles, 1947).

Coates, Charles H., and Roland J. Pellegrin, *Military Sociology: A Study of American Military Institutions and Military Life* (College Park, Md., 1965).

Connolly, James B., *Navy Men* (N.Y., 1939).

Copley, Brank B., *Fredrick W. Taylor: Father of Scientific Management* (2 vols., N.Y., 1923).

Crecraft, Earl W., *Freedom of the Seas* (N.Y., 1935).

Cullum, George W., *Biographical Register of Officers and Graduates of the U.S. Military Academy* (3rd ed., Boston, 1891).

Davenport, Charles B., and Maria T. Scudder, *Naval Officers; Their Heredity and Development* (Wash., 1919).

Davis, George T., *A Navy Second to None: The Development of Modern American Naval Policy* (N.Y., 1940).

Davis, Vincent, *Postwar Defense Policy and the United States Navy, 1943–1946* (Chapel Hill, 1966).

——, *The Admirals Lobby* (Chapel Hill, 1967).

——, *The Politics of Innovation: Patterns in Navy Cases* (Denver, 1967).

Denny, Harold, *Dollars for Bullets* (N.Y., 1929).

Dulles, Foster R., *America in the Pacific: A Century of Expansion* (Boston and N.Y., 1932).

Duval, Miles P., *Cadiz to Cathay* (Stanford, 1940).

Ekirch, Arthur, *The Civilian and the Military* (N.Y., 1956).

Fahny, Aly M., *Muslim Naval Organization in the Eastern Mediterranean from the 7th to the 10th Century* (Cairo, 1966).

The Economic Value of the U.S. Merchant Marine, ed. Allen Ferguson, *et al.* (Evanston, Ill., 1961).

Field, James A., *America and the Mediterranean World, 1776–1882* (Princeton, 1969).

Fishel, Wesley, *The End of Extra-territoriality in China* (Berkeley, 1952).

Fox, Grace E., *British Admirals and Chinese Pirates, 1832–1869* (London, 1940).

Gelber, Lionel, *The Rise of Anglo-American Friendship: A Study in World Politics, 1899–1906* (London, 1938).

Gerth, Hans, and C. Wright Mills, *Character and Social Structure; The Psychology of Social Institutions* (New York, 1953).

Notes on the Revised Statutes of the U.S. . . . . to July 1, 1889, ed. John M. Gould and George F. Tucker (Boston, 1889).

436 Graham, Gerald, *The Politics of Naval Supremacy: Studies in British Maritime Ascendancy* (Cambridge, 1965).

——, *Sea Power and British North America, 1783–1820: A Study in British Colonial Policy* (Cambridge, Mass., 1941).

Gray, Captain J. A. C., *Amerika Samoa: A History of American Samoa and its United States Naval Administration* (Annapolis, 1960).

Grenville, John A. S., and George B. Young, *Politics, Strategy, and American Diplomacy: Studies in Foreign Policy, 1873–1917* (New Haven and London, 1966).

Griffin, Eldon, *Clippers and Consuls: American Consular and Commercial Relations with Eastern Asia, 1845–1860* (Ann Arbor, Michigan, 1938).

Guttman, Allen, *The Conservative Tradition in America* (N.Y., 1967).

Halliday, E. M., *The Ignorant Armies* (New York, 1958).

Hammond, Paul Y., *Organizing for Defense* (Princeton, 1961).

Harrington, Fred Harvey, *God, Mammon, and the Japanese: Dr. Horace Allen and Korean-American Relations, 1884–1945* (2nd edition, Madison, Wisconsin, 1961).

Harris, Brayton, *The Age of the Battleship, 1890–1922* (New York, 1965).

Hart, Robert A., *The Great White Fleet* (Boston, 1965).

Hill, Fredric Stanhope, *The Romance of the American Navy* (New York, 1910).

Hirsch, Mark D., *William C. Whitney: Modern Warwick* (New York, 1948).

Hofstadter, Richard, *Social Darwinism in American Thought* (rev. edition, New York, 1955).

Holls, Fredrick W., *The Peace Conference at the Hague* (New York, 1900).

Howe, George F., *Chester A. Arthur: A Quarter-Century of Machine Politics* (New York, 1934).

Huie, William B., *The Case Against the Admirals* (New York, 1946).

Hunt, Thomas, *The Life of William H. Hunt* (Privately printed, Brattleboro, Vt., 1922).

Huntington, Samuel P., *The Soldier and the State: The Theory and Politics of Civil-Military Relations* (Cambridge, Mass., 1957).

Changing Patterns of Military Politics, ed. Samuel P. Huntington (New York, 1962).

Hutchins, John G. B., *The American Maritime Industries and Public Policy, 1789–1914* (Cambridge, Mass., 1941).

Jane, Fredrick T., *Heresies of Sea Power* (London, 1906).

Janowitz, Morris, ed., *The New Military* (New York, 1964).

——, *The Professional Soldier: A Social and Political Portrait* (Glencoe, Ill., 1960).

——, *Sociology and the Military Establishment* (New York, revised edition, 1965).

Jewell, J. Grey, *Among Our Sailors* (New York, 1874).

Johnson, Robert E., *Thence 'Round Cape Horn: The Story of U.S. Naval Forces on Pacific Station, 1818–1923* (Annapolis, 1963).

Keller, Suzanne, *Beyond the Ruling Class: Strategic Elites in Modern Society* (New York, 1963).

Klay, Andor, *Daring Diplomacy* (Minneapolis, 1957).

Knox, Dudley, *A History of the United States Navy* (New York, Revised edition, 1948).

Koch, Theodore Wesley, *Books in the War: The Romance of Library War Service* (Boston and New York, 1919).

Kraft, Herman F., and Walter B. Norris, *Sea Power in American History* (New York, 1920).

LaFeber, Walter, *The New Empire: An Interpretation of American Expansion: 1860–1898* (Ithaca, New York, 1963).

Laffin, John, *Jack Tar: The Story of the British Sailor* (London, 1969).
Langley, Harold D., *Social Reform in the United States Navy, 1798–1862* (University of Ill. Press, Urbana-Chicago-London, 1967).
Lawrence, Samuel A., *United States Merchant Shipping: Policies and Politics* (Wash., D.C., 1966).
Leech, Margaret, *In the Days of McKinley* (N.Y., 1959).
Lewis, Michael A., *England's Sea-Officers: The Story of the Naval Profession* (London, 1939).
——, *A Social History of the Navy, 1793–1815* (London, 1965).
——, *The Navy in Transition, 1814–1864* (London, 1965).
Lindsay, Robert G., *This High Name: Public Relations and the U.S. Marine Corps* (Madison, Wisc., 1956).
Livezey, William E., *Mahan on Sea Power* (Norman, Okla., 1947).
Lord, Clifford, and Archibald Turnbull, *History of United States Naval Aviation* (New Haven, 1949).
Lossing, Benson J., *The Story of the United States Navy for Boys* (New York, 1899).
Lott, Arnold, *A Long Line of Ships: Mare Island's Century of Naval Activity in California* (Annapolis, 1954).
Macartney, Clarence E., *Mr. Lincoln's Admirals* (New York, 1956).
Mack, Gerstle, *The Land Divided: A History of the Panama Canal and Other Isthmian Canal Projects* (New York, 1944).
McClelland, David C., ed., *Studies in Motivation* (New York, 1955).
——, *The Achieving Society* (Princeton, N.J., 1961).
McCrocklin, James H., comp., *Garde D'Haiti* (Annapolis, 1956).
Major, John, and Anthony Preston, *"Send a Gunboat!"* (London, 1967).
Marder, Arthur, *The Anatomy of British Sea Power* (Hamden, Conn., 1964 [orig. pub. in 1940]).
Masland, John, and Eugene Lyons, *Education and Military Leadership: A Study of the ROTC* (Princeton, 1959).
Masland, John, and Laurence Radway, *Soldiers and Scholars* (Princeton, 1957).
Masterman, Sylvia, *The Origins of International Rivalry in Samoa, 1845–1884* (London, 1934).
Merk, Fredrick, *Manifest Destiny and Mission in American History* (New York, 1963).
Milligan, John D., *Gunboats down the Mississippi* (Annapolis, 1965).
Millington, Herbert, *American Diplomacy and the War of the Pacific* (New York, 1948).
Millis, Walter, *Arms and Men* (New York, 1958).
——, *The Martial Spirit* (New York, 1931).
Mills, C. Wright, *The Power Elite* (Galaxy Paper ed., New York, 1959).
Mitchell, Donald W., *History of the American Navy from 1883 to Pearl Harbor* (N.Y., 1946).
Morison, Elting E., *Men, Machines, and Modern Times* (Cambridge, Mass., 1966).
——, *The War of Ideas* (U.S.A.F. Academy, 1969).
Munro, Dana, *Intervention and Dollar Diplomacy in the Caribbean, 1900–1921* (Princeton, 1964).
Neale, Robert G., *Great Britain and United States Expansion: 1898–1900* (East Lansing, 1966).
Neeser, Robert W., *Statistical and Chronological History of the United States Navy, 1775–1907* (2 vols., N.Y., 1909).

438   Neu, Charles E., *An Uncertain Friendship: Theodore Roosevelt and Japan, 1906–1909* (Cambridge, Mass., 1967).

Nevins, Allan, *Grover Cleveland: A Study in Courage* (N.Y., 1932).

Newell, Gordon, *Paddlewheel Pirate: Ned Wakeman* (N.Y., 1959).

Niblack, Albert, *The Office of Naval Intelligence: Its History and Aims* (Wash., 1920).

Nichols, Roy F., ed., *Battles and Leaders of the Civil War* (4 vols., N.Y., 1956).

Norris, Walter B., *Annapolis: Its Colonial and Naval History* (N.Y., 1925).

O'Connor, Raymond, *Perilous Equilibrium: The United States and the London Naval Conference of 1930* (Lawrence, Kansas, 1962).

Offutt, Milton, *The Protection of Citizens Abroad by the Armed Forces of the United States* (Baltimore, 1928).

O'Gara, Gordon C., *Theodore Roosevelt and the Rise of the Modern American Navy* (Princeton, 1943).

Palmer, Frederick, *With My Own Eyes* (Indianapolis, 1933).

——, *Bliss, Peacemaker: The Life and Letters of General Tasker H. Bliss* (N.Y., 1934).

Paullin, Charles Oscar, *Diplomatic Negotiations of American Naval Officers, 1778–1883* (Baltimore, 1912).

——, *Paullin's History of Naval Administration, 1775–1911* (Annapolis, 1968).

Peck, Taylor, *Round-Shot to Rockets: A History of the Washington Navy Yard and U.S. Naval Gun Factory* (Annapolis, 1949).

Perkins, Bradford, *The Great Rapprochement: England and the U.S., 1895–1914* (N.Y., 1968).

Perla, Leo, *What is "National Honor"?* (New York, 1918).

Pike, Fredrick B., *Chile and the U.S., 1880–1962* (Notre Dame, 1963).

Pomeroy, Earl, *Pacific Outpost: American Strategy in Guam and Micronesia* (Stanford, 1951).

Pratt, Fletcher, *The Navy: A History* (Garden City, N.Y., 1938).

Puleston, William D., *Annapolis: Gangway to the Quarterdeck* (New York, 1942).

Quirk, Robert E., *An Affair of Honor* (Lexington, Ky., 1962).

Rappaport, Armin, *The Navy League of the United States* (Detroit, 1962).

Reuter, Bertha A., *Anglo-American Relations During the Spanish-American War* (New York, 1924).

Richardson, Leon B., *William E. Chandler* (New York, 1940).

Robinson, Charles N., *The British Tar in Fact and Fiction* (London and N.Y., 1909).

Roll, Charles, *Colonel Dick Thompson: The Persistent Whig*, Indiana Historical Collections, XXX (Indianapolis, 1948).

Roskill, Stephen, *Naval Policy Between the Wars: Vol. I—The Period of Anglo-American Antagonism, 1919–1929* (London, 1968).

Rudolph, Fredrick, *The American College and University: A History* (New York, 1962).

Russ, William A., *The Hawaiian Revolution, 1893–94* (Selinsgrove, Pa., 1959).

Ryden, George H., *The Foreign Policy of the United States in Relation to Samoa* (New Haven and London, 1933).

Sapin, Burton M., and Richard C. Snyder, *The Role of the Military in American Foreign Policy* (Garden City, N.Y., 1954).

Schaff, Morris, *The Spirit of Old West Point, 1858–1862* (N.Y. and Boston, 1907).

Schurman, Donald M., *The Education of a Navy: The Development of British Naval Strategic Thought, 1867–1914* (Chicago, 1965).

Semmel, Bernard, *Imperialism and Social Reform: English Social-Imperial Thought, 1885–1914* (Cambridge, Mass., 1960).

Simons, William E., *Liberal Education in the Service Academies* (Teachers College, Columbia **439**
University, 1965).

Smelser, Marshall, *Congress Builds a Navy, 1787–1798* (Notre Dame, Ind., 1959).

Sokol, Anthony, *Sea Power in the Nuclear Age* (Wash., 1961).

Sprout, Harold and Margaret, *The Rise of American Naval Power, 1776–1918* (second edition, Princeton, 1966).

——, *Toward a New Order of Sea Power, 1918–1921* (N.Y., 1941).

Swann, Leonard A., Jr., *John Roach, Marine Entrepreneur* (Annapolis, 1965).

Tate, Merze, *The U.S. and the Hawaiian Kingdom* (New Haven, 1965).

Tong, Te-Kong, *U.S. Diplomacy in China, 1844–1860* (Seattle, 1964).

Tuchman, Barbara, *The Proud Tower* (Bantam paper edition, 1967).

Tuleja, Thaddeus, *Statesmen and Admirals* (N.Y., 1963).

Vagts, Alfred, *A History of Militarism: Romance and Realities of a Profession* (New York, 1937).

——, *The Military Attaché* (Princeton, 1967).

Van Alstyne, Richard, *The Rising American Empire* (New York, 1960).

Varg, Paul A., *Missionaries, Chinese, and Diplomats: The American Protestant Missionary Movement, 1890–1952* (Princeton, 1958).

Veysey, Lawrence, *The Emergence of the American University* (Chicago and London, 1965).

Vollmer, Howard M., and Donald L. Mills, eds., *Professionalization* (Englewood Cliffs, N.J., 1966).

Wehrle, Edmond S., *Britain, China, and the Antimissionary Riots* (Minneapolis, 1966).

Wescott, Allan, ed., *Mahan on Naval Warfare* (Boston, 1918).

West, Richard S., Jr., *Mr. Lincoln's Navy* (New York, 1957).

Wheeler, Gerald E., *Prelude to Pearl Harbor: The United States Navy and the Far East, 1921–1931* (Columbia, Missouri, 1963).

Wheelis, Allan, *The Quest for Identity* (New York, 1958).

Wilkins, Mira, *The Emergence of Multinational Enterprise: American Business Abroad from the Colonial Period to 1914* (Cambridge, 1970).

Williams, William Appleman, *The Contours of American History* (Cleveland, 1961).

——, *The Tragedy of American Diplomacy* (rev. ed., N.Y., 1962).

——, *The Roots of the Modern American Empire* (N.Y., 1969).

Woodcock, George, *The British in the Far East* (N.Y., 1969).

Wriston, Henry, *Executive Agents in American Foreign Relations* (Baltimore, 1929).

Zook, David H., Jr., and Robin Higham, *A Short History of Warfare* (New York, 1966).

Index of Names

General Index

General Index